Hometown Memories . . .

Monday Washdays and Outhouse Roosters
Tales from the Good Old Days in West Virginia's Eastern Panhandle and also Northwestern Maryland
A TREASURY OF 20TH CENTURY MEMORIES

OTHER BOOKS FROM HOMETOWN MEMORIES

Claremont Tales
Taylorsville Tales
Burke County Tales
Catawba County Tales
Cleveland County Tales
Blue Ridge Tales
Foothills-Piedmont Tales
Memorable Tales of the Smokies and Blue Ridge Mountains
Caldwell County Tales
Albemarle Tales
Lincolnton Tales
Montgomery Tales
Lee County Tales
Rowan County Tales
Cold Biscuits and Fatback and other Richmond County Tales
Skinnydipping in the Mule Trough and Other Rockingham County Tales
Lunch in a Lard Bucket and Other Cabarrus County Tales
Rooster in a Milkwell and other Moore County Tales
It Always Rains When Old Folks Die and other Tales from Davidson and Randolph County
A Prayer for a Baby Goat and other Tales from Alamance County
The Mill Village and the Miracle Bicycle and other Tales from Gaston County
Wilmington Tales
Guilford County Tales
Asheville Tales
The Class of '47 Was Me and other Tales along the North Carolina Coast
The Elegant Tarpaper Shack and other Tales from the Heartland of North Carolina
Outhouse Spiders and Tin Tub Baths—Tales from the Blue Ridge Mountains
Wringer Washers and Ration Stamps—Tales from Forsyth County
Front Porch Stories, Back Porch Bathrooms —Tales from Alexander, Davie, Iredell, Rowan, and Yadkin Counties
Crank Victrolas and Wood Cook Stoves —Tales from Green, Lenoir, Pitt, and Wayne Counties
Mules, Mud and Homemade Soap —Tales from Anson, Stanly and Union Counties
Life in the Good Old Days in Alamance, Caswell and Rockingham Counties
Life in the Good Old Days in Catawba, Lincoln and Gaston Counties
Life in the Good Old Days in Buncombe and Henderson Counties
Moonshine and Blind Mules and other Western North Carolina Tales
Ain't No Bears Out Tonight and other Cabarrus County Tales
Two Holers and Model T Fords and other Randolph County Tales
Ham Biscuits and Baked Sweet Potatoes and other Montgomery, Richmond , and Scotland County Tales
Possum Hunters, Moonshine and Corn Shuck Dolls and other Tales from Wilkes County
Chasing the Ice Truck and other Tales from New Hanover County and Wilmington
Steam Whistles and Party Line Phones and other Tales from in and around Roanoke
Squirrel Gravy and Feed Sack Underwear—Tales from the Tennessee Mountains
Miners' Lamps and Cold Mountain Winters—Tales from Southwest Virginia
Cold Outhouses and Kerosene Lamps—Tales from Southeastern Ohio
Coal Camps and Castor Oil—Tales from Southern West Virginia
Brush Brooms and Straw Ticks—Tales from Northwest Georgia
Dust Storms and Half Dugouts—Tales from the Upper Panhandle of Texas
Lessons by Lamplight—Tales from Southeastern Kentucky
Frozen Laundry and Depression Soup—Tales from Upstate New York
Paper Dolls and Homemade Comforts—Tales from Northwestern Virginia
One-Room Schoolin'—Tales from Central West Virginia

Cow Chips in the Cook Stove—Tales from the Lower Panhandle of Texas
Moonshine and Mountaintops—Tales from Northeast Tennessee
When We Got Electric…—Tales from Northwest West Virginia
Outside Privies and Dinner Pails—Tales from Southwest Iowa
Milking the Kickers—Tales from Southwest Oklahoma
Rolling Stores and Country Cures—Tales from Northeast Alabama
Penny Candy and Grandma's Porch Swing—Tales from North Central Pennsylvania
Rumble Seats and Lumber Camps—Tales from Northern Michigan
Lye Soap and Sad Irons—Tales from Northwest Missouri
Almost Heaven—Tales from Western West Virginia
Hobos and Swimming Holes—Tales from Northern Wisconsin
Saturday Night Baths and Sunday Dinners—Tales from Northwest Iowa
Sod Houses and The Dirty Thirties—Tales from Northwest and North Central Kansas
Coal Oil Lamps and Cattle in the Crops— Tales from Northern and Mountain West Idaho
Morning Chores and Soda Fountains—Tales from The Texas Hill Country
County Schools and Classic Cars—Tales from Northeast Iowa
Dust Storm Days and Two-Holers—Tales from Southwest and South Central Kansas
Wood Fire Saunas and Iron Mines—Tales from Michigan's Upper Peninsula
Kerosene Lamps and Grandma's Washboard—Tales from Northeastern Missouri
Picture Shows and Five Cent Moon Pies—Tales from North Carolina's Blue Ridge Mountains and Foothills
Corncob Fuel and Cold Prairie Winters—Tales from Eastern and Northeastern South Dakota
Filling Stations, Shine, and Sorghum Molasses—Tales from The Tennessee West Highland Rim
Down in the Holler—Tales from Southwestern Virginia
Party Line "Rubberneckers"—Tales from Southwest and South Central Wisconsin

At Hometown Memories, our mission is to save and share the memories of days gone by...before they are lost forever. As of this publication, we have created 80 books of memories, and saved and shared over 20,000 stories and 10,000 pictures.
We hope you enjoy them!

Hometown Memories...

Monday Washdays and Outhouse Roosters
Tales from the Good Old Days in West Virginia's Eastern Panhandle and also Northwestern Maryland

A TREASURY OF 20TH CENTURY MEMORIES
Compiled and edited by Todd Blair and Karen Garvey

HOMETOWN MEMORIES, LLC
Hickory, North Carolina

Monday Washdays and Outhouse Roosters

Publisher: Todd Blair
Lead Editor: Karen Garvey
Design and Graphic Arts Editor: Karen Garvey and Laura Montgomery
Office Services Assistants: Laura Montgomery and Tim Bekemeier
Warehouse Manager: Tim Bekemeier
Assistant Editors: Monica Black, Lisa Hollar, Jodi Black, Greg Rutz, Heather Garvey, Brianne Mai, Reashea Montgomery, Hannah Pletcher, Cathy Elrod, and Tiffany Canaday

ISBN 978-1-940376-16-5
Copyright © 2014

All rights reserved by Hometown Memories, LLC and by the individuals who contributed articles to this work. No part of this work may be reproduced in any form, or by any means, without the written permission of the publisher or the individual contributor. Exceptions are made for brief excerpts to be used in published reviews.

Published by

Hometown Memories, LLC
2359 Highway 70 SE, Suite 350
Hickory, N. C. 28602
(877) 491-8802

Printed in the United States of America

Acknowledgements

To those West Virginia's Eastern Panhandle and also Northwestern Maryland folks (and to those few who "ain't from around here") who took the trouble to write down your memories and mail them in to us, we offer our heartfelt thanks. And we're sure you're grateful to each other, because together, you have created a wonderful book.

To encourage participation, the publisher offered cash awards to the contributors of the most appealing stories. These awards were not based upon writing ability or historical knowledge, but rather upon subject matter and interest. The winners were: Dottie Hughes of New Creek, WV; Sharon F. Keefer of Cumberland, MD; and Floyd W. Wakefield of Friendsville, MD. We would also like to give honorable mention to the contributions from Robert E. Drury of Allison Park, PA and Vivian E. Helsley of Green Spring, WV. The cash prizewinner for the book's cover photo goes to Ila Slonaker of Capon Bridge, WV (you'll find their names and page numbers in the table of contents). Congratulations! It was extremely difficult to choose these winners because every story and picture in this book had its own special appeal.

Associate Editors

Andrew C. Agnew, Sr.	Evelyn James
Zona H. Apple	Billy Jenkins
Loretta F. Barlow	Judy (Bergdoll) Jenkins
Janice Cooper Barnes	Elsie Lewis
Iona Crites Bergdoll	Pat McKnew
Rosco E. Bergdoll	Susan Meyer
James Bohn	James Michael
Shirley J. Burkett	Patsy D. Morgan-Ruckles
Eileen V. Capel	Diana Murphy
Louise Smith Crist	Donna J. Pierce
Reba Deremer	John Edward (Eddie) Racey
Robert E. Drury	Shirley J. Ravenscroft
Ruby Froman	Mary Ritchie
Anne Hampton	Barbara Shroyer
Carl Harr	Ruby O. Teets
Vivian E. Helsley	Wayne C. Ward
Beverly A. Horn	Joe Winebrenner
Dottie Hughes	Victoria Younker

INTRODUCTION

We know that most folks don't bother to read introductions. But we do hope you (at least eventually) get around to reading this one. Here's why:

First, the creation of these books is in its fifth generation after we took over the responsibilities of Hometown Memories Publishing from its founders, Bob Lasley and Sallie Holt. After forty-nine books, they said goodbye to enjoy retirement, and each other. Bob and Sallie had a passion for saving these wonderful old tales from the good old days that we can only hope to match. We would love to hear your thoughts on how we are doing.

Second—and far more important—is the who, what, where, when, why and how of this book. Until you're aware of these, you won't fully enjoy and appreciate it.

This is a very unusual kind of history book. It was actually written by 272 West Virginia and Maryland old-timers and not-so-old-timers who remember what life was really like back in the earlier years of the 20th century in West Virginia's Eastern Panhandle and also Northwestern Maryland. These folks come from all walks of life, and by voluntarily sharing their memories (which often include their emotions, as well), they have captured the spirit and character of a time that will never be seen again.

Unlike most history books, this one was written from the viewpoint of people who actually experienced history. They're familiar with the tribulations of the Great Depression; the horrible taste of castor oil; "outdoor" plumbing; party line phones; and countless other experiences unknown to today's generation.

We advertised all over West Virginia's Eastern Panhandle and also Northwestern Maryland to obtain these stories. We sought everyday folks, not experienced authors, and we asked them to simply jot down their memories. Our intention was by no means literary perfection. Most of these folks wrote the way they spoke, and that's exactly what we wanted. To preserve story authenticity, we tried to make only minimal changes to written contributions. We believe that an attempt at correction would damage the book's integrity.

We need to include a few disclaimers: first, many important names are missing in many stories. Several folks revealed the names of their teachers, neighbors, friends, even their pets and livestock, but the identities of parents or other important characters weren't given. Second, many contributors did not identify pictures or make corrections to their first draft copies. We're sure this resulted in many errors (and perhaps lost photographs) but we did the best we could. Third, each contributor accepts full responsibility for his or her submission and for our interpretation of requested changes. Fourth, because some of the submitted photographs were photocopied or "computer printed," their quality may be very poor. And finally, because there was never a charge, "fee," or any other obligation to contributors to have their material included in this book, we do not accept responsibility for any story or other material that was left out, either intentionally or accidentally.

We hope you enjoy this unique book as much as we enjoyed putting it together.

The Hometown Memories Team
August 2014

TABLE OF CONTENTS

The Table of Contents is listed in alphabetical order by the story contributor's last name.

To search for stories by the contributor's hometown or year of birth, see indexes beginning on page 321.

Ronald Abe	111	Dixie L. Brinkman	23
Harold E. Adams	151	Diana Carbonaro Brown	59
Andrew C. Agnew, Sr.	61	Cheston H. Browning	225
Leon Amtower	86	Jerome E. Burch	276
Marlyn Angus	67	Linda C. Burgess	319
Anonymous	257	James H. Burkett	298
Zona H. Apple	28	Shirley J. Burkett	166
Robert Armentrout	121	Sandra D. Butcher	175
John D. Arthur	214	Joe Etta Caldwell	190
Sylvia Baer	91	Marion E. Caldwell	259
Sandra Bailey	172	Eileen V. Capel	95
Ferrie A. Ball	139	Susan P. Carey-Powell	285
Karen L. Barker	97	Janice M. Carper	67
Loretta F. Barlow	164	Cora Carter	102
Janice Cooper Barnes	218	Miller Celia	67
Leonard B. Barron	52	Theodore W. Clark	106
Betty J. Baum	35	Doms J. Clutter	49
Donna Beal	230	Judy Compton	148
Iona Crites Bergdoll	198	Carolyn R. Cooper	64
Rosco E. Bergdoll	313	Gary L. Cooper	211
Sue Bergdoll	291	Barbara Corbett	304
Ethel M. Bland	205	Leoda Cox	255
Mary Alice Blizzard	150	Louise Smith Crist	270
Margaret Boggs	66	EveLina Crouse	94
James Bohn	113	Mary Arlene Currence	149
B. (Bo) Bolyard	55	Freeda E. Davy	72
Maxine M. Bond	317	Verda Davy	145
Forest David Bowers	53	Beverly Day	311
William Euene Bowers	233	Reba Deremer	101
Margaret Boyd	210	Mary Donna Didawick	81
Nettie G. Bright	91	Anna Maxine Dishong	268

Name	Page	Name	Page
Judy Dolechek	206	Harry Handwerk	189
Patsy Dopson	157	Edna Hargett	236
Robert E. Drury	20	Carl Harr	89
Hilda Jane Dunham	318	Jim Harr	228
Jean Catharine Durst	287	Charlotte Eye Hartman	84
Sandra Earp	197	E. Jean Hast	53
Mayo L. Eaton	292	Alma Maxine Hebden	291
Norma Eisner	45	Barbara Heilig	71
Barbara L. Epperson	39	Vivian E. Helsley	22
Bernadine Evans	192	Patricia A. Henson	221
Violet R. Eye	131	Joanne Hesse	207
Gary Fadley	46	Mary E. Higgins	190
Mary M. Fike	316	Susan Kilgore Hill	31
Madeline Fisher	140	Wanda R. D. Himelrick	143
Normand R. Fitzgerald	92	Betty Workman Hohman	155
Helen Cottrill Fitzwater	281	Loretta Hoover	25
Calvin Flanagan	133	Beverly A. Horn	109
Zack T. Fleming	126	Kathy Hovatter	72
Charlotte A. Folk	168	Paul W. Hoye, Jr.	137
Judy Mallow Footen	199	Dottie Hughes	15
Anna Mary Fratz	186	Irene Hughes	76
Ruby Froman	149	Evelyn James	146
George B. Funk	293	Carolyn V. James-McKenzie	63
Jack W. Furbee	180	Billy Jenkins	148
Phyllis Garcia	154	Judy (Bergdoll) Jenkins	201
Darlene Ash Gaston	296	Sharon F. Keefer	17
Maggie Gensel	50	Cecil Kelley	92
Virginia George	136	Jacqueline Kerns	28
Ruth Gift	231	Darlene/Frances Kesner	220
Laura Ann H. Glascock	288	Wilma Lee Ketterman	254
Dorothy P. Glotfelty	196	Stanley Kile	278
Sidney Williams Gooding	293	Cherly Kilgore	117
Carolyn Marie Grapes	189	Lana J. Koontz	195
Ronnie L. Grove	245	Phyllis A. Lambert	38
Kay B. Halterman	135	Robert Eugene Lambert	191
Janet Hammond	315	Robert M. Laughlin	44
Chuck Hampe	216	Alice Sipes Lease	168
Anne Hampton	30	Elsie Lewis	162

Name	Page	Name	Page
Helen M. Lewis	212	Audrey Hedrick Nelson	265
Janet Light	93	Hubert Nestor	284
Raymond E. Litten	299	Glenda D. Kiddy Newcomb	251
Johnny Logan	301	H. Ward Nicklin	99
Viola M. Logsdon	115	Martha Palmer	205
Violet Lowery	138	Elsie Mae Parsons	70
Nina I. Mahoney	241	Marilyn Perdew	285
Phyllis Malone	33	Marlene Stevens Perkins	170
Diana Marine	65	Joseph Petrone	106
William J. Martin	118	Sharon Carr Phares	286
Hazel Mason	253	Donna J. Pierce	161
Mary Ann McCauley	208	Bob Poland	238
Pat McKnew	68	Bud Poland	152
Angeline W. McPeak	208	Faith E. Poland	68
Margaret Meadows	87	James A. Poland	178
Harry W. Meek	107	Linda K. Poole	114
Susan Meyer	234	Paul David Powers	57
James Michael	107	Richard Aaron Pownall	206
Stephen Michael	30	Ernie & Betty Racey	222
Barbara S. Miller	36	John Edward (Eddie) Racey	173
Nina V. Miller	139	Betty Rader	242
Ralph F. Miller	50	Shirley J. Ravenscroft	124
Vicky Miller	229	Betty R. Ream	254
Robert C. Moats	183	Kitty Reeves	32
Harriett M. Moon	150	Therman W. Rexroad	204
Barbara Moore	147	Roseanna Rexrode	290
Vivian Moore	128	Mary Ellen Rich	310
Kathryn Moreland	83	Junior W. Rickard	264
Patsy D. Morgan-Runkles	77	Ralph E. Riley	79
Marna Meyers Morris	34	Carolyn R. Bobo Rinker	26
Norma Lee Muir	256	Mary Ritchie	74
Juanita B. Mullenax	215	Mildred Roach	69
Diana Murphy	48	Roger Roderick	240
Nada Murphy	238	Richard Runkles, Jr.	147
George Myers	44	Eva Sager	314
Clara O. Mynhier	138	Enid Saville	292
Sidney Ray Nazelrod	175	Robert Glen Schoonover	193
Richard Neal	253	Mona R. Schultz	149

Name	Page
Linda Sechler	75
Susan Bailey Shambaugh	202
David Shapiro	112
Wanda Sharp	33
Willard Sheppard	142
John Sherrick	51
Dr. Carleton A. Shore	108
Barbara Shroyer	41
Deloirs Simmons	288
Evelyn E. Sims	209
Kenneth Sims	217
Joyce E. Skidmore	307
Ila Slonaker	23
Ernest Huey Smith	295
Glona Jean Smith	237
John Smith	260
Ruby Nell Smith	294
Virginia C. Harr Smith	213
Arlene Snyder	69
Delores Ann Snyder	247
Donald L. Snyder	95
Hallie M. Snyder	140
Jessie Snyder	185
Maxine Souder	146
Darrah Speis	283
James E. Spinks	236
Pauline Sponaugle	188
Iris B. Stegmaier	96
Bill Sterner	239
Laverne Stewart	138
Don Stilwell	169
Sally Arlene Armentrout Stump	261
Betty J. Taylor	194
Ruby O. Teets	80
Carol Ann Smith Teter	223
Darlene Thompson	78
Jerry Timbrook	158
Donna M. Turner	146
Annabelle Vance	273
Rose Elizabeth Vance	294
Thelma Wagner	144
Floyd W. Wakefield	18
Samuel L. Wakefield	139
Wayne C. Ward	134
Jean Warren	43
Evelyn S. Webster	193
Patt L. Welsh	153
Barbara Walker Welty	171
Betty Wertz	243
Margaret Whitacre	262
Edith Wilson	45
P. D. Wilson	109
Reba Wilt	104
Joe Winebrenner	44
Harold L. Winters	106
Victoria Younker	137
Mark A. Zembower	73
Richard A. Zigler	249
Index A (Hometown)	321

The Tales...

True stories intentionally left just as the contributor wrote them.

First Books, First Cars, and Baby Brothers
By Dottie Hughes of New Creek, West Virginia
Born 1940

My First Book

One day I was going through a large brown envelope filled with mementoes. I opened a little, worn book and began to read *Wonderful Tony*, about a rooster who was friends with a duck. Tony was sad because he couldn't swim like the ducks. He began to help Mr. Robin dig for worms. When Mr. Robin became full, Tony ate and ate. Tony grew and grew until one day, Mr. Hawk picked Tony up, but the farmer shot Mr. Hawk and Tony fell into the pond. His feet touched bottom, and he walked out.

The date in the little book was December 25, 1947. I was seven years old when this little book was given to me by a cousin of the same age. This was probably my first book that belonged to me.

I remember those days in a one-room school when a new box of books would come from the county office. Oh, the excitement of choosing a good book!

There was no television and for several years, no radio in our home. My sister, brother, and I would settle in a corner and to some faraway place on an exciting adventure tour, we would go.

It has been 67 years since that little book was given to me. The desire to read is still great. Luckily, I chose a mate with the love to explore in the land of books. Without intending to, we have passed this love of books to our three children, our grandchildren, and now to the great-grandchildren.

My father treasures books, as his mother did also. My father had the talent of making books and their characters come alive in our imaginations.

I have a desire to visit some of the western states because of the places I've been in Zane Grey's books. Janice Hold Giles takes us to Piney Ridge, and we spend a few days with those wonderful hill people. Corrie Ten Boom, Catherine Marshall, David Wilkerson, and Norman Vincent Peale are some very inspiring Christian writers, but the greatest book of all, the Bible, feeds the soul and guides our life. My oldest son tells me that he remember when he shared the rocking chair with me and his baby brother as I read Bible stories to them.

Books are good friends to be cherished, treasured, and shared with others.

The Night My Brother Walter Was Born

I guess one of my first memories was the night that my brother, Walter was born. I remember a bed made for me on the kitchen table. I guess little three-year-old Bea was there, but I don't remember. Later that night we were taken to the barn by Odell and a bed

Bea, Dottie, and Walter

was made in the feed bins of the stable. It was cool that November 6, 1945 night. I can remember Vance Harris coming to the stable that night. I don't remember Bea going to the stable with us, but I am sure she did.

Later, we were taken back to the house. There was a step down from the kitchen into the living room; they always referred to that room as the house. It was years later that I learned that this room should be called the living room. I remember that right inside of the living room, close to the step down from the kitchen set a table with a kerosene lamp on it. On the table set a pan of water. Grandmother Minnie Michael was sitting in the chair holding a little baby and giving it a bath. I can imagine that Bea and I looked at this little one, wondering about it. Our mother lay in the bed over in the corner of the living room. Grandmother Michael was a small, quiet lady with her wire rim glasses sitting on her nose.

The picture of Thomas and Rebecca (Harris) Rotruck was watching all the happenings of that night. Thomas and Rebecca were the parents of Grandmother Lulie. It seemed like their eyes watched us through the growing up years. Is that why when I first began doing genealogy in the very early 1970s, I chose them to begin with?

It was the custom in those days for a lady who had just given birth to be in bed for ten days. It was during those ten days of bed rest that Herbert arrived back from the service, bringing a wife with him. Mother had been moved to the bed in the little bedroom.

I remember Bea and I were out behind the house playing when we looked up and saw them coming. We hurriedly ran into the house to tell them that someone was coming. There were two more people added to this already full house. I don't remember much after that, but I do remember a few arguments and Judy wanting to return to her home. She was from the city, and it had to be quite a change to come back into these hills with people that she was not used to and did not know. Later, they moved to the Serie house down under the hill from where we lived. Four of their six children were born in that house.

Memories of those very early years are scarce. I remember some time, and it may have even been before brother Walter arrived, but the O'Briens who lived down in the Serie house at that time were there one night. They were hiding candy or something from me in the old sewing machine drawer, and I was to find it. I think Mother bought the old Serie place from the O'Brien family in about 1943. Mother used the money that Daddy sent her from the service to buy those 47 acres.

Years later when I began doing genealogy, I wondered why it was called the Serie place. I went searching in deed books to see who the different owners had been. I saw where often times in deeds it was referred to as the Sarah Rinker place. I remember Odell used to call a sister of Judy's who was named Sarah "Serie." Then I realized that was the way the older hill people pronounced the name Sarah.

My First Car

I have often wondered whatever happened to my little '51 Chevrolet. After I traded it in, I used to look for it like someone would for an old friend. I would look at the cars on the road, in parking lots, on used car lots, and on the street. I never once saw it. Now I hope it is someone's antique car and goes to antique car shows.

I bought my little '51 Chevy in 1959. It was a two door all black car. A spotlight was fastened to the side by the mirror. It was against the law to spotlight deer, and it was never used. It was a straight stick, meaning there was a gearshift. In those days, most cars were like that. The dimmer switch was on the

Dottie's first car

floor and there were no signal lights. I used arm signals when turning.

I bought it from Ludwick's in Moorefield. Galen Whittaker, Gene's brother-in-law had been looking for a car for me. I went to the Grant County Bank and borrowed the $350.00 needed to buy it. It needed the motor overhauled. Gene and his brother, Russ did that for me.

Galen delivered it to Petersburg High where I was going to school. I was not used to driving and very unsure of myself. Judy Bible, a fellow classmate, drove it to her home on Thorn Run, and I drove it the last eight to ten miles to my home.

I have often wondered and felt that God must have helped me drive that car. I made several stupid mistakes that taught me a lot about driving, but not I or the car ever got hurt. One time coming out of the ridges, they had just plowed the roads. I got over too far and slid into this deep ditch. Grandmother was riding in the back, and she fell on the floor. She did not get hurt. Later it was very funny. I had to be pulled out of the ditch.

There was the time that Kathy took the bottle of baby aspirins in the later summer of 1961. Gene was not home, and I went up and got in my little car that we seldom drove. I couldn't get the garage door all the way open. I was scared and needed out, so I decided to back into it. I did not hurt my little car. I got it across the road and ran out of gas. Dovie Rohrbaugh came along and helped me push my car out of the road and took me out to where Gene was to get help.

I traded my little car in on the trailer when we bought it in the summer of 1962. I remember when they brought the trailer and were taking my little car down the road. I watched it go and wanted to cry. I told Gene I felt like crying. He said, "While you do, look out at the trailer." I traded my first car in on my first home.

The Crooked Tree

I can remember back in the late 1940s and 1950s as I walked this road to attend either the Popular School or to catch the bus to ride to Maysville Grade School and later Petersburg High School, we would pass this tree. It was small but nevertheless crooked. Probably at times, we would climb onto the seat and sit a while, pretending it was a horse.

Today the tree has grown much bigger. No children walk by it to catch a school bus but many people drive by, as the people who once grew up in the ridges are returning to build homes there. I look at it each time I drive into the ridges, and I marvel at its beauty as the memories come back.

This tree sits on the curve below the area that was known as the Old Shed. It was always called that because an old shed had sat there at one time. When I was growing up, I heard the story of a man being killed there when he was loading logs on a wagon. In my searching of genealogy, I cannot find out who it was. Even May did not know. If I just knew the year or even a name would help, but when Grandmother was talking of these things, I was not interested and did not remember. Oh, how foolish I was.

The road at the Old Shed would go down Emmie Hill, which was very steep and rough, to the old Alfred house. We would pass it and keep walking and come to Aunt Mag's house. The old goose would meet us at the gate, announcing our arrival. I was afraid of the old goose. Emmie Hill was named after Emma Likins, the mother of Alfred. The ridge people always stuck an "e" on the end of names.

My Memories of Washdays
By Sharon F. Keefer of Cumberland, Maryland
Born 1938

Washday was usually on Monday.

The water may have been heated in an oval, shaped copper vessel that was placed over an open flame in the yard. Once hot, the water was emptied into the manual washer until it was at half or three-quarters filled. Then the rinse tubs were filled.

A manual washer had a dasher that set down inside the washer.

Now in earlier days, the wringer was operated by hand, however, in my memory, the wringer was hooked to electric. The electric also turned the agitator inside the washer. The rinse tubs set to the back of the washer so the wringer would turn and the clothes could be fed down into the first rinse tub where the clothes were rinsed by hand and fed into the wringer, which turned further, and clothes after their first rinse went down into the second tub. Rinsed a second time and then fed down into the clothesbasket. My Mom had a wash stick (broom handle cut to the right length, kept just for washing,) that she would pull the clothes up out of the water.

Keep in mind, the clothes being washed in cold weather the washer would go into the kitchen to be washed, however, when warm weather arrived it was usually done on the back porch. Some ladies were fortunate enough to have a washhouse.

People living in the country never wasted the wash water, especially in warm weather so the porches were scrubbed, and the remaining water went to watering the garden.

Now the clothes were washed but now they had to be hung out to dry on the outside clothesline and you know there was an art to properly hanging the clothes. The straight clothespins were first and later snap pins.

The clothes needing to be starched were put into a starch bath and then the wringer. I remember seeing my Mom put the men's dress shirts into a stiffer starch for the collars and the cuffs. She was very particular about the shirts.

On a winter day in very cold weather, the steam from the warm clothes could be seen and it was very chilling to the fingers as the clothes were hung out. Mom would blow on her fingers to warm them. Also, the clothes would freeze stiff on the line.

The clothes had such a fresh smell and a freshly made bed was so heavenly.

Now when the clothes were taken down from the line, they had to be folded neatly to be ironed on Tuesday.

Supper on Monday after this washday was usually from Sunday left overs. I remember if it was left over beef or pork, my Mom made "Hunters stew," comprised of a broth, onions, carrots, and potatoes.

Tuesday, (no permanent press) the clothes were sprinkled individually with a sprinkle bottle, folded just right, and rolled and placed in the clothesbasket. Covered over when the basket was full with a towel to keep them from drying out. After it set awhile, then standing over the ironing board to iron. I remember the whites were always pressed first.

I was fascinated by my Mom's ironing and when I was large enough she would allow me to press the handkerchiefs and the pillowcases because they were flat pieces.

Can you imagine the time and love it took for Moms caring for a family? Is it any wonder there were more stay at home Moms? Grant you there were some working mothers but how did they handle such a time consuming chore?

I am sure there had to be more about washday but all of my childhood memories, these are what I remember.

Pap's Buckwheat Prank on GrandPap
By Floyd W. Wakefield of Friendsville, Maryland
Born 1930

People just can't live without water. That's why, back in the old days before electricity and running water, when an old timer found a good water spring on his land, he built his house nearby. So it was at our house. I carried many buckets of water from that spring. The springhouse was the only way we had to keep the milk and butter cool between meals. I carried that too.

The spring overflow drained into a pond where the horses and cows drank. The pond water was used for another purpose, too.

My Pap, Lloyd, and his brother, Walt, owned a Frick steam engine, sawmill, and threshing machine. The sawmill was located below the pond. The steam engine was used to operate the sawmill and it used a lot of water to make steam for power. The two men did all the work. Pap could tell how much steam he had by the sound of the puff of the engine.

I played around the sawmill and steam engine. I loved to sit on the bank and watch them work. I was so fascinated by the wheels and engine and how everything worked.

When harvest time came, they shut down the sawmill. They hooked the steam engine to the threshing machine and went around to the farms in the community, threshing their crops of wheat, oats, and buckwheat.

That big steam engine pulling the threshing machine created a lot of excitement chugging along the narrow dusty road. Some neighbors would break stones and put them in the road before the steam engine arrived, knowing it would roll them in and make the road more solid.

Commodore Wakefield in his blacksmith shop

Pap and Uncle Walt sold the steam engine, sawmill, and threshing machine when I was only 7 years old but I still remember them.

It was hard times back then. The WPA was formed. Pap got a job with them running a steamroller where they were building roads.

I spent a lot of time playing around the pond where there were a lot of bullfrogs. I made a slingshot from a strip of inner tube rubber with a slit in it. I used a grain of corn for my ammunition. I was a pretty good shot. I could hit the frog on the chin and roll him. One time I couldn't resist aiming for the red comb on the rooster's head. It hit him right on the comb and down he went. I thought, "Oh my! I've just killed Mother's rooster!" Boy was I relieved when after a while he got up and appeared to be OK.

My mother always raised chickens. We would take eggs to the country store in exchange for groceries or other merchandise. One day I went to the chicken house to gather some eggs. I found more than I could hold in my hands, so I put some in my pants pockets. I hurried to the house, excited to show Mother how many I had found. When I got to the house and began to take them out of my pockets, to my dismay, they were all broken. I handed them to Mother. She took them and threw them back at me! Yuck!

MaCabe, the one room school that we attended through 5th grade, was near our home. Sometimes my brothers and I wouldn't get all our chores done before time for school to start. We would finish our chores and then join the other kids on the playground at recess and go inside when the bell rang, hoping no one would notice.

The country store (Noah Frazee) was ¾ mile away. I was often sent there for something. Along that road my uncle Commodore lived and had a blacksmith shop. If he was working I would stop and watch him as he heated a horseshoe, and then pounded it into shape. Then he dipped it into the water trough to cool it before nailing it to the horse's hoof. I would cringe when he drove the nails, thinking it must hurt the horse's foot.

Sometimes we would visit Uncle Commodore and Aunt Pearl in the evening. She would tell so many ghost stories that we were nearly afraid to walk home in the dark.

I was often sent to the store to get a glass gallon jug of kerosene for our lamps. Carrying that heavy glass jug sure was hard on little fingers. One time Mother sent me to buy a new lamp globe. I chose a pretty globe with a white design painted on it. On my way home the school bus came along. Being a bashful little boy, I climbed the bank to get out of the way. In doing so I dropped the bag with

Lloyd Wakefield on the steam engine and Walter Wakefield on the threshing machine

the globe inside. It rolled down the bank and broke. My heart nearly broke, too.

When I was around twelve years old I had to do the plowing. We had a Number 10 Oliver one-horse plow. I had to begin plowing very early in the spring to get all the fields plowed in time for Pap to plant the grain.

I remember when Pap took the back seat out of our 1925 Dodge Brothers car and hauled 25 bushels of buckwheat to the gristmill at Hazelton, WV, to be ground into flour. I got to go with him and go in the mill and watch while they ground it. During those hard times we ate a lot of buckwheat cakes.

Pap used to tell us about a trick he played on Grandpap while he was a young boy still at home. One evening Grandpap said, "Boys, the buckwheat is ripe. We can cut it down tomorrow." They all went to bed. It was a pretty moonlight night. Pap waited until everyone else was asleep. He sneaked out of the house, got the cradle that is used to cut grain, and walked to the field of buckwheat. The field was about ¾ mile from the house. He cut all 5 acres of buckwheat, walked back home, and went to bed. The next morning Grandpap said, "Well boys, let's go cut that buckwheat." Pap didn't say anything. When they got to the field and saw the buckwheat was all cut down Grandpap said, "Well, I wonder who did that." I don't know if Pap ever told him that he had done it.

Saturday nights were fun in our community. Great Uncle Sam never married. He loved people and he loved music. He owned and could play several instruments, from mouth harp, guitar, mandolin, and fiddle, to organ. He taught several people how to play. Musicians, singers, and neighbors would gather at his small cottage to play, sing, or just listen and visit. Often the crowd would fill his house and some would sit outside on the grass. This went on for several years until television and Hee Haw came along and took its place.

I've seen a lot of changes in my 83 years. Grain is now harvested with modern equipment. The Hazelton Mill still grinds grain. We still like buckwheat cakes.

I can recall the steam engine and all those happy boyhood memories every day. I feel blessed that I own and live on a few acres of the old home place that has been in our family for three generations. I still have that little plow that I walked behind plowing the fields so many years ago.

War Years in the Mountains
By Robert E. Drury of Allison Park, Pennsylvania
Born 1931

I was only ten years old when Pearl Harbor was bombed and our country entered World War II. At that time, I was not aware about the devastation that war caused, so when the army came to our mountains for training, it was an exciting time for me. I marveled at seeing all those soldiers and their equipment go by our house—Jeeps, artillery pieces, trucks, and tanks.

As time passed, I became more aware of how serious this war stuff was. I grew up during the Great Depression, so we really didn't have much. I remember that on many Sundays my mother would have several soldiers in for a chicken dinner. My mother was very patriotic, and this was a way for her to help the war effort. The soldiers talked about where they lived and what their jobs were in the army. They also told me I could help many soldiers by using my bicycle to go to the store to get things for them like gum, candy, sodas, and various snacks. I could also make some money. It wasn't long until I got out my bike and was doing just that. I would go out on the many dirt roads were they were camped. I would also go up to their trucks as they came through town and frequently stopped. When I

Floyd "Buster" Wakefield and his plow and Studebaker

was able to go to their camps, they sometimes gave me "K" rations and canned "C" rations that they often complained about. I really liked them and was very happy to get them.

My dad also did his part for the war effort, although later I did not understand the necessity of it. Every so often at night, our town fire whistle would blow. That was Dad's cue to get his "blackout" sign and go to one end of town where Route 32 entered. Another man would go to the other end of town with his sign. When that particular fire whistle sound blew, everyone was required to turn off their lights, including any automobiles coming into town. The reason for doing this, I was told, was that in the event of an air raid to our capital or other targets, if the planes were unsuccessful in dropping all of their bombs, they would probably then drop them on any targets they could see. I might have been scared a little then of being bombed, but looking back now, we probably lived in one of the safest places in our country.

I saw or heard of many things that happened during the time the soldiers were in our mountains—some were not good. One story was about a couple of soldiers who were bivouacked in the Dolly Sods/Seneca Rocks area. They somehow fell into a rattlesnake den. Both of them men died from the bites. Another story was about three soldiers who drowned in the Blackwater River in the Blackwater Canyon. There was a cable strung across the river, and when the first soldier fell off, a second soldier went into the water to save him. Then another jumped into save the second, and all three were lost. Across the canyon from the current, Blackwater Lodge is a viewing area called Canyon Point. From there, one could see where the cable was strung across the river. It is now down. When you look at the river from Canyon Point (around 1,000 feet from the top to the bottom), it looks like you could easily step on rocks to cross the river. This is actually hard to do even when the water is low. When the river is high, it is practically impossible.

In 1944, a terrible tornado came through our mountains. We still had soldiers camping at various places, and some were between the town of Thomas and Davis, my hometown. I remember at some time in the middle of the night there was a lot of commotion and everyone was awake and up. The next day I saw the devastation. The tornado had hit several West Virginia towns—and Thomas was one. The tornado then came through the soldier's camp and between our town and the town cemetery. Our house was about a half mile from the tornado's path. We were very lucky. I remember seeing all those soldier items—clothes, cans, tents, etc. spread up the tornado's path up the Davis Mountain.

Another startling thing happened during that tornado. My aunt Cora (affectionately called "Cocoa") lived next door with her sister and other members of the family. Her daughter and granddaughter lived in a two-story house on the Bunker Hill area of Thomas. Her daughter's husband was in the Navy and already in the war. For some reason, my aunt decided to stay with her daughter that night. When the tornado hit Bunker Hill that night, they experienced the wildest thing one could imagine. All were sleeping and were abruptly awakened when the tornado hit. When their eyes opened, they were surprised to see that they were no longer looking at the ceiling—they were looking into the night sky! The tornado literally took the whole roof off as though a huge knife swiped through the top of the house and chimney. The chimney bricks were all around their bed, but not one brick hit them. The tornado then crossed the street and demolished a house, killing three people. My aunt Cocoa lived to be almost 100 years old.

Sometime after the tornado, the army moved out, but while they were here, they left their marks. There were many muddy roads, trails, and campsites. Part of the training was artillery shots across Brown Mountain at targets in Canaan Valley. The northeast part of Canaan Valley was wild and uninhabited with the exception of a few hunting camps. A large part of the area was a huge bog because of beavers damming up the streams. Much of this area is now part of the 500th U.S. National Wildlife Refuge. One of the stories concerning this area was that the army had lost a tank in the bog and couldn't get it out. The story goes that the tank is still there. Who knows? Maybe this might be another good reason to visit the refuge. Find that tank!

When the army moved out, it was still a pretty exciting time for me. My school buddy and I would ride our bikes or would walk to all the areas we had found where the soldiers had been. We looked everywhere to find something worthwhile. I brought lots of army items home. Some of the items were canned "C" rations, shell casings, and clothes. One time I brought home a hand grenade. It was really a dud since it had a small hole in it. That didn't make any difference to my mother! Boy, after that encounter I was *very* careful what I brought into the house!

There was one incident I never told my mother—or anyone for that matter. One day, my school buddy and I got on our bikes and peddled up the railroad grade along Blackwater River. We stopped where the Blackwater River exits Canaan Valley. That place is known as Camp 70. We then started looking for campsites opposite Camp 70 on the lower part of Brown Mountain. Then we hit the jackpot, or so we thought. We found a cylinder filled with bags of black powder. We figured that this powder was what they used to fire their artillery shells. But, what good did that do us? We weren't sure what to do with the powder, but I was sure of one thing—there was no way in hell I was going to take black gunpowder back home! My buddy decided to keep one bag. We then hid the rest and went on our merry way.

When we got back to Camp 70, we pondered about what to do next. We knew of a couple of hunting camps in the valley. The nearest one was Snyder's Camp, but we had been to it before. The next nearest one was Bill Burley's Camp. It was located on the other side of the valley. We did have our bikes, so we were able to ride on the old railroad grade most of the way. When we got to the middle of the valley, we had a tough time getting our bikes through that area since the beavers had their way about covering the road with water. Finally, we got though that water and muck, and then in the distance we could see Bill Burley's Camp. It was in an open area several yards from the tree line. We had heard of Bill Burley's Camp many times, and now finally we were going to see it.

Most deer camps were never locked, so we had no problem getting inside the camp. After entering, we proceeded to check it out. We made ourselves at home. My buddy built a fire in the camp stove and then we sat down to eat. Soon after eating, my buddy said, "Run." I soon noticed why, as he took that bag of black powder, opened the stove door, and threw that bag into the stove! We made it out the door before I thought the camp was blowing up. We watched as smoke was billowing out the door, windows, and chimney. It looked as though the camp was jumping off its foundation. When it was all over, we went back inside to check. Wow. After all that noise and smoke, there wasn't any damage. Boy was I happy about that!

Now that I'm in my later years, I occasionally have some dreams about those times. The most vivid one is seeing a dragon puffing all that smoke out of its mouth and nostrils, at Bill Burley's Camp!

The Birthday Man
By Vivian E. Helsley of Green Spring, West Virginia
Born 1945

The sirens sounded, and we scurried under our desks. The lights were turned off, and the blinds were closed. It was the only sound that could be heard until it was announced over the loud speaker, "This is only a drill, and it is now all clear." Going to Flintstone School in the 1950s, this was a regular occurrence and it frightened us.

Going home added to the sense of fear. When playing with my brothers and sisters, we were all aware of an approaching airplane. Mom would tell us all to come inside and be very quiet. We would listen and wait for her to smile and say, "Oh, that's only a (some name of a plane)" and then we were allowed to continue our play. Sometimes Mom would read us a letter from her brother who was fighting in Korea. When the war ended, the school drills ended, but we continued to fear the planes.

My mom was a very special lady. She had seven children, and she knew how to make each one of us feel special. One day after we came home from school, Mom could not be found. We called out for her as we searched. Running out of options, we looked under the house. There in the crawl space and to our surprise, was our mother, busy dying Easter eggs. She was so busy getting ready for the Easter Bunny that she hadn't heard us.

Birthdays were always very special. A cake and a present for the birthday child could be counted on. But our present had to be found.

Vivian's home place

The Birthday Man would deliver the present sometime during the day. On our special day, the Birthday Man would fly over our house and drop a present off just for us. We would listen for the plane to come. When planes flew over our house, we would run outside, looking for the Birthday Man's plane. Then we would run around the outside of our house, searching for our present. Sooner or later, there was a wrapped present delivered by the Birthday Man. We started to look forward to the Birthday Man each year.

As we grew older, it became a game of catching Mom as the Birthday Man. We would take turns watching our mom on those special days. On one birthday, my sister saw Mom's feet as they entered through a bedroom window. It had been fun.

The Birthday Man lived on. My children and grandchildren experienced the Birthday Man bringing excitement to their birthdays, although at that time I thought it was just a nice way to entertain them and make them feel special.

It was only after September 11, 2001 that I understood how truly, wonderfully creative my mom had been. America had been attacked, and we were under a no fly zone. I was an adult now, outside doing some work in my yard, and I could hear them coming; helicopters were getting closer and closer. I could feel my throat closing and my chest tightening when they came over the mountain. As they came into sight, I could see the American flag and USA on the wings. It was at that moment that I knew. I understood why I had a Birthday Man. My mom had used our imaginations to teach us that we didn't have to fear the planes anymore.

Washday at Grandmother's
By Ila Slonaker of Capon Bridge, West Virginia
Born 1923

When I was a little girl, before school age, I spent a lot of time at my grandparent's farm where my mother had grown up. One memory has stayed with me all my life.

When my grandmother washed clothes, we went across the road, which is not far from Slanesville, West Virginia. About a short way across the road was a spring. My grandmother would build a fire over a big iron pot. She then washed the clothes when the water was hot. When she had washed them, she put them in another tub, rinsed them, and then it was my turn to hang them to dry on a big maple tree's limbs, which was the clothesline. It wasn't easy, but it worked.

It was good for me to learn how to do things, even if it was not easy. Today I really enjoy all the things we have to help us.

The Saville farm

Miss Maizie and the Potomac Hotel
By Dixie L. Brinkman of Cumberland, Maryland
Born 1934

To this day, I can't hear the far-off lonesome whistle of a train without remembering some of the best years of my life spent visiting with my aunt, Maizie Kitzmiller at the Potomac Hotel on Ashfield Street in Piedmont, West Virginia. Maizie signed with the Piedmont Hotel Company the third day of August 1934 and at the young age of 24, she made her last payment of $258.27 in April 1937.

There was nothing new or refined about the nostalgic old hotel that Maizie operated with the status of a large facility for over 50

The Potomac Hotel

years. It was just a quiet, comfortable place for those depending on it for their home.

People entering the lobby from the main street of town could always find comfortable old Mr. Dye seated on the settee with his cane, talking with friends who stopped by.

The entrance to the dining room which had tables dressed with white tablecloths, a flower vase, and cloth napkins, was sandwiched between the wide stairway on the left of the lobby and the wall to the right. The entrance to the kitchen that reeked with the aroma of crispy fried chicken was located on through to the back of the dining room.

I'll never forget the time I saw Maizie take off after a thief she caught sneaking out the back door of the kitchen into the alley and bring back the ham she had baked for dinner. She wasn't afraid of anything.

Maizie had the best of help with her kitchen and dining room, but when I was around she'd let me help fill the saltshakers and sugar bowls. I remember one time when my cousin, Hilda was visiting we got the bags mixed up. We put the salt in the sugar bowls. After Maizie gave us a lengthy scolding about not being careful, she handed us a lunch tray to take to Grandmother, who couldn't handle the stair steps and went on with her work as if nothing ever happened.

Maizie was fussy about her guests and made sure Laura Clay had all the glasses chilled for the ice tea and the coffee cups warmed as well as the dinner plates.

After she examined every detail in the kitchen, she would head for her beauty shop on the second floor at the top of the stairs. If things were running late, she'd show up with a bowl of nice hot soup and a light roll for her patron whose appointment had run over into the dinner hour.

Maizie's shop was always a fun place where everybody was welcome. I'll never forget how my friend, Eleanor Bane, and I groaned every time we thought about the time my Aunt Millie, Maizie's youngest sister was visiting from California. Aunt Millie offered to fix our hair while we talked to Maizie, who was down on her knees measuring material spread out of the floor for new drapes. We couldn't run fast enough to Murphy's Five and Dime Store to comb it out.

Despite the noise and pollution from the trains, another aspect of the old hotel was the big porch overlooking Piedmont from Ashfield Street. Grandmother spent a lot of time with her close friend, Ms. Graham there.

My cousin, Harold, and I love to reminisce about Maizie and how anxious she always was to help everybody. "When Melvin and I decided to get married," I said, "Maizie dug

Miss Maizie

out the silver and punch bowl, opened up her dining room, and gave us a grand reception fit for a king." Harold laughed when I told how she tied my nighties all in knots and gave us the best room in the hotel for the night.

Harold and I spend a lot of time going through pictures of the people Maizie cared for: Ms. Patterson; Ms. Joanne; Krista Lambert, the cute little girl that Maizie always wished belonged to her; and faithfully devoted little Laura Clay, who always referred to her as "Miss Maizie" and kept things running smoothly for her at the hotel. But most of all Maizie loved her family. She knew the family tree better than anybody I know.

Like many others, Maizie's life suffered from change. In time, she gave up the old hotel that was still as unchanged as the mountains and moved in with Grandmother and Mr. Dye. She opened up her beauty shop at another location on 2nd Street.

Maizie is gone now, but I can still hear her beautiful voice. She died on September 28, 1999 at the age of 88 and sleeps side by side with her parents in the Odd Fellows side of Nethken Hill Cemetery in Elk Garden, West Virginia.

Dixie L. Brinkman

Sunday Dinner at Grandma's House
By Loretta Hoover of Friendsville, Maryland
Born 1952

In the summer, when the weather was nice and the old country road wasn't all snowed shut, it was not unusual for Grandma and Grandpap to have 30 to 40 visitors or more for Sunday dinner, what modern folks now call lunch. You see, Grandpap had 18 siblings, five children, 19 grandchildren, numerous nieces and nephews, and a lot of friends and neighbors who would stop by all through the week as well as on Sunday.

Grandma would be up early starting to gather and prepare food for the company that was sure to come. While fellowship was going on and Grandma put the finishing touches on the meal, everyone could wash up in the old, white granite wash pan with the red trim on the rim, using water carried from the springhouse in a two gallon galvanized water bucket and homemade lye soap.

The old square table topped with patterned oilcloth was spread with garden vegetables of all kinds: potatoes, corn, peas, green beans, shelled beans, turnips, beets, carrots, parsnips, fresh sliced tomatoes, and little green onions standing like soldiers in the wide Mason jar. Along with the garden produce, either fresh or canned, Grandma would serve up her homemade pickles, spicy brown apple butter, and homemade elderberry and apple jellies in her fancy cut glass dishes. There was always homemade bread, sliced thick and served up with fresh churned butter from the day before. For dessert, my mother always made a huge applesauce cake iced with seven minute frosting in the broiler pan that came with her first electric stove.

Men always ate first, women guests and children next, and then those that prepared the food, usually Mom and Grandma, and whoever hadn't already eaten earlier. After eating, some men smoked in the living room. Grandpap smoked his pipe filled with Cutty pipe tobacco from the brown paper package. A couple of men took naps while others played horseshoes in the yard, and still others spun yarns on the front porch.

While the tedious task of cleaning up dishes and putting away any leftovers from the big meal was ongoing, someone would invariably say, "I'll eat the rest of this so we can have a pretty day tomorrow," while taking the last bites from the once heavy-laden bowl. The women would catch up on the health of all the neighbors, express their sadness when news of a death occurred, rejoice when news of a baby's birth came, question each other about gardens and how many jars of goods each had put up for the coming long winter.

Kids ran through the yard and barnyard, yelling and laughing. Some would sneak into the garden and snatch peas off the vine or pull baby carrots, wiping the dirt off before crunching the fresh vegetable. Some took turns swinging. The swing was nothing more than a rope that was tied to the old apple tree's limb with a wide board that had notches cut in each end to keep it from slipping. Some kids made mud pies using jar lid as molds and decorated them with flower petals. Others dipped their toes in the drain from the springhouse that ran across the road and down the ditch toward the hog pen.

Every now and then one of the kids popped into the springhouse for the coolest, best drink ever. Inside the cool, dark room was stored in brown or gray crocks of various sizes and shapes the fresh milk and cream that had been skimmed from the top of the milk until there was enough saved to fill the tall, green churn for making butter. Around the crocks flowed the cool running water that served as a refrigerator.

When the day was winding down after hours of visiting, one by one the various families would say their goodbyes while my grandparents extended the usual invitation, "You come back now anytime, you hear!" The others would head for home, leaving just our family, for we lived on the farm with my grandparents, Grandma and Grandpap and the couple of people who always seemed to be staying "a few days" to reminisce about the day. Invariable, we would end up on the porch, listening to the "knee deeps" (spring peepers) or the bullfrogs. There we would listen to the oft repeated stories and happenings of earlier years.

Some of the stories that particularly frightened me and the rest of the youngsters were tales of the big cat that roamed the night around the farmhouse and surrounding neighborhood. Some said it was a panther, but few ever saw it. Hunters would try to kill it, tracking it with their hunting dogs, but often the dogs came back severely wounded or never came back at all, only to be found later with huge gashes cut into their flesh. Once it was very close to the old farmhouse and when the dogs frightened it, it ran through the garden fence, tearing down a section of fence while it made its getaway. On another occasion, a neighbor was out late at night and had the sensation that something was following him. He was very sure something fierce was on his track when he heard the big cat's yowl behind him. It scared the poor man so badly that he ran right through the big rose bush in his yard in an effort to get into his house. His face and arms were scratched pretty badly from the thorns on the bush. Often at night, as I lay in bed with my grandmother, we could hear the big cat going up and down the creek that ran not too far from the house. It would make me snuggle a little closer, thanking God that I was inside and not out. Frequently, one of the other kids would come to Grandma's room exclaiming, "Did you hear that?"

On the less scary nights as I lay in Grandma's bed, she would practice my spelling with me when I was very young. She would start with "at" and then all the words that you could spell by adding a first letter to "at." Bat, cat, hat, pat, sat, she would say until I dozed off to sleep. When I was not the lucky occupant in her bed, I could hear from another room the familiar and comforting routine with someone else until I drifted off in quiet slumber in an old fluffy feather bed.

Lest We Forget the Backhouse
By Carolyn R. Bobo Rinker of Smyrna, Delaware

For those of you who didn't grow up in the '30s and '40s as I did and missed the days of the "backhouse." I feel sorry that you were so unfortunate. I will attempt to enlighten you as to just how unfortunate and even deprived you were. It was truly a memorable experience.

I grew up in a small rural community near Mt. Storm, West Virginia. Electricity and indoor plumbing were nonexistent for several years to come. This meant no one had or had even thought of an indoor bathroom. Not even sure we were aware of the existence of such. What everyone did have was a little house in

Carolyn and Wendell Bobo in 1943

the back yard known as the backhouse. For the most part, they all looked pretty much alike, except for the fact that some had two holes to sit on instead of just one. We were only a one-holer family. I was somewhat taken aback the first time I saw a two-holer. I have tried many times to imagine a scenario when you are sitting there and in comes another person and greets you with a hearty, "Good morning!" "How are you this morning?" And then the answer back (with a grunting) would be, "I'm just grrrreeeeaaatttt. And you?"

When I was around nine years old, I was visiting our neighbor girls who were around my age. It was not uncommon for friends to accompany one another to the backhouse and wait outside the open door 'til they were finished. On this one occasion when my friend opened the door to their outhouse, what to my wondering eyes should appear but a THREE-HOLER—two big holes and one little one! I was thinking, Poppa Bear, Momma Bear, Baby Bear? Now get a life-size picture of that in your head. Dad, Mom and one of the kids enjoying a blissful morning relief!

One day, one of my boy cousins and I were listening in on a conversation at the dinner table concerning a prank one of the adults had played on another relative by throwing rocks at the outhouse while he was in there. They were laughing hysterically, and we thought it was very funny, too. It was like a light bulb came on in our heads when we looked at one another. This cousin was notorious for getting into trouble, so this was right up his alley! I wasn't exactly a stranger to pranks either.

Off we went to prepare for our victim, whoever it might be. We not aware of the fact that only two or three rocks had been thrown in the story we had just witnessed. Instead, we gathered an arsenal of rocks ranging in size from a quarter to that of a small apple. Then we hunkered down, waiting with baited breath for our victim to head for the outhouse. To our dismay, it was Manny's dad! He had a temper that few people could match and little or no sense of humor. We let fly with a nonstop barrage of stones. I'm not sure how long we held him hostage. He was afraid to come out for fear of being stoned to death. When he finally did come out, he was so enraged and red in the face he could have easily passed for an Indian! Somehow he managed to miss the humor of the whole thing.

Many years later when Manny and I were reminiscing about the ornery things we did as kids, he said that incident got him a spanking

Students of one of the one-room schoolhouse in 1920s-30s

when he got home that day. Summertime added interest to outhouses. When you opened the door and stepped inside, you might see the big black hairy legs of a wood spider hanging on the edge of the seat that would disappear under the seat with the speed of lightening. Then you were left to sit there and try not to imagine where it went and how near those hairy legs were to your butt!

One more thing you would notice was the lack of toilet paper. No such thing existed. Instead was a stack of old Sears & Roebuck and Wards catalogs. You tore out a page and roughed it up between your hands to make it softer. Guess I should be grateful we didn't have the baskets of corncobs used by generations before us. There would be two baskets—one contained red cobs one contained white. Red ones were used first and then white ones were used just to be sure. Thus, the old saying, "Rough as a cob."

There you have a few of my outhouse day memories. So now, when I have to get up in the middle of the night in a sleepy haze, I'm mighty glad these are not the "Good Ole Days!"

Memories of My Grandparents
By Jacqueline Kerns of Cumberland, Maryland
Born 1933

I just had my 81st birthday, and my favorite memories of the good old days are the times I spent with my grandmother in Green Spring, West Virginia.

I remember sledding on wooden bob sleds that my grandfather made. I also remember playing with my uncle in the woods, swinging on wild grapevines and falling in piles of leaves. My grandpop whittled us whistles out of wood to blow if we got lost.

I also remember Grandma's sugar cookies. She frosted them with powdered sugar and tinted them with a bit of juice.

Grandma didn't have electricity, but we made do. We carried water from an old mountain spring, and Grandma had a springhouse with a stream running through it that she kept crocks of milk in. The iceman brought a block of ice once a week for the icebox in the kitchen.

These were the good old days with my grandparents.

We Came from Rags to Riches
By Zona H. Apple of Berkeley Springs, West Virginia
Born 1927

I was born on August 10, 1927 in Hampshire County, a R.R. village called Okonoko located along the B&O Railroad and the Potomac River. My first memory was when my dad came home from work and told Mom that the stock market crashed, and he no longer had a job. Everything in the country came to a sudden stop. There were Mom, Dad, Grandma, and five kids at home at the time. When he got that paycheck that was it!

We had no modern conveniences at that time. Not only was the Depression bad, but

Carolyn Bobo Rinker at age 80

we had three years of severe drought. There was an island in the river, and Dad and the boys cleared it. We had the wood for the stoves, and they dug it up and planted that and the river bank and watered it from the river. My sister and I filled the buckets and Mom, Dad, and the boys watered it. This was a daily job. The river was so low that we could walk only ankle deep to the Maryland side. The well at home had a rope and bucket; I think that was called a windsal. It never went dry but got pretty low.

During this time, you can't imagine the number of people traveling the railroad from as far away as Pittsburg and Uniontown, Pennsylvania going to Washington to try and find work. They would return about three weeks later with no success. The storekeeper had given Dad credit, and Mom baked bread every other day. When they stopped, which was always, she gave them apple butter, bread, and coffee and sometimes a tomato. There were whole families among the people. Mom always said, "They aren't bums, just people looking for work!" This went on for three to four years.

The only trains for quite a while were passenger trains, as they carried the US Mail and only a few passengers. We would wave at the trainmen, and several times over the years, the cooks would throw off parts of hams, wrapped in B&O tea towels and newspaper. We would have a big pot of potpie then.

With the gardens Mom canned food, and we always raised three hogs and in the summertime ate ground hog and in the fall the wild game. Back then, no one posted the ground and all were good neighbors. The boys went night hunting for raccoons. One night they met up with a black bear. They ran the bear only to knock the back door down!

The winter of 1935-1936 was very snowy, and in March, it started raining. The result was the St. Patrick's Day Flood. Our area was hit hard, as we were near where the South Branch and Town Creek emptied into the Potomac River, and the big runs up the hollow above us. We lost the store, the post office, and six homes. In the morning, Mom noticed that the Edwards family wasn't among us, and they were still asleep. They got them out and 15 minutes later, their home went out and down the river. Our home was flooded but spared. I always felt it was because Mom had fed so many people. Mom felt God brought on the flood so people would be put back to work. The railroad was washed out from Cumberland, Maryland to Pawpaw, plus roads and bridges were washed out, too.

For recreation, up in the hollow were the falls, a big pool, flat rocks, and the long span downgrade of water on flat rocks with algae on them. We would undress and slide down them. We also hunted in the woods for dead pines, and got the roots to start the fires with. They are very rich.

I walked two miles, mostly uphill to a one-room school. All of my teachers were favorites. I loved school. In 1938, that school closed, and I went to a two-room school.

We got electricity in 1938, and things were getting a little better by then. In the 1940s, war was raging in Europe and Asia. After Pearl Harbor, we were in the wars in both places. I had four brother-in-laws and one brother in the war. Luckily, all made it home. I was in Pawpaw High School by then. Everything was rationed, especially gas, sugar, coffee, etc. So we walked to get around.

My girlfriend, Eva, and I would walk to Pawpaw on Saturday nights and go to the movie. Then we would go over to the only "watering hole" in town with the hope of finding a ride home.

It was at that time that this guy in his forties showed up in Pawpaw and got a job in the orchard picking apples. He went by the name Eddie Cooper. He seemed to like us; he would come and sit with us and buy us pop and sandwiches, so he was okay in my book. This Saturday night he told me he was going to move on as the picking apples was done. When arriving to school on Monday morning, the place was all a buzzing about the robberies over the weekend. They felt it was that Eddie Cooper. It seems that it was, and they caught him. His real name was Earl Johnson, and he was an escaped convict from Kentucky. He had robbed a bank there. "Once a thief, always a thief!" as they say.

I graduated in 1944 and married later that year. We lived for two years at Orleans Crossroads and then moved to Martinsburg for four years. Then we moved back to Orleans Crossroads, where we bought our first home. It was a five-room bungalow, fully furnished for $1,500.00. We lived there for 12 years and then bought this small farm in 1962. It had 30 acres and a farmhouse, barn, and one building for $6,000.00. That's to show the difference in prices now.

I had two children and foster children. In these years since I've been a nurse's aide, a waitress, done housekeeping work and worked for 15 years for Morgan County Schools. I retired in 1994. My husband died in 2001.

I tell you, I've seen it all, heard it all. I'm sick of wars, sick of hearing people complaining about the economy. They are never satisfied. I say to them, "You don't know what hard times are!" I'm thankful for what I have. Willard and I came from rags to riches, and we appreciated all that we had. To a lot of others, it is just folly.

Stephen's truck went through a bridge in 1979

My Truck Went Through a Bridge!
By Stephen Michael of Westernport, Maryland
Born 1954

Back about 1979, I was driving a Kenworth tri-axle coal and rock truck. We were hauling riprap rock for the new highway on Route 36 from Barton to Westernport. Part of the road was not finished yet.

We were crossing a little bridge by Harold Reeves' garage. I drove onto the 100-year-old bridge. About halfway across, it I heard a loud bang. My truck's back end went through the bridge and fell to the river, 12 feet below. The front end stayed on the bridge.

When my boss got there, he had his son, my brother, and me get in the bed and start throwing rock over the side. Then after ten tons were removed, we cut the pins at the top and the latches on the bottom of the tailgate so we could remove the rest of the rock. We had to cut the pins that held the bed onto its frame.

We called two riggers from Bellgrove up to pull the truck and frame up over the bridge. It took both trucks hooked together to pull it up and out of the bridge. It took several hours to get the cab and chassis out of the water. Then they had to get the bed up and then pull it up and over the part of the bridge that was still standing.

The road about 200 yards up from the bridge was only dirt, but the State had to open part of the road to Franklin so people could get to their homes. The State tore the old bridge down after that.

I was shaken up for days, thinking about the fall and sudden stop when the truck hit the water. All I could see was sky out of the windshield. My truck was sitting at a 70-degree angle. I am glad that's over. I was 24 years old when that happened. I am now 59 years old, and I still drive a coal truck for BTC Trucking from Barton.

A Wonderful Thanksgiving
By Anne Hampton of Baltimore, Maryland
Born 1946

It was the fall of 1951. It was two days before Thanksgiving and my father was psyched about the turkey. Every year, we would pile in the old Chevy and ride to Ellicott City to the turkey farm, and this year was no different.

We drove down a long, dirt road and parked right at the fence-in field. It was filled with loud, gobbling birds. We all stood by the fence while Daddy, as we all called him, tried to locate the biggest, plumpest bird. He made his choice and the farmer put the turkey in a burlap bag with his head out. The turkey then went into the trunk. We drove the 20-minute ride home. Mom was not real happy since the turkey weighed 45 pounds and she had to cook it!

We had a big cherry tree with a branch perfect for a swing. My dad tossed a rope over the limb and got the bird out of the trunk. By this time, word was out that Mr. Jim was killing his Thanksgiving turkey and kids flocked from everywhere to watch. My father tied the feet together and hung the turkey upside down to the rope. The turkey was still in the burlap bag with just his head out. It went real quick. Dad slipped his knife out and off came the head. The body flopped in the bag for a few seconds as the kids watched in awe.

Mom had the laundry tubs filled with boiling water, and my dad dowsed the bird up and down to loosen the feathers. The smell was "fowl!" We then all started plucking feathers until they were all out. Dad cleaned out the insides, keeping the liver, heart, gizzards, and neck for the giblet gravy. Mom would always act mad because the bird weighed between 38 and 45 pounds and she had a trouble getting it in the oven. The bird went from the tub to the icebox in the kitchen. Mom put damp towels over it to keep it from drying out until Thanksgiving.

Thanksgiving morning came early. Mom got up and stuffed the bird and got it in the oven. She had an enormous roasting pan of aluminum, which I still have. She made a foil tent and started him cooking. The bird cooked for hours. It was the best, fresh turkey with all the trimmings.

We all sat around the table while my dad proudly carved the bird with the sleeves of his white shirt rolled and his one and only necktie on. Mom wore an apron. It was me and my three older brothers at the table, along with my grandfather, and aunts and uncles, and their children.

What wonderful Thanksgivings I remember.

Growing Up in a Coal Camp
By Susan Kilgore Hill of Roanoke, Virginia
Born 1942

I was born in a coal camp in southern West Virginia and lived there until I was seven years old. The camp itself consisted of four-room, square-style houses, all similar, with black railroad ties for fences around the small yards. Everything was owned by the coal company, of course. This was the early 1940s, and there was no indoor plumbing. Each house had an outhouse. We bathed in a washtub in the kitchen and washed our clothes in a wringer washer. We burned coal in a fireplace to heat the house.

A small river, the Coal, bisected the camp, and a train trestle spanned the river. We could see the mine tipple, which cleaned and loaded the coal into the coal cars, from our front porch. A dirt road served as the dividing street in our section, so both dirt and coal dust were constant companions. Dusting the furniture and cleaning the windows and floors were almost daily chores. The school was a series of houses across the train tracks; one grade in each house, down the row through eighth grade.

There was a company store where we could buy practically anything that we needed, from food to clothes to tools. A portion of the miners' pay was paid to them in script, which could only be used in the company store. There was also a boarding house owned by the coal company for the unmarried miners. In fact, my aunt cooked meals there for them for a number of years.

There was a swimming hole in the bend of the Coal River under a bridge and a small sundries store that we called The Fountain across the road. The mountains rose high and close, encircling the camp, providing a beautiful setting for the hardscrabble lives of the people who lived there.

But the mines were booming in the early '40s during the war, which seemed a long way off and continued booming during the '50s. It was an isolated life, but the neighbors were friendly and congenial and evenings were spent visiting with folks who sat on their front porches. We kids ran wild, up and down the dirt road, in the river, and on the railroad tracks. I personally drove my tricycle down a slope into the river one day and was saved by a neighbor. I was also rescued from the middle of the trestle when a neighbor spotted a coal train coming around the bend.

The men worked long hours in the mines and the women just as long in the homes. Bank clothes, as they were called, had to be washed and lunches packed for the men. My dad's lunch box was round and shiny silver with two compartments, one for food, and one for liquids. He wore a helmet into the mines with a light in the front. He had to recharge the battery pack every day so that it would last throughout his shift. It was considered bad luck if the light went out during a work shift.

In later years, the coal company stopped providing housing for the miners and their families and sold the camp houses to any who could purchase them. They had improved the camp by that time by paving the streets and putting in sidewalks, indoor plumbing, and heating. But the coal dust remained, a constant film covering everything, including the lungs of the miners who worked so long and hard to mine the black gold from the mountains. It was many years before the term black lung was used to describe the illness many miners contracted in the mines. In fact, my dad died from complications from black lung.

Indeed, growing up in a coal camp was a unique experience.

Seeing President Truman
By Kitty Reeves of Westernport, Maryland
Born 1939

My name is Mae Catherine Reeves, although I've been called Kitty since my birth on April 24, 1939. I was delivered by Dr. Raymond Reeves (no relation) at the Reeves Clinic in Westernport, Maryland. My parents were Harold Robert Reeves, a darned good mechanic, and Elsa Helen Reeves, a very smart housewife.

Westernport is one town in the Tri Towns, the other towns being Luke, Maryland and Piedmont, West Virginia. Westernport was so named because it once was the farthest port west on the Potomac River. In its heyday, the Tri Towns had a number of thriving, locally owned businesses. What couldn't be found here could be found twenty-some miles away in Cumberland, Maryland, county seat of Allegany County.

Although the Tri Towns are considered a rural area, there are numerous towns and unincorporated areas all around within a twenty-mile radius. In the good old days of my childhood, there was plenty of entertainment, such as circuses, carnivals, county fairs, and the like. Also, each town had schools and churches, which were the centers of community activities.

Outdoor activities such as swimming, boating, and picnicking have always been an important part of life in western Maryland. Places such as Deep Creek Lake, Savage River, and Swallow Falls offered respite from workaday life and they still do.

Kitty Reeves with her father, Harold Robert Reeves, and the dogs

One outstanding memory I have is when my parents woke me up sometime after midnight from a sound sleep to go down to Keyser, West Virginia to see President Truman. My mother had seen in the newspaper that Truman, who was campaigning for re-election, was on a whistle stop tour of the country. His train was due to stop at a railroad crossing in Keyser, so Truman could give a speech.

When we got there, it was very dark, but about 20 or more people had already gathered. Pretty soon, a conductor came out on the caboose of the train and said that President Truman was asleep, and he didn't want to wake him. After some loud grumbling from the crowd of onlookers, the conductor said he would see what he could do.

In a few minutes, Truman appeared wearing a topcoat over his pajama. My father held me up on his shoulders so I could see the President. He spoke for maybe fifteen minutes and thanked us for being there. I didn't understand what Truman was saying, but I was impressed by his "down homeness." I was happy when he beat Thomas Dewey, the Republican candidate.

Chicken Pox and Blackberry Picking
By Phyllis Malone of Springfield, West Virginia
Born 1946

When I was small, I played in the water of an old wringer washer on the back porch. I got the chicken pox and a cold at the same time. I was hospitalized, and my head swelled up to the size of a gallon bucket. They put medicine in my head every half an hour.

We lived on a farm. My brother would take a corn stalk, touch the electric fence, and then touch us girls with it so we would be shocked.

Dad would go to the barn to milk the cows, and the old cat would ride on his shoulder to the barn. Every time my brother would milk the cows, we would catch him sitting there squirting the milk into the cat's mouth.

One summer, my brother took an old purse and stuffed it full of paper. He tied it with a string and then put it in the middle of the road. The campers came down and saw the pocketbook in the road. They got out and bent down to pick it up. My brother pulled on the string and laughed about it.

When I was a child, my parents and the neighbors would get together and play cards. I was only five years old. I would crawl under the table and unlace their shoes. They would have to re-lace them before they could go home.

I was in the first grade, and one day my mom wanted to know who was in my class. As I was naming the names, I told her that one of the kids was named pump handle. She laughed at me, and I got mad.

My favorite teacher was Mrs. Browning. She would take a child out to spank them, beat the coats on the wall, and tell them to yell and cry. Then they would come back in the room laughing.

My dad was a self-taught veterinarian. After my brother left for the Army, he had to rely on us girls, so we all became involved in medicine.

When I was growing up, I learned to drive by driving an old Farmall tractor.

The first phone we had was a rotary phone. When we got a call, everyone on the party line would listen in to the conversation.

When I was growing up, we never had a television. I can remember rock and roll and J.F. Kennedy's assassination. I was coming out of my sister's beauty shop when I heard of the 9/11 attack. It was very horrifying.

My older sister and I decided one day to go blackberry picking. We had our children with us. As I started to put my hand on the bushes, I saw this snake as big as my arm. Needless to say, the berries and the snake stayed; my sister and the rest of us left.

Spankings at School
By Wanda Sharp of Elkins, West Virginia
Born 1939

I lived in the old town of Spruce, a railroad town that no longer exists. The only way to get to it was by foot or in a motor car. I was three when we moved there and the first time I got to go to a town, I was six years old. My first grade school teacher took me home with her for the weekend. She lived at Cass. I seen my first movie that weekend. It was a western starring Gabby Hayes. I also got to go to the company store and had my first ice cream sundae. I thought Cass was a real big city, and I talked about my visit for a week afterwards.

We had no electric in Spruce, only cold running water. We used oil lights. Mother had a gas wringer washer. My younger sister got her arm caught in the wringer. It lifter her off the floor before we got it shut off.

We had a wind-up Victrola. It played 78 records. I remember records by the Carter Family and Bill Monroe and his brother, Charlie. They had one real sad song about a little girl called "I Hear a Sweet Voice Calling." We also had a piano that played rolls. We had a battery radio. We listened to the *Grand Ole Opry* on Saturday night. On weeknights, we listened to Amos and Andy and one called *Life with Luigi*. It was about an Italian boy. He was always writing a letter to his mother. He always started with "Dear Momma Mia."

We had to make our own fun things to do.

We used the old catalogs to cut out our paper dolls. Then we would cut out clothes to fit them. Another thing we would do was sit at the table with a magazine called *Look*. We would open the magazine to the first picture and tell a story using the picture. The first person used it to build up the story to a certain point and then passed the magazine to the next person, and they had to continue the story using the next picture.

I got several spankings at school. I got one the first day for throwing my book up on top of the schoolhouse. One time, I was kept in at recess while the teacher was outside with the other kids. I took her colored chalk and drew all over the walls. I got a whipping for that. One time, I was kept after school and before the teacher got around to the whipping part, someone came to the school and told her that the woman she was boarding with had punched a wire in her eye and needed her. She locked me in the schoolhouse and I waited a while. Then I raised the window and jumped out and went home. I guess the teacher forgot; I never did get that whipping. I never got a one that I didn't deserve, and I deserved a lot that I didn't get.

We got our first television in the Fifties. It was black and white. My dad would sit for hours watching it. It was so snowy that it looked like clothes in a dryer going around and around. Half of the time, he was watching the test pattern and thought it was a picture.

Dad's First House
By Marna Meyers Morris of Cumberland, Maryland
Born 1938

My name is Marna Meyers Morris, and I am 76 years old. I was born and reared in Cumberland, Maryland. My parents were Robert Lee Meyers and Bertha Webb Meyers. I was the youngest of three children; Joyce Lee was born in 1930, Robert William was born in 1935, and I came along in 1938.

This is a story about how my dad came by his first house. At the time, my parents and two siblings were living with my dad's mother, Effie Rebecca Meyers on Sommerville Avenue in Cumberland. My dad's father was deceased.

Marna's parents, Robert Lee and Bertha Webb Meyers

My dad was employed at the bolt and forge shops by the B&O Railroad. He was a blacksmith's helper. My mother was a stay-at-home mom. They were saving for a home and struggling. This was following the Great Depression in the early 1930s.

One day when my dad was at work, a fellow employee asked if anyone could use some building materials. It seemed he had recently built a house, and his wife had just left him. The house was located in Magnolia, West Virginia. A company wanted the land but not the house. The house had to be torn down and removed. The gentleman was looking for someone to tear down the house and remove it. My father was a most anxious volunteer.

Dad had no truck and no money to buy one, so he borrowed an old truck from a Mr. Webber on Maple Street. After working his shift from 7:00am to 3:00pm at the B&O, he would take his borrowed truck, drive to Magnolia, dismantle the house, and cart it to Cumberland. Dad was careful to mark the pieces and draw up floor plans. My dad did not have much formal education, as he only completed sixth grade. He was the youngest of 12 children. He had quit school to help support the family after his father died. He worked at the glass factory for ten cents per hour for a ten-hour day. He made $1.00 a day at ten years old.

I guess you could say that my dad built the first "pre-fab" house in the area. He dismantled the house and carted it to Cumberland. He also went about making his own concrete blocks using a hand mixer and forms He could only make a few blocks each day. I don't know how long this took but looking back, it must have been quite an accomplishment.

My dad had help digging the foundation by hand, but it was eventually completed. He laid the block and reconstructed the house. It presently sits at 21 Blackiston Avenue in Cumberland, Maryland. The house has two bedrooms, a living room, a dining room, a kitchen, a front porch, and a full basement. It is a very attractive bungalow.

I was born in that house in 1938. It's only in my later years that I can really appreciate the life that my parents provided for me; values, fair play, justice, caring, sharing, faith in God and country, fellowship with friends, helping hands to neighbors, security, and trust.

In those days, we could leave our houses and cars unlocked, walk anywhere in town at night, make agreements without a written contract, pray in school, discipline our children, and take a man at his word. I am proud of my parents, my life, and wish we could go back to a time when my dad built his first house.

Handy Hancock
By Betty J. Baum of Warfordsburg, Pennsylvania
Born 1928

My husband and I bought a one-room cabin back in 1964 not far from Hancock, Maryland. We found it in the classified ads of the Baltimore newspaper. We travelled the 120 miles up to see this cabin in the woods. We were fascinated with the location and the beautiful scenery, but most of all the cabin was near the quaint little town called Hancock, Maryland.

What a gem of a town! It had everything. Now, my husband and I were both from the city and this little town seemed to have everything, if not more, than we needed. It was a river town right along the Potomac River, and also a mountain town where the Appalachian Mountains were visible all around. It also had the C&O Canal and a railroad and a railroad station right behind the stores and buildings. There was a library in the park and a creek where everyone would go fish. There were several gas stations that gave away coupons for gifts, a car dealership, several banks, a general store specializing in penny candy, two auto parts stores, two hardware stores, a barber shop and a hair salon, two drug stores, several grocery stores, a shoe store, a clothing store, an appliance store, a dime store, and a feed store. There were several churches, a school, a drive-in movie, a Dairy Queen, several restaurants, and even a Skate-R-Bowl. It also had two doctor's offices, a dentist, and a veterinarian. And all this was in less than a mile. We would come up on a Friday evening and Hancock would be buzzing with activity. These streets were crowded with shoppers and people just out for an evening's enjoyment.

Robert Lee Meyers

Betty's cabin

The little town was known as Handy Hancock.

There were a few special events there during the year that were particularly memorable to me. One was called Canal Apple Days. During this day in the fall, the businesses would set up their goods outside on the street and everything revolved around the apple industry, since the orchards were located on the outskirts of town. There was apple dumplings, apple pie, apple cider, apple butter. Yummy, what a treat.

The other event that sticks out in my mind was the Halloween parade at night. We would travel to Hancock after work just to see this parade. We would go to our cabin first and dress extra warm and then go into town and sit on the curb all bundled up to watch this two-hour parade. Food venders were everywhere with hot chocolate, coffee, hot soups, and funnel cakes. Then we would go back to our cabin and regroup and head back the 120 miles to the city. It would be near midnight when we got home, and then the next day we would get up early and go to work, but it was all worth it. What fun!

After nearly 30 years of travelling back and forth to our cabin in the mountains, my husband and I decided to move there permanently after we retired. We added on to the cabin and are still there today. Hancock is not the same as it was back in the '60s due to the malls that have popped up, but it is still pretty handy today. It has the Rails to Trails where the train tracks used to be. People come from all over to walk and ride bikes along the canal. An antique mall is now one of the big attractions. The river still has boaters and fishermen. There is no longer a dime store, but there is now a dollar store. We now have three parks. The Canal Apple Days event is still in the fall, but it is now held in the park even though the apple orchards are all gone. And the Halloween Parade? It is still one of the main events of the years, and we still go and sit on the curb all bundled up, but we don't have to go 120 miles back to the city and get up early the next morning. We are happy to be able to stay and get everything we need in handy Hancock.

What a Thrill!
By Barbara S. Miller of Keyser, West Virginia
Born 1943

These are my memories of a really wonderful time in my life. Those of us who were born in the Second World War times know about a lot of things said and done from

The Kesecker family in 1961

Barbara, Patti, and Brian in 1948

that time. We were called war babies. Our parents loved and protected us. My mother was Florence Kesecker, better known as Flo and my dad was Cleophas "Cokey" Kesecker. They raised my sister, Patti, my brother, Brian, and me in a strict home. We didn't get away with much. In our day, talking back or out and out misbehavior was not allowed. If we didn't listen, we paid the price. We were put to bed without our supper. It was tough sledding, but we learned to listen. We were taught respect. Years later, I thanked my parents for loving me that much.

I remember Thanksgiving and Christmas in 1949 on E Street in Keyser, West Virginia. Mom and Daddy had the Christmas tree in the right corner of the parlor. I guess I was about five or six years old. The tree was near the window. As I came down the steps, there was a red and white table and chairs in the corner. Then I saw a cupboard with dishes, pots and pans, and everything I could ever need for a tea party. There was a doll on the chair. Daddy had made the cupboard for me. Boy what a thrill! This was my best Christmas.

We later moved to New Creek in the fall of 1950. Growing up in the 1950s was fun. There we had a radio and a record player. Daddy liked his music. He liked Guy Lombardo, Woody Herman, and the Dorsey Brothers.

We didn't get television until 1953; it was a Crosley ten inch. It was black and white, of course. We didn't get a color television until 1957. The antenna was on the roof for the signal. The picture was snowy, but was that ever a thrill. We liked to watch Pinky Lee, Hey! Guess What? He was from West Virginia and was one funny guy. We also watched *The Milton Berle Show*, Danny Thomas' *Make Room for Daddy*, *I Love Lucy*, *I've Got a Secret*, *Cartoon Capers*, *Casper the Friendly Ghost*, and *Mighty Mouse*. I loved *Suzie Snowflake* on WJAC TV, Johnstown, PA Channel 6 at Christmas time. They still show it on occasion at Christmas time. We didn't have time to be bored. Life was great.

Mother and Daddy had a big radio that we kept in the dining room. We would listen to WWVA, Wheeling, West Virginia, to country music. We listened to our local WKYR radio station in Keyser, also. I can remember the song "I'm Looking Over a Four-Leaf Clover;" I can't remember who sang it, though. I also remember listening to *One Man's Family*, *The Great Gildersleeve*, *Ozzie and Harriet*, *The Lone Ranger*, *Gunsmoke*, etc. My imagination would try to figure out what the people on the radio programs looked like.

We got a rotary telephone in the 1950s. My daddy was a railroad engineer, so we had to have it for his calls for work. Telephones in those days were party lines with eight people per line. My friends and cousins would call each other and all talk at once. My old lady neighbor would get on the phone and talk so long that we would have to ask her for the line.

I loved looking at the stars, and my daddy would say, "Bobbi, come look. There's Sputnik going across the sky." We could hear it beeping; what a thrill!

We Think We Have It Hard Now
By Phyllis A. Lambert of Franklin, West Virginia
Born 1946

We didn't have a bathroom in our house until about 1970 or 1971. Oh, those cold, cold little trips to the outhouse. When we sat down it wasn't on a soft, heated seat. We didn't sit and ponder too long, especially at night. In the summer time, we would open the door slowly and look in to make sure there were no snakes and, of course, spiders. We had some spiders that were pretty big. I think our Little Brown Shack Outback is still standing at the home place.

My mom had several wringer washing machines, but her first one was a washboard that she scrubbed our clothes on. She would stand for a whole day, scrubbing until her knuckles would bleed. She also had to heat her wash water in iron kettles over an open fire outside. There were ten kids plus Mom and Dad to wash for. A couple of the older girls, Sally and Arvella would sometimes help her. And we think we have it so hard now.

When we kids were younger and in school,

Phyllis's mom, Ida with her children in 1949

my mom would make most of our clothes, plus her own. There were five of us girls. She could look at the dresses in a catalog and cut herself a pattern. She would cut out the fabric and sew it up. She did a lot of sewing with all of us kids. She sewed by hand until my Grandma Fanny loaned her a treadle sewing machine. Three of us girls learned to sew from Mom. I feel like I kind of got to pay her back a little bit by making clothes for her.

I started first grade in 1951 in a one-room school known as the Dahmer School. My favorite teacher was Mrs. Verna Smith. She was good to all her students. The students would take turns going for water. We would get a bucket full at a time. When we got it back to the schoolhouse, it was poured into a water cooler. We didn't have warm lunches; we packed our own. My brothers, sisters, (Billy, Charles, Delphia, and Butch) and I did our homework by lamplight. We didn't have electricity at that time. When I was to go into the fifth grade, they closed the one-room schools, and we rode the bus into town to Franklin Elementary School.

When I was a kid, my younger brother, William" Butch" Lambert, who was the

Phyllis's family in about 1940-41

youngest in the family, decided we were going to put one of Mom's laying hens to sleep. Some of my older brothers, Bill and Charles Lambert had done it, and it had worked for them. So we thought we would try it. So we caught one and tried it, as it looked easy. We tucked her head under her wing and slowly rocked her back and forth. Well, she went to sleep real easy. Needless to say, she didn't wake up. We didn't get into trouble, but we didn't try it again.

When I was a kid, we had an old wind-up record player. It was a Victrola. It played 78 records, the good ones.

When my mom was still living at home, she liked to play jokes on her brothers, Cecil and Ray Propst. They had chickens running loose instead of in a pen. Well, the chickens would mess everywhere. One had messed on the porch, so Mom got this idea in her head to put a hat over it, and then she hollered for her brother, Ray to come and look. She told him that she had a bird under the hat. If he wanted to see the bird, she would take the hat off, and he was to grab the bird. She took the hat off and he grabbed it real quick, but it wasn't a bird.

My mom used to live in a log house, which is part of it still standing. It is in Propst Gap, Franklin, West Virginia. She was born on July 31, 1904 to John C. and Lovina Lutheria Propst. On September 21, 1929, she married Arthur J. Lambert. They had ten children. She passed on September 12, 1982, and he passed on July 4, 1990.

Barbara's parents, Earl and Gladys Virginia Bowers with Barbara and Philip

Precious Memories to Pass Down
By Barbara L. Epperson of Martinsburg, West Virginia
Born 1942

Riding down a graveled, country road on a hot summer day on a creaking, heavy American Flyer bike held together with baling wire was the reward for a two-to-three hour stint of pulling weeds from our huge garden. My sister and my three brothers were each assigned a number of garden rows to weed or hoe before we were allowed to play. Gardening was a summer-long task until the veggies were harvested.

In between that task, there was feeding chickens, gathering eggs, baking homemade bread, housecleaning, canning fruits and vegetables, mowing the lawn with a push mower, slopping the hogs, and then hours of evening fun.

Our yard rang with cries of "You're it!" or "red rover, red rover, I dare you over!" or "hide and seek." After bath time, which was usually outside in a metal wash tub in the summer, Sissy and I would play ball and jacks, pick-up sticks, X's and O's, or connect the dots while our brothers were busy wrestling or fighting or playing Chinese checkers.

Before the advent of television, our older cousin would walk to our house two or three times a week to tell ghost stories. He had a real knack for scaring us half to death. It was always dark, as he would arrive late and then have Mom turn off all the lights. She would sit with us and pretend to be scared, too.

Our most favorite time was our adventures in a nearby wooded area. My brothers would pull the tops of small saplings down near the ground, and Sissy and I would take turns grabbing a branch and be swished up in the air and tossed to the ground when the sapling was let loose. We would then line up in a row in the field beside the woods and race from one side to the other and fall, panting to the dry, soft grass, with each one of us declaring we were the winner. Many an impromptu ballgame was played in the cow field beside our house, and many a foot stepped in a cow patty during those games.

Then the glorious time of winter arrived. It was magical time for us and the neighborhood kids. Back then, there was always a lot of snow during the winter months before global warming, and the snows would last for weeks and weeks. Twenty or more kids would gather on a favorite hill for sledding on the old-time wooden sleds with two metal runners and a wooden "steering" wheel. We would pack down a sledding lane by stomping up and down a hill until it was icy. There were never enough sleds for everyone, so we would line up down the hill and then jump on the back of the driver as they whizzed by, hoping we would make it to the bottom without falling off. Then came the arduous walk back up the long icy hill.

Barbara Lea Bowers in 1947

When hands, feet, and faces were almost frozen, we'd head for home to savor hot chocolate and warm buttered toast. Sometimes we would open the back door to the wonderful fragrance of roast beef and onions. Everyone wanted to hit the bathtub first, after we finally got indoor plumbing. But the standard rule was youngest first, and then by age to the oldest. My oldest brother always said he got the "soap scum" bath.

Brother John built wooden box traps to catch wild rabbits. He would bait the boxes with fruit or vegetables each night and then check the boxes each morning. If he caught anything, he would prepare it for cooking and then leave to catch the school bus. Baked rabbit stuffed with bread dressing was a suppertime favorite.

Mom and Dad taught all five of us to be good, safe hunters and taught us to hunt squirrels in the nearby woods. Mom would fry up a mess of cut-up squirrel. She served them with mashed potatoes, gravy, and home canned green beans. We did not start hunting deer until we were in our teens. This was like a bonus to augment the hog meat we had butchered earlier in the fall.

Dad worked as a conductor on the B&O Railroad out of Cumberland, Maryland and would be away from home for days at a time. When he was home, it was a special family time. Usually, if the weather was good, we would go fishing. We'd head for the creek (pronounced crik) for a day of fishing. Dad had taken two old car hoods and welded them together to make a boat, since we couldn't afford to buy a store-bought one. Only Dad and one kid could get in at one time. We always remembered whose turn it was the next time, even though it might be weeks later. If the fish weren't biting and it was warm enough we would hop in for a swim. Many a long summer day was spent lazily floating on an inner tube up and down the creek or river.

Just as our tummies were fed with good, wholesome foods, Mom made sure our souls were fed, too. We were faithful in attendance at the little; white community church located just a quarter of a mile from our house. We would all dress in our Sunday best and walk to the church on Sundays. Little cutout figures of Jesus and the Disciples and other Bible figures were put on a blue flannel board at the front of the class as our teacher was presenting the Sunday school lesson. We also attended Wednesday night prayer meeting, and the church was always full.

These are just some of the memories of the good old days that can never be relived, but these precious memories can be passed down to our children and grandchildren through the generations. They can reap the benefits of knowing how to live as we did in those good old days.

Make the Best of This Life
By Barbara Shroyer of Ellerslie, Maryland
Born 1944

Growing up in a small town cannot be beat, especially because there were no electronic games to keep the children indoors. We grew up when it was fun to go outside and play, ride our bikes, play marbles, hide and seek, fly a kite, trade comic books, go camping in the local woods, and simply explore the great outdoors in any kind of weather.

I had one brother who was older by one year and one brother who was younger by 18 months. We were not rich nor did I think we were poor, but it turns out by today's standards, we should have had all kinds of assistance. My brothers took the responsibility of watching out for me and including me in all of their adventures. We built tree houses where no girls except me were allowed. We also built go-carts built out of leftover parts from old bikes and any and all lumber we could find. The guys would ride those things down the hill, and it was my job to pull them back to the top again. It was so good to be included in their games.

The same went with our sleds. We had some of the fastest hills in the neighborhood to ride on. The one hill in particular was an alley, which had ice halfway down, and when we hit that, we really went flying. We kept one person to stop cars when a sled was coming down the hill. It turns out the ice was caused by the open sewer lines that ran down the streets and alleyways, because back then we did not have public sewage. We got so cold from our wet gloves; we would go home and hang them over the coal heat registers, then get dressed again and go back out and do it all over again until dark.

We were not getting into any trouble to speak of, nothing like today. Yes, we did the trick or treat tricks that all kids did, like upsetting outside toilets, soaping car and house windows, or throwing eggs at screen doors and running like crazy. Yes, we got caught and boy did we get punished for it, and yes, we did deserve it. Going door to door for candy was fun. I usually was the one who got the most candy, because I went around the entire town, sometimes twice. We were allowed to go trick or treating for two nights and without fear of something nasty being put in our candy. Some homes even gave us a nickel for the treat.

Barbara's family

We enjoyed trips to Cumberland to Constitution Park or to the Celanese Pool, where we could join our friends and enjoy a picnic with the family. The trips brought our family out of the house to spend a day relaxing, swimming, and having great food. Dad would always bring the biggest watermelon he could find and give it to the kids. During the summer, we could go to the local swimming holes for a swim. There were four places we could walk to, or we would usually ride our bikes. The swimming was great but we always had to have matches along to burn the leaches off of us. On one occasion, the boys decided to build a diving board so we all found big rocks and carried them to the side. However, no one was helping me lug one huge rock, and when I got to the diving board it slipped and fell against another big rock and smashed my finger. I was always the one getting hurt, but I was always included and that made it all worth it.

Like I said, we were not rich, but we had

Barbara with her siblings

good meals and good times together. Every Saturday night was party night. Dad would get a carrier of 16-ounce bottles of Cokes, a large bag of chips, and a stick of bologna. Mom would clear the table, and we would have a card game of setback or high low jick/jack. At 9:00pm, it was Gillette fight of the week that Dad always watched, and then at 10:00pm, it was time for the *Hit Parade*, followed by the 11:00pm movie put on by Alleghany Moon. We only had a couch and a chair, but the boys and I would stretch out on the floor and usually fall asleep.

We had to be separated for a short time due to our mother getting ill, and we were sent to live with our relatives. My oldest brother went to stay with our grandparents, my youngest brother was cared for by relatives in West Virginia, and I went to live with my favorite aunt and uncle in our hometown.

My aunt made a lot of my clothes. Sometimes they were made out of feed sack material, which at the time I thought was beautiful, with all the flowers on it. I went to Sunday school, that was when I realized I didn't have the pretty dresses like the other girls, and they made fun of mine. It hurt and so I would act like I went to Sunday school, but instead I would hide out until it was over and then go home.

My uncle was very protective of me, always making sure I was well taken care of. One time, I was riding my bike from our home over to see my aunt and uncle when a young boy two years older than me caused me to wreck my bike. I told my uncle who it was, and he marched that boy over to his grandmother and explained to her what he had done. Today, that young boy is my husband, and he still teases me for getting him a whipping he never forgot.

To make up for the shortfall of cash we never had, we would sell the *Grit* newspaper. We would also sell our handmade potholders, berries we had picked, and vegetables from our garden door to door. We loved to go to the local store to the penny candy window for a small bag of goodies. Also, we would use the cash to go to the movies in Cumberland on a Saturday. Since our dad was the local bus driver, he would put us on the bus, and we would go to the Garden Theater because it was the closest to the bus terminal. We would watch the cartoons and then a feature film, which was usually a Tarzan movie. Dad would pick us up and take us back home on his return bus run.

When our mother had enough of us, she would say, "Your aunt and uncle called and want to see you guys." We would go and find out it was a set-up to get us out of her hair. One time, we went over, and they were not home, so we got into a game of red rover in the back yard with neighbor kids. We were holding hands, saying, "Red rover, red rover, we dare Johnny over." That was our little brother. He charged us and instead of holding tight, we dropped our hands. He ran into a cherry tree and broke his arm. He walked home and after a trip to the hospital, he came home in a cast and we were in big trouble.

Getting into trouble was nothing new for the three of us. We were always thinking of ways to entertain ourselves, like the time we decided to play volleyball on the bed and broke the ceiling light. Or the time we decided to build a seesaw out of used lumber and forgot to take the nails out of the boards. When my brothers got off of their side of the board and little tubby me was left up in the air, I landed on a huge nail in the side of my knee. Of course, I had to get a shot due to the rusty old nail. Or there was the time we were cracking hickory nuts on the sidewalk and were fighting over the hammer. My older brother said, "You can have it then." He let go of the hammer and knocked out my bottom tooth.

Our family doctor, Dr. John Topper made house calls, and when that super tall giant of a man walked into our home, we three kids would scatter. His gruff voice always said, "Who is sick in this house now?" He would leave a jar of cod liver pills for the three of us. One time, my older brother dug a hole, and I threw those terrible pills in that hole, never to be seen again.

Going fishing was something my brothers loved to do, not me. I was scared of the fishing worms or night crawlers. The boys would hose down an area in the yard at night and then go out with flashlights and shine them on those huge worms and grab them before they would go back into the earth. One time, they made some kind of electric thing to shock those worms out of the ground and believe it or not, it worked. There were worms popping out everywhere. They knew how scared I was of the worms, and they would chase me holding those wiggly worms out in front of them. One time, I ran into the bathroom and locked the door to get away from them and forgot I had left the window open. They went into the garage and got a stepladder and got up to the window and threw that can of worms at me.

Another time, we were fishing at our favorite fishing hole, and I got to go along because I had a basket on my bike, and that was where we carried the worms. Like I said before, I would do almost anything to be included in the boys' adventures. They were good enough to put the worms on the hook for me as long as I carried the stuff back and forth on my bike.

Now that I am older, having raised my children and am helping watch my grandchildren, I think back to the good times we had. I would never think of allowing my children or grandchildren to do the things I called fun. I would never let them go to the swimming holes without an adult. I would never send them into the woods to pick berries by themselves. I would never allow them to go trick or treating without an adult to watch over them. Going to Cumberland before the age of ten on a bus to see a movie without an adult, are you crazy? I would never allow them to go door to door to strange homes trying to sell something.

As I await my 70th birthday, I look back with the many fond memories God has allowed me to share with you. Don't miss a moment of this brief period you have on this earth. Enjoy it with your family and friends. Just remember, you only get one chance on this earth so make the best of it, go out and enjoy it and never put it off. You just might not get that second chance. Just think, someone might ask you to share your good old days with them.

Sister Fell in the River
By Jean Warren of Moorefield, West Virginia
Born 1933

Years ago, what is now Allegheny Street went to the river. There were swings and picnic tables, and the water was over our heads. We went swimming in the summer time and skating in the winter. A T-shaped raft with a long pole was tied up there in the winter.

One December, we decided to get on the raft and push it out as far as the rope would allow. Just as I pushed off, my sister decided, she wanted off the raft. She went to step back on the bank and fell in the river. Everyone on the raft just froze and stared. One girl on the bank was yelling, "Get her! Get her!"

My sister went under twice. My brother, who was the youngest reached down before she went down for the third time. Then we all snapped to and got her back on the bank.

Instead of taking her home to get warm and dry, we jumped on the swings while she stood there shivering. We finally sneaked her through the cornfield to get home to change before Mom found out what we had done.

A Day with Wilma Lee and Stoney Cooper
By Joe Winebrenner of Keyser, West Virginia
Born 1935

As long as I can remember, the love of music ran through my veins, especially what we called "Hillbilly" or "Mountain" music, which now is called "Country" or "Bluegrass" music and I had a mess of it.

I don't remember the exact year, but as near as I can recall it was the summer of 1972 and I received a phone call from a man saying he was Stoney Cooper. I think I said something like, "Hi Stoney, this is Eddy Arnold," because I was sure it was someone just being silly. At this time of my life, Stoney and Wilma Lee Cooper were big stars; they entertained all over the country and we even heard rumors they were invited to the Grand Ole Opry. They were also from West Virginia; that even made it better. When the man on the phone finally convinced me that it was really Stoney Cooper, he said that they were traveling through and were going to have a show at the K of P Campground in Burlington. He explained that it was just him and Wilma Lee, they needed a couple pickers and he had called the local radio station WKYR in Keyser, and they recommended he call me. Curt Dellinger was a guitar picker in the band at this time, so we agreed Curt would play guitar and I would play mandolin. To Curt and me, this was the real deal. The day of the show at the Burlington Campground was a very nice day. Everything went well and we had a good crowd. To a country boy like me, it just don't get better than that.

Swimming in the Pond
By Robert M. Laughlin of Lantana, Florida
Born 1939

When I was a kid, my father used to take me and my friends on a hike to the mountains in western West Virginia. We always passed this swimming hole located on Stoney Run Road. My father would never let us go swimming in Stoney River Pond.

When we got back from the hike, my friends and I would go back to the swimming pond and take a swim. The pond was only three feet deep, so we thought we were in no danger. I am now 74 years old and will never forget swimming in Stoney Run Pond. It is just a memory now.

One day in February of 1975, I was on my way to work. A young deer jumped in front of my car and landed in a snowdrift on Snag Run Road in western Maryland. I had a shovel in my car, and I removed the snow to free the young deer. As soon as I freed the deer, he jumped over the fence and back into the wood! I really felt good about freeing that young deer.

Robert M. Laughlin

My Glory Days
By George Myers of Short Gap, West Virginia
Born 1939

In the summer of 1955, swimming at the lake was a daily thing, and in all truth, it was one of the few things we could do in our little town. The summers were hot and swimming was the best thing for keeping cool.

Our town wasn't anything special, just a town filled with small neighborhoods. But it did have its secrets. I recall one being Mrs. Smith and her many male callers who visited while her husband was at the office. No questions were asked by Mr. Smith until his wife informed him that she had a bun in the oven.

We weren't much into girls yet, so it was just us guys. Our favorite thing to do was visiting at the corner drug store for a milkshake and a soda pop.

Then on occasion or whenever we possibly could, we would sneak off to the places where races were held. We, of course, never raced ourselves, but something about the roar of the engine called us back every time. The whispers of our most secret dreams lay in the humming of an engine. The first time I sat behind the wheel of a car, I was reminded of what true freedom felt like. To this day, I still say that there is no one more free-spirited than a young boy with a racer's heart.

Before that summer was even halfway through, me and my friends had been through things that would bond us forever, things we would never forget. No life changing events happened that year, but even so, I'll never forget it. It was the summer when I was in the best of my youth and the part of my life that I loved the most. The glory days, my glory days.

A Lasting Impression
By Norma Eisner of Summit Point, West Virginia
Born 1936

About 1940, my family of Mom, Dad and two small daughters, would visit my aunt and uncle and their five children in Martinsburg, WV. We would drive eighty miles, a two hour trip usually, no freeways or highways, just two lane country roads. Their apartment was on the third floor with two bedrooms, a living room, kitchen, and one bath. That's eleven people and one bath.

On Saturdays, there was a farmer's market on Burke Street. I loved it; fresh veggies, eggs, home-canned goods, and hanging meat. Saturday evenings, downtown was packed, people in all the stores, sidewalks crowded and even "street meetings" held by different churches on Queen Street. This was my favorite place to visit in the whole world; this Aunt and Uncle owned a candy/ice cream store on the main street! What kid wouldn't love that?

On this fall weekend, Mom and Auntie cooked a huge turkey dinner. I'm not sure if Tom Turkey came from the Farmer's market or some other butcher shop. The evening started out swell. Uncle said grace before the meal, as he always did and we ate, as we always did. I mean, we cleaned our plates. The real fun began around ten p.m. that night. I awoke with a terrible tummy ache; got Mom up to take me to the bathroom; only one problem, there was a line! We waited our turn (some of us couldn't wait). That was embarrassing. It got worse, when we suddenly realized we would need ANOTHER TURN.

That "Terrible Tom" had his revenge. It was years before I could enjoy a turkey dinner. Now, seventy some years later, I still remember Tom, not fondly, but I do remember! That's kind of strange too; I can't remember my zip code or neighbor's name, but Tom made a lasting impression.

The Penny Tree
By Edith Wilson of Cumberland, Maryland
Born 1917

I was born in Rawlings, Maryland on June 27, 1917. World War I was just ending. The stomach flu was killing all the babies. I was about four or five months old when I got the flu. The doctor told my dad to make a box for me because I would die; he couldn't do any more for me. There was an old lady who lived up in the mountains. She dug up some roots, made a tea, dipped a rag in it, and fed me. She saved my life.

I remember the penny postcard and the three-cent stamps. We had a post office. Only two or three people could get in it at one time.

Edith Wilson and her classmates

Edith's Grandma with the cook for the workers in the apple orchard in 1922

I had two older brothers. They liked to do tricks on my younger brother and me. I had a doll made out of a piece of material. My brother cut the head off and said it got in a wreck and lost its head.

We had a backhouse. We didn't have toilet paper. We used *Sears Roebuck Catalogs*. One day, my brothers just put a little snake in the hole to scare me, which it did!

My mom took in washing. She rubbed the clothes on a washboard and ironed them for fifty cents. My dad worked whenever he could get a job, either picking apples or digging for coal in the mines. He got paid a dollar a day. On payday, he gave each of us kids a penny. We could get a lot of candy for a penny.

My older brothers had me and my younger brother, Vernon, bury our pennies so we would have a penny tree. We kept checking, but there was no tree. The older brothers dug our pennies up and spent them. Needless to say, they were always getting in trouble.

We moved up in the mountain in our grandparent's house. Grandpap had an old horse that was too old to work the garden anymore. So my brother, Louis, and I would go to the store and to school on him. Dad told the horse where to go. One day he failed to come to school to pick us up. They finally found him way up at the top of the mountain. They covered him up with dirt and rocks.

Our Best Halloween
By Gary Fadley of Cresaptown, Maryland

I grew up in Western Maryland, in a small Appalachian town called Cresaptown, which rhymes with "dress-up clown," just in case you care about how to pronounce things. Cresaptown, just six miles south of Cumberland on the Potomac River, was a town of only one stoplight, four bars, and a duckpin bowling alley. The summers were demanding on the General Electric fans that spun heavy steel blades, and the winters ate tons of wood and coal, but the people always knew how to have fun.

It was Halloween in 1966, but I was getting too big for trick or treat. After all, I was thirteen years old and trying to act older than that. The prospect of gaining a big bag of goodies, however, was enough to override my desire to act older, so I went trick-or-treating. I don't remember my costume—a hobo, I guess, which was the easiest costume that my poor mother could improvise. And I don't remember whom all I went gadding about town with that night, but I recall that two of them were Cletus and Leonard Hill, my own dear and roguish cousins, whom I had always admired for their creativity in making mischief. Leonard had long forgiven me for my having told on him for smoking, and I had long forgiven him for calling me a chicken sh@#.

Of the pack I was running with that night, I suppose that I remember that Cletus and Leonard were there partly because they always ran together, but mostly because Cletus was dressed liked a girl for trick or treat that year. And he did a very good job of it. He was the tallest and gangliest of the group—sort of an ostrich in dress and high heels. And his gracefully feminine costume in combination with his build was a truly comical sight. Still, however, there was a certain way the moonlight fell upon his bizarrely beautiful visage that rendered him fit for Cosmopolitan. I might have thought Cletus just a little weird for dressing like a girl, but I thought I was even weirder for thinking he was pretty.

So, after making our rounds through virtually every part of Cresaptown, our bags were dragging—our candy bags, that is. In probably less than two hours, we had gained more candy than a kid could get from a lifetime of collecting tonic bottles. But the night was still young; there was still time for mischief.

The people who give apples to trick-or-treaters must know what they are doing. After all, it's not rocket science to know that a kid with a pillowcase full of candy has no use for apples, unless it is to throw them at unsuspecting pedestrians and motorists. For those purposes, however, it is good that at least some houses think to give out apples. It is, after all, quite difficult to create a disturbance by throwing a gumdrop at a tractor and trailer.

Later in the night, after the windows were all soaped, after the phantom doorbell ringers were exhausted, and after the apples were all thrown, we found ourselves at Cresaptown's bowling alley, which was not much more than four or five duckpin lanes, an equal number of pinball machines, and a couple pool tables, but it was definitely a cool hangout. And now that I was a teenager, it was all right for me to be there—especially when Mom didn't even know about it.

I was just hanging out with my older cousins, Cletus and Leonard, and sort of just doing whatever they were doing. They were about fifteen or sixteen years old, so I guess they could do anything they wanted to do. So could I, as long as it made sense, and as long as I came home at a reasonable time. But a "reasonable time" was approaching, because Mom knew about how long it took to trick or treat.

We were hanging out around the pool tables, watching Jimmy Tyree shoot eight ball. He was absolutely impressive with a cue stick, and he was busy taking quarters and dollars off of guys who have to learn the hard way. Some of the people in the bowling alley were in costumes, but not Jimmy. He was much too cool for that. A dozen years later he would die from an overdose of heroin and that would not be cool at all, but he was certainly cool on Halloween night in 1966, with a real leather jacket, playing the part of the bad boy, and absolutely commanding the eight ball table.

There at the pool tables, Gary Von Stein and Wayne Van Meter showed up, and they were also in the mood for mischief, the theme of the night. Not only did they have the inclination, however, but they also had the tools, for they had in their pockets some very serious firecrackers: blockbusters and cherry bombs.

Our exit having gone unnoticed by bowlers, pinballers, and those hypnotized by Jimmy's coolness and eight ball prowess, we were soon outside and behind the bowling alley, contemplating the fun we might have with those high-performance firecrackers. Someone suggested lighting one and dropping it into a bottle to watch the bottle explode, but it was Leonard who came up with the most radical idea when he said, "Let's stick one up a cat's ass and light it."

Fortunate for the town's stray cats, someone suggested lighting one—a firecracker, that is, not a cat—and throwing it into a mailbox. That sounded like fun, so we were soon on one of the quiet streets in that area of Cresaptown that we call the park, which comprises the peaceful and loosely chartered streets on the north side, between Route 220 and the Potomac River. Nearly all the trick-or-treaters had completed their rounds, and the streets had become quiet again. Only an occasional witch, pirate, or mummy could be seen here and there.

We all gathered around a mailbox, giggling as quietly as possible. I had always been afraid of firecrackers because I had heard that they can blow your fingers clean off, so I stayed back several feet. I guess I stayed back as far as I could without appearing to be afraid, lest Leonard should call me a chicken sh@# again. Then he, Leonard, held the mailbox door open, while Wayne lit a cherry bomb. Next, after Wayne lit the bomb and tossed it into the mailbox, Leonard slammed the door shut, and we all took off running and giggling…

Boom! We hadn't run as far down the street as to the next telephone pole when the mighty explosion rang out. It had been even louder than I had expected, and at the sound of the incredible blast, the giggling ceased and the run broke into a frantic sprint. I was at the head of the fleeing pack when Cletus passed me—and he was wearing high heels!

We all regrouped a couple blocks away from the explosion, where we huddled out of the streetlight, in the shadow of a pine tree. And there we had a good but subdued laugh, giggling like a gang of imps.

Then, from there in our little patch of concentrated darkness in an already dark night, we looked up the street toward the site of the explosion, and we saw that no one seemed to be out looking for us. And the several porch lights that had come on in response to the blast were now going off one at a time. After all, a little noise might be rather expected on Halloween. So then, we sneaked back up the street to have a look at the damage, where we saw a mailbox that was delightfully bulged and buckled from the blast, and its door had been blown back open. It was a truly gratifying sight for mischief-makers and called for another round of hearty giggles.

A moment later and a block or two away, it was time to strike again. Whatever was fun once should be fun again, right? But this time it would be even better, for someone in the group had a great idea: Take two cherry bombs and a blockbuster, and twist all three fuses together to create a bomb that would surely mangle a mailbox and make a very memorable disturbance.

So, at the next victim-of-a-mailbox, again Leonard held the door open as Wayne lit and tossed in the powerful trio. Leonard slammed the door closed, and the scramble was on. Again, I was in the lead of the fleeing pack, and then an explosion rang out that rattled the entire neighborhood… BOOM!

Then again, Cletus passed me, but this time, just as he passed me, he broke a high heel and went into a tumble, and it looked like it would be disastrous on the unforgiving blacktop. As he tumbled wildly, his modesty was compromised as his dress flew up over his head, but only for a fraction of a second, for he was instantly back on his feet and running, now with his high heels in his hands. Cletus seemed to be all right, but the rest of us could barely run for laughing.

This time we ran all the way down to Weber's field, the little league field on Darrows Lane, and regrouped there, where in the weeds, not far out of bounds from third base, we lay laughing and discussing the damage that must have been suffered by that last mailbox, cackling like hens and feeling like deviant giants.

Shortly, however, as we lay there delighting in the success of our intended malevolence, we spotted a State Police cruiser coming up Darrows Lane, which caused the pack to disband immediately in several directions. There was suddenly no individual regard for the group; it was every man for himself. And I didn't look back one time as I ran all the way home, and I can't imagine anyone ever running up Winchester Road faster than I did that night.

Because of my incredible speed on the wings of fear, it was actually rather soon after the blast that I lay in the relative safety of my own bed, reflecting on my adventures. And as I lay there on my back, with my fingers smugly laced behind my head, trying to imagine what that last mailbox must look like, I noticed that the moonlight coming through the window somewhat illuminated my room, and in the pale light I could see the wallpaper. This was the room that I shared with my brother, but this was wallpaper that Mom had installed just for me, to commemorate my winning baseball season just one year ago. The paper's pattern consisted of repeated images of baseballs, baseball gloves, bats, and a boy standing at bat. I was a teenager now, but I still remembered how proud and special I felt one year ago, when I was a twelve-year-old baseball champion, and I remembered how I loved my mother for helping me celebrate my fleeting life as an athlete, whether or not I had been much help to my victorious team.

But, as I lay there that Halloween night, that winning season began to feel like ancient history. I found it difficult to think that it had been only a year ago that I was playing baseball with mere kids, and now I was a demolitions expert. Things were happening quickly in my life, and I wondered what might be next.

As I lay there, I imagined that last mailbox to be buckled outward and bulging like a potbellied puppy, that it was probably torn apart at the seams, and that its door would probably never be found. Then I imagined what the lady of the house probably said when she called the cops… "You won't believe this, Officer, but a woman, two boys, a clown, and a hobo just now blew up my mailbox and then disappeared into thin air."

A Day at Bethel School
By Diana Murphy of Paw Paw, West Virginia
Born 1945

I attended elementary school in Hampshire County, West Virginia during the 1950s. Bethel School was a simple, white wood constructed building in my rural community. It had only two rooms, one for grades one to four and the other for grades five to eight. Walking into that first room, I could hear the scratching of the chalk as my teacher; Mrs. Snyder wrote the assignments for the day on the smooth slate blackboard. The tall windows along the opposite wall filled the room with light. My

Diana with her mother, Alice Lease, and her brothers, Timmy and Danny in 1958

teacher opened them on warm days. I could feel the refreshing air flowing over the room.

The students' wooden seats and desks were bolted to two long boards. The boards were long enough for five or six seats and desks, and there were four sets of these in the room. The seat for the student in front of me was attached to my desk. My seat was attached to the desk behind me.

As I worked on my assignments, I was careful to not drop my paper on the oiled wooden floors. Mrs. Snyder gave me a fat brown pencil, and I could smell the sweet sawdust scent as I worked with the freshly sharpened pencil. My favorite scent was the fresh, waxy scent of coloring with new crayons!

I liked sitting near the teacher's wooden desk at the front of the room. I would finish my work early and listen to the other children read their interesting stories around the reading table. All grades had a turn to go to the smooth, wooden table next to the teacher's desk to read aloud. Some of those monotone voices lulled our teacher into dreamland. As my reading skills improved, I eventually read all the books on the two wooden bookshelves in our room.

Sometimes my teacher would ask me to help another student who had difficulty doing her work. I sat next to Karen while her salty tears dropped onto her paper and mixed with the grime on the desktop. By the time we had finished, her desk would be a soggy, briny mess.

The room was heated by a coal stove during the winter. This stove had a tall metal jacket around it and looked like a big open can standing at the front of the room. Mrs. Snyder would periodically add coal to keep the fire burning and bringing warmth to our room.

Before lunch, my classmates and I walked outside to the water pump and took turns pumping cool water over hour hands. On frosty days, Mrs. Snyder kept a metal pitcher of water behind the stove. We held our hands over a basin as she poured a little water over them and gave us half a brown paper towel to dry them.

We sat at our desks to eat the lunch we'd brought from home. I had a green metal lunch box with a thermos of milk. Sometimes I ate cold, sweet pork and beans from a small metal can. Other times I ate a sandwich made of tangy sandwich spread. It was always tastier if my mother had put a slice of cheese on it.

At the end of the day, I heard the clattering of metal lunch boxes and the chattering of students as we packed our bags and put on our coats. Then we hurried out to the big yellow bus for the ride home.

My Favorite Teacher
By Doms J. Clutter of Accident, Maryland
Born 1942

I grew up in a small town in West Virginia called Corinth. I attended a two-room school that was heated by a pot-bellied stove. We had an outside pump for water and outhouses for restrooms.

Mr. Foreman, my second grade teacher was a man I loved dearly. He was so kind and made learning fun. If we would say our multiplication tables correct, he would give us a brand new pencil. If we missed no days of school each quarter of the year, he gave us a nickel. The big reward was if we missed no days of school all year. At the end of the year, we received a quarter. That was a big thing in those days.

I will never forget at Easter we all brought in colored eggs. Mr. Foreman had the older children in the school go out and hide them. He told us younger students, first through third grade, to go out and find the eggs. Mr. Foreman said we could only bring in one egg at a time and lay it on our desks. When we brought in the egg and laid it on our desks, we had to say cock-a-doodle-doo. Of course, the one who got the most eggs got a prize from him.

Mr. Foreman retired that year, and I was

heartbroken when I came back the next year to find out he wouldn't be coming back. This was around 1949.

Mischief I Got Into

When I was a teenager, I went with a group of friends to visit another friend who lived by the Terra Alta Lake. The lake was situated just outside of Terra Alta on the Cranesville Road. There was a Methodist church camp there at the lake. The camp was quite busy in the summertime.

It was evening and we were getting bored, as most teenagers do. We all decided to walk around to the other side of the lake and borrow the rowboats for a ride on the lake. We did not expect what happened.

A dense fog set in while we were out in the boats, and we couldn't find the shore to come in. The campers had no idea we had borrowed the boats. They were having dinner and evening singing. To this day, I do not know how we managed to get to the shore but we did. Needless to say, we never did that again. This was around 1957 or 1958.

Nipping on Dad's Cider
By Ralph F. Miller of Accident, Maryland
Born 1947

I was raised from birth on a farm in Garrett County, Maryland. I have many fond memories of events that transpired around me in my youth.

We were a very resourceful family when it came to harvesting field and garden crops. Our apple orchard supplied us with a hardy crop of Winesap, Northern Spy, Baldwin, and other types of sweet apples suitable for canning and "winter keeping" in the basement. Some years there were so many apples that my father sacked up many feed bags to take to the local cider mill to be made into apple butter and cider. Dad really enjoyed "nipping" on the cider after it had aged for four to five months. The problem was that many others around the farm enjoyed nipping on it, too! In order to protect his cider from being consumed by others, Dad came up with a great idea.

In the fall of the year, our barn was full of fresh miles of hay, loose hay, and square bales stacked 30 high and 60 to 80 wide, tightly packed together to save space. Dad carefully cut out one bale in front towards the bottom of the stack and slid a full wooden barrel of hard cider in the opening. After this, he fashioned a false bale end with two leaves of hay bound with baler twine and placed it in front of the barrel end. The barrel was completely disguised in amongst the mile of hay bales.

Someone had to help Dad lift that full barrel into the hay mile. I believe it was the Carnation Milk man, seeing as he was fairly young and strong and came every other day to load the heavy milk cans into his truck from the cooler. Needless to say, I suspected he was the one because many times that winter, I saw him leaving the cooler house, entering the hay mile area of the farm, and then leaving.

One evening on a cold winter day in January, temptation got the best of me. On my way to do my after school chores, I went to the hay mile and located the cider barrel. There was a small metal cup conveniently located next to the bung of the barrel covered by the fake bale end. I grabbed the cup and drank a container of the cool, clear liquid. It tasted bittersweet. I thought I would have another cup before I finished in the mile. I did, and before I knew it, I had had several more cups.

I was required to fork up loose hay and put it into the mangers below the barn floor. Dad commented to Mom the next day how the hay seemed to be flying in the cows' mangers that evening. Anyway, I wasn't feeling any pain and very soon succumbed to the potent strength of the hard cider. I became very sick and barely made it back to the house. I crawled up the steps to bed. I couldn't begin to sit up and eat dinner. Mom said I learned my lesson about getting into things better left alone.

Anyway, come spring the hay mile was empty and an empty wooden barrel lay in the corner of the barn floor.

Reflections
By Maggie Gensel of Atlantic Beach, Florida
Born 1939

Living in separate regions of the country, miles apart, I still think of my Uncle Buck and the farm where he and Aunt Aggie raised my four cousins. Each time I see a farm, memories flow back to my growing up years and visits to the farm.

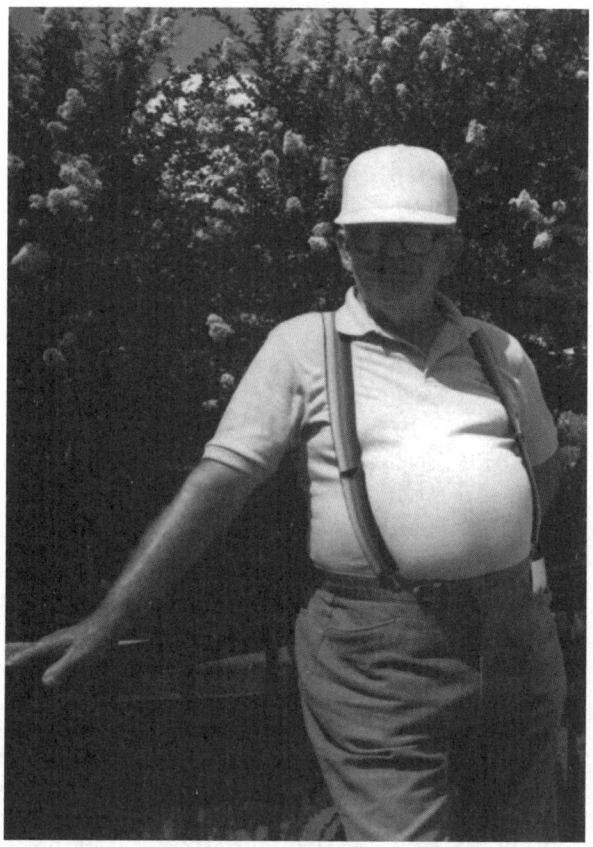
Uncle Buck

I was raised in a town, walked or rode my bike to school, and had the usual pets, a dog, goldfish, and an occasional turtle. To visit the farm meant a trip on the school bus with my cousins and a vacation, even if only for one weekend, to another part of life to which I was unaccustomed.

The bus ride was always thrilling with the kids singing and talking all the way. The countryside changing from stores, town and traffic to rolling hills, green trees and hay fields with their unique smell.

Aunt Aggie always had a pie or cake around with the delicious fresh baked smells. She would do wash in a washing machine on the back porch using a scrub board for stubborn stains and hanging the clothes on lines strung between the trees. Past the trees was the cow pasture and when we were sent to bring in the cows, sometimes we would sneak rides on the back of a slow moving, gentle cow; that is until Uncle Buck saw us and chased us off. What fun to slide in the haystacks in the barn, play hide and seek and other fun games. There were always cats and kittens to play with.

In the summer, when school was over, the visit would be for a week. Some of my favorite times were when we pretended the concrete cow-watering trough was a swimming pool, splashing around in the cool water from the pump, and feeling the green moss on the slippery sides of the trough. Of course, that lasted until again we were chased out, since we were not allowed to be in the unsanitary water. We would take turns carrying the water bucket from the pump to the house. A metal long handled dipper hung from the side for dipping water for cooking and drinking.

The home always smelled clean and fresh and from the open windows, the smell of fresh hay would fill the air. Aunt Aggie was always working, cleaning, scrubbing, and ironing. There was never a need for TV, large meals for the family and the farm hands took time, and any free time was spent at the sewing machine.

At night, lying in bed, the sound of the lids clanking on the pig feeders blended with the sounds of the crickets, frogs, and farm animals, lulling us to sleep. In the winter, the linoleum on the bedroom floors would be icy cold to the feet and we would hurry to dress.

Another favorite game was sneaking into the pig yard without the pigs catching us, climbing the apple trees and throwing apples at the pigs. Mischief? Yes, but oh so much fun! I was afraid of the pigs and would wait for a chance to climb down and run out, especially since I knew we shouldn't be there and before Uncle Buck caught us.

Aunt Aggie and Uncle Buck have since passed on; my cousins are living lives of their own and life goes on, but those sweet memories will never die. Thank you, Uncle Buck, for putting up with another kid and for making my life and world a little broader.

A Lot Like Gramps
By John Sherrick of Ft. Ashby, West Virginia

My first recollection of seeing my personal railroad depot agent, known to me as Great-grandpa Naftzger, was when my father lifted me up and let me peer over Gramps' ticket counter. What I saw was Gramps sending a telegraph message up and down the tracks with the loud clickety-clack of his Morse code sounder happening.

Another thing I can't forget is being around and later working in my father's dairy plant. This plant was interesting because it had a five horsepower electric motor in the milk's homogenizer, two 100-gallon steam heated milk vats, a bottler, a walk-in cooler, and an automatic bottle washer with a conveyer belt. Unfortunately, the invention of the paper carton milk container was known to shut down 300 small dairies in Michigan in the same year. So my dad's 25-year career ended abruptly, and I went on to a technical institute full time.

Once I got my associate's degree from this five semester technical school, I was employed for a dozen years as a technical writer of Department of Defense "tech manuals." Then at the age of 33, I had taken enough accredited semester hours to obtain a BSEE degree from my alma mater, the same technical institute from which I had previously graduated.

Thankfully, my new BSEE landed me a truly challenging engineering job at the Joint Spectrum Center in Annapolis, Maryland, across the river from the Naval Academy. There, I was employed for 31 years as a test engineer, with some interesting field duties, such as the judicious placement of 163 NWS Doppler Weather Radars, which were new at that time. We still watch these on the evening news.

Moving on about having Morse in my personal makeup, I have been licensed as Amateur Radio Operator "W8OHT" since I was 13 years old. I myself have built an SSB receiver and three powerful RF amplifiers from scratch. Hams would say these were "homebrewed." One of my original log periodic antenna designs can still be seen today and is available to all hams to build themselves. It is actually featured in a monthly ham magazine, and it occupies 11 pages of *The ARRL Antenna Compendium, Volume Six*.

As one member of a 400-member radio club and now at age 74, I still enjoy competing with them in most worldwide radio contests that are conducted by the two popular ham magazines. So anytime a member of our club earns a score in a contest, his score is also given to his club. In this way, the clubs around the world can compete against each other. So the score that I obtained just last weekend, for example, of 350 contacts yielding a 47,000-point score, will be credited to my club as well as to me.

What is important to me is how proud my railroad traffic sending great-grandfather would be if he could see me now. I am now able to stand on my own two feet and can even send the Morse code a lot like Gramps. Well, I never warned that a train was at risk of collision, but my most recent log shows that I made more than 40 contacts at a rate of two per minute. So as you can see, I'm not just a ham, I'm also just an offspring! While he was simply doing his job to keep the Pere Marquette Railroad running smoothly, I'm able to do something fun and more importantly, I'm a lot like Gramps.

Time with My Grandparents
By Leonard B. Barron of Berkeley Springs, West Virginia
Born 1930

It was 1930 and the Depression was everywhere. It was my birthday. My dad needed to find work. The plant he worked in building a car called the Dagmar in Hagerstown, Maryland closed. Everyone was suffering. Dad decided that since he helped build the Dagmar and they were being used as taxicabs in New York City, he would see about a job repairing them. The second shop hired him. What luck, now he could bring his wife and son to New York City. Things didn't get much better, and now his wife was with their second child.

Then in the year 1935, I went to Bergoo, West Virginia to stay with my grandparents. My grandfather was an engineer for the Western Maryland Railroad. He drove a big 900 engine to haul coal out of Barton, West Virginia.

Bergoo, West Virginia was a large change from New York City, a lot to get used to for a small boy. Bergoo was a very small town surrounded by mountains. The same road that brought people in was the same way out. There was one store in town, and they had everything from food to a car for sale.

Bergoo was also into woodcutting. There was a huge pond of water that the railroad could use. The train ran alongside of the pond. The train hauling the logs would dump them

Lenny in Bergoo

into the pond, and the logs would float over to the mill where they were cut. The saw blade was six feet in diameter. That made it easy to cut the big logs up in a little amount of time. There was a huge lumberyard close by where the wood was stacked and stored, ready to sell.

Grandma had a large cook stove in the kitchen, and behind it was a large tub where I took a bath. My pap would hunt for food, and one day he brought two rabbits he shot for supper.

My first year of school was in Bergoo. That winter there was three feet of snow. My grandfather drove his engine and caboose by the house that morning and stopped. The brakeman, his name was Logger Davis, waved me to get on the caboose. When I got on board, they took me to school.

During the big snow, I was playing outside and the snow was so deep. I tried jumping over a fence and fell, cutting my chin. The doctor used two butterfly stitches to close the cut.

My best friend was another boy my age who was barefoot most of the time. I never knew anyone that could run on rocks and cinders like he could. He lived in Bergoo all his life. His mother was an excellent cook. She had a cow she milked once a day. Her cornbread still makes my mouth water when I think of it.

On the side of the mountain close to the house was a railroad track where the Shay engine would back up with a coal car loaded with coal. It would stop over the area where a truck was parked. After emptying the load of coal into the truck, the truck drove away.

Every afternoon, my grandfather came through town hauling a load of coal. He would snap the throttle on the engine that would spin the wheels, and he would blow the whistle at the same time. This let everyone know he was home.

My grandfather took me all around the little town of Bergoo. He took me fishing, which I had never done before. I caught some fish big enough for Grandma to cook for supper.

Sometimes my grandparents took me to Webster Springs, about 35 miles from Bergoo. We would go to see a movie and cartoons.

When I think back on the one year I spent in Bergoo with my grandparents, I learned a lot and enjoyed my first time there.

Coal, Corn Silk, and Floods
By E. Jean Hast of Hyndman, Pennsylvania
Born 1943

I was born in Cornellsville, Pennsylvania. My dad moved us to Cumberland, Maryland. When I was five years old, Dad moved us to Hyndman, Pennsylvania just a little past the Mason-Dixon Line. He moved us because he worked for the B&O Railroad at that time and he was a very prejudiced man. I was five years old at that time. Mom would put me down for

Ella Jean's mother, Ella Jean Dwire

Ella Jean's father, James C. Dwire

a nap, and I would climb out the window and go down the alley to play with the colored kids. They loved me and we got along fine. My dad would come after me and spank me with my sand shovel all the way home. That is why we moved to Hyndman. They would tar and feather any black person who came to town. It was so sad!

The house we moved in was by the railroad. We did have an outhouse. Mom had a wringer washer at that time outside in the washhouse. We did have electric but no television. We had a party line phone. We would get on and listen in and the operator would holler at us to get off of the phone.

My dad took us to the drive-in theater. He let me bring home a black cat they were giving away. At that time, the light was in the middle of the ceiling with a long pull string to turn the light on and off. We taught the cat to go ahead of us, and he would jump on the string to turn on the light. I loved that cat, but a neighbor killed him.

My brother, Joe, and I would take our wagon up by the railroad tracks and roll our hands and arms and the engineer would roll off coal to us. We had a heat trolla to heat our house, and it burned coal and wood.

Then I started school. We walked because there were no buses. On the way to school, there was a small grocery store where my mom had an account until payday for milk and bread. I knew this, so on the way to school I would stop and get candy every day. When my mom found out, she asked me why I got so much candy. I said I gave it to the kids so they would like me. I didn't do that again.

Then as I got older, I went down a few streets from us to see friends I went to school with. There was this lady who looked like a witch, but she was nice. I remember her putting these bubble candlelights on her Christmas tree. So one day, I went to visit and she wasn't around. She had a lot of cats. I picked one up and it scratched me. So at that time almost everyone had a cook stove. I was so mad that the cat scratched me that I put it in her oven. Needless to say, the cat got cooked.

We then moved in town to the "blue house." We had a garden, and we would get the corn silk and roll it up in newspapers and smoke it. We thought that was fun.

Then we moved out of town. Mom and Dad were in the process of buying the house, but the people decided to come back to Hyndman. So Mom and Dad had to find a place real quick. Now we called it the home place. It was so awful. It was a double house. But with a lot of hard work, it is now a comfortable, single dwelling.

In 1986, the town was flooded. My mother was running her vacuum and heard the fire siren go off. She went out to get in her car and

Ella Jean with her brother Joe

saw a wall of water. She ran back in her house. Her car was washed away. She ran upstairs and watched houses and people going by. We couldn't find her. She was wondering around. We finally found her and took her to our home in Maryland. I could go on and on about the flood.

One thing though, when we were kids we made swimming holes from Gooseberry to the new bridge, to the black bridge to Black Bottom all summer long and it never, ever flooded. Now they put in a levee and can't be certified. If the Game and Water Commission would let them dredge the creek bed and take out the trees and brush from the water, it would solve the problem and the fish would be healthier.

Harpers Ferry's Cast of Colorful Characters
By B. (Bo) Bolyard of Harpers Ferry, West Virginia
Born 1960

I grew up in a little town on the tip of the eastern panhandle called Harpers Ferry W.V. in the foothills of the Blue Ridge Mountains, bordered on both sides by the Shenandoah and Potomac rivers. The beauty of the landscape is nothing compared to the colorful people of my childhood in our town, long before Maude or Roseanne hit the airwaves. We had our own Maude's, Roseanne's, Otis's, and just plain everyday people being people. Sadly most are gone but live in spirit and memory of those of us who they touched our lives' in some way.

Let me start by describing our little town as best I can. Harpers Ferry proper the lower town started as a point of crossing a ferry service across the rivers. The homes were built of natural limestone, handmade brick, German siding, and grand old Victorians with original stained glass windows that lined the streets and ridge top and cover the other side of the ridge. Union Street divides the two towns of Bolivar and Harpers Ferry. The upper town has much newer homes yet still there are those built before the civil war and used as hospitals. The old jailhouse and town springhouse still stand and all this surrounded by the mountains, blue sky, and winds that echo the past and cry for the future.

This was the home of the Niagara Movement where both white and blacks got along well. During this time people kept hogs, chickens, steer, and even horses which brings me to old Lynn Twyman. He was a black gentleman with a gentle old soul. He was often seen driving his old horse drawn wagon to and from the three schools to pick up the leftovers from the students' lunches for his hogs. He was always polite and willing to give you a lift as he traveled through town talking and singing to that horse of his. As I drive down the main street of town, I can still hear the clip clop of that old horse of his. Best I remember when that horse of his died one winter Lynn lasted till spring, heart broke, and lonely he too pasted away longing for his friend of so many years.

Now every town has their local Otis, lord we had more than our fair share but one stands out in my mind, good old Ollie McDonald. He was a connoisseur of cheap locally made John Brown whiskey and anything else that poured. He kept bottles hid all over town, the bus garage, old buildings, and even the graveyard in the boxwoods. I remember well as a kid hearing singing coming from the older part of the graveyard. One evening and being a nosey brat, I just had to check it out, there laid Ollie drunk as a monkey in an open grave singing and nursing his hooch. I poked around till the streetlights came on and then it was time to be home. The next morning, I had to go check and see if Ollie had made it out of that grave before the next guest showed up for their turn in it and he had.

Now if you think Maude was ahead of her time, let me tell you Maude was tame compared to ours.

I had a friend bless her heart, she was as mild mannered as a newly hatched peep if she liked you. She was a smaller woman in size but had a heart like a lioness. Lord have pity on your soul if you crossed her. She raised three wonderful sons and a beautiful daughter. She was independent, strong willed, and every bit the lady. I'm telling this from her point of view. Her husband a big trucker who when he held out his arm she could walk under it. Seemed he had a mean streak and liked to try and pull out the ole Mr. Nasty attitude with this charming lady. Being of sound mind and madder than a hornet when she'd had enough, she often could be heard saying, "It's better to have a bad stand then a good run." She started keeping a box of d-Con on the back of the stove and daily she'd take a spoonful of it out and throw it away. He'd come home and ask what's for supper, she'd point to the stove, and say, there it is if you feel brave enough to eat it and go back to her seek a wordbook. The grin on her face when she'd tell this story was priceless. May she rest in peace and know I tell this with love for her.

The Roseanne of our town has me cracking a grin thinking about this story. Her husband worked with my dad and they lived down the street. This event happened one summer day long before people had air conditioning. It seemed that her biggest issue with her husband was he would come to the supper table shirtless most days. In the heat, tempers flare so to make her point and drive it home, this good little church lady fixed supper. At 4 o'clock when her husband came through the door, there was supper on the table like it always was and so was the dessert. There also sat his wife buck-naked in the center of the table. He never again showed up to the table shirtless with is hairy chest showing. He came up later that evening and told my parents about it.

Oh my family, my late dad enjoyed making his wine and sharing it. I thought the stuff was only good for stripping furniture but others thought differently. My dad was friends with the local banker, seems they went hunting one time and at the end of the day they met back at the truck. My dad hadn't shot anything but he had filled a couple of five-gallon buckets with fox grapes (wild grapes) to make wine. Being a small town everyone knew everyone else and the chief of police could often be seen at our house with the town police cruiser. One time, Peanut the chief was sampling the wine and got so drunk his girlfriend had to be called to come get him while on duty (rumor has it he was hung over for two days.)

And finally, our local politicians. We once had a mayor who was elected to many terms after being a convicted felon but that is history and he paid his dues. The funny thing about him was he claimed to be a Christian but could often be found drunk as a skunk. My dad and others dads would take him home with them so his wife (a staunch Pentecostal) wouldn't find out he'd been in the vodka again his spirit of choice.

Life in the small town of Harpers Ferry was at one time better than anything Hollywood could come up with. It's the truth, people being people, a colorful cast from start to finish, as wild and wonderful as our state. The beauty of our people being creative in just being their self.

Life is Still Good
By Forest David Bowers of Coalton, West Virginia
Born 1941

I was born in Huttonsville, West Virginia on July 18, 1941. My dad's name was Forest and my mother was Virginia. They were good people, hard working, and religious but not over religious. My dad operated the powerhouse for a coalmine. He was a small but strong and worked as if there was no tomorrow. My mother was a housewife like most women back then. She was a fantastic cook, learning from her mother. Over her lifetime, she fed armies of people.

We moved to Elkins, West Virginia, 20 miles to the north. We lived on 9th Street. Davis Memorial Hospital was behind our house. At the top of 9th Street was Harrison Avenue, the main street into town. The street was up grade approaching a long cement bridge. Under the bridge was the railroad, with four sets of tracks. I remember going across the bridge when steam engines hauling coal, lumber, and stone were going under. There would be a lot of smoke and steam before the engine went under and then no smoke and then a huge amount of smoke and steam when the engine

Third Ward School

came out the other side. That was a sight to see for a little kid!

I remember when the war was over. Church bells rang, fire engines, car horns, railroad whistles, and the tannery contributed to the noise. I was four years old. I can remember it was September 2, 1945.

I started school, first grade, at Third Ward School. It was high on the hill with 15-foot retaining walls. Mrs. Whetzel was my teacher, a dedicated woman. Our playground was rock and dirt and also steep. I can still taste in my mind the peanut butter and honey sandwiches that we were served. Every morning we said the "Pledge of Allegiance" and "The Lord's Prayer."

I remember getting out of school with my classmates to watch President Eisenhower being inaugurated. The television was black and white and the television station was KDKA Pittsburg, The Durmont Television Network. There was one TV on the entire block. The living room was crowded, I remember.

In 1953, my granddad retired from the coalmines and wanted to move away from the farm and all the hard work. My mother and dad bought the farm, and we moved there. I was 12 years old. Our place has been in the family for 91 years.

Things I Remember Well

I spent three years in the Army, 101st Airborne Division at Fort Campbell Kentucky, 1960-1963. We were on alert for the Cuban Missile Crisis. We were issued live ammo and waited to go at Campbell Air Field. We didn't have to go, thank the Lord.

President Kennedy was killed November 1963. I got out of the service a month later.

I remember sitting beside Brenda Lee at the Ice Capades in Nashville.

We went to the Grand Ole Opry several times while I was in the service. Grand Pa Jones, Minnie Pearl, Webb Pierce, Hank Snow, String Bean, Roy Acuff, Johnny Cash, and the Carter Family are among the people I remember seeing. I never got to see Patsy Cline or Hank Williams.

At the Ryman Auditorium in Nashville, the $3.00 ticket seats were behind the columns. I remember we, not knowing any better, moved closer to the front. We were soon ushered back to the $3.00 seats. While we were up front, water was dripping quite a bit beside me on the seat. After we were moved back, it wasn't long before a family of four was ushered to the front seats. I remember well the lady had a brown coat with a fur collar. The water was dripping down her neck. The usher wiped up the water, and she sat there the entire show.

Life was good back then. Gas was 25 cents a gallon, a candy bar was a nickel, and cake was a dime. There were no drugs back then, a lot of booze but no drugs.

I'd best go back to my younger days again. 905 9th Street is no longer there; the hospital expanded to two full blocks. The overhead bridge is gone and so are the tracks. One track remains at the depot. It is a tourist train, which is really nice.

My wife, Jane, and I live on the farm. My son, his wife, and their three kids and my daughter, her husband, and their two girls live here, too, along with one great-grandson. My two sisters own property on the farm. One lives in Charleston, West Virginia. My sister, Jane and her husband, Kenny live on the farm near us.

Times have sure changed over the years, not always for the best, as you know. Life is still good.

Elmer and Clara Powers
By Paul David Powers of Cumberland, Maryland
Born 1952

In 1965, things were tough for my parents with three children. Work was scarce even for a City as big as Baltimore. So Dad took me and my brother to Grandpap and Grandma's Powers's House in Cumberland about 150 miles West, in the mountains of Allegany County! The road after a while gets boring for two boys; obviously, we fell asleep because Dad called out to us to wake up! "Boy's I want to show you something! " We were climbing up a huge mountain that never seemed to end along Route 40 (Now 68)! Up and down, we went through five mountains like being on a huge roller coaster! Reaching the top was scary and awed us at the same time. It was so high up; you could see the Beautiful Blue and Green Valley's spread out for miles.

Arriving in Cumberland, we breathe a sigh of relief to be off those mountains. Alongside the road to the right, there was a motel that is still in operation today, just off Nave's Crossroads! Across to the left was Mason's Barn, a Drive In Restaurant, and A Popular hangout for Teens! Going over the hill into Cumberland, we noticed that entire city was surrounded by mountains-as if it was sitting in a huge crater! We pulled in front of a Green and White House with a White Picket Fence, the sign said POWERS on the door and we knew we were home!

Grandpap and Grandma Powers' house was like taking a trip back in time, like something you would see in a movie or read in a book, old fashioned, quiet, and peaceful, and a huge contrast from living in the Big City! Walking through the gate there was the smell of flowers they were around the house! (Sunflowers, Roses, Daffodils, Marigolds, and Petunias). Flower boxes were lined all along the front porch, some even hung from the porch ceiling! During the day, you could hear the wind chimes and the sound of church bells playing "The Old Rugges Cross, Amazing Grace off in the distance. On hot summer nights, we would sit out on the porch swing and the glider and listen to the crickets sing their orchestrative processions

A Block from the house is Holland Street, which runs alongside of Braddock Junior High School (Today it's called Braddock Middle School). At the top of the street to the left, there is a huge, water tower close to the mountain. The tower looks similar to the tower on Petticoat Junction. (Without the girls bathing in it).

My brother and I were always getting into mischief! In the front of the house stood a huge cigar tree with long pod-like plants hanging down. One day, curiosity got the best of us and we decided to pull a couple of the strange, hangy things down and light them up. I remember taking a few drags of the stinking weed, and coughing and gagging. Grandma caught us! "Boy's you'd better not be in my cigar tree?" Of course, we lied but it was evident that we had been there because we couldn't stop coughing. We never touch another cigar off of that tree. Now there was a green apple tree on the right side of their yard! We knew that tree well, and had many a bellyache more that treat!

Across from the apple tree was Grandma's Favorite Rose bushes. Further to the left was Grandpap's Car, I think it was a Ford, it was light green with huge chrome lights The grill in between looked like an evil smile with two huge eyes on each side! Looked like something from the movie, "Christine!"

To the right of the car was two sheds the bigger one was Grandpap's Carpenter Shop and the smaller one was the shed for the lawnmower! The shop was off limits unless he was there with us. And for good reason, Grandpap had fingers missing on both hands! Grandpap was a Carpenter by trade! It's been said that in his earlier days, he helped build half the houses in North End! I think that was when he was working with Buckhanno Lumber Company, which eventually went out of business! Grandpap was a Master Craftsman, who made all kinds of neat things with solid wood, not partial board like they use today! I loved watching him carve beautiful furniture, cabinets and nick knack shelves for Grandma.

Grandpap was an innovator; he built all of his shop tools, the circular saw, the jigsaw, the drill press, and a number of other tools with washing machine motors using pulley's. The workmanship in the things that he made was incredible, detailed, and intricate in every way. Like the Beautiful Oak China Cabinet that sat in Grandma dining room! It was a site to behold with its curved, swirl designs, shiny brass handles, and glass doors. The kind of furniture a person would put their best china in. I remember dishes sitting on it one with a picture of Jesus with his hands folded and that President dish with John F. Kennedy in the center!

Grandma was funny about her house. She had everyone come in through the back kitchen door; she didn't want her rugs to get dirty. The kitchen was something else, the kind that makes you hungry, even when you are full. My brother and I loved to eat the potato cakes, the crisp bacon and fried eggs, and the most important thing on the menu, drink a hot cup of A & P coffee.

The snacks were good too, homemade cakes, gooey chocolate chip cookies, and Archway Oatmeal Cookies loaded with peanut butter. I would take those little sandwiches, (the two cookies with peanut butter in between) and dip them into my coffee, "hmm, was that ever good!"

In the kitchen was a chrome edged table and four chromed chairs with their red plastic covers! By the refrigerator, was Grandma's Philco AM radio. Grandma played that radio constantly. Grandpap was always complaining, "Clara, turn that damn thing down!", but I don't really think it was the noise because Grandpap was deaf in one ear! He was just cranky and liked to fuss at grandma! But she never paid him any mind she just kept eating at the table! She liked that old radio. Every day like clockwork, she waited to hear Paul Harvey the commentator says, "This is Paul Harvey with News!" (News would sound like a long z). I particularly remember the commercials about Geritol and Exlax, which Grandma had inside her medicine cabinet. One afternoon, after school, I found the box and thought that is was chocolate, I ate what was left of the box; and had the runs for the next two days!

In the dining room, there was an old oak table. It looked close to one hundred years old. On it was the Family Bible with all of the family tree listings, dating back to the early 1800's. Various magazines littered the table, Life and Look magazine, Readers Digest and the good old faithful, TV Guide. My Grandma loved to read those magazines with their weird twist, and the inspirational testimonials.

Elmer and Clara Powers were a contradiction in terms. Grandpap was a white haired, German-Irish fellow, with wired rimmed eyeglasses who liked to chew his Red Man chewing tobacco. Grandpap was a strong-willed man. A man who supported his family of 12 children through the Great Depression of the 1930's. He had the battle scars to prove it.

Grandma was a stout woman, Half Crow Indian who liked to sneak a smoke when grandpap was out. Often when I went to visit, she would send me to Stitcher's for a pack of Winston's for her and a pack of Marlboro's for me! We would sit there in the kitchen puffing away as she looked out the window to see if Grandpap had come home! Funny thing is all those years Grandpap knew she smoked but never said anything!

Grandpap was a Master Fisherman! I remember one night me, my brother Mike and Grandpap went to the garden carrying a flashlight and empty Chock Full of Nuts coffee can! Now coming from the city we had no clue what night crawlers were, but Grandpap did because he watered that garden before dark! I said something don't we need a shovel, "Grandpap said NO they will be on the top of the dirt and you know what... they were! We loved to go fishing with him at Will's Creek, to the C&O Canal or to Corriganville! He had one rule if we went, and that was not talking because apparently, it scared the fish away. But that didn't stop him from catching quite a few with us doing the same! Now back home Grandma was always busy either washing clothes in the ringer type Maytag Washer, or canning vegetables from their own garden,. She had a Green Thumb! Everywhere you could see beautiful flowers throughout the yard.

Grandpap play the Harmonica, stomping his feet, while Grandma clapped to the music's beat! Uncle Bud Powers played his Gibson, Les Paul, (Once had a Country/Gospel Radio Show!). Music has been in our family for generations. From Uncle Bud's Chet Atkins Style Playing, to My Brother Rusty playing Bass with General Store, My Brother Mike, Band, his Son Chris with the Keller Diesel Co. My Daughter Christina, Who is Singing/Playing Guitar, Me playing Bass with Marvalade Mirage, Liberty Temple Church in Mt. Savage, MD, and Today at 61, I sing Classic Rock at Karaoke in the Cumberland Area!

Elmer and Clara Powers died in the mid to late 1980's, in their early 90's! They were Married over Seventy-Five years, had 12 children! They left a Family Legacy that Lives On!

Our Beloved Neighborhood
By Diana Carbonaro Brown of Capon Bridge, West Virginia
Born 1950

My parents, younger brother, Joey, and I moved into our first new home in 1960 in a hybrid neighborhood of both old and new houses. Ours boasted three bedrooms, one bath, a carport, and an unfinished basement. We even had a private line, wall-mounted rotary dial telephone; a black and white wooden cabinet television; and a stereo radio/phonograph, which closely resembled a maple hope chest on legs. Mom's wringer washer was replaced by an automatic, and our long clothesline was upgraded to a metal contraption that looked like an oversized, four-sided television antenna on a pole.

Our new neighborhood was laid out like a sideways E with our street being the middle bar. At the end of the three streets was a large hardwood forest complete with a meandering and very long creek. What more could any kid want?

Close to one hundred kids lived in our 'hood, and we knew one another well. Very few families moved away in the nine years we lived there, but I do remember when little blonde-haired, blue-eyed Robin's family moved. About a year later, we learned that she had been brutally murdered. A predator knew that she was a latchkey child, a term not even in use back then. I was about 12 at the time, and even if my mom had told me Robin had been sexually assaulted, I would not have understood. The word sex only connoted gender to me. The concept of latchkey also would have been a mystery because absolutely no one locked their doors.

Never in all the years we lived there did we ever hear of a break in or of vandalism. And only one mother in the entire neighborhood worked outside the home. She was a divorcee, another new concept for me, as she was the first I knew. The only blended family was possibly the Springmans, with their adopted son and daughter.

We all loved the kind, elderly Mrs. Springman, our local 4-H leader. At least a dozen girls met weekly in her partially finished basement, where we learned to bake bread, make piecrusts, and cook tuna casseroles. She had a large assortment of sewing machines, on which we learned first the basics of threading needles and bobbins, and then the rewarding joys of sewing our own aprons and school clothes. Correcting us mercilessly, she urged us to take our accomplishments to state and local fairs and competitions in the hopes of earning red and blue ribbons.

The Extension Office of 4-H offered our many mothers their Homemaker's Club. Many of our moms gathered regularly to share recipes and learn artsy-craftsy skills. Mom created an exquisite crèche, which we used and cherished. Together, mothers and daughters made excursions to a local German orphanage to deliver gifts and goodies. One hot Saturday, we gathered in our tiny, non-air conditioned kitchen to fry dozens of chickens for some worthy cause now long forgotten. Cackling like chickens ourselves, we laughed and gossiped the day away, moms and daughters together.

Diana with her friend, Anne in 1966

Mr. Maddox (all the parents were always Mr. and Mrs.) decided that his growing family of seven needed eggs, so he and Dad purchased a half a dozen chickens along with some barbed wire fencing. As the new hens free-ranged, the two men went about the task of putting up the enclosure. Too late, a few of the neighborhood dogs, which always ran loose, smelled dinner.

One memorable Fourth of July, Dad took charge when several families got together with all their fireworks, hot dogs, and metal folding chairs. He clumsily dropped the punk, a lit firework starter, in the trashcan holding the goodies. Cherry bombs, sparklers, the whole shebang went off within minutes. It was a grand finale minus the entrée!

Summer nights meant hide and seek, tag, catching fireflies, and softball. But the best part was being old enough that the older kids accepted us into the nightly baseball games held beyond the woods. We'd bike all the way down the next street over, park our bikes at the Cornu residence, take the worn path beyond their house into the woods, and cross two wooden footbridges that were suspended over our gurgling creek to reach the old abandoned quarry that was now a baseball diamond that the older boys had built. Dusk always came too soon. The white softball would continue to blend with the dark until we just couldn't see it anymore. After a familiar, ritualistic mournful groan, we would reluctantly make our way back home. Flashlights lit the way, and it was always quite dark when I finally got to my house. I never remember my folks worrying about me. All the parents knew where we were and who we were with.

In the winter, the Cornus hosted sled parties with steaming hot chocolate and cookies, fire pits, and wooden jump ramps for our more experienced sledders. Winter also meant Christmas caroling from house to house. We'd always be rewarded by the moms with their favorite hot drink and homemade cookies. Because the three streets all went downhill to the wood, it was a perfect neighborhood for sleigh riding, too.

Several years in a row in late spring, we transformed my backyard with tents and colorful booths into a carnival to help fight muscular dystrophy. Encouraged by a TV clown who would later become Ronald McDonald, we were further empowered by the creative kits he sent. One idea I ran with was the fortuneteller's booth.

A new toy that year was the Magic 8 Ball, and I craved one badly. Finally, my birthday came and with it, my greatest wish! Now, Dougie, who lived next door, was an only child whose basement resembled a Toys R Us (which did not yet exist). But even he did not have a Magic 8 Ball. He asked to hold mine and "accidentally" dropped it. My heart was as shattered as my toy.

Now fast forward approximately 24 years and more than a hundred miles away when a man approaches me in one of our family-owned appliance stores. He introduces himself as Doug, and I know before it happens that he has come to make amends. Sure enough, he hands me a beautifully wrapped gift; a Magic 8 Ball.

The saddest day of my youth was when we moved from Carnemaholdubay*. I had only a few weeks left of my senior year, and we were moving into an apartment that I would never call home. That was in 1968.

Forty years later, in the spring of 2008, my mother died. Although she lived about three counties and eighty miles or so away, no less than five families from the old neighborhood were represented and many more posted on her obituary page. Tom Maddox serendipitously was an agent with the funeral home. He was such a comfort as he recalled so many almost forgotten stories and escapades. Mrs. Stanley ("Please call me Helen") remembered how I had babysat her brood of five. Some of the fourteen Holson kids shared their memories of Mom. Mrs. Fisher ("My name is Martha!") held me as she wept for her best friend whom miles and years had failed to separate. All came to honor my mother, but I also believe they unwittingly honored our beloved neighborhood.

*Carnemaholdubay: proper noun; specific neighborhood of the 1960s. Origin: author's cobbling of the first syllables of six family names, specifically Carbonaro, Neihouse, Maddox, Holson, Duvall, and Bainey Pronunciation: car knee mah <u>hole</u> dew bay Usage: Carnemaholdubay Pet Cemetery, Carnemaholdubay Bike Club, etc.

The Old Party Line
By Andrew C. Agnew, Sr. of Burlington, West Virginia
Born 1933

I am going to write about one special memory for me, and it has to do with the party line telephones. We had a party line that was more than a party line. There were probably anywhere from ten to fifteen people on that line. As the story goes, the line was left over from some that Petersburg had had in our area and they had disconnected, withdrawn, and we were left with a number of phones, a number of people with phones, and the phones would still work. So my father became the treasurer and the men in the community every fall and occasionally another time, would walk to the line to make sure everything was still in shape and order. Sometimes they had to do this because someone's phone wasn't working right.

All of these phones rang anytime you rang one of the phones. Each person's ring was different. I remember well that our ring was three longs. That was three long rings, and

Mom knew it was our phone. Mom always answered that phone whether it was her ring or not. Well, she didn't always say hello, but she always picked it up and listened to see who was talking. Sometimes before the conversation was over there would be five or six ladies talking with each other about what they'd done that day, either in the garden or if it was late in the summer, what they had canned or if it was late enough, how the butchering went. And they would let each other know if they needed help or when all of these things were going to transpire and take place.

I remember when I was a youngster, I had an uncle by the name of Uncle Snowden Cannon, and I remember his ring was about a long and a short; we rang one long ring and then a short ring, and they knew it was their telephone. And so one day, just wanting to be a kid, I rang his ring; a long and a short. Well, he answered the telephone, and I said, "Is this Cannon's?" He said, "Yes, it is." I said, "Is this the big gun?" Now, he said, "Young man, I know your mother. I'm gonna' call her and tell her you're playin' with the telephone." Guess what; I hung up in a hurry and didn't bother to call again!

But I remember, too, that there was many times that there was an emergency or a need, and the phone would ring and people would tell us what was going on and that they needed help.

Most of the people on the party line were relatives. I remember Uncle Arthur and Aunt Kathleen; their ring was four longs. I remember Aunt Mae and Uncle Fitzhugh; their ring was two longs. Ours was three longs, and some of the rings were a long and a short and a long or a couple of shorts and a long, but we always rang them depending on who we wanted to be sure to talk to. Nine times out of ten, we would wind up talking to two or three different people besides the one we'd called, because everybody picked up and listened. This was truly a "party line."

I remember some of the experiences that we shared. In the wintertime, if we had snow on the ground I would call my cousins and say, "Hey, let's ride!" and we would get our sleds out, go into the old field that was on a ridge, and we would ride until dark. At dark, we would set an old tire aflame and continue to ride, sometimes until ten or eleven o'clock. Oh, we had a great time. We looked forward to snow and the opportunity to sled ride and enjoy the open field with the snow and the fire and all that went with it. Anyway, it was a great experience.

So these things happened and we were family, literally, and everybody was a part of what our community was in terms of that telephone line. The old phone was wooden, had a crank on the right hand side, two large batteries inside, and hung on the kitchen wall if you were to come into my house.

Incidentally, that is the house I was born in, a house my father built in 1924, and all six of the kids were born in – no, I take that back. Not all six of us. Four of us were born in that house and the other two were born before the house was built. We only had two bedrooms, so we were kind of crowded at times. We heated with wood and coal, we cooked on a woodstove.

My job most of the time in the winter and fall was to get up before school, build a fire in the cook stove, and if it was cold outside, build one in the heating stove, go feed the chickens, milk the cow, slop the hogs, and then come back in for breakfast. Once breakfast was over, we'd crawl on the bus my father drove and ride to school. And sometimes at school we would say, "Hey, we'll call ya' when we

Andrew C. Agnew, Sr. in the 1980s

get home!" We'd use the old crank phone, two longs, or whatever was necessary, to get whoever it was we wanted to talk to.

There are special memories, but the one special memory that stands out in my mind was one Saturday evening when my oldest brother, my brother-in-law, and I were in the kitchen. I was learning to play the mandolin. My brother played the tenor banjo, and my brother-in-law played the guitar. I was about twelve or so years old. We were playing and picking and laughing and joking with each other, having a great evening. Someone, and I don't remember which of us, suggested, "Why don't we call everybody on the line and tell them we're going to play some music." And so my older brother began ringing the phone, and he'd say to those who answered, "If you're on there, we're going to be playing music shortly." And then he would ring another and say, "If you're on there, we're going to be playing music shortly." He called everyone that he could think of who was on that line. There were probably all together some fifteen or twenty of them.

Before long, we started playing music, old-time country music. We played "She'll Be Coming 'Round the Mountain" and others of them that we could think of. We would play those songs, sing, and have a great time. We received a lot of compliments, and we did it maybe once or twice after that and that was kind of the end of that. But what a memory! I was playing music, and I was playing over the old battery operated, long and short ring telephone!

Well, in the fall of the year, as I said, Dad and some of the neighbors would go around and inspect the line to make sure things stayed in order. Then I remember as time passed, the old phones eventually were shut down, and Mother received her first telephone that she could use to officially call outside of the community.

You see, with the phone system that we had with the phones hanging on the wall, if we wanted to call the doctor to come and deliver a baby, we had to call the general store and they in turn called the doctor. This was because they had one of our phones, plus they had one of the phones that they could use to call town or someone else. So if Mom was expecting and it was time for the doctor, Dad would call the general store operated by Mr. Creed Mott and he in turn would call Dr. Wright. Then Dr. Wright would come to deliver the baby. But I remember the babies had been born, and we enjoyed the old phone that still hung on the wall and still hangs on the wall today.

Mom finally got a phone with only three other people on it. Each one had a particular number that meant their phone would ring, but the other two phones would ring, too. So they still picked up and listened. But the old phone still hung on the wall.

Years later, my son and I bought the home place. In fact, I still live in that house and the old wooden, crank, battery operated telephone still hangs on the wall.

Oh, the memories we share when we begin to think about that old phone and the many things it enabled us to do within family and within a small community of people. It was a phone system and a community that knew everybody, and they knew everybody's ring. We were all there to enjoy our fellowship and to share with one another. I sometimes wish we had it back and that some of the electronic equipment that we have today really didn't exist. I sometimes wish we could just crank that old phone and know someone was going to answer and if we need help, they would be there in just a few minutes. But it is a good memory. What a great blessing it was in my growing up years. What a memory!

Unconditional Love
By Carolyn V. James-McKenzie of Charles Town, West Virginia
Born 1948

I remember so well my mother and her ringer washer and my parents feeding a family of seven on very little money.

Leaving for school, I can still see my mom washing all our clothes in a ringer washer. Her scrubbing them first on a wooden and metal washboard. Her hands and knuckles were cracked and bleeding, yet not one time did I ever hear her complain. I am 100% honest when I say that. Never! My precious mom will be 90 this May and she still uses her ringer washer. She always said, "Your clothes gets cleaner!" My brother got her an automatic one and she said, "Thank you, but it's not for me." It sits on the side of her wall never getting used. We didn't have a dryer, so everything was hung outside on a clothesline to dry. In the winter, they would freeze before my mom finished getting them hung.

When we would have to take down to bring into the house, we would stand them on the floor frozen and laugh!

I remember my mom waking and getting up at 5 a.m. The aroma of pancakes, eggs, sausage, bacon, and steak filled the morning air. Dinners would consist of pork chops, homemade mashed potatoes, homemade pork chop gravy, my mom's delicious homemade rolls from scratch, and her barbecue baked beans. These were my childhood favorites.

Today as I pass by the aisles of instant mashed potatoes, pop and fresh rolls, cans or jars of gravy, and egg beaters I'm reminded of all the extra work my mom put into our meals to make sure that we had the best her and my dad could give us.

Maybe we didn't have the latest clothes, games, or toys. What I had was a Mom and Dad that loved us, a home that was built by my dad, and kept immaculate by my mom. And more love then any child could imagine then and still have today. Each one knowing that they are in a family that is built on a foundation of unconditional love.

Now, as I have been reflecting on the past and how deeply my parents loved and still love me and it causes me to weep.

Extra Peanut Butter
By Carolyn R. Cooper of Salem, West Virginia
Born 1938

I was born at home in Salem, West Virginia and grew up in the same house. My parents, Leslie and Lucinda Davis, had seven boys and then I came along, the only girl in the family.

I started first grade and cried almost every day for a while. I walked with some of my brothers about a mile to Harden Grade School in Salem. Most of the time we walked home for lunch and my mom would have it ready. When the weather was too cold or bad, we paid 25 cents to eat lunch at school. Sometimes we would be given three slices of bread, two with butter, and only one with peanut butter on it and I loved peanut butter. The cook was so nice to me and she would give me two with peanut butter and one with butter. There was a rule that we had to eat everything we were given and drink all of our milk. The milk was served to us in heavy white McNicol China mugs that were made in Clarksburg. I hated sweet potatoes. When we had them, I would roll them up in my napkin and stuff it in my empty milk mug.

One time, my dad took Mom and me for a ride. We came to an intersection in Dodderidge County where five roads come together. He said he didn't know which one to take. So we got scared and I cried because I thought we were really lost. Sometimes he would take us fishing. I liked to go but didn't like touching the worms or the fish I caught. So I put on thick gloves to get the sunfish off the hook.

We had a brown dog named Brownie. He was a good dog but he didn't like my dad. Sometimes he would try to bite him. So one day Brownie disappeared and I really missed him. It was many years later when I was an adult that I found out that my dad told one of my brothers to take him away.

Once, when I was about 12 years old, I went to stay a week with my brother, Ed, in his big house in Strasburg, Virginia. He let me drive his car around his chicken farm. One time I got a little excited driving up the long driveway and ran over two pieces of wooden lawn furniture. I put a dent in the bumper too. His wife, Betty, told him, "You can't say anything to her because you are the one who let her drive the car."

When I was in high school, I got my first job as a waitress in a one of the restaurants in Salem. One of my girlfriends was working there too. One Halloween she got the idea to play a trick on people. She got some cow manure in a paper bag. We put it on someone's doorstep and lit it on fire. We wanted to watch what happened when they came to the door but we were afraid. So we took off running really fast and we never heard what they thought. As far as I know, they never knew who pulled that dirty trick.

Later I had several jobs all of which were in Salem and Clarksburg: sewing at the Maidenform, painting flowers on glassware at Harvey's Glass Factory, glass grinder at Salem Glass Factory, and correctional officer for 12 years at the West Virginia Industrial Home for Youth.

I have lived my whole life in Salem within about a half-mile radius in four different houses. I have a lot of good memories and friends from the good old days in Salem.

The Driving Lesson
By Diana Marine of Lancaster, California
Born 1959

I am the caregiver of a 92-year-old woman that was from Maryland named Annabelle Linn Williams Kloss Pond. In my year and a half with her, boy have I heard some interesting stories.

My mother was thirty-six years old and determined to learn how to drive a car. She has had this desire for many years, but my father was always against the idea. He believed that she would not be able to handle the traffic in the city. This summer, however, we were vacationing in Northern Maryland. Outside of our room we were staying in was a big empty lot with nothing on it but weeds. It looked like an ideal place to practice. There was nothing on it for my mother to hit.

Sunday was a bright sunny day, and with apprehension, my father consented to give my mother a driving lesson. He seated himself in the driver's seat with my mother in the passenger seat, and I put myself I in the rear. I wanted to learn too, but of course, I was too young. First, my father explained to Mama the names of the various parts and then proceeded to demonstrate. "First you put your left foot on the clutch to disengage the gears. Next, put your right foot on the brake and take off the emergency brake. The emergency brake is this metal object next to the gearshift. You have to squeeze it to make it release the brake. Then you take your right foot off the brake, and on level ground like this, the car won't move. You put your right foot gently on the accelerator at the same time as you slowly lift up on the clutch. Don't lift up the clutch too fast or you'll stall the motor. Naturally, Papa went through all these manoeuvers very quickly not realizing how baffling it was to Mama. Then they changed seats, and Daddy had to adjust the driver's seat so that Mama could reach the pedals, she being much smaller.

Poor Mama! She put her left foot on the clutch, and Daddy had to tell her to put her right foot on the brake. She had trouble taking off the emergency brake. When she took her right foot off the brake and on to the gas pedal, she let up on the clutch too fast, and the car stalled. Then my father lost his temper and said, "I told you not to lift up on the clutch too soon. Now try it again."

She tried a second time, and again she stalled the motor. Papa was furious and became so enraged that he got out of the car, and said, "Sit there and think about it." I got out of the back seat and climbed into the passenger seat and said, "Mama, let me help you." Slowly, very slowly, I told her the same things that Daddy had told her. This time she listened and understood. When she managed to make the car move, she felt triumphant. There we were driving around an empty field, neither one of us with a license. Several weeks later, a lady who was interested in her progress, decided that Mama should try for a license. Mama was really scared. She had improved, and the helpful lady, Mrs. Thorne, drove her over to the license bureau, a bureau that in this country town did not strike fear into a novice. Mama walked in courageously with her friend by her side. A rather stout man behind the desk was shuffling papers and drinking a cup of coffee. He gazed at the two ladies with an annoying look and asked, "Which one of you wants a license?" Mrs. Thorne spoke up and replied, "The Lady Here." Indicating my mother. The bureaucrat looked at her and asked, "Do you know how to drive?" "Yes"

Annabelle Merne Linn

replied Mama. Then the man asked the lady "Does this woman know how to drive?" "Yes" she replied. "How do you know that she knows how to drive?" He asked. "Because I taught her myself," replied the woman. "Do you have a license?" "Yes." "Let me see it." Mrs. Thorne then produced her own license and showed it to the interrogator. "Well, okay, Lady you get a license. What's your name?"

My mother was so elated that she happily filled out as form and handed over the money. With a license in hand, she then drove the car back to our room. When Mama showed my father her license, he was amazed. "I never thought you could do it. Now I'll have to let you take the family car back home, because I'll be starting a new engineering assignment here. The company will furnish me a car." "Henry, are you really going to be working here?" Mama asked. "Yes, and we'll have to give up our home there and put all the furniture in storage. I start work this week, but I'll get my brother Dan to help you pack up everything. You had better plan on leaving here tomorrow."

Little did I know what a challenge that drive back home would be. I'm sitting in the middle, Mama in the driver's seat. We got out of town all right, then we had a red light at the last part of town, and Mama had to stop. Unfortunately, she had to stop at the light and it was on a hill. I didn't know how we were going to do this, so I held the emergency brake, Mama worked the clutch, gas brake, and shifter. When the light turned green I very, very slowly let the emergency brake out, and once again, we were moving. Not too much longer, we approached another light on a hill; this process went on for most of the trip. When we got to where Uncle Dan was he was waiting outside, and we asked where do we put the car. He said, "We have to go to Baltimore." Mama said, "I am so tired do I have to drive?" My Uncle said, "No, I will drive now." So he drove us all the way to Baltimore. The next day we went to New York to visit my grandfather. We stayed there for a couple days then we eventually got back home. I felt sick and came down with the chicken pox and when Daddy would come home, since we weren't sure at first what it was, small pox, chicken pox or what, Daddy would not come near me. He would say "How you feeling honey?" when he got home and headed into another room. The Doctor sent out a specialist and the specialist thought it was chicken pox. It was raining really hard and there was supposed to be an election and my father's friend was running for office. He got really sick from the weather, the election went on and he won but he was so sick he couldn't take the position and because of his sickness, he died. I was just as sick and Mama said should I take Annabelle to Florida where the weather is warmer. Daddy said yes, it would be better. Off to Florida we went. Thank God, there were no hills. In a few weeks, I was much better. Mama decided to stay in Florida to better her teaching career, and so my father said ok. By the time we left Florida Mama could pretty much finally drive the car by herself.

Penny Found
By Margaret Boggs of Cumberland,
Maryland
Born 1948

Across the street was a country store. It sold the basics: milk, bread, and my favorite coconut candy shaped like a slice of watermelon.

There were not set hours for the store to be open. The lady that ran the store lived up the lane with her daughter and family. If the store wasn't open, we could go to the house and asked her to open and she would.

The store had a wooden porch; when the street light came on we would meet up at the store porch to play hide'n seek, making the store porch our base.

Our town had three other Mom'n Pop stores. Along with the penny candy, you could get a five-cent candy bar and a cold "iced-down" pop for a dime.

We had a unique Post Office as it also had a candy counter within the Post Office.

Walking to grade school would sometimes or back occasionally a penny would be found. It would be a great find, as you knew when you checked the mail on your way home from school you had a penny to spend.

All the storeowners knew us by our first names. It was a great feeling of community. Growing up in that era helps me to keep focused on keeping with the simplicity of days gone by, before computers, Ipod, XBoxes, and cell phones distracts our youth. The best gift to give children is simplicity of life

Waiting Room
By Celia Miller of Chapel Hill, North Carolina
Born 1940

The local dentist was building a new office building. A joker brought an outhouse and set it outside. He put a sign on it saying, "Dr. Quack is in, please be seated." The dentist was highly upset, he rushed outside and knocked it over, but it looked so bad underneath he straightened it up again.

Through a Child's Eyes
By Marlyn Angus of Hancock, Maryland
Born 1935

There have been numerous memories in my 78 years, but I would like to write about one. When I was about five years old, my mother married her second husband, John S. Gough. My stepfather was the owner of the Pimlico Hotel, next to the Pimlico Racetrack in Baltimore, Maryland. The hotel is dated back to 1875. I think John Gough and his father Harry Gough ran the business in the '30s.

I recall a big, grey clapboard hotel with a dining room, a bar with spittoons beside each bar on the floor, and a barbershop adjacent to the dining room. The two waiters, Clayton and Rice, together with my stepfather, wore white jackets. The small ladies room was housed in a storage room where supplies were kept. I remember New Year's Eve party decorations there, also.

The maid would take me upstairs to help her make up the iron beds. There was also a cook who would put me at the kitchen table and spoil me with goodies. John Gough would leave the basement door unlocked in winter so the homeless man could keep warm.

All of this was during World War II. We lived on Cheswold Road off of Greenspring Avenue in Baltimore County. I remember air raid men going up the road to make sure people had their black shades down. Also, John was able to get war stamps to buy food for his business.

In about 1948, he sold the Pimlico Hotel. The new owners had form stone put over it. Later it was torn down and only the Pimlico Racetrack remains. After the sale, John Gough went into partnership with two other men and opened the Surrey Inn on Reisterstown Road in Baltimore County. I can't remember how long they were in business. John Gough passed away in October of 1953. The Surrey Inn was torn down to make way for the Baltimore Beltway.

The Wonderful Miss Sheetz
By Janice M. Carper of Shepherdstown, West Virginia
Born 1931

When I was in Hagerstown High School in the 1940s, I had several excellent and memorable teachers. One teacher, Rachel Sheetz, stood out above all the rest. She was articulate, sophisticated, friendly, and a terrific teacher. No one else could have made Shakespeare or other English authors as interesting as she did. Rachel Sheetz was able to take the dullest subject and effectively use it to educate. We daily had long lists of words to memorize their meaning and spelling— ordinary words, which brought out the jokes and laughter.

We enjoyed her classes. We became familiar with literature and sentence structure in spite of ourselves.

Some of us took every English and journalism class we could take with her as teacher. She shared her love of learning with us. Even her, "Out, damn spot," was memorable!

Rachel Sheetz volunteered to teach at the state correctional unit and even there was able to encourage and help inmates to improve their lives. When she was selected to go to Hagerstown's sister city, Wesel, Germany, she endeared herself to many of the German students while learning German herself.

Her career in Hagerstown was completed at the community college, where she retired at 74. Even in retirement, she voluntarily taught into her 80s while living in Texas near her brother and his family.

When I returned to my home area 60 years after my graduation, I visited her grave. I, like many others, have always credited her with our ability to write well and to love learning. And, even though I was too late to thank her in person, I did offer up a prayer of gratitude for the quality her teaching had added to my life.

Buried with her parents in Williamsport, her tombstone simply gives her name and dates. There is nothing to suggest the effect Rachel Sheetz had on her many students. Her legacy is found only in those of us who remember her. Perhaps, for a time, that is enough.

What do we do With It?
By Faith E. Poland of Keyser, West Virginia
Born 1941

Approximately 72 years ago, my parents, Francis and Ada Moorehead, bought their home in Bloomington, Maryland. The house was previously owned by a Fazenbaker family who were arrested for making moonshine in the basement. Litigation forced them to sell the house, so my parents were able to buy it for $2500.00. During the next few years, improvements were made to the house. During this time, there was no evidence of the illegal activity that had been going on the previous years.

One day, Mom decided it was once again time to wash the outside of the kitchen window. Dirt from coal truck traffic and the steam-fired railroad engines made this job a frequent chore. As she had many times before, Mom propped the stepladder up against the house so she could reach the window. As she reached the step close to the top of the ladder and was about to reach for the washcloth in her bucket of water, the ladder collapsed from under her, throwing her to the ground. After regaining her composure, she went to investigate what caused the ladder to collapse. She found that the ladder was intact but the bottom portion had disappeared down into the ground!

Getting her husband and a neighbor, they pulled the ladder out of the hole and discovered that a barrel containing moonshine whiskey had been buried just outside the basement window. Even though the barrel was now empty, the strong smell of whiskey remained.

This incident provided many hours of "what if" discussion down through the years. They wondered that if the barrel had actually been full of very old moonshine, would have it been any good? What would have it been worth? But the question of the day was, "What do we do with it?"

A Piece of History
By Pat McKnew of Points, West Virginia
Born 1940

On May 11, 1998, my husband and I moved into our log home on a 112-acre farm in Points, West Virginia. I'd look out the back windows watching our cows across the pasture and imagine a civil war battle being fought there or on similar ground.

In the winter, the only heat we had were two woodstoves—one in the kitchen and one in the living room. I would stand in front of the stove and slowly turn around several times 'til I was toasty. I'd sit in the recliner and let the warmth penetrate in my back. Wet socks would hang on nails across the mantle of the fireplace—not for candy, but to dry out.

One day I noticed something white hanging down from between the logs. It looked like caulking. I pulled it out and saw it was paper. Carefully, I unrolled the brittle paper and read it. It read, "*N.C. Course Balt. February 4. The House of Representatives today passed unanimously a resolution declaring that in case the efforts of reconciliation fail N.C.,*

The moonshine house

Pat's log home

along with the other slave states..." That was all that was on that piece of paper.

I was so excited. I got a stepladder and a gutter spike (a big nail) and poked between the logs, fishing out more rolled-up papers. They were from a Baltimore newspaper dated January 23, 1863. The papers had been rolled up and stuffed between logs to keep out cold air. I carefully unrolled each one, read it, and put these very brittle papers in a shirt box.

A few years later in Romney, West Virginia at a Heritage Day festival, I met a woman who professionally restored historic papers for the state. She worked with my papers. I chose the pieces that fit together in an article and mounted them on a black mat board. My husband made a picture frame from weathered barn boards to put them in. It now hangs in our new home on the farm.

Years later, the log home was torn down, moved to another farm, and put back together. We continue to enjoy life on our West Virginia farm. It is home.

Not Much But a Good Life
By Arlene Snyder of Ridgeley, West Virginia
Born 1937

I was born at Patterson Creek, West Virginia in a big, old farmhouse. I went to school in a one-room house with a big, old potbelly stove in the middle of the room for heat. We really had bad cold and snowy winters, we went to school every day, no snow day's off from school, like it is today, a little snow or cold weather it is called (NO SCHOOL). We had a lot of homework to do at home, we didn't have computers and internets, and adding machines like now days. We learned the multiplication tables and the state capitals, which they do not teach today. We took are lunch to school, and we had an outside toilet at school and at home (out house), not a bathroom like today. We took are Saturday night bath in a washtub. At school, we would all get together with classmates and playmates and play. Ring around the Rosie, Drop the handkerchief, play ball, and play tag you run and tagged someone and they was out of the game the one tagged was the winner the last one.

At home, it was fun with all of our brothers and sisters. We had no video games or TV, just an old record player and a radio for news and weather report, and a phone line, and when it would ring, you could hear what they was talking about it was a lot of fun you knew all the news.

So us kids would before dark play hopscotch, jump rope, marbles, and horseshoes. After dark we would play Old Maid, go fish, match cards lay all cards on the table and pick up cards to match, you had to remember where they was to make a match, ones with the most pairs won.

We had to do a lot of things, before we could play anything. Get are school homework done. Feed the animals and water them, get the eggs, and get are lunch boxes ready for morning, and are clothing ready to put on. And whatever mom and dad told us to do.

We had fun times, better then what the kids do now days. Children today are lazy, we was always on the go with lots of happiness and fun, we didn't know any other way, and we was always a happy family. We always said a Bible verse and are prays, didn't have much but a good life.

The Easy Washer
By Mildred Roach of Cumberland, Maryland
Born 1935

I remember when I was a child, I came from a family of 14 kids, we were very poor, but we had lots of fun.

We washed clothes on the washboard,

when I was nine years old we got a washing machine. It didn't have any wringer to it, so we still had to wring clothes by hand, but later on, we did get a wringer for the washer. (I still remember the name of that washer. It was named Easy.) We also had a floor model wind up record player. It took 78 records. We also had table model radio. We listen to radio programs such as "Blondie & Dagwood," "Fibber McGee & Molley," "Gene Autry," "Roy Roger & Dale Evans," "Lone Ranger & Tonto." We never had a TV back in those days. When my mother went to town, she would buy comic books for ten cents. My mother liked to read cowboy comic books.

I can remember when our mother bought grocery, she would buy oleo. It was white when she got it. In the center was a little button. We would push on it and the butter would turn yellow. The more you squeezed it, the more color you would get. We all liked it.

I can also remember stamps were two cents, post cards were one cent.

I also know that our mother had some tokens; this is when the war was going on, to buy sugar, butter, meats, and milk. There were red and blue tokens, since mother had so many children, and got so many, she would trade with her friends.

We used to go to the playground to play in the summertime; it was the only playground to have a real swimming pool over there. It was called East Side Playground.

I can remember our old icebox. We had a man that would bring us a 50-pound brick of ice, when the ice melted, we had to empty the pan of water, and many of times, our pan would run over.

I can remember the rotary phones, we had a four-party lines. I was should glad when private lines came in. I also know when we had a milkman, a bread man, a lady sold country butter, also was a ragman who came once a week.

In the wintertime, we would play games on our living room floor, such as Scrabble, Parcheesi, checkers, dominoes, Life, Monopoly, and many more.

My mother had a Treadle Singer sewing machine. She used to make our clothes for us. She also would bake bread, rolls, and pies. My mother was a very good cook. We used to get the Grit Paper, also the Good Ole Days book; I haven't seen any of them for years.

Didn't Have Money, But We Had Love
By Elsie Mae Parsons of Hedgesville, West Virginia
Born 1935

My mother and father were born and raised in Shanghai, West Virginia. My father was called into the U.S Army in World War I. When he came home, they got married and moved to Ganotown where they bought a farm. This is where me and my sister Sarah still love today. My dad is Charles Edmond (Ed) Parsons. My mom was Sallie Kerns.

They had cows, hogs, chickens, and one mule. Dad used the mule to plow the garden. We always had a large garden, and mom canned a lot of vegetables and made jellies from our produce. When my sister and I were born, we went to a one-room school for grades one through eight. Mrs. Doris Frye was our teacher. When we came home from school, we would help milk the cows. We made a lot of cottage cheese and churn the butter. Mom made homemade bread. We butchered three big hogs each year. Neighbors would help. Everyone would help each other. Mom would bake cakes and pies the day before. The ladies would help with the dinner. I would help Dad sugar cure the meat the next day. Mom and Sarah would cold pack the meat. We made a 40-gallon kettle of apple butter each year.

Sarah and I learned to drive our dad's 29 Model A Ford car, and we still have dad's 31 Model A Ford Truck that we use on the farm today. We still use it on the farm today to feed

Elsie's father, Ed Parsons working in the garden in 1956

Ed, Sallie and Sarah Parsons in 1950

the cows and get in wood. Dad would go to the store every two weeks to get flour, sugar, coffee, and feed for the cows and chickens. Mom would make us dresses out of feed sacks. She would always make our doll baby a dress just like the ones she made for us to wear. We did not have much money, but we had love.

Elsie and Bess in 1989

School Snow Days
By Barbara Heilig of Swanton, Maryland
Born 1952

Sometimes it's hard to remember what life was like when I was young. Other times it comes back with unbelievable clarity. As I sit and look out at the snow, and spend another day home because school has been cancelled, I remember snow days from my childhood. Of course, school was rarely called off because of the weather. If you could get to school, then school was held. I remember the mittens drying on the radiators that sat around the room. Coats and boots were in a small room we called the coat closet. Tall windows that reached the ceiling showed snow falling in drifts on the playground and we always went out. No staying in for us hardy souls. We played "duck, duck, goose, and goose" or built snowmen. Afterward, the playground would be filled with snow people. I would sit inside during the afternoon and could see my snowman watching, wishing to be inside and cozy.

Sometimes there were snow days at home, which were welcomed with great anticipation. No boredom here and no staying inside to play video games or watch TV. Out we would go, bundled up in snowsuits and mittens, hats and scarves to build snowmen, forts, and go sled riding. We didn't mind the cold. Up the hill, we would pull the sled, and down we would fly to the bottom. We had one sled, and there were four of us, so we took turns. Of course, we older ones made the younger ones pull the sled up the hill, and we rode it down. It didn't take them long to figure this out. Sometimes we went down alone; many times, it was two or three together and, of course, hitting the bottom and rolling off onto each other was the most fun. No one ever told us it was dangerous to throw snowballs. My brothers lived for the snowball fights and we, girls, weren't afraid to get our licks in either.

One event that I particularly remember was a snowy day when I did make it to school, but making it home was not as easy. We lived with my grandparents between two hills and often the bus driver chose not to come down into our valley, so we did not go to school. This particular day, the bus driver got to the top of our hill and decided if he went down, he probably would not get back up. My parents were called from the house at the top of the hill (no cell phones) and told that they needed to come get me. Well, they couldn't get to the top of the hill either. Next thing I know, I am climbing on my neighbor's tractor. He bundles me in a big, wool blanket and off we go over drifts and through the blowing snow to my grandmother's house. Here we both get hot chocolate and warmed up. Then off he goes, back through the snow. No problem, that's just what neighbors did for each other. I'll always remember him saying that a tractor ride was better than a bus ride any day. I have to agree with him.

Hillbilly and Proud of It!
By Freeda E. Davy of Purgisville, West Virginia
Born 1935

My name is Freeda E. Davy. I was born on July 25, 1935 to James and Josephine Rinker Davy. I am next to the oldest of 12 children. I had one sister four years older than me. Her and I were real close. We did everything together. Her and I told each other our secrets. We went on double dates together. She is deceased now and I miss her terribly. I had five sisters, and I made six. One was stillborn. I had five brothers, and one died at age 13. One was killed in Vietnam. One died of a heart attack. I only have two brothers left.

We were raised on a farm. We all had our own chores to do—and we did them. We had cows to feed and milk. We also had chickens, hogs, sheep, and goats. We got up early and milked the cows before going to school. One time, my brother and I went to feed the hogs, and I remember that he picked up a rock and threw it at the pig. That pig was knocked right out! He rant to the pond and got a bucket of water. He then poured it on the pig. It came to. We never told Mom and Dad for a long time.

We only went to the store once a month. Mom would write down what she needed and Dad would get it. We had our own milk, butter, cottage cheese, eggs, and meat. Mom always baked bread. I can remember when she was pregnant with my third brother. At this time, she was expecting anytime. She asked me to mix up the bread. She put everything in the dishpan and told me how to mix it. I was 13 years old, and I have been making homemade bread this way ever since.

We walked to school, which was two miles. I went to a one-room school for eight years. I graduated from Romney High in 1954. I went to work for a man in Piedmont. My honey and I were engaged, and I worked for two years. In February of 1955 on Valentine's Day, we got married. Robert told everyone the reason we got married on Valentine's Day was so he wouldn't forget it! We were married for 58 years. He got colon cancer and had surgery. He got along good for several years until the cancer went to his lever. He passed away May 20, 2011 and I miss him dearly.

We had five daughters (now 47-57 in age) and we lost a son at birth. My oldest daughter died September 27, 2013. She had a lot of health problems and had a stroke. My husband worked for Potomac Edison for 32 years and then retired. I stayed at home and raised our five daughters. I lost my best and closest sister in 2010, my husband in 2011, and my oldest daughter in 2013. I was proud of my husband and he was proud of me. We both worked together and got along. That is more than I can say for a lot of them today. It was not easy, but we made it, and I thank God that we did. His dad gave us a piece of land and we built a house on it. It isn't the best, but it suits us and the roof don't leak. I am a pure West Virginia Hillbilly and I am proud of it!

Growing Up on Central Avenue
By Kathy Hovatter of Parsons, West Virginia
Born 1958

I was six years old when my family moved to Parsons—mom, dad, sisters Susan, Barb, me (Kathy), and our grandad, John. We moved into a big, old house on Central Avenue. My parents still live there. Not the same house. Like a lot of people, they lost everything in the 1985 flood.

When we first moved there, it was different. We lived in the country. Most of the time it was just me and my sisters. Now we lived where there was a lot of kids. It was fun to go outside and see who would be out playing.

Back then you didn't have to worry about where or who your kids was with. We played out until dark, a lot of nights we played hide-

and-seek until our moms yell for us to come in.

When we went to school, we walked. No bus came and got us. And our parents never drove us to school. We walk across town to school.

We never missed school for a snow day. If the buses didn't make it, us walkers still went to school.

In the summer, after your chores were done, we could go do what we wanted. We rode bikes, walked, and I loved to roller skate. My Grandma Margie got all three of us girls roller skates. You put them on your shoes and they had a key that you tighten down to fit your shoes. She got them from saving green stamps. I'm sure a lot of people today don't know what green stamps are.

We had a lot of kids who lived around the big block. Sometimes we would play at each other's house, but we were outside most of the time.

In the summer, we were in the river a lot, even when our mom and dad told us not to. I remember one time we were told not to go to the river. And like kids now days, we didn't listen. I was under the water and opened my mouth; thank God, my sister Susan was with me, I through I was going to drown. But she slapped me on the back and I was fine, but I didn't go back in the river for a long time. There was always older kids there who would watch out for us little ones.

When I look back now I know that I was raised so different then the kids now days. Kids now have to wear helmets when they ride a bike and all kinds of pads when they roller skate. I know it's to keep them safe, but I'm glad I had the kind of childhood I had.

"Those were the good old days." Some will say, "The only thing good about them are they are gone." Not me. I miss them days. Some of the best memories I have as a child is playing cards with Janette on her front porch. Having breakfast with Carol Ann and Carolyn Lee. Their mom had homemade bread every day. We played "red light, green light," jumped rope to "Mabel, Mabel, set the table."

When I go to Central Avenue now most of the houses are gone. All of my friends have moved away. We have families of our own. And, hard to believe, but we have grandkids.

I hope that they still remember what Central Avenue used to look like. All the beautiful Oak trees that lined the road. And all the good times we had as kids.

Long Live the Mustang
By Mark A. Zembower of Bedford, Pennsylvania
Born 1957

April 17, 1964 was a date that changed automotive history. It was the day that the Ford Mustang was introduced to the American public. Even at my young age, about six years old, I thought that car was the zenith of automobiles—long hood, short trunk, and sporty-looking. It was unlike any other American-made car at that time. The American public ate it up. In less than two years, the Mustang sold over one million units. At that time, there were only two body styles offered—the hardtop and the convertible.

Then came 1965 and the introduction of the "fastback" model of the extremely popular Mustang. I fell in love all over again, as did many Americans. Performance enthusiasts were chomping at the bit (to use a horse analogy). What a beautiful car! In that same year, Ford Motor Company collaborated with renowned racecar driver and car designer Carrol Shelby to develop a high-performance Mustang. He followed through, much to my delight and other "muscle car" enthusiasts.

The Shelby Mustang GT 350 was the ultimate Mustang. Also in 1965, Ford came out with the Mustang GT, a somewhat cheaper and slower version of the Shelby Mustang. Most of the public couldn't afford Shelby

Mark's grandfather, "Witt" Zembower in 1991

Mustangs, but could scrape enough to buy a Mustang GT.

In 1968, Carrol Shelby came out with the ultimate Mustang—the Shelby Mustang GT 500 KR. The "KR" stood for "King of the Road." With its 428 super cobra jet engine, it could easily outrun any competitor. Once again, the Shelby Mustang was relatively unaffordable to the general public.

The Ford Motor Company, however, had never touted the Mustang as a "sports car" at that time. Ford described it as a "personal car." And it was. You could get a hardtop (or "notchback"), convertible, or fastback. You could get an inline six-cylinder, a V-8, or a high-performance V-8. You could choose an automatic transmission, a three-speed manual, or a four-speed manual transmission. The choice of any combination was yours. Power steering, power brakes, and air-conditioning were available options, as were radios and heaters. A very few Mustangs were ordered with "bench" front seats instead of front bucket seats.

So, if you were a librarian, an auto mechanic, a plumber, a sports writer, a preacher, a brain surgeon, a rocket scientist, a president, a landscaper, an astronaut, a musician, a dental hygienist, a veterinarian, or a fortune-teller, there was a Mustang just for you. Take your pick.

Fast forward to 1969. Ford introduced the Mustang Mach 1. It was the most beautiful car that I had ever seen. It had the newly introduced "sportsroof" body style. There was no other car that came close to the styling of this particular Mustang. Other than the Shelby Mustang, there was no other Mustang that could compare to the high-performance aspects attributed to the Mach 1. I considered it the "poor man's Shelby."

I obviously don't want to go beyond 1969 much. I will admit I owned a 1970 Mach 1 for 25 years. I am, in case you couldn't tell, a "Mustanger." I will offer a few facts in closing. The Mustang has been the only "Pony Car" with an uninterrupted run for 50 years. It was always a front-engined, rear-wheel drive, four-seater passenger car. The Mustang will celebrate its 50th anniversary this year. There will be at least two national celebrations of this historic, iconic car. For its longevity, it should be admired. For its consistency, it should be revered. Long live the Mustang!

Swing Set Mishap
By Mary Ritchie of Frostburg, Maryland
Born 1947

In 1953, when I was six, I lived on Scotch Hill in Lonaconing, Maryland. I had a good friend who lived on the same street. She had a big swing set which set on a hillside and wasn't fastened in the ground.

My dad told me that I wasn't allowed to go there when no one was home. He told me if a window got broken or something else happened, I would get blamed.

One day I decided to sneak off and swing for a short while. I would swing as high as I could. I upset the swing set so I ran home as fast as I could.

When the family returned home, they knew who had done this. They came to my house to make sure I wasn't hurt.

I learned from this incident and never went into anyone's yard when no one was home.

When I was six years old, we had a pet Billy goat, which was tied in the back yard. This goat always managed to get loose.

One time he tore clothes off the clothesline.

Mary with her mom

Students from Scotch Hill

Another time he went over to the neighbor's house and chewed up a brand new umbrella that was drying on the porch. My dad had to buy another umbrella to replace the one that was destroyed.

We all realized that a goat was not a good pet to have while living in town.

Dad was able to find a home for this pet on a farm out in the country.

In 1958, when I was 11 years old, I lived in Knapps Meadow. This is located above Lonaconing, Maryland.

My dad owned a floor model, short wave radio. Short wave meant we were able to get radio stations from other countries.

We would listen to programs like "The Lone Ranger," "Gunsmoke," "Amos & Andy," "Dragnet," and "The Shadow."

The whole family would sit together since this was our only entertainment.

My sister still has this radio in her home. She tells people who would like to buy this that it is not for sale.

Lonaconing had a movie theater on Main Street called "The San Toy Theater." In the lobby on the left side was "The Nut Shop." The Nut Shop sold chips, popcorn, soda, ice cream, and candy.

Sometimes on Saturdays, my sister and I would be given 25 cents each so we could see a movie. Admission was 15 cents a person; and we could buy popcorn for five cents and a drink for five cents.

We would see a cartoon, preview of coming attractions, and a full-length movie.

We would only go once in a while, because there wasn't a lot of money.

Mary with her sister, Cathy

Dirty Water as Bug Killer
By Linda Sechler of Barberton, Ohio
Born 1944

When I was a little girl, I watched and sometimes helped my mother to wash our clothes. Monday was always the day to wash the clothes. She would start to do the wash as soon as the outside farm chores was done, usually around 9 a.m. The washer set on an unheated, enclosed porch in the warm weather. When it got cold, we had to roll the washer into the kitchen beside the sink. We used a bucket to get water from the sink to fill the large round washer tub. It took five to six bucket fulls to fill the tub. The dirty clothes was sorted by colors into five or six loads. Put the soap and bluing in the water. Bluing was a blue liquid that came in a bottle. A small amount of bluing was enough for the wash. Bluing was to make the white clothes whiter. The lever to turn the washer on was at the left side of the tub. Just slide the lever to the right to turn the agitator on then add the dirty clothes. The white clothes got washed first. Then the light-soiled clothes to the dirtiest was the order to wash each load. Each load would wash as long as you thought it needed to clean the clothes. Usually from three to 15 minutes a load. The wringer had two round rubber rollers and an adjustor knob on top of washer. You adjusted the knob for the thickness of the clothes you was putting thru the wringer.

Sometimes the clothes would wrap around the rollers. Then you had to reverse the wringer to get the clothes out of it. Then try to put the clothes thru the wringer again. If some clothes got stuck in the rollers there was a button you pushed to completely undo the wringer to get the clothes out of it. You had to be very careful not to get your fingers in the rollers. After each load washed and was put thru the wringer you put them in the clothesbasket until all the loads was washed. Then empty the dirty water. A rubber hose on the side of the machine you lowered into the bucket to drain the tub. We poured the dirty water over the pine trees in the yard. It would kill all spiders and bugs in the tree. When the tub was empty, we would use clean water and rinse out the tub. Then use our bucket to fill the tub again to rinse the clothes. After they were rinsed and wrung out, they were put in a basket to go outside to hang on a rope line. The rope was strung from tree to tree in the orchard. In the winter, a line was strung across the living room behind the coal stove that heated the house. As the clothes dried, mother would take them down then put wet ones up to dry. We never had a clothes dryer. In winter, she would hang sheets and towels outside on the line. The clothes would freeze solid—no way to fold them. Late afternoon she would bring them in the house to thaw out and finish drying. Monday night we would sprinkle the clothes we had to iron. To sprinkle the clothes we used a soda pop bottle with a cork stopper that had lots of holes in it for the water to come out. Sprinkle the clothes, roll them up, and put into plastic bag to iron on Tuesday.

Mark of the Beast
By Irene Hughes of Cumberland, Maryland
Born 1929

Mom kept shouting out orders as she bustled about getting ready for our summer outing. "Don't forget your bathing suits. There's room for only one inner tube. No, the dog cannot go along this time!" Uncle Joe finally drove into view, announcing his arrival by honking out a tune on his horn. Aunt Mary took up most of the front seat, as she was very pregnant (due in a few weeks). Mary Ann was squeezed between Auntie and Uncle Joe. Young Steve waved from the rumble seat.

I listened as driving arrangements were made. The conversation included Auntie saying, "Oh, I probably shouldn't be going, but this may be my last time to enjoy this weather before the baby comes." Mother added, "Now, don't worry about a thing. I have everything we'll need. Today is our treat." Steve and my brother Frank got to sit in the rumble seat (about which all of us argued). Mary Ann and I sat in our car in the back seat among the hampers of food and cooking utensils for our picnic spot and we were on our way.

We were fortunate to find our favorite picnic spot along Crooked Creek unoccupied that hot, sunny day. The men emptied the car and started a cooking fire while we kids ran into the bushes to change into our bathing suits. Frank yelled, "Last one in's a rotten egg!" I shouted, "Look at the raspberries! The bushes are loaded!" That piqued the parent's interests. "We'll have to pick some before we leave."

The day proved to be as wonderfully happy as we had hoped. We stuffed ourselves on fried chicken, "fixins," and dessert. Finally, we found containers and began picking the berries from truly heavily laden bushes. Suddenly there was a scream. It came from Aunt Mary! "A snake! Oh, Oh, Lord help me!" We all raced in toward her, as my Dad grabbed a huge, ugly blacksnake from her neck and heaved it into the bushes. Auntie's face became a strange ashen color as she went limp. As Uncle Joe held her and asked, "Did it bite you?" She gathered her strength and replied, "No. But it crawled up this loose dress and onto my neck." Oh! I hope the baby won't be marked!"

The ride home was pretty subdued as we pondered what she meant by "a marked baby." I had heard of this superstition among others, as this saying was prevalent in our neighborhood. I couldn't wait for that baby to be born and to get that snake out of my mind.

Two weeks later, Uncle Joe called to say he had called the doctor, as the baby was on its way. We kids were ushered into the living room and told to be quiet. The door opened and the doctor hurried up the stairs with his black bag. Mary Ann said, "See how stuffed his bag is? He's got the baby in there." I shushed her, but I wasn't sure she wasn't right. What seemed hours later we heard the doctor coming down the stairs. Mary Ann again whispered, "Look! That bag is skinnier. He left the baby." Soon, Mom came down and announced, "Steve, Mary Ann, you have a baby brother!" One by one, we were permitted to visit the bedroom. I couldn't wait, and blurted out, "Is the baby marked?" Mom looked at Auntie saying, "It's all we've heard since that encounter with that snake. Aunt Mary laughed and said, "I'm afraid so." Should I show her? Then she gently uncovered one tiny buttock, and there it was—the perfect outline of a tiny raspberry.

Hidden Shoe
By Patsy D. Morgan-Runkles of Harpers Ferry, West Virginia
Born 1945

My first playhouse was our old pigpen. My sister, Nancy, and I divided the stall into two sections and, with the help from mother, we had jar lids and cut out pictures from the catalog for pictures, tablecloth from mom's old dress, cardboard for carpet, and garbage bag drapes. We made mud pies and actually ate macaroni soaked in water to eat as it softened up. To me, the playhouse it was my mansion on the hill.

Having a younger sister, Carolyn who usually got all the attention because of her black, curly hair, I remember her getting these pretty patent leather shoes for Easter. My shoes weren't as pretty as hers, so I took one of her shoes and buried it in the backyard. To this day, no one found out about the shoe and I never told!

I remember roller-skating with the clamp-on skates that always left holes in the side of our shoes. I still have half of the one skate, remember they came in sections. For years, we were the "Roller Derby Queens" skating down the streets of Harpers Ferry, West Virginia. My sisters always followed behind me.

My first cigarette was pages from the newspaper. I rolled it tightly and tried smoking behind dad's car. I enjoyed every puff until dad saw the flames.

Oh yes, I remember mom wearing a pointed bra that would poke out any man's

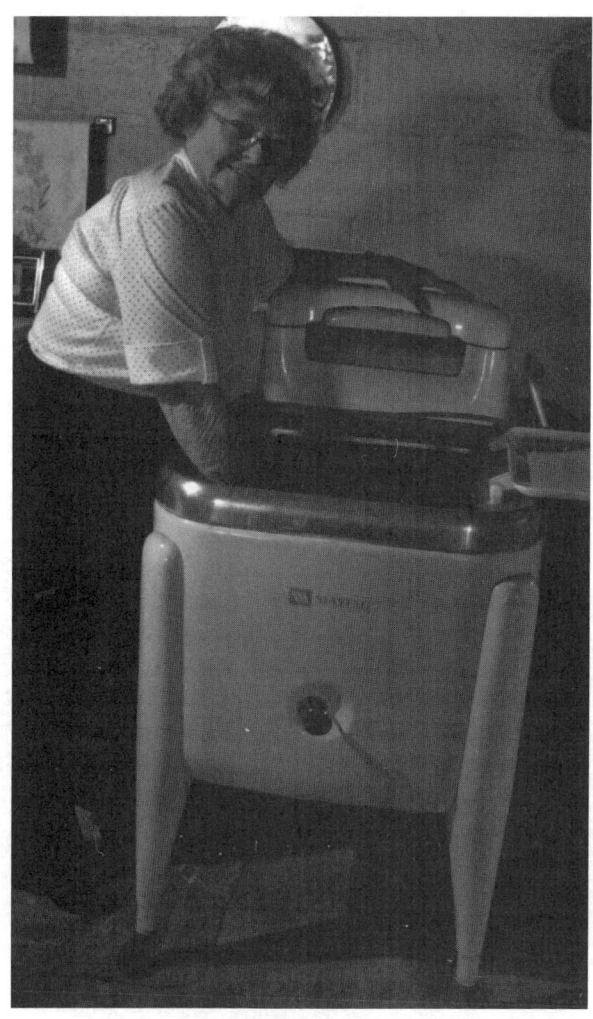

Patsy's mother, Evelyn DeHaven James

eye. I would borrow it for play and stuffed it with old socks, tissue paper, or toilet tissue. Man, did I look like Marilyn Monroe in my eyes. My girlfriend, Diane gave me my first bra for my twelfth birthday. I wore the bra day and night for one month. Mom finally told me it had to be washed.

I loved the sun and would have a contest with my girlfriend, Mary Louise when school was out for summer on who could get the best tan. I knew mom used Crisco oil for frying chicken, so I came up with the bright ideal that if Crisco browns chicken so golden, why not coat yourself in the grease. That I did, and after soaking in the sun for hours, all I got was blisters and a swollen face.

I also remember putting iodine in baby oil and getting a better tan.

My mother, who will be 90 in May, still (to this day) uses her wringer washer. She has an automatic washer, but does not use it. I do have pictures of her washing with her wringer washer.

My first sight on seeing a color TV was when my girlfriend, Diane, and I decided to sneak out one night and peep in the neighbor's window who just purchased the television. Glad we didn't get caught.

With five children in our family, we didn't have many toys, but when it snowed, mom would let up use an old lid from her extra wringer washer to slide down our bank. We also had an old medal rocking chair and we'd all sit in it and fly down that steep hill. The advantages of living on a secondary road.

My fondest memory of grade school, on a Monday morning I arrived at C. W. Shipley School and found a $1 in the hallway, I took the dollar to the Principal's office. He said to come back on Friday and, if no one claimed the dollar, it was mine. Every morning, Tuesday, Wednesday, Thursday, I went to the office only to hear him say, "Patsy it isn't Friday yet," and finally Friday arrived to which he handed me a dollar bill. I finally won the "Lottery"…

Darlene and her graduating class

Dixie
By Darlene Thompson of Asheville, North Carolina
Born 1949

Dixie Elementary in Riverton, West Virginia was not a one-room school, but had four—a cafeteria, an auditorium, and male and female outhouses. I'll never forget the clanging bell and tower to remind us it was time to hit the books. The rooms were consolidated to hold two grades per room. Each room was equipped with wooden desks, inkwells, and storage racks under the desks to hold our books. We were too sophisticated to tote backpacks. The blackboards were slate with both old and new chalk. We were deemed special when the teachers allowed us to clean the boards and dust the erasers. We delighted in flying chalk on the large rocks or the fence in the schoolyard.

We had a dirt playground. No one ever worried about getting grimy at recess. It was a given to be soiled by a game of tag, Red Rover, dodge ball, skipping rope, and other games. It wasn't unusual to be covered in dirt and a few Band-Aids by the end of the school day. No parent ever sued the school for our nicks and bruises. They were merely badges of growing up.

When the classes began, one class would be reading or resolving problems quietly while the teacher taught the next grade. First and second were taught by a jolly, patient teacher, Molly Harper. Not much disturbed her. She provided us with our first adventures of reading, writing, and arithmetic. Cursive writing was a requirement. We learned about Jane and Spot and how they ran. We learned numbers and counting as we completed our days.

The third and fourth grades were taught by Virginia Adamson. She was considered difficult by us because she seldom smiled or laughed. We learned much about hygiene, health, and geography. I still remember all the state capitals. In one of her classes, she had a wonderful story about Mexico and the Aztec Calendar Stone. It made such an impression on me that I went to Mexico to see it when I was 18.

Fifth and sixth grades were taught by a mild, gentle man, Seylon Dove. He took us through civics, the U.S. Constitution, duty to our country, and social studies. In addition, he was the girls' volleyball coach. I still can remember his famous words when we missed a spike. "Get the lead out of your pants!"

The principal, Samson Bland, taught the seventh and eighth grades. He was known to deliver a spanking if a student needed it. He taught West Virginia and U.S. History. He was considered tough but fair. Among these walls, I memorized the first paragraph of the Declaration of Independence, Preamble to the Constitution, Gettysburg Address, and numerous lines of poetry and literature.

The old cafeteria had both good and bad meals. I think most of us hated peas. We hid those emerald gems in our pockets, under the table, in napkins or pawned them off on someone that really liked them. We always said grace before the meals and on Fridays, we sang the doxology. We had a fire escape. It creaked and moaned with our every step. Sometimes doing the drill was more disconcerting than if we had been involved in a real fire.

Behind the school building, was our playground. We enjoyed recess with many games and simply running around the yard. Part of the playground was our softball field. We slid into the bases in a flurry of dust. The volleyball court was directly in front of the girls' outhouse. The school spent a lot of money on volleyballs because the outhouse door was left open. The volleyball seemed to have eyes for that hole.

As the years went by, Dixie closed her doors. During the flood of 1985, the school was spun off its foundation. In time, it was destroyed; only a memorial remains. Dixie never had modern conveniences and fancy attire, but as students we obtained knowledge that took many of us beyond her walls to worlds we would never had known had we not sat within these hallowed walls.

T-R-O-U-B-L-E
By Ralph E. Riley of Romney, West Virginia
Born 1934

Most school memories are held with fond affection. This school memory of mine never held fond affection, but in later years did lose its scorn.

It began in 1952 at Romney High School on a wintry day, after several inches of snow had fallen the night before. I, a junior, was on the way to my Biology class located in the annex building in back of the main school building. Walking behind me on the road that circled by the annex building were two cute, little freshman girls. I was gaining their attention by scooping snow from each guardrail posts with a thin tablet and slinging it over my shoulder at them. They were laughing and making a game of trying to jump out of the way of the cloud of snow that sometimes showered down on them.

However, looking down at me from a window on the second floor of the annex building (like an eagle looking down from its aerie at its prey, ready to swoop down for the kill) stood the principal—a man large in stature but small in temperament. I entered the building unaware of what waited for me at the top of the stairs as I began my climb. When I reached the landing, a giant hand reached out, grabbed me by the arm, and swung me around to a standing position facing the long hallway. My biology book, notebook, tablet, papers, and pencils I had carried under my other arm went sailing in a semi-circle around the floor.

"Bend over!" came his harsh command like that from a drill sergeant. Me? A junior? Bend over and humiliate myself in front of my fellow students that now encircled me, seeming to number in the hundreds? No way! Again, I heard the angry command, "Bend over!" Assist in my own execution? Throw the switch? Pull the cord to release the trapdoor beneath my feet? Again, I refused to comply on the grounds that it might tend to incriminate me. But, after silently asserting my second refusal and begging no plea of mercy, I felt the quick, downward thrust of my arm. It put me at the level of closely inspecting my shoelaces and seeing the rest of the world topsy-turvy.

Looking back, I believe I could have touched the floor with both elbows. Next, I heard an explosive sound—the result of an impact from a gorilla-sized hand meeting my posterior. It drove me two paces forward, but the vice-grip locked onto my upper arm pulled me two paces back. A second assault followed immediately with the same painful results. After assault number three (which I understood to be the limit of corporal punishment allowed by school authorities) I was released with the order, "Get to class!" It was directed not just to me but to the teacher and student spectators that packed the hall.

I was most willing to comply, but first I had to retrieve my school supplies. Luckily, the math teacher who stood in line of fire of them as they'd flown from my arm had graciously gathered them from the floor. After the principal's demonstration of rendering discipline with me as the example, the math teacher handed them to me with a broad grin. I continued on to class.

As I entered the biology classroom, my teacher lamented to me in a sad pseudo-voice that she had no cushion to lend me to sit on. Making no effort to spare my humiliation she grinned from ear to ear. And as I sat down at my desk on a thousand needles, her words contained more wisdom than she had intended them.

But I did receive one compensation from this grueling experience of severe punishment: For several days thereafter I savored in the notoriety of being the only junior, the student body could recall being the exhibition of corporal punishment at Romney High. Even after school hours, I was often besieged by students who weren't there to witness it, to share with them my bold episode. So, I related with boldness the exploit that led up to the ungracious treatment I received at the hands of the principal, each time adding a little John Wayne bravado to the intrigue. And, you might ask, were there any such future encounters between the principal and me? My answer is that throughout the remainder of my junior and senior years at Romney High School—there were none!

Until I graduated from Romney High School in 1953, each time the principal and I happened to meet in the halls between changes of classes, we ever would cordially exchange greetings. Friends.

Playing Possum
By Ruby O. Teets of Fairfax, Virginia
Born 1936

I grew up on a large farm in Mathias, West Virginia. I lived with my parents, four brothers, and four sisters. Mom and daddy had plenty of love for all of us. In the 1930s and 1940s, money was very scarce, but even though we didn't have money, we never went hungry. We always had plenty of food. We had cows, chickens, and pigs and we supplemented our diet with wild game, which at that time was plentiful. We enjoyed dining on wild turkey,

Vincent, Iris, Sandy, and Ruby

rabbit, squirrel, and deer. I don't think we ever ate raccoon, fox, or opossum and I had never seen one of these.

We also had a garden and grew all of our vegetables, which was a great variety. Pear, apple, peach, and plum trees yielded fruit and both fruit and vegetables were canned during the summer to be eaten during the winter. This was before home freezers were available.

We worked hard during the day and in the evenings, after finishing our chores, we had huge appetites.

One evening my mom had prepared a feast consisting of groundhog (also known as woodchuck), mashed potatoes, and green beans. She had steamed the groundhog until it was tender and then browned it in a large skillet of hot lard.

I think that was the first time that I had eaten groundhog and it was really tasty. However, after dinner I started feeling very sick. My mom took my temperature and it was 105 degrees. I was put to bed and excused from all of my farm chores for quite a few days.

But it wasn't the groundhog that made me sick; I was coming down with what was known then as the "big measles." Needless to say, I never ate groundhog again.

Even though I grew up on a farm in West Virginia and had seen a lot of animals, I had never seen an opossum or a fox.

One day, when I was about 12 years old,

mom, and daddy went to visit some relatives and left me, two younger sisters, and one older sister at home along with a girl friend who was visiting us. We decided to take a walk up to the top of the ridge in back of the house.

As we were walking, we saw an animal with gray fur with a little brown tint in it. We thought we had found a fox and we knew that a fox pelt could be sold for several dollars and we thought we would soon be rich. We didn't have any trouble catching the animal but it did growl at us. Our friend was wearing a scarf so we took her scarf and tied around the animal's mouth so it could not bite us.

We took the animal with us back to the house and put it in a crate on the front porch waiting for mom and daddy to come home and share in our good fortune. We thought daddy would be so proud of us, but he wasn't too thrilled, he took one look at it and said, "Take it back up on the ridge and leave it in the woods, it's a possum, not a fox."

There went our dreams of becoming rich.

Sadly, the friend that was with that day recently passed away at age 84. The last time I saw her was at a school reunion several years ago and as we visited, we both laughed as we shared the memory of the time that we went for a walk and found an opossum. She asked me if I had been fox hunting lately.

I now live in a city, my back yard is a wildlife habitat, and I do know the difference between an opossum and a fox. Often I see deer, raccoons, a fox, a coyote, and squirrels. I saw only one opossum, but haven't yet seen a groundhog.

Iris, Juanita, Evelyn, and Ruby

Little Farm Girls
By Mary Donna Jean Johnson Didawick of Berkeley Springs, West Virginia
Born 1937

My sister, Mildred, and I grew up in Morgan County, West Virginia six miles east of Berkeley Springs on a 131-acre farm in the '40s. My dad farmed corn, tomatoes, and grain. Tomatoes were for a cash income and the rest was used for home use and livestock. Dad would cut the wheat with a binder. It would be our job to shock the wheat up. This was to protect it from the elements until a threshing machine came to our neighborhood to thresh the wheat. We would end up with a big straw pile to play in.

Threshing day was a tiring day. We would provide a large meal for all of the workers. The bundles of wheat would have to be brought up from the field and tossed into the machine to

Donna and Mildred in 1942

separate the wheat from the straw. The wheat had to be taken to the granary for storage in bins. We kept one bin really clean with a cover on it. This wheat we would take to the flourmill for grinding for flour for our home use. This mill was located on the north end of town. Dad would buy supplements from the mill to mix with our other wheat and corn for the livestock and chickens. This supplement would come in flowered or printed feed sacks. Of these sacks, my mother would make all of our clothes to wear. Our mother would end up with some odd flour sacks and the women would trade until they received enough to make some dresses or shirts for their husbands.

We had a tomato canning factory next door to our farm. They canned under the label of Stony Ridge Tomatoes. We picked tomatoes all summer in the hot sun. Dad would take the tomatoes to the canning factory for selling. We worked in the factory when we were old enough. We would peel the tomatoes for five cents per 16 quart bucket. We started about the time we turned 15. Before that age, we would roll cans to be filled with the fruit.

My mother had a wringer washer and my sister and I were responsible for the laundry from the ages of nine and ten. She would fix the water in the washer and rinse tubs, and we would take it from there. We put the clothes though the wringer into the rinse tub, and then through the wringer again. Then we would hang them on a clothesline to dry. They would be doing chores on the farm that we couldn't help them do. We had a lot of responsibility for as young as we were.

We had a dairy farm, and we would have to get up early and help with the milking before going to school. Later, Dad put in automatic milkers, but that was still hard work. We had to carry the milk up to the milk house and strain it into milk cans. Then they were put into the milk cooler. All of the equipment had to be washed up and put away. This had to be done every morning and evening, seven days a week.

Dad would mow down the hay and let it dry for a day or two. Then, he would rake it up into rows. We would take the horses and wagon down to haul the hay up to the barn. It was my sister and my job to tramp down the hay so the wagon would hold more for each trip. As little as we were, I don't think we tramped it down very much. Boy was it hot up on those wagons! We would take the hay up to the barn and unload it up in the hay mow. We had a hay fork on a track up in the top of the barn. Dad would insert the fork into the load of hay and Mom would lead the horse to pull the fork of hay up into the mow. Dad would trip the fork and we would tramp the hay to pack it down. Then we would start the process all over again until it was all unloaded. Then we'd have to go straight back to the field again to get another load. We would do three or four loads a day, hoping it wouldn't rain until we got it all into the barn.

Life wasn't easy on a farm with no boys to help, but we managed. We were taught to work hard and appreciate what we had. In the '40s, we didn't realize how poor we were because we all were in the same "boat." Do you think the children of today could handle living in the '40s?

Donna and Mildred in 1942
The Little Farm Girls

My Grandparent's Place by the River
By Kathryn Moreland of Ridgeley, West Virginia
Born 1932

My grandfather and grandmother Collins owned a farm along the West Virginia side of the Potomac River. The farm is now owned by the Allegany Ballistics Factory. There were large fields reaching to the river and a large beautiful farmhouse, which Grandpap built. It had a long porch facing the river with large flowerpots where my grandma always planted petunias. She taught me how to pick off the dead blossoms so that new ones would continue to bloom all through the summer. I always have petunias each summer and remember Grandma as I pick off the dead blossoms. At the back of the house, there was a mountain. In the spring, my Aunt Edna took my sister and me hiking up the mountain where we searched for wildflowers. She taught us the name of each one.

My grandfather raised sweet corn, which he sold to a storeowner from Cresaptown, Maryland. This man would come in a pickup truck; they would fill it with the corn, which he sold in his store. Grandpap had Grandma make him a large apron with very big pockets on each side. He would walk between both rows and pick corn from both sides and put it in the pockets. This saved him time and steps. We always had lots of corn on the table to eat. I remember on Sundays Grandma would cook a big meal and the family would come to eat. I can still see the large platter of steaming corn on the cob in the middle of the dining room table. After dinner, the stringed instruments were brought out and we made our own music. I remember one uncle could play the banjo and mouth harp at the same time.

My parents, my sister, and I lived on the farm until I was about eight years old. We had two rooms in the farmhouse. There was a very narrow road that went from Grandpap's farm down to the next farm. On one side of the road was a steep bank down to the river. On the other side was the mountain. I remember my daddy had a car with a rumble seat, and my sister and I rode there. We thought it was great fun.

The school bus didn't come up to our farm, so when we started to school we walked down to the next farm to catch the bus. We had names for all of the hills and different parts of the road. I remember in one place there was a small waterfall that came down from the mountain, and I remember calling it "grassy knoll." There was a low place in the river where cars could cross over to Maryland and also a swimming hole where I remember my aunt swimming. My dad and his three brothers told about how they cut chunks of ice out of the frozen river in the winter and would ride them down to Cumberland, Maryland.

Kathryn with her Grandma Collins

In the summer, of course there was no air conditioning. Grandma would open all doors and windows at night and close them at 9:00 in the morning. By doing this, the house always stayed cool. I still like to do this.

One morning I was with Grandma in the kitchen and it was pouring down rain. It looked dark outside. I looked out the window and saw Grandpap under the big tree, working on something. I went out and asked him what he was doing. There was a big piece of machinery there and he said, "I'm working on this. I'm going to use it out in the field after lunch." I said, "Grandpap, it's pouring down rain. You can't work out in the field." He said, "It started to rain before 7:00 this morning, and so it will quit by 11:00." Well, I thought that it was not going to quit raining. Grandpap just didn't know what he was talking about. Imagine how impressed I was when at 11:00 it quit raining. The sun was shining by 11:30! I never forgot this, and through the years, I have checked it out many times. Sure enough, if it starts raining before 7:00, it quits by 11:00. They didn't have weather broadcasts then, so they had to have these signs to predict the weather.

On "wash day," Grandma would look at the mountain. If the fog was coming down off the mountain, it meant the rain was going up. If the fog was going up, it meant the rain was coming down. Then she would know not to hang out the clothes. She washed the clothes on big tubs of water with a scrub board. She did the wash on the back porch. I remember Grandma had a churn to make butter. After the butter was formed, there was buttermilk left in the churn, which I loved to drink.

I also remember the barn with horses and cows, a chicken coop, an outhouse, a large garden, and an orchard with apple, peach, and cherry trees. I remember climbing up in an apple tree and eating apples, which were called, spice apples. They were delicious and tasted similar to today's McIntosh apples.

I feel so blessed to have all of these precious memories and many more from my childhood, and to have lived on a farm with a wonderfully loving family.

My Childhood Memories of Franklin, Pendleton, West Virginia
By Charlotte Eye Hartman of Springville, Utah
Born 1930

I was six years old when my family moved from Friends Run into Franklin. When I was eight they rented a little three-room house from Ervin Ritchie. It was by the river and next to the creamery run by Charlie Neville. My mom worked for him testing the butterfat in the milk that was delivered to the creamery by Warnie Kimble from the country farmers. It was fun to see the huge butter vat turn the milk into butter. It was then wrapped up in pound sections and put into a big walk-in refrigerator. The buttermilk was good, too. I can still taste it.

Below the creamery was a field; nowadays it is the home of the community center and several other buildings. Back then there was a sawmill run by B.J. Auld, and later Don

Cleveland Lewis Propst

Bird. Over closer to the river was a little building—a slaughter house where I used to help my grandfather, Cleveland Propst, and my Uncle Wilson butcher for Luther Allen. He had a meat market between the Star Hotel and the theater. My grandfather would call to me as he passed our house, "Come on Shorty." I'd jump on the running board and help him skin the animal. That skill came in handy later on when my husband killed an elk while at college in Arizona.

We ranged our two cows in the field, and it was my job to bring them to the place for milking. One evening, Mr. Ritchie's police dog, Remmie, pinned me on a log pile and wouldn't let me or the cows pass by. Finally, my Dad wondered where I was and came looking for me. That dog finally decided those rocks coming at him didn't feel so good and gave up, to my relief. The dog guarded the chicken house for Mr. Ritchie.

There was a barn crisscross from our house that I was afraid of. A man had killed himself in the loft of the barn. My grandfather, among others, loved to tell ghost stories, and they had a big effect on me. I just knew I was going to see that man's ghost if I got home after dark. My mom said that I sounded like a bomb landing when I hit the front porch.

When I was eleven, I worked folding papers on Thursday night for the Pendleton Times. Nan Shrader set the type and ran the press. Her son, Robert Dice, worked there, also. We were the same age. I made 50 cents a night. Sometimes the folding machine would break down and we would have to fold the paper by hand, plus roll them up with names for mailing. Sometimes it would be very late when I got home, and, of course, I had to go right by that scary barn. This was during the war, so all the mailing to the soldiers made quite a list of names. I was still working there when I was 16 years old. I think we got a raise to 75 cents. When I was in high school, Robert Dice and I were both in Mr. Dahmer's English class. He would tease us by singing a little ditty: "Charlotte lived on a mountain side on a wide and lonely spot. There was no other cot in sight except Rob Dice's cot."

I loved the Saturday nights when all the country people would come to town to do their shopping. It was elbow-to-elbow down the streets. Maurice Bird's restaurant was a happy holiday for those who liked beer. Sometimes there would be a bit of a brawl, which was something to talk about come Sunday morning. The theater was packed. There was always Roy Rogers, Hop-along Cassidy, Tarzan, and a reel on war news. Darius Simmons was the constable of the town. We kids would tease him and tell him we were not going home at the 9:00 curfew. He would tell us he would throw us in jail, knowing very well we would be home, afraid not to be.

Doctor Lambert had an office across from the now Kimble Funeral Home. On the other end of the street was Dr. Sam Johnson's drug store. Dr. Lambert used to pull me in off the sidewalk and paint my throat with something red like iodine. Mom never got a bill. His office was a large room with patients sitting around him in chairs. He was a white haired, heavyset man. He never drove, but made house calls. Raymond Cowger was his driver. Ruth Lantz was his nurse. Dr. Johnson's son, Edwin, was always kind to kids. We would go into the store with a penny and come out with a poke full of candy. At Christmastime, if you were lucky enough to be on the corner Christmas morning, he would pass out quarters.

I remember the times we roller-skated 'til 10:00 at night around the Skidmore garage and Ford garage and played in B.J. Auld's saw dust pile. I learned to swim above the dam at eight years old. There used to be a concrete block above the floodgate that we would dive off into probably a seven-foot hole. It is now gone.

I loved the ole swinging bridge and remember crossing it and making it shake with my friends. I enjoyed climbing up the silo (the barn was Mr. McCoy's, near Orner Judy's shoe shop) to find baby pigeons, climbing up the water tower that used to set on Hauls Hill, and sled riding on Haul's Hill. My brother, Bobby, hit a frozen cow pile with his face. He didn't look too pretty for a while.

Miss Elsie was my first grade teacher at the Friend's Run one-room school. I think it is now a church. Her brother Russell drove her to school. They would pick me up beside my great-uncle Clay Kimble's store. I had a mile to walk. There were four first graders. She would hold us on her lap to teach us to read Dick and Jane. She was a good teacher. I also had her in fourth and fifth grade in Franklin (the wooden building, before it was replaced in 1954). I visited her in the nursing home on Sundays after we retired from California and moved back to the South Fork.

We can go away from West Virginia, but memories still remain in our hearts. Our daughters said, "We are westerners," so after my husband had a stroke we moved to Utah to be closer to them. I get the paper each week and enjoy it; but as I get older, I know fewer people. Time moves on.

Charlotte and her sister, Ruth in 1936

Butter Makin' and Deer Huntin'
By Leon Amtower of Burlington, West Virginia
Born 1944

Remembering the good ole days would make today's generation realize where things come from and how things were in the good ole days. We used to churn our own butter every week. We would put the cream, which came from milking our own cows into a big glass jar, put the lid on with a crank on it, and start turning. It seemed like it would take forever to turn the cream into butter, but then it would happen. Mom had a wooden butter mold that she would fill with the butter, and then she would turn it over and push the handle down from the top. Out would come this perfectly round block of butter with a flower design on top.

In the evenings, my sister Janet and I would ride our stick horses out to get the cows. If we seen someone, we acted as if they were our walking canes. Mom use to wax the hardwood floor, with Simon wax, then Janet and I would put on clean socks and skate all over the floor to make it shine. I used to go down to my aunt Bessie Agnew's to get a haircut. She had these clippers that required her to keep squeezing as she cut. I would be sitting while she was cutting, but then she would forget to keep squeezing, and I would be standing straight up, because it was pulling the hair out, not cutting.

On Sunday afternoons, I used to go down to my aunt Mae McDowell's. We would go around to the back of the house, were there was a well. We would draw water up using a well bucket (about five inches round and three feet long) on a long rope. We would fill buckets by holding the well bucket over a bucket, and pulling the ring to let the water out. We would fill her washer and rinse tub for Monday's wash. Aunt Mae also had a little pitcher pump in the corner of her kitchen that was over a hand-dug well.

My Mom use to tell a story about her brother (Uncle Russel Roberts). He had done something that required a smack'en, but Uncle Russel crawled under the house where Grandma couldn't get him. She asked Granddad to go get him. Granddad got down and was crawling under the house to get Uncle Russel, when Uncle Russel said, "What's the matter, Pop? Mom after you, too?"

Mom use to tell about her great aunt who had a son that she couldn't catch to smack, so she waited 'til he went to bed and went to sleep. Then she sewed the sheet up around him and began beating him! She said they never get to big that she can't correct them.

My first cousin Raymond McDowell had cut an old truck down and made a tractor. It had a bus seat on it. One day, Raymond and Danny Agnew were going down to the meadow to get a load of hay. I sat in the middle. As we were going through some low-hanging branches and leaves, I looked up and said, "What's that hanging on the limb?" They both jumped off, and about that time, my head hit a hornets' nest. All I had on was bibbed overalls—and bees, of course. They both jumped back on when the tractor had got to the bottom of the hill. I went to Aunt Mae's, to get baking soda put on the stings.

One time I was riding Prince the horse. We had just finished plowing out the potatoes when someone started up an engine. Prince took off for the barn. I had to duck as we went into the barn. I had to stand on the stall boards to take the harness off of Prince.

My Dad would take me squirrel hunting. Dad had a 12 gauge, single-barreled Nitro King Shotgun with a wire twist barrel. I had a Red Rider B.B. gun. Dad shot the squirrels; I shot *at* the ground squirrels. We had a big strawberry patch, and the deer would eat the

Leon's parents

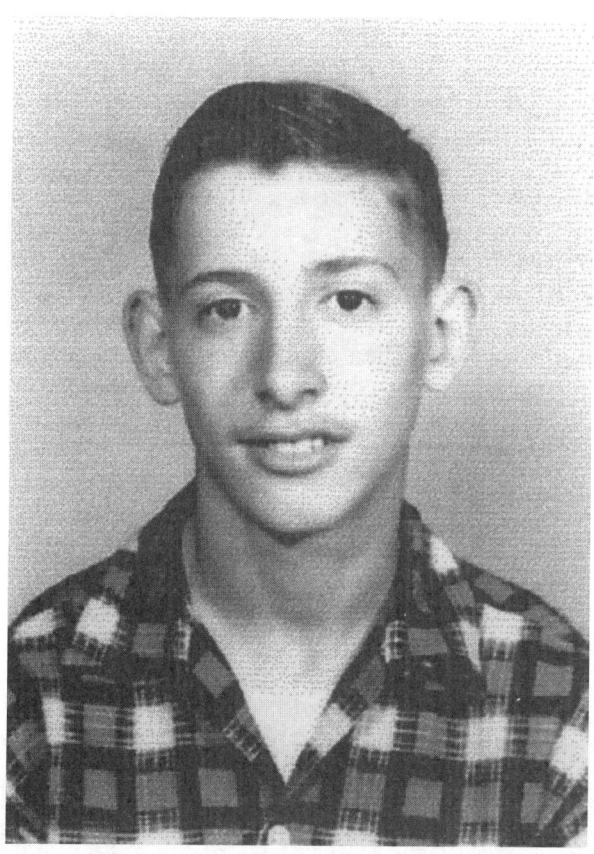
Leon Amtower

plants. One night Dad and Mom went out on the front porch. Mom held the flashlight and Dad shot at a deer. The dog had followed the deer and was barking over on the hill, so Dad went over to see if he had hit the deer. As soon as Dad got there, the dog ran home. Dad turned the flashlight on and a buck deer charged him, Dad shot his last slug and missed. When he would turn the light off, the buck would stop. When he would turn it on, he would charge again. Dad hollered for us to bring more shells, but we had gone back inside. Dad broke open the gun barrel; the sound made the deer ran off. The next day in the mail, we got a postcard with a deer having a man up a tree.

I attended Antioch School. There were six grades—three in each room and one teacher to each room. There was also a kitchen. We played Cowboys and Indians. Every boy always had a knife, so we made whistles from hickory limb when the sap was coming up. We would jump the fence to see who could jump the highest. The further up the fence we moved, the higher it got. We played tag, ball, and marbles. Sometimes the whole school would walk up to the end of Grayson's Gap where the water comes out between two rocks. We would go to Crede Mott's store at lunchtime where you could buy a big Sugar Daddy on a stick for five cents. The school was also used by the Antioch Church for ice cream socials and apple butter making. My mom attended there when it was a one-room school, The first year I went there was the first year they had bathrooms; before, they only had outside toilets.

One evening I went Christmas shopping with Dad to get a present for Mom. We went to the G.C. Murphy store. Dad bought a crystal punch bowl and cups. When we got home, I was excited and told Mom, "Dad got you a pinch bowl!" Another Christmas, Mom and Dad heard something about 2:00 A.M. When they came out to see what it was, there was Janet and I setting on our new sled. They sent us back to bed 'til morning.

We used to have a lot of ice-skating on the pond and sled-riding parties. We would set an old tire on fire at the bottom of the hill. You wouldn't be able to do that now! One time we built a snow ramp to see who could jump the furthest on their sled. Denny Agnew was a little heaver, so he hit the ramp and jumped—but his sled didn't! It stuck in the snow. Denny ended up with a bloodied nose.

Mom and Dad started their housekeeping with orange crates as table and chairs. Today most couples have to have a new car, a new house, and sometimes a new baby, before they get married.

Army Snowball Fight
By Margaret Meadows of Montrose, West Virginia
Born 1933

When I was a fourth-grader each day in our school, Fairview, Randolph County, West Virginia, began with the Pledge of Allegiance to the flag and a prayer to God. Our community had no electric, no phone service, no vehicle transport, and the nearest town, Elkins, was seven miles away. Our teacher came from there, riding with another teacher who taught a few miles beyond Fairview.

One day was to be a very unusual day. World War II was raging and soldiers from the South had been sent to our area on maneuvers. They were encamped about three miles below our school on property of a pioneer family in this region. This family had built a stone house that had become a landmark, which the Army used to pinpoint their position.

It was a cold, snowy day in February and was recess time. The boys had braved the cold to have a snowball fight and we girls were pressed into the middle window to watch. We saw an Army Jeep with a red cross on it come up the road, stop, and two soldiers stepped out to ask the way to Elkins. (There were three roads converging beside the school and the Army had their headquarters and hospital in Elkins.) The two soldiers driving the Red Cross jeep were medics; however, they were very young, so they joined our boys in the fight. We girls pushed even closer to the window to better watch.

Suddenly, I heard a voice say, "Move away and the others will follow." As my mother had taught me to do immediately what I was instructed, I moved to the front of the room. Sure enough, everyone turned and followed. Just as the last little girl turned, a snowball came crashing through the pane, and glass splinters flew across the room, even into the back of the room. As she was a first-grader and very small, she was closest the glass. Her leg caught the largest piece of glass, which cut very deeply across the back. It was bleeding profusely.

Just then, the soldier who had thrown the snowball burst through the door to make sure we were all right. The soldiers took care of the bleeding and carried the small girl to their Jeep to take her to their hospital to stitch the wound. Afterward they brought her back to her home.

It could have been disastrous had our faces still been pressed to the pane. Trained medics—a Jeep for travel—a timely voice? Isn't it a shame that today the doors of schools have been locked to God? The God who was present in our circumstances to see that everything worked so this small girl and all of us would not be harmed by this mishap.

I grew up on lower Cheat in Randolph County, seven miles from Elkins, West Virginia. We did not get electric out our way until I was a junior in high school. We had the wonderful outdoor privy and used old Sears and Montgomery Ward catalogs for toilet tissue. We carried our water from a spring several yards away from the house for drinking, cooking, washing, which included dishes, floors, bodies, and clothes.

Wash day was done, in summer, in tubs of water heated by an outdoor fire, an old wash board, and a copper tub in which the work clothes were boiled in lye. In winter, the tubs were heated by the kitchen stove. When rinsed in cool water, the clothes were then hung outside to dry on a rope stretched between two poles.

The kitchen stove was cast iron, made pleasing to the eye with an enamel covering. It had an attached compartment for heating water and a warming compartment over the top heating surface. We opened the oven door and the kitchen became a nice, warm space around which we gathered while my mom read books to us on cold winter nights.

Our living-dining room held an old pot-bellied stove in the middle. I would dash out of an ice-cold bedroom in winter to dress while one side roasted and the other froze. Mom made our clothes from feed sacks, which had beautiful prints in those days. Sugar sacks became dishtowels and cloths. In winter, the small ones used a bucket with a rolled out edge for sitting (chamber pot) instead of braving the night, cold, snakes, and animals going to the privy (outhouse).

When we went to Elkins, we would have to walk. Sometimes during his lunchtime, my dad, who had a Model T with a rumble seat (a pull-up seat in outside back), would meet us about half way. He and a neighbor had the only cars in our community but would be gone to work early in the morning and not back until late in night. My dad was an electrician—a refrigerator man—and sometimes was gone most of the night trying to get the grocery stores' refrigeration units working so spoilage was minimal.

We walked to school, about half mile from the house. One February day it snowed so fast it was up to my breast by the time school was out. I was five and my sister and brother, who were six and four years older, had to break a road for me to get home. We used candles and oil lamps for light and carried lanterns when traveling after dark. We tried to do school homework before dark, as it was easier on the eyes. We carried our lunch in lard buckets that had a wire handle. Lard was shortening rendered from pigs, which was used in baking products or frying food. Even the very small child had chores. Everyone on farms had gardens so there was weeding and picking food to can. We grew all kinds of vegetables, picked berries, apples, pears for jellies and canning. Kerosene was placed in a can and the bean beetles on the beans were placed in it to kill them.

Lawns were trimmed with a sickle or roller blade mower powered by the pusher. Young children fed the chickens, gathered the eggs, and made sure they were put in the coop at nighttime.

During World War II, each member of the family was given rationing books in order to purchase small amounts of things very scarce because of the war, like gasoline, sugar, coffee, etc. Schoolchildren were given time out of class to pick sacks of milkweed pods, which were used in making parachutes.

My grandfather on dad's side lived to be three months short of 105. He and his brother would come in evenings and we'd sit around our pot-bellied stove while they told stories of their childhood. Would that I'd been old enough to listen well or write down some of their tales from Indians and slavery to the walk on the moon. I even got to see my grandad do the Hoe Down or Russian Bear Dance when he was around 80. That's where you dance squatted down, throwing first one leg and then the other out in front of you. Wow!

Looking back we had less in material things but more in our rich relationships with others and fewer worries. We never locked our houses or cars.

Life on the Harr Farm, Canaan Valley, Tucker Co.
By Carl Harr of Davis, West Virginia
Born 1946

My name is Carl Harr, son of Richard and Mary J. Harr. I am the second born to them with an older sister, Barbara, a younger sister, Phyllis, and a younger brother, Jimmy, who is the youngest. We grew up on the farm that was bought and cleared by our great-grandfather, Seymour Harr, and passed down through the family to my folks. I was born in 1946 and we

Phyllis, Barbara, Jimmy, Carl, Uncle Fred, and Carl's dad, Richard "Dick" Harr

moved from the Red Creek area to the farm when I was two years old. This 270-acre farm was lost to the state of West Virginia in 1966 along with several other farms to create the Canaan Valley State Park. The state offered $40,000 and, after a court case, my folks received $80,000, with a third of the gain going to Bonn Brown, who was the lawyer representing my folks.

I would like to now relate some of the things that happened on that farm that I will never forget. I think they are very amusing stories at the least. My grandfather, Merrick Harr, had built a limekiln into the steep bank behind the barn. It went deep underground, with a vent out the top to draw air. It was brick-lined inside where the rocks were burned to lime. The front was dug out for the lime to be taken out. Well, we did not use the kiln for burning lime and used the dugout place in front of the kiln to throw trash into. The kiln had not been used for many years. My mother asked me and my sister Phyllis to take a jar of water to our Pop, who was working back in the field. On the way, we stopped at the old kiln and I saw a small opening that I could crawl into and gain access into the inside of the kiln. I told my sis to wait and I would do some exploring. I made my way through the small opening and got inside. I was no sooner inside until there was my sister inside also. I reprimanded her, but it did no good. We had found a real nice hiding place. We came out and delivered the water and the next day our mother gave us another jar of water to take to our Pop. We stopped again at the kiln and tried to go in again. Well, don't you know, the thing had caved in just since we had been in it the very day before. The Lord was definitely watching over us. I have thought about this many times since and sis has thought about it many times also.

I want to relate a story about something that happened at the one-room school I attended in Canaan. My first years there, I had a teacher named Hoye Smith. His wife was Louise Heitz Smith. They are both gone now to be with the Lord. But several years ago, she was relating a story that her husband Hoye had brought home from school. She really jogged my memory with the story and it came back to me, because I had forgotten about it until she related it. There was the Cline and Ruth Allman family in the valley (they also lost their farm to the state park), and there were six children. The youngest was just starting to school in the first grade. I was in the third grade at the time and I was sitting right there when all this was happening. It was the first day of school and the teacher had some papers to fill out to send to the board of education listing the students. When he asked the new Allman boy what his name was, the reply was, "Blue Eyes." After several attempts to get another name out of him, all he could get was, "Blue Eyes." So now is the time to call his big sister, Wanda, who was in grade six, to find out what his name was. Well, all he could get out of her was, "Blue Eyes." So Hoye says, "I can't put that down for his name on this form, we will have to put something else." So he asked if there was an uncle that they liked and they said yes. The uncle's name was Hilbert. "Ok, is there another uncle you like?" "Yes, we like Uncle Graydon." So Hoye says, "Do you think it would be ok to put down Hilbert Graydon for his name?" They said yeah, that would be fine. So this boy went home after the first day of school with a new name. They called their uncle Hilbert, Hib, and that is what this young boy was called also. Hib was a very good friend to me as well as his other siblings. He died several years ago and is buried here in Canaan at the Buena cemetery.

I want also to relate some things that happened at the old barn that the state finally tore down because it was in great disrepair and falling down anyway. We had 60 head of beef cattle and several dairy cows. Lots of hay to make and lots of manure to haul. I remember one incident involving my dad with a beef cow. She had some problems after calving and required treatment with a medicine to help her and treat her. Well, he got the rope around her waist instead of her head and she could really resist. When this happened, my dad said the expletive that begins with "sh..." and his false teeth flew out of his mouth into the manure. I dare not laugh because he was really mad now. Another time I will never forget is when we bought twin half Holstein, half Guernsey heifers from my uncle, Harn Raines. They were beautiful but it turned out to be very difficult when it came to milking time.

Jimmy, Phyllis, and Carl

They ended up with the names of Hateful and Fury. We milked by hand at that time and they did not like being milked. Hateful gave my mom a black eye one time with a roundhouse kick. They did not just kick the bucket, they went for you. Fury had her calf and my dad was going to milk her. I was standing in the feed way with a rope on the stanchion to grab her head when she put her head through. Well, she was not having anything to do with that and she would not put her head through there at all. There was a four- to five-foot-high wall separating the milking parlor from another part of the barn. Well, ole Fury decides to jump that wall and make an escape. She did not make it quite over the wall. She got hung up on the wall and could not go over the wall or get back off it. She was stuck there. My dad says, "Aha, I'll milk you now, you son of a so and so." He got the bucket and milked her, with her hanging on that wall. After he milked her, I got on the other side of the wall and pushed her back and she came off the wall. A couple years later we bought a system of used milking machines and the cows seemed to really like them and did not ever kick again.

While I was in high school I was a member of the FFA, Future Farmers of America. My project was a cow that my folks had given me. Well, as bad luck would have it, she lost her first calf. I think it was that she was inexperienced at calving and did not lick off the afterbirth from the newborn's nose. No one was there to oversee it. Well, the next year, I was really watching her. I knew her time was near and I put her in a special part of that old barn where she would be separated from the rest of the cattle. One of my chores was to feed the cattle in the evening after school. For some reason, my sis Phyllis accompanied me to the barn that evening to feed. As luck would have it, my cow was in labor and about to deliver her calf. I am not going to let anything happen this time to cost me her live calf. Both of us are right there with her and I even help my cow by pulling the calf out of her. My sis Phyllis had gotten a really nice, new winter coat for Christmas, which she was wearing. After the calf was out, with sis Phyllis right there taking it all in, my cow gets up from her lying down position. My sis was right behind my cow. When my cow got up her afterbirth water spewed out of her, right onto my sister's chest and the new coat. She blamed me by saying, "You knew that was going to happen, why didn't you tell me to get out of the way?" Well, I did not know that was going to happen, but it did. So my advice to anyone who reads this, is to not stand right behind a cow getting up that has just given birth. You could get a shower. I hope anyone who reads these stories is amused by them. I feel that I and my family do have a wonderful heritage and many fond memories. We lost mom in 2003 and our Pop in 2013. We miss them very much and will never forget so many of the things that happened on that farm. As for me, after graduating from high school, I worked in the coalmines for one-and-a-half years, was drafted into the U.S. Army, and went to Vietnam to the 25th infantry based in a placed called Cu Chi. After my discharge I decided I did not want to go back to the mines.

Some of my long time buddies wanted me to come to the D. C. area and got to work for the airlines. This is what I did and spent 36 and a half years there. I retired in 2004 and moved back to Canaan Valley, the place I was raised and the place I have always called home.

Church Dog
By Nettie G. Bright Lipscomb of Parsons, West Virginia
Born 1938

I was a little girl. I started going to church when I was six years old. I used to walk down off the mountain where I lived to church. It was a good mile one way.

My stepdad gave me a hound dog for my eighth birthday. Everywhere I went the dog went. I named him Buddy.

He went everywhere with me. If he wasn't at home when I left for church, especially at night services, he, the dog, would come into the church, find me, and lay down under my seat. He never bothered anyone else at church.

We had the big, long seats or benches at that time.

The people of the church excepted the dog coming to church. When church service was over, we left the church. My mother didn't worry about me. She knew my dog would be with me.

Boiled Vinegar and Fried Onions
By Sylvia Baer of Frostburg, Maryland
Born 1938

I am 75 years old and I think of times I have had. My father was born in 1898 and back than they went to school to the eighth grade and from there, he went to work in the clay mines. He was only 12 years old.

My father's parents, the father was a carpenter. He made us furniture and toys. We were always glad to see them except when I was sick. My grandmother was Indian, which I am very proud to be, but she would have all doctor ideas that we had to do. I was the youngest of six, if I had a cold I had to inhale boiling vinegar and then she would fry onions and place them in a bag and put them on my chest. With all that being done, the cold would be gone.

We had a potbelly heating stove in our living room and we would take our bath in a wooden tub. In the kitchen, we had a cook stove, which would burn wood, and coal and on the side of the stove was a tank that warmed our water.

We always had wringer washers. My mother used the wringer washer until she was 90 years old. We had an outhouse and, yes, we used Sears' catalog for toilet paper.

We never had a milk man because we had a small farm where we had two cows that my mother would milk. We raised pigs and chickens and every Thanksgiving that would be butcher day to kill the pigs. The meat that we got from the pigs and cows were all canned in mason jars, we had lots to eat. My mother always made her own bread and that was passed down to my whole family, and I still make my own bread.

I went to a one-room school until the end of my third grade. My mother made my clothes out of print feed sacks. We got the sacks from the feed they would buy for all animals. I had to walk a mile to school. In the winter, snow would be so deep that I could hardly get threw and school was never closed.

I remember the first phone was a rotary phone which was a party line and we would listen in on other party. The first T. V. had a round screen. I did see the first moon landing it was a thriller.

Those good old days were hard days, but it made me a better person.

The Day a Life Was Saved on George's Creek
By Norman R. Fitzgerald of Bloomington, Maryland
Born 1941

I grew up in a small town on Front Street in Westernport, Maryland during the 1950s when kids did all sorts of outdoor sports and had a great time doing it. We would sled ride off all the hills in Westernport, snowball battle, skate on ice, build snowmen, and all sorts of things. I loved the outdoors in the winter. I lived along George's Creek and, when the river would freeze over, we would skate and sled ride on the ice. We grew up in the best of times. Kind of like in "It's A Wonderful Life" when George Bailey saved his younger brother Harry from drowning after he's gone through the ice on a coal shovel. This reminded me of the day when my brother Rich and myself, along with some friends were skating and sledding on the iced-over George's Creek. There were a couple of younger children out on the ice that day also. When one of the children called out frantically, "My brother has fallen through the ice, please save him!" We ran to offer assistance and try to retrieve the young boy from the iced-over river. We could see the young boy floating down past us under the ice, looking up at us, but we couldn't get to him because the ice was too thick to break through. We followed the boy under the ice, trying to break through several times, but that didn't work. My younger brother Rich ran frantically for help toward the house, yelling as he ran, "A young boy is drowning under the ice in the river!" My older brother Paul heard the call for help and responded to the call. He ran to the river, along with my neighbor Hilda, who also heard the cry for help. By that time, the boy had floated to the edge of the ice where it was barely frozen over, where my brother Paul and Hilda pulled him from the river, and ran carrying the young boy to my mom's house, where he was laid on his stomach on our kitchen table where first aid could be applied. The boy was blue from the exposure to the icy cold water. My brother and Hilda did chest compressions, expelling the water from his lungs until they saw him starting to response. Soon after the boy responded, I think by that time his mother had been notified and arrived at the scene. The boy's name was Jimmy. The boy recovered completely. Thanks to my Brother Rich's quick response that day, the boy's life was saved. True story.

Grantsville
By Cecil Kelley of Friendsville, Maryland
Born 1933

Grantsville, Maryland from 1920, '30, '40—it is a quaint, interesting old town.

My grandparents, Jack Miller and Ida Johnson, lived there whole life in Grantsville.

Pop worked small coalmine. Mom was a homemaker. They had five children.

They got there needs the town general store belonging to Poly Broadwater.

Grandmother got order every two weeks. One meat store run by Herb Layman, drug store and Post Office. Bank First Nat by Mr. Joe Fay. Town beer room by Fay Miller. M Rodamer town garage. William Winterburg funeral home.

Pop, J. C. Miller, was a coal miner, old fashion way. Black powder squirls new paper. Dug approximately eight-ton day shovel pulled from mine by small ponies. Mine belonged to Joe Paton Coal Company.

J. C. Miller was town cop and Mayor year ago. Mostly Democrat.

Ida Miller was a homemaker. Baked homemade bread, rolls. Old coal wood stove. Toast from hot lids and hot waterside container. Go outhouse for relive you self.

There was gentleman lived on Negro Mountain approximately eight miles tow. He rode his horse town get off. Send his ride home. There was car dealer Bud Bender had the first T. V. in Grantsville much of the time. Joe house Max Smelling were boxing for heavy weight title. There were so many fans there standing room only. County living back then.

Fun back then was fishing along Casselman River for sucker. Always catch all you wanted to get.

Winter clean snow off ice building fire ice skate.

Hunting was for Thanksgiving. Deer, squirrel in the fall. Baseball hall spring summer.

We built own bob sled 14 feet long. Used to come down Nat Highway 50 miles per hour. Our friend state trooper back then would pulled back up for us to ride. If caught doing that now, we would be in bad trouble.

If us kids did wrong, the trooper back then take you home, dad work on you.

Another big week for all was summer carnival came to town. Parade, hot dog, ice cream. Lemon aide.

Mom, Pop only had heat kitchen stove. Stove in living room the old house doing winter snow blow in on sills bed when you got under covers you when for the stoves keep warm.

Christmas time we made popcorn ball to hang on the tree.

Not a lot toys, big stem banana, oranges, nuts, cookies.

We listen to radio a log tem mix Roy Rogers a we could miss news back then. Open Door, Aunt Minney Farm, the Pittsburg Prites, Rosie Rosewell I believe was the sports Ann Koka. Follow Ralph Kinner home run litter. We had lot good ball players old bistate league.

Wringer Washer Mishaps
By Janet Light of Cumberland, Maryland
Born 1950

Yes, I am a child of the '50s. I remember the moon landing, outhouses and chamber pots, my first T. V., which was very small and black and white, Elvis, trips to downtown in my Sunday best, gloves, and hat included, and many more wonders of the good ole days.

But my most unforgettable event includes some of my family. My mother had a great, electric wringer washer. My brother, Donald, was a curious chap and liked to watch this machine clean clothes. He decided he could help, so he climbed upon the washer, removed a wet garment from the tub, and started pushing it through the wringer. However, he forgot to let go and his hand went through too. He screamed for mom, who came to help, but as she did, her dress became entangled in the wringer and they both were stuck. Mom called for my grandmother who was there. Only, to everyone's chagrin, she took one look and fainted! Mom was finally able to unplug the machine and everyone was released. All was well and Donald has a few scars on his arm as a reminder!

Fast forward several years and the second son, Jim, is now a toddler. The machine is still as fascinating as it was to Donald. Jim climbed on to the side of the washer and pushed a piece of wet clothing through the wringer. Again, the wringer gobbled his hand. It had reached his elbow before he was able to get free, but he also was left with scars on his arm and hand.

Several years later, a daughter was born, me! And I really liked watching my mother put clean clothes through that wringer. One morning as I sat at the breakfast table, mom said she was going to the neighbor's house for a moment. "Don't go into the wash room," was her warning to me. To that point I had not even thought about the laundry and that magnificent machine. I waited momentarily and then went into the washroom. Through the window I saw mom enter the neighboring house and I promptly climbed onto the washer. There, in the tub, was my most favorite pink dress. I retrieved it from the water and pushed it through the wringer. That monster started eating my hand, so I pulled with all my might and my hand came out, but with much of the flesh torn off. I ran over to my mom and was whisked off to Memorial Hospital emergency room. I was in pain but my hand healed and I have only two scars on my hand!

When my sister was born several years later, I'm sure that wringer was picking its lips just waiting for its next meal! But my parents put an end to that saga: Enter a new automatic washer, no wringer required!

Growing up in Pawpaw
By EveLina Crouse of Shanks, West Virginia
Born 1952

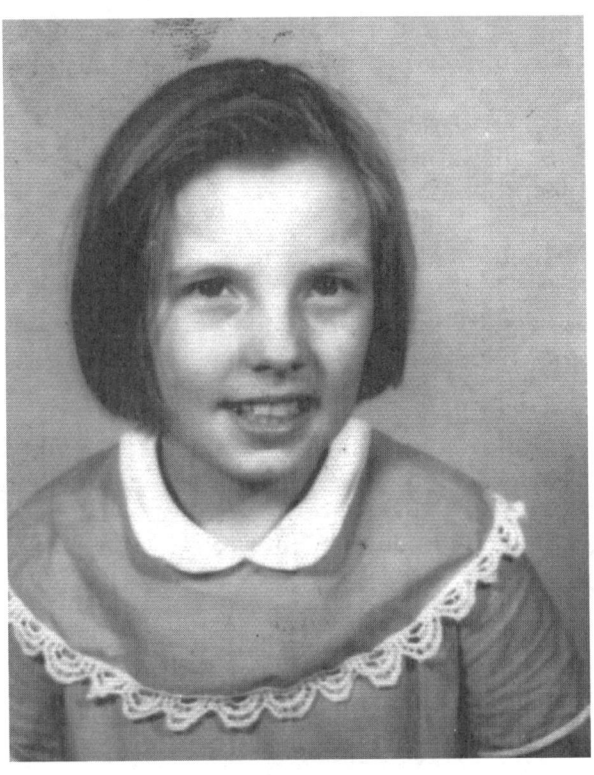

EveLina Crouse in 1962

I was born in an old shanty at Pin Oak Fountain in Pawpaw, West Virginia. A granny woman delivered me. My mom told me. Then when I was one year old too three years old I was walking at a year old, playing in the mud,, picking up sticks, and trying to climb trees at three years old than when I was six years old I started going to school at Pawpaw, West Virginia grade school with my brothers and sisters. Than one day at school was the worst thing ever that happen to me. My younger brother, Bobby Ray, got burned up in our home when it burned down. We will never forget that and then when I was 10 years old my cousin was driving a pickup truck and somebody hit us and knocked us against a bridge and throwd two of us out of the truck against the bridge in Pawpaw, West Virginia. We ended up in the emergency room hurt. It was a terrible accident. Than when I was 12 years old, I met my sweet heart boyfriend, John. He was 16. They were our neighbors. The funniest thing best thing that happened to me was we would go to his house and play games like hide and seek. It was me and my sister, Shelva. She was 11 years old and she liked John brother Jean. The boys would put our scarf and coats on and us girls would put their hat and coat on and we would always pick the wrong person. It was so much fun and we had fun sled riding. That was our two favorite things. One time me and my brother Dennie was pulling me in the wagon upset me and broke my arm when I was 11 years old.

Evelina Crouse, maiden name Kaylor, nickname is Abbigal and Angel. Me, Evelina, when I did something wrong I would go in the woods and hide until my mom went to bed. I had to go to school without books. Had to learn on paper. We had to eat water gravy of the morning and brown beans for supper. We only got a Coke or candy bar once a month. One outfit once a year. My dad left us when I was six years old and my mom didn't have much money.

When I was 11 and 12 years old, I would stay in the summertime with my grandma, Nora Batson, and my grandfather, Granville Batson, in Critter Hollow. Help plant the garden. Go to church on Sunday with grandma and sister RosaLee. We walked three miles every Sunday morning and we would walk back every Sunday evening. We had fun because my sister and one of her friend would play trick on our grandmother. It was so much fun. My granddad was German and my grandmother was Indian. We had a lot of fun staying there.

When I done something wrong my mom ran after me with a hickory stick. Why I was growing up, mom, me, and brother and sister lived in 30 different houses. We moved all the time in West Virginia. My youngest brother Robert would walk to the stores sometime. Then one day my brother, Rodge, was working for a pop man and he got me to help him. I was around 13 years old then and he tried to get me to go with the pop man but I said, "No way brother, you are nuts."

When I was growing up in childhood my mom Virginia Kaylor and me, Evelina, would go to Cacapon Bridge Bingo all the time. We had a lot of fun. Me and my mom when to church on Sunday too. Sometimes that's was my childhood life. That was the good old days back them even those we was a poor families. We still had a lot of fun and loved our family. My mom loved us very much. My dad, Buddy, did too, but he had problems.

Raw Potato in a Bag
By Eileen V. Capel of Ridgeley, West Virginia
Born 1935

I was born 1935 at home, no hospital, in a big, old farmhouse at Blooming Rose in Garrett County.

We heated the house with coal stoves. One in the living room and one in the kitchen to cook on, which we did a lot. The windows in the bedroom had so many cracks in them snow blew in the rooms; it was so cold to go to bed in. Now days all they half to do is push a button and their is heat. There was a 11 kids in the family. We worked really hard in gardens and fields and feeding animals. The oldest kid helped to take care of the youngest. We was a poor family and didn't even know it. But never did go hungry. Mom made nine big loafs of bread every other day and big canners of vegetables and bean soup. Now days they go to the market or McDonalds, we had no such thing. Mom made are clothes out of feed sacks that dad got to feed the cows and horses, it was fun to go pick out what we wanted for a dress or skirt. We got one pair of shoes a year with stamps. Now days they have lots of shoes and clothing.

We went to school in a one-room school; it was so cold to even get there in the snow. No snow day off. For lunch, we had a piece of butter bread and an apple. It was good. We had spring water and a little stream of water run into what we called the milk house, it kept things cold. On the Fourth of July dad would get a big watermelon and a case of orange soda pop and a gallon of orange pineapple ice cream. We thought we was in heaven, it was so good. That is the only time we got it.

We had an outhouse that was a cold job when you had to go and with a Sears' catalog to wipe with, what a job. And we bathed in a washtub, two at a time; we all used the same water. We had a wringer washer and we carried the water after washes was done and put it on the fruit trees. Are medicines was homemade, we didn't go to a doctor. There was many homemade medicines; I will give you a couple of them, to many to write. For cold or croup, we took a half-teaspoon of kerosene on a little sugar. For a headache, we grated a raw potato and put in a bag and put on your head, it worked. Now days everyone goes to a doctor.

We didn't have TV, only a radio to get the news and no phone. We played games. We had youth meeting at church. The cemetery and church was just up on the hill from the house. So after meetings we played Hide and Seek in the graveyard. We would lay down in sinking graves to hide and behind tombstones. Much great fun. And we would dare each one at 11 o'clock to go to the cemetery and get a piece of pine, if you did, you got a nickel. Inside games, we played Rook and Pit and ate apples. Dad liked that. And we played softball a lot to and sled riding, one sled for all kids, it was fun when you got your turn.

And other thing that was fun, there was no funeral homes, everyone one that passed away was kept in the home with flowers and all; we kept running under the casket. Are toys was made of socks, monkeys and rag dolls.

In Memory of Edith Frazee, my mother.

Wringer Fascination
By Donald L. Snyder of Fort Ashby, West Virginia
Born 1942

To start with, I am 71 years old. I remember when my mother used to wash clothes on a washboard. Then when I was about eight years old. My dad bought her a new Maytag Wringer washer and tub set. She was a very happy woman. Also, we had a copycat neighbor that had to have everything mom had, which worked both ways. They papered their rooms and painted to outdo each other and both did very fine cross-hairing and sold couch and chair, table fancy, lace-like dollies. They were really best of friends though. To cut a long story short, she made her husband buy her one too. I was very fascinated by the way the washer worked that I wanted to help her wash. She would let me run the soft clothes through the wringer, but not jeans and blankets because I would get them stuck and pop the wringer rollers and then they would have be reset. Anyway, like I said, I was fascinated by the mechanics of the washer. She always washed on Monday mornings. My dad worked daylight at the railroad in Cumberland and the neighbor washed in the afternoon her husband worked evenings at the old Celanese plant. So that worked out great for me. I would help my mom wash in the morning and then run out to the neighbor's and help her. She also left me run the clothes through the wringers for her. I had a very fascinating day to say the least. It really started in the summertime when school was out so I got to help them both every week. Then, when school started, I would always pretend to be sick on Mondays so I could stay home and help them do the wash. That didn't work most of the time, but about once a month she would let me stay home and help her and the neighbor would yell out and tell her to tell me she was getting ready to wash. This went on for about three years and then I got interested in girls. All, did I mention that I was a boy? My sister never was interested in washing clothes and she was glad I was. Years later I got married and had children of my own. The old wringer washer and tubs were still in the basement and I would take my clothes and the kids over and wash them. I also went to work for the railroad as a machinist. It may have had something to do with the fascination of the mechanics of the wringer washer because I loved doing mechanical things. I washed my railroad clothes in the wringer washer and kids' diapers in it for a long time. My wife couldn't figure out why I didn't let her wash them in the auto electric washer and my mom told her how much I liked using the old wringer washer. I never got my fingers in the wringer once. I was lucky because it happened a lot. The neighbor down the hill had one and she had a son my age and we were friends and I was down there when she was washing on her wringer washer and me and her son was in the basement and she went upstairs and he started messing with the washer and when he pushed a towel in the wringers it started wrapping around the wringer and he tried to pull it back out of the wringer and he pulled his hand in the wringer and he yelled and the wringers popped open. Instead of pulling his hand out, his arm went all the way in the wringer. I shut the washer off. It sort of flattened his arm some, but he was ok.

Toilet Tissue Invitation
By Iris B. Stegmaier of Frostburg, Maryland
Born 1935

I was born in Harrisonburg, Virginia and then, when I was three years old, my family moved from the Smoke Holes, West Virginia to Upper Tract, West Virginia. We were not rich and we were not poor. My father purchased a large farm during the Depression by paying the taxes. We raised 10,000 chickens and I fed them and milked the cow before catching the school bus to ride two miles to a two-room school.

Iris and her sister, Patricia

Iris and her best friend, Joy Lambert in 1950

I raised 500 chickens when I was 11 years old and paid $35 for my new bike from Sears. I then rode it to school at times. I was riding my bike to school one day (11 years old) and, when I had gone approximately a mile, a neighbor stopped me and said, "Do you have a new baby at your house?" I said, "No, why?" She said your father was here and called the doctor. I turned that bike around and went back home and his around the corner of the fence until my aunt and my father came out on the porch crying, "It's a boy!"

I went back to school and my teacher said, "I hear you have a new baby at your house." I said, "Yes, and I'm going to drown him." Jealousy. Well, needless to say, I rode that baby on my bike for hours on end just to keep him from crying. I also had a four-year-old sister.

I remember Belsnukling as a very fun time. It happened two weeks during Christmas. Families would dress up and go to homes and let the people guess who you were and then always refreshments were served!

We loved waiting for the feed for the chickens to be delivered so we could pick out ones for pillowslips, broomstick skirts, or whatever the need. My mother was a great seamstress. I couldn't sew a button on!

I remember my mother making my dress for the junior/senior prom and my best friend one in a different color. What I didn't know was that my friend wrote a letter to two boys in Petersburg on toilet tissue and signed my name, inviting them to the prom, to meet us in the gym, and they showed up. But it turned out to be a fun time and I forgave her. My mother loved flowers and kept them in winter in the upstairs hall and one night my friend had to go to the bathroom, which was downstairs, and she decided she would pee on the X-mas cactus. My mother, after finding out, said it was the only time it bloomed! Another fun thing was box supper socials. Girls decorated boxes with ribbons and bows and the guys bid on the boxes and then ate supper with the one whose box it was. It was supposed to be a big secret, but, if you liked someone, you hinted how your box would look. We went to the movies and the market every Saturday, 17 miles away and thought it was a big thrill!

We always butchered Thanksgiving Day and neighbors came to help.

Threshing wheat was a big day, farmers came and helped, and we served a big dinner for everyone! We had a big garden and hated it when we had to pick potato bugs! We canned all summer along with other chores!

My sister and I were batting a tin can in the back yard and my father was talking with a man and turned and said, "You girls stop that before someone gets hurt." And about that time I hit the can and it hit Tish in the forehead and I took her up to the water trough the cows drank from so daddy wouldn't see it and cleaned the blood off and stopped the bleeding, then took her back to the house and we didn't get in trouble.

I went into nurse's training when I was 17 and my brother really hated to see me go and one time when I came home he took my Boliva watch and we could not find it any place so I had to buy another watch and later my dad found my watch in the hog pen. My brother had thrown it in the hog slop bucket where all table scraps went!

My Daddy, My Hero
By Karen L. Barker of Berkeley Springs,
West Virginia
Born 1961

My name is Karen Stotler Barker. I'm married to my husband Scott Z. Barker. We have to children Bernard Scott Barker and Charles Jefferson Barker. Our children are adults now. My husband and I were married

Bernard C. Stoler in the late 1950s

December 6, 1980. We had our first child September 3, 1981 and our second child April 14, 1985.

I am writing about the most important person in my life. That person was my dad Bernard Charles Stotler, born in 1938. You see my dad passed August 22, 2007. He was my dad, my very best friend, my hero, and the brother I never had. My family was my dad, mom, and I had two younger sisters. When my first son was born, there wasn't a doubt in my mind; I was naming him after my dad.

Daddy was so happy that he finally received a boy in the family. He was so proud of me and my new son. My daddy was determined that, once I was released from Washington County Hospital, he was picking me and my newborn son up. My husband, mom, dad, me, and my son was on our way home. I noticed my dad was taking a different way home. I was very uncomfortable because I had to straddle my legs across the floorboard.

The reason I was straddled across the back floorboard is because my son was eight pounds at birth and I had him natural with no pain medicine, no nothing. Wow! What a birth. I received 27 stitches and the doctor lossed the both of us on the table. I asked them, once I was told this, not to tell anyone about this.

My dad, however, on the way home on September 6, 1981, kept driving and driving. I said, "Daddy, where are we going?" He said, "You sit tight and make sure that baby doesn't fall, you hear?" I said, "He's fine. He won't get hurt." I never spoke of what happened about the birth of my son.

My dad pulled into the Hecks shopping store. He said, "Everyone sit tight. I'll be back in a few minutes." He said, "Lock the doors and don't let anyone get near that baby." I said, "Daddy, the baby is fine, no one is going to hurt him." When my daddy returned with a cart, he had a load of baby food, baby juices, and a bag of baby outfits. He stood with the car door opened and held up all of the outfits. Each outfit different colors, each read: #1 Grandson; Pops #1 Grandson; Grandsons Are #1; Grandsons Are Special. My dad was all

The Stoler family in 1977

teary eyed when showing the outfits.

I knew in my heart that my daddy was extremely happy that he got a grandson. Turns out that I returned to work, after my six weeks, daddy was my babysitter. My dad worked night shift, so therefore he was home through the day. My mom, Leona Stotler worked day shift. I was so happy and was able to go back to work with comfort. My son was the love of my dad's life. When the second son came along, my dad was just as happy. My sons grew to love their grandfather ever so much. My dad babysat the second son as well. He had two now to babysit.

How my dad worked night shift and did what he did is beyond me. My daddy was the best. When my sons grew up to be teenagers, my dad got cancer. My boys took this hard as did his granddaughters, me, my sisters, my mom, and community.

You see, my dad was very well known in the community. He also saved his change at work and donated all of it for the Toys for Tots for Christmas. He had his yard decorated with thousands of Christmas lights. He provided a Santa Claus, which was me, every Christmas and bought gifts, oranges, candy canes for me (Santa) to give to the children. It grew years after year. Soon there were buses coming from the different areas. My daddy always worked very hard. He had a heart of gold. He would pay for my friends' lunches when I went to school in the '60s and '70s. They wouldn't have money for lunches, so he'd find out and pay for a year at a time. We struggled growing up, but he worked two jobs to support us. I was a very sick child growing up. I was in and out of hospitals every couple weeks. My daddy is forever in my heart. I loved him so much. Happy birthday daddy, January 18, 1938.

Delivering the Martinsburg Journal
By H. Ward Nicklin of Hedgesville, West Virginia
Born 1923

My name is Herbert Ward Nicklin. I was born April 23, 1923 in the small upstairs bedroom in a two-story frame house located in the 200 block of South Maple Avenue, Martinsburg, West Virginia. Dr. Claude Thomas delivered me. He told my mother, Lillian Beatrice Nicklin, that I was the second biggest baby he had ever delivered. Sorry, I can't accurately say how much I weighed at birth, but have heard family members say I weighed 12 pounds (sorry, I can't verify the weight). Was told the doctor threw me on the bed and started taking care of my mother. I do have baby pictures up to eight years old verifying that I was a fat, little kid with a double chin. Shortly after birth, my mother entered me in a beauty contest for babies at a county fair in Winchester, Virginia. I didn't win the beauty prize but was selected as the healthiest.

Prior to my birth, Clarence Ward Nicklin, my father, had made a bet with a local attorney named Herbert Hannis. I don't know the details, but believe it could have been an election bet, since Mr. Hannis was chairman of the Republican Party in Berkeley County and at a later date, my father was Justice of Peace and chairman of the Democratic Party. (They were both politicians) If Herb Hannis won the bet, Ward Nicklin was to name his firstborn son Herbert, after Herbert Hannis who was a bachelor. I never did hear what my father got if he won, but it doesn't matter. Now you know my father lost the bet and much to my regret, I became a Herbert. A name I never liked.

Several months after my birth our family moved to 307 South Raleigh Street. At age six, I entered John Street Grade School. By age nine, I was riding to school on my bicycle and learned of a newspaper and magazine distributor in the public square looking for salesman. A man named Mr. Steagle, who I never met, owned the business that was located in the back section of a house known as the Boarman Building. You entered through the side door right on King Street. Magazines and newspapers of every name and description were piled up in this small space before being delivered to stores in town that sold the magazines. The business was managed by Warner Holida, a nice guy who gave me a canvas bag to put across my shoulders, put some magazines in the bag, explained how the system worked, and told me I could earn money by selling them and paying for them later. On that wonderful day, I became a businessman by selling Liberty, Colliers, and Saturday Evening Post Magazines. Didn't have much success knocking on doors and convincing strangers to buy these wonderful books. Had limited success with family and friends, but hit the jackpot when I visited the main office of the Dunn Woolen Mill on Raleigh Street. The Dunn Mill produced cloth for seat covers that was used to cover seats in new automobiles coming out of Detroit at that time—Mr. Prince Dunn, Mr. Frank Dunn, and a Mr. Harlan Eubanks were three top officials at the mill. Each bought all three of my magazines and told me to bring them again each week. Several representatives from Detroit were in the office and they also purchased my magazines. My magazines sold for five cents apiece. Can't trust my memory, but seem to think I got one cent for each one I sold. (It may have been two cents, not sure.) Regardless, these men at the mill gave me extra money and I loved the magazine business. Met lots of other boys who worked for Mr. Steagle, selling magazines and delivering the Washington Post newspapers. All were older than me and definitely more worldly. I was raised in a house where profanity was never used. Many of my new friends both smoked and cussed. Naturally, I wanted to fit in and be accepted. Consequently, I became a social smoker and learned lots of new words at an early age. Incidentally, I began smoking Sunshine cigarettes that were five cents a pack. Must admit I became deceitful at this early age by hiding this smoking sin from my parents.

My father learned of a Martinsburg Journal paper route opening. The boy who previously owned the route owed money to the Journal for papers not paid for. My father paid the bill to the Journal, bought the route, gave me the route with understanding I would have to pay him back, which I did. It was called Route 10 and had about 30 customers scattered around on Virginia Avenue, New York Avenue, etc. The Martinsburg Journal sold individually for three cents apiece. It was printed only six days a week, there was no Sunday newspaper. I delivered to each customer six papers a week. The price was 15 cents a week for delivered papers. To the best of my memory, I got five cents for each customer and had to pay the Journal ten cents for the papers delivered to each customer. All of my customers were given a little card that showed the weeks and months in a year. I had a little card puncher to punch a hole in the customer's card showing they had paid for the past week. Every Saturday morning I started out with my puncher and some change to collect for all the papers delivered the past week. Every customer wasn't always at home and some customers preferred to pay every two weeks instead of every week. I'm happy to say this was a good route. Most customers had the money ready and I had no problem collecting and was happy to receive many tips. Every Monday I had to pay the Journal for last week's papers. Consequently, I had to plan ahead in order to have enough money every Monday afternoon to pay for the previous week's papers. The Journal main office was located in the 200 block of West King Street with the same entrance it has today. All carriers were supposed to pay their bills in the main office every Monday. There bill was supposed to be paid before picking up papers to be delivered for that week. A Richfield garage and service station was located on King Street right next to the Journal building, extending all the way to College Street. A beauty school now occupies that space. The Journal printing press was located in the basement entrance on College Street. This was on the same block as John Street School. Consequently, I could go right across the street from school to pick up my papers for delivery.

Happy to report my Journal route was good to me. I always had a little money in my pocket for candy, sodas, and cigarettes. (I was a chocoholic at an early age and still am.) Even got rich enough to buy cigarettes called Avalon at ten cents a pack. While in the eighth grade decided to sell my route before entering high school. Had built it up to over 60 customers. At that time, a man named Enos Clark was attempting to buy up all Journal routes. He then got boys to deliver the papers and he paid them a fixed amount, depending on size of route. A younger newcomer named Brooke Ettinger was also starting to buy up routes to provide competition. I sold my route to Ettinger, thinking that Enos Clark already had plenty.

At the end of my freshman year my father died. In those days, the corpse was laid out in the house and they put a big black ribbon on the front door signifying a death in the house. We had to move the piano out of the front room in order to accommodate the casket. While visiting for the viewing Mr.

Ernie McKee, who owned the grocery store where we did business, offered me a job in his store. Told me to see him that weekend. Allen Katz, another friend of my father's, offered me a job at Katz store. Told me to come down and talk with him. Which I did. I ended up working for Mr. McKee all through high school and worked at Katz store every Christmas holiday. Enos Clark, the man I passed over when selling my route, contacted me, and said he was looking for a carrier. He offered to hire me to carry Route 4, which was a downtown route and considered one of the best in town for several years. Thought Enos Clark's offer showed lots of class and I have always admired him for teaching me a lesson in never holding grudges.

That's the way it was back in those days. Riding a bike and delivering papers was good, healthy exercise. It helped put money in my pocket and gave me a feeling of independence. It taught me how to get along with people and I learned a lot about life, about business, and my town. What I have written may not be of interest to others, but at age 90 it certainly has been fun reminiscing and writing about the way it was when I was growing up. We lived in a great world in those days and, yes, we live in a great world today. Life is good. Enjoy.

No longer a fat, little kid.

Grandma's Nerve Tea
By Reba Deremer of Barton, Maryland
Born 1942

My parents divorced when I was three and we had to go live with my grandparents.

Every spring, grandma mixed up lime and water and whitewashed big rocks, clothes posts, the outhouse, etc. We had a "slop jar" under the bed, we used at night. We listened to the Wheeling Jamboree on the radio, "Amos and Andy" and "The Lone Ranger." We had a little black phone like the one on the Waltons. It was a party line and grandma liked to listen in on other people's conversations! She would put her hand over the mouthpiece and us kids had to be quiet. Grandpap had a Victrola he liked to wind it up and listen to the big records. I remember one day I was helping mom with the wash; we had a wooden dolly with three

Reba's grandma, Anna Laura Gordon

legs on the bottom and a handle on top. You swung it around, back and forth to wash the clothes. Well, I decided the clothes needed bleach, and poured it on a pair of my brother's brown pants and ruined them!

We had a flood in the middle of the night. The fire whistle blew. Everyone in town was up, but I slept thru it! Someone called us about it, so mom grabbed an umbrella and ran outside, only it wasn't raining! The coal mines had broke loose! We had a huge turtle in the yard that had gotten washed down in the flood. It had bright, yellow paint on its back, someone had done. Our milk was delivered by the milkman, and our neighbor ended up marring him! I used to have to walk down a dirt road to the Post Office to get the mail. One day it was so muddy, like about ankle deep, that my foot came out of my shoe, and the shoe stayed stuck in the mud! My grandma was a mid-wife; she helped the doctor out by delivering babies, giving insulin and penicillin shots. One baby boy was born on Easter; she said here's your Easter Bunny. So he got nicknamed Bunny and it stuck with him. Sometimes after being on a bad case of someone very sick and dying, grandma would come home and have a drink of "nerve tea," she called it, before going to bed. I never knew her to drink any other time, other than that. Sometimes, one of us kids had to walk with her out the road after dark to one of her

Reba Deremer in 1988

jobs; you could hear wildcats up in the woods, crying out. My brother said, she took us with her so if the cat got us, she could get away!

The town we grew up in, Beryl, West Virginia, is no longer. The paper mill took over the whole town. We had a three-room school, two grades to each room, one teacher for two grades, and a hall in the middle where lunch was cooked, and it cost 25 cents. A church, fire department, Post Office, beer garden, and a couple of stores. The kids always got together at the fire hall and danced to the jukebox. That's where I learned to Jitter Bug. When I went to high school we had a dance at night one time where they measured your waist and that's what you paid to get in, mine measured 23 inches so I paid 23 cents to get in. They got Jimmy Dean to come to the school one time for a show. I passed him in the hall; he was so tall and had a fancy, purple, Western suit on! I remember, "Black outs," a man would knock on the door and say, "Lights out until all clear." We would sit in the dark and wonder if a plane was flying overhead looking for lights so they could bomb us! The first hummingbird I ever saw, I didn't know what it was, but I saw this little bird with a big, long beak coming straight for my face and I ducked down and it went over my head! We lived in a double house, hence a double outhouse. I was in there one day and the man next door went in the other side, I was quiet so he didn't know I was there, and my mother came out yelling for me, I had to answer her. Bet he jumped!

We meet every year for a Beryl reunion.

The Drinking Teacher
By Cora Carter of Mt. Savage, Maryland
Born 1938

Well, here I go with my story about growing up on Fire Clay Mt. Road in Mt. Savage, western Maryland around 1940s. It was a great era to grow up. I had a wonderful childhood and love to tell about it.

My dear, sweet mother made everything possible for me. I was born October 15, 1938 in a small, three-room house with no electricity or running water. No ruffles or frills but great memories. I was delivered by a mid-wife who was 73 years at this time her name was Fanny Blank and she delivered all the children on the mountain for years what a gem she was she would take care of my family—mom, dad, brother, and me—for 10 days for 10 dollars that included washing, ironing, cooking meals and she took all the dirty clothes to her house and wash them on a scrub board hung them to dry. Iron them and bring them back the next day, what a wonderful human being she was.

I have wonderful memories of sled riding from a big farm on Bald Knob to where we lived it was about a mile up to Bald Knob and the ride back down was worth the trip. I also cried to some of my friends like Rosita Pope and her sister and they would pull me up on

Cora (Rice) Carter

Cora Rice with her baby doll

the sled (what a sneeky snook was I). We also went swimming in the creek, half the water was from the run off from the sulfur mines and the other was from the Minnow Creek and boy was it ever cold even in the hottest days of summer but my dear cousin and best friend Elmer Rice would play with me every day and when we went swimming I would ask him if my lips were purple and if he said yes we would go home, if not we would stay a while. He and I would take my father's beanpoles that he used to let his pole beans grow up and turned them into a T.P. like the Indians and we would play cowboys and Indians with an old tree stump as our horse and use whatever was available. El and I would have one good fight a day and he would go home and said he wasn't ever coming back but low and behold, the next morning at 7:30 there was El and ask if I was ready to go out and play.

We went to Sunday school on Sunday at St. George's Episcopal Church down in the town of Mt. Savage it was about three miles. We also walked to school, which was about a mile, but we didn't think about the distance we just skipped or ran and would ride our lunch boxes down the hill to the school in the winter. Our teacher was Agatha Witt who came from town in her Model T car each day and she was a drinking woman who smoked cigars and taught us very little she would send us out for recess and maybe an hour or so later she would ring the bell for us to come inside and she was all tooted up and El's sister Shirley would teach us she was just three years older than us surprised we knew anything.

In the summer, we would go to my Aunt Lucy and Uncle Albert Rice's home for a few picnics she was a wonderful cook.

We also went a few times to my Aunt Ruby and Uncle Herb Burns' home for Christmas and how wonderful it was they owned my grandparent Rice's home place, which was eight acres with a house, barn, garage, and washhouse. She had electricity but no running water and a large, old Kalamazoo cook stove and she prepared wonderful food and great friendship for us. It was wonderful and later in life my husband and I bought the farm and more memories.

My mother was one of 14 children she was the first in 1910 and Grandma Lotz had children until 1932. Most of my uncles and aunts came to live with us at some point in time as my Grandpap Lotz was a hardworking and drinking man who wasn't very nice to his children but he always treated me great (I think he was afraid of my mom). After his death in 1952, he was laid out at our home in the living room and people came by to visit and view him and they brought food and would socialize for a while.

I also remember when we got our electricity and we got a radio and every day when I come from school, I would hear the soaps, "Portia Faces Life" and "Maw Perkins." Also, at night we listened to the "Lone Ranger" and the "Screeching Door." Later my Great Aunt Katie (my grandfather's sister) got a T.V. and I was allowed to watch one program a week it was the "Lawrence Welk Show." It was great!

Around the late '40s, Martha (Blank) Orndorff turned her front porch into a store and boy was that great she sold bread cakes, candy, milk, and salt fish, which I loved at the time probably, wouldn't touch them now.

Went to town, Mt. Savage, about once a month. The town was hustling and bustling with the brick plant, movie house, grocery stores, six bars, jail, and confectionary.

Poling to School
By Reba Wilt of Ranson, West Virginia
Born 1932

We were born to George and Rosie Wilt, Reba on April 21, 1932 and Jean on October 6, 1934, the eighth and tenth of ten children. Dad owned the farm located at Keys Ferry, Jefferson County, West Virginia, along the Shenandoah River. He worked the land using his bare strength along with horses and very limited manual machinery. How excited we all were when the big thrashing machine appeared at the farm. It was used to separate the grains of wheat from the chaff, and, when completed, there was a huge straw "rick" which both man and beast enjoyed. Part of the wheat was taken to Clipp's Mill that was powered by a huge water wheel. That wheel is still in working condition and located on Kabletown Road in Jefferson County. It is so beautiful. The wheat was turned in to flour and put in big, wooden barrels.

The flour was used to make bread, cakes, and all other goodies. Our mother was an excellent cook and baker. She would bake all of our bread. We had a large kitchen with a wood-burning cook stove. We did not go to the grocery store for very many things. We grew most of our food. Needless to say, the garden was huge and took a lot of work, but supplied our livelihood. We had a cave in the yard that stored our food for winter. Mother would can hundreds of quarts of fruits and vegetables, and we grew our own potatoes.

There were milk cows that had to be milked, by hand, night and morning. When mother was too busy to help dad, the girls were called on for the chore. We'll never forget that experience. The children learned to milk a cow in a tin cup, we progressed to a bucket.

The milk was carried in three-gallon buckets to an underground cave where a milk separator was housed. It was a hand-operated machine. The milk was poured into the top and there were two outlet spouts below. Plain, blue milk came out one and the cream came out the other. The cream was put in ten-gallon cans, boated across the river, and picked up by a nice neighbor and brought it to Bowers Creamery, located at 110 West North Street, Charles Town. This building is still in existence and owned by the Asbury United Methodist Church, a member of the Baltimore-Washington Conference of the United Methodist Church. Some of the blue milk was allowed to sour and, when processed, became cottage cheese. The cream was put in a wooden churn, turned by hand, and produced butter and buttermilk. Whole milk was also kept for household use. This cave also housed all the canned goods that mother worked all summer to preserve, as well as all the root vegetables.

Pork was our main meat. We would butcher as many as ten hogs a year. We would hang the hams and shoulders in the smoke house after dad would salt them down. What could not be salted down, mother would cold pack. We grew our own corn for the animals, so

Reba's parents George and Rosie Wilt in 1911

that meant pulling weeds from the cornfields. Dad plowed the fields with hand plows and horses.

The farmhouse did not have electricity or running water. The outhouse was so cold in winter with a good supply of Sears and Roebuck catalogues. Need I say more?

Washday was so much hard work. Having no running water in the house, it had to be carried from a pump and well about 50 feet from the house. It was heated on the wood-fired cook stove in the kitchen and then put in a gasoline-powered motor washing machine. After washing, the clothes were put through a wringer into another tub of clean water to rinse. The clothes would be hung on lines across the back yard. In the winter, the temperatures were so cold that by the time the clothes were hung on the line, they were stiff as a board, but somehow there was enough sun to dry them by the end of day. When it was time to do the ironing we would set the flat irons on the cook stove to heat. We took our weekly "all-over baths" in a big washtub by the cook stove.

Three of my older siblings attended a one-room school located up the mountain a couple of miles in the community of Chestnut Hill, Jefferson County. It was grades one through six and was taught by a Miss Margaret Henrietta. That building is still in existence and is owned and maintained by the Chestnut Hill United Methodist Church, which is also a member of the Baltimore-Washington Conference.

By the time the younger children were old enough for school, an elementary school had been built at Millville as well as a high school at Harpers Ferry. Both schools were on the opposite side of the river from where the farm was. We could have walked a couple of miles up the mountain to catch a school bus to attend schools in Charles Town, but we chose to walk a couple hundred yards to the banks

Reba and Jean Wilt in 1947

of the Shenandoah River, unlock a flat bottom boat and pole (not row) across the river to catch the school bus. Every kid knew how to pole a boat. We would tie the boat to a sapling along the bank until we returned in the evening to pole back across the river for home. When the winters were really cold, our bus driver would hold the front seat where the heater was for us. When the river was too high for us to boat across, the teacher would always give us an excused absence. Strangely, no one every complained about our special treatment. We did our homework by an oil lamp.

The river was really our friend but we were taught to fully respect it in every way. It was our swimming hole, a source of food, and a source of transportation. We swam in it all summer. The water was so clear you could see to the bottom. Occasionally, it would freeze over in winter, but not too often.

Some of the children's chores were making sure we had plenty of wood on the porch for the stove—summer and winter—pulling weeds from the garden and helping to milk the cows. The children also created their own entertainment: hop scotch, marbles, hide and seek, and baseball. The ball was made from a sock filled with old rags and sewn very tightly around by mother. She was a beautiful seamstress and sewed most of our clothing using a treadle Singer sewing machine. She quilted beautiful quilts at night using light from an oil lamp. They were truly blue ribbon quality. We lived about one mile from the church. And since we did not have a car, we walked to church twice on Sunday and once on Wednesday for Bible Study. Our Sunday entertainment mainly was getting around the piano singing with mother playing. Dad had a beautiful voice and read music very well. He also played the guitar. On warm summer evenings, after chores were done, we would sit on the porch and sing. What memories!

It was a happy day when electric arrived at the farmhouse. I thought we had died and gone to heaven. Living on the farm was not always an easy life, but it was a great one.

First Love
By Joseph Petrone of Berryville, Virginia
Born 1942

The 1950s was the "golden age" or the "good old days" as some would refer. It was a slow-paced life. I remember them well, as I grew up in a small town Piedmont, West Virginia, population 3,000. Everything you wanted was there in walking distance, the school, grocery store, pool, factory, the bars, clubs, and churches. Not the case today, where a bus or car is needed to go everywhere.

But the thing I most remembered was my first love; a blue-eyed blonde from St. Petersburg, Florida who moved in with her mother close to where I lived. The year was 1955. I was thirteen and she was twelve. We became best friends. We'd climb the hill above my house to pick cherries and plums. Then I went on my first date with her.

First the soda shop; a couple of cokes, five cents each, then to the movie, tickets fifteen cents each, and snacks and drink to watch the western. Then I walked her home.

Later she moved to another part of town and we sort of separated. Eventually she moved back to Florida, got married and I never saw her again.

The Cigar Was For Walking Home
By Harold L. Winters of Cumberland, Maryland
Born 1944

I grew up in a little mining town, named Carlos, just about five miles from Frostburg, Maryland. When I was thirteen years old in 1953, I started working on a farm on Saturdays during the school year and a couple days during the week in the summer. I worked for one dollar a day.

Sometimes on a Saturday, my older brother and I and a couple of friends would go to Frostburg and see a movie. I would take one dollar with me. We would go to the Palace or Lyric Theater; there were two theaters at the time. I paid twenty cents to see the movie, buy a large coke and large bag of popcorn for twenty cents. After the movie was over we would walk up to Parise's Drug store and we would buy a twenty-five cent milkshake, always strawberry for me, and a five-cent cigar. I would have thirty cents left over to bring home.

In case you are wondering about the cigar and me being thirteen years old, back then we usually had to walk to get back and forth to Frostburg, unless we were lucky enough to get a ride. So the cigar was for walking home. It helped to keep the mosquitoes from biting us if it was warm weather. Keep in mind, I didn't inhale the cigar smoke, just puffed and blew it around. If we got a ride, of course we would throw the cigar away, but if we didn't get a ride that cigar would last the whole five miles until we got back to Carlos.

No Children Should Go Hungry
By Theodore W. Clark of Cumberland, Maryland
Born 1922

I am over 91 years old and the "good ole days" were everything but good. When I was just a young kid, depression hit the country. We didn't know what had happened, after a short time, my father lost his job, and we had no income at all. There was no unemployment, social security, or welfare.

My mother would cook a large pot of beans or some other vegetable and about three quarters of the pot was filled with water and seasoned with white fat salt meat. Bread was five cents a loaf, but we did not have the five cents. I went to bed hungry every night. To this day, I cannot eat fat meat.

I wore my shoes until they had holes in the bottom, then my father would cut cardboard to cover the holes. Most of us did not go to doctors or dentists. I never had any of these services until I went into the military service, as we didn't have the money. Most of the houses in our neighborhood had outhouses and no bathtubs. We all took a bath every Saturday in a large washtub. Everyone was very friendly with each other.

For entertainment, we would all gather around the radio in the evenings. We were all scared and didn't know how long our troubles would last or what to do about it. We knew that our parents had very little education, and this gave us the message to stay in school and prepare ourselves for a better future.

I graduated from high school and after World War II; I got some college and have a much better life than my parents. I have seen my son get a good education. I hope that no one ever goes through a depression. This is happening to some countries overseas now. No children should go hungry, and everyone should get an education.

January 13, 1964
By James Michael of Westernport, Maryland
Born 1950

Back on January 13, 1964, I was 14 years old; it was zero degrees cold and windy with two feet of snow. My mom came over to the bathroom about 2:00 am right beside my bedroom, she yelled for me to get up to see the red sky, she said it looked like the town of Barton, Maryland was on fire, but the next day we found out that a B52 Bomber had crashed about ten miles from my home at a place called Pine Swamp in Garrett County Maryland.

My dad worked for Clark Lumber Company, there was a plea made on T.V. for help looking for the five men on the planes, so Arnold Clark the owner and five of his employees including my father shut down for two days to help find the five men. Dad told me they waded in waist deep snow in Savage River State Park; it was ten degrees below zero up there, hundreds of people hunted for the men.

Six men found Major Robert Lee Payne; he was sitting on the bank of the creek in Poplar Lick in Savage. Major Robert Townley's body was found in the wreckage of the plane. The tail gunner Technical Sergeant Melvin F. Wooten bailed out and died from exposure like the other two they found him with injuries in Salisbury, PA about fifteen miles north of the crash site. Two pilots, Major Thomas McCormick and Co-Pilot Captain Parker C "Mack" Peedin, ejected and survived; both are dead now.

My dad took me and my two brothers out to the site about a month after the crash, when the plane went in it took 150 yards of trees out and leveled it. I remember all the pieces of plane, lines, nothing looked like a plane where the nose went into the ground there was a six foot hole in the ground. I remember the Army guys all along the road with M16s on their shoulders watching for onlookers and thieves. We went out two weeks later when all the engines and the two nuclear bombs on board, they were unarmed. All the men were from Turner Air Force Base in Albany, Georgia.

I remember this like it was yesterday. This is fifty years since it crashed; two years ago, Robert Townley's son got his dad's dog tags from a farmer that found them forty-eight years later.

Cobwebs, Dust, Dirt and Two Mad Bad Roosters
By Harry W. Meek of Burlington, West Virginia
Born 1946

We grew up on a small farm in Burlington, West Virginia. Now in those days, the mid-1950s, there were no Kentucky Fried Chicken or any other fast food establishments that we knew of.

So every spring we would get thirty or so baby roosters that we would raise for fryers.

Now we didn't eat chicken every day that was Sunday fare. So on Saturday afternoon myself, my brother Steve, and some of the Rinker kids would catch a couple of roosters put the ax to work, watch them flop, dip them in hot water and remove their feathers and turn them over to mom for further processing.

Now as the summer progressed the roosters got fewer, faster, and meaner. We were down to the last two and we knew we couldn't catch them in the chicken house.

So our step-dad caught them on the roost before daylight on his way to work, and put them in an abandoned outhouse.

Now this outhouse was of magnum caliber, a four-holer, and fairly large inside.

Now by about 2 pm those roosters were ready. Mom gave the word, and myself, brother

Steve, and some of the Rinker kids proceeded to the outhouse. When we got there, every kid stuck an eye on a crack to have a look-see.

Cobwebs, dust, dirt, and two mad, bad roosters. Then my little brother Steve asked, "What are we gonna do?" Now being the oldest and somewhat the ringleader in most of our adventures, I said, "Here's the plan. I'm in charge of the button, so when I yell go I'll turn the button, jerk the door open and you jump in grab a rooster and we'll let you out."

"Ok" said brother Steve.

A- "Go" says I.
B- Door Open
C- Brother Steve in!
D- Door shut and buttoned
E- Chicken noises, Stevie noises, much dust, and yelling of encouragement from spectators.
F- Stevie yells, "I got one, let me out!"
G- We yell, "Catch the other one first!" (Much more of E.) He yells, "I got 'em!"
H- Now we being "Irish" and my brother a redheaded Irishman, we let him out and ran!

Now my brother Steve is my "little" brother who is bigger than me, in a lot of ways. I learned then you could always count on him and sixty years later, you still can.

Dr. Hugh Strachan with Herman

Crossing an Ocean with Seven Children
By Dr. Carleton A. Shore of Cumberland, Maryland
Born 1931

I was born in Kitzmiller, Maryland in 1931 and my grandfather was the only doctor in that immediate area.

My grandfather, Dr. Hugh Strachan had left Scotland with his mother, and brothers and sisters. Can you imagine great grandmother, Sarah, crossing an ocean with seven children, many of them sea sick?

Great grandmother Sarah was the head of the household. Great grandfather, Stewart, and the boys Robert, Thomas, and Hugh all worked in the mines in western Maryland. The Consolidated Coal Company employed between four and five hundred miners. Coal was essential for the industries of Pittsburgh, Baltimore etc. Grandfather Stewart came to America two years before Sarah.

Hugh became an excellent student and a good soccer player. Hugh obtained a scholarship to Johns Hopkins University School of Medicine in Baltimore, Maryland. He received his degree in 1899. Hugh married Lydia Keener Riley and began his medical experience in Oklahoma on a Native American reservation.

Dr. Strachan and wife Lydia left the reservation after completing his internship and first located in Beryl, West Virginia. After several years, the doctor set up his practice in Blaine, West Virginia. He and Lydia purchased a home across the north branch of the Potomac River in Kitzmiller, Maryland. He practiced medicine in Kitzmiller for twenty-one years. He was also under contract with the Consolidated Coal Company, which paid him one dollar per month for each coal miner. This may not sound like much money to attend to their medical needs, but combined with his private practice, he became comparatively wealthy.

An old-timer in Kitzmiller once told me the story of when a small boy living in Vendex became very ill, Dr. Hugh, because of the heavy snow, had to use the rail hand-pump car to travel to Vendex. The doctor had told the boy's parents that if he could keep the boy alive through the night, then he would live.

Shortly thereafter, Dr. Hugh died of a ruptured appendix in 1928 at the Old Allegany Hospital on Baltimore Avenue in Cumberland, Maryland.

The misfortune continued, and in 1929, the stock market crashed. Banks collapsed all over the country. Many Wall Street brokers jumped from windows to their death on "Black Friday." The bank manager in Kitzmiller committed suicide, and the Strachan family was bankrupt.

I can remember hitchhiking from Cumberland to Blaine, West Virginia. (Blaine was just across the north branch from Kitzmiller). Sometimes, I would return to Cumberland via the Western Maryland train. It was a beautiful scenic ride. Blaine was the kind of place where mountain men and women came to raise hell. My father and my uncle always carried a gun.

The Rooster Staggered Out
By Beverly A. Horn of Springfield, West Virginia
Born 1941

When I was young, we lived on a farm close to the river. I was always afraid of the water even though we went there a lot.

One day the neighbor was at the river and the water was up a few feet. They talked me into getting into an inner tube and when I did, the water took me way out in the water and I couldn't swim. I screamed that I couldn't get back, I couldn't paddle myself. After about five minutes, they swam out and got me. I wouldn't go back in the water after that and never learned to swim.

We lived off the farm always growing vegetables and canning them for food in the wintertime. Dad only made eight dollars a week working at a stock sale. He would buy coffee, sugar, and flour for us to use.

The only clothes we had, my grandmother sewed for us, made out of printed feed sacks. There was one in particular with printed horses on it; my grandmother made me a dress out of it. I was very proud of it. We only bought one pair of shoes a year and in summertime, I would put paper in the bottom of them because we wore holes in them and I hated to go barefoot, I still do.

I have a sister who is five years younger than me. She was five years old at the time, and one day she was riding a tricycle, which someone had given her. We had a path from the road down to our house and a big stump was at the bottom with a big curve to go around. She was going too fast to make the curve and upset on her tricycle, she got up off the ground looked at her tricycle with her hands on her hips and said "you dumbass you." We have always laughed about that.

My dad drove a big farm truck with racks on it, and in the summer time always went to a town called Springfield on Saturday night. He would let all the neighbor kids along with us ride the back of the truck to town, there was usually about fifteen kids in all, we had a great time singing all the way.

We had an outhouse we used because there was no plumbing back then. One day I really had to go so I ran to the outhouse and sat down real fast. I looked down and there was a big green snake looking at me. I wasn't long getting out of there.

When I was about ten years old, my dad would make my brother and me get up at five o'clock in the morning and help milk the cows before the school bus would come.

We had chickens and one day my sister was in the yard playing and the old rooster kept flogging her. After a while, she got mad and threw an old washing tub over him and he couldn't get out. About a week later, our dad was outside and could hear this faint squeaking noise, he lifted up the tub, and the rooster staggered out, the rooster never flogged my sister again.

"I Am An Angel and This is My Territory"
By P. D. Wilson of Cumberland, Maryland
Born 1951

My mother's family lived in Shaft, Allegany County, Maryland. Shaft was a coal mining town hence the name Shaft, referring to the Shaft that allowed the miners to go underground to mine coal. My grandfather, Samuel B. McKenzie, was the stable boss for

Emma, Robert, and Iona McKenzie

the mining company in this capacity he cared for the animals that brought coal from the mines. Samuel was killed when he was kicked by one of the very animals he cared for. I lived just across a small stream from my grandmother and my Uncle Bobby (Robert B. McKenzie) who stayed with my grandmother. I spent many hours with them and later in life with my Uncle Bobby. In truth, we weren't that far apart in age.

It was not unusual in the time for families to take in boarders to make ends meet. About a quarter mile from Grandmother's house lived a widow lady named Maim. Maim took in borders and one of these boarders was Tommy Hoet. The boarders were mostly associated with deep mines. The miners were a close-knit family. They enjoyed the company of their fellow miners and there was always the rumor that moonshine was readily available.

My aunt Iona McKenzie and Maim's daughter, Jean, were best friends. They left the area in the late 1950s or early 1960s and went to Washington D.C. to seek employment. Both were successful and were roommates for many years.

In time Maim died. She is buried in a cemetery less than two miles from her home and still rests there. Maim's house still stands in the same spot. The road in front is no longer dirt but has now been paved. The house looks the same.

Aunt Iona and Jean traveled from Washington D.C. via the Baltimore and Ohio railroad to the Western Maryland Station. Many times Uncle Bobby and I picked up Aunt Iona, Jean or both at the Station. It was an old majestic building.

Jean made the trip to Shaft every year on Mother's day to place flowers on her mother's grave. It was a tradition that continues when Jean's health permits. One year she was unable to make the trip and was very upset. Her roommate, my aunt Iona, called Uncle Bobby and asked if he could put flowers on Maim's grave.

Uncle Bobby instead of placing flowers that would die in a few days, planted flowers on the grave. Every evening he took his convertible to the cemetery and cared for the flowers. The cemetery sat on a hill and Maim was buried in a beautiful spot. The flowers flourished.

One evening as Uncle Bobby was leaving the cemetery he observed a man looking at what appeared to be a map. My uncle stopped and asked if he could be of assistance. The

P. D.'s daddy, Samuel B. McKenzie

gentleman said he was searching for his father's grave. The gentleman indicated that his father was a miner that emigrated from Scotland and had boarded in Shaft while he worked in the mines. He never mentioned his name.

My uncle told the stranger to get in the car and he wound back to the top of the cemetery. After parking the car, my uncle walked a short distance with the stranger in tow. Under the shade of a mature oak tree, my uncle pointed to a gravestone and said, "Thomas Hoet, Baker Company WW I." The stranger was overwhelmed that he had located the grave. After Mr. Hoet composed himself, he said to my uncle, "How did you know?" Uncle Bobby stated, "I am an angel and this is my territory!"

My Uncle Bobby died in 2008. I was by his side. To that day, he swore there was not another individual alive in the County that would have known Tommy Hoet let alone where he was buried.

Would Do It All Over Again
By Ronald Abe of Clearville, Pennsylvania
Born 1935

We had a chamber pot in our house of eight people, and every morning it had to be emptied by the oldest or the one with the strongest stomach. Then as I grew older, I became the one with the strongest back and stomach. I didn't mind, it was for a good cause. Three out of the eight are gone, and I miss them! We lived in Mineral City, West Virginia, three miles from Cumberland, Maryland.

We were given castor oil often. Mother would hold us between her legs, and hold our nose closed, until we swallowed. It worked every time. Also, we had a dog, and sometimes he would feel bad, and my dad had a bottle of syrup of buckthorn, and the bottles all looked alike, so one day my twin sister picked up the wrong bottle and took a big spoon of that, well that cleaned her clock for a while.

I remember afternoon radio shows at grandma's house. If you didn't keep your mouth shut, you were out on your ear. The ones she liked were, Ma Perkins with Willie and Shuffle down at the lumberyard, then came Stella Dallas, then Just Plain Bill was at five o'clock, and that was suppertime, and while she cooked we could talk, then you got sent home while they ate. The radio was battery powered and you had to hold your head real close to hear. World War II was going on then and it was hard to get very much that wasn't war. Loyal Thomas out of Washington, DC, and Gabriel Heater out of Pittsburgh, Pennsylvania were the news reporters. It was a sad time then, Roosevelt passed away, and Truman took over and then later was elected to office as President of the United States, so much for radio.

We had two wind up record players at different times, table model, and then floor model. They weren't very good.

I got into trouble spilling ink on the teacher's blouse at school, my backside was black and blue for four days over that, and I caught it when I got home also.

We had a #3 galvanized wash tub, that answered to a lot of calls, bath, canning green beans, heating wash water, for clothes, grinding sausage at butchering time, and many other things, boys went first then the girls. We had a home comfort cook stove with a warming closet on the side to help keep the water warm.

We had a wringer washer, and it had a one-cylinder engine on it, and if your foot slipped off the starting pedal, it meant you had a skinned up shinbone, my mother would cuss when that happened. Then we were able to buy an electric washer.

My mother bought a new 1931 Model A, it had a rumble seat. My brother-in-law also had one until his death last month; it is stored at his house in Cumberland, Maryland. It was a lot of fun to ride it around on Saturday evening, and in parades.

There was a bad snowstorm in 1942. I wasn't very old or big so I remember wading in snow up to my waist. They brought a team of mules in from another farm to clear the road to get the car out. The school bus was stuck in a drift; I didn't have school that day, in later years I moved.

We lived on my grandfather's farm, and we all had chores to do in the summer. One chore I had was to get up at 5:30 in the morning and make sure all the other kids were up and get off to school. I learned many things on that little farm that I still call on in my life today. I learned to put shoes on horses, how to plow the ground for spring planting with a horse, and how to treat and care for sick animals.

I had a girl in school that was a year ahead of me, but I liked her very much, and could steal a kiss at lunchtime.

I got into mischief by talking back to the school bus driver. He told my mother then I was in trouble all over again.

I'll be seventy-nine in March, and have enjoyed my life, and would do it all over again.

Remembering Keyser's Happy Days
By David Shapiro of Keyser, West Virginia
Born 1938

It was Saturday night, December 1955. Two weeks before Christmas and Main Street in Keyser was bustling with shoppers. Cars were parked on both sides of the street. "Not a parking spot to be had." Mayor John Freeland issued free parking for all downtown businesses.

Jim Shay, manager of the G.C. Murphy Co. in Keyser, was busy filling the store counters with new merchandise so not to miss any sales. Don Seibel, assistant manager at Murphy's, was also busy making sure that customers were being satisfied.

Almost directly across the street was Shear's Ladies Shop, owned by Jacob and Ada Shear. Shears sold better quality ladies wear to a prestigious clientele. The Shear family also owned Kaplon's Men's Shop, whose former owner Moses Kaplon died in 1954. Kaplon's was a very well established business, which had three full time employees, Henry Groudan, Harry West, and Ed Miller. Mr. Miller eventually purchased the store from the Shear Family. Jacob Shear's wife, Jenny, owned Jay's Shoe Store, which was adjacent to Murphy's Five and Ten.

Next door to Shears was the Royal Restaurant, "good food for cheap prices," which is still in operation today. There were three movie theaters in Keyser during the '50s. The Music Hall and the Keyser Theater were both on Main Street and the Liberty Theater was on West Piedmont Street. The price of the matinee at the Liberty on Saturday afternoon was ten cents.

Keyser also supported at least four jewelry stores in the '50s. They were Rinard's Jewelry, Clements Jewelry, Ebert's and Bud Paugh Jewelry.

Other businesses that lined up and down Main Street were Minnich's Flower and Appliance, Maurice's Dept. Store, Kessel's News Stand, Gardner's Hardware, Lou's Auto, Peoples Pharmacy, Romig's Rexall Drug Store, The H-P Store, Weese's Appliances and Furniture, Leading Florist and Cut Rate Shoes.

There were also two banks on Main Street- The National Bank of Keyser and the Farmers and Merchants–a hotel which was owned by Ralph Casteel.

Approaching the corner of Armstrong and Main Streets was the Coffman & Fisher Company, which sold lower-priced clothing for men and women. Next to Coffman & Fisher, going west up Armstrong, were Martin's Furniture Store, Workman's Market, and The Army & Navy Store (owned by The Borgans).

Next to the Army & Navy Store was Shapiro's Ladies Store, an architectural achievement designed by Russ Minter and built by Ray C. Coffman of Keyser. In 1958, Robert and Esther Shapiro built Shapiro's Men's Store, which was adjacent to Shapiro's Ladies Store. The Shapiros were known throughout the tri-state area for better quality men's and women's clothing and bridal and tuxedo attire.

The Keyser High School band played for the grand opening of the Men's Store. The band was under the direction of Nunzio Barbera, who later opened up the B-Bop Music Shop in downtown Keyser.

On the other side of Armstrong Street, almost directly across from Shapiro's was Calemine's Shoe Shop, Reno Calemine, who inherited the business from his father, still has the oldest business in the City of Keyser. The shop opened in 1904, and is still in operation today.

Other popular businesses on that block of Armstrong Street were the Green Fern Restaurant, Goldsworthy's Barber Shop and The Wolf Furniture Company. Further up the block were McCoole's Men's Store and Grayson's Sporting Goods.

The upper end of Armstrong Street was also the home of the famous James A. Glaze Merry-Go-Round and Ferris wheel, and the popular Rosemont Restaurant owned in the '50s by "Scratch" and Hazel Stanley. Directly across the street from the Rosemont was the News Tribune, which was owned and operated by John W. Barger, who later sold the business to the Tetrick family.

People were spending freely at that time, as the B&O Railroad, which employed over 1,100 people, was pumping a substantial amount of money into the Keyser economy.

Other important employers in the area were the West Virginia Pulp and Paper Co., which employed over 2,200 people, Penn Ventilator, Tiger Tractor, Keyser Garment Co., So-Rite, which was owned by Paul and Frances Miller, and the Celanese Corporation.

The Osgood Bus Line took workers from Keyser to the Celanese on a daily run. Since Keyser High School was located in the downtown area, students would frequent the local eateries like the Sugar Bowl for lunch, which put additional money into the downtown economy.

Yes, Keyser's fabulous '50s were a time to be remembered. It was a time when prosperity was being enjoyed in almost every household.

Will Keyser ever prosper again like in the era of the '50s? Maybe so, as "what goes around comes around"–like Mr. James A. Glaze's famous Merry-go-round and Farris wheel.

I Would Change Nothing
By James Bohn of Mt. Savage, Maryland
Born 1943

As a small boy growing up in Ellerslie, Allegany County Maryland in the fifties I was influenced by many factors that touched my young life. I was fortunate to have a younger sister and brother living at home with our parents. Dad drove a bus and mother was a devoted homemaker. My age group of boys had a nice woodlot next door to play in and build tree houses, one of which my sister managed to fall out of and impale herself on a sharp stick directly below the limb she was climbing upon.

We attended a small three-room schoolhouse in Ellerslie where the restrooms were located outdoors; the boys had a rainspout hooked to the wall where the urine flowed directly through the sidewall and into the small stream beside the facility. Needless to say, no one went unless you really had to go. Being only seven when the Korean conflict was going on we were not too aware of the war except when dad took the family to the drive-in movies and we watched the news clips shown before the feature, our news before television.

We never had many days off from school as we walked to school and most kids carried their lunches. Seeing a motion picture from the Baltimore Sun titled You Were There, was a thrill to behold. Sometimes a ranger showed up with Smokey Bear literature we were so excited to receive. Now our old school is a church parking lot and there are so many new homes in the area, at one time I could name a person who lived in every house in Ellerslie as I delivered adds for the local grocery on my bicycle, the pay was seventy-five cents which I quickly spent at Zimmerman's candy counter, two for a penny candy; Yum Yum good! It was also where we received our U.S. Mail.

Now being a little older and smarter I was bused to Mount Savage High School eight miles away, where I was placed in classes with kids from the Catholic school, which went to grade eight. My down fall because this is how I met my bride to be. We were in every class together except home economics and gym classes. We were very good friends before we started to date. At times I would walk her home from school and busy myself helping out by removing ashes from the furnace or some other small task as she made dinner for her family, she is a swell cook. Her mother and sister worked in Cumberland, Maryland. I always enjoyed my visits to her home as I was well accepted by them, even her sister. I never had money enough to buy my own car and only got use of the family vehicle on Friday evening providing I had it home by midnight.

My summers off were spent in Levels, West Virginia working on the farm, making hay or picking peaches to help pay for school clothes. We were poor and didn't realize it as most of the people nearby were also struggling to get by. I was accepted to Frostburg State Teacher's College, now a University, where I took classes to become a chemical engineer. After my first semester I was out of funds, and I applied for a National Defense Loan. Dean

Alice Manacure was selected to advise me I was not selected to get the loan because my parents owned their home and could borrow to send me to college, no way Jose, I could never ask, besides I had younger siblings at home, US Army here I come.

Vietnam was going strong and I enlisted in the US Army Reserves becoming a Buck Sergeant during my six years in the reserves. After basic training I married my classmate sweetheart and we proceeded to increase our family size to five by adding three sons to the mix. We built a nice home in Mt. Savage, Maryland, home of the very first iron rail to be made for the railroad, and home of the most reverend Cardinal Moody, his old homestead is still in place on Old Row road in Mt. Savage.

We have also been blessed with eight grandkids and two step grandkids, so far no great grandkids. My father always worried about our surname being carried on as it is not really a common name, but each of my sons has two sons, which I think is a good start on this project for the future. I have no worries here.

Now my wife and I enjoy our time together and anticipate celebrating our fiftieth anniversary together on the 4th of April 2014. It has been a good life together. I would change nothing on another go around.

Joan and Linda riding Queen

The Little Red Pony
By Linda K. Poole of Warfordsburg, Pennsylvania
Born 1942

I will never forget the day my dad bought it. I had been begging for one for some time, of course it had to be a particular color, red with four white feet a blaze and a white mane and tail. I was only six or seven at the time so I must have been thinking about it for a while. One of dad's friends was a livestock dealer who happened to pull into the driveway one day. In the back of his truck was a pony with my exact description down to the four white socks, white mane and tail and blaze. The only difference was the white on her behind with little red spots on it. I was in school that day as it happened, so I didn't know about the surprise. My school was one room with a potbelly stove in the middle of it and an outhouse out back. In those days, we walked to school.

I was walking home when I saw a man leading this pony up the road toward me. You can imagine my surprise. I thought my heart would burst. The closer he got the more I realized it was my dad, Wilbur Bair, of Shade Gap, Pennsylvania. The pony had a saddle on so he lifted me up. He turned the pony around and started walking back home. At the time dad owned the garage at Shade Gap so, he took the pony inside the garage and tied

Linda and a kitten

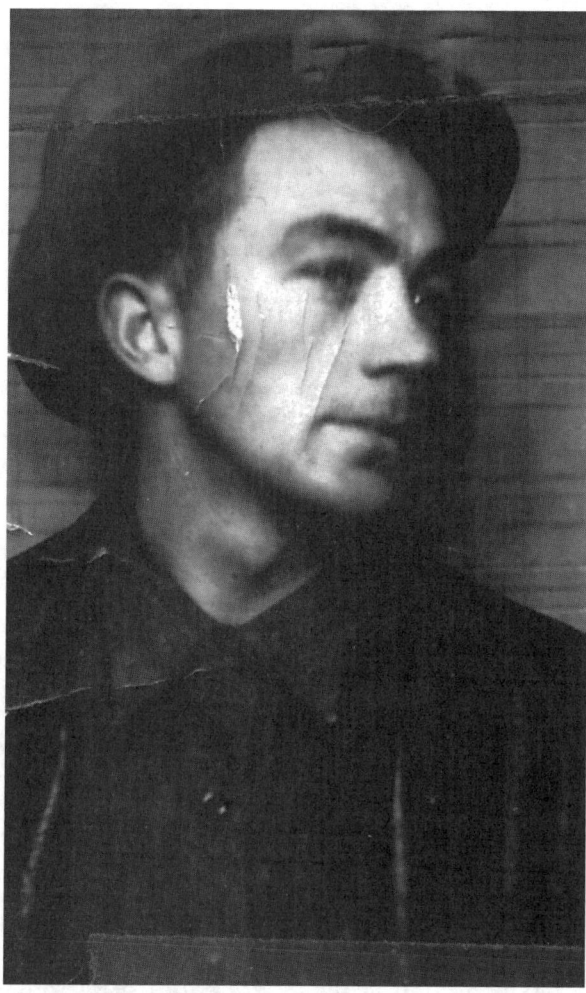
Linda's dad, Wilbur Bair

her to an old furnace that wasn't in use at the time. Queen as I named her, and I were pals for years. I rode her till my legs got so long everyone started teasing me telling dad I should be carrying the pony not the pony carrying me. I don't remember the reason they decided to have her bred, but for months dad, mom and I went around the country trying to find just the right stud pony. Finally, after months of searching they found a red and white paint stallion. They had Queen bred and the following spring she had a really pretty red and white paint filly.

Being a frustrated Annie Oakley, I decided one day to break the filly to ride. I put a bridle on her and jumped on, naturally, she started bucking. Dad was working nearby so of course I had to holler watch me. The filly Taffy and I went round and round till finally she gave up deciding apparently I wasn't going to. The only problem was she was smarter than me. When I would try to rider her later, she would set her feet and not move. There was nothing I could do to get her to move. It was like she was glued to the ground. By this time, Queen was getting old. I was graduating from high school, thinking of getting a job, getting married and moving to the Carlisle area of Pennsylvania. My new husband and I needed a car so I could have one to drive back and forth to work. We had to sell Queen and Taffy to buy one. Reluctantly I knew a local horse dealer who I contacted, who said he would buy Queen and Taffy. He took her home and kept her for quite a while. One day I happened to be at a horse show in Carlisle and saw her at the show, a little boy riding her. I was glad to see that someone else loved her as much as I did and that she was being taken care of. She would have been eighteen or twenty by that time. It made my heart glad that she would have a good home the rest of her life.

Unfortunately, I have been horse crazy all my life and still have them. I rode horses all over the west working at ranches in Wyoming, Utah, and New Mexico. They will never be out of my life or out of my heart. God bless dad and my first pony.

God-Given Memories Last Forever
By Viola M. Logsdon of Hyndman, Pennsylvania
Born 1935

They say you never forget your childhood. Even though I've lived in Pennsylvania since I was fifteen years old, my childhood and memories are of West Virginia.

My great-grandfather came over from Ireland. He married the daughter of a Cherokee Indian Princess and they moved to Flanagan's Hill in the Canaan Valley where he is buried in the Mick Cemetery there on a farm. My grandmother was his daughter Berthany Mick. She married Wesley Davis.

Before my mother was married, my grandmother ran a hotel in Cass, West Virginia, and my mother and her two sisters worked in the hotel.

After that, my grandmother and family moved to Douglas, West Virginia.

I was born there. The railroad stop was called Albert, but the town was named Douglas.

I was born on my aunt Zetta's birthday, which was December 12, 1935. My aunt was born in 1909, my niece in 1946, her granddaughter in 1989, and my grandfather died on December 12, 1940.

Some of our women relatives had unusual names, starting with my grandmother who was Berthany. There was Olive Clo, Zetta, America, Lovie, Peachie, Claura, Chloe, Racy, Arrata, and Dietra Starr. Douglas was a nice town but through the years has diminished to a one-street drive thru.

Just outside of Douglas where the railroad track ran was the old Coke Ovens. They are still there but hard to see for the grass. Tub Run runs alongside of it. We used to live near there.

We had boardwalks; you could run up and down them. They had like a step and then a long run and then another step. I loved to run them. My uncle Walter had an outhouse on the hill behind his house and a boardwalk that ran up to it.

My summers were spent at Aunt Olive's house in Coketon, which is between Douglas and Thomas, West Virginia. My mother would put me on the train in Rawlings and the conductor, Mr. Brown, would make sure I got off in Thomas.

I remember when a tornado hit Thomas. My two aunts and my uncle were walking to Thomas when it struck. They joined hands around a tree while roofs were blowing off around "Tony Row," and the air was filled with debris. They were unhurt. I went to Thomas a few days after and couldn't believe the destruction.

My uncle used to get us kids up early, and take us blackberry picking down to Tub-Run. The berries were as big as your thumb and delicious.

My uncle made homemade brew in his basement in barrels. After it aged, we kids would help put it in bottles and cap it. It was fun. My uncle worked in the mines and he lived down the lane from the B&L store. It was owned by the Coal Industry and sold everything. It was a fascinating store. What was bought was usually put on credit till you were paid. They would put the bill in this container and then they pulled a cord and the container would fly from the front to the office and they would send it back the same way.

Around the track from my uncle's was what we called "our swinging tree." The tree has large limbs you could swing on and it was easy to climb.

My grandmother, my aunt, and my mother were all expecting at the same time. I was born first, my aunt Shirley five months later, and my cousin Jessie six weeks later. We were like sisters and inseparable all through our lives. We went swimming in Snyder Falls in Coketon and sometimes we'd go to Thomas down from the bridge and swim. That place was filled with broken off trees. Our swimsuits were yellow by the time summer was over from the sulphur.

My mother and her sisters used to swim on top of Blackwater Falls. We use to visit there every summer. It's not very far from Thomas.

Thomas cemetery is the burial place of my grandparents, aunt, uncles, and cousins.

Every year as a child, my mother would give my sisters and brothers and I worm medicine. We never had worms, but that was prevention. It was followed with a chocolate cream and a sip of coffee. Even today, I don't eat chocolate cream candy or drink coffee.

Colds were cured with peppermint tea and honey to drink, or mustard poultices or camphorated oil. We also had to hold our nose and take castor oil.

Our skin was clear, no pimples, because mom gave us small capsules fill with sulphur.

My father, mother, and two older brothers went to the huckleberry plains in Canaan Valley. Dad invented a huckleberry picker. It had a handle on top, and you ran it up the bush, the berries went inside. They took washtubs and reaped the bush and filled the tubs. Mom spent the next couple of days cleaning them, and canning them in quart jars.

Mom also had a jar of "gension Violet." It was used for mouth sores. My kids got a sore mouth from a drinking fountain, the doctor said it was a virus and had to run its course. They couldn't eat, their mouth and tongue was covered with sores. I swabbed the inside of their mouth with it, even though the jar was forty years old, and their mouth as cleared up in two days. I still have it. It turns your mouth purple for a couple of days but it works.

I used to take my mother and her two sisters every year back to Thomas to see our relatives that lived in Davis, Parsons, Elkins, and Hendricks, West Virginia. We would make a day of it and visit the graves in Thomas, after they passed away. After they passed away, Shirley, Jessie, and I started going back every year. We visited the few relatives remaining, visited our "swinging tree," even though the property has no trespassing signs because a rod and gun club bought it and we visited the lady who owns my uncle's house now. She lives in Alaska, but travels back to West Virginia to spend her summers. We visited the coke ovens, walked along Tub Run visited with the family who owns the only house left. There name is Flanagan.

Shirley passed away, so Jessie and I haven't been back since together. It's just not the same.

Life goes on but memories will always linger. When I was a child, we were poor but God has given rich memories that have lasted through the years. Simple things like "swinging tree" a wooden boardwalk, coke ovens, berry picking, and a swimming hole meant more than riches. I hope others who live in West Virginia have memories like mine.

Ellen Cocheran "Granny" in 1960

Memories of Granny
By Cheryl Kilgore Concepcion of Inwood, West Virginia
Born 1950

Granny died in 1963. Bits and pieces of memory take me back, forming a pattern, much like the quilts she once pieced together on quilting frames crowded into our small kitchen. I suppose my first memories of her come from when I was very young, perhaps four or five, and she lived next door to us in the coal camp where I spent my younger years. I would stay all night with her and sleep in the giant feather bed that never quite looked neat when it was made up but which was strangely comforting as I snuggled into its ridges and valleys to keep away the night.

She was in a car accident once, breaking her leg, so she came to live with us for a while so that my mother could look after her. I remember my mother's painstaking care of her. The thing I remember most, however, is that I received a Sparkle Plenty doll from my grandmother for helping in her care. Of course I did very little, except aggravate, I'm sure, but I had lain awake nights dreaming of that doll and its long blond hair; I can still remember my surprise and sheer joy when she gave it to me. I had envied my girlfriend's doll with a passion that only a four-year old could muster and had talked of little else for days.

Later, my grandmother, unable, I suppose, to keep house for herself any longer, came to live with my mom and dad and two sisters. What do I remember of those years? Quilts; always quilts. She made so many beautiful ones and promised each one to every relative and friend who came to visit. Using old dresses and cast-off material, she made up her own patterns as she went, and seldom were they color coordinated. Yet they were an interesting array of complicated colors and patterns that mesmerized you into remembering your past as you located a bit of an old skirt here, a piece of the apron that you made in Home Economics class there.

And rag rugs, an even more complicated concoction. They never lay exactly right, but puckered in the middle, a problem she could never seem to solve. And blackberry picking; she would drag me out of the bed while the dew still glistened on the grass because we had to pick the berries before the sun got too hot. We would bundle up in old clothes to avoid scratches and bugs; she with her bonnet and

Cheryl, Susan, and Granny in 1953

I with my hat would take the lard pails and head for the berry patch. When we returned with our buckets full, she and my mom would make blackberry cobbler or jelly.

I remember her stories. About marrying when she was twenty-two; but my grandfather was forty-two. Imagine, he just walked up and asked the folks she was living with–I think her parents were dead by this time- if he could marry her. She hardly knew him but he seemed nice enough, and it was time for her to settle down. They, and she, said yes, and she was off to bear and raise eight children.

Once they moved from Kentucky to Oklahoma- in a covered wagon! It was around 1900 and they could have traveled by train, but no! The men had to have the adventure while the women worked themselves to death. She had three of her children while they lived in Oklahoma. She would tell me stories of my aunts and uncles, about their courting days and their marriages, vividly detailing what they were like when they were young.

Every Memorial Day, her family—my aunts and uncles and cousins- would come home for a reunion of sorts. We would eat together, play together, and climb the steep hill to the cemetery where my grandfather and a baby cousin were buried. My grandfather died twenty years before her. We have picture after picture that we took at the graveyard. Year after year, pictures of all of us lined up in a haphazard, piecework pattern. There are pictures of the gravestones with the flowers lovingly arranged behind them. It seems rather morbid in a way, but somehow it wasn't. For example, once we got caught in a thunderstorm and had to go running down the hill. As one of my aunts slipped and slid in the mud, she cried, "Oh no! My new girdle!" We all got a big laugh out of that.

Granny is buried there now, beside my grandfather, and although we no longer make the yearly trek up the hill as a family, we still try to go when we can. When I make that trip today, I think of Emily in "Our Town." I imagine that my grandmother and grandfather talk to each other as we climb the hill for a quick visit. I imagine they comment on their family's progress as the years pass. The last quilt she made before she died had a note pinned to it, "For Susan. When she gets married or finishes college." I imagine her pleasure and relief the first time I climbed the hill with my husband and later with our son. It seems to me she has a perfect view of the world as we pass before her, a quilted mosaic of her family's lives. Yes, I remember Granny.

The Icehouse
By William J. Martin of Grantsville,
Maryland
Born 1925

During my younger years at New Germany, we did not have electricity. There was not commercial electricity until 1946. Most farmers had a springhouse, which they used to keep milk, cream, butter and other perishables cool. Containers would be set in troughs and water from a spring constantly running caused a cooling effect. Meats were smoked, put in brine or "cold packed." There was never any fresh meat in warm weather, except for an occasional chicken or groundhog.

Most small communities had their own icehouse and New Germany was no exception. Originally, the icehouse was located just south of the McAndrew brother's gristmill near the blacksmith shop. Parking lot #5 now encompasses that area. The icehouse was a basic frame structure about 50' X 50' X 30'. It had a flat roof and a dirt floor. It was of double wall construction. The space between the inner and outer wall being packed with sawdust for insulation. Approximately 150 tons of ice were cut and packed each winter.

Ice cutting was a chore shared by all able-bodied males in the community. Ice was cut in mid-February, preferably on a day when the temperature would be near or below zero. It was a wet, backbreaking job. Word would be passed to all concerned via the local party line that ice would be cut on a certain day. All hands would be expected to be there at daylight with their ice saws, tongs, ice spuds, horses and sleds or wagons. The group would be divided in several teams; one team to shovel snow from and cut the ice; another to drag the ice out of the water and cut it into blocks and load it into sleds; another would be hauling sawdust from the sawmill to the icehouse and yet another team working in the icehouse packing the ice. Younger lads usually worked in the icehouse, putting sawdust between the cakes of ice and tamping the sawdust between the layers. It was also much safer because someone always managed to fall into the water.

The ice was cut when it was 18-24 inches thick, sometimes thicker. A straight edge would be laid on the ice and marked. Then the actual cutting began. A special crosscut saw was used.

A cake of ice about 30" wide and 30 to 40 feet long would be cut, floating free in the water. A special made set of tongs would be hooked up to a horse, which furnished the power to pull the ice out of the water. The horse was equipped with special studded shoes to prevent slipping.

Once the ice was pulled out of the water, another team proceeded to cut it up into blocks weighing 150 to 200 lbs. These blocks were loaded into sleds and sent to the icehouse. The ice cakes were intentionally made very large because some melting always occurred during the summer.

At noon, lunch would be served inside the icehouse by the wives who had brought hot soup, drinks, and sandwiches from home. This was a welcome break for all concerned. There was usually a jug or two of "moonshine" to help fortify the workmen against the cold and wind.

The crew working in the icehouse had to be especially proficient in their duties. The cakes of ice would be laid flat on the floor, making certain that one cake never touched another. If they touched, they would fuse together and be practically impossible to work with. A space of about two inches was left between cakes. This space would then be filled with sawdust and tamped down by the youngsters, me included, working in the icehouse. A space of ten to twelve inches was left between the ice and the inside wall. This was also filled with sawdust. When the floor of the icehouse was covered with ice, a layer of sawdust six to eight inches thick would be laid down on the first layer. The second layer would go immediately on the first until the icehouse was full to the ceiling. About two to three feet of sawdust would be put on the top of the last layer and the door sealed. Anyone in the community would be permitted to use the ice when needed during the following summer. The only stipulation was that the remaining ice be sufficiently covered to prevent melting.

Removing the ice was no easy job either. It first had to be uncovered, then pried loose from adjacent cakes and removed from the icehouse. The ice would be taken to the nearest creek and immersed in water to wash away this sawdust. Probably each cake would have shrunk by twenty percent from the time it was cut until it was actually used.

With the advent of the Civilian Conservation Corps (CCC) at New Germany in 1933, the chore of ice cutting was delegated to the CCC boys. They could cut more ice in two days than a few farmers could in five. They had better equipment. A gasoline driven circular saw that could be raised and lowered was mounted on a sled. This facilitated the first step of the ice cutting operation. Even though the camp personnel had their own refrigeration units, they did use ice from time to time. After the camp at New Germany moved in 1937 the chore of ice cutting reverted back to the local farmers. During this period, a new icehouse was constructed beside the roadway on the east side of the lake. It was closer to the water and sawmill.

When the cabins opened at New Germany, there was no electricity. During the summer months, ice would be dug from the icehouse on Wednesday and Saturday mornings. It then would be washed off and delivered to each cabin, which was equipped with a homemade icebox. These boxes were insulated very well and very solidly constructed.

We finally received commercial electricity at New Germany in 1946. All the farm homes were immediately wired and hooked up. The first electrical appliance to appear in most farm kitchens was a refrigerator. This certainly was a Godsend to the farmer's wife and made her work more bearable. The icehouse was still used for several years in case of power failure, but slowly faded into the past.

My family moved to New Germany in 1931 from the small town of Gilmore in Allegany County. I was five years old. The community from where we came was very close knit, lots of neighbors and lots of children to play with. Most of the parents worked in the coalmine or the mills and the children did not have a lot of chores to perform.

Things were a lot different at New Germany. All of the people were farmers. Our nearest neighbors were a half mile away. The children all had chores to perform before and after school and during summer vacations. These chores included milking, cleaning stables, plowing, planting, gardening, and helping to harvest. The children had most of their time planned for them when they weren't in school. My friends were all usually busy, so I would go and visit them and help them with their chores.

I did not have many jobs to do at our home. My father was Superintendent of Savage River State Forest. We always had a garden and the task of weeding was assigned to me. We had a cow, pigs, and chickens. I soon learned how to milk and also feed the other animals. My most abhorred task was carrying water. Our home did not have running water and I had to carry water from Mr. Swauger's spring near the New Germany schoolhouse. The distance was about a quarter mile and I soon learned that two- three-gallon buckets of water could

One-room school that Bill attended from 1931 to 1937

be quite heavy for a six year old.

Even though most of our free time was taken by helping our parents, we did find time to play. Our playtime at school was very loosely organized. We usually played or did what the older kids wanted to do. Our playground was merely a cleaned patch of woods, dotted quite heavily with pine stumps. We managed to play baseball. Our baseball was usually handmade. A ball of string wrapped with a piece of rubber inner tube sufficed. When one of the stronger kids hit the ball into the woods, the game would be cancelled until the ball was found or until someone made another ball. Our favorite game was Annie Over. We chose sides and stood on each side of the schoolhouse. A makeshift ball would be thrown over the roof and caught by a team member. Then the catching team would all run around the schoolhouse where the team member holding the ball would attempt to hit one of the opposing team members. If he was successful, that member of the opposing team was required to go to the other team. If you were not successful in hitting anyone, the ball would then be thrown to the opposition. The team with the most players over a given period would be the winner.

Dodge ball and fox and geese were also very popular games at school. Each year in grammar school, we were all tested for physical stamina and abilities. This was always done in the spring and was known as badge testing. You were required to run a certain distance, do pushups, chin-ups, and sit-ups in order to qualify for certain badges, bronze, silver, or gold. Usually by the time you were in the sixth grade, you had earned all three badges.

We played a lot of cowboys and Indians during recess and lunch hours. We built forts and Indian villages that were quite impressive. I can't remember how many times I was captured by Indians and either scalped or burned at the stake. The females usually brought ransoms such as chewing tobacco or an occasional corn silk cigarette.

During the school term, we presented plays and skits at the schoolhouse. We usually had one of these programs each month. The front of the schoolhouse was our stage. A clothesline was strung across the room and a couple of bed sheets were used for curtains. About once a year, the grownups presented a play. Everyone in the community attended. In the fall and spring, we had socials at the schoolhouse. All the ladies would make ice cream, pies, cakes, candies, and sandwiches. Homemade root beer and lemonade were available. These items were sometimes sold, but most of the time they were given away. The men usually had some mountain dew stored outside in the bushes on these occasions.

You should be reminded that there was not much entertainment in the area at that time. Most of the farmers had battery powered radios that were usually used in the morning and evening for news and weather reports. On occasion, the family might listen to Amos and Andy, Lum and Abner, or The Shadow. Batteries were quite expensive and couldn't be used for frivolous entertainment. Most of the things we did in the community were done as a group in order to entertain ourselves. Some people had cars but there wasn't any money to spend if you went anywhere. If you were lucky, you got to go to the County Fair every summer. I was usually given a quarter to spend and most of the time couldn't make up my mind what I wanted to spend it on.

Dancing was quite popular with local residents. All the furniture in the schoolhouse would be shoved aside and round and square dancing would be held. Most of the time the square dancing would be done in someone's barn. Young and old participated. Every community had their own orchestra, which consisted of fiddle, guitar, and mandolin. There was always lots to eat and drink at these affairs.

I Have No Desire to Climb on a Horse
By Robert Armentrout of Upper Tract, West Virginia
Born 1943

As I am sitting here at this computer, typing these memories I can see how much times have changed in the short time that I have been around. I take these means to relate to my children and grandchildren, how much things have changed and the different type of life that I lived growing up as a child. I will try to the best of my ability to narrate this in chronological order.

I was born April 1, 1943 in my Aunt Lillian's house (mom's sister) and was delivered by Lillian's mother-in-law, Carrie Harman. I know some people say that your memory of early childhood only goes back to three to four years of age, but my earliest memory is of Kathleen Harman (Carrie's daughter) reaching down into my crib, which was placed across the wheel wells of our tiny trailer that we lived in and making cooing sounds, much as we do today when admiring a child.

This leads me to describing the place that we lived in during the early years of my childhood. I have no idea where the tiny trailer was acquired but do know that my grandfather (Charlie "pop" Armentrout) pulled an old tool shed over from his farm and attached it to the trailer. The trailer served as our sleeping

The schoolhouse

quarters and the tool shed served as the dining room and kitchen. I suppose the trailer also served as a living room. At that time there was no electricity in the ridges and we used kerosene lamps for light and burned wood for heat. We had no indoor plumbing and had to carry water from a spring to cook with, do dishes, and for baths. Speaking of baths, we were only required to take one bath per week and that was on a Saturday night. Mom would heat the water on the stove and pour into a dishpan in which we would do a "sponge bath." It's hard to imagine what parents would do today if their children only wanted to take one bath per week.

Rispa Mullenax Armentrout, born April 11, 1923. My mother, Rispa Mullenax Armentrout, was a homemaker and to the best of my knowledge never had a paying job. I do recall a time or two when she cleaned house for a neighbor. I'm thinking raising six kids was a full time job in itself. There was no such thing as "timeouts" and the switch and belt provided the discipline that was so readily meted out by our mother. Mom's mother (Sudie Lamb Mullenax) passed away when mom was 12 or 13 years old and I suppose life was pretty tough when mom had to grow up without a mother. Mom was a devout Christian and there was not a Sunday missed that we did not attend church. The Bible that she read was dog-eared and well worn, much unlike the Bible that is in my living room.

Mom never learned to drive a car until she was in her 30s or early 40s. There was no need to drive as the things that were needed at that time were either provided for by our few laying hens that we had or by my grandfather "pop." The few things that we needed from the store were brought home by my dad on Saturday after he got paid. We never had a mailbox and the post office was over a mile away in the small thriving community of Kline. I recall many times walking with mom to the post office for the mail. The Kline community at that time was the hub of activity in that area. Not only did they have a post office but there was also a mill to grind wheat or oats and a grocery store, which we kids always loved to browse in. Once in a blue moon mom would have enough money that she would buy us a bottle of pop (five cents) and/or a bar of candy also five cents. There were times when we did not go to the post office for more than two weeks and "Pop's" brother, great uncle, Ott Armentrout would bring the mail to us on horseback.

Clyde Armentrout, born July 6, 1918. My dad, Clyde Armentrout, was, and for as long as I can remember, an automobile mechanic. He had innate ability to listen to an engine running and diagnose the problem. In his teenage years he drove a chicken truck for some of the local poultry buyers. He related several stories to me of heading to Cleveland, Ohio and breaking down in the middle of winter with several inches of snow on the ground. He would dig out his coveralls and fix the problem if it could be fixed with the meager parts they hauled with them. You've got to remember that this was in the 1930s and transportation was not that reliable, to say the least. My dad also served in the CCC camp for almost two years before being kicked out because he had a car hidden close to the camp and he and his buddies would sneak off at night visiting the local ladies or the taverns. I am not sure of the timeframe, but shortly after that (November 1940) he met and married my mother. This was during World War II and consequently dad was inducted into the Army. This was in 1943 or 1944 and he served nine months and was ready to ship across the ocean when the government gave discharges to the married men who had more than two dependents. I guess I was the one that precipitated his being discharged early.

It was very difficult for me to bond with my dad as he worked six days a week and was never around too much as I was growing up. I do know that during his stint in the CCC and Army that he developed a liking for the spirits. He was never an alcoholic, but he did like to drink and have fun with his friends. In my early childhood, mom never mentioned dad's drinking and I can recall the first time the subject was brought up. He had come home from work a little late one evening and headed out of the kitchen to the backyard. Being the inquisitive lad that I was, I approached him only to find him gagging and hacking. I went running to mom, shouting to her that dad was sick and dying. She replied, "He's only drunk as a skunk and will be alright in an hour or so."

As I mentioned before dad worked six days a week and Sunday was his time to be in the woods squirrel hunting. It never mattered whether season was in or not, my dad headed for the woods. For several years squirrel meat was a main staple for the Armentrout family. One evening dad came home with a brand new Iver Johnson 16-gauge shotgun, which he was dying to try out. Previous to this he would only hunt with a single shot 22. As I was about eight years old he told me I could go along with him on this hunt. We were walking around a slate bank next to a rail fence when we both spied a fox squirrel meandering beyond the other side of the fence. Dad crept up to the fence and taking a rest off of the fence he pulled the trigger. He got the squirrel, but when the shotgun went off it knocked him back on his butt. I couldn't help but laugh and after getting over the shock of landing on his butt, he joined in the laughter. After that we referred to that Iver Johnson as the "cripple in front and kill behind" gun.

People were always coming to the house for dad to listen to and/or ride in their car to tell them what was wrong with it. Many a time dad would diagnose and fix the problem for them even if it took several hours. They would always offer to pay him but he would not accept their money. For years and years this was a sore point with mom as we were a very poor family and could have used the extra cash.

Charlie (Pop) Armentrout. My earliest recollection of my grandfather, Charlie "Pop" Armentrout, is the picture in my mind of him running after and catching his two horses to put them in a harness for farm work. My memory of him with the horses was the time when he came to our potato patch to plow out the potatoes. I believe he only had the one horse with him at that time and the horse's name was Frank. He put the collar and harness on Frank and began plowing out the potatoes. It was astounding how well trained Ole Frank was. As Frank would get slightly out of the row, Pop would either holler "gee" or "haw" and Frank would veer right or left depending on which word Pop used. At the end of a row Pop would say, "Come around Frank" and the horse would turn around, ready to being another row. At the end of plowing the potatoes Frank was completely white and soaked with sweat. Pop asked me if I wanted to ride Frank back to his house, which was a distance of about one mile. Being the young and adventurous lad that I was, I readily took him up on the offer. Well I'm telling you, by the time we got to Pop's house, the inside of my legs from my butt down were completely gaulded. I was sore like that for a couple of days and that pretty well ended my horseback riding. To this day I have no desire to climb on a horse even if it is wearing a saddle.

Shortly after this time period Pop bought an old forty-some model tractor and farming in earnest began. I was eight to ten years old at the time and plenty grown-up enough to help on the farm. Pop would pick me up or I would walk the mile to his house and we usually started the farming season by plowing and disking the fields in preparation to planting corn. After the field was prepared it was time to plant the corn. At that time, Pop never had a pull-behind corn planter. He had the old style planter that was held in the hands and gouged into the ground and pulling the handles apart released three to five grains of corn into the small indentation that the end of the planter had made. Once the corn had started growing it was time to plow the weeds out and uncover the corn that the small shovel plows had plowed under. After the corn had matured and a few frosts had set in it was time to cut the corn. This was accomplished by cutting the stalks off with a handheld corn cutter that resembled a machete. The stalks were grasped under the arm until you had an armful and then stacked into shocks. To stack them into shocks we left four stalks standing, each being about two feet apart, two in one row and two in the row across. This provided a support for the corn shock. After the corn was stacked in shocks it was allowed to stand for a few weeks and then it was time to shuck the corn and pile it up in piles. Shucking the corn was accomplished by using a shucking tool that was made of leather with a metal hook attached to the leather band. The band was placed around the palm of your hand and the metal hook was used to grasp the end of the shuck between your thumb and the hook. Once this was done it was time to haul the corn to the corncrib. We would put it in the crib and when chickens were to be fed he had a hand cranked corn sheller that would pull the corn kernels off of the cob. As you can see, Pop and I were very close, and I think that he intentionally done this to fill the void that my dad left, because of his working six days a week.

Survival and Love
By Shirley J. Ravenscroft of Lonaconing,
Maryland
Born 1943

Where will I begin? I will start first with my age. I am 70 years old as of December 30, 2013. I will be married 50 years this September 12, 2014. I have seen a lot in these many years. As for writing about the good old days, I will take these days other then missing my parents to this day. My mother died in 1962, at 41 years of age with cancer and left my dad of 46 years of age with eight children, two daughters and six boys, ages from 19 to 9 years of age. My mother died on August the 11th of 1962 and my dad's birthday was August the 15th. He always said, "Look what I got for my birthday, a dead wife whom I loved dearly and eight children and a home to take care of and to make sure we stayed together."

I am going to start my story of the morning my father came upstairs to wake me and ask me to come down and help my mother bake bread, as her fingers were all infected and dad had to go to work. I was only 10 years old. I protested but dad said mother would teach me. So I got up and got dressed and went downstairs. Mother was sad that I had to do this. We had a big pan with handles on it and mother sat it on a chair for me and then she put a half of a 25-pound of flour in it, then a half bock of lard and told me to mix this together thru my finger till it was coarse, then she told me to put a handful of sugar and salt and work this thru. In a bowl on the table was hot water and I was told to dissolve half the cake of yeast in it. When this was done, I poured it into the flour mixture and worked it till it formed a big dough ball. I then dumped it on to the floured table and kneaded it till it was smooth. I then wash the mixture off my hands and wash the big pan. Then I greased it and put the bread dough back in it to rise. It had to double in size. It was an all day job.

While the bread was rising, she taught me how to cook and fix lima beans for supper. We baked bread three times a week .You always had beans, soup, and mush (made from cornmeal) on bread day. She also taught me how to make pies that day. We always made 8 to 10 pies, all flavors. To this day, I have never forget how to do this.

Before we move to this home in Gilmore, we lived in Detmold, Maryland in a mining company home, which my parents rented. There were four rooms, one upstairs, and three down and we heated it with a coal stove in the middle room and a coal and gas stove combination in the kitchen. Outside in the backyard was a doghouse, coalhouse, and an outhouse. There was 10 of us in this house. In the summer mother and dad slept in the front room, but in the winter we all slept upstairs in one room. At night dad would build a hot fire in the coal stove and the front room was closed off and there was a curtain on the doorway between the kitchen and middle room. We would turn on the radio and listen to it for a while before we went to bed. When it was time for bed, dad would put so many of us on his back and he would carry us up the steps and put us to bed. We always said our prayers and kissed him goodnight. We didn't have much, but we knew we were loved.

We went to a two-room schoolhouse a short distance from where we lived. Grade 1 to 3 was taught by Miss Dunn and grade

Shirley's parents, Roy C. and Mary Kathleen McKenzie in 1941

4 to 6 was taught by Miss Miller. We went home for lunch. I was in the 5th grade when they closed the school and sent us to Central. They were building a new high school right below our home. It was called Valley high School and it was 7th thru 12th grade, now Westmar Middle.

Shirley, Roy, and Marvin

They told my father that they were taking the home we lived in, so dad had to look for a place that had a furnace and an indoor bathroom. The first night mom bathed the boys; she said it paid for the home. They had saved war bonds and they cashed them in for the down payment on the home. They were left with a $25.00 payment on the home per month. Dad was still working in the mines, but shortly after we moved into the house, the mines were closed and dad was out of work. They worried so much about how they were going to make the house payment. Dad got about 60 dollars a week, unemployment, but he had 10 mouths to feed and utilities to pay, so my mother decided she was going to find work.

Mom had only went to the 11th grade in school, so she wasn't trained for anything, so she went to work cleaning for a woman in LaVale and the woman worked her so hard that mother ended up getting sick, so dad said she couldn't do this. So mother decided to sell her baked goods. We went around the neighborhood and took orders for bread, rolls, pies, and cakes. She would bake all this and we would deliver it in our little red wagon and she would save this until she had enough to make the house payment. Dad was out of work for a good while, but he would plant a big garden and mother would can all that she could and then we would set up a stand and sell the rest. We had people come from all over to get the fresh garden food.

Finally, one day our preacher came and asked dad if he would work for labor wages for a Mr. Fuller in Frostburg and my dad said yes. He worked long hours for $1.25 an hour and it was hard work. He asked them to teach him how to lay brick and stone and they told him he was too old to learn, but he proved them wrong and became one of the best bricklayers and stonemasons in the area. He bricked many places all over Allegany County. He bricked my home and built me a stone fireplace the year he retired. He taught my daughter how to face stone and my son also helped him mix the mortar. He was 86 years and 5 months old when he died and I miss him every day. He only went to 9th grade of school but he was very smart. He went from horse and buggy to Space travel in his time. He always said the country really was moving. He loved this country very much.

Fast forward to about 1960 when mother started having health problems. They doctored her for gall bladder for two years and decided to remove it. She went in to Miners Hospital in Frostburg to be operated on. Dad was gone for many hours and I was left in charge. I waited and worried until he came home. When he did, he was crying and he took a hold of me and told me that mother had cancer. When they opened her up she was full of it and they just closed her up and told dad she had six months to a year to live. He said to me that the news knocked him off his feet and he thought he would never get up again but he did. She lived for about eight months and it was a really bad time as she was in and out of the hospital so much. Then they wouldn't let the boys in to see their mother, so dad would go down in the car and get them and I would get mother to the window so she could wave at them. Mother took cobalt treatments, she would go down on the bus and back, and they burned her stomach almost black.

We couldn't get help nowhere. I remember helping dad fill out papers for United Fund to get some help and when they came back, they told him he would have to sell his car. He told them no way, if he sold his car how would he get to work. So we struggled and we got thru it. There are so many details I could go thru but it would take much more than this short story. I am writing about one of the worst things that happened in our lives. As I think of some of the things, we didn't have that people have today and take for granted.

Outhouses and chamber pots, we had outhouses at our home and our schoolhouse. Castor oil and home remedies, we were given castor oil when sick and for other things. Dad made up his own remedies when we were sick. The doctor would come to your house and dad would have us all on the mends and he would say to dad that he should be a doctor. Old radio programs, every night after we were ready for bed we would turn on the radio and listen to several stories, *InterSanctum, Gun Smoke, Long Ranger* and many more. Party Line phone, most everyone had this type of phone and the news went all over town. Saturday night bath didn't have running water so our mother had to carry water and heat on the stove, boys and dad took baths in the same water, then mother heated water for my sister and I and her and we took a bath in the same water. Wringer washer, that's all we had, had to hang clothes outside. In the winter, they froze and we brought them in to thaw and dry, then you would sprinkle them with water and put in the basket and then iron them later.

Homemade clothes and toys, most of our clothes were made or once a year at Easter, mother would order us new clothes from National Bell Hess, some of our toys were made by dad. At Christmas, we were allowed to pick a toy that we wanted and mom or dad would go to town and lay them away at Coffman Fisher, from Thanksgiving to Christmas. No child was allowed upstairs at the store. Christmas Eve Day, Dad would go and get them. 9. Two room schoolhouses with a potbelly stove in the middle of the room. Miss Dunn taught 1 to 3 and Miss Miller taught 4 to 6. We went home for lunch. Iceboxes are what most people had and we would run after the iceman's truck to get a piece of ice. We did the same for our milkman, he delivered milk every day and the cream was on top of it and mother would take it off and make whip cream for ice cream and pies and cakes. Games and playmates, we always played outside till dark and we shared our things with our playmates. Family time, most important to us all, we shared what we did, chores, love, and pray together. As I make note of all these things there is many more. Every day was a challenge and life was not easy, but you never really thought about it as everyone was mostly in the same boat. If you ever watched the Walton's on TV, we were a lot like them. Everyone had to do their share. Life was about survival and love.

John C. and Shirley J. Ravenscroft

The Last Generation with No Worries
By Zack T. Fleming of Kearneysville, West Virginia
Born 1944

I was born August 13, 1944 in Martinsburg, West Virginia. That was the hottest day of the year and I arrived for lunch at 12:01. Dad was in the Army and my mother and sister lived with my grandparents on the small family farm. Since dad was away and didn't know where granddad was when mom went into labor, my sister ran ½ mile down the road screaming for my aunt and uncle that I was on the way. My uncle was a very nervous man and probably exceeded the speed limit for the first time to get mom to the hospital.

I have many memories of my grandfather taking me everywhere in his old pickup truck. He was an old time farmer and did everything by the sign of the moon, from planting crops to butchering the hog. He wouldn't allow a tractor to plow the garden as he said it packed the ground, but had a man plow with a horse. He had several Jersey milk cows and a bull, beef cow for meat, 10-12 hogs, a small flock of sheep, and of course, chickens. He sold the sheep when I was a toddler as I'd venture out in the field and the ram would butt me down. He had a family work for him full time. Uncle Dan helped with the farm chores and garden. Aunt Hattie did the laundry using a washboard and a wringer washer and housework. The washed clothes were always hung outside on a clothesline. Their youngest daughter, "Sissy," helped Aunt Hattie and their youngest son, "Droopy Drawers," helped Uncle Dan in the house when needed. Granny churned butter and they took it in town for her butter and egg money.

Butchering day was always a big event as Uncle Dan had been splitting locust logs for the scalding tank and pots for several weeks. At the crack of dawn, the butchering of at least 10 hogs began and quite a few locals came to help and one elderly lady would clean the intestines and bladders for sausage stuffing. The day ended when all the pots were washed and greased, all the other equipment was washed and cleaned and put away, and the meat was seasoned with sugar cure and placed in the meat house for keeping. Everyone that helped was given a "mess" of sausage and some other fresh pork as a thank you.

Grandfather had a stroke in the barn one evening after he had finished milking and died several days later. Granny found him when he didn't come in for supper. It was one of the largest funerals at the time in the county as he was well known and liked by everyone. I still remember "Sissy" shrieking, "Mr. Carl is dead!" and running through the house in tears.

When I entered school it was technically a two-room school as the big room had folding doors that divided the 1st, 2nd, and 3rd grade from the 4th, 5th and 6th grades with a teacher for each room. Each grade had between three to eight children. Christmas plays were the highlight of the year with the kids singing carols and performing little skits for the parents and community. The teachers didn't hesitate to crack your fingers with a ruler or give swats with a huge paddle if warranted.

The big old house we lived in had a coal-fired furnace in the basement and a little "jack" stove, which grandfather lit on Saturdays to have hot water for the weekly bath. During the week, we had a huge coal/wood range with a "well" on the side for daily hot water. Although we had pressurized water, the kitchen had a hand pitcher pump that was used most of the time. The cistern was our main source and would silt up with soot from the nearby B&O steam engines and had to be cleaned out regularly. The well was used mostly for the livestock.

The big dining room was not opened except on special occasions. The pocketed doors were closed and the room not heated except for Thanksgiving and Christmas. I have vivid memories of all the family dinners of my grandfather's family during the holidays. This one had that day and that one this day and on Christmas my grandfather had the noon dinner and a great aunt the evening dinner. The "johnny house" was used most of the time instead of the inside toilet. It was a treat when the iceman came several times a week during the summer. He would always give us kids a piece of ice to suck on.

My mother was an excellent seamstress and loved to sew. Most of my shirts were made by her from chicken feed sacks until I was about 12, as well as a few stuffed animals when very young. She would go to the feed store and find the print she liked on the sacks and then when empty make clothes for us. Both she and granny would spend hours crocheting this and that while listening to the old AM radio in the evenings. During this period most of us played little league baseball or field baseball or football with the local kids. Sled riding on a hill on our farm was a favorite during winter. We'd build a bonfire out of anything we could scrape up and play until bedtime.

I can't remember exactly when we got our first phone. It was a rotary dial on the Shepherdstown, West Virginia exchange and a real oddity. No party line with direct dial within the exchange with only four digits. When we moved in 1961, we had a party line with two long rings and four shorts. When I called home from South Carolina in 1963 and gave the operator the number, she said it sounded like a circuit instead of a number, but I told her to get the Charles Town, West Virginia operator and tell her the number. No problem, it was correct. After 6th grade, I rode a bus to town for high school. That was considered the 7th through 12th grades. It was a big change for us rural kids with many students, probably 250, and changing classrooms for different subjects. We were allowed to go "downtown" with parents' permission during lunch hour. Most of the boys went to the pool hall and ate a Mexican sandwich and drank a Pepsi and had a dime left over for one game of pool.

It was about 1956 when I saw my first color TV. My sister's husband worked for a NBC station in Wheeling, West Virginia and he took us to the studio to seen this new gadget as it wasn't on the air at the time. If we had time after lunch, there was a sock hop in the gym with the students providing the 45s of the era. I'll never forget the morning in 1957 after "the music died." Everybody was so sad and many of the girls cried all day.

It was in high school that I excelled in mechanics and was FFA farm mechanic of the year my senior year. I had been working in local orchards and on farms since I was about 13. I wanted a "hot rod" but couldn't afford one at the time. I had a 1956 Ford with T-bird motor as the best I could do. Winters seemed much snowier then, but the state didn't have the big equipment they now have. The rule was if you could make it to school, then you were expected to come to school. Some kids we wouldn't see for weeks, as they were snow bound.

The one year that was very bad, I helped a local milk hauler pick up milk from the farms to deliver to the (Sealtest) processor in Chambersburg, Pennsylvania. He'd pick me up about 3:30 AM and we'd start on his route picking up 10-gallon cans and leaving the empties. Many of the lanes were drifted and we'd put tire chains on and try to get in. Sometimes we would get in and at other times we would get stuck and have to shovel our way out. Many of the farmers would load the cans in a wagon and cross their fields with a tractor to the state highways for us to pick them up. It would be nearly 8:00 PM when I got home.

Summers were spent working on the farms and in the orchards. Sunday afternoons were usually reserved for swimming in the local creeks and rivers and a little free time with our friends. Saturday was the only day I could depend on getting off at 5:00 PM unless we had hay down. I'd get my check and go to the local Esso station and cash it and fill up with gas and go to town to just run with my friends and illegally have some 3.2 beer or double date and go to the "passion pit" drive-in theaters with our girlfriends in the summer. I often say we were the last generation to have no worries and a really good time.

Fall was my favorite time of year. I love hunting and would hitchhike home, all of 5 miles, to beat our old 48-model school bus and be out the back door with my shotgun before the bus got to our stop. I'd tend to my livestock when I got in after dark on most days. Upon graduation, two of my classmates and I entered the Air Force in less than three weeks. That was the start of my 20+ years of military service. I got stationed nearby after three years of service when my dad had a serious accident and nobody thought he'd ever recover and mom couldn't manage the place on her own. The little sister of one of my girlfriends had grown up and asked me to take her to her junior prom. I did and that started a new phase of my life.

Dad recovered miraculously and I was then into serious hot rodding and was building big block Ford FE motors. I blew one up in June; we had decided to get married in December, so re-enlisted to get a bonus to pay for a new motor and our future wedding. Within a month after we married I had two sets of orders. One to Vietnam and the other to a top-secret school in Texas. I got the Texas assignment and my new 17-year-old bride and I set off on a journey that took us around the world. We bought all our furniture locally and saw it placed in the moving van out of the store. Once we got to Texas we went to the base credit union and borrowed money for a color TV console. The school was about six months and then I got orders to the Philippines. She couldn't accompany me at that time, so we shipped our "stuff" back to my parents for storage. She lived with them and they used our color TV and liked it so well that when she was able to join me, bought their first color TV.

July 20, 1969 is probably one of my most memorable days. We were watching TV on AFPN in the Philippines when the Eagle landed. I have a Wilkerson sword #258 of 2,000 honoring the moon landing. This takes me to being stationed in the UK and the birth of our daughter, 352 days back in the USA then an assignment to Turkey and then Berlin and a final assignment back to Texas before retiring in 1982 then moving "home" in 1992. This is the end of my "good old days."

Holidays in Coney
By Vivian Moore of Lonaconing, Maryland
Born 1952

Fall time was such a great time in my hometown of Lonaconing, Maryland, Dr. Coney as everyone called it. It was the time of going back to school and getting new school

Vivian's sister, Cecelia, Vivian, and Vivian's brother, Raymond in 1955

clothes, because you only got new clothes on certain occasions when I grew up. I remember going to Frostburg to get a new pair of saddle oxfords, black and white, and my sister got the same, all you could smell was that pungent smell of leather at this store called Super Shoes on Main Street. We always got a book satchel and sometimes a plastic pencil case with a sliding lid. We had to have a black and white spelling book and we covered our books with brown market bags. I remember in 1st grade we got a box of crayons, nice fat ones, and a big fat black pencil. Then one day we each got a square plug of clay and a clay board to play with on a rainy day. That clay had such a good smell that I loved to get it out just to smell it. We had to have two dollars to buy a flutophone in music, then we had to practice our songs every day, "Mary Had a Little Lamb" was my favorite and "Three Blind Mice," I still have mine somewhere. Our moms had to make a cloth flutophone bag for us to carry it to school.

In 1st grade, I cried every day for probably a couple months and stood in the hall and cried for my older sister, who abandoned me and walked upstairs to her class, wanting nobody to know that the red-faced little girl was her sister and my brother ran off with his friends like a bunch of wild Indians. So Mr. Marshall, the custodian, would pick me up and carry me over his shoulder like a sack of potatoes to Miss Myers class. One day she came in and told me, "I have something special just for you if you promise not to cry anymore," by then the crying had gotten very old, I'm sure. She handed me a little package wrapped in pretty paper tied with a ribbon, I wanted to take it home to open it, but all the kids gathered around and urged me to open it. Carefully I untaped the paper and inside there was a lovely little plastic doll in a blue plastic high chair. I was so thrilled; it was just like the ones I had admired at Weber's 5 + 10. I don't remember if I ever cried or not, but I'll always remember that kind gesture of Miss Myers.

Fall also brought on the great custom of trick or treating or Halloweening, as we called it. For weeks ahead, we would rack our brains of what we were going to wear for the school Halloween parade. We checked mom's old rag barrel first to find any old dresses that we could become a princess with a homemade tin foil crown and a stick with a paper star attached for a wand. My brother was always a cowboy or a pirate with a patch on his eye; he was more pleased to have his Roy Roger gun and holster on to show it off in school. The school parade was a big to-do, as we marched down the main street of Coney and the traffic was stopped for a while. The sound of the leaves crunching under your feet and the smell of Fall in the air, what a good feeling it was as we passed all the people and our parents who came out to watch the Halloween parade, all the stores were decorated with pumpkins and tall black arched cats. Then after it was over was the fun fair at school where you could buy a 10-cent grab bag, 20 candy apple or candy cotton and many games to play, it was so much fun.

Halloween night was a big night going from house to house getting a candy treat; some people made fudge and some candy apples. Mrs. Fairgrieve always made us dance or sing for a treat. We took a bar of soap and a tic-tacer that we made out of wooden thread spools, you cut notches in it, and wrapped string on the spool and held it against the window and pulled the string and it made a rattling sound, and we soaped the windows of the people who wouldn't answer the door. The older boys said they threw a bran sack of manure on someone's porch and yelled fire and they would come out to stomp it out, manure and all. Most people had outhouses then, which hung out over the click. The older boys decided to push a couple of the outhouses over and needless to say, it was not done again. Clothes that were on the lines were switched to other clotheslines and one had to go to the neighbors to find their clothes. It was just all-clean fun to us. Fall brings back many good memories to me.

Other childhood memories. The girls in the neighborhood always made there own fun, after the parents were done with the old Sears and Roebuck catalogs we girls would get scissors and make our own paper dolls and we'd even cut clothes out of the same catalogs until it looked like a rat had shredded it. We laid them all out in families and played on the floor for hours with these. On occasions, we would get to buy a book of paper dolls at the store, what a treat. My sister would get Dinah Shore cut outs and I got Cinderella cutouts; we played with these for hours. Once in a while, my dad would go to town and bring us a surprise, but he had the worst taste. I patiently waited for a gift because I was sick and I had so wanted a metal lunch box with a thermos and as I eagerly opened the sack to find instead of the Snow White lunch box he had gotten me a planet lunch box with stars, moons, etc. I thought he bought me a boy's lunch box and then I was ashamed to take it to school, but I did anyway. Playing with dolls and making a playhouse out of dad's workshop was a great venture, we had many good hours in this. In the summer we played Jacks and jumped rope, when it was really hot, we got to get the tin tub out and the hose and that was our way to cool off; oh what good times they were.

I sit back and reminisce about my Christmas pasts and some of my most pleasant memories were of the streets of Lonaconing in the '50s and '60s. Coney always had the multicolored strings of lights strung back and forth the street and it almost reminded you of driving under a canopy of color. It was magical, you rejoiced at the knowledge that the lights were up. Then as Christmas approached, you saved your dimes and nickels to buy Christmas gifts for your family and where better to shop in Coney? We would go up town and go first to Weber's 5 & 10 where we often bought mom three pretty handkerchiefs in a box for 39 cents then we would buy my dad a pair of brown gloves or socks for 29 cents. Sometimes we got mom a small glass lamp filled with perfume, I'm sure it smelled good.

We also had Eilbeck's variety and Coffman Fisher's with the fancy window you could walk around and stand under the entrance to get out of the rain. The best part was being allowed to go upstairs to see the toys, which you did not touch or tryout and you knew this well. The week of Christmas was special because the stores opened till 9:00 in the evening, a rare thing only at Christmas. I still remember the great feeling inside going up a day before Christmas and all the lights were on and carolers would go from house to house singing. Mom would rush in the store for a few last minute gifts and we just wanted to get home before Santa Claus would get there.

We had the best bakery with shortbread that melted in your mouth. You could go into Marshall's Confectionary for a cherry smash or chocolate Coke.

Vivian's dad, Harold Moore, Raymond, Vivian, Mary Alea, and Rheba James

Love's Grocery sold all kinds of Christmas candy bagged by the pound, popcorn balls, and all kinds of Holiday goodies. We had Ternents ready to wear, here's where you could get anything from bathrobes to rock salt. It was possible get all your needs right in Coney. The Saturday before Christmas was the free show at San Toy Theatre sometimes held at the armory. You couldn't wait till the show was over to see Santa Claus who gave you a little box of mixed candy and an orange, what a great treat. Back in days a treat like this was savored just make it last. School was a whole other story. Central school holds so many good Christmas memories, making potholders for our mom, paper chains, and lanterns. I remember at Christmas the cafeteria ceiling would be decorated with popcorn balls wrapped in bright cellophane and before school was out for Christmas Santa would visit and give us a bag of candy and one of those popcorn balls.

Drinking With Daddy
By Violet R. Eye of Sugar Grove, West Virginia
Born 1941

I was born on a cold, snowy, Sunday in January of 1941, in Pendleton County, West Virginia. I'm the oldest of four children born to Delbert and Sheba "Smith" Rexrode. Daddy and mom lived in a farmhouse on the land that my daddy farmed for Rebecca Hiner and her two daughters. The house had eight rooms, but we only got to use four of them. Mrs. Hiner used the rest of the house when she came to visit and also the help would stay there. Mom would do the cooking for everyone who might be in the house at a given time. I was born in our living room, delivered by Dr. Stover, who lived in Doe Hill, Virginia.

We had no electricity, running water, or bathroom. We carried water from a spring, used oil lamps for light, a chamber pot for night going, and an outhouse during the day. We raised a garden for most of the food we had. Daddy was allowed to keep one hog and he would raise pigs to sell. They killed and cured the meat, enough to do from one fall until the next. He would hunt squirrels, raccoons, groundhogs, and quail. We had chickens and turkeys. Deer were scarce and I don't recall seeing a bear until after I was grown.

Mrs. Hiner paid daddy a meager $25.00 a month, so my parents had to make money any way they could. Daddy would hunt skunks, foxes, raccoons, and whatever else that had a pelt that could be sold. Black walnuts would be picked by the wagon load, hulled, dried, cracked, and the kernels picked out. Mom would sell the walnuts to buy sugar and the gifts we got for Christmas. There were not a lot of toys or presents, but we always had a Christmas tree. Mom, my sister, and I would go with daddy sometimes when he went hunting after night. The only light was an oil lantern and we would walk for miles.

My older sister was born when I was 11 months old, so you might say mom basically had twins. She would leave us in the house while she went to the barn to milk and do the other chores. We would take the slats out of the bottom of our baby bed to get out and then we usually made a mess. I vaguely remember one time she was at the barn and I climbed up on the cabinets until I could reach the top one. They had put some worm pills for the turkeys up there out of my reach. These pills being in a small brown bag and red in color looked just like candy so we decided to have some. My sister swallowed hers whole, but I chewed mine up and it burned. Mom heard us screaming and came running. She sent daddy after the doctor who was in Doe Hill, but he wasn't home. While daddy was gone, my grandfather came and he told mom we would be all right.

Grandpap and mom's brothers and sisters would walk from Sugar Grove to our house. Mom was from a large family, having eight sisters and three brothers. My Grandmother Smith died when mom was just 17 and she along with her oldest sister helped Grandpap raise the other children until they left home and married. Daddy had one brother and two sisters and their mother died when daddy was 13. I didn't really have a grandmother in my life until I married my husband, and then his grandmother became mine.

The work on the farms was hard and the days long. I learned how to milk a cow when I was just a few years old and continued helping to milk (my parents sold cream and milk) until I left home. We worked in the gardens and helped in the cornfields when the corn was plowed, and when we got older, we helped with the haying. All the farming was done with horses and simple machinery while we lived at the Siple Place. After the family moved to another farm in Doe Hill, Virginia there was a tractor and baler. A threshing machine would come around each fall after the grain was cut and do the threshing. We had running water and electric lights in this house, but there wasn't a bathroom until after my brother got married and moved in with mom and daddy.

Mom had to go to the hospital to deliver my brother and one of her sisters was staying with me and Joeann, my sister. While Aunt Cleo was getting lunch for the men making hay we poured everything out of mom's sewing basket on the floor and then poured water all over it. We ran off to the orchard and stayed in an apple tree until she calmed down.

Mom has told me about a hot July day (I was probably four and Joeann three) daddy, his brother, uncle, and brother-in-law worked on cleaning out the ditches and filling the potholes in the lane going to the house. Daddy had "home brew" (beer) and the men were drinking this as they worked. Well, Joeann and I drank right along with them. When daddy got us to the house we were drunk! It happened that Mrs. Hiner was at the house that very day and she didn't approve of such things. Mom put us to bed and she said that we started jumping on the bed and screaming until our heads started hurting at which point we cried ourselves to sleep. Mrs. Hiner wanted to know what was wrong with us and mom told her we were just tired.

We would go to Grandpap Smith's every Sunday to make sure he and the other children were alright. This was the only time we had other children to play with. The closest neighbors were miles away and if you visited you usually walked. Daddy would ride a horse to Doe Hill and to the other farms. He had an old car, but money for gas was scarce, and sometimes it wouldn't run or a tire was flat. We would sometimes go places by hitching the horses to a wooden sled and riding that and other times the wagon was used.

I learned a lot about nature living on the farm. As kids we hunted wild flowers, mushrooms, caught minnows in the streams, and there wasn't a tree too tall for me to climb if I could get on the first limb. These adventures weren't without mishaps. I fell out of a cherry tree on to a rock pile putting a gash in my eyebrow and another time I fell off the yard fence, into a Rambler Rosebush, while trying to get flowers from what we called the Bean Tree.

We had a battery radio and Mom would listen to a program called *Ma Perkins* (guess you could say that was a soap opera of the 1940s), and on Saturday nights we would listen to the *Wheeling Jamboree*, that is when the radio played. We did have a wall telephone and everybody on the line knew what was going on at each home because someone was always listening.

I started school when I was 6 ½ years old and went to school at Doe Hill. My 1st grade teacher was Mrs. Edna Armstrong and she taught grades 1-8. My favorite teacher was my 2nd grade teacher, Ms. Audra "Judy" Arbogast. She wasn't married and was young and I thought so very pretty. We are still friends today as we both worked for the Pendleton County School system for many years. Both of us are retired.

I do remember rumble seats. My uncle had a car that had one and also Ms. Leta Hiner had a car with a rumble seat. I rode in both cars when a child. Mom made our clothes from feedbags and any other materials she could get. Homemade underwear are the worst! We didn't wear shoes until it got cold in the fall. Mom washed our clothes on a washboard until we were almost teenagers. I don't remember a lot about Castor Oil, but Cod Liver Oil was something else. I can almost still taste that awful stuff. Mom would fry onions, put them in a cloth, and tie them around our chests when we had croup or a bad cold. Sometimes she would make a mustard plaster and put it on our chest and it would burn for a while. Sounds really nasty, but it all worked because I'm still here.

My brother and younger sister didn't share in many of the things I have shared, as they were too little. My mother is still living and is 93 years old. I have tried to share my early life experiences with my two children and two grandchildren. This is just a small part of my life and I wouldn't change a thing about my humble beginning. I have been blessed many times over and the blessings still continue.

My First Deer Hunt
By Calvin Flanagan of Romney, West Virginia
Born 1946

I can remember how many of my childhood buddies would say that they could just barely sleep the night before Christmas. Me, I slept like a log on Christmas Eve, but on the eve of deer season, I tossed and turned all night, especially on the eve of my first season. Getting to hunt on the first day of the season was really a big problem. Trouble was in those days, opening day fell on a school day, and to get dad to let us play hooky was a major coupe.

My first season started on a bitterly cold snowy morning. I was, at that time, using a single-shot Stevens 410, loaded with a pumpkin ball (rifle slug). Amazingly, it was fairly accurate, but the range was limited. Dad had placed me on a crossing and departed to his stand not too far away. In the late '50s, the deer population in eastern West Virginia had not exploded to today's massive herd, but was strictly managed. Seasons were one week and bucks with three inches of horn could be harvested. Most of the deer you did see were does, which seems to be a trait that still remains.

After what seemed to be ages on the crossing and becoming quite cold, I began to wonder where was dad. I was very hesitant about moving, but in the end, I could not remain on the stand. I hadn't been at the truck long before Dad showed. He started the engine of the '54 Chevy and waited for the heater to warm. We were just about at the point of getting some feeling back, when to my amazement, I caught a movement out of the corner of my eye. Recognizing that it was a deer, I leaped from the truck fumbling for the gun and shells. The buck was massive, at least a 10 or 12 points, and blitzed over the hill. Neither I, nor dad got a shot. All I could think was if I shoot and miss, dad would have my hide, so I didn't shoot. Dad had my hide anyway, since I was a mere 10 yards from the buck. Some 60 years later, I can still see that buck disappearing over the crest of the hill.

Usually deer hunting then was a time for neighbors and family to assemble and work as a team. The elders were the watchers and the young pups, the drivers. This technique was quite productive for all. The marksmanship of some were always questionable, and you could always tell who lived in the country and who didn't by the number of rounds expended to bring in the bacon, which explained the number of shirts with no tails.

My first deer came as a result of one long drive with my uncle on my right and his brother on my left. It occurred with the drive well on its way when on my left seven rapid shots (Winchester 30-30 Model 94). How that machine gun got on that ridge is a conversation topic yet today. I, freezing on the spot, watched as a single deer came trotting down along the ridge towards me and stopped a mere 50 yards behind a tree and peeked out around at me. With a single shot placed neatly between the eyes brought the spike buck down. I believe dad was as proud of that deer as I, and of course, the fellow on my left surely claimed a hit. We all knew the story, seven rounds into the air from a common ailment known as buck-eggers in our part of the woods.

That first buck was not as big as the one I had seen earlier, but from the eyes of a 12 year old, it was as big as any 10 or 12 pointer. From that first season, deer hunting has been and always will be a special time. On my second season, which brought a promotion of sorts for a young deer hunter, I graduated from a single shot 410 to a .303 British Enfield. It was a heavy old bruiser, but it was accurate. It did have some quirks about it, quirks that only a 13 year old would learn to love.

The first day went by without a buck, which meant I would have to score on Saturday. Saturday, we all took up morning watches and rendezvous at mid-morning to begin the drives. Drives that produced little excitement, except for a few does. We had come to the last drive of the season, which was a long wooded stretch. After posting the watchers, the rest of us strung out from the bottom to the top of a ridge and proceeded to move silently through the thickets. I was coming to the end of my drive, the last briar patch was just in front of me, and there the most beautiful buck I had ever seen stood. Some say that I suffered buck-eggers, but I distinctly remember being calm, cool, and collected. I took careful aim and squeezed the trigger, nothing happened. The firing pin snapped, but nothing happened. I stood watching the big buck and my beloved

British would not fire. The buck, having had enough, started to trot around the ridge and after bolting another round into the chamber, the old rifle finally tired. To my amazement, the buck faltered and fell. Dad and neighbors gathered around, showing their respect for the large trophy buck. Oddly, I was not permitted to help in dragging the deer out of the woods. I guess it was the driver's way of showing honor to a successful kill as the one I had made. Some years later, I had the 11-point buck scored, it may not have made the Boone and Crockett, but those 136 points scored high in my book and the center of many conversations.

Later in my teens, I acquired a long bow and as I look back upon my experiences with that bow, I know I will never return to the long bow. I had spent many of long hours in the woods and had several opportunities. Call it what you will, but I believe the deer know when they're safe. One doe in particular knew just how safe she was in responding to a cover scent. Today, a lot of emphasis is placed on scents. Back then, I did not take much stock in cover scents until I saw a doe's reaction to "Doe n' Heat." I was still hunting and the doe was about 150 yards at the opposite end of an apple orchard. The wind must have been just right because she threw her head in the air and came straight at me at the trot. If this wasn't unbelievable enough, she stopped less than 20 yards from me broad side and stared. When I released the arrow she was gone, the arrow eventually passed at its mark and would have been a clean kill, if the doe had stayed in place. The doe left me dumfounded on the side of the ridge. It wasn't that I was a bad shot, it was just the long bow was just too darn slow.

After returning home from my tour in the Army, I was again introduced to bow hunting, only this time with a compound. I was flabbergasted at the speed and accuracy of the compound bow. Since then, numerous deer have fallen and is my preferred method of hunting deer. Although my first deer was small in stature, it was a deer that became a big part of my life. Deer hunting, may it always bring a thrill to my heart and to all those that follow in my footsteps.

Pappy Smith
By Wayne C. Ward of Warfordsburg, Pennsylvania
Born 1946

My name is Wayne Ward and I was born in Fulton County, Pennsylvania on a farm located right over the Maryland line. Our address was Hancock, Maryland for many years and Hancock was our closest town. My grandfather used to plow gardens for people in Hancock in late March and early April. During the other times he farmed, logged, and hauled apples for the Cohill and Dillon orchards outside of Hancock, which are no longer in operation. Hancock is located in the narrowest part of the state and is right along the Potomac River and the C&O Canal and the mountains. West Virginia and Pennsylvania and Maryland make up what is known as the Tri-State area.

When I was a boy around 10 years old in 1956, I went with my Pappy Smith to Hancock to plow gardens. The trip from our house to Hancock was five miles. We would leave at 5:00 am. Pap took his three horses and the wagon, bar share plow, a harrow, and a striking out plow so he could get the ground ready for planting. I rode in the wagon with Pap. He had two black Percheron's named Prince and Doc and one Sorrel Belgian named Bob. Pap would tie Bob behind the wagon and used him to mark the garden out after it was plowed.

Our first stop was at his sister, Addie Bishop's house. She lived near what we called, "The Campsite." Pap plowed three lots there and then Aunt Addie would make lunch for us, usually a sandwich with homemade bread, a bowl of soup, a slice of her delicious pie and a big glass of milk. Then we would go through

Pappy Conard Smith on "Buck" in 1975

134

the park and head up Blue Hill to his other sister, Sally Keefer. We would plow a garden for Aunt Sally and one for Mac Bennett and one for Polly Weller. Then we went over to High Street at the mansion house where Trudy Cullum lived and plowed her garden and last to Jack Deneen's. I got to help hitch the horses and Pap would let me plow and harrow. The horses knew more about plowing then I did. Pap did other gardens during the week. He made $3.00 a lot. That would be about $24.00 a day. He would have enough money at the end of the week to buy his seed corn and fertilizer so he could do his spring planting. On the way home, he would get us each a bottle of pop. What a treat! We did this each spring for five years.

These are my best memories and the best times of my life. My granddaddy will always be my hero. He took better care of his horses than he did himself. They were his pride. I am now 67 years old and I still have the Syracuse two-horse plow, #20 that Pap bought new and used to plow the gardens. I now have a home directly up the hill from the house where I was born and have a team of gray Percherons, Kate and John, and one Sorrel Belgian, named McBride. They are my pride. They have been on wagon trains in Washington County, Maryland, from Clear Spring to Boonsboro, in parades, done wagon rides in Hancock along the canal and even been in a movie. But the thing I enjoy most is using them to plow my garden with Pap's Syracuse plow.

Mr. Carl "Dick" Riggleman
By Kay B. Halterman of Moorefield, West Virginia
Born 1945

How fortunate I was to grow up on a 200-acre farm with my brother and two sisters. It was located about halfway between Moorefield and Petersburg in the very small rural community of Rig. My dad was active in politics and an excellent farmer and my mom was an outstanding seamstress, a hard worker, and active in the community. We had a great life on the farm with lots of friends, neighbors, and relatives visiting and often staying overnight. We had two fishing ponds and a small creek that ran through the farm where we would dam it up and make us a nice swimming hole to enjoy. Seining minnows and catching salamanders were a fun pastime as well. We would also ride ponies, go hiking, play ball, and do a lot of fishing. We would work very hard, getting in the hay, feeding the turkeys and chickens, milking the cows, tending the garden, carrying in wood and working on other chore before we could have our fun time. In the winter, we would make snow cream, go sled riding and ice-skating, build a large bonfire, and invite folks over.

However, this story is not about the good life on the farm, but about a wonderful neighbor, friend, and storeowner, Carl "Dick" Riggleman. He was the owner of a small country store with a big potbelly wood stove and just about anything and everything you could imagine was in that store. If you wanted some place to "hang out," catch up on the latest local news, purchase items, or just enjoy the evening and see about everyone in the community that was the place to be. There were always as many folks "hanging out" there in the winter as well as the summer time because that ole cozy potbelly stove was kept fired up. Dick was a very unique individual; he was a very good-hearted, kind, and just someone you were proud to know. He also collected junk to sell, sold gasoline, was the postmaster, clerk, storeowner, and last but not least, the local news reporter. When you wouldn't have money to buy gas, groceries, or other items, you could just take a piece of junk to him to sell and get a good deal. A few times when I did not have money to purchase gasoline I can remember going out into my dad's tractor shed and finding an item of value such as a tool or a tractor part. Then I would take it to the store and always get enough money to put gas in my dad's automobile if I was going to use it. My dad was very conservative and would occasionally give me a dollar. It really didn't seem to matter what the junk was, Dick would always buy it and give me a fair price. He never turned me down! Also, if I couldn't get my dad's car to go to the big city, Dick would just give me his to use. My dad would later go to the tractor shed to look for a certain tool or tractor part and if he couldn't seem to find it, eventually he would head on over to the Rig Store and it seemed like Dick would always have just what he was looking for. To this day, I am not sure whether my dad had to pay for it or not. I figure he probably paid the same amount to buy it as I did when I sold it, but for some strange reason it was always there waiting for him. Dick just seemed to know what piece of junk to sell and what to hold on to! Many times, I would have no money or junk to sell and Dick would say, "I'll just charge it to you." He would do that for lots of other folks also.

As I got older and had my own car, I would spend a lot more time in Moorefield with friends attending sock-hops, movies, or school activities. On the way home, if I would happen to see a light in the store I would stop by. When I look back, I think he was always just waiting for me to arrive and catch him up on the latest. I would hurry in, hop up on the counter, and sit by that ole warm potbelly stove. He would go to the back of the store and bring each of us out one of those little bottles of Rolling Rock. No charge, just one.

Every year, Dick would always order tons of Christmas candy. This is absolutely no exaggeration; he would order it by the ton. People would come from all over the area to get that delicious Christmas candy, every kind imaginable, at such a good deal. Every year he would have to order more and more. Some years later, I stopped by to "pay up." I wasn't sure if my parents had paid my bill or not, but that was very doubtful. Anyways, after looking around he said, "I can't seem to find it, I think it was paid up." He charged to everyone and to this day, I'm sure many bills were never paid.

I can't ever remember seeing Dick going to church or any social community event, but to me and I'm sure to many others, he was a Saint. He definitely was someone I admired and certainly looked up to. I have many fond memories of hanging out there, laughing, sharing the local news, and particularly just watching how he treated his customers. I say to my fellow West Virginians, we could certainly use a lot more Hardy Countians like Cark "Dick" Riggleman!

Mom's One Lady Band
By Virginia George of Petersburg, West Virginia
Born 1930

My dad always had bees for honey, for as long as I could remember. Now in the summertime swarms of them would leave the hive and go to start a new hive of their own. This would usually take place when the hive became overcrowded. They would keep flying around in the air looking for a place to go, namely a new hive. This usually happened in the part of the day when dad was out in the field working. So when one of us kids saw it we ran to inform mom. Then it was time for mom to get the One Lady Band in action. You would have enjoyed it. Mom would rush into the house to get her musical instruments and then she would come out with them all. She would try to get as near to the bees as she could and then first thing she would play would be the symbols. She had retrieved two of her cooking pot lids from the cupboard. She would take one in each hand and beat them together. After sometime if the bees hadn't settled on a bush or a limb, she would get her next instrument, which would he one of the cooking pots. She would hold it by the handle, and beat on it with one of her tablespoons. If the bees still hadn't left, she then brought out the big brass drum into action. She had brought the dishpan and her big wooden spoon and beat on it. Slowly at first then faster and louder.

I often think now, what if each of us kids played one of the instruments we could have called it the Judy Band. Mom always said the noise was supposed to make them settle down on a bush or a limb. Sometimes they would settle on a bush down low and sometimes on a limb up high. I often wonder if the noise had anything to do with it. I would think they would really fly away, to get as far from the noise as possible.

After they had settled down mom would keep an eye on them until dad came home. But sometimes they would fly away toward the woods. All of mom's playing her instruments couldn't keep them from going. But if they did stay when dad came home, he donned his out of space hood, put a heavy coat on, and tied strings around the bottom of his pants legs. He put on big gloves that reached up to his elbows, then he would get his weapons ready, which was a "bee smoker." He usually put old rotten wood in it and started a fire. It partly worked like bellows puffing smoke out of a small opening in the top. He also had a long handle brush with real soft bristles on it to sweep them into the new hive that he had prepared some time ago, for an occasion like this. Now if they had settled down low it was not much of a task, but if up high he would have to get his ladder, hand saw, and rope and saw the limb off and let it down by rope to the hive.

The bees that flew away before dad got there usually set up housekeeping in an old hollow tree in the forest. Sometimes dad or one of the boys would discover it when they were out squirrel hunting, but can't recall of my dad ever cutting a bee tree. The old home place has no sign of beehives there anymore, but the memories of these days are still fresh in my mind. I can still see my mom and hear the "One Lady Band."

The house that Paul lived in during the "air raid" drills

United in Fear
By Paul W. Hoye, Jr. of Oakland, Maryland
Born 1939

After the Japanese attack upon our military bases in Hawaii on December 7, 1941, our nation became fearful of another attack. This time on the main land of America. The military leaders were fearful of what an attack could do to our industry and the wellbeing of our people. As a result, our nation went into a war preparation state of being. Every area of our society did their best to help with the war effort. On the home front, the authorities were deeply concerned with three targets the enemies may hit. The first concern was sabotage, next espionage, and third was air raids on the factories and upon the citizens. The Axix Powers (Germany, Italy, and Japan) had engaged in all three actions. The world was horrified at the bombing of civilians by the Axix air forces. All cities in the USA and even small towns were asked and encouraged by the federal government to practice air raids. In Crellin, Maryland, we had air raid drills.

In my mind's eye, I can still see my grandparents and me in our little side room of our company house, as we had the drill. The drill started when the siren on the roof of the company store sounded. We then turned out all of our lights and stayed in the "safe room." As a small boy, I was more than a little afraid that we would be bombed. I would listen for the sound of enemy planes and think of our brave fighting men and women fighting to keep our nation free from the enemy that wanted to destroy us.

Later on in life, when I was older and maybe a little wiser, I learned from my reading and from watching my favorite television channel, History Channel, that the Axix Powers did not have aircraft that could bomb the internal of America. So, was it a waste of time for Crellin to have air raid drills? No, it was not. The drills were very useful in uniting our nation in the war effort. By having the drills, we all became one in our fight for preserving our freedom. Now as an adult, I realize that our nation was more united in those dark days of World War II than we are today.

Family Time
By Victoria Younker of Little Orleans, Maryland
Born 1952

I have a lot of memories growing up in the Little Orleans, Maryland area. My father had a sawmill where he would saw crossties to sell. My brother, Johnny and I would skin the bark off when they were finished being sawed and then loaded on the truck and taken to Hancock where they were loaded on the train that was at the yard below where the Bridge Restaurant was. After my father had sawed lumber and crossties for several days, the sawdust would build up under the saw, so my brother, sister, Angie, and I would shovel it out and put it on a big pile. In the summer, we played in that big pile, but always found that black snakes liked it too, it was warm from the sun, and they would like to lay their eggs there. We earned about five cents for our work and when we had saved up 25-cents, we were allowed to walk two miles to a country store in the lower part of Little Orleans next to the Potomac River. We could get so much candy and a soda pop for that 25-cents. The only problem was, it was uphill to get back home, but walking along that dirt road with my brother and sister was and is a cherished memory.

I came from a family of 10 children, so trying to do things to make extra money was just a way of life. My mom would bake bread and make homemade butter to sell to the "city folks" that came from Baltimore to stay in cabins they had built. We also sold eggs and homemade jelly. My parents took in foster children and watched neighbor's children while the parents worked. There was never a shortage of children at outhouse, when the bus stopped at our house, there were at least 8-9 children getting on the bus. Back in those days, most families were big to help take care of the farm and livestock and household chores. All the families living within one mile of my family had an average of 7-10 children and everyone visited each other on Sundays because no one worked on Sundays back then. It was just a time to be with family. And sitting around the supper table and talking (instead of texting) was just how it was done. And everyone ate at the same time and what was put in front of you, no special requests. There were a lot of things we learned to like, we may have doctored it up with ketchup, but we still ate it.

I Remember When...
By Laverne Stewart of Cumberland, Maryland

I remember when I was six years old, World War II began. There was a blackout of the whole city. I don't remember how long that lasted; I only remember how scared my brother, sister, and I were. I remember the Cumberland Bicentennial, I think in 1950. They had a beard-growing contest for any man who wanted to and had a judging contest. I remember when we lived in a 2nd floor apartment that had an icebox. It was wooden and stood on four legs. When you needed ice, you put your ice sign in a front window and the ice truck carrying ice for everyone would deliver a block of ice for a fee. I remember Habeeb's Riding Academy on Baltimore Pike across the road from his house. Mr. Habeeb had a florist shop on Centre Street or Mechanic Street. He had a huge hot house next to his home.

The Sugar Water Solution
By Clara O. Mynhier of Cresaptown, Maryland
Born 1929

I remember when my sister, Helen, and I played beauty parlor. Mom and daddy always went downtown, Cumberland or Baltimore Street on Saturdays. That's when I decided to put my sister's hair up in curlers; she already had beautiful blonde curls. I had no hair setting gel, so I mixed up a sugar water solution. I always remember mom putting her dollies in the sugar water to stiffen them. I put her hair up with the sugar water. Boy was it ever stiff when I took the curlers out. Couldn't even get a comb through it, so we had to wash it all out and start again. Mother never knew what we had done.

Also, I remember when there was this stray dog that hung around the house and we couldn't get it to go home. My dad said for me to ride my bike to the top of the street about a block and turn around, come down real fast, so the dog wouldn't follow. Well I did just that, I put the brakes on real fast and over the handlebars, I flew. I got cut up real bad with stones in my hands and knees. Dad came running and picked me up and used first aid on me. Never knew what happened to the dog, but dad was so, so sorry.

Rain on a Sunny Day
By Violet Lowery of Charles Town, West Virginia
Born 1940

I was an only child that lived in a small part of Jefferson County known as Skeetersville, West Virginia; this was a small development outside of the Shepherdstown area. I was a lonely child and loved to play with my neighbors. You know, I was born in 1940 and wasn't told of all the tricks people could play on you. Down in Skeetersville, there was a set of twins (Jean and Jane), two other boys also, the twin's brother, Robert, and a cousin of theirs named Thomas.

One day the boys climbed a large overgrown Maple tree. We girls could hardly see them. Once they reached the top branches they proceeded to tell us they could make it rain on a sunny day, so they did just that. Little did we know they were peeing on us girls and rejoicing in our amusement of such an ordeal.

As an only child, I loved to play with the neighbors. My mom and dad needed a new refrigerator so they set the old icebox outside the house, not turning the opening against a closed building site. Playing Hide & Seek was the game back then, so I decided to get in the icebox and barely closed the door when I heard a "click." I became excited and started to yell and bang on the closed door. Fortunately, my playmates heard my call and came to the rescue. Just thinking now I could have suffocated myself and be gone today. Thank God for His grace and mercy.

My 12-Gauge
By Samuel L. Wakefield, Sr. of Friendville, Maryland
Born 1950

It was the summer of 1963; I had turned 13 years old in August. My buddy and I worked in the woods that summer for a timber man. My buddy was 16 years old; it was his dad that ran the chainsaw. I ran the measuring pole and carried pulpwood and posts. When the truck came in, we would have to load the whole truck. It was very hard work. My buddy and I earned $2.50 a day for about nine or ten hours a day. We worked six days a week for a grand total of $15.00 a week.

I had earned enough money to buy my school clothes for the year and buy mom and dad a Christmas gift. With money left over my buddy and I wanted to buy each of us a shotgun so we could hunt. My buddy's mom was going to go to Cumberland, Maryland and she said she would get our shotguns for us. We told her what we wanted. My buddy wanted a 16-gauge. I wanted a 12-gauge. When she got back, we were so excited. She had got each of us model 37 Winchesters. Mine a 12-gauge with a 32" barrel. My buddy's a 16-gauge with a 30" barrel. We loved hunting squirrel and competing who could get the most squirrel in a day. I had run out of shotgun shells around Christmas time. My older brother gave me five shotgun shells for a Christmas gift. It was the best gift I could have gotten. I went out hunting that day and got two grouse and one rabbit. Since that time, I have probably killed a truckload of game with that shotgun. After 50 years, I have passed my shotgun on to my son for keepsake.

The Fire Tower Man
By Nina V. Miller of Oakland, Maryland
Born 1932

Sometime about mid-1940s, phone service came to the area where we lived in Pleasant Valley in Garrett County, Maryland. We were on a party line, number 308J3—ring three shorts. Neighbors had assorted numbers and rings of combinations of longs and shorts, one group with J, another W, total maybe 8 or 10, including a fire tower on a nearby hill. Joe was the fire tower man. One neighbor told my daddy that Joe was chatting with a neighbor one day when he heard the ring for the fire tower and answered the phone. The voice on the phone said, "Where are you?" Joe replied, "I'm at the tower." Voice on the phone said, "No you aren't, I am here." It was the boss!

The Lohr farm in the mid 1940s
Richard, Carl, Roger, Nina, and Margie

A Rattlesnake's Snack
By Ferrie A. Ball of Denton, Maryland
Born 1954

One day in the hills of West Virginia (1960), my mother decided she wanted some blackberry pies for supper that evening. In order to accomplish this goal, mom appropriately dressed herself and me to go to the blackberry patch. Off we set with our buckets in hand! When we stopped at just the right spot that had the largest berries, mom started picking her berries, and I sat on a huge rock beside the berry bush. Soon I was filling my stomach with berries as much as mom was filling her buckets!

Mom peeked around the bush to check on me. Suddenly, in a very strange, but firm voice, she told me to come to her immediately. While saying those words, she quietly picked me up from the rock. I wondered what all the "fuss" was about, so I turned around to see what was behind me. It was a fat rattlesnake! This snake was also looking for a nice snack and that snack just happened to be me! Mom and I slowly backed up and started walking toward the house, where it was safe and sound. We both had had our fill of berries for that day, along with a story to tell at dinnertime.

We Were A Lot Better Off Back Then
By Madeline Fisher of Ridgeley, West Virginia
Born 1930

I'm Madeline Fisher. I was born April 21, 1930 on Old Furnace Road in Ridgeley, West Virginia. My parents were Robert and Ella Mae O'Brien. My Grandfather O'Brien came to America from Ireland. I had six brothers and four sisters. There are only two of us living.

As a child, I played house, hopscotch, red light, and other fun games. My dad used a tire and made us a swing in a large tree. I played with the neighbor girls. We had a radio run by batteries; we listened to *Stella Dallas*, *Lone Ranger*, *Paul Harvey,* and the *Grand Ole Opra*. We also had a wind up record player and a rotary phone on an eight party line.

My father was a carpenter and he drove a milk wagon and delivered milk in Cumberland, Maryland. During the depression, we had a cow and my mother made butter and cottage cheese for us. We had an icebox where she kept the butter and cheese. The iceman came twice a week. My mother made most of our clothes; she was a good seamstress.

We weren't allowed to go to movies, but my sister and her husband would take me to see Roy Rogers, Gene Autry, and Wild West movies. My sister also got me my first permanent when I was about 10. Our mother washed our clothes on a washboard until we got electric and then we got a washing machine. We had an outhouse; it wasn't very warm in winter. Mother put water in a large tub in the summer and when it got warm, we took our baths on Saturday.

Daddy played the organ and us kids would sing hymns. We lived in Wiley ford where the airport is. We had two black men as neighbors and they were very nice people. We didn't care that our skin was different. Mr. Burley worked on cars for a living. Mr. Newman worked at the railroad. He was very kind. He would buy material and got my mother to make clothes for children who lived there. He always bought candy, nuts, and oranges, and gave them to all of the children who lived up there at Christmas time. I have eaten jelly bread many times in his house. We never thought of skin color and if people would stop with saying everything is racist, we wouldn't be having the division in our country. God taught us to love one another as he loved us, no mention of skin color.

I went to school in Wiley Ford and my teacher was Miss Lewis; she taught 4th grade and she was my favorite. Mr. Jenkins was my 5th and 6th grade teacher at a two-room schoolhouse at Patterson Creek, West Virginia. Mrs. Schaffler was our cook. We had a pantry with a water cooler and we also had outhouses.

We went to church and Sunday school. Mrs. Effie Abe and Grace Self were two of my teachers. They were very godly women. We didn't have the modern things we have today, but we were a lot better off then children today. They take everything for granted. It is so sad to see our country so divided. We have been so blessed and we have turned our back on God. He will send judgment on us; he did for Israel and they were his chosen ones.

My New Blue Bicycle
By Hallie M. Snyder of Oakland, Maryland
Born 1939

At about nine years of age, I was trying to learn how to ride a bicycle. Oh how I struggled! A kind-hearted friend, Marie Coleman, decided to help me learn. She painstakingly worked with me until I mastered it. My first bike was a used one, but I didn't care. I remember being at the top of the hill of the road, we lived on in Virginia, Woodford Road. Down the hill I went! It seemed fast to me. I hit the next-door neighbor's big tall pine tree head on! The handlebars were never straight after that!

Mom went to work full time when I was 12. It was then she was able to purchase new bikes for my brother, Jim, and I, a red bike for him, and a blue girls bike for me. They were Montgomery Wards bicycles. It seems to me they were called Hawthorn bikes. Jim and I already had a paper route that was divided between us for delivery, the Times Herald, which later sold out to The Washington Post in Washington, DC.

My bike had a large rectangular shaped basket attached over the front wheel to the handlebar. I laid my papers flat in the basket for delivery. I learned that riding a bicycle in snow doesn't work out very well. The snow builds up under the wide fenders and has to be knocked out. Mom had me ride my bike to school. This was so I could get home sooner and get my little sister from the babysitter. This saved her money that was going to the babysitter while mom was working.

One day in my early teens, I hopped on my

Hallie and her bicycle

bike to go for a spin. I headed out the driveway not knowing wasps had built a nest in the springs under the seat. I bailed off and went screaming into the house. My family didn't know what had happened! They found my jeans lying on the kitchen floor. I had run up the steps to my second floor bedroom. I had gotten stung in the rear end.

At the age of 17, I moved to Western Maryland and married Dwight Snyder. My blue bike went with me. I rode close to where we lived. I remember riding it back to the Blue Ribbon Road. After Sylvia, my eldest daughter, was old enough to ride bikes, she remembers her dad fixing my old blue bike up so she and I could ride bikes together. Sylvia came up with this vintage photo idea. She made arrangements with a local studio (Crabtree) to take the pictures. Gary, my son-in-law, worked hard on cleaning this old relic bicycle up for picture taking. He also took charge of hauling it back and forth to the studio. I estimate this bicycle to have been purchased in 1952, 61 years ago.

Hallie's dad, Russell Mize and the school bus he drove

The Bear of a Teacher
By Willard Sheppard of Norfolk, Virginia
Born 1925

I don't remember ever seeing this bear before as we walked into the 6th grade room of Old Mt. Wesley School. He was over six feet tall, hundreds of pounds and bushy eyebrows; horn rimmed glasses really set him off. But I got to know him in a hurry. I still do not know how I ended up in a corner of the room, in a big old time desk. For some reason all I had to do was look at him and back he came to drag me out to the head of the room and wear me out with his belt or rubber hose. I started keeping tabs of the whippings on the wall beside my desk and at school's end; I had a grand total of 30! I did stomp his ingrown toenails at times.

One day he came to my desk and told me he had to leave the room for a few minutes and for me to tidy up his desk. After he left I turned up the clock a half hour so school let our early that day. I found his rubber hose in the desk drawer. I had an old jack knife with a half of blade, so I nicked the hose every few inches. Guess who got it the first time? After the first lick, it shot halfway across the room. But he used it down to the last handful on to the 7th grade. Seventh grade wasn't much better. Another male so-called teacher. He had a bad habit of pulling me out of my seat, clamping my head between his knees, and laying it on me. I took it as long as I could and one day I managed to turn my head and I bit him as hard as I could. He moaned, dropped me, and returned to his desk. I prayed he would have teeth marks till the day he died. I spent another year in 7th grade.

Two months after my 17th birthday I joined the Navy (1942); what a blessing. They took me. I must have been the dumbest kid in the eastern panhandle. My old man refused to sign my papers until the next day. We had a discussion. He was always talking reform school at me until I told him this was a chance to be rid of me, and then he signed.

From Martinsburg they sent me to Baltimore to be sworn in. I had never been on a train, so I stood up all the way to Baltimore. I arrived at Baltimore, found my way to the post office, a man in uniform was standing there, and I asked him how to get to the 3rd floor. He said use the elevator; I thanked him and proceeded to try to pull the doors open. He walked over and said, "Boy where the h*ll are you from?" I said, "Over in West Virginia" and he said, "I thought so. Try pushing that button." I had never seen an elevator.

After about two years, I got back to town on leave. I had changed so much hardly anyone knew me. One day the old man asked me to join a lodge with him. So I went along. Outside the lodge hall, the members were shaking hands and telling lies when up walks the bear. Shakes hands with the old man and looks at me and said, "I don't think I know you." I said, "Well by God, you should. You gave me 30 lickings in one season at Old Mt. Weseley." He looked down over those horned rim glasses and said, "What's your name?" I told him and he wouldn't turn loose of my hand. He dragged me with him until he had met the members and then back to the old man. He said, "Dewey, this was one of the nicest boys I ever taught in school." Teachers never condemn a kid until you know his environment.

There Wasn't Complaining Back Then
By Wanda Rodeheaver Dodge Himelrick of Cayce, South Carolina
Born 1946

I was born at home with a granny woman. There were seven children. I have three full brothers and one-half brother. I have two sisters. We lost our half-brother at the age of 13. We lived on a farm at Hazelton, West Virginia. The farm once belonged to our great-grandfather. There was a picture of him hanging in the boys' room. I always thought he looked scary.

We always had big gardens and truck patches. Mom always grew lots of vegetables to eat. She would can lots of food for the winter months. We also had fresh vegetables to eat. We would go and pick wild blueberries, blackberries, and strawberries to make jelly or jam to eat. I remember one day in early June, mom told us kids to go out to the cornfield and pick strawberries alongside the fence. I was picking berries and saw a black snake. I screamed and ran to the house to get mom. She and I went back out to where I saw the snake, but it couldn't be found. I am scared of snakes.

We didn't have running water in the house. We had to carry buckets of water from the spring and fill the water tank on the stove, also fill up a couple of buckets for drinking water. That was my job to do. We had to milk cows two times a day. When you live on a farm, it takes everyone to get the work done. We heated with coal and wood and also cooked on a wood stove. There was a milk house that we kept and milk and butter and eggs to keep them cold and fresh. We used to take our eggs to the local country store to trade for flour, sugar, salt, yeast, and other things we needed. If there were any money left, we would get about 10 or 15 cents worth of candy. We would walk to the store; that was a three-mile walk one-way. Mom would make our clothes to wear. She would get feed sacks to make shirts or dresses for us. I remember one spring mom had enough money to get some material to make my sister and myself a dress for church. It was the prettiest red organdy I had ever seen. We thought we were millionaires wearing that dress.

We used outside toilets. It was something we done and didn't complain about it. We went to a one-room school. That was a fun time in our life. There were about 25 children going there at one time. There were 1st through 8th grades. We all could hear what each class was being taught, so that would help us as we started our next class. There wasn't very many of the children that finished the 8th grade that went on to high school. Winter was always fun for us kids. We would get a lot of snow, but that didn't stop us from going outside to sled ride. We had one sled, but we would make sleds out of old tubes or cardboard. We would have fun. The playing would be after we had all our chores done. Summer we would play baseball.

We didn't get electric in the house until 1957. That was the year my youngest sister was born. That year we got a TV set. We only got to watch television in the evening about one hour and on Saturday a couple of hours. This only happened if all our chores were done and everyone was there.

I remember one day one summer when mom went to help the neighbor get their hay in before it rained. Mom took the horses and us kids to help out. She got 10 cents an hour and us kids made a nickel a day. We thought that was a lot of money. I babysat four children for one of the neighbors. They paid me one dollar a day. I would save it until I got 10 or 15 dollars, then I would go shopping; I could get school supplies or something for my brothers and sisters.

When I was about 10 or 11, one of the neighbors would get orders to make pine wreaths for the Christmas season. He would have mom make some for him. She would make enough money to make the farm payment and buy us something for Christmas. She would buy us a bucket of hard candy. We would get oranges for Christmas also.

My dad worked in the woods most of the time. I remember he worked for a while in the coalmines. He drove the ponies hauling out coal. He made good money then and we had more food and more clothes to wear. He didn't work there very long because it hurt his back. He had to bend over all day going in and out of the mines with the carts of coal.

There was an old wind up phonograph machine. I think it had belonged to my great-grandfather. We weren't allowed to play it. Mom would let us once in a while if our dad wasn't home. I remember there being an old radio in the living room. We would listen to the *Grand Old Opry* on Saturday night. We all went to bed by nine o'clock every day because we would get up early to get the animals taken care of. You know there wasn't any complaining about things back then because we had each other and a place to stay.

Wanda and her grandson, Samuel Starr

"Back Then You Listened or Else!"
By Thelma Wagner of Hancock, Maryland
Born 1952

I grew up in the southernmost part of Little Orleans, Maryland where the 15-mile creek dumped into the Potomac River. It was a small community of about 20 homes; of those 20, there were maybe 4 that were not related to others. I was surrounded by grandparents, aunts, uncles, and cousins. Living in a small community and being related to boot, whatever you did, others knew about and often that news traveled to your parents before you even returned home, yeah, nothing was sacred! Now of those 20 homes, perhaps only 3 had an inside toilet, ours was not one of those homes. But our outhouse was upscale of its day with a three-seater. Momma, Papa, and baby. The baby had a step so as to reach the seat. On some occasions it had leftover linoleum placed on the floor, now that was class! How could anyone forget that cold updraft during the cold months and sightings of spiders, snakes, and lizards in warm weather? And then the grandest remodeling in our day was electric in the outhouse, no more flashlights to find your way down the path and your own light inside, how great was that?

Back then there was little traffic going by our house, perhaps a few a week. Much unlike today's traffic where there is a few in an hour's time. Neighbors gathered to make apple butter and butcher hogs. If a neighbor fell on hard times, the others would gather what was canned up and harvested in the summer and help the family out.

Christmas time meant a lot of food was fixed as was on Thanksgiving. A tree was found in the woods and chopped down and put up on Christmas Eve, but Santa himself decorated the tree. And Santa never wrapped our gifts. On Christmas Eve before going to bed, each of us kids would say where we wanted Santa to put our presents, in a chair or by the TV, or behind the couch. Christmas morning, lo and behold, there they were! All the presents were exactly where we had requested. Some of the gifts Santa left I remember well and still have a few. Like the Blue Willow tea set or my favorite doll and best of all my brownie camera. That started me on my camera bug days! One Christmas I received a transistor radio. I remember taking it along on one of

Low Water Bridge at Fifteen Mile Creek

our walks up to our grandparents to check on them after a snowstorm. My daddy was more of a wrestler fan, but there was a broadcast that night of a new boxer to fight the champ, Sonny Listin. That new guy won that night and we listened to the announcer all the way on our walk. That guy was Cassius Clay, better known today as Mohamed Ali.

I went to Piney Plain Elementary School. Today it serves as Co. 43 fire station for the community. The school had four rooms to it and a kitchen. Grades 1-6 were taught there. Years before I went there it was grades 1-8, with 2 grades taught in each room. Then grades 7 and 8 were transferred to Flintstone High School in Flintstone, Maryland. The spare room now served as an auditorium. It also served as a room to do exercise or the most famous Maypole dance on May 1st with all the colorful crepe paper. We had plays for Christmas and the adults even put on a minstrel show where they painted their faces black and told jokes. Needless to say, that would not go over well these days. Like many others, I remember the day President John F. Kennedy was assassinated. After lunch and recess, the principal/teacher brought his radio from the office and put it on his desk. No one spoke, just listened to the radio until time to board the bus.

My first year at school the bus did not come across the low water bridge, so the kids had to walk a mile by the road or take one of two shortcuts. If not real muddy then we went along the hillside below the cemetery, through a cornfield, a steep path along the banks above the aqueduct, onto the railroad tracks and down to the country store/post office where the owner of the store/bus driver allowed us to warm around a kerosene stove until time to get on the bus. Another route was to go across a bridge above the train tracks, along the cliffs above the tracks, and then cross the tracks. Trains were running then. In my second year of school, it was approved for the bus to go across the low water bridge and come near our homes to pick us up. Of course, during times that the low water bridge was flooded, it was back to one of those other routes again. And as dangerous as the walk was there was never a child lost. Back then when you were told to not mess around, you listened or else! And that "else" could sting a bit! I don't remember "snow days." I do remember chains being put on the buses to go around all those sharp curves leading up out of Little Orleans and going up over the mountains when we went to Flintstone High School. The only time I remember the bus not coming to pick us up is when it slid around a sharp curve before getting to my stop and nearly going over the bank with students aboard. A tow truck had to be called. That was before cell phone days, so I am assuming someone had to walk to the nearest house to make the call.

Mom filled the washer and rinse tubs with rainwater from 55-gallon barrels that caught water from the roof. On the Friday that was payday, mom left the water in the double rinse tubs and we kids took turns taking a bath. Cashmere soap. Ahh, I can still smell it. We were getting cleaned up to hit the big town of Hancock to get groceries. On some days before payday, daddy would get groceries on time. His name was put on an index card at the store with the total. On payday, the card was marked "paid." No credit check or collateral, just "a man is as good as his word" in those days.

The woods, fields, and L-shaped covered porch were our playgrounds. A tree that grew crooked and had a knothole served as a cook stove. Slippery leaves on a hill served as the sliding board. Once I managed to find a yellow jacket nest. Along with the hurt from the sting of bees was the sting of my brothers slapping my bee-covered face. That night daddy burnt the nest out with gasoline. Dang bees!

The saddest memory was when my cousin and my cousin's wife's nephew were killed in Vietnam within a month of each other. It rocked the community hard. My cousin spent summers and vacations in a summerhouse not far away and the other boy spent time in Little Orleans also. I suppose that was my first experience of death of loved ones. It was also the first time I had ever seen a man cry as both my uncle and grandfather dealt with the loss of an only son and he left behind an only son. Hearts were broken and some never did quite mend. Some nights my aunt would still hug his military photo and cry, this she did until she passed away.

Several years after my parents and brother passed away and the home place was sold, my sister and I rode by after leaving the cemetery, which was not far from the house. Someone was outside and we stopped to talk. After telling him this was our home place, he invited us in to look around. We were amazed at how very small that house now seemed to be. How did it hold five children, not to mention when those five got married and left home, now returned on holidays with their own children in tow? It finally hit me as to what my mom meant when she said of the visits, "I like to see them come, but I love to see them go." Dear mom, now I get it!

Today that small community has a lot more than 20 homes. There is only one family left that is family to me. A lot of summer homes, many people I don't know. Still there is the low water bridge that many years ago was supposed to be replaced so it would not be flooded and the cemetery has many more family members there. The cornfield has long grown up and the area is known for the East Coast Sturgis in the summer. Yep, a lot has changed since way back then, but my memories will always be there.

Fresh Meat for Supper
By Verda Davy of Burlington, West Virginia
Born 1929

Vance and me were married April 28, 1951. We moved into an old tenant house on a farm in Mineral County, W.V. We were dirt poor, but that wasn't new to us. Vance would work on the farm, so he'd always come home for lunch. One morning I seen a squirrel run up the tree in the front yard. Oh wow, if I could just keep that squirrel up there till Vance comes home, we will have fresh meat for supper. I came up with an idea to tie my house cat to the foot of the tree. Sure enough, that kept the squirrel in the tree till he came home for lunch. We had it that evening for supper.

Meat was scarce when you only made $25 a week for 7 days of work.

I Shiver at the Thought of Castor Oil
By Maxine Souder of Mathias, West Virginia
Born 1928

When I was growing up, occasionally, I would get intestinal flu. Most of the time I would get better, but this time it was a stubborn case, so Mom and Dad took me to see Dr. Moyers. Well, he prescribed good old Castor Oil and coffee soup. The Castor Oil was so thick and greasy, I couldn't swallow it. Mom tried several more times without any luck, so she said open your mouth wide, and as I did, she put the nasty stuff in my mouth and held my nose shut, of course it went down. The coffee soup took that awful taste out of my mouth.

If you have never taken Castor Oil, you don't know what you are missing in your life. If you are brave enough, try it sometime. It may not be the same now, as then, but at 86 years old I'm not going to find out, it makes me shiver just to think about those episodes.

Little Children, So Innocent
By Donna M. Turner of Cumberland Maryland
Born 1935

My family and I moved from Wheeling, WV to Romney, WV, when I was in the fifth grade, the year being 1945.

My dad had just become the new First Christian Church minister in Romney. Being shy and backward, I had a very hard time making friends in a new school. One girl in my class befriended me and took me under her wing and we became pals. I'll call her "Krissy." "Krissy" asked me if I'd like to go with her and her mother on Saturday morning to work a few hours uptown in Romney. Of course, I jumped at the chance to be with my new friend. So, with my parent's permission, I said yes. About an hour or so while helping my friends hand out "Papers" on Main Street, my dad came by and told me it was time to come home. I got in the car as told, and went home. Upon arriving at home, Mom and Dad sat me down telling me we had to discuss my "job," I was helping "Krissy" do. Seems one of the Deacons of my dad's church had called and asked him if he knew his daughter was handing out "Watch Towers" for the Jehovah Witness on Main Street. My parents explained why I shouldn't be doing this as the New Christian Church minister's daughter, because our beliefs were very different, but it was fine to still be friends with "Krissy," but I couldn't work with her on Saturday mornings anymore.

Just one of the many trials and tribulations of being a "PK." in small town U.S.A. Believe me, over the years and through the teens, there were many more too numerous to mention. Being a "PK" –all eyes are on you 24/7.

Home Remedies
By Evelyn James of Harpers Ferry, West Virginia
Born 1923

I remember having warts on my hands. My mother, Della DeHaven cut a potato in half, rubbed the cut side on my warts, placed the potato in a box, gift wrapped the box, and placed the box in the intersection of a road. The person who stopped to pick up the box to see what was in it would get the warts. When I got a toothache my father, Franklin DeHaven would go outside and get a brick or large stone and place the stone/brick on our woodstove until it got hot. Mom would wrap the stone in a towel and placed it on my jaw.

For a headache mom would open a handkerchief and cut out a piece of paper the size of the handkerchief, soak the cut out paper in vinegar mixed with sugar, squeeze out the moisture, roll the paper with the handkerchief and tie it around our forehead. Our headaches went away. For sore throats we would mix one drop of kerosene and two tablespoons of sugar, can you imagine this?

I was married to "Curly" (Franklin James) for 55 years until he passed away. He was the only man I dated. I remember my first love letter from him. It was full of grease. When I saw him, I asked about the grease. He said a group of his guy friends were sitting at his mother's table eating French fries and all the guys had a part in writing the letter.

My first trip out of Berkley Springs, West Virginia to Baltimore was a disaster. The bus stopped six miles from my destination and I had to walk six miles carrying a suitcase and wearing high heels.

Cherry Tree Adventures
By Richard Runkles, Jr. of Harpers Ferry, West Virginia
Born 1951

My favorite pet was flown halfway across the US. She was an ACA hunting dog named Patty. When she arrived and got off the plane, she couldn't walk because she was so stiff. My dad rubbed her with alcohol and she was fine. My first love was a girl, Patsy who I met on the CB radio; she was driving down Rt. 340 close to Interstate 70 going to Washington, DC and I was working at a stone quarry in Frederick, Maryland. We dated for five years and have been married for 20 years.

The mischief I got into was when I got old enough to climb trees. We had a cherry tree in our yard and I loved staying in that tree. Every time a convertible car went by with its top down, I would try to hit them with a cherry. This didn't last too long; one afternoon a car stopped that was hit by a cherry and knocked on my parent's door. That was one time I got a good spanking.

We Never Saw That Dog Again
By Barbara Moore of Martinsburg, West Virginia
Born 1945

When I was a small child, my parents worked and my grandmother, who lived down the street, kept an eye on my older brother and myself. The neighbors were mostly relatives because my grandparents came to Martinsburg along with my grandfather's brothers and sister to find work. My grandmother was born and raised on the Blue Ridge and her mother was a Native American. She didn't talk much and she loved to watch wrestling on television. As a young family, my grandparents lived on the Blue Ridge Mountain and my grandfather walked off the mountain for work and would return a couple weekends a month. My grandmother would be there alone with the children so she kept a shotgun handy for protection.

In 1949, I was almost 4 years old; my parents were building their own home from scratch with no help except friends. One very hot summer day I was sitting in the doorway, hanging my feet over what would become our first porch, when my grandmother in her long dress, apron, and barefoot came around the corner with the shotgun over her arm. She motioned for me to draw my feet into the doorway as she quietly walked towards, a chilling and strange sight to me.

A big black dog with foam and saliva dripping from his mouth was running in circles about 50 feet down the street. There was a single gunshot and my grandmother motioned for me to get inside the house. A short while later I ventured out with friends, there was a large very wet spot on the ground.

Richard Runkles, Jr. at age 1

My grandmother warned us not to touch or play around this place. We didn't and it took well into fall for the spot to leave and needless to say, we never saw that black dog again.

Caught That Chicken, Hook, Line and Sinker
By Billy Jenkins of Moorefield, West Virginia
Born 1949

When I was growing up, I had one brother and a dog. I loved to go fishing, but I didn't get to go very often. I was about 8 or 9 and I had an old fishing pole, so I would stand or sit on the front porch and see how far I could throw the line out. One day I put a grain of corn on the hook and threw it out in the yard. But, instead of getting a fish on dry land, , well, about that time here come one of my mom's (Minnie Jenkins) big fat laying hens and took the grain of corn and hook and line and swallowed it. About that time, Mom came out on the porch to see what I was doing and she saw the poor old big black chicken still on the line. I didn't know what to do, so Mom came out and had to kill the big laying hen. She cooked it for supper. I don't know if I ate any of it or not, but I do know I got a big whippin'.

Later on when I got a little older, I got an old bicycle and would ride it down to the river to fish and caught some to bring back home. We ate them and they were good. We had some hard times, but we also had fun times too.

Then, I got my operator's license and an old car and went to work when I was 18. I worked at American Woodmark (cabinet place) for 44 years, and now retired.

I love to metal detect now instead of fishing, and I have a 1957 car I drive.

The Great Cacapon
By Judy Compton of Berkeley Spring, West Virginia
Born 1943

When I was a young girl, we lived in a small town of Great Cacapon, West Virginia in Morgan County. As I remember back in the '50s, we lived just up the hill from the railroad tracks. Being that close to the tracks, we would get some of the men who rode the rails; they were known as "hobos." They would walk up to the house asking for something to eat. They would never come into the house and my mother would fix them something. They would wash up at the cistern. They all were nice and very polite men and they seemed grateful for the food. They always thanked my mother for the food and shook hands with her.

This is one of my memories of living in Great Cacapon. I was born and raised there; I have nothing but fond memories of living there. Back then, you could trust people. You never had to lock your doors or take the car keys out of your car. You knew who lived in the house personally and no one was a stranger. I also raised my three daughters there. The town had changed little from when I was brought up and everyone looked after the kids who ran around in town. Well, that's some of my memories of Great Cacapon. I wish the town were that way again. You never had to worry about anyone doing you wrong.

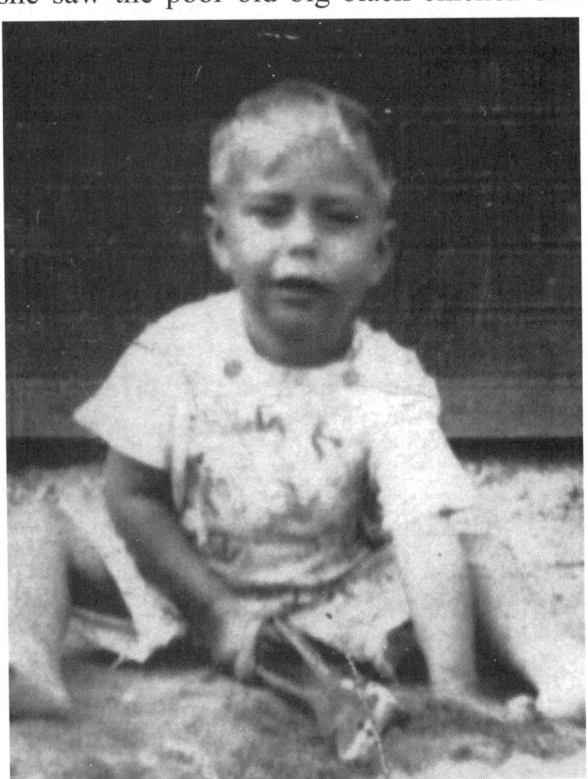

Billy Jenkins age 6

Out Houses, Phones and Hair Care
By Mona R. Schultz of Oakland, Maryland
Born 1933

Do I remember the "outhouse," I sure do! We had the fanciest one in the neighborhood. After the 'spring house cleaning', was done and the "wall papering" done, all the scraps and left over wallpaper were used to paper the walls of the "outhouse." It was bigger than most; a 2 holer, linoleum on the floor, a window complete with curtains made from printed feed sacks, and of course, the usual "Sears Roebuck" or "Spiegel" catalogues for finishing off "your duty". We only had store bought toilet paper when our so called, "rich relatives" came for a visit in the summer to get away from the city, ooh, that paper was so soft!"

You only answered "rotary phones" on "your ring." One lady on our "party line" swore she never listened in on someone else's calls, but needless to say, we knew when she did, because we could hear her canary singing in the background.

For hair care in the old days, the best shampoo in town was made when a bar of soap got too small to handle. Then several saved up bars were put in a small granite pan with some water, put on the old coal stove in the kitchen; melted down into a liquid, then used to wash our hair with "rain water" caught in a barrel outside. This resulted in soft, shiny hair.

I Still Favor the Old Traditions
By Mary Arlene Currence of Mill Creek,
West Virginia
Born 1948

I will always be thankful for all the wonderful home "ARTS" my mother, Mary Ann Chidester taught me. She took in washing and ironing for people (with pay) to help keep us in school. The wash "Rags" and socks were put in a separate pile. My job, at eight years of age was to iron them, match the socks, and fold the wash "Rags" so the corners were perfect. We had an old wringer washer and I scrubbed the socks on a scrub board to get the stains out.

Mom quilted 975 quilts in her lifetime. Her goal was 1000, but she passed away from cancer before she met her goal. She passed the gift of quilt making and old fashioned hooked rugs down to me. I, in turn taught my daughter, grand-daughter and daughter-in-law.

Another "ART" my parents taught me was to plant a garden and can our own food. We also raise our own pork, beef, and chickens. We sugar-cure our hams and make our own sausage and hamburger. Needless to say, we don't buy much at the store.

Mom cooked and canned on a wood stove. In warm weather, it got pretty hot! I followed in her footsteps and have used a wood stove for 50 years. I still do. I pray there will be a few to keep these old traditions alive. Thank you Mom!

My Golden Days at a One-Room Schoolhouse
By Ruby Froman of Pylesville, Maryland
Born 1937

Twenty or less students attended there. Our teachers were outstanding, so we all enjoyed going to school. There was a small room at the school that we used to start our hot lunch program. With the guidance of the teacher, the older girls did the cooking. The government provided milk, eggs, cheese, and dried fruit. We had no electric or running water, so we carried our water from a spring about an 1/8-mile away. It was a good learning experience.

We had a 4-H program in which we enjoyed doing our projects, attending meetings, and going to summer camp. For Halloween, we dressed in our costumes, went across the road from the school for the neighbor man and lady to judge us. Then we went back to the schoolhouse for a party. Christmas time, we made most of our decorations with colored construction paper. Each student learned their parts and invited their parents to come see the program.

During recess, the lunch hour, and a long wait for the bus to pick us up, we had a lot of time to play. We had metal hoops and wheels of all sizes run by a wire handle with a U shape on the bottom or used a stick. Miles and miles we ran around the schoolhouse, schoolyard, or up and down the road. Oh, what fun and exercise! "Handy over" was a special game for us. Dividing into two teams, with one on each side of the schoolhouse, we threw the ball over the roof, as we called "handy over." The other team had to catch the ball and then come around to tag one of our own teammates. The largest team won. Cowboys and Indians, softball, marbles, and rock tag were enjoyed also.

A road bank went down by the school that we would make roads on. Then we carved little cars out of soapstone to run on them. In the winter, we poured water on the bank to ice it up and then slide down. The teacher would take us on a nature hike a couple times a year. In the fall, we raked leaves and then built a leaf house with old boards and fence rails with leaves on the inside and out. It was nice to play in half the winter. When snow came, we played fox and geese and made snowmen and snow angels. Then it was time to move in by the big coal potbelly stove and play Monopoly, work puzzles, or play Mother May I? Our memories and friendships will last a lifetime!

The Moaning Ghost
Harriett M. Moon of Oakland, Maryland
Born 1932

I was born in 1932 in a red brick house, which was across the US-219 road from the one room school where our family got its first years of education. The house was built with brick from the Tile and Brick Factory on the small farm owned by my grandparents. The clay also came from the farm, but a fire destroyed the factory many years before I was born.

My father was next to oldest in a family of seven boys and one girl. When I was a little girl, he told me this ghost story (with sound effects). One afternoon, the rest of the family had gone away, leaving him in charge of things including doing the evening chores. By the time he had finished it was getting dark. He was alone in the house since no one had come home yet. He was deciding what to do next when he heard what sounded like a moan coming from outside. When he looked out of the window, he saw a short distance from the house, glowing eyes, nose, and mouth. His hair stood on end and his heart beat fast. What he had seen disappeared, only to return again along with the moaning sound.

The red brick house

He got up enough courage to go outside to hear and see better. With trembling knees, he slowly approached the place where he had seen the face, which had now disappeared. Just then, there was a slight breeze and the face reappeared and he heard the moan. What he saw came from the ash pile where he had dumped ashes earlier. The "face" was glowing embers and the moan came from a bottle sitting outside. The breeze, of course, is what produced the "ghost."

When the family returned, they got a big laugh from the story of the "moaning ghost."

Such Magic and Wonder Filled Days
By Mary Alice Blizzard of Romney, West Virginia
Born 1920

Looking over the page of "Memory joggers" I realize that I have at age ninety-three, lived, and remember every one of them. However, the one-room school is the dearest to my heart, so I want to share it.

The little white school, with the school bell above the door was at Rada, WV, in Hampshire County. In the four years I attended there, we had two different teachers, Miss Lena Lecherman and Mrs. Georgia Thompson. My school years there were, second, third, fourth and fifth with Miss Lena being there three of those years.

As usual, the teacher's desk was up front and there was two rows of double desks and seats with an aisle between them. In the isle was a long-flat topped stove to warm us on cold winter days. Once in a while, Miss Lena would bring a big kettle of soup or beans-enough for everyone, and keep them hot on the stove until lunchtime. There was two cloakrooms where we also kept our lunch boxes and coats.

Every day, one or two of the older boys walked up the lane to my granddad's house to get buckets of good fresh water from the spring and it would be poured in a crockery water jug with a spigot, so we could easily fill our cups-much prized!

I had two uncles and an aunt in school, with one during my fourth grade, then, my older uncle finished that year and my aunt the next. They were my mother's siblings. It was there in second grade, that I learned the multiplication table through twelve's. The older classes stood in front of the blackboard to read, spell, and recite, so we younger ones learned from them.

Miss Lena was a good teacher, kept order over us twenty-five to thirty students each year, and we all loved her.

At recess, there was usually a ball game or snowball throwing in winter, and some of us girls made play houses under the trees across the road.

In the corner of the yard was a woodshed, which some of the dad's kept full during the winter and the big boys filled the wood box inside. For three years, my brother built the fire each morning and in the evening, he and I swept the floors and emptied wastebaskets. We were paid a small amount for that and we saved enough money to buy a wind-up Victrola, which was used in our home for many years.

Of course, there was the usual two-seater outdoor toilet. A pupil simply raised their hand, the teacher would nod, and you were excused.

Each day started with us saying The Lord's Prayer and the flag salute. Sometimes we sang a song also, and I remember each word to the song.

Miss Lena told each of us good-by as we left at the end of the day. I can still see her standing at the door until everyone had gone. Those were such magic, wonder filled days, with friends and dear teachers.

Hunting, Music & Shine
By Harold E. Adams of Fairmont, West Virginia
Born 1933

Deer hunting in Canaan Valley is a rite of passage for young boys in the Valley. I looked forward to this momentous event. Unfortunately, I would have a long wait. When my mother was a teenage girl, her brother, Hank, was cleaning his gun when it accidently fired, went through the floor and landed at my mother's feet. This single, life altering event would postpone my long awaited hunting adventure until adulthood.

On one of my visits to my Uncle Dick's in Canaan, he took me on a walk through the meadow. Knowing of my love for guns, Uncle Dick allowed me to take his .22 along on this walk. Low and behold, across the meadow near the fence I spotted a deer. Knowing this would probably be my only chance; I took aim at the deer and fired. A startled Uncle Dick simply proclaimed, "Damn, I am glad you missed that deer!"

It wasn't until I got married and moved out of my mother's house that I finally became a gun owner. I then persuaded my Uncle Hank to let me accompany him to Canaan for my first "official" deer hunt. We got half way to Canaan from Fairmont when my Uncle Hank discovered he had packed the food, hunting gear, and booze, but had forgotten his gun. I was beginning to think my mother had put a jinx on my ever getting to go deer hunting. Thank goodness Uncle Hank was deterred by this and some hours later we arrived in Canaan, guns in tow.

The long awaited day had finally arrived. I was staying at my Uncle Joe's and Aunt Ruby's, aka Granny, house along with several of my cousins. We were up before dawn and Granny had prepared a send-off breakfast of eggs, and of course, deer steak with gravy. This was probably the best venison I ever ate, and also probably illegal.

After my first long day of hunting, I returned to my Uncle Joe's exhausted and feeling a little melancholy that I had not "bagged" my first deer. But, my relatives had just the cure for my blues. Out came the banjo, the guitar, and the fiddle. It was a regular "Mountain Music" fest until dinnertime. "Dueling Banjos," "Mountain Dew" and "Boiling Cabbage Down" remain my favorite songs to this day.

After a fine dinner prepared by Granny and including some venison, Uncle Joe said, "I know where we can go and get a drink of moonshine." So, off we went to Ol' Ab Crossland's shack. Now, on the way there, Uncle Joe warns us to be real quiet so we don't disturb the pet skunks that live under his front porch. He also let us know that to get a shot of moonshine, all we had to do is brag on Ol' Ab's hogs. Skunks and hogs, I knew this was going to be a memorable event, one way or another. So, as Ab scratched his hogs behind their ears, we all let him know what a fine lookin' bunch of hogs he had. "Why, probably the finest hogs in the whole valley." Sure enough, Ol' Ab offered us up a drink of shine. Grabbing his old tin cup and wiping its rim with the thumb and forefinger of the same hand that scratched the hog's ears, he poured up a communal cup of shine. Figuring the 110 proof shine would kill any germs; we all took a big ole swig. Obviously, we were right, as I went back year after year to hunt in the valley with my relatives.

Over the years, our hunting progressed and changed with the times. Our deer stand grew to be the largest stand in the valley, holding 5 to 6 people. Each year something new was added to the stand a roof, a chest high gun rest and finally a wood burning stove. I spent many hours in that tree swapping stories and getting to know my cousins and uncles. Our luxurious deer stand lovingly became known as "The Harr Hilton."

The End of the Klondyke Kolts
By Bud Poland of Barboursville, Virginia
Born 1935

This writing deals with life along George's Creek and the residents of Woodland and Klondyke, two small towns approximately the same size and both depending on #17 coalmine operated by Consolidation Coal Company. Each town had approximately 85-95 residents. Consol Coal Company paid the men $2.50 a day to mine the coal. The towns had a company store where they could buy their supplies. Both towns also were supplied their water by a single dam located above Klondyke. In the event of a drought or a break in the water line, the men in both towns pitched in and repaired the damages.

Even though the towns were small, they each had their own church. Woodland had a Methodist Church with a membership of approximately 15 to 20 members. Klondyke had a Presbyterian Church with approximately the same membership. Woodland's minister was also minister for what they called the Midland Charge. This included Midland Methodist, Woodland Methodist, and Shaft Methodist churches and he gave three sermons each Sunday.

During this time, all small towns had a baseball field and fielded a ball team. Midland, Woodland, Klondyke, Carlos, and Midlothian all played against one another. Most of the ball fields have grown over in weeds with the exception of Carlos and Midland. Carlos has many new modern homes built where the ball field was and Midland has a nice modern ball field the likes of which we could have only dreamed about years ago. Midland also has a celebration every August and they entertain their fans with an old-timers ball game at that time. Many of the rules of baseball are altered for that game.

In those days, no one had uniforms, just shirts with the team name sewed on. My brother Jim and I played for the Klondyke Kolts. There was no age restriction. You could be 14 or 60, as long as you could field and hit. The one day I remember vividly was one in which my brother and I convinced our parents to come and watch us play. The game was played on our home field, which was located behind Toad McNeil's Tavern. Most of the time, we only had nine players and sometimes played with less. My brother and I, along with Frank Buskirk Jr., and Jack Burner were classmates between 15 and 17 years old and some of our players were 55-60 years of age. Toad McNeil was an outstanding left-handed hitter in his own right. He supported the team and took care of the field. One way he supported the team was to provide a keg of beer for the older players and cokes for us younger guys.

This particular day, with our parents in

attendance, was a hot and dry day and normally a keg of beer didn't create any problems with the completion of a game. However, this game was tied and went into extra innings and the heat buildup made the older gentlemen enjoy the cold beer even more. When we went out to take the field in the 14th inning (our pitcher, whose name was Sam, and pitched every game because we only had one pitcher) Sam reared back in his warm-up tosses to home plate, he fell over backwards and passed out (guess 14 innings were too much for him). Thus, the game ended in a tie because no one else knew how to pitch. Not only did the game end, but that episode also ended the baseball careers of Bud and Jim Poland, Jack Burner, and Frank Buskirk Jr. with the Klondyke Kolts because our parents saw all they needed to see. However, the four of us continued to play baseball together with Midland American Legion, Frostburg Bi-State League, Beall High, and Frostburg State University for many years to come.

By the way, the only regulation that the Klondyke Kolts had was that we couldn't use the ball field on Sundays. That was the day that all the Judges, elected officials, and law enforcement officials came to the basement of Toad's Tavern to enjoy and bet on the chicken fights and the ball field was filled with automobiles.

I returned and visited the area in recent years and found the ball field all grown over with weeds and trees. Toad's Tavern hadn't fared much better. The sidewalls had deteriorated over the years to the point where they had fallen in and allowed the roof to settle down onto the floor. I remained there for a few minutes and reminisced and thought, although deteriorated, if these walls could only talk, then you would probably have some stories, even though they were true, that you couldn't publish.

Outhouse Adventures
By Patt L. Welsh of Kearneysville, West Virginia
Born 1941

So many memories I have of the old outhouse out back of the house growing up in the '40s and '50s, and believe it or not, our family used an outhouse in the early '60s.

The old outhouse

Standing today like a sentinel behind my house (used only for storage) stands one of the original WPA outhouses built in the '40s during the Roosevelt presidency to give work to others. When my in-laws moved up the road, they moved the old outhouse to where I reside today. A custom I created was to attach a flag of the season, spring, Halloween, Christmas, etc. on the side of the outhouse. Folks would drive by and notice I changed the flag. It proved to be a conversation piece.

As a young girl, my brother had to accompany me after dark to the outhouse located a ways from the main house, for we had no dusk to dawn lights. He used to bang on the side to scare me and/or holler there is a snake and saying he was going to lock me in and "it happened." I yelled and yelled for my mom and sure enough, my brother got a whipping.

Back in the '40s, a Halloween prank was to go tipping outhouses over in the neighborhood and one time my older brothers went on a tipping spree, picked up the outhouse and sat it behind the hole and with no outside lights at that time, resulted an old gentleman falling in the hole. Not a nice picture.

My father-in-law used to dig a new hole covering the old hole with lime and a cover of dirt. One time, a young cousin of my husband was visiting the family; she was always chased by her cousins (my late husband included). Her uncle had filled up an old hole and moved the outhouse to another location. "Yes, it happened," she stepped in the fresh mound of dirt and one of her shoes stuck. She took her foot out and to this day, that little shoe remains buried. She went home in stocking feet.

My sister used to go out and sneak a smoke thinking she would not be seen, but with the smoke and smell radiating out the slats, she ended up in hot water. I never understood why my Daddy made two holes. I never wanted anyone to go in with me and then I understood that one hole was small and the other larger to accommodate adults. Yes, we were poor and couldn't buy a lot of toilet paper (a luxury back then) and used newspaper and even pages of a magazine that you could read before using. No corncobs used as people used to say.

When my husband and I were married in 1960, we lived in a little house before our new home was built. It was three rooms and a path to the old wooden outhouse. One time I went outside and saw a blacksnake in front of the door trying to swallow a frog, I went back inside the house, picked up a rife, went outside, and shot the head off. This is a true story.

Growing up most outhouses was made of wood, cold and drafty, which made you hurry up and get back to the main house. Some families were lucky to erect a brick outhouse, which was a luxury back then. So many memories of the old outhouse standing behind your home. A question I always asked, as a youngster was, why did they put a moon cutout on the door? My father said it was not only for ventilation, but the custom of the half-moon was used to mark a toilet just for ladies and a sun was used for men. It dates back to Colonial times when some folks could not read but understood symbols. I am sure there are other explanations out there.

The Farm in Canaan Valley
By Phyllis Garcia of Waldorf, Maryland
Born 1949

My name is Phyllis Harr Garcia, and I am the daughter of Richard and Mary Jo Harr, who owned and operated a 270-acre farm in the south end of Canaan Valley. This was a beautiful and productive farm of both crops and livestock, but is now part of the Canaan Valley State Park. I grew up with my parents, two brothers, Carl and James, and a sister Barbara. There were always lots of cousins, neighbors, and aunts and uncles visiting and working with us on the farm. The farm work was relentless, but we had a lot of fun too. The funny stories are what I remember most. Here are just a few.

When I was very young, our house was a three-story affair. The lower level was a cellar, the main floor was a kitchen, living room and one bedroom, and the upper level was a loft where we kids slept. Barbara, Carl, and I were playing in the loft, when we saw a bird flying around trying to get out. It was hard work, but we chased it down and caught it. Barbara, being the oldest, was in control of the bird catching operation. She had her hands wrapped around the bird's body with its head sticking up. We had never before, been face to face with a bird and we were amazed to see its facial expressions. It had a mouse-like face and it was smiling with a mouth full of needle sharp teeth. Carl and I wanted to hold it, but Barbara, being in control, would not let it go. She decided we would go downstairs to show Mom. Barbara proudly thrust that poor creature up into Mom's face. Wow! It's a bat. At lightning speed, Mom slapped Barbara's hands, knocking the bat onto the floor where she was on it with her feet stomping it to death. That was shocking, because we thought it was friendly. After all, it was smiling. Amazingly, it had not bitten or scratched us and all we needed was a hard lesson on the difference between bats and birds.

I attended grade school at Cosner School in Canaan Valley. It was a two-room school, which only used one room for education and the other room for play. The only plumbing was a sink for drinking and hand washing, and a sink in the little kitchen for food preparation and cleanup. The Board of Education employed a cook to prepare hot lunches, which I must say, were always very good. Our cook was a robust woman who owned and operated her own farm, as she had no husband. She and one of my uncles were involved in a complicated relationship. They were either sweet with each other or angry and not speaking. One day there was a nice piece of commodity cheese on our lunch trays. To me, cheese was better than candy, because we hardly ever got it at home. At recess, I went to the kitchen and asked for another piece of cheese. Well, the cook and the uncle must have been having a sweet period, because she lifted me up on the counter, gave me a knife, and pushed the cheese (about a 5 lb. block) in my direction. I sat on the counter eating cheese and chatting with the cook for about forty-five minutes. My little seven-year-old stomach was unable to process all that rich, oily yellow cheese, and I became very sick. I never told my mother why I was so sick, but I know it was the cheese. It was impossible for me to eat any more cheese until I discovered pizza in high school. To this day, yellow American cheese does not appeal to me.

My Pop's first cousin, Jack Harr, lived with his mother on an adjoining farm. He and Pop were the same age and had been best of friends since childhood. Jack loved our family and for the entire time we lived on the farm, he visited three times a day. He was there for breakfast, dinner, and supper. He came, but he never ate, because as he put it, he had already eaten "beans and taters." He would sit in the kitchen gossiping and joking with us while we ate. It was always fun when Jack was around.

When I was a little kid, Pop would occasionally treat us to a movie at Sutton Theatre in Thomas, usually a shoot-em up Western or a Jerry Lewis & Dean Martin comedy. Jack would always be invited to go along. All seven of us would load into the car, and just to make us kids laugh, Jack would loudly sing, "Ole Mr. Thompson had an ole gray mule," or any slew of the other ditties he had committed to memory.

One time my brother Carl and I made a chocolate drop out of brown clay and put it in our Christmas hard candy box. We knew Jack had a sweet tooth, and sure enough, when we offered him a piece he went for the chocolate drop. He chewed and chewed, and really tried to eat that wad of clay, but in the end, he spit it out. Everyone, including Jack, thought it was a funny trick.

We kids had a lot of freedom on that farm. When the weather was warm, we played in the woods, fields, and orchard. There was a wide place in the creek where we would go splashing in our birthday suits, or underpants, depending how old we were. We played in the barns, granary, and several other shops and sheds. We never got into trouble for wandering, because we always showed up for dinner and supper. When we were big enough to do farm labor, we all went out to the field together. Mom excused herself from most of the fieldwork because she was too busy with housework, and the garden and all the canning.

We were no longer living on the farm when I graduated from Mountaineer High School in Davis. During my senior year, I knew I needed to do something to support myself, because just staying home with my parents was not an option. We got along just fine, but they always encouraged me to be independent. I wanted to be a beautician and someday operate my own shop. I was in the process of applying for cosmetology school when an FBI Agent walked into my school and changed my future forever. His assignment was to recruit new employees to fill clerical positions in Washington D.C. Just for fun, I decided to apply. He gave me an application form, which I filled out and administrated a spelling test of about ten words, which was probably to see if I could read. The only word I remember from the test is "library." He interviewed me and some of my classmates and neighbors. I got the job, and just two weeks after graduating I started working for the FBI, in the Identification Division as a fingerprint technician. After I started my new job, I learned the spelling test was standard practice for everyone. Now days, they investigate people for about a year before hiring. I left West Virginia on a Greyhound bus with everything I owned in a suitcase and a brown paper bag, and about $250 in my purse. Although this job was terrible in the beginning, it developed into a long and wonderful career.

I'm proud to tell people I grew up in West Virginia. I got a really good start in life, and for that, I am thankful.

That Old Mean Horse Named Pat
By Betty Workman Hohman of Elkins, West Virginia
Born 1941

I was so blessed to have two wonderful grandparents, Jacob and Rhoda Allender Smith, my mom's parents. We lovingly referred to them as Grandpa Jake and Grandma Molly. I was born in 1941 and the early years of my life, they lived within walking distance from our house. We had to wade the river twice to get to their house and could only do it in the summertime when the water was warm and low.

Grandpa Jake had an old, mean horse named Pat. No one could handle her, but Grandpa. One day mom took John and me to visit and decided to take a shortcut through the meadow not knowing Pat was in there. John, who was three years older than me, ran on ahead and was almost to the fence when mom noticed Pat looking at us. In a few minutes, she started running for us. I was only three years old, so mom picked me up and started running for the chicken house while yelling for John to get Grandpa Jake. Mom reached the chicken house a step or two ahead of Pat and slammed the door in her face. We both were crying and the chickens raised an awful ruckus. Grandpa Jake kept that old, mean horse until she finally died. He buried her on the hillside.

I loved our horse, Bess, but I was afraid of her too. I loved riding her when Daddy held onto the reins. On cold winter mornings, when mom had to go to the barn to milk the cows, she would bundle John and me up and make us a nest in the hay to keep warm. One morning after Bess finished her grain, she started stretching her neck up for some hay. Unfortunately, the hay that she was after was close to my feet. I thought she was going to eat me. My screams probably scared her as much as she had scared me.

I was also afraid of cattle, but not our milk cow, Ike. The neighbors on the mountain farm above ours had a bunch of cattle with long horns. They were always getting out and coming down to our house. Mom and John would run and make sure the yard and garden gates were closed and latched tight. I would stay on the couch and watch out the window. I was sure they would come in the house and get me.

One day John was riding his bike on the path by the river, when he heard cattle bawling. He saw a huge herd across the river starting to cross over to our side. A big black bull was in the lead. He hurried home as fast as he could, yelling for mom. The herd swarmed around the outside of our yard fence. Daddy was pasturing a yearling bull for a neighbor in our barn lot. The big black bull started fighting the yearling through the fence. Finally, the bull tried to jump the fence and only got halfway over and was stuck on the barbed wire. My little dog, Tippy, started nipping the bull's legs and when he would kick, it went over Tippy's head. The bull finally tore through the fence with Tippy's help. The two bulls fought all afternoon and the herd scattered all over the neighborhood. Someone alerted the owner and he sent men to round up the cattle and drive them back where they belonged. But not so for the big black bull. It took several men to get him penned up and loaded in a truck. The owner took him to the slaughterhouse.

Daddy worked for the Western Maryland Railroad and was gone all day. We didn't have electric or telephone and lived at the end of the road. Today it would scare me to death to be cut off like that with two little kids. Daddy had an old Model T, but he had to drive it to work. Mom took good care of us and was always warning us to watch out for snakes. Our farm was polluted with copperheads. Luckily we never got bit, but little Tippy got bit every summer. His head would swell up and he would go lay in the swamp in the mud. He always got better. Grandpa Jake passed away at age 92 and Grandma Molly at 91. They lived a good, long life and left behind a lot of precious memories. My four children knew and loved them dearly too. My parents were Charlie and Edna Smith Workman. They were the best parents a girl could ever have.

Grandpa Jake and Grandma Molly in 1944

West Virginia Will Always Pull You Home
By Patsy Dopson of Kearneysville, West Virginia
Born 1937

I grew up in small town in the eastern panhandle of West Virginia. I think most people who grew up in small towns want to get out and see the rest of the country when they are adults. I grew up in the Blue Ridge Mountains with the Potomac River on one side of town and the Shenandoah River on the other side. They meet at the point and continue on to the Chesapeake Bay. Due to the 1936 flood in Harpers Ferry, I was born up the hill in the town of Bolivar in 1937.

My mother, who grew up across the river in Loudoun County, Virginia, would tell us about how deep the snow would get. She said it would reach the fence tops. I never saw any snow that deep, but in the '40s I can remember a storm with a couple of feet of snow and it seemed like we were out of school forever. We had a great place to sled ride. Union Street ran for about a mile from our main street down to the new highway. Until the snowplows came, it was great sledding. The only bad thing about it was walking back up the hill.

The main place to swim when we were teenagers was the stone quarries. Limestone was mined here and when they dug so far down, underground streams would fill them up with water. They were the most fantastic places to swim and dive. The cliffs ranged from about 25 and 35 feet and one large boulder at about 50 feet. Only guys that were considered idiots went off that height. I never even went up there to look down. Later when I was in the military stationed in California, we spent lots of time at the beach. I would tell

Jimmy, Robert, John, and Danny in 1963

them about the great places we had to swim in West Virginia and they would remind me that we were in the Pacific Ocean. Yeah I'd said, but you should see those quarries in West Virginia.

When my oldest brother came home from World War II roller-skating was big. I was about 10 at the time. He would take me along on his dates to the roller rink. I guess after being away for so long he appreciated being home. I don't know what the girls thought. He served in the Philippines and was part of the occupation forces in Japan.

In the '50s, the local historic hotel let us have a large area for a teenage canteen. We spent many happy hours there. We also had sock hops in the school gym. I think that was because the gym floor had been redone and they didn't want it scratched up. Frances, a friend of mine, and I used to go swimming early in the morning before she went to work. When diving, she would always say, "you know me, you go first." One morning she decided to go first and hit her head on a rock on the river bottom. She was taken to a doctor in the next town, about 8 miles away, where she received stitches and has the scar to this day.

The Taylors lived around the lane and across the garden from us. Helen and Webster had a lot of kids. Mildred was the oldest. She and I and Lorelia Goens, who lived next door, were good friends. There was also Aunt Bessie and Granny and Papa Taylor. As kids, a treat on a hot summer day was chips of ice we would get from Mr. Twyman when he brought the blocks of ice in his horse and wagon for

Patsy at the quarry in 1955

the iceboxes. One thing I recall is the Taylor's Christmas tree. It was a large branch of a tree with the individual small branches wrapped in cotton with blue lights. I think it was a reminder of the slavery days. I always said when I grew up I was going to have a tree like that. Last year I finally got my white tree with blue lights.

When my brother, Roy, came home from Korea, I was a senior in high school. We were like kids again having pillow fights and staying up late to watch the *Tonight Show* with Steve Allen. After school, we would take the path down to the river and swim. When he was a teen, a bunch of his friends built a cabin across the river. They called themselves The Border Bandits. They would take off on school vacations and summers. They would catch fish and sell them to their parents. I really envied them. I told him I should come and cook for them, which he knew I couldn't and still can't. He just laughed. I had two older sisters who were into that sort of thing, but I was always playing ball with the guys. My kid's favorite saying was, "What are you burning for dinner tonight?"

The radio programs I liked the most were *The Shadow* and *Inner Sanctum*. The show started off with the sound of a squeaking door, which was really scary. The one that scared me the most was one called Snake Pit. It took place in a mental institution. I saw the movie years later and it wasn't half as scary. One day when I was a child, I walked up the lane to the corner store to get a piece of penny candy. The elderly man who ran the store gave me nine cents change. My mother made me take it back, it was one of those white pennies, and he thought it was a dime.

We spent many Saturday nights dancing at the fire hall in Brunswick, Maryland. Jimmie Dean and his band played there. He had a TV show in DC. He was a lot of fun. He used to jump down off the stage and get in the "Paul Jones" as we called the mixer dances. Patsy Kline would sing down the street at the Moose Club. I remember my mother telling me if you can go dancing on Saturday night you can get up for church on Sunday morning.

Each year the senior class took a class trip to NYC. One thing we were always told we had to do was the parachute drop at Coney Island. I was a Yankee fanatic, so I wanted to make sure I got to see them play. Luckily, they were in town so I got to see Mickey Mantle hit a homerun and I got to walk down the street outside the stadium beside Yogi Berra. I also got Elston Howards autograph. He was the first black player for the Yankees.

We actually had a castle in our town. No one lived there when I was growing up, but some of the older men who lived there would walk around quoting Shakespeare. The thing I remember is having Easter egg rolls there. It was located on Bolivar Heights, overlooking the town. After Harpers Ferry became part of the National Park Service, the castle was torn down. I never understood that. They said it had no historic value, but it was a castle.

One tradition the boys in our town had was swimming in the Shenandoah River on Easter Sunday morning. We would be up on Jefferson Rock having sunrise service and we could see them down in the river. It was called Jefferson Rock because Thomas Jefferson supposedly stood up there and said, "This view is worth a trip across the Atlantic." I have lived in many places in the US, at least 5 other states, but West Virginia always pulls you home.

Eleanor
By Jerry Timbrook of Chambersburg, Pennsylvania
Born 1945

I was born in July of 1945 to Clarence (Timmy) and Lola Timbrook. Dad was a farmer and mother was a schoolteacher. We lived in Bear Wallow Hollow near Augusta, West Virginia, located in Hampshire County. We did not have indoor plumbing, but behind our house stood our outhouse, but I never remember my parents using the term outhouse. They called the little building Eleanor, so when any of us had a nature call, we simply said, "I have to go see Eleanor." I thought Eleanor was a fine name for the little building that stood proudly dressed in red paint.

Of course, we went to see Eleanor regularly during all seasons. It was not a big deal to brush a little snow that had blown through the cracks off the seats. After a snow, we shoveled a path to Eleanor first and to the woodpile second. When making the journey to see Eleanor at night it was simply a matter of carrying a flashlight. When comfortably seated you could turn the flashlight off and have complete privacy even from sleeping bugs or flies that might be tempted to peek. You did have to be careful where you laid the flashlight because Eleanor's décor included two seats.

Eleanor was regularly equipped with last year's Montgomery Ward or Sears Roebuck catalogues. This worked out fine because after looking at the pictures you could simply tear out the page and use it. This practice was commonplace among people in those days. I remember hearing some of the older men saying that they were glad about the catalogues, because now they no longer had to save their corncobs to be used for such a purpose. As I look back, I realize that this may have been the birth of the recycling movement.

Things change and not always for the best. It wasn't long before the texture of the catalogues began to change and shiny, slick, color, less absorbent pages began to be the norm. Somewhere in there, my parents began to purchase the modern TP roll. As a kid leaning toward modernism, I kind of liked the changes because the exhausted TP rolls could be used as telescopes to watch for Indians that might be coming out of the pines on the hillside. The rolls could also be used to yell through and make loud, harsh announcements warning bad guys about what they were in for if they even considered coming near the farmhouse or Eleanor.

One of my fondest memories concerning Eleanor was that she afforded a great place to hide and ambush the Starlings that insisted on building a nest every year in the upper corner of our house under the eaves. At about age nine, my dad started letting me carry his old Remington model 12, 22 with the octagon barrel. I took it with me during most of my farm chores and always when I went to visit Eleanor. When her door was slightly ajar it provided the perfect rest for the rifle to pick off the blackbirds as they lit on the corner of the roof. Thus, Eleanor provided a prototype of the modern hunting blind. The lice laden birds would light for just a second on the edge of the roof just before fluttering under the eaves to feed their young. It was that second of hesitation on the edge of the roof that proved deadly for many a bird. I definitely reduced the population. However, one spring I made a surprising observation. I had shot five birds with worms in their mouths trying to go in to feed the same nest of birds. Then I observed at least two more birds doing the same thing. I was so astonished to see their dedication to communal living that I backed off and didn't shoot anymore for a while. I can't help but wonder if this observed behavior is included in the Audubon Society's Starling Studies program.

"Eleanor"

As I grew a little older, I began to receive some benefits from schooling and I was tall enough to read the paper that had always been posted high on Eleanor's interior wall. It was hard to read because through the years, the rain and snow had blown through the cracks and the water damage to the text was considerable. However, I could make out that it was some sort of inspection certificate. Even though the signature was not legible, it was obvious that long ago some very important person who made his living by scrutinizing such facilities had officially approved Eleanor. It was no surprise to me because Eleanor was fine. She had a concrete floor and hinged wooden covers for the wood seats that had been hand-carved by a craftsman and made as comfortable as wood boards could be. She also had screened vents just in case a foul odor might try to emerge it could be swept away by fresh mountain breeze.

As I recall, it was somewhere late in my high school years, about the time that the great questions of life began to dominate your thinking, that I asked my mother about Eleanor's name. My mother, always the teacher, gave me a great valuable history lesson that day. It seems that in an effort to recover from the great depression, a program called The Works Progress Administration (WPA) was instituted by President Roosevelt's executive order under the Emergency Relief Appropriation Act of April 1935, to generate public jobs for the unemployed. During this time, Mrs. Eleanor Roosevelt took a special interest in West Virginia. One of her goals was that every family has a decent toilet facility, so the effort became a part of the WPA projects. Men, who were very thankful to have a job that paid one dollar a day, built hundreds of such facilities across West Virginia. Each one had to be government inspected and approved and so that is why my parents just naturally called our little facility Eleanor.

Eleanor still stands behind the old farmhouse, though she is leaning quite a bit and the groundhogs keep trying to move into her basement. Occasionally I will mention tearing her down. My wife, Dixie, objects and says, "You can't do that she is an important part of your heritage. We need to fix her up and keep her." I guess she is right. Living with Eleanor all those years seemed perfectly normal to me, but now she really does represent an important part of our history and who knows, the time may come due to unforeseen circumstances that we will need to shovel a path to her again. Besides that, you just know that someday those pesky Starlings are going to try to make a comeback and I want to be ready.

Two-room School, Killer Bees, and the Chicken Snake
By Donna J. Pierce of Berkeley Springs, West Virginia
Born 1953

In 1960, my parents moved into a house on Spohrs Road. It was an older house with a small kitchen, a little room off from it that Mom used for her wringer washer, a play area for us kids, a nice living room with a wooden floor, and three upstairs bedrooms. It was just enough for Mom, Dad, my older sister, Sandy, who was eight, my younger brother, Bobby, who was five, and me, age six. Behind the house there was a little run with a footbridge that led to the cow pasture. There was also an old wooden shed with a dirt floor, which Dad claimed as his, but my brother and I loved going in, and playing in the dirt with his cars and trucks. That always went over big with Mom when we come in looking like we had just survived the Great Depression's Dust Bowl.

Across the road from the house was a field that Dad would plow and plant with corn for the cows and a garden for us. The people who owned the property lived in a newer house just down the road from us, so Dad helped them with the farm. Dad would take my brother Bobby up on his knee and let him drive the tractor. Many times, I would jump on the back and ride on the hitch. If Dad was doing some serious plowing and there were discs or plows on, I wasn't allowed.

Mom took great pride in shining and waxing the living room's wooden floor. Once the weather must have been bad, because we were told to stay upstairs and play while she waxed. We got hungry and so Mom gave us sandwiches and some milk and told us to set on the steps and eat while the wax finished drying. When she finished up waxing, the floor was so shiny we could see our reflections. I started saying goofy things to get Bobby

Donna's parents, Robert and Geraldine Kidwell in 1960

laughing; little did I realize that this would bring down the wrath of Mom. Bobby had just taken a big mouthful of chocolate milk when I caused him to laugh, and the milk exploded out of his nose and mouth, down the steps, and across Mom's shiny-waxed floor. Well, needless to say, our bottoms got a nice dusting off by Mom, and my brother got mad at me. I wonder why?

When school started, we got to go to the Spohrs Crossroads School. It was a little two-room school with two outhouses, one for the boys and one for the girls. It didn't have running water, so we drank from a water bucket with a dipper. We did have electric, though. We would bring our packed lunches, and our teacher would put them in the fridge.

The teacher's name was Mrs. Grove. She was a kind lady, but strict. She had first, second, third, and fourth grades in one room, and fifth, sixth, seventh, and eighth grades in the other room. She would teach and give assignments to one grade and then move on to another one while the first would study or write. She also had us read out loud in a flat or singsong tone, where when we would read out the words it would be in the same volume, neither high nor low.

My brother started his first year of school there, turning six in April, and I started second grade, since I also had a birthday in April and turned seven. He and I both learned to spell "picture" by hearing the third grade class spell it out loud.

Once when I went to use the girl's outhouse, some mean older boys locked me in. Mrs. Grove came out and rang the hand held school bell. I was so scared I would get in trouble that I started crying and banging on the door, sure I was trapped forever and bound to be forgotten. After several tense moments, the door was opened by a girl, and in the doorway of the school stood Mrs. Grove; I was saved. With trembling knees and shaking hands, I dried my tears and went back into the school, ashamed to have been caught crying. The boys were punished and all was right with the world again.

We, my brother, sister, and I had to walk to school sometimes since we were only a mile or so from the school. When winter came, they did run a bus for us, but once the bus broke down, and it had started to snow that morning after we had gotten to school. So that evening

Bobby Kidwell, Donna Kidwell, and Sandy Farris in 1960

we were told we would have to walk home. Since it hadn't been snowing that morning, we hadn't worn our boots, and the snow was already about four inches deep. Now you talk about cold; being girls, my sister and I only had dresses on under our coats. Boy, were we glad to get home! That winter we did get about two feet of snow. I still have pictures of it.

When Christmas came, Sandy and I each wanted one of those Patty Playpal dolls, but they were too expensive, so Mom and Dad got us the Patty Playpal look-a-like dolls that were just as big. Mom always liked to put up the Christmas tree and toys long after we went to bed on Christmas Eve. Mom would tell us that Santa Claus did it all, the tree, the decorating, and the toys. Santa was a busy guy! On Christmas morning, we were so excited about our big dolls, and Bobby got a B.B. gun.

Later, when we no longer believed in Santa, Mom told us that after she had gotten everything decorated and the toys under the tree, she went upstairs to get ready for bed. Then she came back down to get a drink of water when suddenly she spotted two little girls standing near the Christmas tree. She hadn't turned on a light. "What are you girls doing out of bed?" she shouted. The girls didn't move, and then it dawned on her that her girls were in bed and the two standing there were our new dolls!

When summer came again, Bobby and I liked to play on the front porch, but there was a bumblebee nest in one of the porch posts. At about half way up, there was an entrance hole the bees flew into and down at the bottom of the post was another hole that the bumblebees flew to and then walked in and out of. The bees never really bothered us unless we got near their post. Well, Bobby and I felt that it just wasn't right that we couldn't have the whole porch to ourselves. So we hatched an ingenious plan of destruction to rid ourselves of the stinging beasts. Bobby and I stuffed the upper hole with dirt; we packed it as tight as we could. Then Bobby got Dad's hammer and waited for the bees to come crawling out of the bottom. I knelt down beside him to watch. Wham! Bobby got one as it came out. Blam! Another and another. We grinned at each other; we were so smart. He must have gotten at least a dozen or so before the dirt vibrated out of that upper hole. One nailed me on top of the head. I shot straight off the porch, but another one got me on the knee. Poor Bobby was trapped, screaming and jumping up and down as the bees swarmed around him. Mom soon heard our screams and came to the rescue. Mom grabbed him while he was dancing in the yard, and I followed into the house. I don't know how many stings Bobby got, but he sure got the worst of it. Mom doctored us with water and baking soda to draw out the stings. Lesson learned, leave bees alone.

Mom and her family were great storytellers, filling our heads with ghosts, vengeful spirits, witches, devils, lost gold, superstitions, etc., so we were very imaginative children. Although we hated walking to school, we didn't mind taking walks up the same road as long as it wasn't for school. So one summer day, the three of us, Sandy, Bobby, and I walked up to school, and on the way, we repeated ghost stories that were told to us.

Mom had warned us that there was a devil in beer bottles and not to touch them, for if we did the devil would jump out! Bobby and I decided to throw rocks at beer bottles to see if the devil would jump out. We hit a bottle with a rock, ready to run if old slewfoot should come out for us but no devil. So we got brave enough to pick one up. We shook it and peeked in it but no devil there! We threw it back in the ditch. We walked some more and spotted another bottle. We hit it with a few rocks. Bobby ran to pick it up and tossed it up on the bank. "Hey, I want to do something with it," Sandy said. She ran up the bank to where the bottle had landed behind a stump. I ran up the opposite side of the stump from Sandy. Sandy let out a scream, and beside the stump, I will swear to this day, there was a white snake that had the head of what looked like a white chicken! We both flew down the bank, screaming, "It's the devil!" All three of us ran down the road a ways, and then stopped to discuss what we saw.

Did we really see what we thought we saw? Surly not! We decided to go back and check. So, working up our courage we went back. Bobby volunteered to go up the bank first with me close behind. Bobby and I searched and found no trace or sign of any snake, chicken head, or hole for anything to crawl into. The stump was solid and the mystery unsolved. We decided it was the devil after all, who had turned into a snake with a chicken head just to scare us for throwing rocks at his beer bottles. We went home and reported this to Mom. Yes, she said that very well could have been the devil, and now we should leave those dirty old bottles alone. The mystery of what we saw remains to this day.

We Had Plenty of Fun
By Elsie Lewis of Oakland, Maryland
Born 1943

Wringer Washers
I enjoyed washday. We had to heat the water. Then it had to be packed to the washhouse. When the clothes was washed and rinsed, they had to be hung on the line to dry. When dried, they needed to be ironed. Washday was a daylong chore. Most everyone washed clothes on Monday.

Wringer washers replaced the scrubbing board. I enjoyed my old Maytag better than my automatic washer.

Trips to Town
We very seldom got to town. One trip was in December to get our Christmas treats. The National Guard passed out treats. There was a popcorn ball, an orange, chocolate candy, etc. The orange was very exciting, as we didn't often get one.

Sometimes after church, we would go to town for ice cream. We had relatives who lived in Keyser and Hancock. That was like a country away. The most amazing thing was Daddy had only a pickup truck. We would always ride in the back. There were eight children to haul.

Homemade Clothes and Toys

We didn't have many store bought clothes. We got to go get shoes before school started. They had to last as long as possible. They was always black and white saddle oxfords. That was why as soon as warm weather came we went barefoot.

We had dresses made out of feed sacks. We raised turkeys and chickens. Daddy had to go to Oakland and buy feed. We would get to go along and pick out the feed sacks for our dresses. Mother made our dresses. She also made dishtowels, pillowcases, etc.

Toys was usually only received at Christmas. We got maybe one or two. We had out playhouses in the woods. My sister and I each had our own house. We had stumps for chairs and tables. We went to the trash pile and got our dishes, pots, and pans. We also had scraps of material for our curtains. Playing in our playhouses was our very special playtime. We didn't have many toys, but we always found something fun to do after the farm work was done.

We spent many hours playing in the haymows. We had a rafter from one loft to the other. It was probably 15 or 20 feet long and about 12 or 15 inches wide. We would walk that rafter and sometimes jump down into the hay wagon if it was loaded. We made tunnels in the hay with our cousins. We played cowboys and Indians. The oat bin was our jail. The Lone Ranger, Tonto, Gene Autry, and Roy Rogers were our heroes. We didn't have television, but sometimes on Sundays we got to go to Aunt Annie's and watch TV. We didn't spend much time indoors.

I spent a lot of time reading. One time we built a teepee out of burlap sacks. We used thorns to pin the bags together. Sometimes we went to Aunt Mae's. There we had a playhouse under the stairs. We didn't have many toys, but we still had plenty of fun.

Outhouses and Chamber Pots

We are now having a very cold spell. What a joy to not have to go to an outhouse. I was raised on a farm in the late Forties and early Fifties. We had only the famous outhouse. Once you got there in the winter, you didn't tarry long. In warm weather, you could enjoy the *Sears Roebuck* or *Montgomery Ward Catalog*. Once in a while, a spider or other bugs would visit you. Sometimes people would wallpaper the walls. We had to sometimes scrub the outhouse.

At Halloween, it was a trick to upset outhouses. Sometimes there would be someone in one. Then you were really in trouble.

Then there was the famous chamber pot. It was used at night. In the morning, it had to be emptied. The oldest child was the lucky one to get the joy, as my sister says, of emptying the chamber pot.

So let's enjoy our modern bathrooms.

Saturday Night Baths

I had eight siblings. We had only a Burnside stove in the living room and a coal and wood cook stove in the kitchen. Saturday night baths were fine in warm weather, but winter was different.

The water was heated on the cook stove; there were no water heaters. Then out came the steel washtub. It was filled with the water. It was sat by the cook stove for warmth. If you was lucky to be the first one to bathe, it was fine. Usually the youngest got to go first. But as each child was bathed in the same water, it got a little less warm.

After our bath, our mother would curl our hair. She heated our hair with a hot poker and wrapped it in strips of rags. Our hair was beautiful for church the next morning.

After I was married in 1959, I had to bathe my children in the washtub. We don't realize the times of yesterday was hard, but back then we didn't know it was a hard life.

School

I went one grade to a one-room school. Then I was moved to a two-room school. My favorite teachers was Mrs. Rechart and Mr. Buckel.

The mobile library come once in a while. It was exciting as I enjoyed reading.

In the spring we had a fun day. We would get to bring our pets. I had a pet lamb. Most of our pets were farm animals, as most of us lived on farms.

We had a bucket of water from the spring. We each had a tin cup that folded. Then there was the outhouses, one for the boys and one for the girls.

We played games at recess. We played hopscotch, red rover, and fox and goose. We played easy over, where you threw the ball over the school. If you caught the ball you run around to the other side and tagged the other team.

There was a maple tree grove next to the school. In the spring when they tapped the trees for maple syrup, we got to go to the trees and get some sap to drink.

Farm Chores

Farm chores had to be done before we went to school and then again when we got home. We only had two or three cows to milk by hand. We had to go and bring the cows in to the barn. Some mornings, it was chilly. Then we would get the cows up and stand in that spot and warm our feet. After milking, we had to run the milk through the separator.

In the spring, we ordered our chickens and turkeys by mail. When they arrived, we had to teach each one to drink by dipping their beaks in water. We had a house called brooders. We had maybe five or six separate ones. Each one had a stove in it that had to be kept burning. If there was a thunderstorm we had to stay with them or they would get in a pile and smother.

Summer was the busiest. Hay had to be made. I would usually drive the team of horses. We had a hay loader pulled behind the wagon that pulled the hay on to the wagon. When the wagon was full, we went to the barn. The team had to be unhitched and hooked to a rope that pulled the hayfork up to the loft.

Turkeys and chickens had to be fed. Turkeys was our larger flock, sometimes we had around 100. Hogs had to be fed; we only had four or five of them, mostly just enough to butcher in the fall.

We had a lot of sheep, maybe 50 or more. In the spring we had to shear them. Daddy done his own shearing and he did it for the surrounding farms, too. We also had a few angora rabbits that was sheared for their fur.

Gardens had to be planted, hoed, weeded, and then canned. We had no freezer. The jars of food is what we ate in the winter.

Threshing was a community job. One farm had a threshing machine. The farmers moved from farm to farm until each one was done. If it was your farm, there had to be a large noon meal cooked for the men. That meant several pies, cakes, meat, and more.

In the fall, we had butchering to do. We made the sausage into meatballs for Mom to can. The winter was slower. We just had the milking and to feed the livestock. Remember, we had wood to keep in the house as we only had the cook stove and a Burnside it the living room.

Farm life was hard but we didn't realize how hard. It was life in the Forties and Fifties. We learned how to work. We worked hard but had a lot of fun. We had reunions to go to in the summer. Oh, the table after table of home cooked farm food.

Swimming

We went swimming in a big farm pond. We was only allowed on one side. This was done after our farm chores was done. No way would I get in that pond now, but back then it was a lot of fun.

Favorite Pet

We always had a pet. Our pets were pigs, cows, and lambs. We had a milk cow named Polly. We could ride her like a horse.

We always had a pet lamb. We had to bottle feed them until they got big enough to eat. I always took my lamb to school on pet day.

We had a pet calf one time. It got big enough to butcher, so we wouldn't eat one bit of it.

You Might Hear Our Voices in the Wind
By Loretta F. Barlow of Arlington, Virginia
Born 1941

My name is Loretta Fern Thompson Barlow. I was born in the Macksville Post Office building in Pendleton County West, Virginia on September 17, 1941. My grandmother was Mary Susan Harper. She was the Post Master, taking over for her husband, Henry Elmer when he was unable to work and passed away. When my grandmother broke her hip, my mother, June Thompson took over the store and post office until it closed on May 10, 1951. The mail carrier for the Harman Hills rode a horse to make his deliveries. It was exciting to see Lester ride up, pick up the mail, and head out for deliveries. The original store and post office is still there, as is the first post office built by Henry in 1901.

They had a small store in the same building. I remember as a child baby chickens were shipped by mail. As kids, we made sure all the air holes were popped out so they could breathe. We also had feed shipped to the store. I was allowed to pick out the feedbags I liked. Once the feed was used, my mother used the

The original post office/store

cloth to make my dresses.

Why we lived my first eight years at the post office is unclear. We had a house on the property, which was built by my grandfather around 1900. Getting the keys and going into the house, which had a parlor filled with musical instruments, was a favorite until we were caught. Sadly, our generation was not the musical part of this family and could not sing and could not play.

My first grade teacher was Ms. Mollie Harper, who lived across the river from our house. We had to cross a swinging bridge to get there. Her sister and niece lived with her. The niece had this beautiful dollhouse with a butler, maid, and family. I spent as much time as I could with Ms. Harper and her niece. The niece taught me how to draw, and we made clothes for paper dolls. Ms. Mollie owned a player piano, and I spent a lot of time playing the songs that came with it. I even tried to convince my dad that I had learned how to play until he caught me pumping away.

As kids, we stayed outside as much as we could. Our favorite outfits were for me a WAC uniform and my brother wore an Army uniform. We were cowboys and Indians sometimes, too. Summers were spent swimming in the river and building a place, we called our house in the woods. We installed moss for carpet. Learning how to swim was not from lessons but from being shoved off a river ledge and dog paddling our way back to the top.

We grew up with the stories of the legends of the Seneca Rocks, Seneca Caverns, Princess Snow Bird, the Hell Hole, and the Cave Schoolhouse. We climbed the Seneca Rocks with no climbing shoes and no ropes. We sat on the Gendarme, which fell on October 22, 1987. We had no fear ever of heights or snakes.

My last trip to the Seneca Caverns was for a class reunion for my brother. We were eating at the new restaurant when a storm came up, making it as dark as night. A few minutes later, the storm was gone, the sun came out, and a double rainbow appeared. It was almost heaven, West Virginia giving us a view of the joy and beauty of the area that remains in our hearts.

My grandmother made black cats from oatmeal boxes for Halloween. She went to school with me one year dressed as a witch. Our school had an upstairs for assemblies and lunches. In the winter, we would go to the top of the hill across the highway, hop on the sled, and cross the highway to the lane to the house. Traffic was not an issue back then, but it was not the safest thing to do.

My dad made things from everything; the hood of an old car became a boat to cross the river. It leaked a lot, but we dumped water and used it often.

We grew up with cows, pigs, chickens. We grew a garden, canned food, and picked

Loretta's grandmother, Mary Harper, her mother, June Thompson, with Dallas, and Loretta

fruit that grew in the orchard. We helped with making homemade soap for the laundry and apple butter in large outdoor kettles. We had chores, but we had fun.

We did not have a television until a few years before I moved away. I would ride my bike to the neighbors' and watch one or two shows a week. We had a crank phone, which was still in use for several years after I moved away. Dial tone replaced them in 1977. Explaining to the long distance operator how to call home was our inside joke. We knew everyone on our line and which ring was his or hers. We listened in if we thought it would be interesting. I am sure they did the same. No one ever complained; we just took it in stride.

When my dad worked at the sawmill, he brought home two baby squirrels. He built a cage, and we fed them with an eyedropper until they got big enough to care for themselves. Then we returned them to the woods.

I had a dog, Ginger, that went everywhere I did. Ginger could spot snakes and kept me away from them by standing in front of me and backing me up. My dad always had coon dogs and others as well.

Every Saturday night we had relatives of my grandmother's show up with their coon dogs and musical instruments. My mother played the guitar and sang, and the relatives played the banjo, fiddle, mandolin guitar, organ, and one played the accordion. Our little store rang with music on weekends. The men would take the dogs and go hunting. The older kids spent the rest of the night telling ghost tales and trying to scare the smaller ones with their stories. Come day light, we would hear the men returning and the dogs barking.

I have been gone for many years, but with all my memories I can travel back just by closing my eyes. I do visit when I can and things have changed, but the people remain the same. Sadly, the booming little village with a mill and post office and store are just memories and for the purpose of 911 calls, Route 33 from Franklin to Seneca Rocks has been named Mountain Drive. Our house is now #21074. In our minds, it will always be Route 33, with a mailbox that says HC73 Box 14.

Many of the homes are empty, some have new people, and I realize even though I moved away, my heart is still in Macksville. I am sure if you go near the woods or river, you just might hear our voices in the wind. The world we lived in growing up, the wonderful teachers, our parents, grandmother, and all those relatives made us very special people.

Two of the teachers, Ms. Sadie Propst and Ms. Louise Bowers, are still living and making a statement for West Virginia women. They both represent the best in their profession along with the others, grade school teachers Ms. Mollie, Ms. Joy, Mr. Dove, and Mr. Bland. Ms. Mollie taught us to read, write, do arithmetic, and patience. Ms. Joy taught us a little bit of everything and showed us how to be our very best. Mr. Dove took us to exciting places in geography. Mr. Bland taught us West Virginia history and to not chew gum in class. The result of chewing was putting you on your tiptoes with your nose in a chalk ring. They prepared us to go from a four-room school to high school with knowledge and respect for who we are today. We were always will be Montani Semper Liberi (Mountaineers Always Free).

In Those Days, Everybody Worked
By Shirley J. Burkett of Points, West Virginia
Born 1938

Here are some facts of life when I was a kid. We had an outhouse, which was built by the WPA. At night, we used the chamber pot, which we called the slop jar. We never had toilet paper. We used catalogs. We would use the soft sheets first, and then we would crinkle up the stiff ones to make them soft. I made my own sanitary napkins. Later, we bought Kotex. I would send my dad to buy them for me, because I was too shy to buy them myself.

We had a party line. Our number was two long rings and one short ring. We had a record player, which had round tubes for records. The only song I can recall was "There's No Bananas Today." We were the first family in our five family area to have a black and white television. There was no color TV.

I took a bath every night. I would take a pan of water in my bedroom, which was very cold. At nighttime, a glass of water would freeze in there. I also did my homework in the cold bedroom.

My mom washed our clothes on a wringer washer every Monday. Sometimes I would draw the water up with a well bucket for

Shirley's dad, Thomas Pownall and her uncle, Bob Pownall

her, which I thought was fun. Later on, Dad put water into the kitchen sink but not in the bathroom.

My mom canned all of our food. She baked bread three times a week.

I also cleaned the baby bottles out with little rocks if they weren't washed right away. We didn't have bottlebrushes back then.

We had bad weather back when I was growing up. The snow would be on the ground for most of the winter. The roads would be packed with snow. I don't recall any snow plows. I know we never had any snow days for school. We would stand up at the road waiting for the bus. We didn't know what time it would pick us up. We would stoop down and put our dresses around our legs to try and stay warm. During high school, we could only wear jeans at football games on Fridays.

At grade school, we played out in the snow and sometimes it would be pretty deep. We would play fox and geese. I never got any spankings at school.

I only had one dog named Bubbles. She was white with long wavy hair. I know when she died it was like having a human burial. We all cried as Dad dug the grave to bury her.

At six or seven, I sat down by a rattlesnake that was all curled up. Mom hollered at me, "What are you thinking?"

Dad worked at the B&O. Mom and Dad raised seven of us kids and also took care of his mom and aunt, Mary. My dad only had gone to the sixth grade, as far as I can recall. He had to quit school to go to work to help his mom, but he could do math. He could build, too. Every time there was a new baby on the way, he would build another room onto the house. Mr. Ambrose, who lived down the road, would hear Dad hammering and without knowing he would say,"There's going to be an increase in their family."

All of us kids were born at home. Dad would let Dr. Daily know when to expect the call. Dr. Daily would make house calls also. I only remember one time that we were all sick and he came and gave us some medicine. I don't remember any home remedies.

I went to work on the orchard at the age of ten going on eleven. I was never told to do it, I wanted to. Making fifty cents, an hour sounded good to me. I could help Dad by buying my school clothes. Mr. Cline would send a ton truck with racks on it and pick us up and bring us back home. I would get myself up, pack my lunch, and was ready to go. Now Dad would be put in jail for letting me work at that age. I say if you don't start early going to work; you are not going to make anything of yourself. In those days, everybody worked to feed their families. If you didn't work, you didn't eat. Now people eat and don't work.

I would help Dad in the garden. I loved to use the push plow up and down the rows of potatoes, beans, tomatoes, onions, or whatever was in the garden. I don't think any

Shirley's mom, Gladys with her children

of the kids now days would know what a push plow is. We still have one and at the age of 75 ½, I still love to push it through the rows.

A memorable thing about my grandparents is they raised nine kids while farming. They sold hay, eggs, milk, cottage cheese, chickens, butter, and buttermilk in Fort Ashby. They went to Cumberland once a week. Granddad would carry milk up through Fort Ashby, West Virginia in a wire basket in each hand.

I can remember that the barn where Grandma milked the cows was spotless. It was concrete, and you could have eaten off the floor. The cows would be brought into the back. They did their business, and then Granddad let them in the barn. He had them well trained. Grandma would sing while milking the cows. She mostly sang all day long. It broke her heart when Granddad sold the farm to the Fort Ashby Fire Company and didn't tell her until after the fact. He sold it back in the 1960s for $20,000.00; it was a two story house, an apartment behind the house, a large barn, and I don't know how many acres. The apartment is still there.

Christmas time was the only time we got oranges. We could only have a cedar tree, but later on, we got live pine. At Christmas time, we only got one toy. My brother, Richard got a wooden tractor or trailer. He busted it up with a hammer and put it under the stove to hide it from Mom and Dad before they even got up on Christmas morning.

My brother could get by with anything. One time he pulled his sled across in front of me when I was sled riding. My one side of my face was scabbed up for days. He said I wrecked on my own. Mom believed him, of course. He laughed about it years later.

I loved Elvis. They wouldn't let him do much shaking on TV back then. Now you can do most anything. That's what makes me so mad.

Dead or Alive
By Charlotte A. Folk of Frostburg, Maryland
Born 1931

Many moons ago, when I was a child of about ten years old, I was walking with my mom on an old country dirt road in Garett County. It was one of those beautiful summer days when the sun was hot and a cool air was blowing. We were taking our time and enjoying the shade of the large trees along the road.

All of a sudden, Mom grabbed my hand and hollered, "Run, Charlotte, run!"

Mom had seen a snake in the road, so we went back the way we had come. The only problem was Mom was going so fast that I tripped and fell, and she dragged me through dirt and rocks. Both of my knees were raw. As she calmed my fears, she decided to go back and see if the snake was dead.

I was screaming and crying all the way back to the snake. It was a big old rattler. Its tail was straight up in the air, going back and forth, back and forth. Now the old wives tale or what we believed was that even though the rattlesnake was dead, his tail would still move until the sun went down. Never will I forget that day when the snake that was dead was still moving as if he was alive.

Today I am 83 years old and a wife, mother, grandmother, great-grandmother, and great-great-grandmother.

Christmas Gifts Both Good and Bad
By Alice Sipes Lease of Paw Paw, West Virginia
Born 1925

I was just a young girl during the 1930s living near Paw Paw, West Virginia with my family in a four-room house that was cold and drafty. It was Christmas morning, and I woke before anyone else. I crept expectantly to the small Christmas tree my mom had decorated a few days before and found a present with my name on it. I quickly opened it and found a new coloring book and crayons. I don't remember what I was expecting for Christmas or even if I expected anything, but I remember feeling very excited about the new crayons and coloring book. Shivering from the cold, I hurried back to my bed and snuggled under the covers to color a picture.

Another Christmas memory happened at school. We had exchanged names and brought our gifts to give. Most of the other children received some type of toy or candy, but I received a piece of fabric for a new dress. I remember my disappointment. Looking back,

I know the mother of that child who drew my name meant well. I needed the dress, but oh, how I wanted a toy at that moment!

Another school memory is walking to Camp Hill School from our house behind the Camp Hill Cemetery in Morgan County, West Virginia. The school was about a mile away and my older brother, Ernest and I had to walk through the cemetery. That was scary enough! We were also bullied by some mean boys in the area, which really frightened me. I was in the first grade at that time.

I also remember my mother putting old socks over our shoes whenever we had to walk through snow. We had no boots, so she did what she could to keep our feet a bit warmer. Later, the Camp Hill School burned, and then we just had to walk through the cemetery to meet the big yellow school bus, which took us into Paw Paw to the town school.

At the Paw Paw School, I remember being in a St. Patrick's Day play and wearing a crepe paper costume. I saved that costume for many years.

Sometimes the mothers would make homemade soup for the students. We would bring our own bowls and spoons that day. I don't know how they knew which bowl and spoon belonged to which student, but it was a good lunch compared to what we carried from home. In those days, no one was concerned about health department rules for kitchens. Mothers did it for their children.

The Goat Who Stayed for Dinner
By Don Stilwell of Princeton, West Virginia
Born 1930

From our front porch, we could see the carnies' house high on the hill, overlooking the road to our farm. However, to visit this unique family, we had to ride in the wagon about five times the distance as the crow flies. Their home was at the end of a dirt lane. My father and I visited about once a month to sit and talk, exchange stories and news, and watch their performing pets. In addition to their home, there were several barns, sheds, and fenced-in animal cages at the edge of the woods. Retired carnival people, the Flagherties still had their trained menagerie. They kept a small terrier-type dog, white with one black eye as well as black at the tip of its tail. The owners would tie a colorful collar around Dog's neck. Mrs. F. would play a few measures of dance music on an ancient piano, and Dog would stand on its hind legs and proceed to whirl and twirl about the yard. My dogs, Flossie and Boyd, were more intriguing and fun to watch than Dog, and I soon lost interest. Next to the barn, was a fenced-in pen imprisoning a fearsome brown bear who paced back and forth, growling, and snarling. Inside the cage was a strange looking bicycle, which Mrs. F. said the bear could ride. I never waited long enough to observe this feat. The cage and Bear smelled rank, and I had no reason to admire him, nor did I want to stand close to watch his frantic antics. Doves in the barn flew down to Mr. F.'s call and would proceed to roll and tumble through the grass before soaring into the trees to circle and return to their loft.

That particular day, as I drank the lemonade prepared by Mrs. F., I heard a new sound coming from the barn. At first, it sounded like a baby's cry. But it grew louder and more pitiful by the minute. The curiosity for a six year old is quite compelling, and I ventured past Bear, seeking the source of the cries. There in the cool shadows of the barn stood a large brown and gray mother goat. Standing behind her was a small, winsome kid, bleating for attention. When it saw me, Kid Goat waddled around Mama and came to me. I whispered to him and scratched his bony head. I quickly named him Billy and called for him to follow me to see my father.

Mr. F. told my dad that Kid Goat was seeking a new home. I heard these words and just knew his new home had to be with us. "Can he live with us? We have a lot of room. Can he go home with us, please?" My father and Mr. F. consulted for a few minutes, and soon we were back in our wagon heading for home with Billy ensconced precariously on my lap.

Billy lived with us for at least four years, growing taller and more adventuresome with every passing year. He was as curious as I was when he came to live on our farm. He frequently wandered off to explore the various buildings and animals on the dairy farm, often scaring the chickens and ducks. He would chase the newborn calves around the orchard or tease the cows before milking time. Once he even butted my father, who was leaning over picking tomatoes in the kitchen garden.

Unfortunately, the Great Depression was straining our family budget and resources, and my father, still upset by Billy's unruly behavior decided to sell him. I overheard the family discussion the night before the buyer was to appear. The next morning, I found a piece of rope, tied it around Billy's neck, and led him forth into the woods to save him. Needless to say, my father was angry at Billy's disappearing act (I am certain he learned it from his carnie mother) and at the loss of the potential buyer's money.

One evening the following winter, we had a rich stew for dinner with mashed potatoes, green beans, biscuits, and the most tender of meats. It wasn't long after that when I missed Billy. One evening, I found my father in the barn, scraping a large hide stretched over a frame for drying and tanning hides of rabbit, deer, and squirrel he hunted to feed our family. I knew without having to ask that Billy was the goat who came to our house and stayed to dinner.

Marlene Stevens in the 1950s

The Best Neighborhood in Frostburg
By Marlene Stevens Perkins of Frostburg, Maryland
Born 1947

Located on a quiet corner of Frostburg surrounded by woods on one side, the Frostburg State College on the other, and Braddock Park on the third sat a cluster of houses filled with kids. Every house had at least two children, usually several. Long before the college had expanded to its present size, children played ball there and explored the surrounding woods. Here is a typical day for these adventurous kids.

Early on a summer morning, about seven o'clock or so, the neighborhood kids would begin to stir. After jumping into clothes, shoes optional, and a quick breakfast, out they would go to the neighboring houses. No one knocked on the door but stood on the porch and gave a singsong, "Hey Mary and Martha!" at the top of their lungs.

Early morning was the best time to go into the woods to look for strawberries. We would run across the ball field, wade through the sewer creek that ran a strange foamy orange color and trudge through briars to the abandoned house foundation where wild pink roses and big fat juicy strawberries grew. We would pick our fill of the berries and then usually stop by the Braddock Stone.

Every child had been told the story of General Braddock, who during the French and Indian War marched with his men through the area and left the carved stone. We would not think of defacing it in any way. We would stand there and talk about the story of the stone. It is now located in the Frostburg Museum.

Our bellies full and our faces stained from the strawberry juice, we would often go up the side of the small mountain to slide down the slagheap that was high over our heads and great for sliding down. We would get covered in coal dust, but we didn't mind. Though the mine was open, we never went inside as we had been warned of the danger of getting lost in the mine.

On our way back, we would stop at a neighbor's small farm that we found fascinating. This neighbor boarded horses and kept pen after pen of rabbits. We always chose a favorite that we called the Easter Bunny. He also gave pony rides for half hour at 25 cents. What made it really fun was the neighbor did not want us there because our dogs, who were with us constantly, would scare the rabbits. So we had to quietly sneak into his yard to see the baby bunnies. He usually caught us and gave a yell. Laughing, we would run as fast as we could, thinking the faster we ran through the woods and back to our houses, he might not be able to identify us. Of course, since this happened at least once a week there was little doubt who it was. He never complained to our parents but kept up the game for as long as I lived there. Then it was lunchtime.

After lunch, we frequently had a game of softball. With so many kids in the neighborhood, it was easy to get enough kids for a game. The field was at the bottom of the yard of what is now called the Fuller House on the present college campus; then it was almost in my backyard. If we didn't do that, we might go to the Braddock Park and ride the merry-go-round. It was always best when the big boys came because they could make it go fast.

Twice a year, at the beginning and end of the summer season, they would have a party in the evening at the park. All the moms would make something sweet, and we would go for the evening to play bingo and dance to records. I learned how to do the dance the Stroll there. The evening would end with a kids' movie outside projected up onto the back of the pavilion. Usually popcorn was served. I really looked forward to those evenings.

Or after dinner on summer nights, we went to the ballpark to watch the boys' Little League play. We all had our favorite team and had a great time cheering for them. The night would close with a game of hide and go seek played until the streetlights came on. That was our time to go home. After a good night of sleep, we were ready for the next day to again explore our neighborhood.

Winters in Frostburg in the Fifties were fierce. Heavy snow and howling winds were common. Since most of us in the neighborhood walked to school, the schools were rarely closed. We would bundle up with boots, heavy scarfs, and thick coats and for the girls, thick pants under their skirts since pants were not allowed for girls in the elementary schools.

Winter was also great, because the city would close off College Avenue or Hill Street for a couple of hours one or two evenings after a snowstorm so the children could go sled riding. Both streets are really steep, and we would go flying down the snowy hill. Kids from all over town would come to sled ride. We would stay out until we were nearly frozen. When we returned home, we would stand over the floor register. The hot heat from the coal-fired furnace would warm us in no time.

One special event that happened to us is when Hurricane Hazel hit the eastern part of the United States. We got what we called the tail end of the hurricane. When it got so windy, we got big cardboard boxes and flattened them into big pieces of cardboard. We then stood in my side yard and held the cardboards up in the wind, which was so strong. The wind would pick up the cardboards and carry them up the hill to the next street called Bowery. We would run up the street, bring them back to my yard, hold them up again, and let them go. We had little competitions to see whose cardboard went the highest, farthest, or fastest. We did this for two days until the wind calmed down. I don't know how safe it was to be in wind like that, but we had a great time.

All of the events are true as I lived them in the mid-Fifties. I have changed any names or neglected to mention them because I do not have their permission to include them in this essay.

It's Not Just an Amish Thing
By Barbara Walker Welty of Bakerton, West Virginia
Born 1953

Jefferson County, West Virginia has long been known for its rich farmland. George Washington, father of our country and his brothers built several plantations here throughout the county. Rich, lush orchards full of sweet blossoms in spring, golden straw fields ripe for harvest, deep green hay fields waving in the breeze, herds of beef and dairy cattle grazing, horses of every breed found on farms for their hauling, pulling, and riding.

Anyone who has farmed or grew up farming knows the heart of the farm is the barn; it's the lifeline of the farm. Everything happens there, life, death, and money making. The spring cleaning of the barn and the spreading of the manure is the smell of money, crops it will feed to be harvested in a couple of months for the long winter to come. The land, soil, and animals come before anything else. They depend on you for everything almost. There are no holidays, no rain days, and no vacations; somebody has to be there for the stock's every need.

While a lot of farms are now housing developments and shopping centers, one farm on Job Corp Road is now the new Driswood Elementary School. Driswood Farm was owned and operated by Pete Walker and his family and named for his late wife. One cold winter evening all the cows had been milked, placed in their stalls till morning, and the lights turned out, and the family had settled in for whatever each's plans where that night when somebody noticed the lower part of the barn was on fire, smoke was rolling. Panic stricken as they were, Pete was told somebody called the fire company, and that's when things really got scary.

Pete entered the burning barn to save his girls; all 72 head were chained in their stalls. The flames had already blocked the normal exit the cattle used, and they had to be forced out the other end of the barn. Cattle are animals of habit and don't take change well, let alone when you add fear of fire, panicked people, screaming, and yelling. All the cows were out but one, and as Pete went to unchain her she backed up, penning his hand, and she was still chained. Somebody forced her up into the stall, and Pete freed her as the roof was dropping all round them, embers lighting anything that wasn't lit already.

By the time the barn was leveled to the ground, half the county had shown up to help in any way they could (this was long before internet was even thought of). Friends had brought pickups and cattle trailers, and each left that early morning with ten head. Pete's girls were farmed out and silence fell over the acreage. It looked like the farm was done for. Little did the Walker's know that from the ashes of the barn while still hot and smoldering for days, plans for a barn were rising like the phoenix from the ashes.

Within 30 days friends, family, and strangers helped with a new barn raising. Food to feed the workers came from every corner of the county, and finally the girls (cattle) were brought back home. On New Year's Eve, the Walkers were once again a farming family with milking going on. Unless you have a love of the land and understand truly how the silence on a farm is deafening, unnerving, and even eerie at times, these memories of Barbara Walker Welty would mean nothing, but to her and her family there's no words that can express what the community gave her and her beloved Dad (Pete) Walker back. Years later, she still can't thank each and every one enough for the love they were shown during the time of the fire.

A Special Note from the Writer

We had a current resurrection of community out pouring to help a member and friend in need just this week. The Boswell farm had been without water for over 30 days. This winter has been one for the books, with frozen ground and snow once a week. There was little chance of hand digging the 200 foot of line and replacing it. The little village of Bakerton got together and helped out by supplying man power and equipment. Now these type of things don't happen anymore like they once did, and when they do it's news and heartwarming to this writer. There is hope for this country we live in and our life style in the country, this County of Jefferson, and the state of West Virginia. Thank you for being good-hearted Christian people willing to lean a hand and get dirty. God bless you all.

Written by B. Bo Bolyard

No One Had Idle Hands
By Sandra Bailey of Baltimore, Maryland
Born 1942

My story begins in western Maryland. I was born in the town of Cumberland, Maryland and lived in Ellerslie, six miles outside of town. I was lucky enough to have both sets of grandparents, with whom I shared many fond memories. Being the first granddaughter on my father's side, I received

Sandy with her mom and dad

Sandy with her grandmother

a great deal of attention, as some of my aunts and uncles were still at home.

When I was approximately three years of age, my aunt was watching me at Granny's, just across the street from our house. She was returning me home and walked me to the front steps and then proceeded back across the road. I had a German shepherd dog, Laddy, and when my aunt was out of sight, I decided to take him and wander. When my mom discovered that I was missing, the family searched and searched, to no avail. News traveled and soon most residents of Ellerslie joined the search. I was found hours later, soaked to the bone with the exception of the hat on my head. When asked how I became wet, I replied, "Laddy helped me cross the stream." The team found me in Corriganville, a good distance from my home.

I grew up with my cousins and friends, sharing many great moments with them. One particular day stands out as our Granddad Miller would place us in a wheelbarrow and push it up the tram road. He would point out different plants, trees, and animals and explain a little about each. He was an engineer on the railroad, and sometimes when my aunt, cousins, and I would take him supper, we would ride back to the crossing on the train with him. It was very exciting for us.

I had the best of both worlds, as my mother's parents lived in Romney, West Virginia on a farm. My mom, brother, and I spent a great deal of time with them. They both taught us many things about farming and living with and off the land. My grandmother was an excellent cook; many tasty meals were shared. My grandfather showed us how to take care of the orchards, pruning and spraying the trees and tilling the ground around them. He also taught us how to butcher cows, pigs, squirrels, rabbits, and other animals. We would hunt for wild mushrooms to accompany the meats.

My mother and grandmother at harvest time would can fruits, vegetables, jams, etc. They would make apple butter in a copper kettle over an open wood fire. In the same kettle, they would deep fry pork rinds. They would also make homemade butter, cottage cheese, homemade breads, and pies, etc. No one had idle hands.

Sleigh riding in the winter on our Flexible Flyers or riding old Doss, the family workhorse in the summer made contentment for both children and parents. There were no televisions, computers, or cell phones, but here we are, survivors!

Old John and the Box Turtle
By John Edward (Eddie) Racey of Augusta,
West Virginia
Born 1950

When I was six years old, I hadn't started school yet. I never started until I was seven. I am the second of four boys. My dad never had an automobile and never drove a day in his life. He lived to be 86.

Dad and I would go to Romney, West Virginia to get things we needed. Since he couldn't drive, we would walk to my uncle's, which was about a mile and a half away. We would catch a ride with him to Romney, where he worked for West Virginia State Road. We would stay all day and ride home with my

Eddie Racey at age 7

uncle after work. While we were in Romney, we would go to the hardware store and to get groceries. At lunchtime, we would go to a little store owned by Jeff and Ethel Stickley, and get a pop and ice cream. Of course, they had penny candy, which was a real treat.

We lived in Kirby, West Virginia and I still do. I went to the Grassy Lick School, a three-room school with grades one through six. My first and second grade teacher was Mrs. Polly Billmeyer. My third and fourth grade teacher was Mrs. Rosa Wilson. My fifth and sixth grade teacher was Mr. Lincoln Cox, and he was also the principal of the school. He and his wife, Nellie, owned the grocery store, Cox's Store, which was also the post office. It was just down the road from the school. This building is still there. We bought groceries, gas, and kerosene there.

Another store across the road from the school was Roy Haines' store, where we could get homemade sandwiches. They were made by Mrs. Haines. We could get other groceries there, too; they even had salt fish. This building no longer remains.

The school is an old Medal Military Surplus building. It still remains and the community of Kirby turned it into a community center, the Grassy Lick-Kirby Community Center. We have reunions, holiday parties for the kids, and a fall festival to help support the center there.

At home, we got our water from a spring and carried it in buckets to the house. We had a pitcher pump in later years. Mom had an electric wringer washer and a clothesline. We had an outside toilet. We had no phone except we had a line to my grandmother, about two miles away and a wall phone, which I still have. When my mom was young, they had the community switchboard in their house where my grandmother lived.

In the 1950s, we had a company called the Bunny Bread Company. They delivered bread and cookies. They came to our house once a week. We had a cow. We sold cream to a creamery in Romney. They came to the house to pick up the cream.

My older brother got a car in 1966. It was a '51 Chevy; now we had a way to go places.

We never had a television until 1969, which was the year I graduated from high school. My parents didn't get a phone until 1975, which was the year I got married to Melinda Timbrook, who lived across the hill from us.

I walked about a fourth of a mile to meet the school bus in the winter. I remember the snow banks were so high I couldn't see out the windows of the bus. If the bus met someone, they would have to back up to a wide place. We lived on a dirt road, so if we saw a car or truck in two or three days we were lucky.

We butchered two hogs every fall and cured the hams. We would sell one to get a roll or cheese or sometimes maybe a roll of bologna.

Since Dad didn't have a tractor, we had a workhorse we used to pull out trees for pulpwood. That is what Dad did for a living. We also used the horse to cut hay, plow our fields, and rack the hay. We did about everything with the horse.

When I was seven, we had this workhorse

Blanch and Old John

called Old John. We had a homemade wooden sled that had runners made from young hickory trees about eight feet long. We laid boards on it to haul our potatoes from the patch and rocks. We used it to butcher the hogs. We put a 50-gallon barrel chained to the end so we could scald the hogs and then put clean boards on to cut them up.

Just a little story, one time I was riding the sled without the board, sitting on a cross piece of the sled and Dad was walking. We were about to go across the bridge over the creek when Old John saw this box turtle on the bridge. He got excited and turned the sled and me around. I fell down through the sled, and I still had ahold of the reins. Across the hay field we went. My dad was screaming, "Let go of the reins!" About a hundred feet down the field, I finally did. I never got hurt, just shook up.

Memories of Riverton
By Sandra D. Butcher of Broadway, Virginia
Born 1938

My remembering of Riverton, West Virginia was my beginning. My grandmother was the daughter of John and Ellen Warner. She lived in that house until someone came and set it on fire, not caring it was a big part of the lives in history of the area during the War Between the States of 1864. My great-great-grandmother was Phobee Warner and my great-grandfather was Zebebee Warner.

Pack Warner was a teacher at the one room school. We attended the Solman's Chapel Church, which is still in use. The church is located on Route 33. There was a one-room school there. It had two outhouses, one for men, and one for women. They are still standing. The school itself was moved to be used as a home. On a part of the land, there was a cemetery where both soldiers and Indians were buried. They used stones to mark where the graves were. None of these had names on them.

Yes, there was castor oil as a daily medicine for different things we do daily.

I remember my great-aunt had a wooden washer and a wringer. Also, there were outhouses, and chambers were used at nighttime.

As for cattle and other farm animals, we had cows for the milk we drank. We had chickens for the eggs, which we used for cooking and eating.

We had hand cranked wall phones. Saturday night baths were in washtubs.

Growing Up the Mountain Lake Park Way
By Sidney Ray Nazelrod of Oakland, Maryland
Born 1957

Being born in 1957, I was one of the WWII baby boomers. The town I grew up in, Mountain Lake Park was a recreation town in the late 1800s up until the First World War. At the time of this story, the area was residential and the reminders of The Mt. Lake Hotel and various boarding houses were in a state of decay. Sadly today most are a faded memory just as the adventure that I am about to tell you.

My parents, Paul & Joyce Nazelrod, met during WWII while my father was in the Civilian Conservation Corps. My only sibling was my brother, Paul Jr., who was born in 1944. I feel I was a surprise to all when I was born, especially brother Paul. My father eventually, after his time with the C.C.C., settled in at a very good job for a company called DeLaval, which was for milker equipment. Dad was a traveling salesman for the whole Eastern Coast of the United States, which meant he was away from home most weekdays. He left early Monday and returned late Friday. While this proved to be a good financial move for our family, it left my mother to be what was known as a "Sales Widow" and my older brother Paul was to be the "Man of the House" in Dad's absence.

In the early 1960s era everyone knew everyone. My brother Paul was known by friends and family as Sonny. To me he was "Big Brother." Big Brother was more like a young father to me than an older brother.

Big Brother had a group of friends his age that put some folks in the mind of the "Our Gang Comedy." Big Brother made special time for me throughout the 1960s.

This one very special event comes to mind. While I was small then, he and I talked about

Sidney Ray Nazelrod in 1962

it many times over the years. It was 1962 in the early spring and Big Brother had a day off from school. I was only five then, and we decided to go fishing. Big Brother asked most of the gang if they wanted to come, but all seemed to have plans. While my mother really didn't care much for the idea, Big Brother and I were heading for another adventure.

We finished lunch, got a couple of fishing poles and Dad's tackle box, and then headed for Mountain Lake. This was a manmade lake of about 25 acres, which was a big attraction during the Victorian Era. While the lake was only about 10 blocks away, it seemed like 50 miles to this 5 year old. While exciting it was also scary. Mt. Lake just had a new highway go through the middle of the town, which caused concern because of the increased traffic. Big Brother was careful, sticking mostly to side streets where a lot of the neighbors would yell "Hi, Sonny." Some even came to the curb to chat and find out about this younger Nazelrod. Being shy, I'd say "Hi" and mainly wait impatiently while dreaming of catching the "Big One."

About a third of the way there was Martin's Store. It was also known as C.P. Martin & Sons. It was a second generation general store, an old two story boarding house where the bottom floor had been opened up for a storefront. You could buy a beefsteak or a gallon of paint with much in between. Britten Martin was the owner at this time and while some kids liked him, others didn't. Mr. Martin was a no nonsense man. Yet I liked him and he liked the Nazelrod boys. He had a group of employees as colorful as the rainbow: some family, others long time employees that had been there, and a couple that were there even after Mr. Martin's passing.

That day Mr. Martin spied our fishing gear and asked how many we were going to catch. Big Brother and I enjoyed one of those wonderful 5-cent Coke Crass sodas. I had a cherry and Big Brother had a lemon-lime. We talked about the Pirates baseball team, Big Brother's graduation, and future employment plans. That day Mr. Martin told Big Brother, he had a job there if he ever wanted it and yes after graduation Big Brother started working there.

The old wooden floors of Martin's store and the different smells gave it a charm of its own. It was dimly lit with a couple of yellowed hanging light bulbs and what light the few windows let in. Most of the meats sold there came from local farms, while the canned and dry goods came by railway. The goods were picked up in Mr. Martin's 1940s Chevy pickup, also used for the delivery of groceries from the store. All patrons had to do was call the store by 11 a.m. and your order would be delivered that same day.

After finishing our soda and the free Tootsie roll Mr. Martin gave us, we marched on. Heading and hoping for that big catch. We came to the Mt. Lake Hotel. It was one big awesome building with a large open porch and many rocking chairs. We sat and rested in a rocking chair, enjoying the shade of the porch and the large oak and maple trees that surrounded it. The old Hotel was in declining condition. Even the neon sign, when lit, read "Mt. Lake otel." The H was burned out.

After resting a bit, we headed for the lake as excited as I could be. A trout run stream and a large fresh water spring called "Crystal Spring" fed the lake. We stopped at Crystal Spring where out of a large stonewall there was a pipe we could get cold water to drink. Big Brother and I headed for the banks of the lake where he helped me bait my hook and cast it into the water so I could catch my Big One. In its heyday, this lake was used for paddleboats, swimming, and of course fishing. Probably ice skating in the winter too. In the wintertime, ice would be cut off the lake to be used at local hotels and on the dining cars of the B & O Railroad during the summer. They stored the ice in structures at the lake in layers with sawdust. We could see the outline where it once stood.

The frogs, lizards, and dragonflies were out in full force. The lake in spots was loaded with lily pads so there were a lot of places for the fish to hide. We carefully fished, getting nibbles but not one catch. Being a typical 5 year old, the "When" and "Why" questions started at a steady flow. Big Brother was good with the answers and both were having fun as we worked our way around the lake. As it started to get late in the afternoon Big Brother said we should head home. Being disappointed about not catching one fish, I wasn't happy about leaving. Big Brother suggested we go back fishing our way home on trout run. In the past, seeing some of the local kids doing that, it would make the feeling of failure not as bad in my heart.

About a third of the way fishing here and there was Parson's Esso Service Station. We walked to it and Big Brother suggested we split a Grape Crush soda. This was one of a very few places that sold Crush Products but it was oh so good. Near the station was a bridge that many fished off. This would be our final chance to catch something. Since the new highway came along, this was a side road and no longer the main thoroughfare. After just a short while our neighbor Mr. Everett "EB" Bray stopped and said, "You boys want a ride home?" Mr. Bray worked for the B & O Railroad and had stopped at Parson's to fill up. Mr. Bray drove a 1957 dark green Chevy pickup. He said throw your poles in the back and hop in. Big Brother said we would just ride in the back. Being disappointed yet tired I was glad for the ride. Mr. Bray said his standard "okey dokey" and we were off.

As we sped home, the cool breeze felt so good. We saw some of Big Brother's friends who yelled and waved at us. Also, the neighbors, the Johnston's, Ken, & Hazel Martin out in their yards all waved. Even old grumpy mechanic Ray Kight waved and smiled. I felt like we were in a parade float and then we were home across the street from our house. We thanked Mr. Bray for the ride. He said "Sonny, Sid Ray (that is what my name was most of my youth-I hated it then but yearn to hear it now), Mrs. is baking tonight about 8:30. We will have fresh rolls and lemon cake and you are welcome. Just come on over and you don't have to knock, just walk in." I loved to knock at the Bray's because they had a wooden homemade woodpecker doorknocker. We told him we would if Mom said it was ok.

We first placed our fishing poles and tackle box back in the garage where they were kept so there would be no problems with Dad.

As we walked in the front door, the smell of Mom's pot roast filled the air. Yum Yum! Mom asked, "Well where is that Big One?" Big Brother said it was still in the lake. I was so disappointed, feeling like a failure. I looked up and it was 4:55 p.m. Oh boy! Time for my favorite T.V. program: Paul Shannon's Adventure Time on WTAE Channel 4 Pittsburgh. Adventure Time was a children's program featuring comic skits, jokes, and music with an audience from all over the Pittsburgh viewing area, but my favorite feature I loved the best was the Three Stooge's short subject films.

This day Big Brother and I watched them together and laughed at the mayhem. This helped heal the hurt of our fishing failure.

It has been 52 years since that day and a lot has transpired. The Mt. Lake that we fished in was drained over 25 years ago for fear of lawsuits. Crystal Spring is so overgrown with brush and weeds it is almost impossible to find. Parson's Esso is gone and the side road leading to it is closed, with the bridge we fished from removed. The Mt. Lake Park Hotel was closed, the furniture auctioned off (I now have two of those rockers. Maybe they are the ones Big Brother and I rested on). The Hotel was razed and now a modern church stands in its place. Martin's Store is gone and in its place is a beverage store, the building remodeled and looking nothing like the original store.

Mr. Martin, Mr. Bray, and most of the people we waved or spoke to that day have passed away along with Paul Shannon and his Adventure Time show.

Mom and Dad both quietly left us. Most recently, the one who I shared this experience with not only that day but many times since, Big Brother, passed leaving me with many good memories. I am now the last one in my family.

To those reading this please don't feel sad because at about the same time as

Big Brother's passing our granddaughter announced that she will have a baby girl in August. While still missing Big Brother, my mind jumps five years in the future when a bright 5 year old will have the "What" and "Why" questions flowing. I will say to that 5 year old, "Let's get my dad's tackle box and those poles and let's head for the pond on our property," where we now live. Then we will start another adventure time generation with new memories.

Homemade Lamps, Chamber Pots, and Optometry School
By James A. Poland of Frostburg, Maryland
Born 1933

My name is James Poland, and I am 81 years old; I go by Jim. I have been an optometrist for over 50 years, and I just retired in June 2013. I have one brother who is two years younger; his name is Francis Poland, and he goes by Bud. We were born in 1933 and 1935 respectfully. As I said to him, I think that this was made for people of our age, because I can relate to virtually every one of those topics listed. We were born and raised in a coal-mining town in western Maryland called Woodland of about 100 people, at most. It is close to Frostburg and Cumberland, Maryland. As far as my brother and me, we were raised by two hard working and loving parents. My father and both grandfathers were coal miners. My one grandfather was a blacksmith, so he shod all the horses and mules that went underground on the little track, and the other grandfather was in a different mine, six miles away, he was kind of a supervisor. My father was one of the miners who went all the way back a couple of miles underground to dig coal and dump it in the little wagons that came out of a small track. We lived in a five-room house, three down and two up, and we had no central heat, just a potbelly stove that would burn wood or coal. The heat that would come upstairs to our bedrooms was just by a vent in the floor.

We had an outhouse, and the only running water we had, was in the kitchen sink. We did have outhouses and chamber pots. In fact, I have two chamber pots in my basement right now that I brought from my parents and grandparents' homes. They are still in very good shape. My Grandmother Poland died in 1984 at age 96. She would not call them chamber pots or pee pots or slop jars. She insisted on calling them piss pots.

The outhouse carries a tale that I am told is true. There were two guys walking along and one said he had to go in the outhouse so he did. The other waited outside. After a long wait, the one outside wanted to see what was taking so long, so he opened the door and there was the first man with a stick, and he was digging down in the outhouse. He told his friend that he had dropped his coat into the hole and he was trying to get it out. The other man said, "Well, surely you're not going to wear that coat now." He said, "I'm not going to wear my coat, but my lunch is in the pocket."

We had one of those old Philco round top, table model radios. When the war was on in the early '40s, my grandfather would come over and my father and he would sit beside the radio listening to Gabriel Heatter. He would tell of all the ships that were sunk and all the planes that were shot down, and my father and grandfather seemed to be running a race about cursing the Germans and the Japanese for being in the war against us. I learned to curse just like them.

We did have a party phone line. I brought it in the house when I first got a job. I think there were seven parties on the party line, and it caused a lot of problems. You knew that when you were talking to someone you could hear someone breathing that was listening from the house next door or down the street a little bit. There would always be somebody listening in. A lot of people would take a long time and after they took such a long time, the person listening would start cursing and telling them to get the hell off the phone.

I still have a wind up record player sitting in my dining room right now. It looks very nice; the wood is still in brand new shape.

There was such a thing as spankings in school and usually the parents would side with the teacher. We had a two-room school for six grades. Each one of the rooms had a potbelly stove. Ms. Riley taught the first three grades in one room and Ms. Manley taught fourth, fifth, and sixth in the other room and by the way, we had outhouses there, too. When I was in the third or fourth grade, the Board of Education moved us to a little bigger town a few miles away, and the school bus picked us up and they did have first through sixth grade. The principal/sixth grade teacher would ride the bus because it was convenient for her. My father didn't like the schools being taken away from our little town, and he used to go in and curse a little bit at the schoolteacher.

When we were young, of course, we had to wash up during the week, but on Saturday night our grandfather across the alley had a bathtub, so we went over there with our clean clothes and took a bath. When I was probably eight, nine, or ten years old, my father closed in the side porch and put in a bathtub and commode so we thought we were doing pretty well then.

I remember the wringer washer. As the story goes, the preacher was walking down the street and saw a little boy who was just learning how to curse. He was shouting every curse word that he could. The preacher scolded him and said when you curse like that it gives me cold chills up and down my back. The boy said, "If you'd have been in our house when my mother got her tit caught in the wringer washer, you would have froze to death."

My grandfather bought the first television in our little town of Woodland. We used to go, especially on Saturday night, and watch a show called *The Hit Parade*. It was an hour program and all these singers would sing a certain favorite song of theirs, so it was interesting and entertaining.

Yes, we had homemade clothes and toys. In fact, about everything in our houses was homemade. I remember one time my mother wanted a floor lamp and my father said, "Okay, I will make one." It is sitting down in my basement now. He brought home a pole from the coalmines made out of ash, he made a base out of a big piece of wood, run the wire up, and found a lampshade somewhere, and that was our homemade floor lamp. He made a lot of things, all the chairs and stands and things.

My father had a 1931 Chevrolet coup. It was black and dark red with a rumble seat. That was great to get a ride back there. Two or three people could sit in it. Of course, there were no seat belts, but it was a big thrill. My father would not let me drive his car even though he taught me in it. I think he felt he couldn't afford to fix it if I wrecked it; but my grandfather did let me drive his. The cows were left out to graze and you never knew where they would go, and when I got home from school, I would take my grandfather's car, go around to all the favorite finding places, and chase the cows back home. We did have to milk the cows, which was interesting and fun sometimes.

Bud and Jim

Our parents and grandparents went to town every Thursday. Town was Frostburg; it was maybe five miles away. They would not go in the same car; they would go separately. I remember I went with my grandfather a lot. He would give me a dime every time they went to town, and he and my grandmother would put everything they bought on the kitchen table and check it off to see that they weren't cheated at the store. Every item had to match.

We live in a snow belt here. I remember a picture of my brother. He was standing on a very deep snow. So deep that he was standing next to a telephone pole, and if he wanted to, he could reach up and touch the wires.

I do remember Elvis. He would be just about my age. In fact, we were at Las Vegas one time and he was in the audience of a show, and when we walked out to the lobby, he was right at my elbow. Of course, he had some bodyguards around him, but I could have touched him.

My brother and I both played baseball, basketball, and soccer. In fact, I expected to be playing center field for the Pittsburgh Pirates. The coach at the high school that we went to was named Ebby Finzel. He became like a father to me, and he taught all three sports that I played. I learned a lot from him, and he was a role model for me.

My grandfather had two cows and three pigs, and my father had about 30 chickens. I remember when my mother said she wanted a chicken dinner, he would go grab a chicken and lay its head down on the block and take a hatchet and whack it off. He would throw the chicken's body over in the grass and it would flop around until it stopped and then he would hang it on the clothesline for an hour or two until it bled out. He would take it in, and my mother would take off all the feathers at the kitchen sink while he was pouring the teakettle of very hot water over it.

We used to run around with girls to see what they were made of. We used to play a game called spin the bottle. Whoever spun it had to kiss the person that the neck of the bottle pointed to. I did marry my high school sweetheart, Judy. We've been married 58 years now. We have three children, Jeff, Jay, and Joni. The combined total of grandchildren is six. Each one of the kids had two children.

I got a job during high school and then after with an optometrist by the name of Dr. Walter Jeffries who became a mentor to me. He would teach me how to cut lenses and insert them into frames and things like that. At that time, I had no interest in going to college, but I worked for Dr. Jeffries for two years. When the Korean War started, I was in the reserve so I requested active duty. I was on board a ship out of Norfolk, and I went to optical man school since I had experience in optical things. I was put into an optical shop on ship. Our shop repaired binoculars and telescopes. The big ships would come in and bring their binoculars and we had to fix them. We would go over on the aircraft carriers and repair their gun sights for all the big guns they had. I decided to go to optometry school, so I started to college in Frostburg. I had pre-optometry courses. Judy and I got married and moved to Chicago while I went to optometry school. She got a full-time job, and I got a part-time job while I went to school. Jeffery was born a few months before I graduated. We came back to Frostburg, and I went into practice with Dr. Jeffries until he passed away, and then years later my son went to optometry school, and he came into practice with me.

Yes, those were the good old days!

Van Camp: Lost and Found
By Jack W. Furbee of Bourbonnais, Illinois

Many settlers came to the Ohio Valley traveling through the roughness of western Pennsylvania to Fort Pitt. They then went south via the Ohio River to claim their land grants, often surveyed from the river east into the hills of Virginia.

One such settlement had its origin with the first generation: Steven (1763-1829) and Rachael (1770- 1855) Van Camp, having settled temporarily in Lancaster, Pennsylvania. Shortly after their marriage in 1792, hearing of land opportunities along the Ohio River, they obtained rights to one thousand acres of land. It was about two miles south of Fishing Creek where there was a settlement later to be called Martinsville in 1838, named after its founder Presley Martin.

Approximately one hundred and forty years later a part of the original Van Camp claim was my ancestral birthplace and home from 1934 to 1958. During this time, I attentively listened to my elders who had been born and reared on Van Camp property. From Steven and Rachael Van Camp I was the sixth generation of Van Camps and one of the last to grow up in Pleasant Valley along Point Pleasant Creek. It was so named from the Van Camps' attraction, love, and appreciation for the area.

As with most pioneers, Van Camp families were large beginning with the eleven children of Steven and Rachael. Within a few generations, scores of Van Camp families populated Pleasant Valley resulting in the community, Van Camp. The original Van Camp claim was divided among members of the large families; some acreage was deeded to other settler families through payment for work such as clearing land. One of the many second generation Van Camps was John Squire (1793-1873), my great great grandfather who married Margaret Martin from Tyler County. They developed a large homestead along Point Pleasant Creek including many barns for raising sheep. John Squire's many siblings received acreages of land deeded from the original Steven and Rachael claim.

Although part of Virginia, a southern state, several Van Camp cousins of the third generations from Steven and Rachael became Civil War soldiers in the Grand Army of the Republic enlisting through Wheeling, Virginia, one of the largest cities in northwestern Virginia. John Marshall (1837-1919), grandson of the original Van Camp in the area as well as my maternal great grandfather, enlisted in the Union Army September 8, 1862. He fought in the Gettysburg campaign. Near Casinova, Virginia, he was seriously wounded and hospitalized. On May 3, 1865, he mustered out at York, Pennsylvania. John and his wife Margaret Ann Martin Van Camp (1849-1927) raised a large family on the original Van Camp homestead of whom my maternal grandmother was one.

Resting in the Van Camp Cemetery are four Civil War veterans with two having been wounded and one imprisoned. One of the soldiers died shortly after the war. Each of these young men entered the service from the Old Dominion State, Virginia. They returned as veterans to a new state, West Virginia, formed by President Lincoln on June 20, 1863. My ancestral connection to Van Camp inspired me to apply for Civil War veteran markers for the graves of these valiant patriots who left their small community of Van Camp to serve in a great and noble cause. As of this writing, I have erected two markers on the graves of the soldiers, one having been wounded and the other having been both wounded and imprisoned. It is my honor to continue my labor of love until all four graves have been marked by beautiful granite military monuments.

In 1998, I began my research to rediscover the Van Camp community since current residents seemed unaware that such a place existed. Maps no longer listed the community. Stopping at scores of modern homes built on Van Camp farmland, I asked the owners if they knew of Van Camp: the post office, store, church, and school. Disappointed at the negative response except for the cemetery, I began my unmitigated effort to find Van Camp again.

On July 28, 2001, a faithful Van Camp group gathered in Pleasant Valley on the banks of Point Pleasant Creek just below the cemetery and church location along present day Route 180. After extensive research on my part, the State of West Virginia had erected one of their spectacularly beautiful historical markers. Upon removing the temporary covering, we stood in awe. Van Camp was back! After a short dedication ceremony, we spent time in the cemetery overlooking modern homes where once a post office, store, church, and school had served a successful pioneer community. We could almost hear the cheers of our forbearers as we entered our cars to return to our homes in various parts of the country. Van Camp was lost but now it is found.

A Civil War Story: John Marshall Van Camp stepped cautiously along the ice covered Fouch Run, Point Pleasant Creek, and finally Paden Fork Creek. Having fought in the Civil War during severe winters when he built roads and bridges for the Union Army in eastern Virginia, his winter walk of one half mile was somewhat reminiscent of military life. Passing the Van Camp Methodist Episcopal Church on a knoll above Point Pleasant, he recalled that recently an extended religious meeting was cancelled due to high water and ice. He walked slowly and steadily on the precarious ice surrounded on one side by wooded hills and on the other by meadows where he and his boys cradled wheat only months before. Soon the Van Camp Post Office appeared above the confluence of Point Pleasant and Paden Fork Creeks. Following buggy and wagon tracks, he climbed the icy creek bank to enter the post office.

"Good morning, John. How can I help you this cold morning?" asked Josie, the elderly postal lady. She had managed the Van Camp Post Office for decades prior to the Civil War. It was one of about ten post offices in Wetzel County, Virginia. Knowing each patron's incoming and outgoing mail, she was aware of what John wanted. It was time for his regular military benefits, both pension and disability. While Josie found his mail, he chatted with several Van Camp friends sitting near a "potbellied" stove in the Van Camp store, part of the post office. One Civil War veteran from among his farmer friends spoke up after releasing his tobacco juice into the stove, "Did Uncle Sam pay you today, John? He doesn't give us much, but he's on time."

Intent on getting home John thanked Josie for getting his mail, bade his friends a "good day," and followed the icy path back home. Eager to get home where he would open his mail, the deserving Civil War veteran looked at the envelopes he had just received from Josie. Limited in his reading and writing abilities, John recognized the handwriting of Lavina, his sister-in-law. As usual, she addressed her frequent letters to "Van Camp, Virginia." Proud of his new state, West Virginia, John planted one foot on the bank and one on the slippery ice questioning the address as he thought, "Virginia? This is not Virginia anymore!" He felt a sense of reverence and patriotism stirring within him as he honored both his old and new state.

Van Camp, Virginia, an early nineteenth century Appalachian community having a post office, store, school, and church, gave many of her sons to the Civil War effort from 1860-1865, one being my great grandfather, John Marshall Van Camp 1837-1919. Along with him, several of his Van Camp cousins enlisted in Wheeling, Virginia. Two were wounded and one was imprisoned. One contracted a disease and died soon after the war. All were buried in the small Van Camp Cemetery on Route 180 between Paden City and New Martinsville, West Virginia.

In the winter of 1876, John Marshall and his wife Margaret Ann sat by their fireplace in the ancestral Van Camp home, grateful that John returned from Civil War service. Wounded and still healing, he spoke quietly to his wife, "Maggie, did you notice the letter from your sister was addressed to Van Camp, Virginia? Does she remember that our address has changed?"

By the light of the fireplace, they read the carefully scripted address on the envelope together, affirming the Virginia address. Margaret endeavored to explain her sister's error. "Homesick for Virginia, Lavina forgot our new address. We were part of Virginia from the beginning of our country. Actually, I miss our old state. When you were away in the army, our dear President Lincoln recommended a new state, West Virginia. We have had our new address since June 20, 1863. Our post office is now Van Camp, West Virginia."

To make her point even clearer Margaret continued, "Have you ever considered that our youngest children were born in Van Camp, Virginia?" John Marshall looked deeply into the blazing fire remembering the birth of three children while he was a soldier in eastern Virginia. "They were Virginians for a while. Now they are West Virginians," she affirmed proudly. As John thought further, he realized that he enlisted from his revered home state, Virginia, in 1861; he was discharged in a new state, West Virginia, in 1865.

The winter evening had grown cold; the log house needed someone in continual attention to keeping the fireplace burning. Sam, the eldest, brought more logs and laid them on the fire. It was time for bed, but the Civil War veteran and his wife sat more closely beside the fire to reminisce. Their lives had been changed by the War Between the States.

"John, do you remember when we decided to name our fifth child? You had returned from the army hospital in Casanova, Virginia. Still suffering from your injury, you held our new daughter saying, I know what her name will be!"

Leaning back in his chair by the fire while enjoying his well-seasoned corncob pipe, the proud soldier said, "Maggie, no doubt the army nurses and doctors saved my life in the Casanova military hospital. The head injury was nearly fatal leaving me incapacitated for weeks."

A little girl played at their feet near the fireplace when her mother, Margaret, said, "Sweet heart, come to Mama." As she held her daughter, she reminded John of how Arma's name was chosen from John's Civil War experience.

"Arma was chosen because you loved your country, left beloved Van Camp, and fought for the Grand Army of the Republic. The middle name, Casanova, was chosen because you believed the doctors and nurses in the military hospital saved your life," the proud wife and mother recalled.

The aroma of combined tobacco and wood smoke added warmth to this unique Civil War story. John sat quietly by the fire while Margaret held Arma Casanova more tightly in her arms. "Maggie, do you think Lavina will get our West Virginia address correct in her next letter?" John inquired, leaning closer to the fire.

"John, Lavina loves the state of her birth. It will take a while for her to recognize her new state, West Virginia," Margaret replied.

Nearly one hundred thirty-five years later to preserve the Van Camp story, it was my privilege to apply to the state of West Virginia for a state historical marker, which now stands along Route 180 at the center of the community. The resting places of the Van Camp Civil War veterans are marked in the cemetery by military markers which I researched and erected, a labor of love. I consider myself fortunate to have lived my first twenty years in this pioneer community, my maternal grandmother being a Van Camp, daughter of John Marshall.

After raising a large family of eleven, on May 21, 1893, John Marshall Van Camp and Margaret Ann Martin Van Camp decided to name their twelfth and last child Martin Presley Van Camp after Presley Martin, founder of Martinsville, now New Martinsville, West Virginia, as of 1871.

A Lifetime of Work at Millstone
By Robert C. Moats of Aurora, West Virginia
Born 1940

I did not know they made any kind of car but a Ford 'til I was nine, and then I realized the garage above us sold Dodges. They quit making Studebakers around the '50s, then the price went sky high because everybody wanted an old Studebaker to sit in the back and that was about all they did.

In the late 1940s there was a family called the Stemples that lived at the top of Cheat Mountain. When they would find out that my dad didn't have work we'd walk to Cheat Mountain and walk up their road and mow the road bank. It always took two trips to do the road. We would mow with scythes, rake it up with a pitchfork, and throw it over the hill. Sometimes they wanted trees cut so we had to bring an ax. One time I helped Fred Stemple get stones and dump them in the holes and soft spots in the road because they didn't want mud on their vehicles.

That was the first house I saw with a refrigerator. The motor was on top. The entire refrigerator was six foot tall including the motor and maybe three feet wide. There was a tiny icebox in the middle. I always brought a jug of water when we worked on the road and I thought that was wonderful that I'd get three ice cubes in a quart of water.

One summer I remember a strange weed that we had never seen before began growing in our potato patch. We begin pulling them out but they kept growing back. We decided to feed it to the hogs but it made the hogs crazy. We decided to feed it to the cows but it made the cows dry, or stop giving milk. My dad decided we would pile it up at the end of the field and when it dried we would burn it. The day came for us to burn a pile of it and those weeds made a blue smoke that lingered for a couple of hours. The next time we begin burning some of it Fred Stemple's nephew came to our farm and told us that we couldn't burn those weeds because the smoke was going to his dad's farm. We explained to him that we couldn't feed it to the cows or the hogs and there wasn't anything else to do with it. He tried to explain to us that the weeds were a plant called marijuana that people in the city smoked to get high. We told him that he was crazy, that people smoked tobacco. Finally, he got us convinced that the marijuana was a drug and we couldn't burn it. We took it way out in the woods and dumped it. As best we could figure the marijuana came in the fertilizer we had bought that year.

When I was 10 years old I started working at a truck stop named Mill Stone on Route 50 in Aurora, WV. The restaurant was originally an army barracks with 5 cabins. The owner of the truck stop's husband had died and they needed someone to pump gas in the summer. I started with fixing their white fence. When I was 12 or 13 years old I started feeding their cattle. Eventually, I pumped gas, mowed the grass with a push mower, fed the cattle, and helped serve in the restaurant. When there was a blocked up blizzard I had to walk to the truck stop on the top of the fence posts.

I remember they couldn't decide what to name the restaurant. They decided on Mill Stone because Casey, the owner of the truck stop, got two millstones, I believe, from the old mill in Brookside, WV. First they put down old electric poles. Then Casey got everyone who would listen to him to come help him set these two big millstones on top of the electric

Robert's father, Ward Moats with a girl who worked in the kitchen at the Millstone

poles. They brought them to the restaurant on a wagon. They had to pull the stones off the wagon with chains. The stones must have weighed 10-12 tons. First they blocked it up then they stuck a pole through the middle of the millstone. When they tried to lift the stone the pole broke and one guy didn't let go of the pole and was lifted eight feet off the ground. My brother Elmer was lying in the field laughing at the guy "lying in the air." Finally they talked Casey into setting the stone against the pole but 3 grown men couldn't stand the stone on its end. They had to dig a hole under the stone. Elmer and I finally got tired or it was dark so we went home. When we got back from school the next day they had finally gotten the stone into place, but I don't know how they got the second stone set.

The owner of the truck stop, Casey, bought Mr. Lipscomb a wrecker so he could tow the trucks (18 wheelers) up the hill (Cheat Mountain) during winter. Lipscomb would pull them down and up the hill. The parking lot at the truck stop would be so full that a vehicle couldn't get to the pumps. They would be parked 3 deep. I would tell the truck drivers to park in a line starting with who's going to leave first so there was enough parking space.

There were 12 motel rooms. Most trucks had two guys to a truck. There would be 5-6 guys in one room. They would put the mattress on the floor and they would sleep on the springs and the mattress. When too many truck drivers came in we would tell them we didn't have any more room and they would say, "There's got to be room for me." They would go knock on the back glass and see which room had the least people and he would go in that room. They all worked for different companies but they all knew each other.

There was one girl that worked in the restaurant. She would make buckwheat cakes and sausage for breakfast and there would be four to five cakes on a plate. They hardly ever had pancakes. Sometimes they would be started serving before I got there at 7am.

When the guys would come in for breakfast there would be at least 5 guys that came in at once. I would have to take out ten to twelve plates at a time because when I came out of the kitchen there would be ten more guys coming out of the rooms. When I would carry the plates out of the kitchen I would ask "Who's turn is it?" and ten hands would go up, whoever hadn't had breakfast. This would go on 'til practically noon. The place would be so full there wouldn't be practically no room for anyone to come in and sit down. I had to do the dishes because there was only twenty or thirty plates that didn't have a seam in them

Robert Moats

and you couldn't serve buckwheat cakes on a plate with a seam because the cakes wouldn't come off the plate.

At the same time I was doing this I had to pump gas. Now when I came in from pumping gas I had to wash my hands in the men's room and then wash them in the kitchen so the girl who worked in the kitchen could see me wash.

Once breakfast got under control the Greyhound bus came. It was supposed to stop for five to seven minutes but it was already a half an hour late so everyone on the bus would come in to have lunch. And guess what they would have? Buckwheat cakes. Everyone who walked in the door would smell them and had to have them. When the Greyhound bus would finally get out the truck drivers would come back for lunch.

The old restaurant had a holding tank just for the wash water from the kitchen. It would get stopped up or greased up. It would take two people to move the lid with crow bars. Then you had to take a bucket to dip the grease out of it. We would dip out seven to eight gallons of pure grease. Once the can was filled it would take two men to load the garbage can. The owner's brother, Melvin, would help my dad move the lid and I got to dip the grease out. When I was finished I would set garbage cans around the opening and they would put the lid back on it in the morning. Then I had to scrub the garbage can out with water. We called it the grease pit.

In the early seventies the restaurant closed because Route 38 was finished and it took the traffic off of Route 50. The restaurant was torn down and the motel was changed to living quarters. The 12 motel rooms are now rented as 5 apartments.

I worked there until I moved to New Jersey. When I moved back I became the maintenance man and I still work there as the maintenance man.

That Life Prepared Me for the Future
By Jessie Snyder of Hagerstown, Maryland
Born 1940

My childhood days were nothing like they are today. My parents, siblings, and I lived two miles out in the mountains. We were called mountain kids. We had no neighbors for miles around, except our grandparents across the road.

We went to a one-room schoolhouse with a wood stove. We could bring soup or something else and put it behind the stove, and it would be warm by lunch. We did ride the bus because the school was ten miles away. We went no matter how high the snow. The bus had chains on the tires.

We did not have a lot of fun times. Our dad rented a room in Hancock, Maryland for the week because he worked there and came home on Friday nights. My siblings and I had to do the work. Our mother was sickly. We had no running water or electricity. We carried the water from behind our grandparents' house. On Sunday evenings we had to fill the iron kettles with water for Mom to wash on Monday. My brothers would light the fire under the kettles so it could get hot. They did this before going to school. I remember brushing out teeth with salt and baking soda.

In the spring when we came home from school we changed our clothes and went out to the truck patch, as it was called, better known as the garden. We had to get it ready for planting. We would throw rocks off so the neighbor could bring his horse and plow the ground. When Dad was home on Saturday we would plant the seeds. As they grew we had to pull the weeds. I hated doing that.

My parents didn't go to church but they let us go. I am glad they did. We walked two miles to catch a ride to church. I remember I had a red coat, and where we waited for our ride there was a farm there. They had one of the biggest bulls I ever saw. He would run back and forth inside the fence until we left. I was so afraid he would get out.

The school had a medical box on the wall with tape and gauze and iodine in case someone got hurt. I got hurt. One day I was going down the steps, and Billy Fisher was coming up swinging a croquet mallet. He hit me above my right eye. In these days I would have had stitches. My grandmother doctored me by putting some kind of salve on it until it got better. I still have a scar from it.

As I said, we didn't have much time for playing but we did find ways to entertain ourselves, like taking a box of oatmeal to the corncrib to eat. It would fall down through the cracks. If Mom found out, and she usually did, we were punished. My sister and I would pick a mossy place in the woods, close to the house, and make a playhouse with whatever we could find. I remember one Sunday after church we went to the woods looking for teaberries. My sister stepped on a yellow jacket nest. She screamed all the way to the house with the bees stinging all the way. We had a wagon wheel we ran down the road from the top of the hill. Once my brother got inside the wheel and rode it down the hill. The wheel hit the bridge abutment. His eye got bonged up. Our grandmother took care of him.

Our grandmother was a tough old lady. She could handle hot coals with her bare hands. Our grandfather was tough also. He was an Indian with rough brown skin, and he was a hard worker.

We didn't have any store bought toys. For a sled we used a cardboard box or just slid down on our butts, wearing our coat out. I remember a tire hanging from a tree. I fell out of it once, and it knocked the breath out of me.

We butchered every Thanksgiving. We had this pig named Red Jim. He weighed 500 pounds. We made our own butter by churning it, and made our cottage cheese and buttermilk. We made apple butter in the copper kettle. We mostly ate from the garden and canned everything we could. We dug a big hole in the ground by the garden and put our root vegetables in it for later in the winter. In deer season my brothers would go deer hunting early. Usually they would have their deer before going to school.

On Sundays my dad walked seven miles to catch a ride with the then Blue Ridge Bus. Sometimes we would walk with him. It seemed a long walk back home.

Our grandparents never really had us to their house very much unless they had company. We would sneak in the back door and sit on a bench and listen to the adults talk. Kids were to be seen and not heard. We girls did help Grandma bake cookies for the holidays or some special occasion, which was rare.

We had chickens of different kinds, even bantam roosters. They would chase my sister and flog her. She had a habit of going outside and just screaming for no reason. Our grandmother would run to see what was wrong. Usually it was nothing but one day she saw these two snakes in the woodpile, but by the time Grandma got there they were gone. It's a wonder we didn't get really hurt bad. We would run around barefoot all summer.

We moved to town when I was fifteen. What a change of living. I never did learn how to ride a bike. I tried. I was babysitting at seventeen and I got on a bike that was parked on a gravel road. I got on, put on the brake, and went over the handlebars. I was sore for a week.

I am glad we grew up back then. Little did I know how that life prepared me for the future. I am so glad I was taught to be respectful, especially of our elders. We were taught manners and how to live on our own. I am so thankful I learned to eat everything, learned how to iron clothes with a flat iron, and learned how to bake bread from scratch. Things like this is what I call the good ole days.

A Carefree, Loving Time
By Anna Mary Fratz of McHenry, Maryland
Born 1932

I was born in 1932 on a farm in the country in western Maryland. The farm was located in the Sang Run area because of the ginseng root harvested here. We raised mostly what we ate and bartered for meat with friends and relatives. We would trade a half of a beef one season for a half of a pig the next butchering season.

I didn't feel poor. It was such a carefree, loving time with family, especially cousins, and friends. Nothing was sold publically on Sundays, so we visited with family and friends after church. Once in a while, some of Dad's family would stop by and tell us of faraway places like Ohio or Connecticut and leave us wide eyed!

We had no indoor plumbing; a hand pump from the spring pumped cold water into our pitcher. A coal and wood cook stove heated any water we needed. We had an outdoor toilet, and for some reason Dad called it a "snipe house." Dad always kept lime spread on the toilet base so there was little odor. The door to the snipe house faced the barn, away from the house, and I would let the door open when I went in to read. My reading in the snipe house was not the best thing. When the preacher and the house painter were at our house they each (at different times) came around the corner

Anna Mary Fratz

and there I was! I was probably nine or ten years old.

Also, when company came Mom always warned us not to giggle or make noise with the chamber pot lid that was above the dining room in an upstairs room. Mom always kept the "pot" very pleasant smelling with "germicide," as she called it. Probably in today's terms that would be Lysol.

On Saturday mornings, it was bath time. A large, round galvanized tub was placed in the kitchen near the coal cook stove, where the water was heated. The oldest, my brother, got the first bath. No one was other than the bather was allowed in the kitchen during bath time. No oops allowed! My sister was the second bather after hot water was added to the existing water. I was third after more hot water. We never thought of sanitation; I guess the added hot water to each bath was the logic. By the way, during the week, each person would take a wash pan with water, soap, washcloth, and towel to their bedroom for between tub baths. Mom called that "sponge bathing."

Also, in my youth there was serious use of laxative called Fisics (not in any dictionary!). It was not unusual for a family to drink a glass of warm water daily with castor oil in it. It cured sluggishness. Epson salt was really known to clear the head. If any child or adult got ill, especially with headaches, the question always was "have they had a fisic?" in my growing up years, my mom believed in the power of laxatives. When I was dating my husband-to-be one night I had a headache, and I told him when I went home I'd probably take a laxative. He assured me I was doctoring the wrong end! Although after marrying him, his mom never failed to ask if I had given my sick child a fisic. It could have been he didn't "fess" us to his upbringing.

Also in my youth, we were never allowed in the barn to see animals birthing or being treated for illness. In fact, when our aunts were expecting our cousins, we were told they had swallowed watermelon seeds. I think that's when we kids started "who can spit the watermelon seed the farthest?" We didn't want big bellies.

Also on that note, we had an elderly preacher who also was a veterinarian or vet. He didn't have a car so Mom would go get him, bring him to our house where he treated the cows, and then she would give him a meal and then take him home. On one occasion, at the table, he was telling that he had given the cow an injection. I was always mouthy and I said, "How and where?" He said, "In the rectum." I asked, "What's the rectum and how's that?" My mom and sister started kicking me under the table, and I asked them why they were kicking me. It got worse; the old preacher's name was Phenis and I left out the H in his name! I had never heard of that word either! My sister has been known to say she hoped my children someday would embarrass me the way I embarrassed her and Mom. Knowing my sweet dad, I'm sure had had a good laugh when he got away from the situation. I did have seven children, no embarrassment, just blessings and fun!

We had no electricity until I was in high school. To get the money, my mom went to work in a restaurant near where my dad worked in the garage. Evenings we would listen to the battery radio as daddy peeled us all apples. Sometimes I would play the piano, and my sister and I sang or we women (girls) would crochet or embroidery.

My mother had chickens and sold eggs to the neighbors for ten cents a dozen. Also, it was Mom's job to go to the feed store and get chop for the cows and grit for the chickens, because the feed sacks were printed, and she made our clothes from the sacks. With some of the egg money, Mom gave me $1.00

Anna Mary Fratz in 1951

piano lessons. As a result, my love of music, especially gospel, has been such a blessing. I have sung at church services, baptisms, weddings, ordinations, and for the sick. I still use music to calm my spirit and soothe my soul!

Two funny stories have grown with me. My mother-in-law told me this one: we had only party telephones lines, possibly three to five parties on one line. There was a man in the area where she lived who had a speech impediment. He had put Vick's Salve on his hemorrhoids. He picked up the phone and another party was on the line. He yelled "Hello Anee-body. My arse is on fire!" Of course, everybody knew him and knew it was him!

We had a couple nearby in town that had the post office and a small store in their home. They would also sell eggs and homemade butter for nearby families. One day one of the farmer's wives came in to the store and asked if they would give or exchange her pound of butter for another pound of good butter. It seems as though a mouse had fallen into the cream before she churned the butter. So the storeowner's wife took her butter to the back of the store in the kitchen, rewrapped her butter, and gave it back to her. Story has it later she came back in to the store and exclaimed how good the butter was! It proves what you don't know won't hurt you.

Hard Times
By Pauline Sponaugle of Circleville, West Virginia
Born 1939

To start the story I lived way back in the woods on a small farm owned by John Sponaugle. He had cows and sheep on the farm. He let us live there for free. The place was called Black Ridge. I lived there with my mother, a brother, and a sister. My daddy didn't want us. There was hard times. My mother always had a garden she planted every spring. She canned up food and kept it in a cellar. We had a bunch of apple trees. We made apple butter in a copper kettle, and we canned that also.

We went to a one-room school with grades one to eight. We had a wonderful teacher. When the weather was a deep snow, my mom would make a path to get to school. It was a half mile to school.

My mom and brother cut the wood off the place. We had a wood heating stove where she did all the cooking. She would also tap the maple trees and boil it down to make maple syrup. My mom made our clothes from flour sacks. We had no electric, and we had an outhouse where we had catalogs for toilet paper. We also had a well where we drew water.

My aunt Sallie lived about two miles from us. We had to walk through the woods to get to her house. She had eight kids. Her husband left her with all the kids to take care of. We would go there often. Another aunt and her husband lived down over the hill from us. He had an old Model A car. He would take us to the doctor. They had four kids we would visit.

We moved from there when I was fifteen to an old store on Hunting Ground. We ran the store. They had electric there, and we took care of the store. Then I left there and got married. We had one son. I had to leave my husband; he became an alcoholic. He had 160 acres of land and cattle and sheep, but he wouldn't take care of them anymore. He had a right room house, which I really loved, but I had to leave. He burned the house and barn and grain house. We had electric there but no bathroom. We had an outhouse. We also had an old telephone. Our ring was four shorts and a long. It was a party line.

My son and I went to Harrisonburg, Virginia. I was over there for 31 years. I finally come back to Hunting Ground. My son built his house here. My ex-husband died in 2004. I live in a trailer he had across the road from my son. He has three kids, and one died as an infant. I loved living back in Ridge and Hunting Ground. These are my roots. I worked in Harrisonburg at a tube factory for 15 years and other places too. I left and would come back to my husband sometimes, but nothing worked out. I had to stay away. I am 74 now and will be 75 in July. I have arthritis and a lot of health problems. I want to be buried here on the mountain.

Thank You, Daddy!
By Carolyn Marie Grapes of Romney, West Virginia
Born 1936

The year 1935, the setting is the beautiful little village of North River Mills, West Virginia, and the young, just married couple was renting two rooms to call their own, not too far from their parent's homes in Hoy and Slanesville.

Work was scarce. The young bridegroom worked for anyone who needed help on his or her farm or business for just $1.00 a day.

The Hampshire County Board of Education had just closed the North River Mills one-room school and needed a bus driver to transport children to Slanesville School. Edgar Lorain Grapes was the happy young man to receive the position, and it paid $35.00 a month! Also, he was able to continue work for a local farmer during the day.

There were two little sisters to be picked up and delivered each school day, and although the young bus driver learned the names of, and enjoyed all his passengers, these two little girls were especially appealing to this young man as he and his wife were looking forward to the birth of their first child.

The school year passed, the summer wore on, and the young couple welcomed a baby girl born in the mother's home in Hoy so that her mother could care for her. The couple had not decided on a name for their baby and the young father said that he would like to name her after the names of the two little girls that he had enjoyed transporting to and from their new school.

The baby was named Carolyn Marie. Oh, how happy I am that their names weren't Anastasia and Drisilla! (-names of the stepsisters from Walt Disney's Cinderella)

The Two-Room School
By Harry Handwerk of Grantsville, Maryland
Born 1940

I was born in June 1940 in Jennings, Garrett County, Maryland. I started to school in September 1946 in first grade. I went through sixth grade in June 1952. Then I went to Northern High School until June 1958.

The county closed Jennings School in 1956. We had about 60 kids in the six grades. There were two teachers. The "big" room teacher was also the principal. He had two paddles, a little brown one for little offences, and a big green one for big offences. The next principal used his big, wide belt. I got

Harry Handwerk and his classmates from Jennings School in 1946

to sample his belt. He said he gave me a "strappin'."

We had two outhouses, one for the boys and one for the girls. The girls' outhouse had some knotholes in the backside. They would plug the holes with toilet paper. The boys would punch the paper out. I don't remember anyone being punished, just threatened.

The teacher in the "little" room was always a woman. She was one of the best teachers anywhere. She taught things that were not in the book. She taught on moral issues. She taught common sense. She taught some religion like a Sunday school teacher would. She would have a box of tissues on her desk. Sometimes she would have to clean some kid's snotty nose.

Some of the parents didn't like her because she would ask a lot of personal questions. She would pry into your personal home life. Sometimes she could make you feel like you could fall through a knothole. She could not be a teacher now because of the things she taught.

Bobby Eats the Horn Soap
By Mary E. Higgins of Davis, West Virginia
Born 1935

This story is an excerpt from my husband's autobiography, which he wrote (up to age 12) before his death in November 2012. He was a great storyteller. He was born and raised in Littletown, West Virginia. I was born and raised in Grafton, West Virginia.

Bobby O. was probably my best pal in grade school. He was inventive, brave, and mischievous. He was a combination of Huckleberry Finn, Opie Taylor, and Dennis the Menace. He would bite the heads off of chub fish we caught—I mean RAW, right out of the water! He would grab a wasp by the back without getting stung. He once jumped from a railroad bridge, a 20-foot leap into some 4 feet of water. It took days for the mud to settle in the stream.

He and I joined the "Jr." band about the same time, during our 5th or 6th grade stints. Both of us came up with old, used coronets. The instructor was a former Army Captain with the disposition of Captain Bly. Bobby and I seldom practiced, so our weekly performances were hardly reason to consider

Bobby O. is in the middle

us as candidates for the Boston Pops orchestra.

All I can recall at the rehearsals was the raspy voice of the director screaming over and over "Do it again! Do it again!" Plus the constant banging of the baton on the music stand. After 3 years of horn tooting I managed to get kicked out of the band because I went squirrel hunting when I was scheduled to be with the band at a bake sale event. Wonder why I forgot about the bake sale?

Bobby nearly got us banished from the 6th grade band because as we were sitting together one day in class, he decided to use our trumpet cleaning soap to blow bubbles. Our teacher, Mrs. Kimble, nearly lifted innocent me out of the seat by the hair of my head. Bobby got whacked on the head with a ruler. So much for child abuse in school.

Skipping School to Help Mom
By Joe Etta Caldwell of Keyser, West Virginia
Born 1938

When I was younger, times were quieter and slower paced. I grew up in New Creek, West Virginia, six miles south of Keyser and the Maryland line. Everyone knew everyone in New Creek in those days in my neighborhood. There were a lot of kids in the neighborhood, and we did a lot together.

In the summer time, we played in the creek, catching fish and crawdads, and in the winter, we slid around in our boots on the ice if we didn't have skates. Just a little way down the creek there was a swimming hole. Young and old enjoyed that.

Some of the grownups would get together and go sled riding up on a steep field near Route 50 near John K. Sanders. Any kids who would want to go just got permission from their parents, and the other parents would watch out for them. A couple of old tires were burned to keep everyone warm. Black smoke would roll up but no one cared. When it started to get late we would go home, and Mom would have hot cocoa for us.

The Swisher family had a large, white store in the middle of New Creek. Later the big drafty place was replaced with a smaller store.

New Creek Grade School was up the alley from the store on the hill. For a long time the kids were allowed to come to the store for candy, but after a while, no one was allowed off the hill until school was over for the day.

If a child didn't listen to their teachers, they got a paddling by the teacher; the teachers were in charge at school. Sometimes a parent whipped the kid at home for getting a whipping at school and showing disrespect for the ones in charge.

My mother and we three kids lived at Grandmother Liller's for a while. We had a happy childhood. Mom was strict with us but showed a lot of love. We never doubted that love.

Grandmother was very special to me. She was the first one to tell me anything about the Bible. To this day if I drop anything more than once I remember Grandma saying, "Get behind me, Satan."

Grandmother had an icebox on the porch, and the iceman would deliver a block of ice from Keyser, West Virginia. An icebox was a little cupboard that kept food before people had refrigerators. I can't remember what ice cost, but I do remember the large tongs the iceman carried the ice with across the swinging bridge.

Grandmother had an outhouse also. It set down a little path. You made a real quick trip in the wintertime. Of course, with an outhouse you had to have chamber pots to use at night.

When I was older and dated, the boys had to be out of the house by 11:00 p.m. If not, Mom said she would rattle the chamber pot lid. We believed her.

There really was such a thing as Saturday baths. We were getting ready to go to town in Keyser and to church at Rees Chapel the next day. We had a pan of water through the days for anyone who wanted to wash their hands.

Mom had a wringer washer and two tubs of rinse water to do the wash on Mondays. My sister and I loved to get to miss school to do the wash. If Mom had a lot to do such as canning, cleaning, or just didn't feel well she would let us skip school. There is just something nice about line dried clothes and sheets. They smell so good!

We had a radio for a long time and would sit real quiet to hear it. We didn't get a television until I was thirteen.

Met My Wife at Highland Drive-In Theater
By Robert Eugene Lambert of Monterey, Virginia
Born 1940

I was born in 1940, the 10th child of Zella and Mattie Mae Vandevender Lambert at Hall Bush Hallow near Circiville, West Virginia.

My parents passed away when I was around five. At that time my brother, O'dell, and I were moved to Sandy Ridge to live with Harry and Carrie Jane Sinnett.

We went to school in a one-room school at Cherry Hill. Mr. Botkin was the first teacher. He had eight classes, then Charles Linenburg, who took over until the school moved to Franklin.

The winters back then were really cold and snows were really deep. We walked a mile to school. I remember my brother and I slept upstairs. It was so cold we had to put our heads under the covers to keep warm. We also had an outside toilet.

We had to go out on the mountain to feed the cows. We would ride the horses, old Prince and Dan, and play cowboys and Indians. Our dog was Fido.

We walked to the neighbor's to watch TV on weekends because we didn't have one. One time when Harry was gone we decided to learn to drive the car. I drove it through the garage door.

In summer, we picked strawberries, cherries, apples, beans, corn, and potatoes

Robert and Dottie in 1960

for Harry to sell at Harrisonburg. One of my favorite things to do was go to my neighbor's, Chap and Will, and listen to their stories and drink cider.

When I was a junior in high school, I met my girlfriend, Dottie Lou at the Highland Drive-In Theater. I graduated in 1961. We were married and 53 years later, 2 children and 2 grandchildren later, we still live in Highland.

Giant Strawberries, Piggies, and Poppies
By Bernadine Evans of Kitzmiller, Maryland
Born 1937

I live in Kitzmiller, Maryland along the Potomac River. It is so close to West Virginia you can throw a rock across. This little town is pretty dead now, but it was a pretty booming place at one time with trains running four times a day going to Ohio, Elkins, WV Baltimore Coal trains still run up here, along with log trucks and coal trucks. They're stripping all the mountains off.

But when I was a little girl, it was different. Daddy worked in the coal mine. Mommy was home with the kids all the time. That helped us to feel safe. We lived in a very little place, one store. You had to walk everywhere you went; there wasn't any cars. No one had enough money to buy one. Some people had cars, but they didn't live here. They just came to see what other people lived like. But we were happy. Everybody looked after one another like family. Health nurses came and brought medicine. There were some that brought babies. We were little. We never knew where those little kids came from, but that was okay. We just had more kids to play with.

I can still see that little town. There was a river just across the tracks. In the summer we swam, and in the evening we would take the soap and towels and go over there and bathe and go home and get in bed and Mommy would read to us from an old Bible she found somewhere. It was so brown and worn you had to be very careful or it would fall apart. But Mommy would read us to sleep. They were very peaceful nights.

My granddad lived just up the road, and we walked there. I loved him very much, but he was very busy. He worked in the mines but he had a garden. He chopped wood. He had an old white mule he plowed with. I can still see him in my mind over in that field working. But Granddad wasn't well. They had to carry him out of the mine on a stretcher sometimes. But he would rest a few days and go back to work. My granddad grew poppies. They were so big they looked like big feathers, real fluffy. He grew strawberries as big as apples, but you had not bother them. He said he would give you some but you better not touch them. Grandmother raised piggies and cooked good food. I remember the table in her dining room was so big with a lot of dishes and people, all family and friends.

Then there wasn't much going on in this part of the country at any time, only work. My mommy and I worked to gather dishes and keeping up fires. You had to keep wood in the cooking stove and heating stove going to keep warm and for cooking food and baking. I had three little brothers and an older sister. I liked to cook and bake cookies.

There wasn't much to worry about in those days. No one bothered others or stole from you. We helped each other. We had a movie house. It was twenty cents to go to the movie and ten cents for popcorn. There were a lot of good family and western movies. Ice cream cones were five cents. If you were lucky, you would get a cone with a stare; you would get a free one.

There is no stoplights in this town. We have a fire station, post office, and a very little restaurant. Bat your eyes and you would miss it as you cross the bridge to West Virginia. It isn't much other than a few houses. It was a spot for miners to hang out with five beer joints at one time, but not anymore. They were all torn down. No drinks allowed anymore.

Snake Tales
By Robert Glen Schoonover of Elkins, West Virginia
Born 1927

I was born November 30, 1927, the youngest of eleven. When I was about seventeen my parents took in my nephew and two nieces, as their parents were in the service. We lived in a six-room farmhouse. We had no electricity or plumbing. Of course, we had the little brown shack out back. My nephew was only about six years younger than me. I was seventeen and he was eleven, and I had to go to the backhouse. We kept a box for catalogs and newspaper in the corner of the toilet. My nephew was playing with a stick about three feet long, tossing rocks in the air. He wanted me to leave the toilet door open so he wasn't alone. He was standing just in front of the door when I reached for a piece of newspaper to tear some off. When I picked up the paper there lay a garter snake. I was deathly afraid of snakes. I said something and my nephew stepped inside the door with his stick. I said for him not to bother the snake until I got out. He took his stick to punch the snake, and I yelled at him. In his excitement he got the stick under the snake and flipped it right onto my naked lap. That may have been the first time the phrase "to moon" someone was said. I was screaming, and of course, my entire family came running. I don't think they ever quit laughing.

I grew up and got married. My son-in-law and I went turkey hunting and each killed a turkey. We were in my backyard cleaning the turkeys. I had cleaned up mine and had the guts on a newspaper. We always saved the heart, liver, and gizzard. I was cutting the gut from the gizzard and when I cut it off, there was a ground snake about sixteen inches long that popped right up in my face. My son-in-law said he heard some bad words come from me and looked and I was halfway up the path, my knife up in the air and more bad words. When I went back to the turkey, I saw that the snake was dead but to me a snake is a snake. I called a good friend who worked for the Department of Natural Resources to come see this. He was going to a meeting and couldn't come but had us take a picture of it.

Moonshine for the Chickens
By Evelyn S. Webster of Lost City, West Virginia
Born 1934

You have to be old enough to remember the days before the automatic transmission to appreciate this story. Mom and Dad had gone to visit a neighbor and left my sisters and me at home. I'm sure we were supposed to do some chores, but we were about the age to think about learning to drive, so we decided that we would start the truck that was in the shed just to prove that we were smart enough to do it. Our problem was that we didn't realize that you needed to engage the clutch when you pushed on the starter, so when we pushed on the starter the truck would give a little jump but not start. Lucky for us the shed was open on both ends and after a few pushes on the starter we had jumped forward a little, so we

The snake in the turkey guts

tried to push the truck back but we couldn't do that either. We must not have moved it too much or maybe Dad just thought he put it a little farther in the shed. At least we didn't get in trouble. Later we all learned to drive and got our driver's license, but we weren't self-taught. We took Driver's Education at school.

We had a little joke between us and the neighbors on the party line. All of us knew when one neighbor was listening. She would breathe very loud and her little dog, Billy Boy, would bark when she was listening. Now we text, e-mail, and do Facebook for all the world to see.

We walked about a mile and a half to meet the bus to go to school. We were fortunate that we got to go inside a little store and gas station to wait for the bus. One day the waters were getting up, and we came back early. We went in the store to wait for our dad to come get us. The storekeeper's wife made us pimento cheese sandwiches with "store bread," a treat then. Now it's a treat to get homemade bread. They were so good. They are still my favorite sandwiches.

My grandpa had a few laying hens that supplied eggs for the family. One time he put a jug of moonshine in the grain house where they sometimes would keep a few jugs of water for the chickens. It was one of the daughter's jobs to tend the chickens, and when she watered the chickens, she mistakenly got the moonshine jug, not knowing it was not water. She poured it in the chicken water containers. The chickens were a lot happier after they drank than Grandpa was when he found his moonshine was missing, but he didn't say much since it was an innocent mistake. He must have had the moonshine for "medicinal purposes" or to give the men who helped on the farm a little sip so he wouldn't have to give them as much cash, since he was known to be very frugal and not known to indulge.

Soon after we got electricity in our rural neighborhood we had the first radio, and the neighbors would come to our house to hear the *Grand Ole Opry* on Saturday night. My dad also liked to listen to a program called *Inner Sanctum Mysteries*. It started with a door opening, making a terrible screeching sound that I thought was very scary, but I couldn't make myself not listen. One night it was a story about a black cat that had poisonous claws and lived in a basement. I was sure that cat was lurking in our basement, just waiting to attack me with those poison claws. I made my trips down to the basement and back very quick and never once saw or heard that cat.

Beware a Sunny Spot in the Road
By Betty J. Taylor of New Franklin, Ohio
Born 1927

I was raised on the farm of Grandpa Sponaugle. This was the former Lumber Mill across the river between Hendricks and Hambleton. There were three families of us in the small houses. Grandma and Grandpa Sponaugle, Uncle Brian, Aunt Vista, and family lived in the big house, which looked like an old hotel. Uncle Buck, Aunt Vista, and family, and my parents, Arthur Moore and Breciy Moore, lived in two smaller houses.

We walked to school in the winter. It was pretty rough with the bridges across the river covered with snow and ice.

There were ten of us brothers and sisters.

Betty's parents Arthur and Breciy Moore with baby Roscoe

My sisters and brothers would go into the grocery store and wait around the heating stove for the school bus. There was a huge gym across the street with a large porch. One day I was accused of stealing some jellybeans. The owner of J C Penny sent a note to my parents. They really gave me the dickens about it. To this day, I never touched the jellybeans! I never went in that jar again! After that, I waited for the bus on the gym porch in the cold.

One day after school was out my sisters, Dorothy and Arjetta were to take some tickets from Hambleton School to Hendricks School, so I had to tag along, and it was cold and snowy, and very late when we got back across the swinging bridge to home in Hambleton. My brother was looking for us. My mother had gotten worried and sent him to look for us. When we got home, my sister got a smacking with a switch. I was too little for that. Haha.

I was the one elected to go to the chicken coop to collect the eggs from the nests. Since I was familiar with them, I spotted a sturdy nest that a chicken had made along the creek on the way to Hambleton, so one day Mom sent me to the store and I saw the eggs in the nest. With my bloomers (Mom always made them out of feed sacks), I knew I could take the eggs to the store. I would get some candy with the egg money, but alas, on the way to the store (I had put the eggs in my bloomers) the eggs started breaking and running down my legs. Ugh! When I got to Elk Creek, I took them off, threw them in the river, and cleaned myself off. No candy and poor chicken, no babies.

On the way home from Hambleton I saw a nice sunny spot in the road and being barefooted I stepped on it. A big black snake was sunning himself in it and I ran like crazy to get home!

I can't forget Simon. He was an African American man who lived in a small cabin on Grandpa's property. He would walk to Parson's once in a while. My mom would give him something to eat occasionally. Us kids would run to the road and speak to him. He would always have pieces of candy or nuts to give us. I never knew where he came from. We loved Simon. He passed away and was buried by his little cabin.

However, despite all the bad times, I loved the farm, all the fun we had playing hide and seek, and other games with the family.

Dad finally bought a house in Hambleton and we left the farm and didn't have to cross the swinging bridge any more.

I went to Parsons High and married my love, Everett Taylor, and we had three lovely daughters. I never forgot my time on the farm. Everett served in WWII. We then went to Akron, Ohio, where Everett worked at B. F. Goodrich until he retired.

I still have two sisters who live in Parsons, Bonnie (Jo) Gainer, and Arjetta Piggott (lucky ones). I loved Parsons and going to town on Saturday to watch the cakewalk and the people walking by.

Beautiful West Virginia with its green hills and rivers, those were the days. I loved them. West Virginia is heaven.

Tale from the Outhouse
By Lana J. Koontz of Green Spring, West Virginia
Born 1947

I grew up in the very late '40s and the '50s. Looking back, the '50s were my very favorite decade. During the time the '40s slide into the '50s, most everyone had something in common - an outhouse. There were a few who could afford the luxury of inside plumbing such as a bathroom, but until that happened we used an outhouse.

Growing up I spent a lot of time at my grandparents' home (James and Amanda Wilson.) They had an outhouse about 300 feet from the house. There was a wire fence between their property and the neighbor's. The neighbor's daughter and I were good friends' and we played along the fence and, of all places, the outhouse at the end of the fence. Whenever my mom couldn't find me right off, she always looked down the toilet hole for me. Thank heavens I was never there.

One day I dropped a knife down the toilet hole. I got the bright idea to get a long stick and get the knife out. So I stirred and stirred; never did get the knife out but really stirred up a smell. All the neighbors came out to see why the smell was happening. I wasn't too popular for a few days.

Every once in a while a new hole was dug and the outhouse was moved. So this outhouse was moved about 50 feet, and the wire clothesline ran through it. My grandmother had papered the ceiling with wallpaper. This looked good for a while until the rain dripped through, and the paper came loose from the ceiling. One day my mom, Anneva Koontz went into the outhouse, and my brother, Randolph Koontz and I got the idea to pull on the clothesline. What a sight! Mom ran across the garden in disarray of pulling her clothes on, screaming that a big bird was after her. It was so funny, up until we got a tongue-lashing.

Another story, around Memorial Day we always took my aunt down to a cemetery along Route 522 about eight miles out of Berekley Springs, West Virginia. So me, my mother, my grandmother (Amanda,) my aunt (Aretta Wilson,) and her mother (Lillian Allen) all visited the cemetery so my aunt could put flowers on the family graves. Of course, we needed to use a restroom, and they had an outhouse. My aunt said she wasn't going in that flea bitten thing, so she went around to the back of it. I wasn't about to go out in the open, so I went in among the cobwebs and just as I was going to sit down, I looked over to my fight and there lay a snake on the ledge. I ran out of there screaming, and my aunt came from around back to see what was going on. My mother laughed so hard. She said my feet were tangled around each other, and I was trying to run and couldn't. My aunt's mother got so mad at my mother for laughing at me.

Another time a bunch of us went to Lost River State Park for a picnic, and when we went to use the outhouse, my mother was looking for something to come down on her head. Well, my sister-in-law, Wanda Koontz took a stick and shook it under the stall and made my mother believe it was a snake. We got a good laugh, but Mom didn't think it was funny.

Another story, over in the Lost River area we would visit relatives. One time we stopped to visit some, and they had the prettiest outhouse (the Miller's Outhouse) I had ever seen. It was spotless, papered on the inside, linoleum on the floor, the seat just shined, the outside painted, and flowers planted around it. Sometimes we would stop just to see how pretty the outhouse was.

Another friend, Virgil Mullins had an outhouse until he could get a bathroom installed in his house. One time his grandson, John came to visit, and he was from the city. He wanted to use the bathroom, and when he was told, it was the outhouse he said he would wait until he got home.

Castor Oil: It Sure Did the Job
By Dorothy P. Glotfelty of Oakland, Maryland

I remember the good old days more than I remember today.

I grew up on a 100-acre farm in Western Maryland in 1937. We did not have electricity and there was no indoor plumbing. We had an outhouse with 2 holes and a Montgomery Ward and Sears catalog for "wiping." In the winter, the snow had to be brushed away before we sat down or we would have a cold rear end. At nighttime, we had a chamber pot to use so we didn't have to go out after dark.

We lived in the woods and never knew what kind of critter we might meet up with since it was pitch dark. In the mornings, my sister and I always "discussed" who was going to empty it (the pot) since neither of us wanted to do that job, however it always got emptied and rinsed out, ready for the next night. Sometimes it took a lot of rinsing, especially when my dad thought we needed a good cleaning out and gave us a dose of castor oil. Ugh. It sure did the job.

Saturday night was bath night in a tin tub, which was also used on washday to rinse our clothes. Bath water was heated on the wood-burning cook stove. The tub was always placed in the kitchen next to the warm stove. Everyone used the same water and the oldest one always got to bathe first. The rest of us always said, "Don't pee in the water." Saturday night after we were all spit shined, we got to listen to the Lone Ranger on the radio and to the program with the squeaky door, which always scared us but we listened anyway. No TV.

We did not have a telephone. Our neighbor 2-3 miles away had one with a party line: different amounts of rings for different people. Our little short neighbor lady didn't pay any attention to the amount of rings. She would jump up on her little stool and listen to everybody else's conversation and then pass it on to everyone she would see. Another thing we did for entertainment was listening to our wind-up record player, which stood on the floor about 4 feet high. We had great big records, 33 1/3 and 78. We did not have many, but we played them over and over and enjoyed them each time we heard them.

I went to a one-room school for 7 years and had the same teacher. There were a total of 18 students in the whole school. There was an outhouse and when we had to use it we wrote our name on the blackboard—only one student out at a time. In the winter, there was a "pot-bellied" stove, which was "fired" by the oldest boy. In those days, the teacher was allowed to punish the unruly student and sometimes the "bad" girl or boy would get a spanking. My mother always said, "If you get a spanking in school you will get another one when you get home." And believe me; they had a way of finding out if there had been any spankings. I often wondered how they found out. I was lucky enough not to get a spanking but I did get my hand bent back and hit with a ruler.

Clothes washing day was always on Mondays. My mother would start up our wringer washing machine with the gasoline motor. Blue smoke would just fly. We lost a lot of buttons in that wringer but they were always replaced. Tuesdays was the day for ironing. Everything had to be ironed. Mom would fire up the kitchen cook stove in order to get the irons hot.

We always cooked a big pot of beans and baked bread. Nothing is better than homemade bread with beans. We always had fried bread with homemade butter dripping from it. Most everything we ate was homemade. We always had a huge garden, growing all our vegetables. When it was harvest time, we canned everything we could.

My dad would go to the apple and peach orchards and bring home 8-10 bushels of fruit to be prepared for canning. Sometimes we would dig holes and bury the apples and cover them with straw. They would keep all winter.

On our farm, we had a lot of different animals. The day my dad went to the feed store was a real treat. We got to go and pick out our dresses. The feed came in beautiful print bags. My mother made us dresses from those bags that lasted forever.

We only had heat in our house on the first floor. Upstairs where we slept there were freezing temperatures. If it snowed during the night, sometimes the snow would blow in through the cracks and it would be on top of our blankets. We had so many blankets on our bed we could hardly turn over. It never took long to get dressed and get downstairs where it was warm.

All these memories are very precious to me. I'm glad I can still remember them.

Horseshoe Curves and No Guard Rails
By Sandra Earp of Keareysville, West Virginia

When growing up in Poolsville, MD, I remember living on a road called River Road. Well I found out why it was called that. Our clothes and socks would get stained like red mud. Ha Ha!

I liked living there with my mom, dad, and two sisters, Geneva and Anne. We also had our little dog called Jack. We had few chores but the one that stands out was feeding and collecting the eggs. Every time we would be met with one rooster that would flock and run at us. The scratches would hurt and bleed. Mom said we were mean to him and that's why he did it. The only thing we would do is get the eggs.

Some cold day Mom and Dad would build a fire at a small pit and put a wash tub on it to heat the water. Daddy would then chop heads off some of the chickens. He would then dunk them into the water to scald them. We kids helped pluck feathers off. I remember the blood on the snow and the smell like it was yesterday.

I remember the day my uncle gave me an old guitar with maybe five strings. I would pretend I was on the Grand Ole Opry, playing and trying to sing. Ha Ha! My sister would sit and be my audience. We would play with Mom's sheets on the clothesline, pretending they were teepees.

We did have a TV. Black and White TVs you could buy colored film that was blue, clear, and green. It was blue at the top, then clear, and then green at the bottom—that was our color TV.

Every Friday night we had a hot dog with chili for dinner. I don't remember why.

When my parents would go shopping at the big grocery store in Rockville, Daddy would always stop in the town of Poolsville to buy him and Mom banana boats and us ice cream cones. We would then stop someplace out of town to eat. Then on to Rockville. We would also go by and see my mom's folks. I really loved my grandfather.

Mom would sell the eggs and Dad would cut and dry some type of grass to sell when he would go back to Virginia every May 31 for a family reunion. It was used to make some sort of medicine. With the money, Mom and Dad would go to Sears and Roebuck to buy our school clothes. We got 1 pair of shoes each and 3 dresses, plus socks and underwear. They would get coats and boots at the Goodwill or hand-me-downs. Mom always took very good care with the clothes. She would wash them in the wringer washer and starch and iron them.

Dinner was beans and cornbread a lot but I didn't mind. Daddy's seemed to smell better. It was the onion in it.

I have a lot of good memories of carrying water in a wagon in buckets and our little washing to water the garden about ½ mile from the house. We had to go real slow. It seems like 3 hours to haul and water. We would be so scared to go through the dark woods. But we made it.

Up and down one mountain in Virginia called Paint Hick there were horseshoe curves and no guard rails. Daddy said that if you were to go over the edge straight down no one would find you for two, maybe three, days. I think it was on that same mountain that we would gather wild grapes. Talk about good jelly, it's the best. We ate a lot of homemade biscuits with white gravy. Mom would also make fried potatoes loaded with onion only using a cast iron skillet. She might have used country ham in it if she had any. Mom was a good cook and made pies and cakes. My daughter takes after her. She loves cooking.

Daddy did have the crank up record player, which I still have, and works with old 33 records. I still play old music. Bluegrass is my favorite. I wasn't a coal miner's daughter but life was the same. We had love.

Once there was a black snake that was sunning itself on a small wooden bridge leading to the outhouse. We were scared to go across the bridge. My great grandmother on my mom's side had a chamber pot in her large bedroom where we also slept with her and the other females. She would tell us to use this pot—do not wet the bed. She had so many quilts and blankets on the bed that myself, my sister, and my mother slept on, that once you were in bed you stayed because you couldn't move. But we stayed warm.

She also had a cast iron stove, and boy she could cook a lot of food for every meal. Our family was huge. I don't know how she did it and have everything done on time.

I lost my parents but never would I lose my great memories and good times with them, back when things were at a slow pace.

A Doughy Lesson
By Iona Crites Bergdoll of Moorefield, West Virginia
Born 1928

When I was growing up times were hard. We always had enough to wear and enough food to eat. We always had lots of love.

I was born in 1928. My mother (Ida Crites) was a part time cook at Toll Gate School near Moorefield, WV, and at a one-room school at Durgon where I went to school. When I was 12 years old, my mother had to go to cook and she said I could stay home from school that day if I made up bread and fixed supper for my brothers and sisters and Mom and Pop. There were 5 boys and 5 girls and me and our parents in our family.

I liked to cook so I stayed home that day.

Iona's parents, Strite Eugene and Ida Crites

After they all left, I started to mix up the bread. I was short so I stood up on a chair to reach the table. I emptied a big 25 lb. bag of flour in a big dishpan like I saw my mother do. I put in the homemade dry yeast and lard and the rest and I mixed and mixed it up.

I waited a little while and it didn't seem to rise so I thought I must have done something wrong, so I carried it outside and under a big tree behind a shed and dug a hole and put it in. Boy was it heavy. I covered it up and went back into the house to rest. I rested a little and I wondered what to do, so I decided to make up baking powder biscuits. So I hunted some more flour out in the pantry.

I put flour in the pan and put baking powders in it and mixed it up. I rolled them out and baked them and fixed the rest of the supper. They turned out pretty good so when my folks and brothers and sisters came home they were all hungry. I set the table and put them on the table with the rest of supper. They all ate them and enjoyed them. They ate them ALL. I was proud of myself.

My dad (Strite Eugene Crites) went outside to do the evening work and he noticed something white out behind the shed under the big tree. He went on out to see what it was and here it was the big dish pan of bread dough I had mixed up the first time and I never gave it time enough to rise. When the sun came out hot that day and the dough and ground got hot, it raised the bread and it caused it to raise and it came up through the ground and raised up the ground and ran all over the ground.

My dad came back in the house and he said, "Girl, I thought your mother told you this morning to mix up bread today."

I said, "Yes, Pop, I did."

I said, "Didn't you and everyone eat some for supper and enjoy it?"

He said, "Yes, but come with me."

He took me by the hand and we went outside, out behind the shed and under the big tree and there was the bread dough raised and come up through the ground and run all over.

Needless to say, I got a "whippen" for wasting the flour. The next day I didn't ask to stay home. I was ready to go back to school.

Then when I was growing up as a young girl, we had to walk to school and back home to Durgon School about 4 or 5 miles, until they brought up a little bus in later years. I would walk down to the little Durgon store down the road about a mile and a half. We had chickens and they laid eggs for us and I'd take the eggs down to sell. I put them in a little bucket wrapped up so they didn't break and walked down to the Durgon store and sold the eggs for Mom.

My mother would need a couple things like a little piece of longhorn cheese or something. She said, "If you have any money left you can have it." One day she didn't want much so I had enough to get a little pack of crackers and a little jar of peanut butter.

I had some neighbor children to walk with me, so we stopped along the road and sat on a culvert and ate some and talked. I didn't want to take it home because we wanted some for the next evening when we came home from school. So I hid the crackers and peanut butter in the culvert. I took Mom's longhorn cheese home and she didn't ask me anything about it.

I was thinking about my crackers and peanut butter all the next day. Well, the next day we walked up the road and stopped to eat the rest of the peanut butter and crackers, and here that day the State Road men came up and mashed the culvert clear shut.

So we never got the rest of our crackers and peanut butter. I cried about it.

We really had some good and funny times growing up. There are only 3 of us girls left. We had to work but we had lots of fun and love.

My Place of Peace and Contentment
By Judy Mallow Footen of Berkeley Springs,
West Virginia
Born 1952

Country roads take me home! I can't hear that song without thinking of the farms and the mountains where I was young. There wasn't a lot of money but there was plenty of love! I was fortunate to live in an area where we were surrounded by lots of family: brothers, sisters, cousins, great aunts, and great uncles. Most of the farms still had outhouses and of course in every kitchen was the old cast iron wood-burning cook stove that burned all day long summer and winter. In the summer, we picked berries of all kinds, which were made into jams, jellies, pies, and cobblers. In the fall, we picked apples, pears, and gathered nuts, which were made into delicious fall and winter treats. We would walk miles to the little country church singing hymns as we walked along. We could have gone in the car with the older people but it was so much fun walking the five or so miles to the church that we chose to do so.

A special place was the farm of my great aunt and uncle. It was a place of peace and contentment. An ice-cold stream meandered its way out of the springhouse and down into the meadow passing underneath the weeping willow tree. The cows grazed in the field, the chickens clucked near the barn and the honeybees gathered their nectar and hurried back to the hives scattered across the hillside. The barn was across the road and the old family cemetery was at the top of the hill surrounded by its picket fence. A picket fence also surrounded the house. The yard was entered through a gate, which had an old plow hung on a chain, which made sure that the gate was closed after everyone who entered. Across the front of the house was the porch. The porch was the gathering place but also a work place. During the canning season, the women would come to sit and break the beans, shell the peas, or peel the apples. On Sundays, scriptures would be read, hymns sung, and instruments played. It was also, where babies were rocked and announcements of family happenings were made. In the evening, the men would gather with the women to listen to the sounds and sights of the coming evening. In the background, the quiet sound of the spring flowing into the watering trough brought a sense of relaxation.

You could enter the house into the kitchen. It is the place that I think about when I need to think of the most calming place that I know. The floor was pine, covered in flowered linoleum, which was again covered with rag rugs that had been patiently braided from whatever garment that had become too worn to wear. Nothing was wasted. When plastic bags were produced to hold store bought bread, the bags were cut into strips and braided to make outdoor rugs to get rid of the red clay mud that was constantly waiting to invade. Rocking chairs and oak chairs were placed close to the old chestnut table, which was covered in brightly covered oilcloth. The wood stove gave off the scent of cherry, oak, and maple, and the quiet snap of the burning fire along with the quiet ticking of the mantle clock soon put all who entered at ease. The milk separator sat in the corner (it always fascinated me with its many bowls and arms) and the slight odor of fresh butter, buttermilk, and cottage cheese lingered in the room. On the top of the stove, freshly made rolls and bread were rising, waiting to be popped into the oven. These would be served with fresh butter and honey from the hives outside. A beautifully carved German mantel clock ticked and tocked softly from its alcove above the door. The atmosphere belied all of the hard work that occurred there and the room beckoned to all that entered it. Water was hand carried from the springhouse and heated in the cistern of the cast iron stove. This was the hot water source for dishes and baths.

If you walked through the kitchen and onto the back screened porch, you would see a bench sitting next to the door. There was a ladle placed next to the bucket on that bench. When you wanted a drink, you would dip the ladle, throw that water out the door, and then dip again. Drinks were taken straight from the ladle! Next to the bench was a wonderful old porch swing that was long enough to stretch out on for a short, midday nap and directly behind the swing was the wood box. It was the duty of everyone to make sure that the bucket had water and the wood box had wood and no one had better be caught taking a nap when either one of those were empty!

My uncle did not believe in changing the time. He would get up at four in the morning spring, summer, fall, and winter, and make his way to the barn. He was tall and thin and wore suspenders to hold up his pants. He would carry a kerosene lantern, which he hung on a peg on the rafters to light his way as he milked each cow. The quiet swish of the milk hitting the galvanized pail was accompanied by the soft meow of the barn cat, which would willingly open its mouth to get a fresh squirt of milk direct from the cow. After the milk was carried inside to the separator, my uncle would tend to the garden, which was lovingly guarded, and weeds were ruthlessly destroyed if one should dare to invade.

My great aunt and uncle lived well into their nineties. They had celebrated over seventy-five years of marriage and they had spread their message of love of God and family to all who had entered their wonderful home. They were a special blessing to all of us.

How Daddy Lost Babysitting Privileges
By Judy (Bergdoll) Jenkins of Moorefield, West Virginia
Born 1954

I lived in a little place called Durgon, West Virginia. I was the youngest and littlest of my family. I have a wonderful big brother that is so special to me and a big sister that is so sweet and kind. I am the youngest. I was real little. My mother (Iona Bergdoll) had all three of us at home.

The day I was born, my dad (Scott Bergdoll) was off work and went back over a big hill to deer hunt. He took a big seashell along and you could blow in it and it made a loud noise and you could hear it from a long way off. He had one and my mother had one at the home. He said to my grandmother (Ida Crites), "If she gets the baby, blow the horn and I'll come home." My grandmother would go for miles to help deliver the babies. My sister was 3 years older than I and my brother was older than my sister.

Well, my grandmother sent her outside to play with the neighbor children. My grandmother blew the horn for my dad to come home. He heard it and returned the blowing of the horn to let her know he heard it.

It was about the time for me to be born. Back then, a woman did not know if it would be a boy or a girl. They just took what they got and were happy.

My older big brother was in first grade of school. His reading book was about Jim and Judy, so he told my mom, "If you get a boy I want to name him Jim, and if you get a girl, I want to name her Judy." So my dad had just shot a big deer, and came dragging it home and hung it up outside. He came in the house and I was being born. So I was real little but my mom named me Judy, not Judith, just plain Judy, like my brother wanted.

My sister says she doesn't remember much about that day but she sure does remember the big deer with horns that Daddy killed. My dad (Scott Bergdoll) was so proud and said he got 2 deer in one day. The big deer and the little "dear." We lived 5 miles from one town,

Judy's parents, Scott and Iona Bergdoll with their children in 1959

Petersburg, WV, and 8 miles from the other little town of Moorefield, WV.

I had asthma so bad when I was a baby. They couldn't lay me down flat, so they would put me on their stomach or chest to sleep. My mom and dad would take turns watching me at night. If they would lay me on their chest or stomach, I would go to sleep and breathe better. Well one night it was my dad's turn to watch me so my mom could get some sleep for a few hours. I was lying on my dad's stomach and went to sleep, and Dad was tired too from working hard, so he went to sleep too. I rolled off on the floor behind the bed. My mom woke up and couldn't find me. She woke up Dad and said I was gone. They thought someone came in the window beside the bed and took me.

My mother started crying and praying. Then my dad heard a noise and looked under the bed and there I was on my hands and knees asleep and it didn't hurt me any.

But needless to say, my mom didn't let my dad watch me anymore at night.

About my grandparents, Strite Eugene Crites and Ida Crites, they were wonderful caring people and hardworking folks.

My grandmother (Ida Crites) was known as a Mid-Woman. She would go for miles in the snow, sleet, hail, or rain to deliver a new baby and then she'd go back and care for the mother and child for a week or more. They would come and get her on horseback and say, "Ida, it's time," so she'd go. Sometimes she would get home and not even get in the house until another one would come and get her to help deliver another baby. At times, they really kept her busy. I don't know how many babies she delivered but she enjoyed it and was never known to charge for her service. She also had 6 girls and 5 boys of her own. She also cooked at a one-room school called Durgon School. She would walk down 5 miles and back 5 miles. Once in a while, someone would bring her home but not often. She also cooked at another school, Toll Gate School, close to Moorefield, WV, for several years. She passed away Jan. 11, 1964 with a heart attack. Then the home place burnt down in April 1966 due to lightning striking it.

My granddad (Strite Eugene Crites) lived in a small trailer until he passed away March 11, 1972, but my granddad (but I called him Pop) worked for area farmers for 50 cents or $1 a day. He also helped build the main highway on Route 220 between Moorefield and Petersburg, WV.

We had some very rough and cold winters back then. We had deep snows and ice. We loved to play in the snow and make snowmen and snow houses. It would stay cold and freeze for weeks at a time. We would have one snow and then another snow on top and then another one. We loved to make snow cream to eat, that's ice cream. It was GOOD. We also had fun sled riding off big hills and skating on ponds.

We also had fun times in the summer too. We would go barefoot and wade in cool water in the streams. We'd go fishing and had lots of picnics and enjoyed friends and family and neighbors coming to visit. We raised chickens for eggs, a cow for milk, cheese, and butter, and a hog to butcher for meat. We raised a garden and would walk over the hills and pick berries.

We had a wonderful time and I met a wonderful man named Billy Jenkins and we got married. We have been married 34 years and as the song goes, "And if I had it to do all over again, I'd do it with you." With the same man.

At the End of Crack the Whip
By Susan Bailey Shambaugh of Paw Paw, West Virginia
Born 1952

I grew up in Paw Paw, WV (Morgan County) in the '50s and '60s. We lived about a mile out of town and were considered country kids. My older brother and I had lots of kids to play with. My younger brother missed out on

Kay Wintermoyer, Susie Bailey, and John Bailey

much of this, as he was 10 years younger than me.

Our cousins lived next door and there were 5 of them and the other neighbors had 3 kids that were the same as family. We spent all our spare time running from house to house and all over the nearby cherry orchard and woods. All the parents could yell or swat us if need be, and there were plenty of times when we needed it. They also all fed us, gave us cool drinks in the summer, and brought us in out of the cold in winter to warm up and have hot cocoa.

Some of my best memories were sled riding down the road by our house. Our parents would go out and start an old tire burning at each end of the hill, while we kids went back and forth packing the snow down to make for a better ride. We knew we had to roll off our sleds at the last neighbor's driveway or we would go into the highway. We also went ice-skating as often as we could and I ended up on the end of crack the whip more times than I wanted to, because I was the youngest of the bunch. For those who don't know what that is, everyone takes hands and starts skating around in a line going faster and faster until you break the chain. Needless to say, the ones on the end usually go flying across the ice, rarely still standing.

In the warm weather, it was all about kick the can, riding bikes, and playing baseball in the cow field behind our house. Evenings were spent sitting on the front porch visiting with friends and family, catching lightning bugs, and playing hide and seek. Sometimes we would make homemade ice cream (by hand cranking), and fortunately there were enough adults that we didn't have to crank much.

In the summer, we spent as many nights out under the stars as we could. We would take blankets and pin them across the clothesline to make our tents and that's where we slept. We would listen to the whippoorwills, crickets, and frogs, tell ghost stories, and see who we could scare back inside before the night was over. Of course, wash day would come and we'd have to take down our tents and help with that. I always got stuck washing socks on the washboard before Mom put them in the wringer washer. I hated that job, but continued to wash clothes in the wringer washer until 1973, when a year after I was married my husband bought me a washer and dryer. When my mom saw how easy it was she soon had them too, and the wringer washer was put in the building where it still is today!

I remember getting my first record player for Christmas around 1960. My mom bought some of her favorites like Marty Robbins, Johnny Cash, and Johnny Horton (I still enjoy them today). But, I also got Oh Boy, At the Hop, and of course Elvis. I still have some of them today, except the ones I wore out. I'll never forget watching the Beatles on Ed Sullivan. My cousin Ruth Noland Long and I were so excited. We sat on the floor singing and giggling and my dad and Uncle Donald Noland made fun of us, and called them longhaired hippies, and saying who would want to listen to that caterwauling.

I was so ready for the moon landing. I had asked for a tape recorder (the old reel type) for Christmas and gotten it, so I was set up in front of the TV watching Walter Cronkite and taped the broadcast. I still have it somewhere in my attic. I don't know if it would still play or not.

I have a lot of good memories from my childhood. Riding my bike or walking down the highway to visit my best friend Vicki Brown Campbell (who is still my best friend after 56 years). Spending time at my grandad's, staying at the cabin on the river that my dad and family built, getting the milk delivered and put in that silver insulated box at the driveway, and sometimes sneaking in an order for chocolate milk (until Mom caught us). The whole family going to the drive-in movies. Taking car rides on nice days, fishing, swimming in the river, and everywhere we went, Mom would pack us bologna and cheese sandwiches to take along. We usually got to buy chips and soda at a nearby store, and that was such a treat for us!

I have some not so good memories too, of Outdoor toilets, getting beat at school with a thick wooden paddle, having to share a party line with nosy neighbors who listened in on everyone's calls, castor oil, methylate, mercurochrome, bomb drills, and summer canning. I always had to wash the jars, because I had the smallest hands that would fit inside of them easier (at least that was Mom's excuse).

I've went from Black and White TVs, to color TV, Console TVs to Flat screens. From records to albums, to 8 tracks, cassettes, from CDs to Mp3 players. I went from rotary dial phones, to push buttons, to portables, to cell phones. I've seen doctors who made house calls, and said that you could settle up later, to having to pay for a test before they'd give it to you. I've heard sonic booms, seen countries

John, Wade, Butch, Wilma, and Susie in 1954

change their names, found out Christopher Columbus didn't discover America, been told that Pluto was no longer a planet. I have to get my son, daughter, or granddaughter to show me how to operate my DVD player, cell phone, computer, and just about anything electronic.

I've spent 62 years in this same area. I have traveled all over the U.S. and had seen some beautiful places, but I'm always glad to get home. This is where I have made a lot of memories, and I hope that I have many more to make, and I hope I leave some good ones behind for those I love!

The Day the Ku Klux Klansman Came to Church
By Therman W. Rexroad of Rawlings, Maryland
Born 1917

I am 96 years old. I was born in Flintstone, Maryland in June 1917. We moved to Keyser, WV, and then to Black Oak, MD, which is now where the Potomac Edison Substation

Therman Rexroad and his team of horses

The church building committee

is located. I was in the 7th grade when we moved to Black Oak, MD. I was married in 1938 and my wife and I just celebrated our 75th wedding anniversary on November 4, 2013.

I had a farm and had to milk the cows and plow the fields. I had a dog that would take the cows down to the river and sit on the bank until the last cow came out of the river and he would bring them back home. When we first had a television, we had to have an antenna at the top of Fort Hill and run wires down to the house. Birds would fly through the wires and twist them and I had to go up the hill and untwist the wires to see television.

We used a washboard to wash our clothes. You had to heat the water on the stove to wash them.

I went to a "one room" schoolhouse in Gerstell, West Virginia. There were approximately 20 children that went to school. My wife went to a "one room" school on Twenty-first Lane, off of McMullen Highway, near McCoole, Maryland. Approximately 15 to 20 children attended.

You could flag the train down in Black Oak and ride to McCoole and then walk across the bridge to Keyser. I think the cost was 30 or 35 cents. At one time, there were 11 trains you could flag down and ride to McCoole, Maryland.

We had to "cold pack" the meat we butchered to keep it. You had to put the meat and salt in the jars and put the lids on them and put them in a pot to boil. When it boiled for a certain length of time, the heat was turned off and they started to seal.

I went to the "old Dawson Church" in Dawson, across the railroad tracks. They decided to build a new church on down the highway and at one of the nightly services;

a member of the Ku Klux Klan entered the church. No one knew what he was going to do; it was so quiet you could hear a pin drop. He walked up the aisle and put money in the collection plate and turned around and walked back out.

When they started to build the current Dawson United Methodist Church on McMullen Highway, I helped dig out the foundation with my team of horses and a plow.

We had a group of young people at the church called the "Epworth League." One of the games we played was called the "Hen Cackling Association." Everyone sat in a circle and if you wanted to join, you had to stand up, wave your arms, and cackle like a hen. While you were standing, the person next to you would slip an egg on your seat. Then everyone said you did a pretty good job, look what you did.

Another game, everyone sat in a circle and one person started whispering to the person next to him, and he was to pass it on, but you could only say it once, if you did not hear it right, you just said what you thought you heard. What eventually came around was nothing at all what it started out as.

The Potomac Edison eventually bought everyone out in Black Oak. We had a home built on Carman Drive, off of McMullen Highway, in Rawlings, Maryland in 1958. My mother died in 1970 and we had to move to our current location to live with my father on McMullen Hwy., in Rawlings, Maryland, as he did not want to move in with us. Our mailing address is Rawlings, Maryland, although we live in what is called Dawson, Maryland.

The Delco
By Ethel M. Bland of Riverton, West Virginia
Born 1939

I was born at home (a doctor was with my Mom,) In the Dolly Hills near North Mountain. I had three sisters, two older and one younger than me. My Father worked in the woods cutting timber then later started carrying the mail, which he did for years; first on a horse and later in a Jeep.

We had to go outside to the outhouse. We didn't have running water; we carried it from the spring. We had no electricity so we used kerosene lamps. We cooked on a wood cook stove.

After I was up some in age, my Father and a neighbor went to Ohio and brought each of them a Delco. It had twenty-four batteries like a car. It had a motor that you had to start every evening and let it run awhile to charge the batteries and then we got lights like electric lights. Later we did get real electricity.

I had to walk to school about one-half mile to a one-room school. But we had all grades from first to eighth. We all got along good and made good grades. I finished the eighth grade and then started high school at Circleville, which I graduated from.

I look back and remember all of this. Kids today would never make it like I did then. We had to walk if we went anywhere.

The Thirteenth of Twenty
By Martha Palmer of Gerrardstown, West Virginia
Born 1937

I was born in Morgan County, West Virginia on March 17, 1937. My parents were Martha Irene Bishop Unger and Calvin Sherman Unger. I am the thirteenth child in a family of twenty. I was named Martha Rebecca Unger. We lived along the railroad track behind the Sand Mine in a little place called The Factory.

My parents were hard working people. My Dad worked at the Sand Mine and my Mom sewed almost every night to make our clothes. I remember my Dad spading up fields to plant vegetable gardens that we canned to have enough food to feed us all.

I had a very happy childhood, did not understand how poor we were because there was always love. We had no indoor plumbing (outhouse out back) and we took a wash pan of water to our bedroom to bathe

We walked the railroad track to school and back. It was about one and one-half miles to two miles one way. What a long way for a first grader.

I have very fond memories of playing in the woods and swinging on grapevines with my brothers and sisters. We didn't have toys like other kids did but we learned to be creative and make do with what we had.

My Father was also a minister and pastored a church. We all loved going to church, as that was the main event of our social life. I thank God that our parents taught us the love of God and the importance of living a Christian life.

In the winter of 1946, we moved to Ridersville on Route 9. It was there that the last two children were born.

It seemed when I started to school in Berkeley Springs Grade School was when I began to see how poor we were compared to other kids. Other children made fun of our clothes and shoes, but thanks to our faith, we learned to deal with it.

I suppose the highlights of my life was growing up in a large family were summers and Christmas time At Christmas, there was no tree or toys, but my Mom would make the younger ones new outfits and we would have a program at church. It seemed that the long, happy days would never end. As of now, there are ten of us still living and I thank God for each one.

Riding the Sled with Dad
By Judy Dolechek of Keyser, West Virginia
Born 1948

My story takes place on Gilmore Street in Keyser, West Virginia. Back in the day, it was about the prettiest street in the west end of town. There were several children my age to play with there, or we would shoot marbles at the side of my house under Mrs. Newhouse's umbrella tree. (She was our neighbor who supplied me with Hostess chocolate cakes each Saturday to accompany my TV cartoon time.)

Speaking of trees, the street was lined with them. If I remember right, I can count seven plus an empty lot across the street that had fruit trees, and a green hedge around the entire lot. Not even the lot exists now. It has a house on it.

The winters were very special to me. I love snow and we definitely got more snow then than we do now. My Dad enjoyed it too, and I recall one day, Dad took me to the top of Gilmore Street to sled ride.

It had snowed for a couple of days and traffic was almost non-existent. Dad looked at me and said, "Go get Uncle Don's sled."

Needless to say, after Mom dressed me like I was headed to Alaska, we headed up the hill. The time was unlike other times, Dad said, "Let's go to the top." I was excited because usually we only went halfway up the hill. Once we reached our destination, I was mesmerized by the view. I could see the trains running on the B &O tracks; I could see Memorial Bridge, which linked Keyser, West Virginia to McCoole, Maryland, and the lights from downtown lit up the sky.

Once we boarded that sled, and received the go-ahead from the people watching traffic on St. Cloud Street, we took off. We flew down the hill, crossed St. Cloud Street, passed our house on Gilmore Street and we were still going. We were fast approaching West Piedmont Street, which is also Route 46.No one was watching traffic there because no one had ever made it that far on a sled. Dad told me to hold on and lean to the left, so I did. We immediately slid on to the sidewalk and slowed down on bare cement. After that ride, we called it a night.

That was one sled ride I'll never forget and neither will the kids that lived on Gilmore Street at that time.

Uncle Don's sled is in my attic to this day.

The Frozen Pond
By Richard Aaron Pownall of Jarrettsville,
Maryland
Born 1940

My name is Richard (Dick) Aaron Pownall. I was born and raised in Springfield, West Virginia. My parents had seven children all delivered by a mid-wife at our home. Our home was a small one-story house in the valley overlooking fields and a mountain. I remember my Mother would bake delicious hot cinnamon rolls and doughnuts.

We had an outhouse, which had three holes. My Mom, Dad, and I could all use it at the same time. In the late fifties, our family got our first television. We had a crank phone in our house for which you had to remember different crank sequences to call neighbors.

Growing up I had fun with my sisters and brothers. As children, we played in the fields and the pond. I played cowboys with my toy gun that I got one year for Christmas. My younger brothers had pedal cars that looked like a lot of fun. In the summer, we waded and fished in the South Branch River. In the fields, we made forts and caves in the fodder shocks, which are bundles of corn stalks. In the winter, we sleighed down the hills. One winter day the pond froze over and my Dad told me not to go near it. I did not listen and fell, and cut my chin. Needless to say, Dad was not happy with me.

I attended Springfield Grade School for eight years. One fond memory was of my first grade teacher, Mrs. Blue. She sewed my britches that I split open while playing on the merry-go-round. As I got older, I enjoyed helping my neighbors on their farms. When I was ten years old, I started going hunting with my Dad for squirrels. I remember the floods that occurred about every eight to ten years that washed away the trailers and camps by the South Branch River.

When I went to spend the night with my Grandmother, she gave me a glass of warm water and kerosene to drink before bed to keep the bed bugs from biting.

On November 9, 1955, a tractor-trailer loaded with frozen turkeys crashed through the Springfield Presbyterian Church. Town folks were given free turkeys.

I went to Romney High School for four years. My first wife, Agnes, was my high school sweetheart. She helped me with book reports. I didn't like to read then or now. During my high school years, I worked on a peach and apple orchard. After serving in the Army in the Vietnam War from 1967 to 1968, I moved to Jarrettsville, Maryland. I would often come home to Springfield to visit my family and go deer hunting at Thanksgiving.

"Alligator in the Bed"
By Joanne Hesse of Moorefield, West Virginia
Born 1938

When we moved from Dad's (Jim Davey) home place down to the Johnson house, I was in school, don't remember what grade or the year. But we walked about two miles to a one-room schoolhouse called Forest Hill. Grades one through eighth in Hampshire County, West Virginia.

The Johnson house was very large, eight rooms plus a summer kitchen. We kids used to walk the railroad tracks on Sundays, see who could walk the longest without falling off. This time we met dad's brother John Davey and his son, Floyd (Speed.) Mom, Josephine Davey, and Speed were all the time picking on each other.

Before bedtime that night, Mom told me and Arbutus (my oldest sister,) to go upstairs and put the alligator in Speed's bed. The alligator was mounted and hung on a wall in another room. So we went up the back stairs so no one would see us, put the gator in Speed's bed and covered it up. We go back down the same steps. Later it got to be bedtime and Speed went to bed first. We had kerosene lamps and lanterns.

Next, we heard all this yelling and screaming. We kids started laughing and Mom hushed us up. Here comes Speed down the steps whiter than the white shorts he had on. So scared he could hardly talk. Finally, Mom got him calmed down, and he said, "There was an animal in his bed." Mom tells him "he must have dreamed it." Speed said he'd never gotten in the bed yet. Mom took him up the stairs to bed and she checked the bed, nothing there. Meantime, while Mom is calming Speed down, Arbutus and I got back up the back stairs and removed the alligator. He never forgot it.

So one time Speed and Uncle Davey came back to the Davey Farm and Speed use to have nightmares. He'd kicked the glass out of a window upstairs. Next day, Mom put him on the porch roof to put the glass back in.

Mom loved to whistle, she'd been to the well getting water and she got almost to the porch, Speed yelled to her, "A whistling woman and jumping sheep ain't fit for a man to keep." Mom made him repeat it.

She sat the bucket of water down, and removed the ladder. Then she told Speed, Just for that you can stay up there until I say you can come down. It must have been at least two or three hours before Mom put the ladder up and let him come down.

They were all the time trying to get the best of each other and it was all in fun. I know when them two got together we had lots of fun just watching them.

This was in the 1940s so we had to make our own entertainment, no bathroom, no electric, no T.V. and no phones.

Looking Back
By Angeline W. McPeak of Augusta, West Virginia
Born 1923

Looking back to the childhood days, I often think of the many things we did to entertain and amuse ourselves.

We made believe a lot, pretending to be some movie star or playing doctor and nurse; making mud pies, playing paper dolls and all those good things kids used to do, plus getting into a few spats or just being kids—mischievous.

There is one vivid memory that I recall, which took place in the early 1930's with sister, Gladys, age six and I, age nine. The older one always had to look after the younger; that is why I was at the right place, at the right time.

This incident took place in the chicken house. The barn, chicken house, and "John" were connected all in a row, wide cracks prevailing. Anyone in the "john," which happened to be me, could look into the chicken house with a good "birds'" eye view. I had the best seat in the house.

This day, Gladys, or shall I say "Rev." was in the chicken house holding service for the chickens. Now, to get in tune with the story—picture this! Some of the hens was on a nest, some just strutting around or standing still on one leg, making little noises like chickens do, and after laying an egg, well, you have heard that cackling sound too, which in this case could have been a big "Amen" in chicken language, if one's imagination could go so far. You have never seen such contented chickens as Rev. Gladys did her preaching, pointing her fingers at them, holding onto her Bible, which was the Sears Roebuck Catalog turned upside down. Every now and then, she would give the Bible a big whack and nod her head back and forth at those chickens. Of course, service included singing, "In the Sweet By and By and When the Roll is Called Up Yonder," also praying.

Believe me, some of the Evangelist of today, had this been in their hey-day, would have been running scared, as Rev. Gladys really presented some stiff competition. Come to think of it, they would have had nothing on this gal. Rev. Gladys could have put them to shame when it comes to preaching to chickens, that is!

As I look back now—HEY! That kid was pretty good and I can enjoy that beautiful memory.

Dreams of Yesterday
By Mary Ann McCauley of Gerrardstown, West Virginia
Born 1938

I think about the old days a lot. My grandfather was the constable in 1930. I currently live on the land he owned. It was an apple and peach tree orchard. My father inherited the land and it began as a farm. We had cows, chickens, hogs, goats, and horses. There must have been a lot of Indians around here, because my father found many arrowheads on the property.

The closest store was 2 miles away, so we did not get much from there. My father and my Uncle Bill would go to the store on horseback in the winter when we were snowed in.

We had a huge garden and my mother canned everything. She cooked on a wood

Sherman, Gladys, and Angeline

stove. The stove would heat the whole house. I did not know we were poor back then, but we never went hungry because we always had food to eat from our garden.

We had no running water in the house, and an outhouse out back, the Sears Roebuck Catalog for toilet paper. I know you have heard of this before, it is true!

Monday was washday. We would take water down back to a big iron kettle and start fire under it to heat the water. We then carried the hot water back into the house to wash our clothes. It would take us all day to wash. Also, on washday we always had a pot of beans on with a piece of side meat and maybe slice of pie.

In the spring, we would go out to the orchard and look for land cypress for our supper. I loved going out to our smokehouse with my mother to get meat for supper and I would get a piece of dried ham to chew on. Mom would bake bread and kill a chicken or two on Saturday for Sunday dinners. We most always had company on Sunday and the dinners were so good.

Chicken feed came in pretty printed bags and my mother would make all my dresses from them. I would get one pair of shoes for school. The rest of the time, I didn't wear shoes.

I love to help my father on the farm. He didn't have a son to help, so I guess I was it. When Daddy would come in to eat, he would take off his hat, wash his face, hands, and brush his hair. He didn't have much. I still have that brush he always used. He did this in a pan of water on the back porch.

I made myself a tree house in an old apple tree. I would spend a lot of time in there daydreaming. Well, my dreams are about gone now, but when I die if they say they don't have running water and I have to go to the outhouse, well, I'll be right at home.

My Safe Haven
By Evelyn E. Sims of Hedgesville, WV
Born 1938

I was born on a very blustery cold, snowy day in February 1938 in Gerrardstown, WV. As I was born, the doctor told my parents that I was a bleu baby. Since I was so frail, the doctor worked several hours to save me. Later we moved to Hedgesville, WV.

We were poor and I was next to the youngest of five. My father worked on the orchard making 9 cents per hour. Earlier in his life, he had a car wreck and had a steel plate in his head. When he would drink, he would go completely out of his mind. He would beat my siblings and me. He would not remember anything that happened.

With my father drinking, he used up his money and therefore it left us little for food. Mom was a very sickly and frail lady and could not do much work. We had a garden and grew food, but it was not enough to last all year. I would go to bed at night with such a gnawing hunger that it was hard to sleep.

I had two friends at school and sometimes they would give me a nickel so that I could buy a candy bar, a box of pretzels, a pack of peanuts, or a bottle of pop. I have always been grateful to their kindness. A teacher noticed that I was undernourished and my lunch was an apple butter bread sandwich or some fat meat fried hard. My teacher went and talked to the principal and they asked me, "If I would like to work in the lunchroom in exchange, I would get my hot school lunch free." I said, "Yes!" I worked in the lunchroom making Kool-Aid, cleaning the tables, and helped clean the floor. I did this for the rest of my schooling.

Evelyn E. Sims growing her own food

I have been so thankful for my school friends, my teachers, my principal, and the wonderful ladies that cooked the mouthwatering food that was served each day.

I had someone that really cared about me, someone to teach me the knowledge I needed in life. I had a nice warm meal each day and I was able to keep my mind on my classroom learning so much better. I realized that school was my safe haven.

The Mountain Lion
By Margaret Boyd of Cherokee, Oklahoma
Born 1948

For its time, Cherry Run, West Virginia, had a large rail yard. I remember steam engines slow moving as they stopped at the water tower. When I saw a diesel for the B & O railroad for the first time, I thought it was the strangest thing I had ever seen.

I was born and grew up within forty yards of the one room school. The school and our house were built in a clearing on top of the mountain. It wasn't exactly one room since there was another room of equal size that was the lunchroom with a small kitchen. Most weeks I volunteered to help in the kitchen in exchange for free lunch.

The classroom accommodated usually thirty students in six grades. There were wooden desks with inkwells, lift-up writing surfaces covering the storage area and the seat for the next desk was attached in front. The iron legs were screwed into the creaky wooden floor.

At the back of the room stood a potbelly coal stove. Students sat alphabetically which put me first in the row where the heat didn't reach. One year during warm weather, the teacher we had that year held classes beneath the poplar tree behind the school at the edge of the cornfield. She also took us on nature walks. I learned to recognize spearmint plants and I would chew them. The teacher pointed out asparagus growing along the dirt road. Each week, I checked on the asparagus and when it was about a foot tall, I'd pick it to take to my Mother to cook. There was unlimited access to walnuts, plums, pears, peaches, persimmons, apples, grapes, blackberries, cherries, and the wild cherries from which Daddy made wine.

Most of the students were related to each other and nearly all walked to and from school as much as three miles one-way. It took me less than four minutes.

Like our house, the school had no running water. The outhouses were approximately ten yards down the hillside. The water well with hand pump were about eight yards from the schools entrance.

One fall, a mountain lion had been spotted around the area a few times. Before lunch, one day two boys were sent to pump water so we could wash our hands. When we heard the animal roar, we knew the mountain lion was nearby. Before the teacher could start toward the door at the back of the classroom, the door opened. The two boys stepped inside, both trembling but still clutching the pail. Their eyes were wide. All color was gone for their face as they stammered to tell what they had seen. There was no telephone to call for help as the big cat paced around the schoolyard. We were forced to remain inside after school. After about an hour, the owner of the general store drove up to find out why his son wasn't home. The mountain lion fled down the hill.

A telephone was installed the next year on a private line. A party line would have disrupted class throughout the day. The telephone didn't ring often but most times when it did ring, the call was for the cook to get one of her recipes.

A couple of months later as I walked up the hill after a Christmas play rehearsal, it was dark and the snow, several days old, made a crunch sound as I walked. I heard footsteps crunch the snow in the tree line to the right of the road. I'd take a few steps then stop and the footsteps did the same. I believed the mountain lion was stalking me. I could barely breathe. When I reached the clearing where our house is, the woods were farther down the road. I quickly ran to the back door and safety. Despite several men hunting it, the mountain lion was never caught and probably left the area.

The school was also the community center. In the fall, most of the village joined together to make apple butter. The women gathered in the kitchen to wash utensils and gossip while the men were in charge of stirring the sliced apples in two blackened vats over an open fire. They used wooden paddles as they told tall tales. As a young child, I imagined the large pots were a witch's cauldron.

Due to the remote location in Morgan County, hiring teachers was a problem that led to the closing of the school.

During the summer months after my chores were done, I sometimes sat on the hillside between the school and the house Daddy built in the early 1950s. Back then the trees weren't tall or thick. I could see the Potomac River and Maryland on the other side. I watched as a farmer on a green tractor plowed a field alongside US 40. I was fascinated with the sound of the eighteen-wheelers as drivers dropped a gear or two to haul heavy loads up the mountain.

When I stopped sitting on the hillside, I was probably fourteen. I heard a gunshot from a careless hunter and a second later, the bullet whizzed past my ear. It was loud and terrible close.

Sadly, the school was donated to the volunteer fire department to be used for training, and trees have overtaken the entire school grounds since I moved away in 1966.

The Car
By Gary L. Cooper of Salem, West Virginia
Born 1939

I was born at home in Sully, West Virginia where my parents, Benett F. and Mabel Harr Cooper, lived. We also lived on the top of the Alleghany Mountain above Harman and one year in Lockbourne, Ohio where I attended the first grade. Then we settled on the farm my parents bought in Canaan Valley in 1948. My sister, Janice Lee was born soon after we moved to the farm.

Even though there was lots of hard work to maintain the farm, it was a happy time. Both sets of grandparents and some of my uncles were all farmers who lived within a few miles and we all helped each other quite a bit with the big jobs. My maternal grandparents, Frank and Caroline Harr, lived on Freeland Road less than a mile away. We helped them too.

When I got a brand new red two-wheeled bicycle, I was so happy and proud. The next day my friends and I really had fun racing each other on the state road. It was all fun and games until the last time that evening when I played "chicken" again with one of the other guys. We ran straight into each other and my new bike got the worst end of the deal. We had to load the bicycle pieces and the broken fork into the back seat of one guy's car to bring it back to my house. Needless to say, my parents were quite upset about the bike that I had only one day. My Dad had a lot to say that night and he said that he would not pay to get it fixed. So I worked and earned a little money to buy a new fork. After that Wayne Bonner, a neighbor, and I would jump off the school bus and run to get our bikes. We would race to the top of the hill near the lime quarry and wait for the bus to come back out on the state road. Just after it passed, we would race down the hill past the water pipe. We would pass the bus long before we got to Stingtown and the driver would shake his fist at us. He told my Mom what we were doing and she told me to stop so I didn't get killed. It was so much fun that we did it several more times but the driver didn't say anything else to my parents.

At first, we had two workhorses on our farm. They were named Harry and Doll and our Father bought them when I was just a little fellow. They were white where most of the workhorses were black or brown. My Dad did the plowing, mowing hay, raking, etc., with the horses until he was able to buy a tractor and then a hay baler sometime in the 1950s.

I was always interested in machinery and got even more interested in cars and trucks when I got to be closer to getting my driver's license Asa Pennington owned some land in Stringtown and I kept noticing this old vehicle that had been parked in the tall grass below his store. It was an old car (Model A) that had been cut off and looked something like the one my uncle had on his farm. I got after Dad to buy it but he didn't seem to think we needed it. Every time I would go into Asa's to get a bottle of pop, I would ask him about that old car. He said a lot of people wanted to buy it and he was not selling it. Then at the beginning of the next summer, our tractor broke down and it was going to take a few weeks before it would be fixed. So I went back to Asa's store and told him that old car would help us a lot on our farm. He agreed to sell it to me for thirty dollars. Asa helped me get the thing started and I began the three or four mile ride up hill to our farm. My Mom and sister were in the car following me home. I had driven only a short piece when Mom honked her horn so I stepped on the gas pedal. I thought I was going to slow so I gave it more gas. She kept blowing the horn and I drove even faster. I didn't realize the thing was on fire until I got to the house, and that's why Mom was blowing the horn! The fire went out soon after I turned it off but a little damage had been done. I fixed it up and I named it "the jitterbug," It was a big help to use it to pull many trailer loads of hay that summer and we used it on the farm for many years. I tinkered with it quite a bit. It was fun to work on it and even more fun to drive.

I even drove that old jitterbug up on Bald Knob. Janice and a friend of ours were with me and we started up the old dirt road toward the Canaan Valley Ski Resort is now. It hadn't been very long before that the gas pipeline had been built right up over the top of the knob. It was really steep and I didn't know if we would make it all the way to the top. We did make it but we were holding on for dear life. On the way, back down we got caught in a thunderstorm. Since there was no top on the thing, we got off and huddled under a big tree. We got soaked anyway and thankfully, the tree didn't get struck by the lightning.

Over the years, I have had many cars and trucks and always enjoyed working on all of them. I became a backhoe operator and spent many years at numerous jobs all over the state of West Virginia. One of my jobs was helping to build the road into the Canaan Valley State Park. Unfortunately, in 1968, the state government took my parents farm to become part of this park, and they moved to Harman. I often think about our farm, our relatives, and old neighbors. There were lots of good people and good times in those good old days in Canaan Valley.

Willye Florence Shobe

Willye Florence Shobe
By Helen M. Lewis of Hyndman, Pennsylvania
Born 1941

Willye Florence Shobe was born Oct. 7, 1899, and died Oct. 27, 1992 at the age of 93. Funeral services were held at Harper's Chapel Brethren Church of South Fork, where she played the organ for many years. Rev. Lee Cullers officiated Willye's funeral services, which were under the direction of the Basagic Funeral home in Petersburg, WV. Willye is buried at the Shobe Family cemetery. Willye was never married and her occupation was that of a schoolteacher. Willye was the daughter of Phobe Margaret Graham Shobe and Ross Graham Shobe. Phobe was born April 29, 1866, and died March 16, 1940. Ross was born Dec. 31, 1872 and died Sept 17, 1938. Ross's father was John Armentrout Shobe who was born 1839 and died Oct 14, 1907. He married Catherine Armentrout. Willye had one sister, Clarice Virginia Shobe who was born April 4, 1895 and died Dec. 25, 1988. Clarice is buried at the Harmen Family cemetery. She was married to Max Clement Barger.

Willye F. Shobe and her family raised Kirk Armentrout from the age of two years old. After becoming a schoolteacher, Willye bought a farm on the South Fork Rd., Moorefield, WV. Janie and Kirk Armentrout lived in Willye Shobe's home while all of their children except Thomas John was born. Willye was like a second mother to all of the older children. She helped take care of the farm animals, work in the gardens, butcher, can, and cook, sew, help the children with their homework and always made sure they were in church every week. Since Mom, neither Dad, nor Willye had no driver's license or automobile, we had to walk one mile each way to church and back in all kinds of weather. Mom would often "catch" a ride to town to get a few groceries and the grocery store would deliver her and the groceries back home. There were eleven of us living in Willye's house. The home had three rooms downstairs and two bedrooms upstairs. There was no running water in the home, no bathrooms, and no electricity until 1952. A large pot-bellied stove heated the house, which was in the middle room downstairs. Everyone had chores to do before and after school… carrying water from the well, splitting, and carrying in the wood, working in the garden, cooking, sewing, and helping to take care of the farm animals.

Willye loved to crochet. She fed and milked the cow and slopped the pigs and hogs. There were always chickens to feed and eggs to gather as well as cottage cheese and butter to make. Willye died at the age of ninety-three of colon cancer. She is buried on the Graham family property, Keller Ridge Road, Rt. 220, south of Petersburg, WV.

NOTE: Strite Eugene Crites, the father of Janie Crites Armentrout, has ancestors who are related to Willye Shobe's family. His great grandfather on his mother's side, Martin Shobe is also listed as an ancestor of Ross Shobe, Willye's father. Doris Armentrout Stanley discovered this data when she was typing the family history of the Janie and Kirk Armentrout family.

Fried Chicken made with Cream
By Virginia C. Harr Smith of Columbus, Ohio
Born 1921

I was born in our farmhouse on Freeland Road, Canaan Valley, West Virginia. I lived there on the farm with my parents, Frank and Caroline Kesner Harr. Altogether, they had four boys and four girls and I was the seventh child.

My father worked as a foreman in the woods and he was gone away a lot before I was born and when I was a youngster. I can remember one time when I was about six years old; one of his nephews had a car and was going to drive him back to work. My Dad had worked at several lumber camps in West Virginia but this time he was working farther away in Maryland. They decided that we would go on a picnic and my Mother, my baby brother, Charles and I went with them to Deep Creek Lake. It was a big day for me riding in a car that far and we ate our dinner beside the huge lake where my father was meeting some of the other men. On the way back home through Davis, we stopped at Cleon Raese's Store. (Sometimes my father would take excess potatoes, eggs, and dressed chickens in a wagon to sell to Mr. Raese for his store.) I can still remember that in the store was the first time I had ever seen electric lights! I kept looking up at the ceiling where there were about six light bulbs hanging down on wires. I was amazed at how the store was so lit up and I couldn't take my eyes off the bright lights.

Sometimes we would visit my grandparents, Raleigh Barker "Buck," and Mary Elizabeth Griffith Harr, who lived a few miles away on the Back Hollow Road. One day, when my father was helping his parents with the farm work, my mother fried chicken and fixed up a big dinner to take there. The rest of us stayed at home while she walked with my youngest brother, Charles to my grandparent's house and carried the dinner to them. We didn't get chicken very often. It smelled so good but she wouldn't let the rest of us kids have any of it. After she left, we were very mad. My siblings, Mildred, Emery, "Pete" and Raymond, "Buck, came up with a plan. So we went to the henhouse and they caught a chicken. They got the axe and proceeded to kill it and we cleaned it up. When I went to fry it, I couldn't find the lard or any grease so I decide that maybe cream would work. I fixed the meal and it was the best chicken we had ever eaten! We ate it all and my parents never missed the cream or the old hen.

Life on the farm was very hard work and everyone had to help. We raised oats and hay for the cattle and sheep and worked in the big garden every year. We had fruit trees in the orchard. Sometimes the whole family would go to the huckleberry plains (also called Dolly Sods.) We would take sandwiches with us and it would take us all day to walk there and back. We would pick lots of huckleberries and fill our tummies and our buckets. Then we poured the berries into larger handmade containers. They were round wooden vessels with tree bark on the outside; two of them were connected by a rope that was draped over each of the two horses to carry home. (One time an awful thunderstorm came and we had to put buckets over top of our heads to protect us from the hail.) Lots of meat, fruits, and vegetables were preserved and kept in our cellar for the cold winters.

There were many huge maple trees on our land. In the spring, we tapped the trees and let the sap run in the buckets hanging on them. We poured them into wooden barrels and when they were full, we hauled them to Granddaddy and Grandma's farm. There the liquid would be cooked outside over a hot fire for many hours. The maple syrup was delicious and sometimes all of the kids got a maple sugar egg at Easter.

Breakfast was always a big meal with buckwheat cakes, maple syrup, and sausage and eggs before we walked almost a mile to Cosner School. The original Cosner School had burned down and they had school for one year in the Buena Church and that is where I attended first grade (1926-1927.) The next year the new one-room school building was ready and was built on the opposite side of the road from where it had been. It had a stove near the middle and had two coatrooms and a window on the side of the building near the road (later became Route 32.) We didn't have a kitchen so we always carried our lunches. Water had to be carried up the hill from Golf Teter's house. We made cone-shaped cups out of paper and drank water from them. I went from the second through the eighth grade in that building. My teachers were Mr. Russell Hinkle, Mr. Gene Graham, Mr. B.R. Meadows (from Montrose,) Mr. Bill Smith, Mr. Hoye Smith, and Miss Mildred Eshelman.

During my seventh grade at Cosner, I passed the test for eighth grade so I graduated. I returned for the next year and mostly read library books. During this year, my brother, Buck, and I were janitors and helped to clean the school and build the fires.

After, Cosner a school bus started to run to Davis where Buck and I attended high school. He had stayed with our sister, Mabel and completed one year of high school in Sully so he graduated from high school in 1938. My graduation in 1939 was held in the Davis Theater located near Coffman's Store. I remember around 1936 or 1937; our basketball team was playing for the State Championship. Our principals announced that win or lose; the whole school would get a day off. The team lost the game and he went back on his word. He didn't let us off. The students went to school the next day and decided to go on strike. With the band, playing almost all of us walked in a group from Davis to the Thomas High School. It was quite a sight. The police were called since they were expecting trouble. The Thomas teachers walked with their students to class and the bathroom since they were afraid they would join the Davis kids outside. After awhile, we all walked back to Davis without incident. The town kids went home and the ones that rode the country bus went back to class because they really didn't have any other place to hang out. The next day there were lots of kids standing in line to turn in their signed excuses? Since there were so many, the principal just told us to return to class.

My parents and all of my siblings are gone now. I miss them a lot but I have such fond memories of the times we shared at home in Canaan Valley.

This Is the "Hole" Story
By John D. Arthur of High Springs, Florida
Born 1936

My name is John D. Arthur, and everyone in Beryl, West Virginia called me John Dale in 1945. I remember when we first went to Beryl to live; it was a few days after Christmas, 1945, my mother, little sister, little brother and I. We moved in with my Grandpap and Grandma Gordon. I was 9 years old, my sister Reba Jean, was 4 years old and my brother Sam was less than 1 year old.

We all lived in an old Coal Miner Co. house right behind the Presbyterian Church. It was a double house that my grandpap was able to buy and fix up, because he never bought anything on 'tick' as they called it (credit) at

John D. Arthur

John Arthur with his Grandpap Gordon

the Co. store or anywhere else. He was a coal miner for the Masteller Coal Co. from the age of 13 to age 62, when he was forced to retire because of the Black Lung. The house had five rooms and a path on each side, and the path led to a double outhouse, one hole on each side. My grandpap rented out the other side of the house. In about 1948, he rented it to Mr. Mash Bowers and his wife Dorthey. They had two sons, Bobby about nine and Billy about five.

Then came the day when the outhouse hole filled up and we had to dig a new hole and move the outhouse over and lime and fill the old hole the rest of the way up. My grandpap, Mr. Bowers, and I had just completed digging the new hole and were in the process of moving the outhouse over the new hole. Mr. Bowers had just told Bobby and Billy to stay away from the hole. While we were moving it, here comes Billy running from Bobby, looking back over his shoulder, and in the old hole, he went right up to his armpits and his dad who was closest to him, grabbed his arm, and pulled him out. Then he yelled for his wife to come and get him. Then said jokingly, "I don't know if it would be best to make another one, or clean this one up." Ha, Ha, Ha, Ha

Childhood Memories
By Juanita B. Mullenax of Petersburg, West Virginia
Born 1938

In the spring of the year of 1947, our dad purchased thirteen acres of land and an old abandoned homestead that had set empty for many years. The evidence of this neglect could be seen at first glance with all the weeds and brush that encumbered the surrounding house right up to the perimeter of the building.

Naturally, all sorts of critters had established their claim of ownership by their very existence. One of the worst culprits was the deadly copper head snake. For many years, our pet dog and even the cats would bring us a stunned trophy and we would, in most cases, have to finish the kill. Needless to say, there were many close calls for us six kids running barefoot day and even after night to have been bitten, but miraculously, we survived. I would say the one time when I was most threatened was when we, the family were picking huckleberries. They grew plentiful against our hillsides and we periodically picked, canned, and made numerous delicious cobblers, etc. Sometimes a simple meal was a cobbler and milk. Anyway, we came upon a patch that was simply loaded with this luscious fruit. After picking around the outer-edge of the patch, I automatically got up and started to step into the center of the patch for closer reaching. With my right foot in mid-air, I glanced to where I was going to step and stared right into the beady eyes of a coiled deadly copperhead. His tongue was darting outward and he was poised to strike. I danced off that ridge barely touching the ground and didn't stop until I reached the safety of our home in the hollow below. You would be right if you guessed that I picked no more berries that day. Oh yes, Dad killed the snake.

A small stream meandered from the mouth of the hollow above the house and traveled alongside as it followed its path onward. A drinking and cooking supply of water was a hand-dug well. We drew it up bucket by bucket on a chain. Once a year we cleaned and limed it for purity and our health's sake. Consequently, we heated water for usage of cooking, cleaning and bathing in the reservoir of our cook stove that was fueled with wood from our own private stock of mountain land.

Our weekly baths occurred on Saturdays by filling a big aluminum tub that we used weekly for washing our many loads of dirty clothes. We also had the pleasure of using a washboard for this chore. The reservoir only held, like 5 gallons of water, so we continuously heated several pans of water on the cook stove as this project evolved with all six of us kids getting our weekly bath. Otherwise, throughout the week we would "wash off" in a wash pan. Today when I think about it, it doesn't sound very sanitary, but it didn't seem to leave any scars or discontent or otherwise, with any of us.

In the summertime, we would gather a cake of soap, a washcloth, and a towel. We then would walk about fifteen minutes to a near-by creek and in a favorite, not-so-deep 'swimming hole' sheltered by overhanging tree branches, we would wallow and splash to our heart's content as we indulged in our soothing body cleansing bath. This would occur sometimes as many as five times a week.

Some might say that we lived 'pretty rough and pretty poor', but I sincerely consider that we were very privileged to have had the necessity of what we had to survive and enjoy!

My Teacher Broke Three Yardsticks on My Rear
By Chuck Hampe of Berkley Springs, West Virginia
Born 1951

A time I have always considered a private time is using the bathroom, or in this case the outhouse. Mom called it a "privy." As I child I was sometimes puzzled at some that had more than one place to let one go. I had used some two holers, but this one time I opened the door, there was three. Apparently, this family enjoyed sharing the experience. Using the outhouse is also, where I learned about the bucket of red and white corncobs. Using two red ones and then the white one to make sure you were clean and finishing with a few pages from a Sears catalog.

As rebellious child, I always seemed to be in some kind of trouble. In school one day, while in the third grade something happened on the playground and I got the blame. The teacher gave me a "tongue lash-in," then, she told me to bend over. She started smacking me on the rear end with three yardsticks. After the first hit, the spanking hurt like crazy. The second swing broke one of the yardsticks and I started laughing. This made the teacher lose her temper and she hit me even harder until the other two sticks broke. As she stood in front of the class with what remained of the three broken yardsticks in her hand, the other kids started laughing. She was embarrassed to a point where she threw the sticks on the floor and left the room.

One particular bad winter in 1962, the snow was about two feet deep. The road crew was plowing the road, which went right past our house, but they were pushing it up the hill. Why they didn't go down the hill is something we couldn't figure out because the whole length of the road was only about an eighth of a mile. As a result, the plow got stopped at the top of the hill. The school bus stop was also at the top, so in order for us to go to school we had to carve steps in an accumulation of six feet of packed snow, make a path across thirty feet, and make steps at the other end. Of course, we continued shoveling the path as winter weather occasionally gave us more snow. We were so very happy to see spring that year.

When we were boys, my brother and I had one bike we shared. If we traveled together, I usually did the peddling. He rode on the handlebars. One afternoon in May, we were riding past our neighbor's house. He had a collection of scrap metal. Someone had given him an old bicycle frame with wheels and handlebars, no sprocket. He saw us riding by and called out for us to come over for a minute. He asked if we would like to have this bike. We looked at it trying how to figure out how to make it move. I asked if he had a short piece of rope. He obliged us and helped us tie the bikes together then, reached over to retrieve a seat from the pile. We told him, "thanks," and we were on our way. The next challenge was stopping it once we got it going. Since it had no fenders, my brother simply put his feet against the tire. After flipping it one time, he learned not to use the front tire for stopping.

People would stare as we rode by, but we didn't care, we were having fun. We rode around that way most of the summer that year.

With way too many choices to watch on TV these days, imagine growing up with only three channels to choose from. We had a pipe outside with two antennas attached to it. One would pick up the major channels, but to pick up the local news and weather, someone; usually me, had to go outside while Mom or Dad were watching to tell us when the picture was clear; all this effort just to watch Batman and Daniel Boone.

One Must Never Give Up
By Kenneth Sims of Hedgesville, West Virginia
Born 1945

As A child, I had three goals; to become a teacher, own a little red wagon, and be a farmer. I have leased farms and raised all kinds of animals, but I have never owned a little red wagon.

It was a cold, blustery winter day in

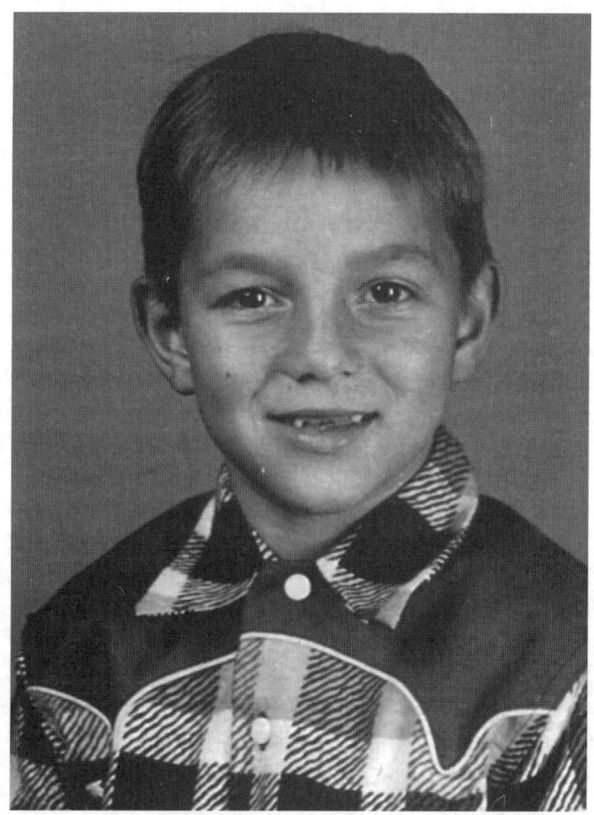

Kenneth Sims at age 7

December. After lunch, I walked into my first grade classroom and there was Santa. This was my first encounter seeing Santa, even though I had heard a lot about him. I ran over to Santa and climbed upon his lap and talked to him. He asked me what I wanted for Christmas. I replied, "I want a little red wagon; that is all I want." He told me, "Not to give up hope," as if he knew my parents did not have the extra money to buy gifts. I was the youngest of eleven children. My Father was a coal miner and Mom ran the house and the farm. We bought things we needed or received "hand me downs." We learned so much about life from our family conversations. I feel really blessed to have had the family I had.

Christmas morning arrived and I rushed into the living room looking for my little red wagon. There was no little red wagon. I received a pair of bib overalls, and a pair of black high top Converse sneakers. Oh, how I hated both of those gifts. I remember Santa's words, "don't give up hope."

The following year, when Santa came to school, I made my way to Santa and climbed upon his lap and once again, I told him I wanted a little red wagon. Once again, he told me, "Not to give up hope." Christmas morning came and I received a pair of cowboy boots and a western plaid shirt. I was pleased and happy, but it was not my little red wagon. This ritual went on all through elementary school. In high school, I saw Santa, he told me, "I was too big to sit on his lap, but I could tell him what I wanted for Christmas." Santa looked at me, and said, "I know what you want. You want a little red wagon." He told me once again, "Not to give up hope."

I graduated from high school and still no little red wagon. I went on to college and became a teacher and still no little red wagon. However, I never gave up hope. I met a lovely lady and we got married. Two years later, our daughter was born. I held her for a while and handed her back to my wife. I told her I needed to go buy a gift. I went to the store and bought her a little red wagon. Not for me, but for her. Another forty years passed and I never received my little red wagon. I never gave up hope, and continued to wish and pray.

Each year, as I would read the story, <u>Dragon's Red Wagon</u> to my students, I would tell my class how the dragon and I were similar. He was always wishing and praying and hoping for a red wagon. Even though no one made wagons for dragons. Little dragon kept saying, "One must never give up hope." "When I am not hoping, praying, and wishing, I just cry a lot!" As the story goes, there was a forest fire. The dragon agreed to go, but he couldn't cry no matter how hard he tried. Then his friend whispered into his ear, to tell him about that little red wagon that he was never ever going to have. He welled up in tears and put out the fire. As a reward, the next day all the forest friends worked together to make a little red wagon with these words painted on the sides, Dragon's Red Wagon. They asked him if he liked the wagon. He said he did and it was the best wagon ever! He also said, "One must never give up hope, wishing, and praying." After I finished reading I asked, the children the moral of the story, and all of them said, "One must never give up hope."

The following day, a teacher walked up to me in the hallway and said, "There is something special in our room for you." I walked into the classroom and saw that a little girl had cut out, colored, and glued paper together to make a little red wagon. It had four wheels, a handle, with the words, on the side, that said, "Mr. Sim's Little Red Wagon. It took for me sixty-two years to finally receive my little red wagon. The students reminded me, "One must never give up hope."

I may never receive a real little red wagon but this paper wagon was made with so much love, it was more precious than a real one. I have this little red wagon in a display case sitting in my bedroom. It is one of the first things that I see when I get up each day, and I say to myself, "ONE MUST NEVER GIVE UP."

Favorite Kittens
By Janice Cooper Barnes of Waldorf,
Maryland
Born 1949

The first seventeen years of my life was spent in the southern end of Canaan Valley, West Virginia. Our land was located directly across from the Buena Chapel and Cemetery on Route 32 and my parents, Bennett F. and Mabel Harr Cooper, bought and settled on the sixty-eight acre farm in 1948. Up to that time, they had lived in a few places in West Virginia. They lived in Sully (on Middle Mountain) where my only sibling, Gary L. Cooper was born, also on top of Alleghany Mountain above Harman. After the State took the farm to be developed as part of Canaan Valley State Park, they lived below Harman.

We lived about a mile from the farm owned by my maternal grandparents, Frank and Caroline Kesner Harr on Freeland Road, and my Mother was raised there. We all called my grandparents Pop and Mom Harr. My Uncle Pete lived there also. We would go in the car to see them often for short visits and then I got old enough to walk over by myself. Times were great in the summer when my aunts and uncles visited their house from Ohio, Pennsylvania, and Virginia. I would spend all day over there and often stayed nights too with my cousins. Sometimes we had to do several chores but we got to play a lot and explore the whole farm.

It was good to see these relatives who mostly came to Pop's only in the summer. It was even better that they would cook or bring different foods with them like sloppy joes and scrapple that we had never eaten. Sometimes we would have big picnic dinners in their front yard. The wooden sawhorses would be brought out and long boards placed over them. So all we needed were a couple tablecloths and we had a very large picnic table. There was lots of cooking done and other aunts and uncles brought prepared food from their homes in Hardy and Randolph Counties. There would be big galvanized tubs filled with bottles of Nehi soda pop that was cooled by the cold water pumped from the well. Another tub was filled with cold water and watermelons.

We also went often to my Granddaddy (Abraham) Cooper's farm on Route 72 between Stringtown and Flanagan Hill. This is where my Dad was born and raised. He had three brothers and one sister who were all farmers nearby and we would go often to visit or help out with their farm work. Throughout the year at holidays and birthdays, we would have family get-togethers with lots of great food and visiting relatives.

One of my jobs on our farm was to feed the chickens, pump water for them, and gather the eggs in an old wooden basket. One day I got so excited that I hurried to the house to show my mother what I had found in the hen's nest. I didn't even know what it was but I had it carefully cradled in my little hands, and then clumsily fell up the step from the porch into the living room. Fortunately, I didn't break the membrane. My mother said it was a soft-shelled egg and it didn't happen very often. She explained that sometimes hens laid an egg before the shell had completely formed and probably it was because the hen didn't eat enough calcium or oyster shells.

I have always loved kittens and it was so exciting to locate the newest ones when I was growing up. One evening at milking time when I was pretty young, I could see from the barn door a black and white cat walking along in the grass with her little kittens trailing in a straight line behind her. I was ready to run and catch them when my mother stopped me. I'm so glad she did because it was actually a mother skunk and her babies!

We had one particular tomcat that was my favorite. I called him Mustard because he was yellow/orange and white. I can remember when he was born in our barn along with his three brothers and sisters. Of course, they were outside cats. Mustard lived a lot longer than the rest and he spent a lot of time out on the farm catching rodents to supplement what little milk we gave him along with scraps of food we threw out. He was probably three or four years old when he met with a "cat-astrophe." First, he went missing for a couple of days, after a couple more days, my Dad "fessed up" and told me that he may never come back. He said when he had been mowing hay in the meadow with the tractor; he didn't see the ole cat crouched down in the tall grass. He said this was typical of what they do because when there is a loud noise coming at them, and they don't know which way to run so they will crouch down. He said he thought the cutter bar probably cut him and he took off running toward the woods. It wasn't Dad's fault but I was very sad. Then after a full week, the cat came dragging himself slowly to our doorstep. He was so pitiful looking with dried blood on him. His right back foot was cut off along with part of his tail. Part of his front left paw was missing too, so that he had only one claw. He was so weak and he could hardly walk. I cleaned him up, fed him for the next several days, and gave him lots of tender loving care. He lived several more years and continued to be the best mouse catcher out of the other cats. He usually went with me to the chicken house to do my chores. When I opened the door to get the grain, he pounced on the many mice that would scatter out of the big metal barrel. He always caught at least one mouse and sometimes caught two if they were little ones. I was always glad he adapted so well that he had one claw on his left paw. He used it like a hook with his other good paw.

I remember one summer at Pop Harr's barn there were more than twenty cats and kittens and my cousins and I were in heaven! Some of them were wild but in just a week or two, we tamed them one by one. We loved dressing them in our doll clothes. It was even funnier when the kittens sometimes wanted to run away and we chased them down so that no one knew we were using the doll clothes that had been carefully hand sewn by Mom Harr, our Grandmother.

Pop and Pete milked the dairy cows twice daily in the barn. They would give the bigger cats some warm milk but not very much was spared since they sold the milk to the Carnation Milk Company. There was one kitten we called Punkie Pete that was really scrawny and malnourished. He was one of several in his litter and the others pushed him out of their way, and the momma cat must not have had enough milk to go around. My cousins and I felt so sorry for him and knew he needed more to eat. We also knew that we couldn't ask Pop for any milk. I knew how to milk cows and helped with the milking at my home so I came up with a plan. We got a pint jar and walked down to the pasture where Pop's cows were grazing during the middle of the day. It isn't good for the cow if you don't milk her dry but this was a very important mission. I knew which cow was the gentlest and went to find her. I wasn't sure she would let me milk her in the pasture but she cooperated and I was able to fill the jar. We sneaked back up to the barn mow and put some of the warm milk in one of our doll's baby bottles. Punkie Pete ate hungrily from the bottle several times that day and the next. Sometimes after that, we would let the other kittens nurse a little bit and then take them away from the momma while he took his turn. He survived but was always the runt of the litter.

There were times when I wished I lived somewhere else. Especially when I was a teenager, I dreamed about living in town or somewhere new and more exciting. Soon after graduating from Mountaineer High School, I moved to the Washington, D.C. area and started a job where I have spent most of my years. Sometimes it was more exciting, however now I look back on these country memories, and I wouldn't trade them for all of the other experiences.

The Green Spiral Notebook
By Darlene M. Kesner and Frances Robinson
of Petersburg, West Virginia
Born 1942

My parents were George W. and Breatrice V. Nesselrodte. We lived on the South side of Petersburg, West Virginia in Grant County on Route 220 in Franklin Pike across from the little white church (Saint Johns,) is on the right and our home is on the left on Middle Mountain.

Dad and Mom met at the sawmill camp at Northfork. Mom was the cook there and Dad owned the sawmill. March 28, 1928, they got

The Nesselrodte family in 1947

married and moved to Middle Mountain and raised their family.

Dad and Mom provided our family, by running his own sawmill, his first mill was in Northfolk. He moved the mill to where he got his timber. They raised and sold hogs, chickens, sheep, wool, and eggs. Mon was a housewife and mother of twelve children, two dies at birth. She raised a garden and canned food and made our clothes. One time Dad was moving his mill to another place but when he was moving his steam engines on an old dirt road, and they got to close to the edge and it rolled down over the hill, so he had to get the other steam engines to pull it back up.

All the families on Middle Mountain in the fall at harvest time got together and did their wheat and oats; they butchered hogs and made apple butter for the winter. We would start out with our family then, went to Harley and Verlie Sites, Nelley and Alvie Alts, Martin and Beakey Alt, John and Margie Rateliff, John and Ethel Borror, John and Anna Mayers, and Nancy and son Georgie Kesner. He was the photographer for all their friends and family.

On May 19, 1938, my Brother "Bud" or Stanley Nesselradte was in the newspaper, win Marble Crown tournament that was a big thing when we was kids.

When we were kids, we made our doll babies out of corn shuck that was the body and the corn silk was the hair, and to make our cars and trucks, we used old cans, boxes we put holes in them, put a stick thru them, and took corncobs and cut them and made wheels. We also played in a dirt road and made mud pies.

After supper, when it got dark, we sat around listening to the radio. Gabriel Heater, he was the newsman. We also listened to the Grand Old Opry, and on Saturday night, then on Sunday after breakfast, we would go into the living room and listen to preaching on the radio.

We used to take a bath in a wash pan and sometimes we got into a big washtub and took a bath behind the wood stove.

And we had outhouses and chamber pots in the house at night and we used old catalogs to wipe with, the secret was to take a page and keep balling it up until it was soft.

Mom made our clothes by hand. She used feed sacks and flour bags. I remember them well that had a rooster on the back of them.

On school days, Mom would pack our lunches; she made us jelly bread, baking powder biscuits with jelly or apple butter, French toast, and cookies. Our dinner buckets were King Syrup cans with handles.

My niece found a little green spiral notebook that had prices in it from 1942 and 1943 when they wrote thing down in the book that they got from the store.

Broom 69 cents, hair barrettes 10 cents, six plates 2/25 cents = 75 cents, one mixing bowl 20 cents, two teacups and saucers 22 cents, one mixing spoon 15 cents, two spools of white thread 10 cents, cloth four yards $1.80, four pencils 5 cents, six cans of milk 50 cents. 1 pound of coffee 23 cents, 1 box of baking powder 10 cents, sugar, two pounds 16 cents, washing powder 25 cents, cough syrup 35 cents, hack saw blades, 10 cents, kerosene one and one-half gallons 16 cents, one ax handle $1.25, two quarts of oil, 18 cents, two pounds nails 12 cents, thirteen gallon of gas $2.75. December 23, 1942 (I guess this was for Christmas,) two postcards two cents, twenty-five cents, , one dozen oranges, thirty cents, one, one-pound gingersnaps, twenty cents, flour, ninety-five cents, soap toilet, five cents, sugar, two-pounds, sixteen cents, and they sold seven dozen eggs @ twenty-four cents. We also found the receipt that they bought a sewing machine in 1952, it was $139.00. They made payments of $16.00 a month and we still have the sewing machine.

It was Easter time, and Mom would take onion peeling and eggs and boil them together and they were pretty. That's what we did when we were kids.

Then we all grew up and two of my brothers went into the Army and some moved to Winchester and four of us stayed in Petersburg. We all stay in touch even our children. Also, we still have the home place and a family commentary. It stays in the family.

Dad & my Brother, Two Mysterious Characters
By Patricia A. Henson of Big Pool, Maryland
Born 1942

"**Daddy's Fun**" We used to live in Everett, Pa. when I was about 3 years old. We lived near the river and it was a gathering place on Sundays for people, we did not know that came to swim. When our aunts, uncles, and cousins would visit, they would swim also. I remember one evening my daddy's sisters were coming to visit. We liked to play down where the people went swimming at, and so my daddy thought he would play a joke on them. He liked to sit down and read the paper and they knew this. One evening, he knew they were coming for a visit, so when they got there, they saw my daddy down there reading the paper, so they went down. They sat down in their chairs and started talking to him. After a while, they figured out why he did not talk to them. Earlier, he had stuffed his bib overalls and had his shoes there also, and stuffed his shirt also, and fixed the newspaper in what appeared to be his hands. He made it appear that it was him sitting there. What a laugh and what teasing for a long time my aunts had to bear. Memories are very precious things to have.

"**Good Neighbors**" What to do when you have no TV to watch? Well, if you were us kids, you would go to your neighbors'. Right, Right! Our neighbors knew which nights we would be coming to their house to watch TV. It was when we could see "Amos & Andy," "I Love Lucy," or "George Burns and Gracie Allen." They were our favorites. Oh, we didn't go inside their house to watch TV. We just stood outside and watched through their bay window on their front porch. We were so excited just to do that, even though sometimes we had to wear our coats and wish we had a drink or snack like they were having, but we got to watch our favorite shows. After our shows were over and when we were ready to go home, we would peck on the window and wave good-by to them. This let them know that we were going home and then they could shut their curtain and were probably glad no one was looking at them through their window. That's what I call good neighbors to some kids who were less fortunate than they were.

"The Mystery Lady" When I was not yet a teenager and we had no TV to watch, we would go over to our other neighbors house. It was not to watch their TV, for they had no TV either. They were Bill and Bessie, brother and sister, and well up in years. When we were not watching TV at our other neighbors, we would go to their house and go out to the side of the road with them to sit under a big old pine tree with its roots growing out of the ground. These roots made a good place to sit on, since we had no lawn chairs. We would watch for the cars that would go by and wave to the people in the cars for we knew most everyone around. There usually weren't many cars to go by, but one evening as we sat there talking to our neighbors, we heard a noise and then we saw a lady come running down the road by us. She had on heels, "the source for the noise," a hat, a dressy dress, a pearl necklace and gloves, and carried a large purse. She sure did have on the makeup! No one knew who she was even though we thought we knew everyone in our little place called "Shanktown." It was between Big Pool and Big Spring, Md. After she passed and went around the curve in the road, we were trying to figure who that lady was. Before long, she came running back by again and this time she waved at us. We were sure baffled by that lady. When we could not figure out who she was, us kids went home. What a surprise awaited us there. There, bent over in laughter when we came in the door, was our oldest brother, Amos. He still had the dress on and was still trying to get all that makeup off. I'll never forget that "Mystery Lady" that made our evening so long ago, so puzzling and yet so much fun.

"Swimming Fun" We kids liked to go swimming at McCorys Ferry in Big Spring, Md. It was about 2 miles or so from our home and we had to walk. My brother, Buck, had an unusual thing that he did each time we got to go swimming. He would wear what we called his "Mackinaw Coat." No matter how hot it was, he wore it to and from swimming. I still don't know why. Also, that happens to be where I was baptized as a teenager. There were other people swimming there also. It sure was a fun thing to do.

Country Picnic
By Ernie & Betty Racey of Rio, West Virginia
Born 1947

As the summer months begin in the little rural village of the Eastern Panhandle of West Virginia, excitement of the biggest entertainment for the community known as Grassy Lick is coming the last Saturday of July. The folks here are happy to be able to have a Modern Woodmen of America Insurance Club that was organized in the mid-1800's, and it has its own meetinghouse and grounds located in the mountain village.

School is out for the summer before Memorial Day in the mid-1950's, and as young children are anxious to earn a few coins for the "big picnic." We help with all chores on the farm and offer to take the extra eggs and homemade butter to the local store to sell, getting a small reward for that long walk to the nearest store in Kirby, W.V.

Finally, the big day is here and folks came from near and far for the M.W.A. Picnic. It was like a large homecoming with the folks that had went to the city for employment and all the cousins and their cousins came for the big day. Folks came from all the nearby hollows and hillsides early in the day, some arrived by foot and others came by horse and farm wagon and, of course, the city folks had their new shiny automobiles.

A big softball game started early in the day when a couple local teams played in the recently mowed hay fields across the Grassy Lick Rd. Following the games, the big horse-joisting tournament will take place with lots of beautiful horses entering the competition. The men on their speediest horses would race down the field with a wooden spear held over their heads trying to get as many hanging rings as they could in the quickest time. Later in evening was the annual horseshoe competition. As a young child, it was just impossible to take all this in and of course, in the center of the main grounds were lots of activities with food and people catching up on all the news, as we didn't have telephones, television, or internet.

The members of the M.W.A. club had built several nice concession stands, including the main hall, which opened with big drop-down windows at one end. From the building, the most exciting gifts ever seen by a young child were being sold. My dad always made sure that my older brother and I got a couple special gifts, one that was always a box of cracker-jacks and in that was a real neat little gadget plus that yummy snack. Among the special toys to purchase was popguns, wooden paddles with a ball attached with a rubber band, harmonicas, paper fans, little glass banks, and dolls on a stick and they also sold big slices of ice cold watermelon from a big tub of ice. Also, in the same booth was a wooden spinning wheel with numbers and if it was a match with the wheel, you were a winner. A small both was set up for the ball throw which had wooden milk bottles all lined up for the three wooden balls to try to knock all off the board for a prize.

Another small board frame building with a little red panel truck parked in the back with several hoses running in the open doorway was selling the first sodas that I remember ever tasting. The wonderful drink was seltzer water with coke flavoring and served to you in paper cups. Later years, it was served in glass bottles and more flavors were made all from the Coca Cola plant in nearby Romney, W.V.

The big kitchen building was next in line, that's where the first hotdogs in the area were served, and the most delicious hamburgers you ever ate were being fried on the big grill top. The gallons of vegetable soup made by the neighborhood ladies was the best found in Hampshire County.

Across the end of the food area was another large building with openings all the way around with benches on the outside where you could sit and eat some of the real ice cream, homemade cakes, or pies that were sold inside the building. Also, a five-gallon crock of fresh lemonade was ready for the thirsty attendees.

On the hillside stood the open stage where a big-name country music group would appear to the delight of the crowd. Not only did they sing and play; they also had some comedians or even a sharp shooter one year. There were always some locals that got up front to do some clogging to the music and were joined by a few that were feeling good from some homemade corn liquor. There would be two sets of entertainment for the evening and by 11 pm, it was time to say goodnight and start the walk down the dark road to my grandmother's house to spend the night. Needless to say, that all the special events and an overly full tummy kept me awake the remainder of the night. As I listened to the frogs croaking, and a neighboring farm's bull bellowing, I planned my morning trek back to the Woodmen grounds to search for a dropped coin, or perhaps someone even left a gift behind, or who knows what kind of treasures a child may find to savor for next year's picnic.

Summer at Pop's and Mom's Farm
By Carol Ann Smith Teter of Red Creek,
West Virginia
Born 1948

My parents are the late Earl Conrad Smith, born on a farm on Rich Mountain near Harman, West Virginia, and Virginia Crue Harr Smith born on a farm in Canaan Valley a few miles from Davis. I have one sister and she was born in Elkins.

In April 1948, my parents moved from West Virginia to Akron, Ohio, where my Dad found a job at the Fruehauf Trucking Company. Then not long after that, he got a job with the General Tire and Rubber Company and worked many years. I was born one month after their move to Ohio.

We were far from well off. My Mother and Dad had married during World War II and shortly after they had my sister while working on a farm at Valley Bend. Not seeing much future there, many West Virginian's headed to Ohio to find work. My Mother tells how Dad was so proud; he had found a "modern house" for them. It ended up having indoor plumbing, which was a step up from the outhouse they were used to in West Virginia. Times were very hard and my aunt and uncle and their two children moved into our house and lived upstairs for the next ten years. I think of our life as a page from the "Little Rascals." We had little money but had a good life.

Our Grandparents, Frank and Caroline Kesner Harr, and my Uncle, Emery. "Pete" Harr lived on the family farm on Freeland Road in Canaan Valley where my Mother grew up. My Grandfather's parents, Buck and Mary Elizabeth Harr were some of the first settlers in the Valley, coming there in a covered wagon from Fairmont. They lived on a farm at the Southern edge of the Valley.

Pop, as we called our Grandfather, was a large man who had spent many years working in the woods during the timber boom in West Virginia. During that time, my Grandmother was left to care for the farm and their eight children.

In the early 1950s, there was an outbreak of polio and it was a big problem especially in the hot summer weather in the city. Because of this, my parents decided it would be best for my Mother, sister and me to leave the city for the summer and stay on our Grandparents' farm in Canaan Valley. So our summer adventures began and continued every summer for the many years.

When we came to the farm to spend the summer, there was still no running water in the house. They did have electricity but cooked on the old Home Comfort Stove that they got from my Mother and Dad when they moved to Ohio. It was almost like stepping back in time and we loved it. Every day was an adventure.

We would wake up early to the sound of Pop, clanging the milk buckets and the smell of kerosene as my Grandmother, Mom or Mom Harr, started the fire in the cook stove to prepare breakfast. Breakfast was the same most mornings consisting of salt cured ham or bacon, gravy, eggs, and homemade bread. Pop would top it off with a large bowl of oatmeal.

About once a week, the Sunbeam Bread truck would drive in Freeland Road to see if pop wanted to buy anything. He didn't get to the grocery store very often so usually he would buy sliced "store bread" and sometimes a small cake.

One of our jobs was to carry water in from the well out back of the house. We would have to pump each bucket and carry it into the house filling the teakettle, the reservoir in the stove, and the large dishpans that were set on the cook stove to get hot. Two buckets would be filled to set on the cabinet with a large metal dipper from which everyone would drink.

Pop, Carol, and "Harry" the work horse

After the breakfast dishes were finished, Mom would send my sister, my cousins, and I to the garden to gather things for dinner; digging new potatoes, picking lettuce, radishes, onions, and whatever else Mom wanted to prepare. There was always a dishpan full. We spent lots of time sitting at the well cleaning and rinsing the lettuce, each, and every leaf.

Mom would also send us to the cellar to gather the canned goods she needed. There was a well-worn path through the woods to the cellar. It was great fun choosing the canned carrots, beans, pork loin, blackberries, peaches, jams, etc.

Another of our chores in the evening was to walk with Pop down the road to bring the milk cows in for milking. When we got a little older, he trusted us to get the cows by ourselves. We usually went barefoot and had to be very careful not to step in fresh cow manure as we walked behind the cows.

As Pop and Pete did the milking, we

would spend time in the haymow playing with kittens. It was great fun to play with the many kittens. It was also fun though dangerous to try to walk the rafters in the barn mow or jump into the calf's pen that was full of hay below.

After supper, we would finish the day by carrying kindling and wood into the house for Mom to use for the next morning's fire.

Our summer wasn't all work. We had lots of fun picking wild strawberries and red raspberries, playing in the run (small stream) that passed near the barn, painting rocks from the run, playing in the sand pile, playing ball and badminton, and swinging on the rope swing that hung from the huge maple tree in the front yard.

We only got a full bath once a week when Mom would build a fire outside and heat water in a huge iron kettle out in the yard. We would carry buckets of water to a large washtub behind the smokehouse and take turns taking an outside bath. Other days we would use a small wash pan to "sponge off."

Every now and then, we kids would sweep and clean the spider webs in the two-seater outhouse. We put glass jars of mountain laurel, some new magazines, and our painted rocks, to make it "pretty." I often wondered in my later years what Pop and Pete thought of our decorations!

One real treat would be to help make hay. This was before Pop got a tractor. My sister and I would ride his two workhorses, Harry and Kate, and hook up a chain around the hay shocks to haul them across the field. Pop would take the hay shock and place it with a pitchfork around the tall pole that would form the big haystack. They would also haul hay to the barn and lift it up into the mow by using ropes and four large hayforks.

My Uncle Buck raised cauliflower for several years on Pop's farm. When it was ready to be sold, my uncles and Pop would spend days cutting off the heads by hand and hauling them on the wagon into the woods where huge piles of wooden crates were waiting to be packed. We would grab the saltshaker and run to the woods to spend lots of time sitting on the wagon eating raw cauliflower.

The evenings brought new adventures whether it was playing tag, kick the can, catching lightning bugs in mason jars, or catching toads in old buckets. A lot of time was spent sitting on the front porch swing. There was talking, snapping beans, shelling peas, or just watching it get dark. The dew came out into the meadow, the cows were grazing in the pasture, and a line of baby skunks following their mother were seen going down the dirt road in front of the house.

The summers always ended too soon. My Dad would come and spend the last week before taking us home to Ohio. Mom, Pop, and Pete would stand in the yard-waving goodbye to us. Pop, the tall and sometimes harsh man, who would yell at us for slamming the screen door, finding, and eating his candy, and saying we were the orneriest kids he ever saw, would have tears flowing down his cheeks wishing we didn't have to leave. And we were wishing the same thing!

As the years passed, I married a country-boy who I met at a Canaan square dance. Ironically, my parents met at the same place in 1940. We now live on a farm only a few miles from my Grandparents' farm. We raised three daughters who could handle farm chores as well as any boys. I taught first grade for over thirty-three years and was blessed to retire in 2013. We have seven wonderful grandchildren whom I hope enjoys farm life as much as I have for so many years.

Growing Up in the Appalachian Mountains
By Cheston H. Browning of Spring Hill, Florida
Born 1942

"Oh My God," my Mother cried as she flung open the door of Grandpa's old four-door Pontiac. She had just scolded my two older sisters for not telling her I had fallen out of the car. They told her they were afraid to tell because Dad had ordered them to "keep quiet and enjoy the ride."

Having a ride in a car was a great treat in 1946 because our family didn't own one. Occasionally, Dad would borrow Grandpa's car when he finished work at six p.m. for a spin through the mountains of Garrett County, Maryland. The name of our town was Oakland, population one thousand four hundred and was the county seat, which attracted many people from small towns in West Virginia, as well as Maryland.

Cheston with his father in 1954

I start these memories with falling out of the car because that is as far back as I can remember. I'll never forget seeing my Mother crying as she ran back to rescue me. I was crying too because of a serious hole on the right side of my forehead. The blood was pouring from the wound as my Mother picked me up. It was a very dark night and I have no idea how they got Dr. Baumgartner to come to his office to stitch me up. The closest hospital was Cumberland, Maryland, fifty miles away. Doc, ("Bummy" as we called him,) with the help of my parents, held me down and sewed nine stitches to close the wound. He did not believe in numbing, telling my parents that numbing created nasty scars. I'm now seventy-one years old, and the scar is quite visible.

My Father was a meat cutter at Smouse's Store in Oakland. He would walk to work each day, which wasn't too far from our small duplex. He worked six ten hour days and was off on Sundays. Oakland was a busy little town and most of us were poor. We had no idea we were poor because most of the families lived similar lifestyles.

We grew up riding our bikes to the elementary school's playground, where we'd play for hours. Saturday afternoon, we'd go to the movie matinee, which cost ten cents, and another ten cents for a delicious bag of popcorn.

As we got older, Dad joined his father at his small grocery store. There were about seven grocery stores in our area and all of them charged and delivered.

Our family bought a tiny bungalow in town, which had two tiny bedrooms upstairs, and one small bathroom. My parents had one bedroom and my sisters had the other. I was nine years old and shared a bed in the hallway with my baby brother, Ed.

I mowed four yards in the neighborhood and went to work with my Dad when I was ten years old. I filled the egg cartons, weighed and bagged candy, swept the floors, and helped keep the produce department filled. He taught me how to run the cash register when I was twelve years old. I had to stand on an orange crate to see the register's numbers.

We had blizzards in the winter. Those of us who lived in town went to school. Country kids didn't make it when it was bad. There were no cancellations back then.

A milkman delivered quarts of milk to our home very early in the morning. You always had to shake the bottle before using, to mix in the cream on the top of the milk.

I feel like we grew up in the happiest era of history. School was fun and we respected our teachers. At home, we never locked a door and our front door had no lock at all. My Dad and I would lie down on the sofa and listen to "Amos and Andy" and "Our Miss Brooks" on the radio. We had state parks and a big lake for swimming. We would sled ride down steep hills in winter. I was a member of our area's first Little League Baseball. I enjoyed scouting where my favorite memories were scout camp and the drum & bugle corp. We had a youth football team and played against other small towns.

I still remember wooden toys, and a play set with a wooden sliding board. I have pictures of these. We got along fine with our wooden toys and were oblivious of the fact that metal was scarce due to the World War II. I'll never forget the old medical remedies, which were used in the 1940s and 1950s. As a child, I suffered with asthma and was sick often. Castor oil was the most memorable medicine used by many. It had the worst taste of anything I ever swallowed. Your parents would mix it with orange juice or soda pop and try to force it down. I can still remember throwing up castor oil and getting sicker than I was before I took it. Dr. Raymond's Bile Salts were given when our bowels were not normal and believe me they cleaned you out fast and it was a painful ordeal. Sal Hepatica was given for an upset stomach, before Alka Seltzer came along. When I would get a serious asthma attack, my parents would run the hot water heater to maximum heat, then take me to the bathtub and run the hot water. I would kneel and they would use towels to capture the steam. I would breathe the steam into the lungs and then exhale. These treatments would last for thirty minutes. After the treatment, I would take a bath to remove all the sweat, then was dried, and tucked under thick, handmade quilts on my bed. The treatments made me feel better. It was sometime later vaporizers came along and I would stay in bed and inhale Vicks salve vapors. Luckily, my asthma disappeared when I went away to school in the 1950s.

Pennsylvania Electric built a seventy-mile lake in our county called Deep Creek Lake, to provide electricity for the area. It was and is a beautiful lake with many inlets. Very few citizens in our area could afford to build homes around the Lake. Rich people from Baltimore, Pittsburgh, and Washington D.C. bought properties and built beautiful vacation homes. The new lake brought a lot of tax money into our area, and by the mid-fifties, Oakland businesses began to prosper. New schools and highways were built.

My family was very fortunate to get rid of charging and delivering groceries. My Father and his brothers built a modern supermarket and joined a new grocery co-op called Foodland. With the help and ideas of the co-op, our family soon became the primary supermarket in the area, and one of the finest Foodland markets of the co-op.

A memorable teacher I had in the fifth grade, Mrs. Jackson's, was so interesting and talented. She changed my life. Prior to her class, I just played around and didn't take studying seriously. Mrs. Jackson treated me like I was very special. She told me, I had a lot of talent and she wanted me to use it. She encouraged me to study and make good grades. She had me join the band and take the lead in our class play. She would see me working in the store with my Father and I always spoke to her and offered help if she needed it. In Mrs. Jackson class, I also met my first girlfriend. She was the prettiest girl I'd ever seen. Her name was Carolyn, and she joined our class from a country school she had attended for four years. Carolyn was the smartest in our class. I would sit with her at lunchtime and walk in and out with her at recess. For five years my one and only girl was Carolyn. As we got older, I rode my bike five miles to her house. We met at the town movie very often, and attended birthday parties, learned to dance, and rode the bus together. I would call her a couple nights a week. I would walk down to the Ford dealership and use the pay phone.

After I went away to school in the mid-fifties, Carolyn and I parted. We wrote to each other for a while and then it was over.

I have to mention fast cars, for they were an exciting part of our lives, especially in the 1950s. In our area, Chevys, Fords, Studebakers, and pick-up trucks were king. Guys would add loud mufflers, white wall tires, souped up carburetors, shine the bodies, and peel out to get attention. Races would happen late at night at strips that were long and straight, which were scarce around our mountain town. Gasoline was twenty-nine cents a gallon and these hot rods had huge V-8 motors under the hood. I never got into the hot car era because my Dad wouldn't allow it. I got to drive the store trash pick-up truck and

Cheston and his buddy, Bill in 1952

later a Dodge my Grandfather used to haul goats to his goat farm. My Dad, who couldn't afford it, bought me a small motor boat to use on Deep Creek Lake when I came home from school for the summers.

All four of us children, who grew up in the happy days of the 1940s, 1950s, and 1960s are still living, happy, and enjoying life. My Father taught me the grocery business, and I ended up owning my own supermarket in Cumberland, Maryland where I was quite successful.

Me And My City Slicker Brother-In-Law
By Mr. Jim Harr of Jackson, Ohio
Born 1953

My name is Jimmy Harr, and I grew up in Canaan Valley, WV in the late 1950's and early 60's. I was the youngest of my parent's four children and I believe that I caught the tail end of an era that is gone forever. We lived on a family farm of 270 acres and I learned much about life through the "hands on" experience that the farm life offered. My dad needed us on the farm and we all pitched in. He handed us responsibility long before we can imagine today. I learned to drive a John Deere tractor before I could lift a hay bale. I also learned to handle a gun. Two things were drilled into my young mind at an early age. One, you let your clutch out slow, or you'll jerk your uncle off the wagon, and two, don't you point that gun at anybody! These were the basic "need to know" things in my world by the time I was eight years old.

We also played with the farm animals. We learned how to hypnotize a chicken and to rock them to sleep with their head under their wing. Two of my siblings and I rolled in laughter the day we painted the cat's butt with my sister's lipstick. The cat was ashamed of himself and my sister was livid. (She still bristles over that one.)

It was the oldest sister that left home after high school in 1961. The lure of the big cities on the East coast and Ohio, were ever present and claimed so many of the graduates in our area. My sister landed in Baltimore, and within a couple of years had found a feller and married him. His name was Jim and his integration into our family had its curious moments. Their trips to the farm were always welcome adventure for me, because it gave me an opportunity to educate my brother-in-law. He was ten years my senior and I'm sure was very much a man in his city world, but on the farm he was my equal. I was about eleven and I quickly learned that we had two things in common; he liked to drink a lot of pop and he liked to shoot guns. I'm sure that the city offered lots of pop, but nowhere to shoot and he was eager to explore. The farm offered plenty of open space, and as long as we had pop and .22 bullets (lots of .22 bullets), we had things to do.

Of course, there was always the can shooting off the fence posts that is for beginners, but the ultimate quest was to kill a groundhog. This was an achievement that eluded us for years, although we pursued it relentlessly. One time we climbed an apple tree that hovered over an active groundhog hole. We sat up in that tree for two solid hours and finally the groundhog stuck his head out. There he was, not fifteen feet away! I motioned for Jim to take the shot, which he did. Don't you know that he missed him? How could he miss? I could have spit on him! I was about ready to quit on him that time. Of course, we had already missed hundreds before and this one would be no exception.

We discussed many ways to force a groundhog out of his hole. I had heard that you could drown them out, but that it required several barrels of water hauled from the stream. We just didn't have the equipment to do that, so we decided on trying a second option. I had heard that it was possible to smoke one out, and this we proceeded to do.

We decided that the essential ingredients for this would be a few rags soaked with a little gasoline. Now, the mixing of gasoline and fire was another of the lessons that most farm boys learn young, and at least I knew enough to be careful. What I didn't know was that gasoline vapors are even more flammable than gasoline, and I was about to find that out. We had an active groundhog mound in mind and there we set up our experiment. It was a three hole complex which we knew contained a resilient groundhog that we had shot at many times. This time we intended to get him. We placed the gasoline soaked rags in two of the entrances, and I stationed myself with the gun at the third where I expected the groundhog to make his exit. I wasn't going to trust Jim with another sure-shot opportunity like this. What I expected was to light each rag and let the smoke fill up the tunnels, forcing him out at the only hole without fire. What I didn't know was that the vapor from the gasoline had already made its way through the tunnel system and was already exiting at the hole where I was standing. When all was ready, I raised the gun and gave Jim the signal to light the first rag. Boy did I get a surprise! It only lasted a millisecond, but the fire shot out of that hole like a rocket, right in my face. I don't know what the groundhog looked like, but I know that my eyebrows were gone for some time. Of course, Jim thought it was hilarious, and I am sure that I am famous in Baltimore to this day. We never saw the groundhog again. If he survived, I think that he moved out, perhaps looking for a mate that would accept a hairless partner.

In the years that followed, we both grew up. I now pastor a small church in the hills of Southeast Ohio. Jim eventually became a Baltimore city policeman and carried a gun for many years. Thankfully, he never had to use it. He would probably have missed anyway. He has now retired and moved to Leadmine, WV, where he continues to live with my sister. We moved off the farm in 1966 after the state acquired it for the Canaan Valley Park. The groundhogs continue to live there in abundance unabated by the likes of us.

Granny's Holler
By Vicky Miller of Danville, West Virginia
Born 1958

Places that you will always remember. That place for me will be my grandpa & grandma's. It was my second home. When I was young, 4 or 5, I remember when my dad came home from work, just about every evening saying, "I want to go to Mawmaw's," so we went most nights. I was an only child until around the age of 5 ½. Then my sister was born. I remember my dad took me to Mawmaw's to stay, and on the way there, there was a little store. We stopped and Dad got me a coloring book and some crayons, while I stayed at Mawmaw's, while Mom was

Vicky Miller

in the hospital to bring me a baby sister.

I always wanted to go to Mawmaw's because I have an aunt just 4 years older than me and an uncle a year younger, so I had someone to play with. I also liked going because Grandpa smoked a pipe and I liked to smell it. I called Grandpa-Poppaw.

. Mawmaw also had an old barn. It had stairs, we use to go in there and play. WE- meaning my aunt, uncle, and me. I might have been young, but I liked the way it was designed. I imagined having my house made like that old barn when I grew up.

There was a smokehouse out back. Mawmaw said they use to smoke meat like a lot of people use to. They use to have animals. Mom said she use to milk a cow. I think I remember Mawmaw telling about a mule they use to plow the garden with.

They didn't have any running water. There was a well. It was up on, like a porch, which was attached to the smokehouse. On the other side of the building was a cellar where Mawmaw stored her canned food and potatoes for the winter. She built that when her cellar under the house was unsafe to go under there. It used to be cool in under the house even in the hottest days of summer. I remember being in there a few times. Mawmaw didn't want us to be under there, she was afraid it would cave in on us.

No running water meant you had to go to the well to get a bucket of water. Mawmaw kept a bucket on an extra table in the kitchen;

we had to use an aluminum dipper to get a drink. Everyone used the same one, we weren't afraid of germs back then.

Mawmaw didn't have any electric either, so she had gaslights. You had to use mantles; mantles are a little cloth sack you put over the end of a gas light and it burns to make light. Mawmaw used a cast iron, iron; you had to heat it on afire to iron clothes. I think she ironed everything.

Poppaw & Mawmaw later on got running water and electric. Poppaw got a television, he use to watch the girl's Roller Derby. He also liked the show, The Monkeys-the singing group.

Mawmaw's house was L-shaped, had three bedrooms, a kitchen and a living room. How they raised 10 children in just two bedrooms. Mawmaw's bedroom had room for two full size beds. Mawmaw didn't have a bathroom either; she had a two-seated outhouse. Two can use it at the same time. I guess with that many kids it came in handy. One of my aunts married a guy and when he came home in from Indiana, he always wanted to use the outhouse. He said it made him think of the old times.

Poppaw & Mawmaw's bedroom in the back of the house was called the backroom. Where in our teenage years, is where we would go hang out, while the adults would be in the living room or on the porch when it was warm enough. I remember in the summer Mawmaw use to build a gnat smoke to run the bugs off

I use to like to sit on that old porch. I liked to go out there, especially in a thunderstorm and watch the lightning. I think the porch was my favorite part of the house. Just like that old barn, I imagined when I was older to have a house like Mawmaw's.

Sometimes my dreams take place at Mawmaw's. Later in life, Mawmaw became Granny. I saw a while back on Facebook, one of my cousins was talking about the holler where Granny's house is. His dad and mom still live in the holler. He called it Dad and Mom's holler, but it will always be Granny's holler to me.

It was the place we met at on holidays or if some out of state families came home for a visit. I miss those days. Been years since we been together at that house I'll never forget.

A Fourth of July Celebration
By Donna Beal of Lighthouse Point, Florida
Born 1953

As an eight year old, I remember the Fourth of July as being a day busy with family gatherings, parades, picnics, and fireworks.

Our family started the day early by going to church. Memories of tears rolling down my mother's cheek as she proudly sang, "God Bless America" with the rest of the congregation still linger. We were the children of World War II veterans, very proud of our country and glad to be free. After services, we would hurry home, because the rewards of a long week of preparations were about to be reaped.

Old double washtubs were placed under the elm tree. Two chipmunks, tamed by the feeding of five children, chirped excitedly overhead, anxiously watching the activities below. Big blocks of ice were chopped into smaller chunks to chill the soda, juice, beer, and baby bottles that would soon be consumed by the day's guests. For my siblings and I, this was the only day of the year we would be allowed to drink soda; two each, one grape Nehi and one orange Crush. Heavy wooden porch furniture, freshly painted white, was arranged in the side yard under the maple trees. My oldest brother, a boy scout, hung our flag on the front porch railing, insisting that the remaining scouts stand at attention and recite the Pledge of Allegiance.

Aunts, uncles, and cousins spanning three generations arrived with a flurry of noisy greetings, kisses, and hugs. As a casual observer, one would think we had not seen each other for several months rather, we had all just worshiped together at Saint Michael's only hours before. To our close family, it seemed appropriate to tell each other how happy we were to be together.

Soon, the men had horseshoes set up on the sunny, flat part of our front yard. The sound of clinking and ringing, as some lucky player scored a point, was cheered by the children. We may not have known the rules of the game, but we knew by the laughing and backslapping that something exciting had happened.

My uncle Rance, a small man not much taller than some of his nephews, was always telling us funny stories, which would send us into fits of giggles. Secretly, we were all sure he would rather be playing with us than talking with the adults. Traditionally, he acted a drum major leading the younger nieces and nephews in a parade up and down our dusty unpaved street. He played, "Yankee Doodle" on his harmonica while the rest of us kept time with clanging cymbals made of pot lids, wooden spoons banging on pots and waving small flags. Our off-key voices joined together, paid tribute to every soldier whoever fought a war for our independence. We were being taught the real reason for the 4th of July.

Meanwhile, card tables were being set up under the shady branches of the big oak tree in the middle of the side yard. Soon we were enchanted by the tinkling sound as pennies were anted up as Great-aunt Mattie held court at her annual game of Penny Poker. She saved her pennies all year in a gallon jug she used as a doorstop, just so she could challenge any member of the family who was foolish enough to fall into her trap. She would even finance the older cousins if it would guarantee her an opponent. Poker wasn't the only trick she had up her sleeve, she also challenged anyone to Bridge, or Canasta, bidding, and counter-bidding as the cards were dealt out. She allowed the little ones to win at a make believe game designed to build our confidence; after all, we would be opponents in future years. Feisty and crafty at 70, she loved winning.

In the midst of all this commotion, luncheon was served. Traditional favorites were Aunt Martha's pickled eggs. Served in the big glass jars in which she prepared them, they gave off the aroma of vinegar and beets, which accounted for the deep crimson color that stained our fingers. Happy squeals of eww or yuk accompanied the peeling away the red layers of egg white until we came to the yolk, which was no longer the familiar yellow, but now an icky shade of brown no artist could or would want to duplicate. Aunt Virginia's creamy, white potato salad, and Aunt Peggy's macaroni salad all added to the feast of blackened hotdogs and hamburgers cooked too long on the grill. Each family brought something to contribute to the meal; sweet watermelon, cantaloupe, cakes and pies, made our patriotic gathering a culinary delight. Roasting marshmallows on bent, opened metal clothes hangers was always a dangerous feat, not only the risk of losing the gooey glob to the hot coals of the fireplace, but a carelessly discarded wire produced a painful sensation on bare feet.

Firecrackers exploding and the sulfur smell reminded us of the Revolutionary War, which was one of the reasons for celebrating our nation's independence. Blankets spread out in the grass cushioned unsuspecting children as we were lulled to sleep to the music of clanging horseshoes, tinkling coins, laughter, and love. Catnaps provided the youngest child and the oldest with the stamina to stay awake for the fireworks displays at sundown. The magnificent starburst of red, white, and blue accompanying the greens and golds deserved the ohhs, ahhs, and applause. After the fireworks, which never lasted long enough, the family would gather around the fireplace and sing the old hymns and songs taught by one generation to the next.

Over the years, as time and distance has changed the way we celebrate the 4th of July, that feeling of love and pride of being an American family has never dimmed.

A 25-Cent Steak Fed All Five of Us
By Ruth Gift of Keyser, West Virginia
Born 1923

My name is Ruth F. Gift. I was born in Piedmont, W.V. January 29, 1923. At 91 years of age, I remember almost all the subjects you asked about.

To begin with, way back when, I remember my mother talking about the Depression of 1929. Her mother had her money in the bank in Lonaconing, Md., and lost it all. She couldn't even get in the bank, the doors were locked. She had to deed her farm to her son so she would have a place to stay.

I remember we had a two party telephone line and we had to go through an operator to make calls. Our number was 288-J.

We did not have a radio until 1933. My younger brother and I were so excited we could hardly wait until 6 pm to hear "The Ralston Straight Shooters are on the Air." We always had school—didn't know what a snow day was, and we had to walk home for lunch every day.

My older brother got a car with a rumble

seat when he went to Potomac State College in 1933-34. It was such a treat for my younger brother and me to ride around town in the rumble seat.

When my mother needed ice, she put a sign in the front window letting the ice man know how many lbs. of ice she wanted that day—usually 25 lbs. My kid brother and I, along with the neighbor's kids would run to the truck and patiently wait for Buss Hamilton to chip off ice for us to suck on. What great days!

We got our milk from a man who lived on the outskirts of Piedmont. He would leave two quarts of milk and take two clean empty bottles.

Many times my mother would give me 25 cents and tell me to go downtown to the A & P and get a quarters worth of steak for supper—no tax then. We had plenty of steak for the five of us.

My mother would go to downtown Piedmont every Saturday evening. She always dressed up and always wore a hat. Every woman always wore a hat back then. Piedmont was a thriving town and had a store for anything you needed. There was a wallpaper store at the end of the Westernport-Piedmont Bridge. On Main Street was Obed Beach, photography studio, MacGuinies Shoe Store, the Ryan Sisters Dress Shop. (Their brother had a dental office over the shop; Joe Coury's Bar and Grill, Wagner Furniture Store, Charlie Peter's News Stand, Walter Lyon's Meat Market, Suter's hardware Store, Drane's Drygood Store—where my mother bought the material, buttons etc. for the dresses she made for me. The Potomac Edison, where the electric bills were paid, and where we bought new appliances when needed. My sister took cooking lessons there and became a great cook. The other side of Main Street had Dixon's Clothing Store, The First National Bank, The G. C. Murphy 5 & 10, and The Cut Rate Drug Store where we gathered after school to have a coke for a nickel, Mrs. Codire's Hat Shop, The Abramson Clothing Store. There was always the Rendezvous where young adults would gather for beer and dancing. We also had Francis Shoe repair, an Acme Grocery, we had Dr. Paul Wilson, Dr. James Wolverton Sr., Dr. Pennell was another Dentist.

My favorite teacher was Miss Ruth Jackson, who later married James Goldsworthy, who became our principal. She taught English and coached me when I was in the Mineral County Junior Literary contest, which I won 1st place for 2 years and 2nd place one year. She was the most beautiful person I have ever known.

I remember World War II. I graduated that year-1941-I had two brothers in the fourth Marine Division who fought in Iwo Jima and other battles. After the war ended my younger brother stayed in the reserves, so when the Koran conflict started he was called back into service. He was in the unit that was trapped at the Chosin Reservoir. It was sub-zero weather and his unit had no food or supplies of any kind. Everyone had frozen limbs. My brother had frozen feet. When we saw him in the Naval Hospital I thought he would lose his feet-but with good care, he just lost a big toe.

During World War II, I had a friend stationed in Chamblee, Ga. in the Army. My older brother, who was still in the marines, got me a ticket to visit him. I took the train to Atlanta, and then had to take the bus to Chamblee. When I got on the bus, I went to the back seat. The bus driver came back to ask me to move up and I told him that I was fine, but he told me I would have to move further to the front, because black people couldn't sit in the front. The black people in Piedmont were so nice I didn't think of them as black, but I did move up to the center of the bus.

During the war we had to have ration stamps or tokens to buy gasoline, meat, butter, shoes, nylon hose and cigarettes to name a few. I still have a couple coupons in my cedar chest.

After I came back from Georgia, I applied for and was called to work at the West Virginia Pulp & Paper Co. in Luke, Md. (Now New Page). I started on what was called the Sealing Machine. I got 57 ½ cents an hour for day shift and 59 ½ cents an hour for second shift. One girl would feed a ream of paper into a machine that would wrap it; another girl put a label on the ream. One girl put reams in a carton and two girls put tape around the carton, then a man put the carton on a skid. The paper was for use at our bases overseas. The day the war ended, so did our jobs. I was fortunate to pass a test for a job in the Control Lab where I worked and retired with 41 years of service.

I Thought I was Someone Else
By William Eugene Bowers of St. Peters, Missouri
Born 1937

In October 1911, my father was born in a log house on a 125-acre farm on Friends Run at Hwy 33. He started out working as a schoolteacher where he taught my mother in a one-room schoolhouse in Buffalo Hills. After they got married and started a family, he couldn't afford to go to school in the summer and also raise a family, so he then went to work for Ben Smith in a sawmill and planer mill that was run by water power.

On April 17, 1924, the town of Franklin, WV was 50 to 70 percent wiped out by a very destructive fire, as they had no water line in town at that time.

I was the third child born out of ten children. Until I was four years old, we lived in a four-room house by the manmade race that supplied water to the water wheel. We then moved to a farm on Friends Run. I always went to Ben Smith's house all the time, and they nicknamed me Buck Smith.

On the farm, we had a four-room house with a spring outside of the house with a hand pump to bring water inside the house. We had an outhouse. As we had no electricity, we had an icebox that we kept food cold by cutting ice out of the pond in winter. We stored the ice in sawdust to keep the ice as long as possible. We used kerosene lights. We had a battery-operated radio that we charged the battery, with a generator ran by a windmill that we had put in a tree.

When I got old enough to work on the

William's parents, Virginia and Roy Bowers

William's dad, Roy with Earl, William, and Marty

farm, I mowed about 20 acres of hay with a team of horses. We had an orchard with apples, cherries, and pears. We also grew potatoes and raised corn for the stock. We milked 6-8 cows that we kept, putting the milk and butter in a springhouse with water running through it to keep it cold.

In 1944, my father was drafted into the Navy. He was away being examined for the Navy the night my sister Mary was born. He spent 18 months in the Navy before returning home.

While my father was in the Navy in 1945, we had a big snowstorm. The snow drifted in against the back of our house so high that if you went up above the hill above our house, you could not see the house. We tunneled out the back of the house. We carried the snow through the house to dig the tunnel to the woodshed and outhouse. We found some of our chickens in the snow bank. All the chickens were okay except the combs on the roosters were frozen off.

In 1945 when I started to school in Franklin Town School, the teacher asked our names. By then, everyone called me Buck, so I told my teacher my name was Buck Smith. She knew my family, so she knew my last name was not Smith. She had to go to my older brother to find out my actual name, as I was very insistent that it was Buck Smith. To this day, over 70 years later, all my family still calls me Buck, even though that is not my name.

In 1948, the Franklin Town School was found unsafe, so they opened up all the one-room schoolhouses in Pendleton County. We were lucky as one schoolhouse was on our property, so we only had a quarter mile to school.

When we weren't busy on the farm, we cut logs for the sawmill, and put the lumber in stacks to air day. We then put this lumber into a dry kill that was used to fire the boiler night and day until the lumber was dry enough to be ripped and planed.

On Saturday nights, we had a kettle to heat water for baths. We also heated water to wash clothes. We had a gasoline powered wringer washing machine, hanging the clothes outside on a line to dry. We had no phone or electricity until 1953. We also got running water in the house in 1953.

The first TV I saw was in the showroom floor window at Franklin Ford garage. We went to town on some Saturday nights. I would get 25 cents to go to the movie and buy popcorn. I would walk to the end of our farm to get a haircut for 25 cents until I went into the service in 1954.

We had chickens, so always had eggs. My mother would fix fried chicken for Sunday dinner.

When we were teenagers, my three cousins and I went to Elkins to the fair. Coming back home to Franklin, the headlights on my 1936 Chevy went out. We had to drive across Long Mountain using a flashlight to guide us.

I left the farm in 1954 to go into the US Air Force where I spent the next 20 years. My father passed away in 1964. My mother is 98 years old and still lives on the home farm. Although I now live in St. Peters, Mo., I still go to Franklin WV in September for the family reunion. All ten of us children are still living.

Franklin got its first fast food restaurant in 1999. We had three other restaurants in town, but Mean Gene's Burgers was the first of this kind.

Davis, Thomas and Canaan Valley Surviving Change
By Susan Meyer of San Antonio, Texas

When I was a kid in the 1950s, our little town of Davis, West Virginia, seemed to bustle with activity. Since my father was a businessman our life centered on that. Our old Victorian house was on one corner, his car dealership, garage, gas station on the other. The business was on William Avenue (Main Street) and as you went north on that street (Rt. 219) there were other businesses--four bars, one museum (history artifacts of the area), a barber shop, a hardware store, a corner grocery, telephone company and across from the phone company, the National Bank of Davis. That building complex held the bank, a drugstore, the US Post Office, five or six apartments, and the Masonic Lodge. My four older siblings (2 boys and 2 girls) were raised in the 40's, so their memories were quite different than my younger brother's and mine were since we grew up in the 50's.

As well as those businesses, there were 4 small grocers, two more gas stations, two small motels, a grand large hotel, another barber shop, a dentist and a doctor, a boarding house, a couple of restaurants and a new state park and lodge with cabins named after our river, Blackwater Falls State Park. We also had a large edifice that housed grades 1-12 that my father attended and that my siblings and I would attend. We knew and dealt with most of the businesses at that time and rarely drove anywhere to shop, but might have ordered from catalogs (Sears, JC Penney etc.)

Families were very active in the community whether on town council, PTA, band boosters, voter registration, the new ski industry, or working to get more jobs for the area. Since the railroad had helped to deplete the timber in the area, the jobs in the area were mainly centered on the mines. Those jobs were better paying jobs, but very dangerous and not all could or would do that work. By trying to center on tourism for the area, many hoped that would pan out. My ancestors had settled in Davis after Henry Gassaway Davis brought the railroad from Pennsylvania.

My family always attended the boys' basketball games where one brother would excel on the hometown level, then at the college level and as a small college coach. My youngest brother did really well at this as well, but didn't pursue it like our older brother did. Of course, there were school programs that our parents attended to show support to all of us and the obligatory fudge or cookies for school dances. Some of us belonged to the high school band, or church choir or school chorus.

When my brother Fred and I were young, we spent lots of time playing together and with friends who lived close by who were our ages. We built forts in the dining room with my mother's chairs, rolled marbles or cars down the hallway, even rode the oak bannister down the stairs (that's where I stashed candy wrappers). I even did a little roller-skating in the downstairs library that became a bedroom for my grandmother and eventually my mother. Our beautiful front porch had a large family swing and a great glider—both places for naps in the summer with the large windows open to enjoy a mountain breeze. We would take our bicycles and ride all over town, but we weren't allowed to ride on William Avenue, where it became a state road. My mother thought it was too dangerous (I wrecked once trying to ride with no hands on the handlebars and it was on the part of the newly paved road). I also crashed a few times on roller skates in places I wasn't supposed to go.

Fred and I never learned to swim because my mother was leery about us going to the town dam or in any other place that wasn't too safe. I went in the water once when staying with my uncle and his wife and lost the hearing in one ear, so I guess some of her fear had a foundation. Also, my older siblings had each other to go everywhere with, so they did learn to swim and learned to dance. However, we did have ponies we learned to ride and that was always something we enjoyed in the summer. We had a wonderful white boxer as well that my brother spent many hours enjoying.

During the winter, we spent lots of time outside in the snow building forts and tunnels, because the drifts next to the house would get pretty high. Sled riding was kept on two or three streets and we made sure we could go as often as possible. The best time to enjoy the snow was when school was canceled. It didn't happen as often as it does now, but we made sure we got outside. Only illness, kept us from playing outside any time of the year.

Changes: Now, things are quite different. The town seems to be surviving on less population and really little or no industry. Jobs are related to the tourism primarily—two state parks now boast that Davis and surrounding towns are a great area to visit. The parks are about 12 miles apart and are quite different. Both are spectacular!! Blackwater Falls State Park is older (more than 50 years) and more rustic, her lodge and cabins very quiet and remote. Activities here center on picnicking, hiking, biking, and nature at its best. Our gorgeous state flower, the rhododendron blooms in late June, and none are more spectacular than here in our local state park. The newer Canaan Valley State Park, although nearly 40 years old, has a newly renovated lodge. It is more modern in design, but its emphasis is still on nature. This park has a golf course, indoor and outdoor pools, a rock wall, paintball area, and grand vistas of Canaan Valley. Driving through either park is a slow adventure, as you can be guaranteed to see deer at nearly every turn.

Some businesses in the local area center more on arts and crafts and both communities (Davis and Thomas) are less than three miles apart. There are artisan galleries in both towns along with two coffee shops and an array of restaurants that seem to survive even when tourists are not in the vicinity. Now, the town has two Bed and Breakfasts that do well all year round. The old bank building now houses the post office, a massage therapist, and a shop offering handmade goods and herbs along with a few apartments. My father's garage is long gone over 40 years now, though a partial structure remains. Our home is now a busy bed and breakfast named after our ancestors (The Meyer's House).

There is still one dentist, but no doctors and only one grocery store with no owner in sight (the best part growing up was the personal touch). There is a dollar store that is much appreciated in this economy. There are still a few churches, but most with a declining older group attending most Sundays. I'm not sure how active the community is, but they still have an active volunteer Fire Department and many will make sure needs are met within the community when tragedy strikes. I will say that the Tucker Community Foundation, which was started nearly 30 years ago, has pursued many grants and much needed scholarships for students in the area. This foundation has also worked to establish much needed financial assistance for the local area—libraries, charitable organizations, cemetery funds, etc. This is one area that my father and other deceased business leaders would be extremely proud of—giving back to the community—helping young people pursue their dreams even if they have to leave the area.

Many of the people who have moved to our area upon retirement are very involved in getting local history from the older generation of families who settled the area. Although I don't consider myself quite the older generation, my original family members are no longer here and they were early contributors to the growth of the area. Because of this, I was able to participate by telling my Meyer family story as well as my Hivick's family story. It was important that they not be forgotten in their pursuit of life in early Davis history. My great-grandfather Meyer was one of the first teachers and went on to be a successful businessman and town father. The Hivicks were all involved with the railroad that came into the area in the late 1880's, so it was vital to be sure both families' stories were written as I knew them, rather than have any conjecture about them.

Our area of Davis, Thomas and Canaan Valley are now part of the bigger picture when it comes to homeland security and where people may go when/if they ever need to leave the Washington DC area quickly. New highways that have recently been constructed will make it much easier to leave that area. But more than that, our area will be vital to the individual's way to relax and enjoy what God has created with the beauty in our area. The story in my great-grandparent's day was that a large dam was to be built on the Blackwater and it would flood the Valley. It would be a great way for the towns to have electricity. My father had hoped this would be built also and pursued it as a means of providing jobs for the area other than mining. Most of us are grateful that hasn't happened, but sorry those jobs didn't come to fruition. We need the solitude and beauty to surround us and keep us mindful that God created this for all of us.

Quite a Funny Sight
By Edna Hargett of Fairfax, Virginia
Born 1943

Entertainment was a rare commodity growing up in Sir John's Run, a tiny hollow tucked away on a mountainside two and a half miles from Berkley Springs, West Virginia. It was a poor area, but for kids blissfully unaware of their circumstances, it was bucolic. My three brothers, restless as all kids are and always keen for some healthy troublemaking, were forced by time and circumstance to find ways to keep themselves amused. Televisions were still rare in that part of the country, and personal computers and video games were in short supply.

Living near the railroad tracks offered unique and rewarding opportunities for involving oneself in the pursuit of harmless pastimes, with shock value carrying the highest value. As luck would have it, they lived within a short bike ride of the train tracks—and just happened to know the train schedule by heart. Being a mite ornery, from equal part nature and nurture, they hatched a plan. And again, as luck would have it, they happened to have the kind of pal all restless kids should have—one willing to be talked into anything. This particular kid may not have been the brightest cookie in the jar, but he had guts. Whatever it was, he possessed something valuable for this particular plan.

Anyway, they offered up a dare—to stand on a tractor alongside the railroad tracks, which weaved through a largely unpopulated area, wearing nothing but a straw hat. He got to choose the expression on his face. I can only imagine the level of disturbance it conveyed. In the bushes sat my brothers, as they report to this day, snickering away.

The turning heads and dumbfounded looks of the train's startled passengers, befuddled and undoubtedly disgusted as they passed by the unholy sight, would have been priceless. For those passengers, it was likely the highlight (or lowlight) of a long trip. For my brothers, it was a rare moment in time in a certain place that they've never forgotten.

The Big Blues
By James E. Spinks of Mechanicsville, Virginia
Born 1933

In the late 1940s in Jefferson County, West Virginia, there was an all-black semi-pro football team known as "The Big Blues." Its members, as I recall, was made up of former players from the all-black segregated county high schools in Charles Town, Harpers Ferry, and Shepherdstown and Storer College in Harpers Ferry. Some players maybe had no prior school affiliated experience. The only two places I remember they played their games were on Wysong's Field out where the B & O and N & W Railroads crossed and on the old Legion Field on River Road.

Other than their blue jerseys, from which they got their name, it was my impression that not all the players had full football equipment; some played without helmets and/or pads. I don't remember if they even had a coach or any kind of a substitution system. I do remember there was a lot of loud banter between the teams and that it was raw football they played. When they hit, it was so loud that you would involuntarily wince and cringe.

I can recall only one player from the Big Blues team. He was from Charles Town and his name was "Funny" Newman. It was rumored that he was prone to take a little drink of Four Roses now and then. I suspect he may have taken a nip before a game just to combat the cold. For whatever reason old "Funny" played with complete abandon and without regard to the physical beating and suffering he endured on those cold autumn Sundays long ago. He was a delight to watch!

My clearest memory of the old Blues has to do with a player from Storer College. For the life of me, I can't recall whether he was playing offense or defense when he shouted in a clarion voice (which still rings down through the years): "Every man get a man; every good man get two men," and as he pointed his finger at the opposing team, he yelled, "I got these three!" GO BLUES!

Days when it was Safer, but Much More Inconvenient
By Glona Jean Smith of Petersburg, West Virginia
Born 1944

I remember when I had to walk to the Crites one-room school. Estel Sites was one of the boys in the older class and I was one of the youngest girls. Ms. G. Alt was our teacher. We carried the water into the house and heated it on the stove to do dishes or anything else that we needed warm water for. We cooked on

The old copper tub used for canning

a woodstove winter and summer. It really got hot in the house when you were baking bread, pies, or cookies. We would build a fire outside in the summer and do the canning in a copper kettle. It would take hours to do one turn of beans and you had to keep the fire at the same level the whole time.

In the summertime, there was hay to make, which we did with a horse pulling a mower. Then you had to let it dry. Then it was back to the field. After Dad would use the dump rake to pile it in rows, we would have to pile it in shocks. Next came putting it on the wagon and taking it to wherever we were going to make the haystacks. We would make a big round base and then tramp it down, add more hay, and then more tramping down. You were really hot, tired and had scratches all over you from the hay by the end of the day. Dad was so used to the old stubborn horse, so when we got our first tractor, he did not push on the brakes hard enough and the tractor did not stop. Dad started yelling "Whoa, dang you, I said whoa!"

I can remember having a wringer washing machine that my mother used to wash our clothes in. It sat in the middle of the kitchen floor. She would then rinse our clothes in a big tub before hanging them out on the clothesline to dry. Sometimes, our clothes would freeze on the line as soon as they were hung up.

The "good old days" are fine to remember, but let me have today's convenient ways. Except it was much safer back then and even when we were young, we could walk for miles and be safe. If we got thirsty, we could knock on a door and they would give us a drink, or we could just go to the well, pull up a little water, and then go on our way.

My Life in Tucker County
By Nada Murphy of Woodbridge, Virginia
Born 1936

Thinking back to my life in Tucker County in West Virginia in the late '30s and '40s and part of the '50s, I remember that the people of that old mountaintop were the best in the world. They are still some of my friends, although I don't see them very often.

I remember washing clothes for the family on a scrub board and wringing them by hand. The white clothes were boiled to get them white. Bluing was added to white rinse to get them to look whiter. Lots of my clothes were made from feed sacks. Some of them were very pretty. Ironing was done the day after washing. Everything had to be ironed. The irons had to be heated on the woodstove. We did not have electric in those days.

We grew most of our food. We done lots of canning to provide food for winter. We grew lots of dried beans, potatoes, and apples. We had cows and churned our own butter and made cottage cheese and buttermilk. We had pigs and chickens, which were part of the food chain. We picked lots of berries for jam and jelly. We made apple butter in the fall in a big copper pot on the open fire. Friends and family would join in this fun. Always a good time.

School was a wonderful experience for me. It was a one-room school with grades from one though eight. One teacher taught all the grades and did a great job. The school was heated by a potbellied stove in the middle of the room. We got our drinking water from a farmer's well. Christmas time in the old school was such fun. We always had a program and invited our parents.

Growing up on Limestone Mountain in Tucker County was sometimes very hard. Money was hard to come by. Some of my growing years were during the war and lots of things were rationed. Gas, shoes, and sugar to name a few. You had to a stamp from your ration book to buy these things. A wood or coal stove heated our home and our meals were cooked on a woodstove. Cutting wood was an ongoing thing. Every farm had a crosscut saw and a good ax.

Our local church was a highlight for me. It was through my Sunday school teacher that I turned my life over to the Lord. The roads through the mountain were not hard serviced until sometime in the '50s. Lots of snow in the winter made for some interesting trips to school. One time it snowed and the bus driver could not get through, so he hitched a horse to a sled and come for us. He covered us with a smelly old tarp and got us home. Those days growing up without much made me tough!

Hobos
By Bob Poland of Keyser, West Virginia
Born 1942

The first home that I remember was located at 266 W. Fairview St. in Piedmont, West Virginia in the late '40s. The house was lost in a fire many years later. West Fairview St. ran parallel to the Potomac River and the Baltimore and Ohio railroad at a point close to what was then The West Virginia Pulp and Paper Co. and the Piedmont-Luke, Md. Bridge.

Not very far from there, the B & O started its steep 17-mile grade up the mountain and points west. Also close to our house was what used to be a coal tipple, long since removed when Fairview Street was constructed. The interesting thing about this particular tipple was that the coal arrived there by a tunnel, which was said to travel from the railroad, under the west end of Piedmont, to a point above the town that we called the "first flat" on "Old Baldie," or the mountain directly behind the Luke paper mill. Many people have contributed this mountain being bare to the pollution of the paper mill. My father, who grew up in Piedmont, often told me that in his youth, the mountain was covered with chestnut trees. It fell to him, being the oldest of ten, to supplement their garden provisions with squirrel and game from this forest. He told of a chestnut blight killing the trees, and then later, a forest fire clearing the mountain of the blighted and dead wood. Through the pollution abatement projects of the West Virginia Pulp and Paper Co., now New Page, this mountain is reforested and is green once again. Missing is the chestnut native to the mountain and in abundance is the Autumn or Russian olive planted there.

As for the tunnel, we were never able to confirm that it did indeed go under the town because the tunnel had collapsed about 50 feet or so from the entrance. Our exploration ended there. On the flat, at the supposed other end, however, there was evidence of mining activity by a couple of old mining cars, some rail, and coal piles lending credibility to the tunnel story.

Let me attempt to tie the details together. The trains coming down steep grade would stop at the bottom to allow the brakes to cool. In those days, it was common to see "hobos" riding the trains. When the trains stopped, they would get off and seek out this tunnel, especially in colder weather. They probably had heard that it was a place to obtain some shelter.

At times, I can remember seeing strangers in our town. They would come to our house and ask for handouts. I'm not sure about any kind of markings that they placed on the houses that they visited to denote whether that house was friendly or not, but it is said that they had a code for doing so. We never had any trouble with the men who came. Most of the time they were hungry, needed clothes, or asked if there was any work for them to do. They came and went, and for the most part kept to themselves.

Our parents always told us to be polite, but not to stop to talk with strangers, and by all means not to go near that tunnel. We moved from Fairview Street in 1954, and sometime later, the tunnel was closed over by a concrete retaining wall. The tipple probably operated in the early 1900s. There was no trace of the wooden trestle, or any part other than the tunnel itself.

Most of the people that would remember this have passed or have moved on. My memories of Piedmont are fond. It was a nice town to grow up in.

The Memory of Coach Imphong
By Bill Sterner of Hancock, Maryland
Born 1954

I grew up in Pittsburgh, Pennsylvania where life in general—even in the '60s and '70s—was a little fast-paced and certainly less personal than smaller, rural communities were. My high school had 3,000 kids and I was involved in so many extra-curricular activities that it was a relief to my parents when I got my driver's license and could get to practices and rehearsals myself. I received my teaching degree from Lock Haven (PA) State Teachers College in 1976, a great school located in a tiny town by the Susquehanna River. From that, I got a taste of small town life and knew that it was for me.

My first teaching job was in a very rural school in Warfordsburg, PA (Southern Fulton County). The only downside was they didn't offer football—a sport I had played through high school and college. Of course, I wanted to try my hand at coaching, so I began attending games at nearby Hancock, MD high school—an even smaller school than the one I taught in. In fact, Hancock is the smallest public school in the state of Maryland with just under 160 kids in grades 9-12, but they played football, and that was an attraction to me. Soon I was coaching at the school, and finally in 1982, coaching and teaching there.

Of course, in a small community, traditions run deep and an icon in the community happened to be a former Pittsburgh guy and retired teacher and coach by the name of Paul Imphong. Now Imphong's big claim to fame in Hancock was that he had founded the football program through some amazing work by him and his wife, Dottie. Paul coached them up and disciplined them and Dottie fed them, patched them up, and sewed their uniforms.

Paul and Dottie sort of took me under their collective wings, and when I became the head football coach, Paul would call me to help calm my nerves every game day. Many times, I ate lunch with Paul on his porch or in his home office and Dottie was always very accommodating. He also made it a habit to show up and watch every opening day practice from the time he retired. "Best day of the year; opening day of practice." Paul used to smile. As the years went by, Paul was there every August 15 as another new edition of the Hancock Panthers rolled out onto the practice field. I guess to him, it was part of his family.

We had a ceremony and named the football field after him, he was inducted into the Hall of Fame for our county, and through it all, he credited everyone else. "You know," he told me once on his porch, "you and the other fellas have made way too much out of what I've done. I was a football coach and teacher."

However, life and age has a way of catching up with all of us, and one year, a neighbor of the Imphongs contacted me to say that Paul was very ill and wouldn't be there on our opening day. He was too weak to drive and too sick to leave his home. He and Dottie had crept into their nineties, and to me it was amazing they still were living on their own. However, I wanted Paul to still be a part of our football program.

The night before practice, one of our coaches, John Blake, had the idea to transport our entire team (31 kids) to Coach Imphong's and do our warm-up for practice in his front yard. That way, Paul could enjoy yet another opening day of practice. The next morning we showed up at Coach's home and I knocked on the door. The local press and television had caught wind of our plan and there was quite a "circus" in Mr. Imphong's front yard.

Dottie answered and looked quite surprised to see all of us there. "Dottie," I said, "We would like Coach to come out on the porch." She quietly turned away and soon Paul emerged with his cane and dressed proudly as always. His eyes welled up as we told him we decided to bring practice to him.

The team warmed up counting in cadence, and afterwards, every player individually shook Coach Imphong's hand as he stood proudly giving each boy a word of advice. His eyes were alive and his voice quite strong as he thanked each player for their commitment and dedication.

However, the best was yet to come for me, and it solidified my belief that these simple folks who dedicated their lives to this small community were the most genuine and wonderful of human beings. And I realized that fact when Dottie took me aside and quietly said," Coach Sterner, I certainly don't have enough lunch meat to feed these boys." She quietly counted each youngster in the yard. "But I will if you can run me to Pittman's Grocery. Paul isn't allowed to drive anymore." Of course, I told her we weren't there for lunch but how wonderful that in their nineties, these dedicated folks were thinking hospitality even when they were being honored.

Forty years I have stayed here, as a coach and athletic director and I owe much of that learned allegiance to Coach Imphong. In his quiet, lead-by-example way, he helped me to see the value of loving and dedicating what you can to make things better for those you come in contact with.

If it is true as H.D. Thoreau once said that "The hero is commonly the simplest and obscurest of men," then Coach Imphong was a hero to countless young people in this community.

Uncle John's Grey Nightmare
By Roger Roderick of Oakland, Maryland
Born 1943

I grew up in the Appalachians, a country atmosphere with people bout 50 years behind modern times and inventions. It lent itself to great experiences with very interesting, make-do folk: full of fun, humor, and resolve.

One such person was Uncle John. He had one of the best looking grey Percheron teams on the mountain, one of which was also known to be probably the mountain's worst balker, by everyone but Uncle John, who was a big man with a big rep for accomplishing the task set out to do.

Problems seem to occur to all of us, regardless of stature and resolve, and I guess the same is true with critters. Whatever the reason, on a brisk spring day, Uncle John hooked up his team and sled and set out on a mission of cutting a load of firewood. Everything went well; he got a nice load of firewood cut, loaded, and was heading home. Then, for a reason unknown to man or beast, his fine dapple mare decided that last piece was a little too much, balked, and would not move!

Being a problem-solving man of resolution and stature, John went to the woods, cutting a sturdy two-handed hickory sapling and waded

Roger's dad, Stan Roderick

Great-Grandpap Roderick with his horse, Bob

in on the contrary bovine with stealth, vigor, and strong vocabulary. After having worked himself and his fine dapple into a worn out, sweating froth and frenzy, getting nowhere, John decided to give 'em both a break. He set down on the sled and lit up his old kawoodie pipe. It was then that his next plan began to materialize. FIRE! With this in mind, he began to gather tender and kindling, placing a small heap under the belly of ole Perch.

Now then, in a short time things begin to happen. A little heat in the right place, and forward compulsion started. That navigating equine pulled her load of firewood just enough to place that locust sled with its load of dry wood plum middle of Uncle John's fire and balked permanent!

As Uncle John drug his empty spreaders home, I'm sure one thing had to be perfectly clear: sometimes the bullet just don't fit the pistol!

My Life as I Remember It
By Nina I. Mahoney of Ranson, West Virginia
Born 1936

I was born May 13, 1936 at Millcreek, Bunkerhill WV. I'm the fourth child of seven; I have three sisters and three brothers. In those days, your mother stayed home to take care of the house, and she kept a clean house. My father worked at National Fruit in Martinsburg WV, making applesauce and apple juice. In those days, we didn't have much, so there weren't any toys for us kids to play with.

The most I remember is when we lived on Swartz Street and our grandmother, my father's mother, lived on Burke Street, about a block away. It was Christmastime, and I'm not sure where my parents were at the time, but my oldest sister came in the kitchen where my siblings and I were under the table to put us to bed. She told us we weren't getting anything for Christmas. We got up the next morning, and sure enough, there wasn't anything for us. At that time, the war was going on and we couldn't go outside. It was a hard time for people.

I'm not sure what happened, but when I was nine years old, we were taken from our parents and placed in a foster home in Jones Springs, except for my oldest sister who was placed in a home down the road from us. It was about an hour drive from Martinsburg. This home also had other children in this home. Still no toys for us to play with because when the Salvation Army gave us toys, they took them and placed them in the attic so we couldn't play with them. We had to go barefooted, and the only time we wore shoes was when we went to school. When we went to school, we were picked on by the other children because we didn't have nice clothes like they did.

We were moved to another home and we just had each other to play with. After that, we all were separated and put into different homes. I was placed in a home on Moler Avenue. Us older kids would take a barrel and roll down a steep hill and we would also swing back and forth across the creek at the bottom of the hill because there still were no toys to play with. On Saturday nights, we would get a bath in a washtub. We had to go to our neighbors to carry water for drinking, bathing and for washing laundry. There was a small electric heater that was placed in an old wringer washer to heat the water with and we heated an old flat iron on the stove to press our clothes with. In the summertime, it was so hot, and we didn't have air conditioner or a fan. We were made to stay outside until they called us in. As I got older, I had to help do the housework.

As I sit here trying to remember my childhood, I remember one more home that I was in; I was there for a few years. When I was first placed in this home, I was told the man of the house was sick and that he spent most of his time in bed; and he did. The first two weeks I was there I only remember him eating one meal at the table. We had ham and dumplings, and they were very good. While we was at the table eating he said, "Susie, (that's what they called me) you and I are going to live the longest." That night he must have gotten worst, because the next morning when I got up I was told he passed. We got through all of that; I believe was around 1952 or 1953.

By that time, I was in high school. We still had out accommodations. She did have a small hand pump in the kitchen for water. The stove for cooking had one-half of it wood and the other half was gas, it also had a place built in the stove for heating water. Later on she had a small restroom installed; it just had a commode and small sink. In 1954, we got our first black and white television and it didn't get that many channels.

They still had one daughter living at home at the time. Their niece would come over to visit with their daughter. One day she brought a friend with her and they went out for a ride. That is how I met my first boyfriend. We got married February 26, 1955. A week after we were married, we moved to Colorado Springs, Colorado. He was in the Air Force, and that's where he was stationed. After we had our first child, we had orders to go to Germany, where I had my second son. In 1958, we were still in Germany when my first daughter was born. My husband nicknamed her Sputnik after the first satellite that went into space.

At that time, the United States and Cuba was having problems and we had to be ready in a moment's notice in case there was a war. They were sending the wives and children somewhere else. In 1959, we were sent to Ohio where I had two more children. We stayed there until 1964. While in Ohio, my husband was in a car accident on November 25, 1963. On February 25, 1964, he died of his injuries.

I moved back to Inwood, West Virginia and lived there for a little while before I moved to Winchester, Virginia, where a friend of mine introduced me to my second husband. The only thing that was good out of that marriage was he gave me my last child. I left Winchester, moved back to Charlestown, WV, bought a mobile home, and rented a lot from my brother in-law. That's where I raised my six children. Once my children were on their own, I met and married my third husband. We had a good relationship and it didn't last long enough; he passed away November 1995.

That pretty much brings us to today and that story is to come.

Lost on the Mountain
By Betty Rader of Thomasville, North Carolina
Born 1941

I grew up on the mountain that lies east of Riverton, known as North Mountain, the side that overlooks the beautiful Germany Valley with a full view of Spruce Knob far to the west. My home sits almost up under the limestone rock ledges known as the Dolly Hills. Our home can be seen from numerous vantage points when there is no foliage, and a beautiful site it is. I am the only daughter of Gale and Elsie Warner and I have five brothers, the late Dale Smith, Richard, Robert, Carroll, and Jerry Warner.

We grew up listening to this story as told to us by our mammy who was Mary Huffman that raised my mother, Elsie Smith Warner. The Huffman's settled in this area in the 1820s-1840s and were a diverse family of hard-working and self-sufficient people. The original large tract of land has been divided several times and most of it is still owned and cherished by descendants of the Huffman family. Our mother, Elsie, came to live with the Huffman family when she was five years old in 1920.

This is a true, sad story based on facts and has been told and retold many times, and I believe the dates are accurate. We heard this particular story many, many times when we were young and would break out crying, saying we didn't want to be lost on the mountain like little Adie!

George and Anna Whitecotton were the neighbors of our Huffman family and they had 11 children; five of them died while they lived on the mountain. Four died from diphtheria, a contagious childhood disease of the time. Two of these children were buried in the same coffin and they are all buried in the local Huffman Family Cemetery. The twins Andy (probably Andrew) and Adie (probably Ada) were born in 1886 and had been inseparable since birth.

It was May 11th in 1891, a beautiful

spring day; actually, it was the first day warm enough to shed the shoes. Adie and Andy were barefoot, and the little sister and brother were excited to be allowed to accompany the adults to the mountain to help build a fence. The task at hand at this particular time was the rebuilding/repairing the line fences that separated the land and defined the areas that belonged to each family. Back then, neighbors helped each other to complete this arduous, backbreaking chore, and it usually required several days, even weeks. The men and many others of the family that were old and strong enough to work went to work on the mountain. As was the custom of the time, they carried parcels, bags, or buckets that contained their dinner and jugs or jars of water with them so they could eat at noon and continue the work instead of taking the time to walk back home to eat their midday meal.

Adie and Andy 'helped" and played, enjoying the sun and fresh air. For some reason, Adie decided she wanted to go home. Ordinarily, Andy would have been by her side, but for some reason he declined to walk home with her. She started home by herself. That evening when the workers returned home, they were shocked to hear that Adie was not there. She had not returned from the mountain!

The word went out among the neighbors and a search party was immediately formed. The search went on for days. They roamed the mountain practically day and night, but no sign of Adie was found. There was great speculation as to what might have occurred; could she have possibly been kidnapped, or maybe killed by a wild animal? However, there were no answers; little Adie was surely gone!

The following year, neighboring farmers, Elmer Wimer and Garnet Huffman were on the mountain, possibly hunting or looking for a certain type of tree branch that made good fishing poles. They were on the west (Franklin) side of the limestone ledges that run across the mountaintop known as the North Mountain Trail. There they found what they believed remained of little Adie. They returned with their sad parcel to the Whitecotton home, and her Momma identified the pieces of the material to be that of the little dress she had been wearing that day.

Little Adie's remains were brought back over the mountain and she was buried beside her sisters and brothers in the Huffman Cemetery; it is listed in the Pendleton County Grave Register as the Wimer-Weese Cemetery. It is located on the property that is owned by the family of John and Etta Weese. A pile of stones with a little white cross marks the spot where Adie was found. I personally have not seen it, but my brother, Richard Warner, and many other people I know has been there several times. It is located off the Skidmore branch of the North Mountain Trail.

The Whitecotton family left the mountain sometime between 1893 and 1897, moving to the Buffalo Hills area of Pendleton County. Their youngest daughter, Kate was born there in 1898. Records show that George and Anna spent their last years with their eldest daughter, Pearl who lived in the Upper Tract area. Andy, the beloved brother, lived to be 65 and never marrying. He died in 1951, according to the local grave register and is buried in the Cherry Hill Cemetery in Upper Tract where his parents are also buried.

All the people who lived and were involved in this sad story are gone now. My grandparents and my mother and daddy kept this story alive for us. So if you are fortunate enough to have an older member of your family still with you, ask them to share their memories and what stories they remember from their past. Hopefully their memories will provide stories that have a much happier ending that this one; however I believe all of them need to be passed on so they will never be forgotten. I recently told my youngest son Rob this story. He will remember it; and along with all you readers will be able to pass it on.

A Castle without a King
By Betty Wertz of Warfordsburg,
Pennsylvania
Born 1935

Nestled on a hillside overlooking the town of Berkeley Springs, West Virginia stands a mysterious castle. It echoes with stories of death, a faded love, wild parties, and disgrace. Berkeley Springs is a town with two names. There is its post office name of "Berkeley Springs," and "Bath," the name George Washington gave it in 1776. Bath is still the official name of the town because of the warm mineral springs that flow unceasingly at 74 degrees and produces 1,000 gallons per minute.

During the end of the 18th century, Bath attracted traveling preachers because of its gambling, quarter horse racing, and general partying. The most appealing oddity is the Berkeley Castle, and the story of Colonel Samuel Suit, a Civil War Veteran who made his wealth by distributing his well-known whiskey. He packaged it in various containers, including the famous brown jugs and cut glass decanters. His wealth began in Kentucky and led to his namesake of Suitland, Maryland where he was a Maryland Legislator.

Suit hobnobbed with Presidents Hayes and Grant, one of which sent him to Bath, England where he visited a castle owned by the Berkeley family. Suit mentally sketched the castle, and after two marriages, he fell in love with 17-year-old Martha Rosa Pelham, daughter of an Alabama Congressman.

The castle in Bath, England remains within the Berkeley family since its reconstruction in the 12th century. Traditionally believed to be the scene of the murder of King Edward II in 1327, its details are too graphic to describe. An email from house manager, Martha Houser said she was unaware of the existence of Berkeley Springs Castle. She thought it bizarre that there are two names of Berkeley, Bath, and Castle, intrigued with the details of its structure.

In 1877, Suit met Rosa at the spa in Berkeley Springs, and promised to build her a castle if she married him. Together they chose a site along Warm Springs Ridge. The property spreads over five acres, divided by what are now Route 9 and Sir John's Run Road. Because of their age difference of 24 years, friends questioned the marriage, but in 1882, the couple wed in Washington D.C. In quick succession, Rosa bore Suit three children.

Suit's dream was to make Berkeley Springs, West Virginia, a spa to rival any other on the East Coast. For years, the hot springs in that area drew the rich and famous because of the waters. Three large hotels already graced the site, but Suit foresaw even further developments. In 1885, Colonel Samuel Taylor Suit began laying the foundation for the castle, designed on a one-tenth scale of the Berkeley Castle in Bath England. Crews, making eight cents an hour, toiled for three years hauling the hand cut silica stone, up the mountainside by horse and buggy. The total price of construction was $100.000.

Suit died at age 58 and never lived in his dream castle. His will stipulated that Rosa must finish the castle and never remarry or she would not receive his inheritance. Rosa, only 27, was a wealthy widow with three children, a castle to finish building, and her husband's business of which she knew nothing about. During May 1891, she returned to Berkeley Springs to finish the structure.

After the mourning period for her husband, she began entertaining guest with lavish parties. Rosa began selling off her belongings to feed her extravagant lifestyle. It was in the early 1900s when she was evicted from the castle, owing a debt of $40,000. She moved to a small house in the Oakland community of West Virginia, and later Greenwood, where she raised chickens. Still wanting to entertain, she allegedly served wine in mismatched coffee and teacups. When her son heard of her plight, he moved her to a remote place in Idaho. Martha Rosa Suit died in 1947 at age 85.

The castle had numerous owners and opened for visitations and weddings. Today, it is a private residence but still a hushed monument of the Suits. There is a four state view from the castle because of its unique location. Leading South from Warfordsburg, Pennsylvania to Berkeley Springs, West Virginia, the total distance is approximately 10-12 miles. The Maryland and West Virginia state line meet over the Potomac River Bridge. In less than 30 minutes, travelers cross over three state lines, and in another 40 miles, they are in the state of Virginia. In 1863, West Virginia became a state.

In the early 1900s, Edith (Henry) Unger, my mother, and her older brother delivered milk to the castle at ten-cents a quart for Rosa's 13 cats. They entered through a tunnel off Sir John's Run Road, leading to a wine cellar. No one has found the hillside tunnel, now overgrown with brush. Berkeley Springs was her birthplace and where she died at age 97. Listening and remembering the stories of the elderly resemble an unread book. When they are gone, so is the history if it is not preserved.

The annual Apple Butter Festival attracts

Apple Butter Festival in Berkeley Springs, WV

thousands each October. The center of town at The Morgan County Courthouse is the gathering place for boiling the butter. It is a two-day event with plenty of food, vendors, and entertainment. Berkeley Springs had its share of grief in other tragedies. In 1903, three local men, who worked for the telegraph company, were on the Duquesne Limited and scheduled to arrive from Cumberland in Western Maryland to Berkeley Springs on Christmas Eve. The train wrecked in Connellsville, PA, killing 60 passengers, crew, two Berkeley Springs residents, and one from Hancock, Maryland.

In June 1926, there was a premature sand mine explosion a few miles from the town. It killed five men, and injured seven. One of the deceased was my mother's brother, Irvin Henry. The funerals of the men numbered nearly 2,500 mourners. All the men in both accidents were husbands and fathers. Several men rest in the old Greenway Cemetery on a hillside of the small town of Bath one of which is my Uncle Irvin Henry.

An old motto is, a man's home is his castle, and he is king. If this is factual, then after the accident, all the homes of these men were a castle without a king. Fires consumed hotels and the Morgan County Courthouse. In 1974, a pre-dawn blaze engulfed the 120-year-old Washington House, five businesses, and killed 13 people. It was the sixth hotel fire in Bath since 1844. In 1898, the famous 400-room Berkeley Springs Hotel, burned to the ground, yet the town revived to its present day of antiques shops, bookstores, restaurants, and a new hospital.

The drive to Berkeley Springs is well worth the time. The bathhouse and springs entices tourism, the Silica sand mine still operates, and the old Greenway Cemetery holds burial services. In addition, the stately castle is a constant reminder of a past one-sided love story.

Ramps (The Kind You Eat)
By Ms. Ronnie L. Grove of Berkeley Springs, West Virginia
Born 1944

In 1977, I went to work for Charlie Stiles at Business and Tax Services in Berkeley Springs. I had two wonderful co-workers, Estelle Unger Ditto and Linda Sue Householder. We soon became fast friends.

As spring approached, we had a conversation concerning ramps. Ramps are a spring tradition in much of WV. They grow wild and are very much like a green spring onion except the odor they leave behind is unbelievable. Much like wild mushrooms, they have a short harvest time in the spring.

My parents, Sue and Gus (Gilbert) Grove were living in Preston County, WV at the time. Ramp Festivals were held at several places in Kingwood, Terra Alta and the surrounding area. If possible, my late husband, Ronie Grove, never missed one of these festivals. I, too, liked the ramps but would not eat them because "ramp breath" makes "garlic breath" smell like perfume, not to mention it hangs around for days. I even refused to sleep in the same room with my husband for a couple of days after he had partaken of this great delicacy. They are so strong the odor can even be detected in perspiration. As we discussed the issue of ramps, I told the girls of this personal experience. I'm not sure they believed the "stink" was as bad as I said.

Estelle's husband, Tom, "Weedle" Unger was a mail carrier and she said one of his customer's gave him some ramps every spring and told him if they were cooked, it would eliminate the awful foul breath. I told her I didn't believe there was anything that could cut such stink. A few days later, Estelle came to work and said, "Well, Tom came home with ramps yesterday evening. Fried them with some potatoes. Can you smell them?" I said, "Not if you are in another room." We laughed and started to work. As luck would have it, the boss was away that day and my brain was cranking.

Finally, I was able to get Linda Sue alone and asked her help to pull a prank on Estelle. Linda Sue called one of Estelle's clients and explained the situation, gave me a thumbs up, and we sat back and waited. In a few minutes, Estelle's phone rang, she answered it, and her client is asking some questions about her account when all of a sudden we saw Estelle's face go red, dead, and very quiet. It was at that point we knew the client had said, "Estelle, what is that terrible odor I smell?" After what seemed like forever, Estelle responded with, "I don't know about you, but I smell a rat."

I'm not sure who got whom, but we all cracked up and the story has been told many, many times over the years. Both Estelle and Linda Sue are in a better place now, but I have many fond memories of both. However, I think this is one of my favorites.

Eggs

My then four-year-old nephew, Kyle Fike, came for an extended visit. As I was still working, he would spend evenings and nights with me and I would drop him off with Grandma and Grandpa (Sue and Gus Grove) on my way to work the next morning. That first morning, Mother asked him if he would like some eggs for breakfast. He said, "Yes." Next question, of course, was, "Would you like them fried or scrambled?" After considerable thought, he looked up at Mother and very sweetly said, "Fried, because, you know, when they are scrambled, you just can't be sure how many you are gettin.'"

Flashlights

When my nephew, Christopher Grove, was about four years old, he loved to play with his dad's flashlight. Since this, of course, ran down the batteries, my brother was constantly telling him to put the light away. "It's not a toy." I bought him a small penlight. He was thrilled until the batteries went dead.

We were playing cards when he came into the kitchen and very nicely asked his dad if he could barrow the big flashlight, adding, "I only need it for a minute." Chuck said he could, but not to be fooling around. He picked up the big flashlight end went into the living room. Since none of us knew what was going on, we sneaked a peek and saw him place the big flashlight on the carpet facing the penlight. He then turned the big light on and said, "You see that? Now you do it!"

Airport

I started to lose my hearing when I was ten years old. The loss was slow but continuing, and by the time I was 35 it was becoming quite profound. Hearing aids helped, but only because I was very good at lip reading. My sister, Jennifer Grove Bryan, was living and working for American Airlines out of Dallas. She was coming home for a visit and I was to pick her up at the airport in Hagerstown, MD.

As most people know, employees fly free, but they also fly standby. You are never sure of arrival time. To make matters worse, she also had a hearing problem. This was in the days before everyone had a cell phone and there was no texting, and if you couldn't hear, you were at the mercy of the world. I was at the Hagerstown Airport at the appointed time, which was maybe 9:00 P.M. It was a very small airport at the time and I could sit in my car and watch each plane land and taxi right up to the door for passengers to disembark. I thought when she got off I would then go inside and get her.

It got later and later and no Jennifer. Knowing the last flight came in at 10:00; I thought I had better go inside and see what was happening as that time was drawing near. I went to the counter where two girls were working. Both had customers, but in a second, one was free and offered to help me. I asked if that last plane was the last one they were expecting for the evening. She said they had one more coming in from Pittsburgh. That was the wrong direction for Jennifer, so I started to leave; thinking standby had caused her to not make her plane as originally planned.

Then I had a thought that caused me to turn back and say to the girl, "My name is Ronnie Grove. You wouldn't happen to have a message for me?" She asked me to wait while she looked. All of this had been a normal voice level conversation and we were doing well. However, upon hearing me announce my name, the second girl excitedly said, "I'll handle that," waited until she finished with her customer, and she came to the counter, leaned forward as close as she could and with extremely exaggerated facial expressions she very slowly and loudly said, "YOUR PARTY HAS BEEN DELAYED." Etc., etc., etc. I thought I would die trying not to laugh in her face but I now knew my sister did not make her flight and she would be arriving the next day. I also knew what had taken place before my arrival.

I came back home and stopped at my parents because I assumed my sister had called them to explain things and to get the message to me. I came into the house and said, "Okay. Exactly what did you tell the girl at the airport?" Right away, my mother said, "Talk to your daddy. I had nothing to do with it." It seems when daddy called to leave the message, he asked the girl not to make an announcement over the PA system because he knew I would not be able to discern that. In doing so, he must have put too much emphasis on the situation and the poor girl thought she had to draw pictures to relay the message.

My family and friends still get a hardy chuckle when I retell this story. The exaggerated facial expressions alone made my wait worthwhile.

A Thanksgiving Midnight Baby
By Dolores Snyder Smith of Winchester, Virginia
Born 1937

I, Dolores Ann Snyder, was born right at midnight on November 27-28, 1937. The doctor told my father that he could choose either day for my birthday. Since Thanksgiving was on November 27 in 1937, he chose the 27th, and the doctor noted on my birth certificate that I was born at 11:59 P. M. on November 27, 1937. My father, Edward Lee Snyder, loved to tell me that I was named after his favorite movie actress at that time-Dolores Del Rio. The house in which I was born was on Raleigh Street and had been changed into two apartments. We lived in the first floor, which had originally been a slaughterhouse. When I married in 1959, I married a renderer and my dad got a big laugh about that.

Dad also loved to tell my older brother, Edward Lee Snyder, Jr. and I about my first Christmas. He had been employed at the Interwoven Stocking Company in Martinsburg, West Virginia, but due to the Great Depression, he had been laid off. He did have a Christmas Club of $5.00. With that money he bought my brother a tricycle, me a rattler (since I was only four weeks old), and he had enough left over to buy a large chicken to roast for Christmas dinner. He said that was the toughest chicken he had ever eaten.

I later had three sisters, Shirley, Carolyn, and Barbara. When Shirley was born in 1939, Shirley Temple was a very popular child star; and my brother kept telling everybody that Shirley Temple had been born, so my parents named the baby Shirley.

My father quit school in the fifth grade since his father kept him out of school so much to help on the farm and also with his sawmill. Even though my dad never weighed more than 155 pounds, at the age of ten he was using a mule team to haul trees to the sawmill where they made crossties for the railroad which was being built in Berkeley County. My mother, Elsie Elizabeth Unger Snyder, also had to quit school after she finished eighth grade since her father had died, and she had to provide for her mother and younger siblings.

Because my parents did not have much education, it was very important to them that all of their children graduate from high school and get as much additional education as they could. When I graduated from Martinsburg High School in 1955, I was in the top ten of my class and wanted very much to go to college. I had worked at the Interwoven Stocking Company during my senior year of high school from 4:00 to 9:00 P.M. on Monday through Friday and on Saturday from 7:00 A.M. to 12:00 Noon. I also won a one-year scholarship to Strayer Business College in Washington, D. C., (now Strayer University). My parents helped me with $100.00 a month to help pay for my room, board, and other expenses from August to December.

When I came home for the Christmas holidays, they told me they could not help me any longer. The day after New Year's, my dad drove me to the train station in Martinsburg to catch the train back to D. C. At that time, he handed me a $5.00 bill and told me that he was sorry; that was all he had. I left Martinsburg with my return train ticket to D. C. and $5.00. I knew when I got to Washington I needed to pay the Young Women's Christian Home where I was living $65.00 for January's room and board. I lived only two or three blocks from Union Station and could walk from the train station. I dropped my suitcase off at my room; and, after eating breakfast, I walked the twenty-six blocks to Strayer College.

When I got to college, I ran into a good friend I had made at school; and I told her I was going to have to drop out of school. Before that day was over, one of the men, who ran the school office came to me and offered me a part-time job in the office so I was able to finish my one year of college. At this time, there were no student loans, very few scholarships, and no community colleges for students like me.

Our family was poor. My father's mother, Fannie May Whittington, and his sister, Isabelle Virginia Snyder, made most of the clothes that my three sisters and I had out of feed sacks. We did not have a phone or a television. We would listen to the radio to Amos and Andy, the Lone Ranger, and other such shows and to the news. I remember at four years of age listening to the scary news of the bombing of Pearl Harbor, the sirens that would warn us to turn off all lights in the house, and the rationing of sugar, gasoline, tires, and other items. Dad would go out into the county to dig up sassafras roots to make tea and land cress to eat.

In 1942 when I was about four years old, my father bought an old house on Bowers Street for $2,500.00. After his death, we found a record he kept of the payments he made on that house. Many years when we were small, he could pay only the interest on the loan. It took him until the mid-1960s to finally pay off that loan. The house had an outhouse in the backyard, no basement, a water pump in the kitchen, but no hot water. We took a bath in the tub we used for washing clothes in the middle of the kitchen floor on Saturday nights. Water was heated on the woodstove we used for cooking.

Over the years my father and brother dug out a basement by hand, turned the pantry right off the dining room into a bathroom, dug the drain field by hand, installed hardwood floors throughout the house, and put siding on the outside of the house twice. My parents lived in that house until their deaths—my mother in1982 and my father in 1999.

When my father was 80, he had a stroke, which made it impossible for him to drive any longer. After my mother's death, I would go to Martinsburg two or three times a week to take him for a ride in Berkeley County to see the farms he had once lived on and helped his father farm. During one of those drives in the early 1990s, we drove past a sign that pointed to Swinging Bridge. That brought back memories when I was a little kid and our family used to go out to Swinging Bridge to have a picnic, play in Back Creek, and walk across the Swinging Bridge. When I told Dad I wanted to go see it, he asked me if I knew why they went out there every summer. I told him "No." He then proceeded to tell me that was the Snider home place. He told me that his great, great grandfather, Jacob Snider, came to Berkeley County in the 1700s with Lord Fairfax and received the land grant to that property and the property remained in the Snider family name for over 200 years.

The Faulkner family in 1944

That conversation resulted in my doing a lot of work on the genealogy of the Snider family and the other branches of my father's and mother's families as well. We spent the 17 years after my mother's death discussing the family he remembered, the property and businesses they had run, and visiting various cemeteries where family members were buried.

Lightning Bug Hunts and Fishing with Grandpa
By Richard A Zigler of Charles Town, West Virginia
Born 1955

I grew up in Frederick, Maryland. There are some things that need be remembered for what they were and what they weren't, but as a farm kid, I went to school and worked at home and had fun when and where I could. Not much help to you there, huh?

During the '60s, we had a lot of stuff going on. One recollection is of "The Great Lightning Bug Hunt." I remember that while I was in elementary school. An officer from Fort Detrick came to our school and announced that the government was going to pay for the capture and turning in of lightning bugs for the amount of five bugs for a penny. The bugs had to be put in an airtight can, wax paper lining the bottom and between each layer of bugs and a sheet of wax paper on top. The bugs were to be frozen, alive and frost free. This was potentially the greatest ecological catastrophe to befall Frederick County to date. Lightning bugs disappeared from parks, fields, streams almost entirely within a week, until it sunk in how much work was involved to accumulate enough bugs to get enough money to buy even a pack of five-cent gum. The program died almost as fast as it started.

The military wanted the bugs to study bio-illumination. The need for a non-electric source of light for the upcoming space program, as well as military use, was in full swing. The bugs were dissected, heated, electrified, and doused with a myriad of chemicals to no avail. Word is that some poor shmuck of a lab assistant accidently knocked a vial of the substance onto the floor and it broke allowing it, the bug juice, to be oxygenated, causing it to glow. The results of this program can be seen everywhere that has self-illuminating glow-in-the-dark status. The most noticeable product to come from this are the glow-sticks sold at stores everywhere. I never got any royalties from that either.

During the November of 1965, there was the "Dwayyo" scare that lasted about a month. The Frederick News Post had a writer that had hit upon a scheme to increase circulation by doing a twist on the War of the Worlds theme. The Dwayyo is something of a European first cousin to werewolves, and was allegedly sighted at Thurmont, Gapland Park, and Adamstown as well as other locations. People freaked out in some cases. It was a wonder that nobody got shot or killed because of the frenzy that some were whipped into.

As a kid, I also remember visiting friends that lived in town during the winter. At that time, milk was delivered to individual homes daily or weekly. It was left on porches, usually in insulated boxes, but not always. If left unprotected, the milk would freeze, during which the cream separated from the milk, rose to the top, and forced the paper lid off the top of the bottle. As it froze, the cream made a column of frozen cream left exposed to the predations of every cat and dog in the neighborhood. Another thing about this delivery system was personal interaction of milkman and customer. I know of at least one milkman that would occasionally knock on the door and wait until the lady of the house came to retrieve that milk. He would then hand her two bottles, about eighteen inches apart. If the customer wasn't thinking about it, and was scantily dressed under her housecoat, she would reach for them both at the same time and let go of the front of her robe. "You never stare. Just take a good, but quick look, then turn and leave. If you turned and left, it was an accident. If you stared, it got you in trouble, most of the time." That is what is what I was told by one milkman who just happened to do this occasion.

The community that is now Amber Meadows was the Clem Farm when I lived near Frederick. My father rented it for a few years. When we were making hay and putting it into the top of the dairy barn, we would occasionally be treated to a game of chase. On one team were the Lab Coats, or "Labs." The people that were to capture the goats and/or sheep that were in the pasture across the road from that farm on the Fort Detrick property. On the opposing team were the animals, or "Critters," to be corralled and captured for whatever purpose the Labs needed them for. We would take timeout of our activities to watch when things looked like the end of the game was at hand, but we knew it usually wasn't.

First, the participants would spread out in the open pasture with the Labs chasing individual players of the opposing team. This may have gone on for 5-15 minutes before the Labs would think to go to the fence and form a perimeter of evenly spaced people. They would then make noise, slowly move towards the Critters, and methodically herd them towards the receiving area at the barn. Usually a Critter would bolt for the fence and all the Labs would chase after it. Chaos would prevail until the original surrounding tactic was resumed.

After a couple of false starts, the game moved in favor of the Labs. All the Critters would be huddled just outside the gate to the barn and then the fun REALLY began. With his legs apart and the lab coat hanging below his knees, like an apron, a Lab would make a lunge for a Critter only to have it dash between his legs. The Critter's horns would catch the coat, blinding the Critter as it made a mad dash for freedom. The Critter was then running open field with an inverted Lab riding on its back or being dragged while being pummeled and thrashed by hooves and weeds. If a Critter escaped through the legs of a Lab, and was unobstructed by a lab coat, the Lab would sometimes watch the disappearing Critter from the vantage of his head between his knees only to have a second member of the Critter team rush through the same gap striking the Lab player in the back of the head, flipping him completely over. Usually the labs finally won, but in many instances, it seemed that it was a stalemate, in which case the game was credited to the Critters as a win. We always rooted for the Critters. The Labs did not enjoy our enthusiasm.

One of my maternal grandfather's best friends was Ford Hedges who lived up the road from us. They always seemed to have a friendly competition going on during gardening season. Though it was before my time, I heard about this one instance often enough that I can imagine the minute details in my mind. It seems that one year Pop, my grandfather C. Raymond Crum, had an extraordinary potato crop going. There was one potato in particular that had been partly uncovered while weeding and it was huge.

Grandma said that if anybody came to visit, Pop always took them for a stroll down past the garden and would "inadvertently" scuff dirt away from this behemoth of a tater. He made certain that Ford got to see it on a regular basis. Well, Pop hand watered that tater, sprinkled manure around it, and kept it weeded all summer long. He shook out straw over it so as not to damage it when it was inspected or showed off. It was being groomed for the fair, and Pop knew he had the prize spud of the county.

When the fateful day arrived to have it removed from the earth, old Ford Hedges was there. Grandma Hellen and my aunts and uncle were there as well to witness the triumphant king of the potato patch remove his magnificent specimen from the ground that had nourished it all summer long.

He cleared all the straw away to fully expose this solid nine-inch diameter monster of a potato. He used his pocketknife to loosen the soil around it and dug a shallow trench around it. Gently he removed the loosen dirt and ever so gently pulled it out of the ground and then he almost cried. Grandma said she almost wept for him, or maybe it was the pain from biting her tongue that brought the tears. The beast was a solid nine inches across but only about two inches thick. It had grown down to a rock and spread out to make a disc. Ford said that he couldn't bring himself to do anything except pat Pop on the shoulder and walk away a few steps as he felt his friend's devastation, but that sympathy only lasted a day and for at least a month, everywhere that Pop went, and Ford showed up, the tale of the tater had to be told.

My grandfather taught me some of the finer points of relaxation and how to enjoy a lazy afternoon. Pop liked to go fishing. He would take me to the creek in the upper pasture to the old milldam where the trees gave a cool shade as the water slowly slid by, where life seemed to have no hurry in it at all. On one occasion, he stopped by and asked if I wanted to go fishing with him on a particularly hot July afternoon. I readily agreed, as we had nothing to do right away on the farm.

We settled in between a couple of roots of a large maple tree and readied our fishing lines. Pop cast out his line to about center stream. I dropped my line closer to shore. I immediately got a bite and reeled in a nice bass. I put it on the stringer and commenced to re-bait and drop line again. I caught several fish of varying size and species, but he never caught anything.

As the afternoon wore on, I got curious about his line and pulled it in. To my surprise, there was no hook on the end of the line, just a weight and bobber. He woke up and eyed me with a smile on his face. I told him that I was surprised that he had no hook, much less any bait, and that he would never catch anything like that.

He leaned over, took his fishing rod back, and cast again. He gave me a wink and said that he had needed to get away from the house and that this was as good a way as any with no questions asked. Then he imparted a line that I will never forget, "When you need to relax, go fishing. And remember, there is fishing and then there is *fishing*." He pulled his hat back over his face and dozed off again.

Glenda, her sister, Louann, with their grandparents, Charles and Ethel Dayton in 1954

Growing Up in the Tri-Towns
By Glenda D. (Kiddy) Newcomb of Oakland, Maryland
Born 1948

Growing up in Western Maryland in the 1950-60s meant a small-town, all-American experience and this experience is even more in focus in a place called "The Tri-Towns," Luke, Westernport and Piedmont. The Tri-Towns looks like one town, a mill town, until you look closer. One of the three (tri) towns, Piedmont, is in West Virginia.

The towns are nestled in a steep valley where Georges Creek empties into the Potomac River, which is also the boundary between Piedmont, WV and the two Maryland towns. Each town spreads up the adjoining hills to the point where you can see most all of the three towns from any hill and each town became an integral part in shaping this small town girl.

I will start in Luke where both of my parents grew up and where both grandfathers worked at the Luke Paper Mill, or "the mill" as all locals referred to it. It was like a little United Nations in my parents' day. Many families were first generation immigrants who came to work at "the mill" with names like Diaz, Mazzone, Krumpach, Alvarez, and Walsh. My dad liked to tell the story that within five minutes, he and his little buddies could run through peoples' yards and be cussed out in four languages.

In Luke, in the '50s and early '60s, there were stores, a jail, and a train depot where you could catch a train to the big city of Cumberland for shopping. However, the center of all activity was the Devon Club, owned by the mill, where you could duckpin bowl, play pool, play cards, read, get a fountain snack, or attend a movie. I spent every Sunday afternoon at my Granddad Dayton's house until after dinner. My friends and I saw the current western or mystery at the matinee for a dime. My friend Christa got all the horses and I got all the good-looking cowboys. Remember Guy Madison?

Afterwards, we would play around town pretending Dracula lived behind the ornate wooden basement door at the Westvaco Club up on Luke Hill. We always wore our crosses to ward him off. Then for fun we would return to the spiral fire escape attached to the Devon Club, inch our way up until it got too dark, and our imaginations got the best of us; don't forget Dracula!

Luke also meant family ties. I spent many weekends overnight at my grandparents' house. Granddad usually had cherry-vanilla ice cream cones when he returned from the card room at the club. I attended a private kindergarten—not yet public, at Luke school where my Aunt Katherine had once been. May Queen and my parents and their siblings had attended school grades one through eight. Both grandmothers had sisters who also lived in Luke and I often accompanied them to Bingo on Saturday nights. They took me for good luck. My granddad Dayton had been mayor of Luke for several years, so every aspect of life there was familiar to me.

However, Westernport was home base. There I lived most of my life until high school graduation. Here was the old neighborhood. Our house, on Miller Street, was one of the first in what was a new "after the war" development. Johnny Green's old ballpark became Green's Addition. Soon it was filled with young families with children.

There was never a lack of things to do, and most of it was outside. I especially enjoyed the springs, summers, and falls. We played softball on the vacant lots, badminton in Strong's yard, road our bikes everywhere including in Philos Cemetery, and later road skate boards on the neighborhood driveways. When it rained we played monopoly in McBee's basement, played Jacks and cards on everyone's porches (people had porches not decks), set up school in Strong's basement, or housekeeping in my basement. We would take a break in the afternoons for a pop-cycle or soda at Schimer's, the neighborhood grocery where the cooler was on the porch. It slid open at the top and the opener was along the side. My dad also swore by their homemade ham salad. At dusk, we caught fireflies in a jar and played hide-and-seek. No one ever worried about trespassing in a basement stairwell or shrubs. Every mother's eyes watched out for you. Then it was time to come in for baths after which it was relaxing with family and friends on the porch till bedtime. Life was simpler then.

I have great memories of school. Hammond Street School, long ago torn down, was an all-wooden structure where I attended elementary school until third grade. At which time we transferred down town to Bruce High School, which in turn moved to the new building on top of the hill a few streets above my house. Because we could see the school from our kitchen window, in winter we watched for the smoke that came from the cafeteria chimney. No smoke, no school. Snow day! My favorite memories of Hammond Street were at playtime. We could go to any one of the three neighborhood groceries for candy. Hence, the many trips to our dentist, Dr. Whitworth.

My best memories of downtown Westernport are of the library, Girl Scout meetings and dance classes at the Union Hall. Jeanne Biggs and I spent many Saturdays loading our arms with books to fill our heads with wonders. It was a challenge to see who could read the most. She won. Also, Girl Scouts was a big part of my early learning and socialization. Mrs. Harris and Gertie Grove taught us many of the basics I treasure today, like hard work, truthfulness, teamwork, and resourcefulness. Some of the friends I made then I still value today. One of the biggest perks was the annual springtime trip to D.C. organized by Boy Scout leader Alton Fortney, who had been a leader since my parents were scouts. Over the years, we scouts from the diminutive Tri-Towns saw nearly every building and monument worth seeing in Washington.

Jeanne and another friend, Terry Reeves, and I also spent many hours in the Union Hall with the Oldfields, two retired professional dancers, learning the basics of ballet and jazz. She had been with the Russian Ballet and he had been a dancer on Broadway. With no organized sports in school for girls, these lessons fostered in me a lifelong love of physical activity, primarily dance. We also learned poise and confidence much needed by these small town girls.

Last but not least in my small town odyssey is Piedmont. Though Piedmont was across the river and in another state, it was an integral part of Tri-Town life. There we shopped, went to the doctors (Wolverton and Berry), went to church, and used the public swimming pool. There were upscale lady, men, and children apparel stores. You could buy furniture and appliances, go to a bakery, have lunch, and of course, go to the 5&10 Cent Store. The 5&10 was my destination every Saturday morning to check out what new Ricky Nelson 45s they had in. I still know all his songs by heart but have long since lost the 45s.

The Trinity Methodist Church was a big part of my childhood. Looking back, the choir was my favorite activity. Led by Miss. Betty

Glenda Kiddy, Louann Kiddy, and a neighbor in 1955

Jean Withrow, who was also my high school music and chorus teacher, my heart soared to the classic hymns we sang. She was a hard taskmaster, but I loved every minute of it. I have fond memories of singing carols in the town parking lot around the beautifully lit community tree, very Currier and Ives.

However, here in Piedmont, I also became aware of one of our society's ills that small towns had a way of hiding. When I went to Brownie meetings in Piedmont Elementary, we played with the "colored" Brownies before the meetings, but separated for the meetings and we never did activities or took trips with them. It was not uncommon to see "colored people" on the streets, but never in places like stores or church, my own school, or the community pool. I asked my mother, progressive that she was what this was all about. She explained to me what discrimination was. Of course, this was the beginning of the era in our country where the struggle for civil rights was displayed on TV every night. What had been hidden or accepted in our small town was relevant then and still is today. As an adult, I was introduced by the writings of Professor Henry Louis Gates, a native of Piedmont, to the other side of this story.

These are just a few of my memories of a wonderful childhood in a small town. It seemed to have everything I could have wanted or needed to produce a successful life, family, friends, a great education, and the sense of community. When Hillary Clinton said it takes a community to raise children, she must have meant life in the Tri-Town during the 1950s and 1960s. I will always cherish the memories.

Being a Pastor
By Richard Neal of Martinsburg, West Virginia
Born 1932

On June 1957, my wife Carroll and I moved from Springfield, Ohio to Charles Town. I had graduated from Hamma Divinity School, a Lutheran seminary on the campus of Wittenberg College, been ordained, and accepted a call to be a pastor of St. Thomas Lutheran Church. Our telephone number in the parsonage was 750. When I wanted to phone someone, I would pick up the phone and Nina Vickers at the telephone office would say, "Who are you calling, Pastor Neal" I would tell her and she would connect us. We lived in the parsonage on South Seminary Street for 46 years.

Good Ol' Wheat Threshing Days
By Mrs. Hazel Mason of Winchester, Virginia
Born 1926

My memory takes me back to the summers that my siblings and I were at our grandparents' farm during wheat threshing time in the early 1930s. On one special day, early in the morning, we could hear the big steam-driven engine from a distance clanking and snorting down the dirt road and blowing its whistle at intervals as neighbors followed to help with the harvesting of the wheat. The men were wearing overalls and straw hats to protect themselves from the sun and carrying special wooden type rakes to use in their work. We kids were not allowed to go near the wheat fields, but watched from a distance for a while.

In the meantime, Grandmother was in the kitchen preparing fried chicken, ham, green beans, sweet potatoes, corn on the cob, cucumbers and onions, sliced tomatoes, and potato salad. There was delicious, ice-cold lemonade. She also made her famous rolls and apple pies on her wood-burning cast iron stove. I never could figure out how she knew how long to bake anything in the oven without a timer. After placing the tablecloth on the table just right, my sister and I put Grandmother's best dishes and glasses in place, making sure the silverware and napkins were on the correct side. By lunchtime when the men came in from the wheat field, the table was full of good food. To us kids, it was like a picnic.

With the grain in the bin in the barn and the straw in shocks in the field, the men were finished for the day. They would help another neighbor another day. Giving three more toots on the whistle, the steam engine drove down the lane. At the close of the exciting day with all the people and activity, it was hard to go to sleep, but has left us with happy memories.

Stories of Old
By Betty R. Ream of Swanton, Maryland
Born 1935

My dad, Bruce Sweitzer, Sr., grew up in the early 1900s close to the tiny town in Garrett County, western Maryland. Swanton, a little larger now, is located along a section of the Baltimore and Ohio Railroad, better known as the B & O Railroad. This part of the railroad was known as the "Seventeen Mile Grade." It began at Bloomington, Maryland, which is at the foot of Backbone Mountain, continued through Swanton, and ended at the Altamont Bridge. At Swanton, there was a small station and a siding track. Also, a mail hook for pickup and delivery via train was there. Mrs. Lohr was postmaster of the little post office in one side of the Arthur Green Store. Swanton was also blessed with a two-room school and three churches.

The men and boys of the community liked to hang out at the store and tell tales. Of course, they wouldn't gossip like the ladies did. One afternoon as some fellows were lounging around at the front of the store, another man they all knew came walking up from the railroad tracks. He told the others that he had just come from down the tracks, and as he passed a small shed, some "thing" was making an awful noise inside. He admitted he had been too scared to investigate the building and discussion followed as to what could be in there. It was decided they would all return with the fellow to check it out.

The man who reported the noise had gathered his courage, so with some support from the other guys, he went to the door of the shed. He turned the wooden knob, and began to open it. As soon as daylight shone in the opening, a buck sheep crashed out and knocked him down so quickly he didn't see what hit him! He was glad the others were with him or he might have believed it was a ghost! They found that someone had put down a board that leaned into the window opening. The sheep had walked the plank and fell into a place he didn't like! All were glad it ended well, especially the sheep! The story seemed more exciting when my dad told it and I was only eight years old back in 1943.

Old Arthur Green Store

Growing Up on a Farm in Grant County
By Wilma Lee Ketterman of Petersburg, West Virginia
Born 1949

When we got a telephone put into our home, it was a black party line phone where you had to dial the number you wanted. We had to share the party line with about four other families. It was hard to use the phone with so many people talking so long on it when they did get to use it.

When I went to school, children who lived some distance off the main road had a bus shed to wait inside for the school bus when the weather was cold or bad. My favorite bus driver was John Greenwalt. We got on the school bus at 7:30 each morning and got home at 5:00 each evening. Our mother would have a good supper ready for us when we got off the school bus. My dad was also home from work, so we all got to eat supper together before we had to go do our chores. I went to school at Dorcas Grade School where there were two grades in the same classroom. I went there through the eighth grade and then I transferred to Petersburg High School where I graduated in 1968. Dorcas Grade School closed its doors in 2013. It is now the Dorcas Community Center.

In vehicles, the headlight dimmer switches were on the floor by the clutch. We didn't have turn signals in our vehicles, so we used hand signals. One time we had a Studebaker that would only start when the weather was warm. When we were growing up, we never got new clothes. Someone, usually a relative,

School bus shed

Down in Black Oak Bottom
By Leoda Cox of Keyser, West Virginia
Born 1923

My name is Leoda (Kimble) Cox. I'm 91 years old. One of my fondest memories was going to school in a one-room schoolhouse on 21st Lane in McCoole, Maryland. It had two outhouses—one for girls and one for boys. There was no water inside the school, so we took turns carrying it from a well, which was a good ways from the schoolhouse. We used a long pole placed through the handles of two buckets. It took two kids to haul it. The school was heated by a potbellied stove. Recess was the best part of the school day. The boys would play marbles or kick-the-can or join us girls to play games such as flag relay, block tag, red rover, jump rope, and hopscotch. I don't remember how old I was or the name of my teacher, but I do remember she was always bringing baked bean sandwiches for her lunch. We kids mostly ate peanut butter and jelly sandwiches.

When it was warm, we went barefooted; only during the winter, we wore shoes. We got one pair of shoes a year, and when they wore out my mom would sew cardboard bottoms on them at night so we could wear them the next day. I remember my mom got a job in Cumberland, Maryland once and she would buy me a dress. It would cost between 25 cents and 50 cents.

When school was out for the summer, I would stay with my older sister and cousins on their farm on Black Oak Bottom. There was plenty of work to do and also a lot of fun things to do. I helped feed the animals and I also worked in the garden pulling weeds. We picked berries, blackberries, raspberries, and strawberries. We kids always came back with purple or red faces. We probably ate as many as we picked. Boy did the berries make good cobblers!

My sister didn't have a washing machine, so the clothes had to be washed on a scrub board. There were two washtubs, one for washing, and one to rinse the clothes. She used homemade lye soap to clean them. There was no electricity, so we used kerosene lamps. We usually just went to bed when the sun went down and we got up at sunrise. We played in the haystacks and in the barn loft. We caught lightning bugs and put them in jars. They

would give us their clothes when they outgrew them. Their hand-me-down clothes were new to us.

When I was young, I would run off from working with my mother and three sisters in the house to go help my dad and brother outside. If I got to the tractor before my brother did, I got to drive it. Now as I am older, I wish that I had spent more time in the kitchen with my mother learning how to make homemade pies and bread as good as my mother did. She was a great cook.

My dad always told me about a road called Shady Death Road. It was 8/10 mile long and located between the Baker Rock Church and the Durgon Run Road. It got its name from the old days when wagons were pulled by horses. An elderly lady was riding in the wagon with a blanket around her when she passed away on that road. The road was narrow and it was shady where the sun never hit it. She probably died of pneumonia.

In his younger days, my dad chewed square snuff. He bought it by the case. It would come in glasses with a lid on each glass. Those glasses are what we used to drink out of and although they broke easily, we always had plenty of snuff glasses around.

were something to see at dusk lighting up the cornfields. They looked like thousands of tiny stars blinking on and off.

There was a river that ran by the farm. We had a flat-bottomed boat which we would take rides down the river in. One time they left me alone in the boat and it drifted down the river. They ran and caught it. It's a good thing, because I never knew how to swim. Of course, there was an outhouse. One day, my cousin and I were in it. We looked up and there was a very large blacksnake above us in the rafters. We sure didn't take time to look at the catalog!

When I got older, a friend and I went to work in Baltimore, Maryland in an airplane factory. This was during World War II. I guess we were some of the "Rosie the Riveters."

Norma's parents's anniversary

Growing Up in Pekin
By Norma Lee Muir of Lonaconing, Maryland
Born 1936

My name is Norma Lee (Colmer) Muir and I was born on December 21st, 1936 in the little town of Pekin, Maryland. The town is now known as Nikep, two miles from Lonaconing from where we got to the mall. We had a post office in town for about a hundred years in different homes during those years. We had a schoolhouse, which I went to for four years, and it was very nice in the day. We had a potbelly stove and a water bucket, which we all drink from in a dipper. The teacher was Miss Ella Wallace and she lived about a block or so from the school. She walked down every day and women always wore dresses in those days. Then in the fifth and sixth grades, we went to Moscow School that was almost a mile from Pekin. Both of them schools also had outhouses, water buckets, and potbelly stoves. Then in the seventh grade we went to Central High School for the next years of school

My dad, Peter Colmer, had a store in our town for about 40 years. We also had a gas station and a Sunday school; all are gone now. The public buses ran every hour from Cumberland Maryland and took about an hour then. Most people never had cars, so they were always full coming from Cumberland on weekends. There was a movie theater which was always full and only cast about 15 cents to 25 cents and then. The Celanese plant was outside of Cumberland and a lot of people from the area worked there. My dad ran several of their shifts to the north. Also, Cumberland had a lot of stores and a theater that we attended. I liked to go down on the bus with my mother, Elizabeth Colmer, on Saturday to get lunch and go to the movies.

My five sisters were all born at home with Dr. Hogsan coming down. There was also a midwife to help with the birth. My husband David was also born in Pekin and had four sisters and two brothers who were born at home. Most families had six to eight children. Everyone had wells and had to get water for work, washing, and drinking.

I was going to school during the World War II and we had our raid drills when we had to get underneath our desks. My mother's two brothers were in the war. My husband's two

David and Norma Lee Muir in 1957

brothers also were in the war, along with quite a few men from the area. Later when I was a teenager, I met my first husband, Charles T. Shroyer and he went into the Army in October of 1952. He took basic training and came home on leave in February of 1953. We were married on February 15th and he left to go to Korea. He became a medic and was killed in action on July 18, 1953. He was only 21 years old and I was only 16. They brought his body back here in October of 1953 and he is buried in Laurel Run Cemetery.

When I was 18 years old, I married my second husband David on June 11, 1955. He was in the army also for two years and got out in October of 1953. We moved to Baltimore, Maryland and he worked at the Chevrolet place it for two years. We had our first daughter in Baltimore and then we moved back to our old hometown. When we were in Baltimore, we had a "rabbit ears antenna" for the TV and got stations. Back here at home we did not have TV until they ran a cable around the early 1950s. The first ones were only black and white. Later we had three more daughters and they are all grown up and married now. One moved to Florida and one to Wyoming. The other two live close by.

We have 8 grandchildren and 14 great-grandchildren. My husband's brothers and sisters are all gone. Also, most of our neighbors we knew are all gone, along with my mother and dad. Most of our family is buried in Laurel Cemetery in Maryland. My husband retired from West Virginia Paper Company about 20 years ago. We still live in our little town and love it.

Mr. Crite's Bear
By Anonymous Contributor of Romney, West Virginia
Born 1941

The time was the late 1940s. Mr. Crites, then an old man living in a small town in West Virginia, had since retired from a traveling circus and built a pen behind his living quarters for his pet black bear. On a dare (and wanting to prove a stupid act of bravery to my playmates) and knowing the sleeping bear was chained and inside his bear house, I crawled across the fence enclosing the pen and proceeded to look into the doorway at the sleeping bear. When the bear looked up at me, I tore out of there as fast as I could, feeling the bear's hot breath on my neck with every step until I dove across the fence. Laughter from my friends told me that the bear had not moved from his resting place, but Mr. Crites had seen what had happened and gave us a stern warning, saying, "Boys that bear is friendly but you're gonna make him mean by pulling stunts like that."

As would happen, one morning bright and early, the bear got loose and proceeded to follow the only person walking along, an inebriated man who was staggering down the sidewalk. Picking up the pace when he realized the bear was nearby and gaining ground, the man (probably sober by then) made it to the nearest residence. After pounding on the door profusely, the man was admitted into the house and the town police who didn't want to shoot the old man's pet summoned Mr. Crites. The situation was resolved when Mr. Crites arrived and taking hold of the broken chain quietly and calmly said, "Come on bear," and led his long time pet back home. After the bear escaped a second time, Mr. Crites had to part company with his pet bear and, as far as I know, that was the last pet bear allowed in town.

Bang, Bang
Bang Bang, already an old man in the late 1940s, was a harmless, odd sort of character who lived several miles over a mountain from a small West Virginia town and usually walked to town carrying a cigar box full of candy. Bang Bang got his nickname by simultaneously shooting children whom he came across with his hammer thumb, gun finger, and a loud verbal "Bang, bang." After winning the gunfight, Bang Bang usually offered the loser a piece of candy and went about his way in search of a new victim.

One day Bang Bang was making his customary trip to town when two ladies in a Model T stopped by the roadside and offered him a ride. Bang Bang graciously declined the ride, explaining to the ladies that he was in a hurry to get to town. A few miles later, Bang Bang walked by the same Model T parked along the road and the two ladies outside staring at a flat tire. Bang Bang, still in a hurry and not knowing anything about automobiles, walked quickly by the distressed Model T, beating the ladies to town after all!

Betting Brothers

Working at a small town family business, my two uncles, Jim and Willie were always trying to outdo each other one way or the other and would make a bet on just about any challenge. After betting which one would complete their delivery and return to the starting point first, both uncles departed at the same time from the same work place in West Virginia and were driving to the same place in Virginia to deliver their load. Jim had completed his delivery first and was high tailing it back when he was stopped by a state trooper and given a ticket for speeding. There was no way he was going to let Willie win the bet, so he ingeniously informed the officer of the wager and asked him to remain there to catch his brother and keep him there for a while. The officer complied. Willie was stopped and given a speeding ticket while Jim went on to win the bet…that time!

Chicken Run

Delivering a load of baby chicks after a 1950's hard rain, I came upon a small stream that I had to cross. Spotting a farmer on the other side of the stream and unsure of the depth of the water, I got out of the vehicle, yelled to the farmer to get his attention, and asked if he thought I could cross safely. Without hesitation, he replied that he didn't have any trouble crossing the stream earlier. Confident that the stream was low enough to make a safe crossing, I plowed ahead only to have the front end of the vehicle dip below the water. The engine sputtered as I floored the gas pedal, but luckily, it kept running as water from the front end poured over the hood while the vehicle pulled up the embankment on the other side. Keeping the engine running to dry off and a little hot under the collar myself, I got out of the vehicle and asked the farmer why he told me that he didn't have any trouble crossing the stream. Pointing to his tall tractor, the farmer informed me that he had no trouble at all, but then added that it was earlier in the morning before the hard rain and that he was driving the tractor. Needless to say, I waited until the stream was considerably lower before attempting a return crossing.

Electrified Car

My uncle bought a brand new car in the late '40s and parked it along the sidewalk in front of the building where he worked. It was at a time when denim jeans still were made with rivets and some of the older teenagers had no more respect than to find a seat on his new vehicle. After several scratches appeared, my uncle asked the boys to stay off his new car. However, his request fell on deaf ears. They finally got the message when a few of the boys had a hair raising electrical shock from the vehicles battery that had been wired to the chassis. No new scratches appeared!

Five Point Duck

Cole, my teenage grandson, called his grandmother to report that he had shot a five-point buck. Excited to spread the news, his grandmother called our other son and reported that Cole had shot a five point duck.

Fun with Freddie

Owning a small retail department store after the Freddie Krueger movie had become popular, I purchased a Freddie Krueger sweater, hat, outfit, glove, and mask to decorate a complete Halloween window display and decided to make it scarier with a live performance that, on first appearance, would look like a mannequin—until the mannequin moved.

After dressing as Freddie and assuming a mannequin pose, I stood quite still on the mannequin stand, which had been placed in the window. In short order, I spotted an elderly couple across the street, and noticing the lady paying particular interest, I waved up and down with both hands to draw her interest. Startled and pointing in my direction, the lady quickly nudged her husband to look. When her husband looked, the lady was bewildered because the mannequin stood perfectly motionless. She kept staring until I waved profusely again and again. She quickly alerted her husband to look, but alas, every time her husband turned to look, the mannequin was still perfectly motionless.

This went on for a few more times with each time her husband becoming more agitated until finally he motioned for her to get in their car, which was parked close. I don't know if he thought she was crazy or not but as they pulled out of their parking place, she looked back one last time while I turned in her direction and waved profusely with both hands as a farewell gesture. At that point, she quietly admitted defeat by simply lowering and slowly shaking her head as her husband drove away.

Still in the Freddie Krueger costume, I moved the mannequin stand outside on the sidewalk that evening and assumed the mannequin appearance just as school was dismissed. Spotting a small group of boys approaching, I stood perfectly motionless; noticing that one of the middle school students whom I recognized was eyeballing the Freddie mannequin and especially the glove. "That's really cool," he said, feeling the glove, which I was wearing.

Without saying a word, I squeezed his hand as he dropped to both knees while taking a distressed breath, gasping, and exclaiming, "I can't breathe! I can't breathe!" Only then did I let go, still without saying a word. The boys continued to glance back once in a while as they continued on their way, probably to make sure Freddie wasn't right behind them.

The Hayride

Thirteen years old in the early fifties and excited about my first hayride, I found a seat between two young girls wearing skirts. Since it was late fall and chilly, someone had provided a rather large wool blanket that completely covered our legs and extended to our waist as we sat on the straw. The girl to my left said something that drew my attention in that direction as the hay wagon started moving along the road. No sooner had I turned to answer her than a hard haymaker slap on my face from the girl sitting to my right quickly returned my attention in that direction.

Somewhat shocked and hurting, I managed to ask, "Why did you slap me?" "That's for feeling my leg!" she replied, "and don't do that again." With both of my hands in plain sight on top of the blanket, I raised them into the air and explained that I couldn't possibly have been feeling her leg. However, she refused to listen to reason, and an apology was totally out of the question as she stubbornly replied, "Well, it had to be you because you are the only one sitting here."

Being a farm boy and knowing full well that snakes are fond of hay and that it was probably a snake that had crawled up and across her leg, I found great satisfaction in not causing a hysterical reaction by keeping my mouth shut while the grin on my face erased the pain of the slap rather quickly!

My Experience in a One-room Schoolhouse
By Marion E. Caldwell of Oakland, Maryland
Born 1944

My first four years of schooling (1950-1954) were at a one-room schoolhouse near Altamont, Maryland. Wilson School had approximately 19 students, ranging from grades one through seven. Because we were such a small school and all the students lived within walking distance, we were like a family. I walked to and from school about one mile each way, rain or shine. At that time, girls weren't permitted to wear pants to school—only skirts or dresses, regardless of the weather. To keep our poor knees from freezing stiff, we wore snow pants over our skirts until we got to the schoolhouse.

During the winter months, students would take turns bringing in coal from the coalhouse nearby to keep the potbelly stove warm in the center of the schoolroom. We also took turns carrying buckets of spring water from the nearest neighbor's house to fill the crock water cooler that we drank from.

Winters in Garrett County could be quite harsh, and everyone always looked forward to warmer weather. Each spring we would all practice for weeks to compete against another school in important Olympic-class athletic events like sack races on what was called "Play Day." That was the only day we rode a bus.

Also, each spring we would occasionally lock the school up and spend a day hiking through the woods and along the tracks behind

Marion and her classmates saying the Pledge

the schoolhouse, looking for flowers to dig up and bring back to plant around the school. After one such outing, we returned to find that our teacher, Mrs. Martin, had locked the keys inside the school. One of the boys had to take a hatchet and bust a hole through the door into the cloakroom attached to the school. I was one of the smallest students, so I was elected to crawl through the hole and get the keys.

For such a small rural school, there was no shortage of mischief to be had. While most of us carried our lunches to school, one of the girls lived close enough that she went home each day for lunch. Sometimes several of us would walk home with her at lunchtime. Her parents always had cigarettes lying around, so we took a pack or two back to school with us. We girls had a roped-off area down in the woods as our playhouse. We would smoke and think we were big shots, until one day one of the girls forgot to hide the cigarettes. She had a pack in her blouse pocket when she was with the teacher at the front of the class. The teacher saw the cigarettes and asked our little enclave if we had been smoking. Of course, we all denied it, but then the teacher ordered me to come up front so she could smell my breath. She said she liked the smell on men, but on young girls, it was disgusting. She told me that she was going to call my folks and tell them. For weeks, I was scared to death every time the phone rang. Thankfully, she never called (I can only assume she knew that the guilt would probably be enough to stop the behavior), and I never told my parents.

Mrs. Martin went out of her way to keep our school days both educational and fun. I remember that there was a wind-up Victrola record player that the teacher had brought in. At lunch or recess, we would dance the Virginia Reel, and as the machine would wind down and the music would slow, someone would need to run over and wind it up again.

Every week we had a spelling test, and at the end of each term, the teacher would bring in big boxes of penny candy. For every 100% we had gotten throughout the term, we could pick out a piece of candy. You can bet we studied!

By the end of my fourth year at Wilson School, we had only about nine students spread out between grades one through seven. After that year, the school was closed and torn down. My uncle bought the materials from the school to start building his home, located nearby. Oh, how I wish I could go back and relive just one day, but I at least have some great memories of my time there.

My First (and Last) Attempt at Smoking
By John Smith of Parsons, West Virginia
Born 1947

I grew up in a large blended family of eight kids. I was number seven. All my older siblings started smoking as teenagers, and as a curious lad of four or five, I thought it looked cool. I liked the smell of tobacco. I knew how to light and smoke a cigarette because I had seen it done thousands of times. It was something older people did. I also knew I wasn't supposed to do it. Put all that together, and the appeal was irresistible to me. I was going to try smoking!

The smokers always kept their smokes close at hand, so the opportunity to steal one never arose until my oldest sister came visiting. She was a smoker like all my older brothers and sisters, and she preferred unfiltered Lucky Strikes. One day, she got careless and left her cigarette pack where I could reach it. I saw my chance and waited for the right moment to make my move. Once everyone was out of sight, I stole a cigarette from the pack, grabbed a box of matches, and headed down over a nearby hill at high speed to a large set of boulders. This was my hidey-hole, and it was a good one. I could see everything in front of me and I was invisible from the back and sides to any prying adult eyes. The backside where I could not see was protected by tall, dry grass, which would give away anyone trying to sneak up on me.

Once safely hidden, I did what I had seen my siblings do. I stuck the cigarette in my mouth, struck a match, held it to the end of the cigarette, and took a draw. Nothing in my young life had prepared me for the sensation of swallowing fire, which is exactly what it felt like. When the heat and smoke hit my throat, my body instantly rebelled. The gag reflex stopped anything from getting to my lungs, and the horrendous coughing fit expelled all signs of the tobacco invader. My first thought beyond recognition of pain was, "What is the fun in this!"

I wish I could have seen my face! I

know the expressions ran the gamut of pain, surprise, disgust, chagrin, and disappointment in mere milliseconds. My throat burned and the taste was utterly disgusting. The grand experiment was an utter bust. Friends, at that moment, I was cured of smoking! I stubbed out that cigarette, gathered my wits, and went back to the house and I have never smoked a cigarette from that day to this one!

Climbing

My mother and older sister told the following story to me. I grew up on a farm, and was a healthy, active lad with a tad more desire for excitement than I should have had. That adventurous streak started when I was very young, and its primary manifestation was my desire to get to the top of tall things by any means possible. By the time, I was three or so, I could climb anything with enough handholds.

There was a dug well in the yard with a hand pump in it. Over the well and pump sat a 40 foot metal windmill with a ladder up the side. The tower wasn't connected to anything, but it was tall and it had handholds. One day, I started climbing it. My mother suddenly missed me because it was "too quiet," and she asked my younger brother where I was. He said, "Up a twee (tree) I weckon (reckon)." That got people looking up, and Mom finally spotted me about halfway up the windmill ladder. She managed not to scream and startle me, but she told me in no uncertain terms to stop climbing.

My older sister got the job of retrieving me. She climbed the ladder to where I was holding on, cradled me between her arms and body, and walked me down to safety. That very day, Dad took the bottom ten feet of the ladder off the windmill, but that was only a temporary deterrent. By the time I was five, I was climbing the tower again by using the X-braces to get up to the ladder, which I used for the rest of the trip to the top.

Another climbing adventure took place in an old wooden corncrib. As usual, I was as high as I could get inside the crib. I decided to cross to the other side by crawling along a 2x6 rough-sewn oak joist on my hands and knees. About halfway across, I lost my balance and fell off the joist. I was wearing a pair of suspender overalls and, somehow, the suspenders caught on the head of a large spike nail. True to the nature of "suspenders," they suspended me in mid-air! Talk about a wedgie!

Once again, I had to rely on my younger brother to sound the alarm. He listened calmly to my shouted instructions and wandered slowly off in search of help. Despite my loud attempts to impress upon him the need for swiftness in his mission, it obviously wasn't an emergency in his eyes. Eventually, one of my older brothers came to my rescue and got me safely down. Thanks to God and the strength of Montgomery Ward's denim, I was completely unharmed!

Feed Sack Clothes and Homemade Lye Soap
By Sally Arlene (Armentrout) Stump of Moorfield, West Virginia
Born 1942

Aunt Willye's family consisted of a mom, a dad, and one sister. Dad had one brother and two sisters. His mom and dad died very early. Dad was the baby of four children. The four children were put in separate homes. Dad was two at this time. Aunt Willye's family took Dad and raised him. At an early age, Willye bought a 100-acre farm four miles from Moorefield on South Fork Road. Willye took Dad with her, and shortly after Mom and Dad married. Then we all lived together. Willye never married.

Mom and dad had eight children while living at Willyes. Mom told us that we were found under cabbage leaves when we were babies, so when we got big enough to hoe the garden, we were very careful and looked under all of the cabbage leaves. The smaller children used hoes that had the shorter handles that had been broken. We were told that at one time our dad had a cart but traded it for a milk cow that had twins from one of the neighbor farmers.

Willye raised chickens to eat and sale. Dad worked at several jobs as we grew up. Mom stayed home, had, and raised babies. Mom had several of us at home. She had a boy first and then six girls and two more boys. I remember when she had the first of the two later boys. She was in the bedroom and they called my older brother in to see his first brother. Big brother came out screaming and

James, Helen, Sally, Diana, Charlotte, Doris, JoAnn, and Stanley

crying and said, "You lied! It's another girl; it has a dress on!" It was just a gown; all of us at that time wore gowns when we were born.

The next child, a boy, was born after we built a house in town and moved. The oldest boy stayed back with Willye and worked on local farms. Finally, the oldest boy got married and moved. He left Willye at home by herself. He went back often and visited with her often, along with some of the rest of us.

Yes, we had the outhouse. It had lots of old newspapers instead of toilet paper. Yes, I remember the castor oil. Mom would throw us across her lap, hold our nose shut, while another kid would hold our legs to keep us from kicking. Yes, we had spankings at school and then someone would tell on us and we got another one when we got home. Yes, we had Saturday night bath in the washtub with lye soap. We had a wringer washer in which several of us would get an arm stuck in the wringer. We had homemade feed sack clothes made by our grandmother. We also had feed sack sheets and feather bed mattresses and pillows. We had long, wool socks and sweaters to help keep warm on cold nights. Sometimes the snow would blow in around the windows a couple inches deep. We had snakes crawling up the eaves of the house and coming out into our bedrooms.

We got one toy each for Christmas; sometimes it was a little purse or a little doll. There were no store-bought toys any other time of the year. We swam in the river and got full of leeches. As children, the older ones got to go to town once a year, besides going to school. We had a neighbor man that would put his cattle racks on the old pickup and load up his several children, stop by our place, and load us up and take us to town to watch the yearly parade. We usually had chicken to eat once a week, and that was on Sunday. Willye would walk us older children to church one mile each way while Mom stayed home and fixed Sunday dinner.

We were just country folks. Back then, we had breakfast, dinner, and supper. At one time, a lady asked my dad how he fed all those kids. He said, "Just add more water to the gravy." I can't remember of anyone at our house ever going hungry. I remember when we got electric. I was young. We never had TV, phones, or lights. We used oil lamps. We did our schoolwork before dark, went to bed, and got up at daylight.

Growing Up in West Virginia
By Margaret Whitacre of Clear Spring, Maryland
Born 1927

My name is Margaret (Unger) Whitacre, and I am the sixth child of 20, all single births. My first memory as a child was when my father, Calvin Unger, had been let go of his job at the PA Glass Sand Corp, a company that mined rocks out of the mountain in Berkeley Springs, West Virginia. We were living in one of the company houses at that time. The rocks were mined out of the mountain there and ground up for sand. While we were living in this house, the upstairs had only two bedrooms. My father and mother, Martha (Bishop) Unger, put up a line across one room and hung blankets on it to make it two rooms. Three boys slept on one side and seven girls in one bed slept on the other side.

We had to move from there to a house out of town off the main highway beside a railway track between Berkeley Springs and Hancock. I was six years old at the time, and we were enrolled in a small country school, which had two classrooms, no water, and no bathrooms. The children were assigned turns to go to the next house to carry water back to the school to fill the reserve water cooler in the hallway.

Calvin Unger family

There were two outside (back houses) on the grounds.

When I was in the third grade, the state started the school lunch, which were fixed in the clothes room at the school. The only thing I remember having was soup, beans, and milk. That was the first time I remember having pasteurized milk; it tasted awful. We had a cow at the time at home, which was given to us by my mother's parents.

By 1934, our school averaged about 30 students. A tuberculosis outbreak in the community started about this time. I was in the third grade and had a very dear friend, a girl of about my age, who lost her father with the disease, caused by the sand dust from the mine. They took her out of our classroom when she was in the tenth grade in high school; she later died with the disease as well.

When I was in the third grade, my teacher, who was a wonderful person, bought me a new pair of shoes and a pair of boots. She walked all the way to our home to give them to me. I was at home sick with appendicitis. Another time a sub teacher bought several new dresses. She then took several of the girls in school to her house, let us try them on, and gave each of us one dress.

My father at about this time lost his job because the State Administration changed politics. He was working at this time for the West Virginia State Road Commission. Hard times really hit. He was getting $25 a month from being in France during World War I. He had to sign a note at the grocery store not to let the bill go over $25.

My father always put out a nice garden. He then started putting out fields of tomatoes and we sold them to the canning factories. At one time, we were canning them at home and the canning factories gave us their labels to put on the cans, making them their brand. My older brother planted a patch of popcorn. In the winter, we shelled it, and us kids went around in the spring and sold it to neighbors. Then he went to the CCC Camp and the government sent my parents a check each month. I think it was $7.

My father would go huckleberry picking with some friends, and us kids would take the berries around and sell them to neighbors. We went into the cornfields in the spring, gathered land cress, and sold them to neighbors, too. We picked blackberries in the summer and Mom canned them for winter food. I remember at one time she said that we had about 400 quarts of berries canned.

By July of 1941, my parents had their 16th child and the town photographer took a picture of all of us. It made the papers of the Washington area, saying the Ungers were looking for a name for their 16th child. (Their second child, a little boy, died of an ear infection at 6 months old). We received gifts and clothes from all over the area because of this news article.

My father and another man in the church we went to signed a contract with a fruit grower that together we would pick all his fruit and help pack them. Soon my older brother joined the Navy for 28 years and the next brother went into the Army.

We walked to church many Sundays with the most of us barefoot. Those railroad ties get real hot in the summertime! In the winter when a deep snow was on the ground, we kids would walk around in the woods to find rabbits hiding in a hole in the snow. We would kill them with a club and take them home for dinner. I remember one time our neighbors gave Dad a big turtle; he killed it and Mom made soup with it.

Sometimes we had shoes and sometimes we didn't. If love could have bought us shoes, we would all have shoes made of gold. I married a man at 17 years old, with parents approving. At that time, there were 17 of us; three were born after I left home.

Lots of Memories through the Years
By Junior W. Rickard of Hedgesville, West Virginia
Born 1944

Well, I didn't think of myself as an old-timer yet, but now at 70 years old, I do remember when I was in those bygone years of my childhood days. It was in the later years of the 1940s in the mountains when I was a little, but I remember some of the things that happened then. Of course, we were poor. We lived in a little house with no electricity or running water except what we carried by bucket from a spring in the ground down from the house. It's still there today.

I don't remember seeing any vehicles at the house. We had to walk about everywhere. I remember going with my brother Neal on Saturday mornings up the path to the turn of the mountain with a wagon to get ice for our icebox. We would then pull the wagon back down the path with a block of ice covered up with a burlap sack to keep it from melting. It cost 25 cents.

Back then in the '40s, the only past time or entertainment we knew of was listening to the WWVA on a floor model radio with a battery that had been heated up on the stove to get it charged to play the radio. Tubes had to heat up in the back. On the same stove, my mother heated water up to wash the clothes on Monday. She washed them with a washboard in a tub of hot water all carried from a spring. Rubbing clothes by hand over a washboard

Junior's brother, Wayne, a friend, and Junior

Junior at about age 2

is hard to imagine today with six or seven children!

Our old house wasn't much to look at, but it was our home. I remember one time, two blacksnakes crawled out of the side of the house and my sisters were scared to go upstairs to bed that night. Sometimes at night, we would hear noises on the roof. They would talk about bobcats up there looking for chickens that may have roosted there. I didn't know it then, but my oldest brother was called up by the army to go to fight the Japanese in the '40s.

Yes, I remember the first school I went to was called Smith Schoolhouse. I believe it was a one or two room school. During the first grade of school, we moved to Martinsburg to the housing projects on Wilson Street. Then we started going to a new school on Win Avenue in about 1950.

Sometime during the early 50's I remember visiting with my second cousin and seeing for the first time a TV—black and white, of course. I could not understand how he knew the very next thing coming up on that TV. How do you did he know that? That puzzled me at the time.

During the early '50s, the most respected person we knew was my uncle, who was a pastor who cared enough to take us to church each week with his family. Back then, you could easily get ten or more in the car; it all depended on how you seated them or hid them. We didn't know about seat belts back then in the good old days, but I don't remember anything about people getting hurt in vehicles, either. Also, growing up in the 1950s, if I said a bad word, I got my mouth washed out with soap and water. I learned my lesson well.

When I went with my mother uptown in Martinsburg on Saturday, the sidewalks were so crowded in places that we'd have to step out into the street to get by. People would stop and talk. You couldn't get around them. No one ever heard of malls are shopping centers back then. Most jobs were in the orchards or the mills in town. I got a job where my brother worked on the orchard at the foot of the mountain, digging around fruit trees at 30 cents per hour and later I got a better job at Catrows for 70 cents an hour, cutting thistles in the fields and laying off rows for potatoes behind a workhorse.

Here in the projects at Wilson Street is where I met the girl who would later become my wife. Punkin. We only had one date with her mother going with us to the movies to see a western. Sometime later, when I was staying with my sister and brother-in-law, my girlfriend called me and asked me to come get her if I thought anything of her. She was running away from home. Punkin was only 17 and I was only 19, so in my brother in law's car with no reverse in the transmission, I went to get her. Within a period of a couple days, we were married in Williamsport, Maryland with my sister signing a paper that allowed me to get married. That was November 21, 1963. It was very important thing to get married instead of living together or "shacking up," as it was called back then. To celebrate, we went swimming in the Back Creek that day.

Something happened to me that night that was so clear to me. I stepped outside in the dark, and something moved in front of me on the ground. There was a white cloud just above the ground; there was no way to explain it. The next day was November 22, 1963, and that is when we heard the saddest news we had ever heard on the news. As of today, we are still together after 50 years with lots of memories of the years we've spent together.

Signed Junebug & Punkin

Those West Virginia Hills
By Audrey (Hedrick) Nelson of Dry Fork, West Virginia
Born 1947

Let me begin by introducing myself. My name is Audrey (Hedrick) Nelson and I am one of eight children who grew up on a farm at Red Creek, West Virginia (also known as Flanagan Hill), near Canaan Valley. We all attended a two-room schoolhouse through the eighth grade and were then bussed to the nearby town of Davis for junior and senior high.

Our first home, however, was on a farm at Eglon, West Virginia, about 30 miles from Canaan Valley. This is where I and four of my siblings were born. In 1950 when I was the age of three, my father obtained the job of mail carrier and we moved back to Flanagan Hill, which was the birthplace of both my parents. The last of the children were born there.

Our home was a small, three-bedroom house, heated only by one woodstove, and was, therefore, very cold and drafty. With all ten of us sharing beds, we managed to keep warm and toasty, most of the time. The house always felt warm after a trip to the outdoor toilet, or "John" as it was called. We lived in this house until 1960, when we moved across the road to a new house, which my father had built with lumber from the farm. This was a two-story home with four bedrooms and an "indoor bathroom." It remains the family

Audrey's mother cleaning ramps

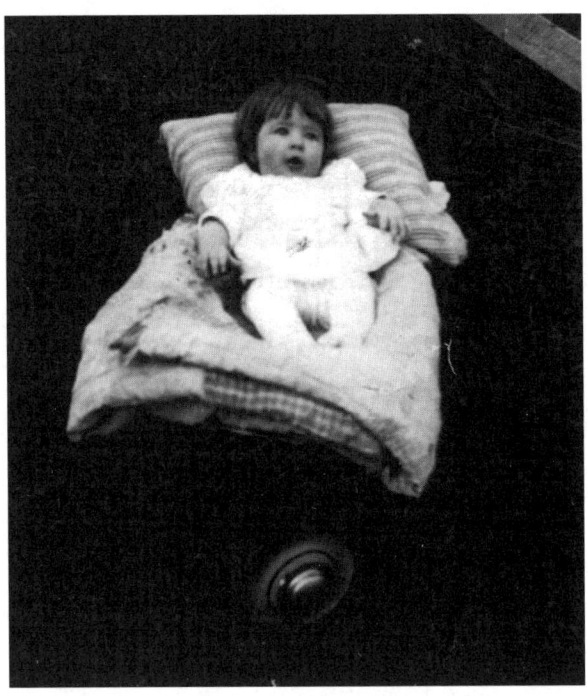
Audrey (Hedrick) Nelson

home place today.

I was a very precocious child, who loved to climb everything in sight and gave my parents several grey hairs. Mother told me that when I was three or four I came up missing. After some searching, they found me sitting up in the cab of a grader, which the Department of Highways parked at the schoolhouse. As is the case with several children in a family, there are bound to be many mishaps while growing up.

While still living in Eglon, my two older brothers, Jim and Richard, were wrestling and Jim flipped Richard over his head, resulting in a broken leg. As I mentioned earlier, I loved to climb, and at the age of nine or ten, I climbed up the door facing in our old house and then proceeded to swing back and forth through the doorway. My brother, Richard, thought it would be very funny to give me a push. Down I came, resulting in a broken arm. I'm sure they all heard me screaming across the road where my paternal grandmother ran a small country store. My mother had one scary fall at our old house one day as she was doing the weekly washing on the back porch with the old wringer washer. She leaned against the porch post, which gave way and she fell into the yard. Mother always wore frameless glasses; when she fell, the glasses cut a huge gash in her cheek. We were all very scared at the sight of all that blood running down her face.

Other mishaps occurred between the boys and the tractor. Again, Jim and Richard came to odds over who would be driving the tractor. Richard was told not to be driving it, but when Jim got off to get something, Richard jumped up in the seat and would not get off. Jim tried to jump up to get him off, but he fell in the process. The tractor ran over his leg and arm and then came to a stop. When Richard went to move the tractor, he jerked it. This resulted in a very badly bruised arm for Jim. Needless to say, Richard was not able to sit down easily for several days. On another occasion, Jonathan, the youngest, was driving the tractor at the age of 12. He was driving too fast and not paying attention. He drove the tractor into a creek in the hollow. He was thrown off, but was not seriously injured.

One of my favorite recollections while living in the old house was when Dad bought our first black and white TV. He put up an antenna in a tall pine tree near the house (which I climbed many times) and the first show we watched was The Lone Ranger, on a very snowy picture.

Our maternal grandmother, Maudie Hedrick, lived in a small house about a quarter mile from our house. This was the gathering place for many family members for Sunday dinner after church. My Aunt Kate, who never married, lived there with her mother and her Aunt Della, who also had never married. Aunt Kate was the cook and custodian at the two-room schoolhouse for many years. She was a wonderful cook, and many of the students still speak of the wonderful lunches she prepared with just the "commodities" provided by the county school system. One recollection of my grandmother's house was the time I came down with the chickenpox. I had gotten the virus from some cousins I had visited. Mom did not want all the other kids to get it at the same time, so I was sent to stay with Grandma for two weeks until I was over the "Pox."

Another wonderful memory of Grandma's place was at Christmas when I was about eight or nine. With eight kids in the family, we did not get too many toys for Christmas, but this one year, "Santa" brought us a sled, a tricycle and a red wagon. We had gotten up early to see what Santa had brought. Of course, we wanted to show everything to Grandma, Aunt Kate, and Aunt Dell. So, with someone pulling the sled, another one pulling the wagon, and someone riding the tricycle, while others rode, we proceeded down to Grandma's house. We woke them all up to show off our "booty."

There are many happy memories of growing up in the country—swimming in our favorite hole at the river in the summertime, skating on a frozen patch of ice near the schoolhouse, playing "Fox and Geese" in the snow, and sledding in the winter. Our favorite sledding place was the "Back Hollow Road," which intersected with Route 72 right at Grandma's house. It is a wonder that some of us kids were not injured because "Back Hollow Road" had a very steep grade as it came down to the intersection. We never knew if a car would be coming along Route 72 when we ended our speedy slide down the slope. I do recall that one of the siblings (can't remember which one) did end up in the creek, which ran by Grandma's house, when he could not get stopped as he entered the intersection. He just sailed over the road and into the water.

Growing up, however, was not all fun and games. As I said, we grew up on a farm, so we had plenty of "chores" to do. We had cows to milk (Dad sold milk to a local dairy), pigs to slop, chickens to feed, eggs to gather, and lots of "weeds" to pull. We always had a large garden every summer, which provided us with lots of food. However, this entailed weeding, hoeing, and then digging up the vegetables and potatoes. Everything was then canned or frozen. We also picked lots of berries in season, which could be frozen or canned. Strawberries grew wild, and I loved picking (and eating) them so Mom could bake a strawberry cobbler. We also picked a lot of blackberries, which were very plentiful back then. Our favorite place to go was on the land, which is now Canaan Valley State Park. We would drive about two miles up the "Back Hollow Road" where we would park and then walk about two miles up into the Valley where the Park Lodge sets today. We took several milk buckets and spent the day picking berries, eating our packed lunches, and occasionally "skinny dipping" in a pond nearby. The pond was usually covered with green algae, so we were a pretty sight when we came out. We also picked some "cattails" before carrying our berries the two miles back to the car and home. The berries were then to be made into a cobbler and canned. We also expended a lot of sweat in the summer, making hay. Our farm had 40 acres and there were several meadows of hay to be put away. We also butchered hogs and a beef, which had to be canned or frozen (nothing like fresh pork ribs and liver and onions).

My brother, Richard, bought an old 1934 Plymouth when he was around 21 and restored it to its former glory, but also turned it into a "hot rod." I went with my boyfriend (and future husband) several times when Richard took his "hot rod" to a spot about five miles from home where there was a nice straight quarter mile of highway for drag racing. Can't remember how many times he beat the competition. When I married, my now ex-husband and I owned many of the muscle cars. He taught me to speed shift, as almost all of the cars had a standard shift. Over the years, we owned a '66 GTO. a '69 Chevelle (350/396), a 454 '70 Chevelle, a '69 Trans Am, a '69 Camaro, and a '66 Camaro (which would really move). We also owned a

The Hedrick children

'73 Nova, which we had ordered and bought brand new for $3,400. Think of the prices of cars today!

Another car that we owned was a '69 or '70 Barracuda, which presented us with an unusual problem one day. Our son was only about a year old and we had offered a friend a ride with us to Ohio. We had the car loaded with all his baby stuff and Bob had just a small space to sit in the backseat. We had stopped at Mom and Dad's on our way, and after visiting a little while, we all got in the car to leave. When Larry started the car, the carburetor caught on fire. Bob had a heck of a time getting out of his cramped spot in the back seat, but luckily, no one was hurt.

Dad worked many jobs to raise his family and put three kids through college. He farmed, of course, and built a sawmill. He logged and sold the timber. He also had a mail route. Once he was was a dozer operator. He worked as a welder for several years in Washington, D.C. and was a State Inspector of unsightly junkyards. For all his efforts, he produced two engineers, several carpenters, a teacher (myself, who never taught, but worked in Hotel Management), a real estate agent, two homemakers, and a minister. He was very instrumental in acquiring funds, and with the help of Senator Jay Rockefeller (then Governor of WV), was able to establish the Flanagan Hill Community Building.

After college at Shepherd University, my husband and I lived in Akron, Ohio for four years, where our son Eric was born. At the first opportunity, we moved back to WV and I worked at the Canaan Valley State Park for 36 years. Although the State Park displaced the homes and farms of several people at its inception in 1967, it provided a source of employment for many people. Besides myself, my sister Rose worked there for 15 years, my brother, Jonathan worked for four years, and my youngest sister, Judy is still employed there after 27 years. All of the siblings live very close, except for two of the boys. In the past few years, I have traveled to several places and other countries, but it is always good to come back to those WV Hills, especially in the spring when the ramps are coming up. I know that a feast of ham, beans, fried potatoes and ramps are being prepared at the home place for a wonderful Sunday dinner with the whole family.

Adventures on the Alcan Highway
By Anna Maxine Dishong of Corriganville, Maryland
Born 1926

I am Anna Dishong and my husband was William Dishong. He died February 14, 2014. We would have been married 70 years in June of 2015. We had a very good marriage with five children, Bill, Greg, Donna (Beal), Janet (Householder), and Roger. It was in the newspaper that we were the most traveling family in Frostburg, where we lived. My husband was a salesman for Armour Meat Company, were he got three weeks of vacation. After a while, where Bill was out of high school, he got five weeks.

As for traveling, we had all of our kids to every state in the union and every province of Canada except Labrador. We visited many national and state parks. Our favorite was Yellowstone National Park. We camped every mile of the way. Once in a while, we'd get a motel to get a good shower and shampoo to feel a little better to go the next hundred miles. We never made plans, just enjoyed the sights, and followed our noses.

We were in Alaska twice, once in '63 and once in '65. Dishie and I slept in the back of the wagon, Donna slept in the front seat. In the back seat, we had padded the floor with laundry and Roger slept in the middle padded area. Dishie had built a box big as the roof and mounted it there and Janet slept there. In the daytime, we kept our luggage up there so the kids would have room to move from back seat to the back of the wagon. Then at night, we emptied the box and put the things under a pup tent.

On one trip to Alaska, on Prince Edward Isle, we were swimming and all of a sudden, we noticed these people signaling to Greg. Of course, we all went over to see what they wanted. They saw him diving under the water for fun. They asked him to dive down and get them oysters. So he and Bill spent the rest of the evening getting them oysters, which they put in their mouths and swallowed raw. One woman's husband about turned green every time she did that. It's really not my choice either.

We tried to get a motel that night, as it was rainy and cold. The motel was filled but the manager rented us a small cabin. It was just like a little house. In it was a foot pump organ, so we played and sang and really enjoyed ourselves.

One day Bill had gone into the water and got a bunch of little fish called periwinkles for the fun of getting them. Then when he went to bed, he forgot about them. Seeing the bag that looked like nothing inside, Greg threw it into our stove. That happened to be the night Bill slept close to the stove, and he couldn't believe he was smelling this terrible smell so plainly. In the morning, Greg told him what he'd done and they really had a word battle.

It was amazing such simple things could keep the kids occupied and enjoying themselves. No need for TV or games. Well, one game was cards and a game of tossing horseshoes. Of course, another thing that took up their time was looking for what they knew as nonpoisonous snakes and catching them to wear around their necks, mostly to get the attention of other campers. Even the girls got into this deal. They got a laugh to hear the people scream or be scared of them coming into their camp with those snakes. You had a hard time convincing them they wouldn't bite and weren't poisonous.

One time I had a real scare with Roger. We had camped at a park about 45 miles from where we lived. A group of adults were talking, telling jokes, etc. Roger was up in this other section of the park where they usually played. He was with some other boys so we felt he was safe. He was in the sixth grade. Little did we know they were on the ridge of the hill above a dried up creek and were jumping over the lumps of grass. Roger went to jump over this bunch of grass that didn't have sturdy roots, and he fell down over the edge about 60 or 80 feet into this dry creek bed. We didn't hear any of this until we saw two Boy Scout leaders leading him to our camp. When they told us what had happened and we saw Roger bleeding, we about croaked. We piled into our car and headed for the closest hospital. It was back in Cumberland, about 35 or 40 miles away. Dish was driving all the speed he felt safe to do. When this little Studebaker flew past us and waved and laughed, Dish wasn't too pleased. We took Roger to Memorial Hospital, and he had bruises and cuts over 80% of his body with a couple of deep gashes in his arms and legs, which needed stitches. While this was being done, we went to eat.

When we came back Roger asked me, "Mama, am I gonna die?" I said, "Of course not, why would you even think that," he said. "Well, the priest came in and anointed me for death." Mom said, "No, that's to make you feel better, so listen to the doctors and nurses and you'll be home with us in no time at all." He missed some school, but his teacher came after school was out for the day. She'd come to the house and teach him and give him homework for her to check the next day. He was bedfast. When she no longer needed to come I asked what we owned her and she said, "Nothing; it's just that I wanted to come so he wouldn't get back in his classes and lose a year." I was never so surprised to get such an answer. We did give her a gift of some money.

Another funny thing I remember was when we got off the Alcan Highway, which at that time was dirt. They told me in some travel books I'd ordered that it was a 35 mile per hour road. Dishie always took good care of a car and hated to see anyone mistreat a good car no matter how old. Our car was anything but new, and he got a few miles up on the rough road and said, "We are turning back." I said, "Oh no, we're not, cause you knew it was a 35 mph roadway. They were showing off when they called it the Alcan Highway."

One time when we turned off onto a smooth road at a little town, Janet woke up and said, "What's wrong?" She thought something was wrong because there was no road noise and it was smooth. Another time I was the navigator and we got on the top of this mountain, and there was an old time gas pump that you pumped the gas up into this top glass bowl and the hose just poured it into the car's tank. It was a dollar a gallon. Dish had originally passed it up to find a cheaper price. When we got to this little hill, there were no stations or anything in sight. As Dishie expressed it, it looked like the pictures of the Burma Road during the war. When the guy put in the gas he squinted his eye, put his hand above his eyes as it was facing the sun, and he said, "I think it's around $7.00." Dishie said, "At $1.00 a gallon, you better be sure." Gas at that time was something like 26 cents a gallon.

They repaved the road constantly where it washed out. One time we followed the bulldozer and a truck that was repaving it, etc. The best road we found out was the coal-covered road. Dirty yes, but much smoother and we learned it held up longer.

One time was we were on this road for quite a while and we came to the Yukon River with no boat or bridge in sight. Dishie thought we would have to go all those miles back to where we turned off the regular road to go into the Yukon and see the Yukon River. This was it and there would be a ferry every 20 minutes according to a pamphlet that Dishie had no time to read in his opinion. I said, "You would have known that if you had read the pamphlet." He did not think it was funny.

At another time, we were visiting on an Indian reservation where a friend of Dishie's worked. Dish had given Greg a Mohawk haircut. That seems to be back in fashion, though. At that time, it was just a joke of Dishie's to please Greg. Anyway, while looking around in there we noticed some boys gathered together laughing at Greg's haircut.

Once, Dish stopped to help a Michigan car. You didn't pass any car that was having trouble, at least Dishie didn't. The guy said he was a teacher and had never seen under a hood. Dishie asked the guy if anyone else had stopped and he said, "Yes, they said it was my plugs or points." Dishie said, "Have you had them changed?" and the guy said that he had just before he left home. Dishie asked him if he had the old ones and the guy said yes. So Dishie put in the old ones and looked at the new ones. The guy that had put them in didn't wipe the grease off of where they went in. The guy remarked that he wasn't a drinking man but he had some Hague & Hague, one bottle that he'd bought for a friend back home in New York. He said, "If I make it up this mountain we are stopping to have a drink." Well, he made it and they stopped, and every time we came to the top of a mountain, they would stop again. Dishie said it was the smoothest part of the Alcan.

I remember one time we had seen several bears in one day. We stopped to camp and a car stopped and the man said, "Are you folks afraid of bears?" I said that we had seen a lot of them, and we avoided them but seeing them didn't bother us. "Well, a big one just crossed the road heading for the creek," he said. Well, at the time, Dishie was at the creek fishing, so the kids ran over to warn him. He came back shortly and I was really glad. I tried not to show fear in front of the kids, because I didn't want them to be afraid of being there.

That night, Roger asked, "Daddy, if should we move?" Dishie said, "Look at that campfire. Bears are scared of fire." Roger said, "Are you going to build one in back?" Dishie said, "You don't have to be afraid. He would have to go over me to get to you."

Once we were watching a mother bear and two cubs. The cubs got into a trash barrel and got to wrestling and squirming inside it and upset the barrel. Another time a mother bear and her two cubs were sniffing at a barrel and up the tree, the cubs went and were lying across the tiptop limbs. It was so pretty. Then she merely gave a little sound and down they came and on down the trail. We'd seen other mother bears that if the cubs didn't obey her, she'd cuff them, and they rolled on down the trail very obediently.

School started after we came home, and our kids were famous in the other pupils' eyes because they had been to Alaska. They asked them questions and wanted to see the pictures.

Come with Me: A Trip Back to My Childhood
By Louise Smith Crist of Hagerstown, Maryland
Born 1928

We travel north on Route 220 from Franklin to Ruddle on a paved highway. At Ruddle, we take a left onto a gravel road and follow it for two miles, past several homes and the Presbyterian Church perched on a knoll. I remember both the post office at Ruddle, where we got our mail, and there was always the pickle barrel with salty pickles for my papa, big rolls of cheese, and the penny candy glass enclosed case for my admiration. Mr. Harold, the postmaster, usually gave me one piece of candy if I said I had been a good girl.

I attended church twice every week – once each Wednesday evening when my mama practiced the hymns she would play on the pump organ on Sunday and once on Sunday. Mama had been the church organist since she and Papa were married in 1917. She was about 20 years old then, and she was organist until she died at the age of 84. She had me singing along with the music she played, and my love for singing carried through my high school years in the school chorus. She also had me singing "Jesus Loves Me" at the age of six for a Sunday school program.

We continue on the gravel road until we come to a white two-story frame farmhouse built in 1918 by Papa and Uncle Sam Hedrick. Everywhere you gaze you will see all the necessary buildings: wash house, cellar, chicken coop, woodshed, outhouse, smokehouse, springhouse, and a large two story log barn built much earlier with no nails; only wooden pegs were used in building the barn. One of my memories was to climb up into the haymow and jump down onto the mow below filled with hay. What a thrill, but Papa said, "Not again unless someone is with you."

Papa had inherited quite a large acreage of farmland and woodland, and we had plenty of acreage for two gardens, a potato patch, and a cucumber patch beside the creek, which ran behind the barn leading to the pigpen.

My greatest fear was of snakes, and one day as I went to the cucumber patch to gather cucumbers for our supper, I encountered a coiled copperhead just waiting for me to put my bare foot in his mouth. I managed to sidestep the snake by going farther into the patch and yelling for help, but no one came. I remembered that where there was one snake there usually were two, and I ran into the creek and over to the barnyard and back to the house. Lesson learned never to go into the cucumber patch barefooted.

Our farmhouse was built along the creek (two creeks adjoined beside our smokehouse and where Papa parked the cars) and at night, the rippling of the water put me to sleep in my upstairs bedroom in the summer time when our windows were always open to feel the fresh country air. Doors were never locked, for we trusted our neighbors.

Summer was my favorite time of the year on the farm. Papa plowed the garden with a single blade plow pulled by Old Queenie, and I was allowed to ride bareback. When the plowing was done and the harness unhooked from Old Queenie, she made a beeline for the creek, and as she leaned over to drink my arms were too short to hold onto the bridle, and I slipped off over her head into the water. Papa was always there to help me out of the shallow water and with a smile.

When garden vegetables were ready for picking, we all helped Mama, who canned them and placed them in the cellar for good winter eating. One memory of garden ripe tomatoes: At a very young age, I had my tonsils removed. The only hospital was 50 miles away in Harrisonburg, Virginia. The doctor told me not to eat anything too salty for a few days after going home. Did I listen to him? No, I wanted a ripe red tomato from the garden and took my saltshaker behind the house, and what a surprise. My throat did burn. And Mama said it was the best thing I could have done since it helped heal my throat, but I wouldn't have eaten it if I had been told to do so. Philosophy: I didn't understand it at the age of seven.

Louise's parents in 1917

We had about twelve to fifteen chickens and two roosters in a chicken house that was open so the hens could have the run of the grassy hillside around them during the day and then go back to the nest to lay eggs. My job was to gather eggs each day. I was cautious checking out the hen nest before reaching in for the egg, because sometimes the black snake had gotten there first and was enjoying his feed. Papa told me that black snakes were not poisonous and that they had to eat too. Papa also had put a large black snake on the rafter of the smokehouse to catch mice and varmints that might attack the hams placed there after butchering in the fall. Any eggs not used for our meals were taken on Saturday, along with pounds of country butter, to Franklin to Bowman's Store to barter for yeast, spices, and sugar.

Mama baked bread every week, sometimes twice a week, and she baked all our pies and cakes too. She was an excellent cook, baker, seamstress, could sing like a robin, and was just a jack-of-all-trades mother. Until I was a freshman in high school I did not have a catalog dress; however, National Bella Hess had a pink cotton that I wanted, and Mama ordered it for me. What a disappointment – I received a purple taffeta instead and was told the company stressed if the item I had ordered was not available then they would substitute, and they did. Mama's dresses seemed and were A-Okay. I remember a special yellow chiffon dress she made for me and visiting photographer friend from Ohio took my picture with my pet collie sitting on a fallen log under the maple tree at our farm. I kept the picture, had it enlarged and framed, and it is hanging in my bedroom. I am now 86 years young and that picture brings back such wonderful memories.

I remember watching my papa and neighbors cut old potatoes with growing sprouts, preparing them to be planted for the year's new potato growth. We grew every item needed to supply our needs from year in and year out, sometimes sharing some to our needy neighbors who were not as fortunate as we were.

Mama worked day and night. In the winter she was the first one out of bed to start the kitchen stove fire as well as the wood potbelly stove in the living room. Those two were the only heat we had in the winter; our bedrooms were cold. I took a hot water bottle to bed each night to warm my feet. I slept on a straw mattress, covered with quilts and a comfort made by Mama. Each morning I crawled out of bed onto a cold linoleum floor and hurriedly trotted downstairs to get warm by the stoves. Mama always had a warm breakfast for us all of ham, eggs, gravy, and homemade bread, and hot chocolate she had made for us.

Papa taught school in a one-room school and on snowy days rode Old Queenie through the snow for $600.00 a year. I attended school from the first through the fourth grades with my papa, and it was a memorable time. I learned the lessons ahead of time while sitting there on the wooden seat desk and following along as the lessons were taught by Papa. It was good for me!

Louise Smith Crist

In the fall we stirred apples to make apple butter in a copper kettle over a metal rack with a wood fire underneath the kettle. Apples were peeled the night before on our hand turning apple peelers and then cut into snits to put into the kettle. Papa and Mama took turns from early morning until late afternoon using the long handled stirrer to keep the apples from burning or sticking to the kettle. Yummy, when the sugar and spices were added and they said the apple butter could be put into large crocks to store in the cellar for our use later in the year. I was allowed to drop one penny into the copper kettle after the butter was scooped out and just like magic, the penny turned bright copper! I still don't know what the magic was, but Papa said that was the fun of it.

Late fall was also our butchering day when several friends and neighbors came to assist Papa with hanging the slaughtered pig to bleed out before cutting up the various parts to be used for hams, sausage, spareribs, liver, etc. One neighbor always took pig's ears, feet, and jowls. Mama and a neighbor sat in our kitchen astride the sausage grinder, grinding the meat into sausage while Mama made it into sausage balls and canned the meat to save for our winter meals. Before butchering was over, someone was jokingly pinned with the pigtail, unknowingly. Mama always had pie and cake and coffee to treat either before or after all the hard work was done.

We had no electric lights or radio, but we did have what Mama called co-oil lamps and a battery radio that we listened to a program called "Only the Shadow Knows" and a squeaky door sounded announcing the program. In later years we got a wind-up phonograph to play records on (probably 78 rpm).

My papa decided that we would probably all be grown before the electric company would string the wires through our countryside so he purchased a gasoline motor and placed it in a small building across the creek from our home and strung wiring over to our house. Each evening for three or four hours he ran the engine, which made enough juice to give us light to study by. We had no excuse for unprepared lessons the next day at school.

My papa loved his home brew beer and made a batch and then bottled it with his manual bottler, and placed it in the springhouse cold water to be available when he had to spend time in the evenings getting the gas engine going. Mama wasn't too fond of this idea, and sometimes one of the bottles was heard popping its cork on its own, and she would say, "Well, that's one less."

We were blessed with several springs on our property, and one of them was piped into our kitchen for drinking and cooking water. Only the teakettle provided hot water for dishwashing and baths. Also, Mama used a wringer washer each Monday and carried water from the springhouse to heat in the oval tub on the wood stove.

Not all of the farm life was work. There were times, mostly in the summer, when I could have my cousins as playmates, and Mama would fix special treats for us. We also had Saturday night jamborees when my mama played the pump organ, my papa played the banjo, Uncle Fred played the violin, and Cousin Hansel played his fiddle. He was recognized years later as THE fiddle player of the county.

This had been a wonderful memory lane for me, and to have lived the memories so vividly now at age 86 is a gift that cannot be bought. Thanks for the opportunity to share them with you and for going with me on the road to my childhood farm life in West Virginia.

(No persons listed in this memory trip are still living except me.)

Kris' Kindlin' or Pelzin'
By Annabelle Vance of Mathias, West Virginia
Born 1935

As our forefathers settled in the hills and valleys of Hardy County, West Virginia, they brought with them their customs and traditions. One such custom was the Christmas celebration known variously as Kris Kringling, Kris' Kindlin', Pelzing, and Bellsnickling. Once a very common practice, it remained a popular activity through the decade of the 1940s but by the 1950s it was on a fast decline. Today, only the older generation is familiar with this once popular Christmas tradition.

The celebration was brought from the Rhine Valley with the Germans who immigrated to Pennsylvania and made their way into the eastern panhandle of West Virginia and on into the Shenandoah Valley, including what later became Hardy County, West Virginia.

Pelznickel and Kris Kindle had their origins in the Rhine Valley. There, Pelznickel would visit the children on the day before Christmas. He often carried a switch in his hand. He would question the children about their behavior, their studies, and other pertinent questions. If the children were able to convince the dreaded Pelznickel that they were deserving, he would promise them that Kris Kindle would remember them the next day. Kris Kindle would make his visit while the children slept.

Pels is a word meaning fur. Translated from German into English Kris Kindle is Christ Child. This establishes the connection to this celebration of Christmas.

Some years ago when I was a graduate

Hostess Jean Snyder plying her knowledge of how to identify the Kris Kindler, John Heatwole as Mrs. Rabbit

student at West Virginia University, I finally was able to enroll in Dr. Patrick Gainer's Folk Literature class. One day as he discussed folk traditions, he asked if anyone knew what Bellsnickling was. Having participated in the custom since I was a young child, I raised my hand. I was sitting in the front row and noted the lack of another hand on either side of me. Sure that there must be several others in the class who were familiar with the custom, I turned a bit in my seat but I still didn't see another hand.

It was then that Dr. Gainer looked directly at me and said, "You're from the eastern panhandle, aren't you?" Of course, I answered in the affirmative. He paused briefly and then said, "I suppose you wonder how I know that." By now my interest was really piqued and I certainly did want to know how he could identify me as being from the eastern panhandle. He then gave us information that was very surprising to me. This custom was unique to this section of West Virginia.

In my hometown of Mathias the time for Kris' Kindlin' or Pelzin', as it was known locally, was two weeks before Christmas and the week afterwards. The participants would decide on the evening "to go Kris Kindlin'." That evening they would disguise themselves in many and varied ways, limited only to the imaginations and materials on hand. Very often men dressed as women and women dressed as men. Some would use pillows as stuffing to make identification even more difficult. In the earlier days masks could be bought. These were made of tough paper-like material. In our family we would fasten the mask to a triangular piece of white cotton flannel, which would cover the head and thus hide the hair. We would also make the eyeholes in the cloth very small as the eyes were often used as helpful means of identification.

Once dressed and masked the Kris' Kindlers were now ready to begin visiting their neighbors. Upon approaching a neighbor's house, in disguised voices they would seek entrance by asking, "Do you let the Kris Kindlers in?" After all had entered and the greetings made, the hosts/hostess would begin the task of trying to identify their visitors. Some were very adept in making identifications. My mother told of a time that a hat gave the disguised away. The hostess said, "That is Pat Patterson; that is Sally Doc's hat." Pat was working on the new road that was being made in the area and was staying at the home of Dr. and Mrs. Moyers at the time!

When a masked visitor had been correctly identified, the mask was removed to acknowledge the correct identification. If some remained unidentified at the end of a reasonable time, they, too, would remove their masks and reveal their identity. The host would then offer a treat of their Christmas "goodies" to the Kris Kindlers and soon the group would be on their way to the next neighbor's house. Sometimes one or more of those visited would quickly don a disguise and join the group.

While this is a dying tradition, it still lives on in Mathias. On the night of December 28, 2001, a small group of Kris Kindlers set out to visit and were invited into seven homes in the community. Most of the hosts/hostesses were familiar with the custom and reminisced on the days when they had enjoyed participating and thanked the revelers for their visit.

A first time participant was John Heatwole, a folklorist and resident of Bridgewater, Virginia. John is the author of numerous books on local lore and traditions. He has collected many stories about this custom throughout the area, but this was the first experience for him. He noted "the gleam in the eyes" of those visited and "the sense of community" revealed in the delightful reception of those visited.

Those enjoying the evening as Kris Kindlers or Pelzers in addition to John, dressed as Mrs. Rabbit, were Elnora Hawse, who as Mrs. Claus turned the tables and offered homemade cookies to the hosts and hostesses; Janie Eayres, who made a "mean-looking" devil; and Frances Hite, who was disguised as a man. Jim Vance represented Father Time, and Annabelle Vance wore the crown and carried the torch as Lady Liberty. It was difficult to determine who enjoyed the evening the most – the visitors or the families visited. The activities of the evening brought back many memories of the "good old days" when this was a common, fun activity enjoyed by both young and old.

How do we get invited into homes today? We start our visit with a family who is expecting us, arranged beforehand. We then ask them to call another family and ask them if they'd like to be visited by a group of Kris Kindlers. This is the built in safety factor which was not needed in the "good old days."

An interesting experience happened some years ago. We left our vehicles parked and walked a short distance along the road to the house we planned to visit. As we slowly walked along, a car passed us by and slowed down. Very shortly afterwards a car came slowly by in the opposite direction. Soon a car from the first direction came creeping by. By that time I realized that it was the same vehicle all three times. The confused driver was certainly trying to figure out who and what this motley crew was. He's probably still trying to figure out the mystery!

I have many happy memories of "the good old days of Kris Kindlin'!"

A note: John Heatwole has since passed away.

Shoot, Boys, Shoot – A Blast from the Past
By Loring "Jim" Vance, Jr.

We got an invite to Odell Comb's place on New Year's Eve. We were to take part in shooting out the old year and shooting in the New Year.

It was to be my first experience with this celebration although my brother tells me that Daddy Barr and some of his buddies at the Natwick Company used to shoot their guns at Moorefield in Cat Alley half a century ago. This is right where the ball diamond was situated.

So Belle, Janie, and Enora joined us on a trip to Big Ridge to the site of Odell's sawmill on the hill. A huge bonfire greeted us as we migrated up the incline. Revelers and shooters mingled a short distance away and welcomed the warmth of the burning bonfire, which penetrated the chill of the night – the last embers of 1999.

Conversations abounded and Elnora quickly did her thing and energetically engaged with anecdotes about family and friends with Roland Combs, Pete Funk, and me.

Ray Schmitt was there with his camcorder to record the festivities for posterity. He was accompanied by his wife, Judy. All in all there were twelve to fifteen gathered to enjoy the night's doings, most of them from the Parker Hollow area.

Odell frantically apologized for such a hastily called celebration but circumstances had prevented him from calling earlier which meant that he did not have his ducks in order. Odell said that this tradition is possibly hundreds of years old. He remembered when a group of revelers would go from house to house seeking entrance, being fed a bountiful meal and washing the victuals down with the host's best squeezings. The latter being in the form of home brew, homemade wine, or applejack might be just across the road.

During the early days of the 20th Century, shotguns were fired across the house to insure good luck for the coming year. In keeping with this tradition, the idea was to blast the evil spirits out of the last century or year and hope that there was enough firepower to carry good luck over into the next year or the 21st Century.

When Odell was ready and the seven or eight shooters were lined up, he invoked the poem and shouted, "Shoot, boys, shoot!"

It was like Waco revisited as the high-powered rifles blasted away at the Big Ridge. It surely was loud. I perceived that evil spirits did not like noise.

Odell said that he did not remember when this tradition began, but he remembered it as a boy in the twenties. He also recalled that the first guns were of single shot powder and flint type so each man had to shoot and reload after each discharge. No live bullets were used since they wanted noise.

The Poem
Awake, awake, my neighbor dear
And to my wish ponder near:
The New Year is here right at your door;
And the old will pass to come no more.

I wish you a Happy New Year;
That you from bad luck may be clear.
That you may ever be content
And you and your family be ever blest;
That health and plenty may abound
By you and all the rest around.
That you may be able
To feed the hungry at your table;
Your barns with grain be stocked,
Your fields and meadows with corn be shocked;
Besides that blessed hand
That gives and takes at His command;
All which have may be destroyed
Upon which our minds are much employed,
To which thanks must be given
That we are now amongst the living.
And now before I make an end
Too much time I must not spend,
Shall I salute you with a gun
Or would you wish the report to shun?
Since you give life I do declare
The noise shall throughout the air;
With apples and cake it would be right
To satisfy the appetite;
With whiskey, bounce or apple brandy,
Or any good liquor you have handy,
We will receive the thanks of thine,
So here is the end of this happy wish of mine.
SHOOT, BOYS, SHOOT.

Boone's Ballroom
By Jerome E. Burch of Fairmont, West Virginia
Born 1937

This story is about a group of young teenage boys who grew up in the 1950s in the city of Thomas, West Virginia. Thomas was a booming coal town in the early 1900s but was well past its heyday of crowded streets, bustling businesses, and hard-working coal miners drinking and raising hell on Saturday night. In 1949, the Davis Coal and Coke Company started closing their coalmines, and by 1953, the coal tipples were no longer operating. As the coalmines were closed down the people living in coal company houses started moving to Cleveland, Washington, D.C., Baltimore, and other large cities in search of work. As the families moved out of the houses, they were torn down and the lumber salvaged. In 1920, the population of Thomas was 2099. The population of Thomas in 1960 was 834.

The smaller of the towns owned by the coal company were the first to lose stores and places of entertainment. Thomas still had a theater and stores of various types, but there was not near enough entertainment possibilities for active young men to occupy themselves. There was football and basketball in high school, plus studies, of course, but still that was seasonal. For that reason, many of those with time on their hands took to the woods, and those adventures and a mountain man's cabin are what this story is about.

The cabin was actually built by a group of men in 1945, shortly after World War II, who evidently had time on their hands also. Among those in this group of 20 was a young man named Daniel Pase who acquired the nickname of Boone very early in life because of the time he spent in the woods hunting, fishing, and trapping. Boone was a direct descendant of Jacob Christian Pase, who brought his family from Clearfield County, Pennsylvania in 1880 and occupied a hunter's log cabin on what is known as Pase Hill until a better house could be built. The cabin I refer to was first named the Mule Packer's Camp, because almost everything needed to construct the cabin had to be carried in on the backs of those building it. As time passed many of those instrumental in the construction of the cabin moved to the cities in search of work or died, but for Boone this was his home. He spent a great portion of his high school and early adult years staying in the cabin, hunting, fishing, and trapping every winter. As time passed and because he was always there, the name of the cabin changed to Boone's and there are few living at this time who can remember it being named the Mule Packer's Camp. If a person asked the question where are you going when you or others were going camping, the answer was always Boone's. For me and those who will be mentioned in the following paragraphs this hunter's cabin was the best source of entertainment to be had at that time in our young lives, and Boone Pase had a very big part of those times. The door to Boone's cabin was always open.

There were many who used this rough old log cabin as a place to spend their leisure time, but for the sake of this story, the names of just a few will be noted. Stanley Sedmock (Stan, Spank) was the leader of the pack. Hobert Cleveland Smith, Jr. (Hobe, Smitty, June), Jerome E. Burch (Jerry, Burch), Franklin P. Martin (Junnie, Bug), and George Huffman (Huffman, Big George) made up the rest of the cast. Spank was two years older than the rest of us with the exception of Bug, and Spank was one year older than he was, therefore it was natural he be the leader. In addition to that, Spank was a natural born leader and none of us questioned his leadership. All of us in this band of self-proclaimed frontiersmen played high school football for Thomas High School and in the case of Smitty, George, and me, Mountaineer High School, which was the result of the consolidation of Thomas High School and Davis High School in 1955. We spent most of our free time at Boone's and from time to time a cabin nearby. As a rule we always went to Boone's after each football game, especially those played at home, and that is the case for this story.

The trip from Thomas to Boone's was, as I recall, a journey of approximately seven miles. We would walk a gas line owned by the Columbia Gas Company, which came through Tucker County and passed near the city of Thomas. We each carried a pack on our back with enough provisions for the weekend and, if hunting season was in, a shotgun or .22-caliber rifle. If fishing season was in, we carried fishing line and hooks. In those days, the practice was to cut a sapling and wrap fishing line around the small end, attach a hook to the fishing line, put a garden worm on the hook, and you were in business. Don't get me wrong, there were those with bamboo fly rods, but the outfit I described was adequate to fish for native brook trout in small streams and beaver dams.

As I recall, this particular day was a warm fall day with only a few clouds in the sky and only a whisper of a breeze. There were streams and beaver dams to cross as we journeyed toward our destination. At one point, we had to cross beaver dams, which were built on Pendleton Run, now known as Pendleton Creek. The swimming pool in Blackwater Falls State Park was constructed in Pendleton Creek three or four miles downstream from the gas line. We started up a hill, known as Slip Hill because of the muddy conditions caused by small spring drains, which kept the earth wet all of the time. We always stopped at this location to eat a snack and drink from the spring near the bottom of the hill. As we enjoyed our Vienna sausage, crackers, coffee, and perhaps a candy bar or a piece of pepperoni, Spank kept looking in the direction of Thomas. The daylight hours were waning and almost gone. Spank rose to his feet as the black clouds began to move in and said, "We best move along. I think we are in for a storm."

Boone's Cabin

We were about three fourths of the way up Slip Hill when the storm hit. As a rule, flashlights were not needed because a person could use as a guide the light coming through the opening in the trees created when the trees were cut for the gas line, and we usually arrived at Boone's before dark. Needless to say, not one of us had a flashlight. In any event, Bug somehow was in the lead and he said, "Watch out, there is a big log here, and I almost fell over it." About that time, he evidently fell flat on his face. Big George was next in line. When he got to the log, or at least what he thought was the log, he put his foot down and walked the length of it. I was next in line and when I started up the log, it moved and I realized it was Bug. George had walked up his back before Bug could move or say a word. Spank took the lead, and after going a short distance he decided we best stop, build a fire, and wait for the storm to go through, or spend the night and continue our journey in the morning.

As it turned out, that was to be a long, exceptionally wet, uncomfortable night. The fire did offer some warmth, which made the situation somewhat better. The only light we had was what was created by the fire, which made finding wood difficult, but with all of us carrying wood, we managed to keep a good fire going. There was thunder, wind, and lightning, as well as the hard, driving rain. Sometime after midnight, lightning hit a large tree very close to us. The sound of the thunder and the concussion caused when it hit caused an immediate reaction from all of us, and we ended up in a hole created in the ground when work was done on the gas line to repair leaks. I doubt any of us would have slept, but all of us were most certainly awake the rest of the night.

When it started to break day, Big George said to me, "What are you going to do?" I said, "I can see well enough to get to Boone's and I'm starting now." George said, "I'm going with you." The others chose to stay until there was additional light and they could see well. George and I arrived at the cabin about one hour later. Building a fire was a difficult task because everything was soaking wet, but I finally found some almost dry hemlock twigs and got the fire going. When the others arrived, the cabin was semi-warm, there was coffee on the stove, and George and I were in top bunks under blankets while our clothes dried by the stove. The others were appreciative of the fire and the warmth it created. They had a cup of coffee and did as George and I did. If I remember correctly, we even slept a little, taking turns feeding wood to the fire.

Those who frequented Boone's Ballroom and kept it up moved to other locations and it was neglected until if finally fell down. Boone's nephew and a few of his friends built a small cabin next to the spot where Boone's cabin once stood. It is still standing but vandals and hooligans have done much damage to it. In addition to all of that, there had been extensive timber cutting in that area, and where there was once a magnificent stand of timber there is mostly sapling size timber. Also, there are 166 industrial wind turbines proposed for Dobbin Ridge, which is very near where Boone's cabin was erected.

This is just one story about time I and some of my good friends spent in Boone's cabin at the head of Elk Run, which empties into the North Branch of the Potomac River near what was once a busy logging town named Henry in Grant County. There are many, many stories about Boone and his cabin, and I am thinking about writing a book, which will contain as many as I can collect.

Man of the Cloth
By Rev. Stanley Kile of Franklin, West Virginia
Born 1925

Asked to describe the Rev. Stanley Kile, Carole Hartman said, "He's caring, down to earth, sincere, produced a wonderful family… anything you could think to say about him that's good would be true.

Indeed, Rev. Kile is one of those rare individuals of whom an unkind word is never heard. He has ministered to the spiritual well-being of people in at least two counties, Pendleton and Grant. He bore large family responsibilities from his teen-aged years and went on to embody the work ethic of country folks through his adulthood.

Stanley Kile was born on Kline Road below the Schmucker Schoolhouse on June 12, 1925, the sixth of eight children, five boys, and three girls, born to George Arthur and Cleta Mallow Kile. Stanley's grandmother Mallow was the sister of Dr. Robert Thacker, a dentist in Franklin, who was the grandfather of Franklin resident Larry Rexrode, the former owner of the Pill Box Pharmacy.

George Arthur Kile, born in 1896, was the son of Ulysses Simpson Grant Kile. George Kile owned the Ford Motor franchise in Petersburg until the big flood of 1924 wiped him out. He moved back to the family farm where he had been born and raised in "a little hollow down below Upper Tract," as his son puts it. Two of George and Cleta's children were born in Grant County, the others in Pendleton.

Through eighth grade, Stanley attended

the two room Schmucker School, which stands in the Kline area. While attending school and for a couple of years thereafter, he was the janitor. He made $118.00 a year, which was good money in those days, for building the fires, sweeping and oiling the floors, and washing the windows.

After finishing his sophomore year at Franklin High School, Stanley went back to running the family farm after his father sustained a broken back. He recalls those as "the horse days, not the tractor days. Getting an acre and a quarter done was an excellent day of plowing with horses. Each one of the family members had chores. You had to do that, regardless." Stanley ran the farm "for a good many years," until his brother, Arlin, took it over, and he makes his home there to this day.

Stanley Kile has always loved to trap, hunt, and fish. He owns an exquisite hunting rifle of undetermined age but is an heirloom, which belonged to his great-great-great-grandfather. He remembers trapping his first mink when he was ten years old. He sold it to Homer Dove of Dove's Store in Mozer for $35.00. "I thought I was gonna be a millionaire," Stanley says.

He had a good coon dog but no flashlight. Instead, Stanley used a lantern. He discovered that by setting the lantern on his head, "the old coon would look directly at you. With a flashlight, it would not look at you because of the beam." He also remembers getting 25 to 30 foxes a year in the wintertime.

Stanley was a charter member of one of the county's first 4-H clubs, when D.W. MacFarlane was the county extension agent. His first project, in 1935, was a heifer his dad had bought along with a bull. They had been shipped to the east from out west during the Dust Bowl. Stanley took the heifer for his project and won at least three blue ribbons. He went to Jackson's Mill when there were only two cottages and most 4-H kids slept in tents.

He also remembers a big annual even, a cattle drive that started in the Broadway/Timberville, Virginia area and came through Kline en route to the Sinks, where about 150 head of two-year-old steers were pastured for

Rev. Stanley Kile

the summer. Each of the men who drove had a dog and a horse. The dogs kept the cattle on the road. A man from Harman named Blake Cooper led the drive. He wore a patch over one of his eyes.

Growing up, Stanley attended the Mount Hope Lutheran Church until he was seven or eight and then started going to the Methodist Church in Upper Tract. The Kile children walked about a mile to get to the Lutheran church; they rode to the Methodist church. Stanley was active in youth programs and services.

After leaving the farm, Stanley, as he puts it, "entered the stream of life" by going to work for Ben Snyder who had a saw mill in Franklin at the present location of Craig Hott's feed mill. After Snyder moved to Lewisburg to go into road contracting, Stanley cut timber for almost a year on Bullpasture River in Highland County. The largest tree was a yellow poplar, which yielded 5,500 feet of lumber. It was huge and went straight up for a long ways before there were any limbers. It didn't take long to fell the tree because one of the first chainsaws in use in the area was the instrument of choice.

Like many working people in the country, there was no such thing as a job that Stanley was too good for, and there was no job he took on that he didn't do well. "People say they can't find work," Stanley reflects. "In my 89 years, if I wanted to work, I found it. It might not have paid much or made you rich, but it was there if you looked for it."

Kile next went to work for C.F. Burgoyne and the Pendleton Produce Company. Burgoyne contracted chickens and turkeys and hauled live poultry all over, from Baltimore, Maryland to Pittsburgh, Pennsylvania, Cleveland, and Cincinnati, Ohio. Stanley hauled feed in Pendleton, Highland, and Randolph Counties for several years until Burgoyne went out of the business.

Working as a cement finisher, Stanley helped build the Hanover Shoe building and worked on road construction on Interstate 81 before going to work at Hott's Mill, where he mixed the feed. After about five years, he went to work for the highways department, serving for five years as a bridge supervisor when Lon Simmons was the state road chief in the county.

Stanley next went to work in Mount Storm for VEPCO, where for another five years he did "anything that needed to be done." Reflecting on his work history, Stanley says, "You'd work till a job was through, then you moved on to another one."

Working for the Wilson Consruction Company out of Huntington, Stanley "did the fish hatchery in Reeds Creek and the Petersburg water treatment plant." He went on to do work on water and sewage treatment in Moorefield, Berkeley Springs, Norton, Huttonsville, and Camp Horseshoe.

Over the years, Stanley and his wife, the former Jessie Ruth Hartman, a Reeds Creek native, have been active in the church. They married and went on to have three children. Stanley became a certified lay speaker, performing those duties at Harper Chapel on Route 220 and the Walnut Street Methodist Church in the county seat.

In 1988, he was challenged to serve three Methodist churches on the North Fork and for 12 years, he did so. While serving as the pastor, active youth groups sprang up throughout the valley. In the meantime, Stanley had taken ministerial courses of study through the state United Methodist Church Conference and became a full-time licensed pastor.

He had come to the calling of pastor... a bit later in life than most (in his early 40s), but his years of service to the church were rewarding and productive. Those very active youth groups in the North Fork produced two people who became pastors.

In 1981, the Kiles moved from Reeds Creek to Maysville in Grant County to serve the South Branch charge, which consisted of seven churches. Rev. Kile traveled about 40,000 miles a year to serve those seven congregations. There were times when he visited ailing parishioners at hospitals in Cumberland, Maryland and Harrisonburg, Virginia on the same day.

In 1985 he became the first local pastor to be named the state United Methodist Minister of the Year.

Today he reflects on the highlights of his career. There was the time when 28 people were baptized in the North Fork on a single Sunday afternoon. The next Sunday, 18 more were baptized. Some of them were older folks.

There was the time in 1985 when he conducted Circuit Rider Sunday. He rode on horseback and preached to members of all seven churches gathered together that Sunday at the Corner Church in Cabins. "It was a wonderful day," he says. Ruth nods her agreement and adds, "A lot of food, too."

Two people are in the ministry today who were church members when Rev. Kile preached in Maysville.

Over the years, Rev. Kile presided over more than 1,000 funerals and more weddings and baptisms than he could count, even if he could remember them all. Asked if the number of weddings is at least 500, he replies, "Oh, yes. There's been a bunch. As for baptisms – a pile of 'em."

He remains active in the church, teaching an adult Sunday school class in Reeds Creek and conducting a church Bible study class twice a month. He has always enjoyed singing in the church and continues to do so. He continues to field requests to conduct weddings and preach at funerals.

The Rev. Stanley Kile says that he and Ruth enjoyed "a great ministry and great time together." He credits her for raising three exceptional children. The oldest is Teresa, who was born in 1957 and is married to Roy Bowers. She served two terms on the board of education and helps manage Bowers Garage in Sugar Grove and Brandywine. Their son Elwood was born in 1961, and is the assistant manager of the Reed's Creek Trout Hatchery. He is married to Robin who is a teacher and Author. The youngest is Matt, born in 1973. He is one of the county's outstanding volunteers (a fireman and a fire inspector), with his wife, Cathy, owns, and operates one of the county seat's most popular restaurants, the Fireside Café. Rev. Kile and his wife have three grandchildren and two great-grandchildren.

Helen, Lennie, and Dorothy in 1935

Reflections
By Helen Cottrill Fitzwater of Oakland, Maryland
Born 1927

Ever hear of Buzzard Run, Lynn Camp, or Beeson?
Well, I really didn't reckon you had,
But just in case, thought I'd ask.
That summons up memories of some fifty years or more.
I wasn't much more'n a toddler when
We'd spend long summer days on the farm,
In the backcountry, a fer piece from town.
We breathed the pure an' clean air
Not yet contaminated by the wastes of the world;
Waded in the sparklin', clean streams
Fed by the cool trickles from a crevice
Between the moss-covered rocks up on the hill.
The sun come up o'er the tree-lined horizon
With a special warmth the glow,
Neighbors was thoughtful and kind;
Never askin' for nothin' in return,
We'd set in evenin's as whippoorwills
Echoed their call among the quiet hills,
Or listen to our elders tellin' stories
Of haunted houses that stood nearby.

Now my sister and me, we'd run a barefoot;
Never fearin' snakes, lizards, or any other crawlin' things.
We'd invent our own pastimes-
A hoop rollin', walking on stilts, catchin' lightning bugs,
Or playin' with stick people made outa elderberry stems-
In the corncrib or up in the woods.
At times we'd become adventuresome,
And roam off a ways to the cornfield or pasture across the crick,
Where Blackie, Brindle, and Jersey grazed.
Now Blackie wasn't all that friendly
And there was times she'd put me over the fence
Without so much as a twitchin' her tail.
A favorite pastime was a hikin' to the mailbox
Our one link with the outside world.
Oh, well, we did have a battery-operated radio;
And I remember listenin'
To the ongoing saga of *Amos and Andy* and *Lum and Abner*,
Just after the daily news with Lowell Thomas.
And I remember hearin' the long and short rings
Comin' from the crank box phone hangin' on the livin' room wall.

Life was fulfilled and happy then;
No earth shakin' decisions to make
Or worldly problems to solve as we'd swing merrily
On the grapevine swings.
Now Dad worked real hard on the farm
To feed and clothe us kids.
Mom did her share and more as she struggled
With little more 'n life's necessities.
Her home cooked meals – smoked ham,
Wild greens picked outa nearby fields,

Warm milk fresh from the cows,
Hot biscuits or cornbread a drippin'
With home churned butter and honey or jam –

Was the best eatin' a "fellow" ever had.
She made things outa almost nothin',
Lovely feed sack dresses for school.
She'd dye 'em with walnut hulls or pokeberries.
Sometimes she'd leave 'em white and trim 'em
With scraps of flowered material.
We was a close-knit family, with plenty of love to go 'round.

A one-room school,
Mt. Harmony, was where I got my first formal learnin',
Then on to Pennsboro High,
'Twas two miles o'er the hill to the bus.
Walkin' that trodden path, a chawin' on sassafras leaves
I'd dream big dreams and imagine fabulous things.
It was pure joy just to be alive
And drink in all the beauty of God's creation.
I can almost vision the orchards
Aboundin' with the best tastin' fruit
One coulda sunk his teeth into;
Blackberry pickin' time, and even the raw scratches
From the jagged briers –"Ouch!"
Keepin' a constant vigil for copperheads
That might be lurkin' nearby'
Persimmon trees a laden with succulent fruit;
Mulberries hangin' from boughs low enough to pluck off,
Fields of millet and wheat a swayin' in the soft breeze.

Now and then I'd hear the call of crow on wing'
Serenades of other feathered friends that nested in the branches
Of thickets and grassy fields;
And the steady cluck, cluck of the ole settin' hen
As she turned her eggs in the nest
Over in a remote corner by the barbed wire fence,
I can almost hear the steady hum of the horse-drawn mowin' machine
As Dad and neighbors brought down the tall grasses
For hay to feed the winter through.
There was a zigzag rail fence where bobwhite strutted in the sun
As swallows darted from rickety barns.
We'd gather nuts in autumn's warmth,
Bury apples and potatoes in straw-lined mounds of soil;
And wait for the first snow to clothe the grass;
When we'd make an icy treat from thick cream, vanilla, sugar,
And the clean white snow – ummm.

Now and then, I trek back to Beeson.
Mom an' me and sometimes other kinfolks
Traipse over the hill and descend on Buzzard.
The old homestead glares up from its crumpled heap.
"Look out for the well!" Mom yells,
As I step too close for comfort to the old hand dug well
Lined with rows of moss-covered stone.
We lazily saunter through fields with bubblin' gas wells
Where Dad and me hunted 'possum in years gone by.
A hawk swoops down and plucks a mouse from the grass.
Soft rain begins to tumble and I bare my feet
To relish the soft red clay oozin' between my toes.
A deer darts in front and leaps the rail fence
To the safety of the nearby woods – probably headin' for Mom's garden.

Uncomplicated and peaceful – a brief respite
From the hustle, bustle, and wearisome tasks of the day.
Such is life on Lynn Camp, Buzzard Run, and Beeson.
Speak of wealth –
I feel I'm wealthier than most,
Because I have experienced all this – and more –
During my early years which were
The "Good Old Days" with Mom and Dad and us five young-uns
Over on Lynn Camp and Buzzard Run, near Beeson,
Back in the beautiful hills of West Virginia.
I have a myriad of memories
Encased in love…

Great-Grandmother and the Hobo
By Darrah Speis of Cumberland, Maryland
Born 1920

This is a story told live by my great-grandmother, Goldie Speis:

"Do you want to hear about the time I fed a hobo?"

"Sure!"

"Well, the year was 1935, and I was fifteen years old at this time. I lived with the Shaffers, who had hired me to be, well, sort of like a nanny, though I did all sorts of jobs for them."

"How did you start working for them?" I asked, interrupting my great-grandmother, Goldie Speis' story. "And how old were you when you started working for them?"

"Mr. Shaffer was building a cottage down the road from my family's log cabin, and whenever he passed my house he would see me working in the yard. One day he approached my parents and told them that he was looking for a girl that could work and help his wife watch over his children and wondered if I would be interested. My parents told me what he said, and I knew that they had already decided I should go even though I barely knew the man. I was fourteen when I moved in with them. Now remember," she added with a look at my shocked face, "this was Depression time, and my family had barely enough to eat as it was."

"Was it a big change moving into their house?"

"Oh, absolutely." "How so?"

"First of all, they had a brick house, which is still there today on Fayette Street. It had two floors, six rooms, electric, running water, and a bathroom."

I laughed. "You didn't have a bathroom at your old house?"

"No, we had what was called a back house, which was a good deal back into the woods and if you needed to go to the bathroom when it was dark out, you just went in the woods instead of walking that far in the night. Regardless, my home life was a good life, and after I left, I always missed playing baby dolls with my sisters. We would go into our log cabin's cellar and find potatoes that had smaller potatoes growing off of them, giving them a look of a baby with a head and limbs. We would pretend that these were our babies, since we didn't have any real dolls to play with."

"Wait, didn't you have school?" I asked.

"I went to school until I was halfway through the ninth grade. Then my dad caught my brother smoking and decided to pull him and myself out, proclaiming that I didn't need an education to pin 'hippins' on a baby anyway."

"So what about the hobo?"

"Right, so I worked for the Shaffers and their four boys, all under five, mind you: John, Charlie, Bobby, and the baby, Jim. Every Sunday they would head off to church, and I would stay home to fix breakfast for them.

One day when they were off to church, I heard a loud knock at the back door. I opened the door and there was a large man, in my mind I see him to be around 60. He was wearing a large overcoat down to his knees and a felt hat with about a two-inch brim on it. He looked ragged, and everything he had on was far from new, yet he seemed well educated. He told me he had just hopped off the train that was two blocks away from my house and that he was very hungry, and he'd asked if I could fix him something to eat. So I invited him in."

"Weren't you afraid?"

"No, I was very naïve and didn't even think it could be dangerous, so I set him a plate and started making him what I made for the Shaffers every Sunday morning, which was ham, eggs, home fries, and orange juice. Now you can bet that the Shaffers were surprised when they came home and saw a hobo sitting at their table. Mrs. Shaffer asked him to go out and sit on the back porch – they had a table and chairs out there – and then she would bring him some breakfast.

Once he left, she turned to me and said that she didn't blame me for feeding him, and she would have done the same thing. She was always very kind to me, she also taught me to cook and dressed up my country English – but she sternly said I must not bring a hobo in the house again, so she helped me fix his breakfast and he was on his way. Later she said that there would probably be a blue chalk cross on the sidewalk outside the house, which was a universal sign to hobos that the home was kind and you could get a meal there. Sure enough, when I went outside, there was a blue cross on the sidewalk! It was then my job to scrub it off."

Moatsville Memories
By Hubert Nestor of Moatsville, West Virginia
Born 1930

I was born and raised on a farm in Moatsville, West Virginia, with my brother and six sisters. We worked on the farm and did everything by hand. We hoed, shucked, and cut corn on 20 acres of property. We milked the cows by hand every morning and evening. We had a cream separator to take the cream out of the milk. They sold the cream and fed the rest to the hogs. We raised hogs, chickens, and workhorses. Dad loved to break horses. We stacked hay outside once the barns were full. You set your pole and stacked the hay around it to make a haystack. We raised most of our food. We bought coffee, flour, salt, and sugar at the store. Christmas time was the only time we had store-bought bread. Mom made biscuits for breakfast and cornbread for dinner and supper.

When I was five years old, my brother and I stopped at the neighbor's house with the horses and wagon. He told me to stay in the wagon. The neighbor's house was at the top of a very steep hill. My brother was going to get a rock to chock the wagon wheel. Before he got the wagon wheel chocked, the horses' neck yoke broke. The horses could not hold the wagon back now. The horses started running very fast to keep the wagon from running over them. Mom and my sister heard the commotion of the galloping horses and wagon coming down our dirt country road. They ran to the road and opened the gate to try to head off the horses. Mom waved her straw hat to slow down the horses. The horses ran through the open gateway into the field. My sister grabbed me out of the wagon. There were only three boards left in the bed of the wagon, and I had been sitting on them. The horses finally stopped once they had run into some rocks. That is the fastest ride I ever got in a wagon.

I attended Phelps School, which was a one-room schoolhouse. We had reading, writing, spelling, history, and math classes. One teacher taught each grade separately. Primer was the first year you went to school. Then you went to first through eighth grades. You were supposed to be studying your lessons if your grade was not being taught at that time. The recitation bench is where you sat whenever the teacher was teaching your class. All of the kids walked to school.

One day one of the boys picked a pawpaw on his walk through the woods to school. He brought the pawpaw to school. While sitting on the recitation bench, he put it in another boy's hand and smashed it. The juice went all over the recitation bench. The teacher was not amused. They had either a paddle or a switch to discipline the children and they weren't afraid to use them.

The older kids did the janitor work. The janitor got the coal for the stove, swept the floors, and cleaned the blackboard, desks, and outhouses. My sister and I were janitors.

At recess, we played a game called base, threw balls, and went sled riding. The teacher would ring the school bell to let us know recess time was over. If we were sled riding and at the top of the hill whenever he rang the bell, we were to come in. One day one of the boys knocked another boy onto the sled at the top of the hill after the school bell had been rung. Down the hill they went. Of course, they were late getting back to class. The teacher told them they had to spell all of their spelling words correctly whenever he taught their class. If they didn't, they would get a whipping. They both studied their spelling words diligently. The one boy was not the greatest speller, and the teacher asked him if he was sure, that is how he wanted to spell one of the words. They both spelled all of their spelling words correctly.

Hubert with his siblings and parents in 1944

Building the Road in Long Stretch
By Susan P. Carey-Powell of Frostburg, Maryland
Born 1960

I remember when, in the summer of 1913, Route 40 in the Long Stretch area, five miles west of Frostburg in Garrett County, Maryland was first macadamized. It was water bond macadam. The old roadbed was dug up with picks and shoveled out by hand with shovels. Most of the stones for the base of the roadbed were from the farms in the area. The State paid fifty cents a load for them delivered on the job. There was a specified size for the load of stone. The stones were broken by hand with hammers in the grade on a pike by the road and then forked into the grade. There were only a couple of machines used on the job; a steamroller operated by Sam Otto, and a water wagon and a dump wagon that John Carey from Long Stretch hauled with his horses. The coarse stone were put in first and rolled down and then the finer stone. The same coarse limestone, and then it was rolled, and then a finer grade of limestone which was watered and rolled. Then the limestone dust was watered and rolled until it formed a hard surface. The stones that were in the old road were broken by hand with hammers and put back in the road.

This part of the road in the Long Stretch area was not let to a contractor; it was built by the State. A man by the name of James Crump was in charge of the work for the State of Maryland. Mr. Crump was from Frostburg, Maryland. There were others from Frostburg who worked on the road. There were a lot of men and boys from the Long Stretch area who worked there. We worked nine hours a day. The men were paid more per day than the boys were. I do not remember what they were paid. We went home, ate supper, and went to bed.

None of the boys working on the road caused their parents any problems. In those days there were not laws prohibiting a boy from working, and the boy took what he was offered and he learned to work and grew up to be a useful citizen. He was an asset to his country instead of a liability.

Then the next summer of 1914, the State let a contractor by the name of Bamberge and Chapman build the road. It was rumored they were not hiring any local help. Sam and I took a lunch and went out one morning, and the gang boss put us to work. At noon, the headman came, and he asked, "Who are them two you have there?" The gang boss replied, "I just hired them this morning." He said, "Pay them. You know we are not hiring any local help."

In a couple of weeks, World War I started, and a lot of men they had working were called to fight for their country. Every day you would see some going down the road to answer their country's call.

While we were working on the road, a girl from the state of Montana rode a bronco to Washington, D.C. She was on her way back home. She came over the top of Long Stretch Hill in a fairly fast gallop and was still at the same pace when she went over Laymen's Hill. She had a big shepherd dog following her. When we last saw them, the dog was far behind. That pony could travel!

By William W. Murphy, born March 18, 1896, neighbor and close friend to John Carey.

Hay Rides and Snow Skis
By Marilyn Perdew of Cumberland, Maryland
Born 1954

Our family lived on Beall School Road off of Route 40 from 1964 to 1966. I was nine years old when we moved up to Garrett County when Daddy got a job with the Boys Forestry Camp.

My two sisters and I had chores we rotated each week. We lived in a house where we hauled water in three large milk cans from a mountainside spring that didn't freeze during the coldest winters that we had ever seen or lived through.

We even had a three-seater outhouse. My sisters and I would use the outhouse at the same time or wait outside to be on the lookout for the wild critters! We moved to another house that only had a one-seater outhouse. We sure hated emptying the chamber pot. However, to get out of that particular chore, I would trade with my sisters and milk the goat twice a day. My younger sister had no strength in her fingers, and my older sister had long fingernails. We needed the milk for our infant brother.

We even used a round, galvanized tub to

take our weekly baths on Saturday evening after supper. We would help each other with rinsing out our hair. Mom would put several pots and pans on the stove to heat our bath water while we ate supper and then did the dishes before we would begin our Saturday night bath ritual.

The day before my mother went to the hospital to have my baby brother, I was helping her to do the laundry in an old wringer washing machine. I literally got my arm caught in the wringers. Mom got the washing machine stopped by the time it was almost up to my shoulder. We made a quick trip to the emergency room down the mountain in Frostburg at Miners Hospital to find out that I would be bruised but no broken bones.

We had identical 19-year-old twin boys who would plow up our garden each year in exchange for the hay that they would harvest. They would even store it in our barn. They always made sure that we had enough for our goat and chickens. They would even haul away our trash/garbage every couple of weeks. They would let us girls steer their new tractor, but the best time was when they would come to the house and pick up the whole family with their tractor pulling a wagon full of hay. The hayrides included all of our neighbors and would be fun, with singing by all. We always had hot cocoa and marshmallows for roasting whenever the boys would take a break before we all would be returned to our warm homes during the fall.

My two sisters and I were given snow skis for our first Christmas living in Garrett County. However, we didn't get any snow until January 1st. We had to wait a whole week before trying out our skis. I spent more time going down the little hill beside our barn on my backside. I so enjoyed trying to ski, but soon discovered that I was better off sledding. My sisters did much better on the skis.

My sisters and I played outside all the time and rode our bikes to our closest neighbor who was about five miles away. It may have been only about two miles away. We were free, just as long as we kept our mom informed as to where we were going, and then she would tell us what time to be home so we could do our evening chores before we sat down as a family for supper. We even had a party line on our telephone and only had a black and white TV.

My Best Friend
By Sharon Carr Phares of Circleville, West Virginia
Born 1945

Virgie Bell Warner was the first person to die whom I really loved, except for my dad. My dad died when I was five, and all I can remember is seeing him lying there in the casket. I thought his legs were gone. I cried and they had to take me outside.

My mother had died when I was eleven days old, so when my dad died I went to live with my grandparents. That's when I met my aunt and best friend, Virgie Bell.

I would tell her little nursery rhymes and she would laugh and laugh. She was always so happy. I slept with her and snuggled up close to keep us warm. It was so cold in the house in the winter, and the snow blew in around the window. She would wet on me sometimes, but I still snuggled up close.

You see, Virgie was different from me. She couldn't run and play or talk very well or even feed herself with a spoon. She was born on August 4, 1913 and was a lot older than I was in years, but she had the mind of a little child and a twisted body with crooked feet. The Lord really blessed me to have her as an aunt, friend, and playmate. Spending time

Sharon Carr Phares with Virgie Bell Warner

with Virgie made me understand that although some people may look different from me, they are special in their own way.

When I was 15, Virgie got sick and had to go to the hospital. Of course, that was a scary thing for her because she was never away from home. When I went to the hospital to see her, she had all kinds of tubes in her. It was a horrible thing to see. I came home and prayed to God to take her home.

That night an angel sat on the foot of my bed, and when the phone rang the next morning, I already knew she had gone home to see her Lord and Savior.

I can see her up in heaven now, with a brand new body, running and jumping and enjoying her new life. She went to her heavenly home at the age of 48 years.

Grandfather's Life
By Jean Catharine Durst of Grantsville, Maryland
Born 1935

My grandfather, Christian A. Beachy, nicknamed Bud, was born March 24, 1870 in a log inn known as the Thistle Inn along the old National Road about two miles west of Grantsville, Maryland. He was the son of Arron and Catherine Folk Beachy.

As a young man, he was privileged to meet Lloyd Lowndes, governor of Maryland and the owner of a large dairy farm, Bloomfield Farm, near Rawlings, Maryland. The governor, it is said, "took a liking" to the young man and offered him an opportunity almost too good to be true. He proposed to send young Bud to the University of Maryland to study dairying and animal husbandry, all expenses paid. In return for this, young Beachy agreed to live at Bloomfield Farm and manage the Lowndes dairy operation at Rawlings. Being a clever and sensible young man, he accepted. Upon completing his studies, he moved into the house on the farm with his wife, Mary Ann Keim, whom he married in 1895.

Their first three children, all girls, with my mother as the third, were born there. The young couple worked together in the dairy. However, when Governor Lowndes died in January 1905, Bud found himself at odds with the new ownership and in March of 1905, he purchased a farm on Negro Mountain, near his home place. The family moved onto the farm and another child, a boy, was born in 1908.

In March 1908, while working in the woods on his farm, Bud was injured in an accident when a tree fell on his leg. The men rushed him to the house, where he was placed on a couch, known as a daybed, and the doctor was summoned from Grantsville. Dr. Bowen examined the leg and pronounced it beyond his abilities. He immediately set out making arrangements to transport his patient to Johns Hopkins Hospital in Baltimore, Maryland.

The daybed was picked up and carried to a spring wagon, which carried Beachy to West Salisbury, a distance of about ten miles. This ride in March cold must have been horrific. At the railroad station in West Salisbury, the daybed was transferred to a boxcar, still with no heat, and he made the trip to Baltimore.

He remained in the hospital many weeks but in spite of the best treatment available at the time, the leg developed gangrene and in June had to be amputated. He returned home in July to Mary Ann with a wooden leg and a grim determination to keep his farm and provide for his family.

Christian's training at the university stood him in good stead. His skills with animals, especially horses, became widely known, and his help was in great demand. He also became the neighborhood butcher. He acquired the help of a competent overseer, Harry Kolbfleisch. Harry was invaluable in all areas of the farm work. He married and remained in the family's employ, becoming a lifelong family friend.

Bud developed a profitable outlet for farm products of all kinds by establishing a huckster route through Frostburg, Maryland. My mother had many memories of riding with him in the spring wagon and helping to make deliveries.

His years spent with the governor had kindled a deep interest in politics and after serving in several unofficial capacities, he decided to run for office and served as Garrett County Treasurer from 1912 to 1914.

Bud and Mary Ann continued to run their farm and raise their family, having welcomed a second son in 1913. However, they mourned the loss of their first son and a daughter, both to pneumonia. They lived long, fulfilling lives. They belonged to the Springs Mennonite

Church in Mary Ann's hometown of Springs, Pennsylvania. They most often attended the Oak Grove Mennonite Church only half a mile away.

Bud died in December 1947 and Mary Ann in January 1952. My husband, William Durst, and I are currently living on the farm and plan to leave the remaining acres to our seven children, eleven grandchildren, and four great-grandchildren, which now totals six generations.

The Centennial Parade

The Centennial Parade
By Laura Ann Hendershot Glascock of Berkeley Springs, West Virginia
Born 1972

Hello, my name is Laura Ann Hendershot Glascock. I am 42 years old and live in Berkeley Springs, West Virginia. I have a few pictures of the Centennial Parade I participated in in 1976 in Hancock, Maryland.

My grandfather is Lewis Jackson Hendershot, Sr., the owner of Lou's Pony Farm in Hancock, West Virginia, which is right across the Potomac River on the West Virginia side. He used to take his ponies around the panhandle and give pony rides on a merry-go-round.

On a nice day in June of 1976 the whole family and some friends known and unknown to me, were involved in dressing up like colonial days and celebrating the centennial year by being in this parade. My cousin and I were five years old. I do remember this day. I wanted to drive the buggy, but my Aunt Rhoda said the boy had to drive, which was her son, Gabriel, my cousin. We were so cute! Our cousin, Ernest Beattie, is standing beside the buggy with us, but I'm not sure where he was in the parade. I can't remember who the other boy in the buggy was, or some of the others who participated. My sister, Shelia Hendershot Foltz, was riding with Tony Fox on a two-wheel cart. My cousin Angela Snyder was driving a wagon with one of the Emerson boys. Two black and white ponies are pulling my grandparents, Lou and Hazel Hendershot, and Grandma is holding my cousin Gus Golden. Grandma didn't go around the horses much, so this was exciting for me to see her participating! I'm not sure who the man riding the cow was, but he sure was entertainment! It looks like we started at the north end of Hancock, Maryland and went south down Main Street to the park.

I remember being in two or three parades in Hancock, Maryland. I won 1st Place in the Halloween parade when I was around ten years old. I might be able to dig up a picture of that too. I was driving a two-wheel cart with a black and white pony, Prince. He was an awesome pony. He put up with a lot with all of us kids riding him wherever!

I have fond memories of growing up as a kid in the eastern panhandle of West Virginia and in western Maryland.

The Simple Pleasures of Life
By Deloris Simmons of Franklin, West Virginia
Born 1944

My name is Deloris Simmons, and I was born in 1944. I was one of four children born to my late parents, Mabel and Luther Harold. My family and I lived in what many would consider a two-room shack located on "The Thorn" in Pendleton County until I was a sophomore in high school. Then we moved to what's known as Simmons Mountain. My grandparents lived with us too.

Memories include the fact that I had to share a bed with my family, and I recall that during the winter months we would use at least four to five comforters to stay warm, as the snow would blow in under our bed. Winters back then lasted easily from November to April, and there was always much more snow than there is today.

Deloris's parents, Mable and Luther in 1930

The youth of today take for granted how easily they have clean clothes to put on. My family carried water from a stream known as Thorn Creek, where we would heat it on the wood burning kitchen stove so we could wash our clothes on a washboard. We did this once a week.

Each day there were chores to be done, which included getting in the wood and feeding the cows. We did not have indoor plumbing obviously, so I used an outhouse until I was in the eighth or ninth grade. Saturday evening was bath day, which meant carrying more water from the stream to be heated so we could bathe.

There was no television or radio until we moved to Simmons Mountain, again when I was a sophomore in high school. When we did get a phone, it was one that's called "an old ringer phone" by most today. It was a party line, and we knew the call was for us when we heard ringing consisting of two longs and two shorts. It was almost a given there was no privacy when a call came in or went out.

There were neighbors within walking distance, and so as children during the days, we'd often play games like duck, duck, goose; hide and seek; and kick the can; and at night sometimes, we'd gather at a neighbor's house and play the card game Setback. Thorn Creek provided water for necessities, but it also held our swimming spot, "The Rock Hole," where we'd swim in our underclothes because there were no bathing suits back then.

The town of Franklin was not far away by today's standards, but back then, if we got to go to town, we were so excited. It usually happened once a month or less.

Christmas always meant I'd get a new dress, and I wore feed sack dresses to school until sometime after the fifth grade. Each Sunday we'd go to church, and I was given a nickel to put in the offering plate.

Discipline that meant getting spanked was done with a wooden paddle. I attended a four-room schoolhouse, and I recall huddling by the stove in the winter to keep from freezing to death. To get there and back home again, quite often we had to kick our way through a many a snowdrifts.

If I got a cold, my Grandma Nellie would make some home remedy to treat it. If I got the croup, she'd make a plaster of kerosene and lard, or what she called a mustard plaster, for my chest.

I was raised on beans, potatoes, and homemade bread. We would plant a garden, work the crop, and put away as much as we could to be sure we had enough food to get us through until the next growing season.

Deloris with her sisters, Nina and Helen in 1954

289

Living life was not easy, as we had none of the comforts of today, but it was good. We learned about the importance of family, work ethic, helping others, and were raised to be thankful for what we had and how to enjoy the simple pleasures of life.

Growing Up Poor
By Rosanna Rexrode of Petersburg, West Virginia
Born 1949

Rosanna with her siblings

My life began from the love of a soldier, Herbert Andrew Leatherman and a young Italian girl, Judy Delores Allessio. I was the second child of this marriage born at home. I have an older sister and four younger brothers. We lived in a three-room house until I was ten years old. We did not have electric, a telephone, or indoor plumbing, and used wood to heat our home.

We raised our food by planting a garden to can, and raised hogs, chickens, and cows for milk, and during hunting seasons, we had rabbit, squirrel, and deer. We churned our own butter, made cottage cheese, and baked our bread.

We had enough to live on and all we needed, but times were hard with my dad cutting pulpwood with the use of two Belgium horses. Later in life, he found employment as an orderly at the local hospital where he worked the night shift so he could cut wood during the day and have time to get some sleep before going back to work each night. My mother stayed at home raising the six children but always helped my dad in the woods. I recently realized that my sister, Rosalie, brothers, Paul, Norman, Gary, John, and I were never left home alone. We went with our parents to the woods, sometimes we worked but a lot of times we played. I remember having the measles and laying on a wagon in the woods while, they cut wood.

My father served in the US Army during World War II and was captured at the Battle of the Bulge. He was a POW for five months. He never wanted to talk about his time in the war. He met my mother during a train stop in Clarksburg, West Virginia and when she did not hear from him, she thought he had forgotten her. When he was released from prison camp and completed his tour of duty in the service, he stopped in Clarksburg to surprise his sweetheart. They married and moved to a place we call the Ridges. Without a car, they traveled by train to Keyser, West Virginia and were picked up by a family member to go live in the country. I often wonder how my mother felt leaving her family to move to the mountains where very few owned a car. Later, when my father bought a car, they traveled occasionally to her home, a two-hour drive,

Judy Delores Allessio and Herbert Andrew Leatherman

to see her family. Sometimes her sisters came and visited with her a short time and a brother came to hunt.

When I was ten years old, we moved to a house with more room. We lived there until 1967. My parents built a home and moved in June, the week I graduated high school. I shared a bedroom with my sister, and my brothers all shared a room, two in a room. Since the home had four bedrooms and indoor plumbing, electric, and a telephone, we thought we were rich. My son now owns the home and has done a lot of remodeling, but nothing can take away the memories. The one thing he has kept is the rotary telephone and the same phone number.

We were very close to our cousins who lived near us growing up. We walked to the school bus together and played together quite often. I remember playing paper dolls with my cousins when they were teenagers, and we couldn't wait until a catalog date ran out so we could cut new dolls, clothes, and furniture. We made a house out of a cardboard box or a shoebox and furnished it from the catalog.

All six children graduated from high school and two have completed college. We all live within 25 miles of each other, married, and have families of our own, and recently two of my brothers built a home and moved back to the Ridges. My parents are buried within sight of our home where I grew up. My memories of growing up poor make me appreciate what I have today.

Driving the Tractor
By Alma Maxine Hebden of Oakland, Maryland
Born 1925

My father told me when he was a young man there wasn't any entertaining things to do. The Streets in Oakland were dirt and on Saturday evenings, they would rope off a ring in downtown, and the young men would box for entertainment.

We use to go to Sunday school, but my sister and I would play sick sometimes and stay home when we were teens and get the tractor out and run it all over the farm and my father would complain to my mother that the tractor was drinking gas but he couldn't find the leak. That's how we learned to drive.

The only place there was to go was to church and they baptized you in a lake. My oldest brother dammed up a stream and would baptize us young children every week.

My uncle lived next to us. He played musical instruments, and we all learned to play a guitar. On evenings, he would sit on his porch, and play his violin and we would play guitars and sing with him.

When my mother was young, there weren't any jobs for women, except if someone was having a baby, she could take care of the baby for a week or two at seventy-five cents per week. My first job, I made three dollars a week cleaning and taking care of a big family.

Signs and Wonders
By Sue Bergdoll of Moorefield, West Virginia
Born 1950

This is a funny statement that our son said when he was learning to read.

One Saturday, on our way to go grocery shopping, we passed a local fire station that was advertising a dance that night. Our son said, "Mom, what is a sausage dance. My husband said, "What did you say?" He said that there was going to be a sausage dance. The further we went down the road we were trying to figure out what he saw, so we turned around and went back to see what the sign said. The sign read square dance here tonight. Now after forty years when we go by the fire station we always think of the (sausage) square dance and laugh.

Our church was holding a baptism in the river, which our son had never seen before. The preacher put you under the water, no sprinkling. The next day, I was washing clothes in an old wringer washer and steel tubs with rinse water in them. I had gone inside to get some clothes, and when I came out, I saw my son with a cat in the rinse water. I asked him what he was doing. He said he was baptizing his cats, like the preacher was doing the day before at the river. I didn't know whether to cry or laugh. I have the washing machine and tubs and I still think about our son baptizing the cat.

Train # 34
By Mayo L. Eaton of Paw Paw, West Virginia
Born 1943

Hello, I'm writing these words to express myself as a person born June 22, 1943, at Okonoko. West Virginia. A black lady, Mrs. Spencer from Paw Paw, West Virginia, delivered me. I enjoyed life as a kid, worked hard in gardens, and fed animals during the day. Just to go fishing in the Potomac River at Okonoko in the 1940s and 1950s. I helped at the Post Office for my grandfather. Took mail off train number thirty-four every morning. For towns of Levels Points, Slanesville, North River Mills, Cold Stream, and Spring Gap, West Virginia. Especially in the spring, little chicks would come on the train for people.

School at Bethel West Virginia, was a two-room school, four grades in each room, first to eighth grades. The principal; kept sticks ready if you were bad. Hitting a softball over a big white oak was a crazy thing us boys liked.

As kids, we liked to take a bath at the Falls. Water there was nice to swim in the hole.

My favorite teacher was John Martin. I loved math.

Trains run day and night at Okonoko. Coal was big in the 1940s and 1950s and still is today. My dad was a railroad conductor for years. As a kid, I never knew that I would be working for thirty some years as a railroad engineer on the B & O. Chessie, and CSX Railroad. I retired in 2003.

I remember working on a farm for three dollars a day at ten to twelve years old. Had my first car at fifteen years old, 1947 Chevy, I paid one hundred forty dollars for it. I worked for one dollar per hour on farms to get it.

Hunting in those days was great, I remember one time, I asked my grandfather if I could go turkey hunting with him. He said, "Grandson, some other time." He went across town hill, came home in the afternoon with a big turkey.

When I was in the first grade, my mother gave me a dollar to pay for something and I lost it. You would have thought it was a million dollars.

I learned to play basketball with an apple bucket on the building.

Rumble seat in my aunt and uncle's car was a joy to ride on Sunday morning to grandmother's and grandfather's home in Okonoko, West Virginia. They would be singing hymns as I sat in the back rumble seat.

Red Fingernails
By Enid Saville of Romney, West Virginia
Born 1922

When I was thirteen years old, I decided I was old enough to wear makeup, so I bought some lipstick and fingernail polish. I got all made up and my mother and dad didn't object, but we had a neighbor who visited us almost every day and he was always drunk. When he saw me, he said, "Why are you putting that damn stuff on your face and fingernails?"

He left and went to the grocery store and bought me an old time Valentine with this ugly old girl with a lot of makeup on. It said, "You powder and paint to look what you ain't you're the talk of the town don't you know it." I got a big laugh.

The next time he stopped by drunk as usual, he sat down by the fire and went to sleep with his hands on his knees and fingers splayed apart. I painted his fingernails bright red. When he woke up and went home he didn't realize his nails were painted until he was at the grocery store the next day and the clerk said, "I see you have your nails all painted up," He said, "That damn girl." He sat down with his penknife and scraped it all off.

The clerk at the store told me about it. We had a big laugh.

The drunk never told me about it or said anything more about my makeup. He still

Enid's parents, Virgil and Flo with their children

visited us almost every day since our house was between his house and the grocery store.

A Saturday Routine
By Sidney Williams Gording
Born 1938

Small rural towns in the 1940s and 1950s were struggling to meet their basic obligations of fire protection, policemen, water, and sewer provision. Cultural additions fell to the bottom of the heap. In Moorefield, a group of civic minded women who were members of the Women's Club worked together to provide a library and service to the community. This library was housed up a long flight of stairs over the McCoy's Grand Theater.

Each Saturday-and it must have been open only on Saturday-I would walk to town with several books tucked under my arm. On the way, I would stop at the home of a shut-in relative and add her two to three books to my armload. Once at the library, Mrs. Starkovitch would choose replacement books for Mary Kittle by checking the card in the pocket and judge how long it had been since she last had the book. They were light fiction popular at the time. Mary Roberts Rinehart is an author who comes to mind. For being the library courier for Mary Kittle one Christmas, I was given a whole box of candy. That was a treat of the first order and I doubt that I shared it with anyone!

There was always a group of ladies at the back of the library room, chatting at a desk where they pasted pockets and created accompanying cards for books added to the collection. I am not aware of a budget for books or staff-all were contributions of time and personal books.

The children's section had a limited supply. I must have read every one, a favorite being the *Little Lord Fauntleroy* series (Pink covers!) A highlight of the summer when I was a rising fourth grader was a collection of books loaned by the State Library Commission for fourth through sixth graders; I will always remember the pleasure of reading *Johnny Tremaine* and *Caddie Woodlawn*. A prize was awarded to the one who read the most from this collection. I lost to our minister's son, Tommy. Although this first library experience came from a small collection and a dedicated group of women, it planted a seed, which led to my becoming a career librarian with a lifelong love of books. The small upstairs library became the Hardy County Public Library, an important community asset.

Pin Up Poster
By George B. Funk of Pennsboro, West Virginia
Born 1940

This story could only happen in a small town like Beryl, West Virginia. When everyone knows everyone, there are many stories that come to mind and often thinking their own, I have settled on this story.

Johnny was not only my best friend but he was also my cousin. He had a younger sister named Reba. Since her sixteenth birthday was fast approaching, I wanted to do something special for her. I thought what would be a greater present than to fix her up with a friend of mine from Maryland.

So everything was arranged for him to come to the party and since he was a nice fellow that played the guitar and sang, I thought he would be the perfect person for a sixteen-year-old girl. He also brought a present, which was a full-length poster of him, in his blue and white cowboy suit, holding his guitar.

I thought, "Wow! What a cool guy. Not only a boyfriend, but a poster to put up on the wall to remember him by."

So the day of the party, my friend showed up with a large tube all wrapped pretty with a big bow. I could see Reba's eyes light up when she was handed the present. She opened it very carefully and unrolled the poster, took one look and returned it to the tube and very quietly left the room not to be seen again that day. My friend and I had a piece of birthday cake and a glass of milk and finally left.

Well Reba received two of the coolest gifts I could think of for a sixteenth birthday. She hated them both, so for almost sixty years I have had this hanging over my head. So all I can say is Reba, I still love you and happy sixteenth birthday.

Sincerely,
P. Joe

Springrun School
By Rose Elizabeth Vance of Petersburg, West Virginia
Born 1921

When I went to Springrun School, we had to walk three miles. There were two rooms. We only used one. When the weather was bad, we had to go anyway. We had to carry our water from up Springrun. The hatchery wasn't there then. We hung our bucket on a pole it, it took two to carry it. We had a water cooler to put the water in with a spigot on it. We play ball, prisoner base, and tag. We had recess in before noon, hour off for lunch recess in afternoon. We carried our lunch and used outside toilets.

My teachers were Ira Shobe, Conway Brake, and Miss Daisy Brake. Thomas Sites was a great teacher.

I would go home with some of my friends and stay overnight. Miss Ira Shobe rode horseback to school and let us kids take turns riding.

They closed Springrun School and moved it to Dorcas. Our address was Masonville, W.Va post office-moved to Dorcas

I wore handmade clothes made out of feed sacks. The ones with flowers made dresses and the white ones for underclothes.

When I got out of school, I went to work over in South fork, for three dollars a week. I didn't stay long; soon as I got away home, I came home because I was homesick.

One summer my brother and I raised corn and harvested it.

We washed our clothes on washboard. Put the whites one in a big iron kettle, boiled them, washed them, and out of that water, rinsed them and even hung them out on line to dry.

We took our bath in washtub. We had telephone that ran off battery. We did have a radio. We listened to stories on radio. Ice before had to buy. Dad worked at the Petersburg Tannery. We had a little blind brother we helped our mom take care of him. He had spinal meningitis when he was a baby. He lived to be fifty-eight. We had to feed him, bathe him, and he told us when he had to go to the bathroom.

My dad had a Model T truck. He made a big bed on it in summer he took us to Charlie Ruggleman's store. We would eat candy, drink sodas, and get chewing gum. Sodas were five cents and a stick of gum was a penny.

I snuck out to go with a next-door neighbor's son and my dad didn't want me to. I married him at ministers and had four children. We had two girls and one boy passed away at two days old. I was only married for nine years. I raised my children with the help of my dad, mother, and brother Alvin with the help of the Lord. We walked to church every Sunday. I am ninety-three years old. I have two grandsons, four great grandchildren, two great-great grandchildren, and another one on the way.

Memories of Clintwood
By Ruby Nell Smith of Elkton, Maryland
Born 1940

We moved to Clintwood, Virginia after school was out. It was a move up in school with indoor restrooms and each grade had their own room and teacher a hut that the soldiers use with round top. Mom lived there, dad was in C.C, camp, so he met mom, Nomel Bryant. My dad's name is Charlie Rufus Christian. Mom was born on March 11, 1924 and dad was born on June 30, 1918. They

Ruby's parents, Charlie Rufus and Nomel Bryant Christian

Ruby's grandparents, William Harris and Della Mae Bryant

were married on March 12, 1940 and I was born on December 23, 1940. We went to the Church of Christ and had egg hunts at Easter.

We lived on the hill above my grandparents, William Harris Bryant, (February 22, 1898-March 16, 1963) and Della Mae Bryant. (September 4, 1900-December 22, 1979. Well grandpa's leg was lost when a railroad car ran over it and blood poison set in before Mom was born in 1923. Mom had three sisters, Nellie was born on February 22, 1918, Dovie on April 1, 1920, and Marie on August 16, 1922. She also had three brothers that passed away young and four brothers that were younger. People say the seventh brother, could blow in the mouth and heal Whopping cough. That was Uncle Emory. Harold was the sixth son, then Terry the fifth, and then Uncle Jay was the fourth. There were lots of grandchildren and great grandchildren. Grandpa passed away at sixty-five on March 3, 1963 and Grandma at age seventy-nine on December 22, 1979.

My grandma could sew by hand and it would look as if she had used a sewing machine. She also had eye problems so; she counted money by feeling of it.

Mom lived to be eighty-six and passed away on April 26, 2010. She taught my mom that she could sew the other girls small families. Marie lived to be eighty-four years old and had two sons. A niece came to live with her at age ten until eighteen. Aunt Dovie just one son but two of the boys, Mom's brothers, had big families. Uncle Jay and Uncle Emory (September 3, 1934,) Uncle Harold (September 17, 1931,) and Uncle Jay (September 11, 1929.)

Well my sister, Della Mae and I would walk to Clintwood, which was two miles to town in the summer and get ice cream, frozen custard. That was a treat. We lived in a two-room house on that hill and had a nice garden, lots of vegetables and chickens. Dad would order baby chicks, one hundred in the late spring and raise then. We love chicken. Aunt Marie's house was over the mountain, so we would walk there on the way back, climb apple trees, pick apples for pies and apple jelly. I fell out of the tree once. My ankle swelled up and dad took me to the Norton Hospital in my uncle's car. Mom would yell for us to come from the apple orchard for supper.

Curtains on Fire
By Ernest Huey Smith of Elkton, Maryland
Born 1932

When I was two years olds, my mom passed away. I was the youngest of five, Mom was twenty-nine and had TB, dad had to work, some of the family wanted some of the children to be adopted out but dad said no, but my oldest sister and I went to live with our grandma in West Virginia. I set the house curtains on fire at about four years old and hid under the house until they put the fire out and found me. My sister called me her baby. A midwife delivered me and my brother. We had the wrong date of birth because in the Bible, dad wrote it in the Bible so mine was the fifth and the midwife had it on the fifteenth and my birth record and middle name. Lucas, my brother's birth in Bible was a week to ten days off, April 30th. So we have to go by our driving license and birth record. Our social security card too, when it came later.

Anyway, when I was about six, dad remarried, Dad was born in April 1900 at that time and was thirty-eight when he remarried. Our stepmom was very good to us and a

Ernest's step-mom and dad, Edna and Jim Smith

good cook. My other sister, Claraisa, at that time was about twelve or so, and we three boys were younger than her. We didn't have any manners, reaching across the table; she stuck a fork in our hands.

My dad passed away in 1967 at the age of sixty-seven and a half. My stepmom died at age seventy-two but before that we had moved to Maryland but my two brothers had went into the service. Harold next to me went into the Army. But Bill four years older than me went into the Navy, then later into the Marines but they said I had a busted eardrum. I was so upset. I was fifteen at this time.

I was in thirty feet of water and almost drowned and they gave up on me but my brother begged them to go back down, then that time they felt me with their feet. Well thank the Lord; he had better plans for me. I accepted him and he changed my life at the age of twenty-four.

Two years later, I married a young lady also from Virginia. That was fifty-five years ago. A lot of people didn't have a lot of schooling' I remember cars didn't have seatbelts back then in them.

We moved into our house at Farr Creek with four rooms and a bathroom I put in three or four years later. Just town water was in the kitchen.

I remember my dad used to swear off drinking for five years than he would pull a big one. My stepmom didn't like that drinking; also, my parents moved to Farr Creek in a four-room house and path but later a bathroom and used the round bathtub for clothes and a wringer washer.

Boo Bunny
By Darlene Ash Gaston of Johnstown, Pennsylvania
Born 1945

Growing up in Berkeley Springs, West Virginia in the late 1940s, 1950s, and 1960s. Near grandparents, aunts, uncles, and cousins were almost heaven.

My earliest memory was in 1949 when I was four and a half years old. On Easter morning, a pink toy bunny, he joined a doll, Irene named after my grandmother, Ash and a brown teddy bear with a bell in his ear.

Boo Bunny was my favorite and went everywhere with me.

One hot summer day, I had to go to the outhouse. I don't know how it happened, you guessed it, Boo Bunny fell down the hole. I went screaming down the path, Mother got Boo Bunny out of the hole, got out her wringer washer, pumped water from the outside pump. We washed him, he never looked the

Darlene's parents, Freda Johnson and Joseph Ash in 1945

Darlene Ash Gaston with Boo Bunny

same again but he was still my buddy. When hanging by his ears to dry, I thought when I get married and have children; I want to be smart like my mother.

Many times, I prayed that prayer when rearing my two sons and now for my grandchildren, praying to keep them on the right path to God.

Our Dad, Joseph Ash would at Christmas take my sister, Bernice and I downtown to see Santa on the fire truck, how happy we were with snow falling to receive an orange and candy.

Daddy told me he talked to Santa and if I was good he would bring me a watch, on Christmas a beautiful jewel watch was mine that I still have. He also taught me to ride a bike and drive a car. He made it easy to believe in a heavenly Father.

My sister, Bernice and I grew up loving and playing with cats. One summer our mother cat had kittens, brought them in the house one by one, and left them on my pillow. We were so happy when we went to bed and discovered kittens.

Our special cat was grey and white. Teddy would let us dress him in doll clothes. He would hold a doll bottle with milk, look around to make sure everyone was looking, drink it then let it drop when he finished.

He rode in our bicycle basket, one day he jumped out and ran into a culvert. Every day we went calling him and two weeks later, he came home, he had lost weight but it was a happy reunion. Often we would ride downtown and he was happy to be back in the basket on the bicycle.

Sometimes we took him in the grocery store or drugstore with us, other times one of us would wait outside with him still in the basket. An older couple from Washington, D.C. on vacation thought it was cute. They took our picture with him in the basket.

Another cat was Bang Bangs. We had gone down to my granddad's farm one Fourth of July to pick huckleberries. When we came home, mother cat had kittens. We named one Bang Bangs since he was born on the Fourth of July.

Every evening, he would walk up to the bus stop to meet us, one day we didn't have school but walked outside and saw Bang Bangs walking to the bus stop, we called to him and he came back and got an extra loving.

Every Sunday, we would go to the country about fifteen miles away to granddad's James Johnson's farm. At Easter, we would have Easter egg hunts with cousins, Richard, Billy, Danny, Cindy, Sherry, Regina, and Lloyd. There were cookouts for birthdays. Sometimes we would help make homemade ice cream by putting salt on the ice and cranking the handle of the old time ice cream freezer.

The winter of 1961 was really cold and snowy. Our dad and Uncle Andrew Johnson worked on the state roads. One evening after school Dad said, "We are going down to grandpa's farm your cousins will be there to sled ride." You never saw homework get done so fast.

Grandpa, Uncle Beverly, and Andrew, Garvin, and Buddy had the fire going with old tires, while our mothers, Freda, and Aunt Hazel, Jetti, and Opel made hot dogs and hot cocoa for us.

Ours was a time of fun. We lived in the best of the good old days.

We were blessed to have Sunday school teachers, family, schoolteachers, and friends who cared for and helped to teach us to become the Proud Americans we are today.

Twenty-five cents!
By James H. Burkett of Point's, West Virginia
Born 1936

My name is James Burkett. I grew up in Point's, West Virginia. Just like everyone else in the area, we had an outhouse. It was really cold going outside, there was a big crack, and the wind would blow in the outhouse.

Home remedy was Vicks Salve and you only got ginger ale if you were sick.

I helped daddy to plant corn and get the hay in, my brother, Jack helped also. I remember Jack got tired of sowing the corn and he put some corn under a rock, dad found out when the corn started to grow around the rock.

My dad also worked at the B & O railroad tracks shop. My dad and mom also had a small store. They sold groceries and beer. I would help filling the coolers and pump gas. I also helped in the store. I wasn't old enough to sell beer but I did anyway. The law never caught me-but today I wouldn't get by with it. That was in the 1950s.

A couple of friends would come in and want me to pump them gas when I went out to pump their gas I suspected them taking money out of the cigar box that I had the money in. We didn't have a cash register at the time later dad got one. Get back to the cigar box, I started to place certain objects on the box to

James "Pete" Burkett

tell if they were in it or not, they saw what I was doing than they didn't want any gas, so I knew than that they were taking money out of the cigar box.

I worked on the orchard when I was twelve years old. One other thing that happened when I was young, Jack, and I went out to help Sam Martin pick up brush out of his orchard, which we worked all day. We thought we would be making a little bit of money, when we got done, he handed my brother a fifty-cent piece for us to split.

Talk about being mad, Sam's brother paid us twenty-five cents per hour. Jack was old enough to drive and the next day we were coming by Sam's house and his chickens were out in the road. Well Jack never slowed down, chickens went flying every place, and I knew not to say anything because he was still mad about working all day and only getting fifty-cents to split.

I also milked cows for my mom; she sold milk to the family's around the area. There were no milk trucks then. She also peddled her items from the garden to Cumberland. I would

Jack and James

go with her to watch the truck sometimes. She always told me not to give anything away. This day she had some apples on the truck, here came a little boy. He was dirty and looked hungry, so I gave him an apple about five or ten minutes later, there was a bunch of little boys around the truck, boy did I get in trouble. My mom had to make money any way she could because my dad passed away at the age of fifty-two. Mom had four kids to support.

I had a sister to pass away when she was fifteen before my dad passed away.

Winters were real bad. We lived in a two-story house the snow would blow in the cracks of the windows. My brother, Jack, and I would pull our jeans in under the covers to get them warm before we would put them on. One time, the window was up a little, and I told Jack to put it down and he said why the snow blows in anyway.

We had a party line; it was hard to get your call through because all of the old ladies would be on the line telling each other what they were doing and what they were going to have for supper. If you did get the line open, everyone would listen to what you were talking about.

I went to a two-room schoolhouse. The teacher would whip you if you did something you were not supposed to do.

I read a lot of funny books. I always said I got my reading education from the funny books. I wish I had some of them funny books now.

If you needed a haircut, Miss Nixon would cut your hair. She never cut my hair.

Things that happen back than don't happen today, that what's the matter with kid's today, they can do anything and the teachers and parents can't do anything or say anything to their kids, or they will say I'm going to report you to the law or my teacher. I don't think there is anything wrong in using a paddle, as long as you don't abuse the child, just let him know there is something's you just don't do. You just can't let them do anything they want to do-put the parents in jail if they abuse the child, don't punish everyone else for trying to make your child listen.

Getting back to things that happened, my jeans would have holes in the knees, so I made a promise to myself that when I got a job; I wanted to wear a white shirt, a tie, and a suit, but when I got old enough and money enough, guess what everyone was wearing holes in their pants on purpose. (Bummer)

My grandma had a gasoline washer that made a lot of noise and would shake the dishes off the table.

They had oil lamps and when you went to visit at night you didn't know who might be sitting in the living room around the fireplace so you had to be sure you knew not to say anything about anyone. I also had a great dog-named Lassie.

My Early Years
By Raymond E. Litten of Hedgesville, West Virginia
Born 1928

My dad and mother went together for eight or nine years. They married and lived at his home place with his mother. I was six months old when they moved to the house in Cherry Run in May 1929. When my dad moved to their house, my granddad came to live with my dad and mom. I have said that not many people my age lived in a house with a man who was alive when Abraham Lincoln was alive. When Dad bought this house there was no electricity in it. My granddad paid to have the house wired so they could have electric, so with this he helped my dad. The first thing electric things bought were a washing machine and an electric iron. My granddad lived here and died here January 3, 1932.

When I was 12 years old, I got a job as a water boy at an apple orchard. I got five cents an hour, 50 cents a day. I worked there until March 1945 when I went to work on the railroad. I saved money and bought my school clothes and my new bicycle. The next three years I rode my bike from Cherry Run to Sleepy Creek to work.

December 7, 1941 we all know what happened. I went back to being a water boy with a raise to seven and a half cents an hour, 75 cents a day. Wow! 1943 and 1944 to the spring of 1945, I worked with the men at 25 cents an hour until I went to work on the railroad for 66 cents an hour. A big jump, $5.28 a day.

When I started high school, I was the only one to get on the bus here at Cherry Run. My first year I did well enough, but I had trouble with the other boys there. I was a dumb kid from Cherry Run. I passed to the 10th grade. 1943, that year wasn't much better for me. I wasn't passing. So in the spring of 1944 I quit school and went to the orchard to work. My daddy wanted me back to school.

That fall I went back to school to the 10th grade again, but things weren't any better for me. I went nine days, got off the bus a couple miles from home, and walked home. When Daddy got home, we had a war. He said I had to go back to school. He wanted to know what I was going to do. I told him that Mr. French was going to give me a job on the railroad when I turned 16 in November where my daddy worked. He didn't want me to go to work on the railroad. I don't know why. He had worked there about 25 years then. He was very disappointed with me. He wanted me to get an education, as he didn't have a school education.

I kept after Mr. French for a job. I don't know to this day whether Daddy was the cause for Mr. French not putting me to work, but I kept after Mr. French. Remember, this was wartime, and the railroad hired some of us boys. Finally, Mr. French told me he had an opening. All I had to do was get a release form from the high school and from Daddy to sign my papers. My daddy said no. So Mr. French, he and Daddy were the best of friends, told me to get two railroad people to sigh my paper. I waited on Mr. White's store porch and waited for men to get off from work. I asked Mr. Weigle, another good friend of Daddy's and Mr. Pickett, our neighbor, to sign my papers. I had put them on the spot, so as to say. They looked at my daddy and they said nothing. They took my papers and signed them. There were never so hard feelings between them and my daddy ever!

On the 15th of March 1945, I went to work on the Baltimore and Ohio Railroad, pushing a wheelbarrow. I stayed on the railroad 40 years and almost two months, retiring May 8, 1985. I was 56 years old. My retirement brought an end to the Litten railroaders for the Baltimore and Ohio from 1868 until 1985, a hundred and seventeen years. The railroad was good for me. I never had any regrets for quitting school, except my daddy wanted me to get an education.

Now about girlfriends. I had a few friends who were girls, but no dating girls. I tried to date a couple, but no one wanted to go with me until I met Dorothy. I knew her for a couple years. She was a sister to Esther Starliper that was married to my cousin, Harry (Tom) and was with them a lot.

Christmas 1948, I was at their house as I was for several Christmas. Tom and I were always close as cousins. He had no car. I would take him around, sometimes to the wrong place (beer joints). Dorothy was there that evening, and I asked her if she would want to go to the movies. She said she would, but we didn't go to the movies. We just rode around. She was the only girl who thought I was good enough to go out with and finally marry.

Dorothy and I went together the year of 1949. She thought I would give her a ring for her birthday, May 3, but I got her a watch. In July, I did give her an engagement ring.

The fall of 1949, Tom and I were laid off at the railroad through the winter. We went on an orchard in Berkeley County and picked for a while. We quit that and went to cutting timber in the Sleepy Creek Mountain. I didn't know anything about cutting timber. I worked at it for a little while. Someone was off sick on the railroad so they called me back. I worked a week. The fellow came back to work so I was laid off again, but this was all right it made me eligible to draw unemployment benefits. You couldn't quit a job and draw unemployment.

Dorothy and I had set November 5 to get married. She wouldn't get married until I was 21 years old. She didn't want Mom's wrath. When we got married, her Uncle Norman had already got me in trouble. He was full of devilment and him and Carrie was up visiting Mom and Dad. Carrie and Mom were first cousins. He told Mom we were already married, that he had married us, he was a preacher. Mom went all crazy, and Daddy believed it too. He told Daddy better. My dad's niece, Georgia Shields, was here for the weekend, and she got Mom straightened out.

So when we got married I wasn't working. I received $3.50 a day unemployment, $35.00 every two weeks. We hadn't decided where we were going to get married, only that it would be Maryland. Charles Pickett that lived in Hancock, our neighbor's son, wanted us to get married in his house. I went up there a lot.

The day Dorothy and I went to Hagertown

to get our license at the Washington County Courthouse, as I was parking Aunt Brownie was walking on the street right there. We got out. She knew why we were there. I asked her where Uncle Nute was. She said he was at the Western Maryland train station. They were going to catch the train up to Big Pool. At this time, they had an apartment over in Hagerstown and would only come over to the home place when they wanted to. We went to the courthouse. She went along, and we got the license. We went to the railroad station and got Uncle Nute and they came home with us. We went up by Hancock so we could take them home at Sleepy Creek. He wanted to know who we were going to get to marry us. We still hadn't thought about a preacher in Maryland. I told him about Charles Pickett's invitation. He said he would like for us to have Byron Kesecker to marry us. For me, anything Uncle Nute wanted me to do I would do. Dorothy said it would be all right with her. We were going to drive right by the Methodist Church and parsonage anyway, so we stopped at the parsonage and knocked on the door. Mrs. Kesecker came to the door She was glad to see Uncle Nute. They had known each other ever since they were kids. Uncle Nute told her why we were there and introduced us to Mr. Kesecker and her. We went in and made the arrangements. Rev. Kesecker was glad he had brought us to him. We went on home.

On November 5, 1949, Dorothy and I were married in the Methodist parsonage. My daddy and mom, Mr. Bowers and his wife, Audrey and son, Roger, was the only ones with us. Both Harry E.S. Litten and Bowers was our witnesses. Dorothy has put up with me almost 52 years, one more month.

We started housekeeping in Tomand Esther's two rooms upstairs. We had already had our furniture in there. Dorothy quit her job in Martinsburg at McCrory's. We only stayed there two months. Things weren't working out with this arrangement. Dorothy didn't like me taking Tom places, especially the beer joints. I didn't drink, and she didn't want me to get started. But I had learned long ago that I didn't want to be like Tom and Uncle Nute. If I had went along with Tom I would have been as big a drunk as him.

So in January 1950 Dorothy and I were staying at her uncle Cecil and his wife's. Dorothy was taking care of Muriel, who was about to have her third baby. I heard Roy Payne had an apartment empty over his store. So Daddy and I went out to see Mr. Payne about renting the apartment. It was a good place to live. We stayed there 15 month, until May 1951.

1950 started out pretty well. Dorothy and I was satisfied with things. We had a garden and Pop Silver gave us a couple of pigs. I raised them there at Mr. Payne's. At butchering time, I sold one of them to Elmer Payne. Larry was born August 27, 1950. We were down at Mom and Daddy's a lot those last days before Larry was born. We were there the Sunday or two before he was born.

Dorothy and I ended up living on the old home place where I was born. It was 35 acres that I didn't know what to do with. For starters, there was no electric, never! The kitchen was in terrible shape. Why did I bring Dorothy to a place like this? Like I have already said, she was the only one to see anything in me. So she was satisfied with it. We all went to work, Red, Irvin, and Daddy. Dorothy and I moved in in May 1951. We had rented Mr. Payne's apartment for 15 months and paid him $75.00 rent money, the only rent I have ever paid to this day.

Lola Elaine Litten was born October 21, 1954 in City Hospital. Sandra Lynn Litten was born February 2, 1959. Clarence Edward Litten was born July 31, 1052.

Farming and Moonshine
By Johnny Logan of Oakland, Maryland
Born 1951

I was born in Ellijay, Georgia, Gilmer County, in the north Georgia Mountains and moved to Deer Park, Maryland in 1995 after retiring from the US Navy. Deer Park is a little town in Garrett County, Maryland in which Oakland is the county seat. Garrett County is the most western of Maryland and is most like where I grew up than any place I've ever been. There is one exception: the weather. We had some big snows in Gilmer County, Georgia but here it is simply a way of life. From November to April, we are pushing and plowing snow.

My daddy, Claude I. Logan, born

Johnny, Vanessa, Susan, Mama Belle, and Coatus "Bub"

December 7, 1911, and my mama, Belle Wood Logan, had seven children, one girl, Shirley, followed by six boys; Joe, James (Bo), Billy, Coatus (Bub), Fairley, and myself, the youngest. We lived out in the country on the west end of Gilmer County on the Tails Creek Road (282) on Mountain Town Creek. I was born after the family had moved from the old Sutton place to the house on Mountaintown Creek. My daddy and Papa Logan had hired it built and bricked, a six room house with a room for a bathroom that was never plumbed until years later. This is where we lived when I was born.

We heated the house with only a fireplace and wood cook stove in the kitchen. The back of the house never got any heat. Mama would pile so many quilts on us that we couldn't hardly move. We didn't have running water in the house. We used a spring across the bridge on the side of the mountain until Daddy got us a well dug, then we used bucket, rope on a windless and drawed our water from the well.

When I was about seven or eight, a man came around selling Home Comfort pumps and sinks and we got water in the kitchen, but still no bathroom, not even an outhouse. You just went off from the house and did what you had to do.

I started school at Tails Creek Elementary when I was five years old. I cried to go with my brothers. They let me go too. We carried our lunch in a big brown paper sack, biscuits, jelly, and fried pork. We would go outside and eat most of the time, the four of us, and sometimes we would ask if someone wanted a biscuit if we thought they didn't have anything to eat.

We raised most of our food on the farm. We always had hogs, milk cows, and game chickens. Mama made butter and churned buttermilk and would plant a big garden every summer. Mama would can everything from the garden, and we picked all the blackberries we could, and she made jelly and jam and canned the berries, jam, cobblers. Mom would can green beans, blackberry, and other vegetables and fruits in half-gallon Mason jars, as they seemed to be plentiful from Daddy's moonshining operation. However, if the family didn't eat it the hogs or dogs would. We always had a slop bucket for the scraps to feed the hogs along with what we called shorts.

Liquor and Lumber

Papa Logan owned a sawmill, and Daddy and Uncle John Thomas helped to run this saw mill, which was moved from one tract of timber to another as needed. Daddy also had another line of work at times, which was making moonshine. We had cornfields to feed the stock with, get our cornmeal from for cornbread, and to support the moonshine operation. Gilmer County was noted for its good corn liquor.

There was a story that a big shot out of Atlanta came up to Ellijay and stopped in front of the courthouse and asked some of the loafers setting on the bench under the shade tree in front of the courthouse what was the biggest industry in the county and Holbert Roger and Rusty Nickleson jumped up and hollered, "Liquor and lumber, in that order!"

Papa Logan always kept yokes of steer for logging. He would find a set of twin bull calves, buy them, and sometimes bring them to our farm for my older brothers to get them used to the yoke. When the calves got to about 500 pounds all my brothers would yoke them up, and those calves would just have a fit pulling us around, hanging up in trees, running over everything. Seems like the last yoke we broke were Billy and Bub steers and Fairley and I helped them. It's a wonder we didn't get killed. I know I was just seven or eight years old. I stayed out of the way a lot.

I remember the law (Feds) coming to our house three different times and searching for moonshine. On two of these times, they found what they were looking for. I think they were here times before and can't remember; I wasn't born. One of those times cost Daddy a year and a day in Tallassee Florida. He called it his college days. Those guys would walk around looking and searching for it and ask us kids (we would follow them) where Daddy and Mama had hid it. We wouldn't say a word. We sure didn't tell them they were getting hot.

In the summer when we wasn't working in the garden or corn field or picking berries and carrying water we stayed in the creek swimming and fishing, having mud fights and all. We would play in the creek until we were blue and shriveled up. Our best swimming hole was the baptizing hole. A lot of people came there to swim and bathe. Us boys were all the time into meanness but we didn't bother no one. We didn't have any in sight neighbors. We ran that 300 acres up and down both sides of the creek.

We never had a car so we walked everywhere we went or someone would give us a ride. We attended Pleasant Grove Baptist Church where Papa Logan (his name was Johnny W also, I was named after him) and Grandma Mid were members. Mid was Papa's second wife. I don't remember Mama Logan; she died before I was born. Between Papa Logan and Mama, they would see that we had rides to church. We would also attend revivals in the community during the summer.

We rode the school bus to school, Tailors Creek Elementary was a three room school with first, second, third, fourth, fifth, sixth, and seventh. Some of my teachers were Mrs. Holt, Jeff Hampton, Mrs. Martin, and Mrs. Puckett. I have gotten paddlings from all of them.

Some other memories I have of my childhood days are Thanksgiving Mama would always cook a big turkey and cornbread dressing with green beans, corn, mashed potatoes and gravy, also potato salad and nanner pudding, cakes and pies. She would invite Earnest (Peanut) and Mildred Buckner. They had about six girls and us three youngest brothers would be so bashful, but we all had a good time.

Christmas we didn't get many presents (gifts) but we always had plenty to eat. Mama would cook about the same meal as Thanksgiving with maybe a ham. We would have apples, oranges, and nuts. We didn't put up stockings. We put up a big cedar tree with lights and a star at the top. We didn't ask for gifts. We knew money was hard to come by, but we did aggravate Mama wanting firecrackers and she and Daddy would get us some. We loved to shoot those things.

I learned how to milk the cows very young, before and after school, we milked the cows, fed the hogs and chickens, and in the evenings, we would also have to get in the firewood for the fireplace and cook stove. We killed hogs when cold weather came and rendered out the lard. Those cracklings in cornbread were good and the meat skins too.

Our toys were things we made: a lard bucket lid nailed to a sawmill strip to roll around, Spam cans to excavate with or just roll, an old car tire around that we found in the trash pile.

Mama and us kids would pick beans for George McLure for fifty cents a bushel for school clothes. We used to also find muscadines and shake them out. We had fun doing these things.

Sometime around 1963 Mama bought a car after going to work at the new chicken plant in Ellijay. A year or so later Mama and Daddy divorced. I guess she just couldn't handle Daddy's drinking anymore. By this time, all of my siblings had left home. Shirley married Cletis Davis and had four children. Joe married Francis Panter and had two children. James joined the Coast Guard; Coatus joined the Navy. Fairley was working and would later marry Suell Quarlls and would have two children. In July 1965 my brother, Billy, the fourth child of us seven was killed in an

Uncle Jim Sellers, Claude Logan (Johnny's daddy), and Jess Crawford in 1937

Susan and Johnny Logan in 1984

automobile accident. He was 21 years old. Eunice, his wife, was pregnant and later gave birth to a son.

In the fall of 1965, I went to live with Mama. She had moved to Pickens County, Georgia. Daddy had gone to California to live with my aunt. Thanks to my mama, she put me through high school and on May 26, 1969, I graduated from Pickens County High School. I belonged to the Future Farmers of America in high school. Mama just had four acres of land, but we had a hog and I showed one of them. Farming was in my blood.

I got married at 17 and we had two boys, Jason, born March 12, 1970 and Terry, born February 28, 1972. I had several different jobs including cutting pulpwood, working at a chicken plant and a yarn mill, and operating a service station. This marriage failed, and my life was going in the wrong direction when my brother James convinced me to join the Navy.

On December 17, 1974, I went to basic training in Orlando, Florida. While in boot camp, I volunteered for submarine duty and went to sub school in New London, Connecticut and then torpedo school back in Orlando. I was command advanced to 3rd class out of school. I had found my calling in life. I went on to serve on one diesel sub World War II type and four nuclear submarines. I was advanced to the rank of Master Chief Petty Officer TMCM (SS). The last two submarines I served on USS Sea Devil SSN-664 and USS MG Valleyo SSBN658(G) I served as Chief of the Boat (COB). I retired from the Navy in June 1995 as the Command Master Chief of Submarine Group Six in Charleston, South Carolina.

I met my wife, Susan Hinebaugh, in 1984 through a Navy buddy, Bob Dixon. We are now in our 29th year. Our daughter, Vanessa, was born July 24th, 1986. Upon my retirement from the navy, we moved back to Garrett County, Maryland.

Susan and I still raise cattle and keep up one of the family farms that her Uncle Arlie passed down to her and we grow a lot of what we eat in the garden. We have five grandchildren that we love very much, ranging in age from 22 years to two years, Lindsey, Taylor, Clay, Brandon, and Bridgett.

My mama Belle worked very hard to keep us kids fed and clothed. I owe my work ethic and my Christian upbringing to her. We might have been poor, but we were so rich because we were loved and taught right from wrong and to respect others and that God was the only redeemer. Home is "the hunter is home from the hills; home is the sailor home from the sea."

Growing Up in a Small Town
By Barbara Corbett of Berkeley Springs,
West Virginia
Born 1939

The small town of Great Cacapon, Morgan County, West Virginia lies in a small valley below a scenic overlook called the Panorama. It was said to be once inhabited by Indians and was called Kak-a-pon. Several families in later years while digging in the soil found arrowheads, beads, and other objects. It is surrounded by the Potomac and Cacapon Rivers. The Cacapon begins in Wardensville, West Virginia, flows into the Potomac and down through Washington, DC, where it then flows out into the bay. In 1936, there was a flood, which hit a lot of places. Cacapon was flooded in some places up to Main Street.

Cacapon was a very pretty town with well-kept homes. Today some are still well kept while others are in bad condition. It had four grocery stores, Noland's, Ball's, Kidwell's

Barbara's Grandpap Michael

(once housing the post office), and Munson's; two churches; a gas station; a canning factory; a ball field with a grandstand; Compton's trucking; Stienbaugh's Garage; Barker's Restaurant; and a train station.

The train stopped in Cacapon for passengers and at times, hobos who rode in boxcars would jump off and wander around town looking for a meal. They were harmless, but it was still scary when they knocked on your door. The station and tracks were on the bottom section of town below Main Street. The tracks are still used today.

Above Main Street was High Street. Some houses set in back on High Street and more were out in a section called Creek Road, while others were in what was called 'up the hollow.' A small part of town once had an operating sand mine in back of it with a few houses for workers to live in. It was called Hazeltown. The mine no longer exists, but more homes are there. A former judge of the Supreme Court, William R. Rehnquist, once resided in Cacapon.

Today one store, two churches, and a new post office are still there, plus a fire station and a school, which is used only for Head Start and other functions. The gas station and one store are still standing but in bad condition and the rest are gone. A small airplane crashed in a field next to the bridge entering Cacapon. I don't think anyone was hurt badly or killed but it sure had the town residents in a tizzy.

The school held country music shows featuring Bud Mesner's band from Pennsylvania and the McCumbee Brothers band from Berkeley Springs, plus well-known country music stars and other types of entertainment. It had several school programs a year. The students from the upper classes got time out of class to help build and paint scenery and other props, although all classes participated in the programs. Some programs were held in the grove across from the school. I had a good singing voice, and one year I was an angel sitting on a decorated ladder, singing "O, Holy Night."

We were also fortunate enough to have several carnivals come to town when games and rides cost five to ten cents and food was not costly. There was always an Easter egg hunt in the grove with candy and money filled eggs hidden for the children to find and a prize for the largest family attending. The Gene and Delores Kidwell family always won.

We had a sheriff and a constable in town, Mr. Munson and Mr. Zimmerman. Mr. Zimmerman had two sons, Henry and Paul. Henry had a sort of heavy foot when driving. One Saturday night, some of the older guys were going through town, probably going over the limit. Mr. Zimmerman stopped them and asked, "Where are you going in such a hurry?" They replied, "Trying to catch up to Henry!" He said, "Go on, but slow it down." My brother Bob was one, along with Jack

Barbara's Grandma Clark

Barbara's parents, Ralph and Viola Clark with their children

Henry, Zane Barker, Lewis Ridgeway, and an Avery boy.

In the old days, some local men would gather every evening on the porch of Balls Grocery, sit on benches, shoot the breeze, smoke, and drink soda. They also gathered at Mechem's Gas Station.

My family, Clark, was large – parents, three sisters, myself, and four brothers. Daddy was a B&O track foreman and Mom sometimes worked at the canning factory in town and outside town at a hospital and a nursing home. She was mostly at home raising us and caring for our home. They moved around a lot, wherever the railroad sent them, living in seven different towns and in four houses in Cacapon before buying their last home. We never went hungry or without decent, clean clothes.

We raised chickens (supplying eggs), hogs, a cow, two sheep, a goat, and two ponies. Daddy also fished and hunted for food. We had one of the nicest vegetable gardens in town, raising everything but a few necessities we'd need from a store. If we wanted to go swimming at the local swimming hole, Mom would get us up at 6:30 to go weed and hoe the garden before it got hot.

We bathed during the week in a basin, but on Saturday night, we got a 'tub' bath. Before a certain age, the girls bathed in the same water, drawn by hand from a well and heated. Then, in clean water, it was the boys' turn.

Mom had a wringer washer, getting the wash and rinse water the same way. She not only had large laundry loads to do, canning food form the garden and helping with butchering plus whatever else. She could chop the head off a chicken, pluck off the feathers, take out the entrails, and cut it up like a pro.

Bless her heart! In later years, they did get a small freezer so she could freeze meats and vegetables, an electric stove and dryer. Daddy also put in running water and a sink and a small bathroom.

Mom had some home remedies. For the croup, there was Dr. Drake's Glesco and castor oil followed by sucking on half an orange. Yuck! For earaches, there was heating sweet oil in a small spoon and letting it drip into your ear. I always told her she caused my hearing problems of today. She had to keep coal oil on hand, because when the roads were tarred and chipped and it became hot, the potholes got hot and bubbled, and we'd stick out toes in to burst the bubbles. She'd give us a rag with oil on it to clean out feet before we were allowed inside.

When Elvis made his first movie, "Love me Tender," Daddy and Mom took Linda and two of her friends, Sally and Erma, and me to the drive-in to see it. Elvis died in it, and those three girls cried all the way home.

On Christmas Eve, which was Daddy's payday, Mom and Daddy went shopping for gifts and groceries. When they came home, we always had fried oysters and stew. We always got gifts from Santa. One year Daddy built Linda and me a kitchen set with stove, sink with a window above it, and refrigerator from dynamite boxes from the Berkeley Springs sand mine. He painted them red and white, and they all had imitation parts. Oh, what memories!

When Julia, the oldest, got married, she lived in a small apartment having only an icebox to keep food cold. Her husband and his dad worked at the sand mine and would get ice in Berkeley Springs, stopping on the way home at Niners Bar for a few beers, and by the time they got home, there wasn't much left of the ice block!

Bob and Dick, my oldest brothers, had little 'go rounds,' like all siblings. They were in the garden picking tomatoes, got peeved, and Bob left. Dick threw a tomato at him. When Bob started throwing back at Dick's feet, Dick kept jumping up out of the way. Bob got wise, drew back, and threw. Dick jumped in the air and got it smack dab in the face.

Marlene would always go to see the Avey girls after supper, and I always wanted to tag along and she'd get mad if Mom made her take me, until one night I fell and broke my collarbone. After that, she always let me tag along.

David had a dog that was always getting sprayed by polecats. When it happened, he'd take Pepper to the postmaster, Mr. Avey, and sell him for a nickel. In a few days, he'd go back, telling Mr. Avey he'd better take Pepper back home to care of him. Of course, the smell was gone.

David and a few town boys like to tilt outhouses at Halloween, until one night, the owner was in one and yelled. That ended the tilting of outhouses.

Larry loved baseball. Until Mom got him a real bat, he'd use any old board he could find, and if he couldn't find a ball and we had a rubber doll, guess what he used for one. He played Little League, and one evening he was washing and dressing for a game. He asked Mom for a washcloth. She had done laundry that day and told him they were on the clothesline. He replied, "I can't wash with a wet cloth."

Linda was a tiny girl, weighing only four pounds when she was born. She was kept on a pillow and a hot water bottle was used to keep her warm. She liked to pretend that Daddy's vise in the smokehouse was her spigot until one day she twisted it too far and it fell and cut her forehead. She still has the scar.

I got into a bit of trouble in the seventh grade. Two girls didn't come to school one day. After lunch, Barb, Susie, and I decided to go to the dam, knowing they were there. We didn't use the metal swinging ladder to go down; we went through a field and across the dam. Well, one of the boys, Bubby, told the principal where we were, and they came out. They saw us, but not Joyce and Peggy. He made us climb that ladder. Believe me, I never skipped school again.

My playmates and friends growing up were Barbara (Cookie), Marggie, Susie, Jean, Joan, Kay, Mary Jane, Peggy, Joyce, Jeanie, and Mary Ellen. As teenagers, during evenings in the summer, we'd walk around town, go to the school ground to swing and talk, or go to the Stinebaugh Garage for a soda, a candy bar, or ice cream. When a little older, Susie was the only one who had her license and a car. Some of us rode to high school with her and ran around on weekends. All the kids in Cacapon had two hills we could sled ride on, using old rubber tires, burning, to keep warm.

Two of the most memorable people in my life were grandparents who visited with us. I was dating and at the time, short skirts were in style. When I came downstairs, Grandma Clark said, "Honey, you'd better put some sugar in your shoes." When I asked why, she replied, "To coax that skirt down a bit!" Boy, if she were alive today! Grandpap Michael liked hard tack candy, which he kept in a small paper sack. At night, he'd sit in his rocker and the small children would get on the floor. He'd roll several pieces at us, and if you got one, okay. If not, you tried again the next night.

Well, that's my story of growing up in a small West Virginia town. I am a widow living six miles from that town. I have two children, Jay and Jill; in-laws, April and Clayton; and an adorable granddaughter, Cora, age three; and two sisters and two brothers still surviving.

Our family had its ups and downs but it was a wonderful life!

My Large Family was Great!
By Joyce E. Skidmore of Oakland, Maryland
Born 1928

I was the youngest of nine siblings; all passed away, three brothers and five sisters. I loved being part of a large family, but it is so sad when they all go!

I was born in the oldest village in Garrett County, which was Selbysport, Maryland on the Youghiogheny River. Growing up there was one of my most wonderful memories!

We lived on the east side of the river on Old Morgantown Road (East). My home was a big, old, rambling house built around a log house, which was approximately 200 years old. My ancestors who came over from the Old Country around 1750s built it. When it was finally torn down about 20 years ago, you could see the original log house and the old fireplace. A buyer of the house was purchased by someone in Virginia and the log house reconstructed there. A large bridge connected the east side of Selbysport from the west side.

At one time, the village had a railroad station, a post office, a large store with groceries, a hardware store, a milliner shop, a photographer shop, a blacksmith shop, a tannery owned by my ancestors, a Methodist church, a two-room schoolhouse.

We went to school there for grades one to five, and then to Friendsville, about two miles away for grades six through four years of high school. There was no eighth grade then. Everyone loved our teacher in Selbysport, whose name was Jenny Timney. She was a good teacher and a lot of fun. She would sled ride with us, and at Christmas and other occasions, she would have family get-togethers at the school with food and games. If we got in trouble at school, we were in trouble at home. We were taught manners and how to act properly. Miss Timney checked our ears, fingernails, and posture every day! Our small church would have family socials and programs for holidays.

In the summer, we would swim in the Youghiogheny River. We had two swimming holes called Mill Race and Snake Dam. What fun we had! In the winter, besides sled riding, we played fox and the geese in the fresh snow, dug tunnels, had snowball battles, and a lot of other games we made up.

Later on, in the early '50s, our village was separated and a flood control dam for the Pittsburgh area was built, taking a lot of houses, the railroad station, tracks, the post office, and our main road to Friendsville. Another road was built from Addison, Pennsylvania to Friendsville. Our church and school were saved and a few other businesses, like the blacksmith shop. In order to visit our friends across the river you had to go to Friendsville first and take another road to the west side of Selbysport. A few people had to use a boat. There are still a few people living in Selbysport.

I entered seventh grade when Pearl Harbor was bombed and World War II started in 1941. I graduated from high school when the war ended in 1945, so you see my teen years were spent in wartime. Quite a few of my classmates left school and enlisted in the service, even some of the male teachers. I had two brothers who joined the Army and one brother wanted to but couldn't because he had rheumatic fever when he was young and had a bad heart. He was so disappointed when they wouldn't take him. Two of my sisters were Rosie the Riveters and worked in a defense plant in Baltimore, Maryland until the war ended.

We were all very patriotic and even when "The Star Spangled Banner" was played in the movies, we would all stand up with hand over heart. Almost everything was rationed such as sugar, shortening, gas, silk stockings, and a lot of other items. We bought savings stamps for 25 cents each at school, pasted them in a book, and when it was full, we turned them in for a $25.00 War Bond by the government. We wrote to all the soldiers we knew and gave them rides as the hitched-hiked a lot, met the trains when they came home, and saw them off when they went to war. We cried with the mothers who lost their sons. We had a close-knit community and everyone helped everyone else.

After high school I went to Catherman's Business School in Cumberland, Maryland, studying secretary science, typing, shorthand, bookkeeping, and other subjects.

I married my high school sweetheart and lived in Friendsville for a while and then we moved to Ohio for work and lived there for a while. My children were born there, two beautiful girls and a handsome little boy. We moved back to Oakland, Maryland where my husband put in a bowling alley named Oak Lanes. It was very successful and we eventually put one in Friendsville and one in Kingwood, West Virginia which we eventually sold an bought a motel on Deep Creek Lake

Joyce with her 1st grade classmates in 1934

Selbysport School students at a picnic in 1930

which we named the Beachcomber. My husband Alan died suddenly when he was 38 years old and our children were twelve, eleven, and six years old. I kept the motel from when he died in 1966 until 1971, selling it and going to work in Oakland as a clerk for Selective Service while the Vietnam War was going on. My mother stayed with me to help with the kids.

When our community college was built in McHenry, I worked for the Dean of Students and after that with the Garrett County Commissioners for the Roads Department as secretary. I retired from there in 1990, but worked part-time jobs until 2002. My children grew up, were married, had children of their own, and eventually my oldest daughter and her family moved to Kentucky, my other daughter moved to Massachusetts, and my son still teaches here in Oakland, where I moved to 20 years ago, after living on Deep Creek Lake at McHenry for 31 years.

I looked over you list of items you wanted to know about, so I'll list them here:

Outhouses - everyone in Selbysport had outhouses when I was growing up there, also chamber pots. It was hard to make yourself trudge through snow and cold in the winter to go to the two-seater outhouse.

Saturday night baths – we had a large galvanized tub with water being heated on the coal stove. We had to carry water from our spring, as we had no pump. The water was good to drink.

Needless to say, we had no central heat. The downstairs was heated by a big stove called Warm Morning. Upstairs there was no heat. My mother, Emma, would heat the 'sad irons' on the stove, wrap them in a towel, and put them at our feet. Of course, we always had a 'bed buddy.'

Washing clothes was done on a washboard by hand and hung on a clothesline to dry. When they were dry, you would sprinkle them with water, roll them up for a while, and then iron the wrinkles out. I always thought this was strange, wetting them again. We heated the old 'sad irons' on the coal stove to iron with.

My mother was a beautiful seamstress and she would make most of our clothes. They were beautiful. She even made hats. When we were real young, we wore what was called 'panty waists,' which were tops buttoned onto our underwear and long, tan cotton stockings in the winter that were always wrinkled.

Home remedies – I remember my brothers going in the woods, cutting some cherry bark, and my mother making cough syrup. She also fed us onion juice for coughs.

Entertainment – we made up most of our games, which we called: red light, green light; handy over (throwing a ball over the roof to someone on the other side); hide and seek; tag; and Mother, may I? We were never bored. In the summer, we had huge rocks in our barnyard to play house on and a creek across the road where we caught crayfish under the rocks. We would dam up the water, and we would swing on the wild grapevines out over the creek.

Wind-up record players – we had a large Victrola and would dance to big band music, mostly the jitterbug. We had records by the Dorsey Brothers, Harry James, Frank Sinatra, Perry Como, the Andrews Sisters, and others. We would make that old house shake when we danced.

When we were older, we would go to the movies in Friendsville, mostly western and war movies. We would cry in some of the war movies and some we learned to hate the ones where we were bombed and attacked by the Germans and Japanese. Of course, these hate feelings are all gone now. They had Bank Night on Wednesdays where they might call your ticket number and you'd win money.

Rumble seats – my cousins in Uniontown, Pennsylvania had a car with a rumble seat, which we loved riding in.

My grandparents had a hotel in Oakland named Hotel Frantz, which was next to the train station. I loved visiting there.

Up Home at the Mountain Cabin
By Mary Ellen Rich of Berkeley Springs, West Virginia
Born 1940

I was born in Amaranth, Pennsylvania, about ten miles from Hancock, Maryland. My father worked on the sawmill there in the early '40s. Around 1942 we moved to Sparrows Point, Maryland, where he got a job at Bethlehem Steel.

My parents were both from Great Cacapon, West Virginia. My mother had quit school at 16 to become a maid during the Depression. She said she made $3.00 a week. Nevertheless they had to sell their most prized possession, their player piano, to pay their electric bill and for food.

My father worked at the CCC camp, where he helped to put up buildings and clear trails at Cacapon St. Park. There he met and became fast friends with George Dawson, who later became my uncle. My father married my mother, Martha Dawson. After the war, George also moved to Sparrows Point, where he lived right next door.

Mary Ellen's mother, Martha in 1958

We would come up here every weekend that we could. My father would come home from his 3:00 to 11:00 shift on Friday night and say, "Would anybody like to go 'up home' tonight?" Everybody would be ready on a dime. It took about three hours to get here, and we would pull in around 4:00 a.m. When we were about 15 miles from the mountain and just after crossing the Hancock Bridge into West Virginia, my mother would wake us up to point out the spot where the 'red-haired lady's body was found' (a local murder mystery that was never solved). Then we knew we were almost home.

We had a small mountain cabin at Mt. Nebo, just past Great Cacapon. My two sisters and I would go straight to bed to snuggle and keep warm while my parents would fire up the old cook stove. When it warmed up, we would have some breakfast and rest a while. After that, we would head down the mountain to visit with my father's brother, Tom, and his wife, Nellie. They lived on the Capon River, and we would swim there in the summer time.

Once when I was about nine and my sister, Betty Jean, was 14 she decided to swim to the other side with me on her back. She got very tired about halfway across and placed me on a slippery round rock so she could run up to the house for an inner tube. The water was over my head, and I kept slipping off to the side. I have never been that scared before or since. She was only gone for a few minutes, but to me it seemed like hours. Of course, my parents never heard about this adventure.

I can still remember the smell of Nellies homemade bread and soup beans and how good they tasted after three or four hours in the 'crick.'

Tom and Nellie lived in one of the oldest houses in Morgan County. There was a part of the house that they called 'the old stairs.' My sister and I used to sleep up there because it was kind of spooky. One cold winter morning, we were surprised to wake and see snow on the foot of the bed. We weren't even cold, because we were under several big old homemade quilts. The snow had blown in through a crack in the window.

Also at Tom and Nellie's there was a secret pathway that led down the hill to the main road. From the main road, it looked to be impossible to navigate. Actually, it was quite easy. It looked like a completely vertical sheet

Judy, Betty Jean, and Mary Ellen in 1958

of rock to passing cars, and people would stare to see someone standing in the middle of it.

Some of my cousins used to play a trick on passing motorists. They called it playing pocketbook. They would tie a string on an old wallet, lay it on the side of the road, and then climb about halfway up the side of the cliff. Sometimes a car would turn around and come back for a second look. When they reached down the joker would pull the string and laugh loudly. Not very nice, but it seemed hilarious at the time.

Another time we had a picnic at a fire tower. My sister, Betty, ended up marrying the fellow who manned the tower. Sister Judy also married a man from this area.

Then on Saturday nights, there would be a square dance at the Sycamore Inn in Largent. A lot of families and kids of all ages from near and far would gather there. That was some of the most fun of my teenage years.

The man who owned the place at that time lived across the road in a big house on the hill overlooking the inn. He also had a very nice grandson who was just my age. We used to sit on the porch swing and watch the festivities down below. Our last date was to see the movie "Picnic' with William Holden and Kim Novac at the old Berkeley Springs drive-in. I wrote to him for a while after he joined the Army but then we lost track. I think of him now and then and wonder if he remembers me.

Then the next summer I met a tall boy (six feet eight inches) at the yearly festival at Mt. Nebo. He was a lot of fun and a great dancer. After that summer, I never saw him again. I heard he moved out west.

We usually celebrated a second Christmas at the mountain house and would leave the tree up until we came back around Valentine's Day.

I remember bringing my homework from school with me and doing it at the kitchen table by the light of a kerosene lamp. We had no electricity at that time and no indoor plumbing. The only problem was that you had to watch out for copperheads and rattlesnakes on the way to the outhouse. Actually, my aunt and uncle found a copperhead under the couch when they stayed at the cabin one weekend.

Then in the summer of 1959, there was a strike at the Bethlehem Steel. We moved up here for the most of that summer. My father got a temporary job on the building of the New Fisher's Bridge. In September, the strike was settled, and we headed back 'down home.'

I soon got a job in the office at Bethlehem Steel where I worked for the next five years. In the meantime, I married and we bought a farm in Doe Gully. After two years, we moved up here and were chicken farmers for two years. It was a hard life, and we sold the farm. We moved to Berkeley Springs in 1965 and have lived her ever since, for 49 years.

My parents dreamed of retiring up here but they both passed away at the age of 54. They are buried at the Mt. Nebo Church cemetery about two miles from the old mountain house.

Wonderful Days with True Friends
By Beverly Day of Great Cacapon, West Virginia
Born 1954

My favorite memory is when all the kids in the row where I lived would meet at my house early in the mornings during the summer months and on weekends. We had a special place to play which we created ourselves.

I lived below the old sand mine quarries in Great Cacapon. We would meet and go up in the quarries to play for the day. There was a large pine tree area, which we played under. Under these trees was our special play place. Back then, people would dump their garbage up there, and we would find all kinds of treasures: broken chairs, pots, pans, bowls, old rugs, and tables. We created what we thought was a palace of our own. We would work hours digging and decorating our palace.

Right below the quarries at my friend's house was an old pigpen. We had it fixed up like a house, so when it rained it was our shelter. We had old curtains hung, old rugs, and an old table and chairs, and it was certainly a special place to us.

Then at the end of my yard was an old building with a window that had a screen in it. We used this as our restaurant. The boys became cowboys, and they stopped by to order their lunch. The menu was very special made mud pies made the day before to be hardened for the next day's menu.

We stayed outside all day only to go to the door to get a drink, but usually we took a jug of water with us.

The outhouse was our bathroom. I remember they all liked my outhouse. My mom had put a commode seat on and linoleum on the floor, and she used a bucket of water and a broom to clean it each day and to keep the spiders cleaned out. Our outhouse was the nicest and cleanest in the row.

We entertained ourselves for hours, and we didn't know what "I'm bored" meant. After dinner, we would meet outside again. We would walk below the house to the ball field and look for pop bottles worth two cents each if there had been a game. When we found enough we would go to the store to cash them in for a bag of chips at five cents or a bottle of soda for ten cents or ice cream for ten cents or a candy bar for five cents. If we didn't find enough for everyone, we would buy things we could share. We didn't get soda or candy very often so it was a real treat to us.

My uncle had made me two pairs of stilts so we would meet in the evening down in the road and all take turns seeing who could walk the farthest without falling off.

Many days in the summer while the kids played our moms would meet at whoever's house that needed help with the harvest they had picked out of the garden that day. Bushels of green beans would be broken on someone's front porch. They worked together as neighbors and friends. Whoever needed help all of them would be on the front porch helping.

We didn't have much, no fancy toys, but we didn't even realize that. Our imaginations were the toys we needed. Our imaginations took over and what one of us didn't think of the other one would. Sticks became guns for the cowboys and you would be surprised what we could do with a pile of rocks or leaves. We would play all day with things out of the garbage, dirt, homemade stilts; we played games of red rover, red light, hopscotch, jump rope, and I remember my first hula-hoop. Wow, what a prize possession.

We were happy. There was little to no fights or arguments among us kids. We were true friends. We got along and had fun. We needed each other.

There was an elderly lady who lived near us all. She had a cookie jar and kept homemade cookies. Our parents only allowed us to go there one time a day so we wouldn't be a bother. At the end of the day, we would meet there and line up for our cookie. They were so good. I wonder now who looked more forward to it. She was alone and I'm sure she waited for us to come.

When we finally came in at dark, Mom would have a pot of something wonderful cooked on the stove. You never said "yuck" because that was what we had to eat that day, and I was hungry after playing outside all day. My mom could take a little bit of nothing and make the best food. That's why I like everything today. We couldn't say I want something else to eat. That's what we had. I remember when Mom could she would make our big treat. It was homemade cocoa made with Hershey's cocoa, not a packet, and buttered toast to dip in it. We looked forward to that very special treat.

I tell my grandchildren these stories. To me they were wonderful days, and I believe they were. Believe it or not, my husband and I have bought my home place and have lived here for years. One of the boys put a house right below me and one of the other boys bought his home place next door. We have stayed close. That's what true friends are. What wonderful memories we made as children growing up together in Hazel Row in Great Cacapon, West Virginia.

Life on a Hillside Farm
By Rosco E. Bergdoll of Moorefield, West Virginia
Born 1947

We raised a lot of our food and meat. I helped both my father and our neighbors in the '50s and '60s with farm work. I earned the trust of the neighbors, and we shared our machinery and tools so that each didn't have to buy them.

My dad and I built a wooden sled to transport our supplies and vegetables and potatoes. Our neighbor had a very large horse, and he said if we built the sled and let him use it to haul his hay in his barn, he would let us use his horse when we needed it. I had helped him feed the horse, the horse liked me, and he knew that I had helped workhorses before. The horse's name was Duke. We all gathered up leather and made a special harness so we could also use a steel wheel wagon that we had. I still have the wheels of the wagon, but a very large tree is growing up between the spokes. I also had a dog named Pooch and two sisters that helped. When we went down a steep hill I would stop at the top and wrap a chain around the sled runner and the chain would cut in the ground and hold the sled from running up on the horse's heels. With the wagon, I would put the chain around the spokes of the wheel and fasten the chain to the frame. When we got to the level land, I would stop, unloose the chain, pull off it, then gather it up, and take it for another trip.

In school, we had to have a Future Farmers of America (FFA) project. Mine one time was raising pigs. Dad got me a sow and after

Rosco's dad, Scott Bergdoll with his children

Rosco with his dog, Pooch and horse, Duke

she had pigs, they turned out well. The FFA teacher said I should keep her for more pigs since she took good care of them. We made a special pen for her to lie in so she wouldn't lie on the pigs or push them against the sides of the pen. It worked good.

Well the sow got bigger and bigger, and we decided that we would have to kill her for our winter meat. That sow must have weighed 500 pounds or more. The neighbors would go around and help each other butcher each year. Well it came time for them to be here and they showed up. I couldn't stay and see them kill her so I went to the house. After a long time, I heard them fussing and fussing and I decided to come down and see what was going on. They couldn't get the hog down in the scalding barrel, they lost a lot of their hot water, and they had to end up skinning her. One man came over to me and said, "Boy don't you ever let a hog get that big again. I have butchered many of a hog but that was the hardest I ever had to do."

Well, after they left, my dad and mother had to cut the meat up. When it was time to grind the sausage someone told Dad to jack the old car up and tie a rope through the wheel and tie it to the handle of the sausage grinder. He did this and it seemed to be a good idea. Dad started the car and the wheel began turning, and he sat down on the bench the grinder was attached to and told me to feed the pieces of meat into the grinder. Boy, I said, this is great, but for some reason the rope got twisted and it threw Dad off the bench and beat the grinder down in the dirt until the rope broke. We had to take the grinder apart and wash it and grind the rest of the sausage by taking turns turning that handle. What a tiring job. Dad said he wasn't hurt, but I knew he was.

Another farmer had a dairy herd, and when a dairy cow had a calf, they would keep the calf for about a week and then sell the calf so they could put the dairy cow back into the rest of the herd. The farmer told us he would sell us the calf for I think seven or ten dollars. So we got it put it in the back seat of the car and got it to our farm. We fed the calf, powdered milk, and it grew to a nice size. We made a rope halter and began to lead it around. Dad decided he was going to get on its back, so I got it close to a fence so Dad could get on, and when he did that calf jumped backard and I was holding the halter, and it came off and Dad went flying up in the air. It hurt him I know but he said, "Don't tell anyone. They will make fun of me."

Dad, the horse, and dog are gone now, but the memories will be with me forever.

Two Terrible Floods
By Eva Sager of Hyndman, Pennsylvania
Born 1926

I am Eva Sager. My husband was Earl Sager; he is deceased. We have two daughters, Laverne Blank and Donna Sager. We lived in Hyndman, Pennsylvania, where floods in 1984 and 1996 destroyed our home, our car, our buildings, and our possessions with five feet of water in our kitchen and the rest of our home.

The first flood was in 1984. We had picked up our grandchildren Kevin and Jodi. Kevin had gone to the school for band practice, and Jodi, nine years old, was riding her bike when she heard there was a flood coming.

She came running and screaming, "Nan, there is a flood coming!" I ran downstairs and I saw water everywhere. She said, "Let's run," but it was up on our front porch; I knew we couldn't get out. It burst open the door, and our living room was full of water. We ran upstairs. Earl was in the car when across the street was a new mother and a week old baby. She yelled at Earl to take her baby, and she gave the baby to him and she fell down. Along came our neighbor and he was in a truck. Earl put the baby in the truck and went to the railroad. The water was too high and our neighbor took the baby and mother to a house across the street upstairs. The house they were in was washed out on the street.

Our home shook and went off the foundation. I had a fire rope and I tied the rope around my nine year old's arms and told her "We're going to drown," and I wanted her to be together. We screamed and prayed for I had never seen so many cars, homes, trucks, etc. I went to put Jodi in a tree outside the bedroom window but the tree was washed away. They screamed across the street, "Don't go out on the roof!" for the porch was gone.

We were in an off side home from twelve o'clock until six. A high lift with a huge dipper took us out the window and to our family who didn't know we were still alive. I will never forget the screaming for help.

With not a chair to sit on or a plate to eat from, we struggled on for four months. Our son-in-laws and many others put us back a home where we went back December 16th. We stayed at our daughter's where we used an old truck to go for repairs to our home for there wasn't a store to purchase anything. We lost our car, all our buildings, our home, and our possessions. For many years, we worked to make our home livable.

Here we go again, hard to believe.
Second Flood
On January 1996, we were in bed and our phone rang. It was our daughter, Donna, who stopped at a store for a soda. Someone told her a flood was coming. Unbelievable. She saw a huge truck pull in, and she ran to it and asked them if they could get her mother and dad for we lived in a flood zone. Earl and I grabbed a coat and shoes and the phone rang again. It was our daughter saying get out it's a bad flood. There was ice and snow everywhere. We went to the front but there was water everywhere. The two men pulled up and asked who goes first. I said take my husband who was feeling bad. I was scared. They took him and came back after me and the water was above my waist. The two men were taking me and a log lodged against the lamppost. The one screamed let go but I held on to both of them with water under my chin

and my purse with the side out. They took us to the street light where my family was.

Our home again was destroyed, our car, our carpets, and places you could bury a car in. Again, we were shocked hurt, and didn't know where to turn for we had used our savings in the '84 flood and we didn't know where to turn. Again, our son-in-laws worked night and day, as they could. The government was of little help. There was so many involved and hurt. There were seven homes in our area washed away and dozens damaged. We lost a friend and a great-nephew who was trying to save cars and tools. Bodies found twenty-some miles down creek. Garage and all.

We stayed again at our daughter's and spring came before we could get back in our home. We lived in fear every time it rained or snowed. We would run to our daughter's night after night, time after time. We had lived there for 58 years. We started looking and found a small home three miles out of Hyndman, Pennsylvania. We were only here three months before my husband passed away and I live alone. How lonely can you get?

Sliced Apples, Popcorn, and Sled Rides
By Janet Hammond of Moorefield, West Virginia
Born 1947

Life was never boring for me. I was the oldest of six children. I was raised in a small house at Durgon, West Virginia where three of us kids slept in one bed. We were poor in a lot of ways, but rich in other ways. We always had chores to do. Sundays we always went to church twice, morning and at night, rain or shine. Sometimes my dad made his own tracks in the snow. Mondays was washday, done with a wringer washer and rinsed in a metal washtub. We even had to haul our water from a neighbor's spring for years, and then we got a well dug of our own. What a blessing that well was. We hung all of our clothes on clotheslines, so that meant everything had to be ironed. I did that all day on Saturdays. A lot of our clothes were made of printed feed sacks.

We fed chickens, milked a cow, threw hay out for her in winter, slopped hogs, and helped make cottage cheese and butter. We always had a big garden, weeded, picked bugs off potatoes and beans, picked the vegetables, and helped get them ready to can. Washing all those jars was a job. We canned all summer and fall it seemed. We helped the neighbors pick up potatoes in the fall. They would give my mom and dad small and cut ones, and Mom would can them. We canned outside a lot in washing tubs over a hot fire.

We always butchered hogs. That was always done on Thanksgiving Day. We very seldom ever had beef. We ate a lot of wild meat too, deer, squirrel, rabbit, groundhog, quail. We canned it mostly. We even canned fish if people brought us a lot.

We raised strawberries, so of course we had to pick strawberries. Mom and Dad would grade them. We would sell the big ones, and Mom would clean and mash some for jams, ice cream, and short cakes and freeze them. We picked huckleberries, raspberries, and blackberries to sell house to house in town to buy our schoolbooks. Back then, you had to buy your schoolbooks. We picked up walnuts wherever we could and I had black hands a lot when hauling them. My dad would crack them with a walnut cracker and all of us children and Mom and Dad would sit and pick them out. We would sell the nice pieces to a candy store in Cumberland, Maryland. That is what we bought our Christmas presents with. Mom used the small pieces for cake, cookies, and candy.

We looked forward to hand-me-downs from friends and relatives.

Mom and Dad always made Christmas special for us by going to a country store at Durgon and Rig and buying pounds of bulk candy. They would count us all out equal pieces, put in a brown lunch bag with our name on it, and put it under the Christmas tree. They would put in an orange, an apple, and a popcorn ball. That was special to us. I traded a lot of my candy to my brothers if I didn't like a certain kind and they did. We were each given $5.00 at Christmas to buy Mom and Dad and all four brothers and sisters gifts with at the Ben Franklin Store. Mom always got a lot of Blue Waltz Perfume; Dad got fingernail clippers or a comb; and the rest got candy, a pencil, crayons, or something for their age, but we were so proud of our purchases.

We shared a lot of good times as a family eating sliced apples and popcorn, sled riding or going fishing at the gap bridge in Petersburg, West Virginia as a family. Mom would sometimes cook hot dogs or fry potatoes in a skillet along the river for us. We always had fun going for rides and getting our nickel frozen custard ice cream cone at Mr. Hardwood's ice cream place in Moorefield. We took baths by a wood stove, no bathroom for years.

I would not trade the good old days that I grew up in for the present days. We didn't have the stress of being persuaded to drink, smoke, or use drugs for we never ran around without our parents like young children do today. Yes, things were harder, but we had more family time, and we had loved, shared, and enjoyed what we did have.

Cranberry Swamp
By Mary M. Fike of Frostburg, Maryland
Born 1941

My Mom's Story
Cranberry Swamp

My maternal grandparents owned a farm in Garrett County, Maryland, not far from Frostburg, Maryland, and on this farm was a swamp called Cranberry Swamp, and in this swamp grew blueberries, serviceberries, and cranberries. Everybody in the area went to the swamp to pick berries. My mom always said that in this swamp lived a white frog and no snakes, but I was always afraid to venture in anyway, for fear that there were snakes.

When the blueberries were ripe in August, as I remember, we went to the swamp to pick. We would put on our big rubber boots and long sleeved shirt and trudge in, a whole gang of us, and we didn't come out until our buckets were filled. Mom would can the berries and when she had all we needed, we would sell the rest to local markets.

I no longer pick blueberries and the property has been sold three times. My grandparents owned it, then one of the sons took it over, then my brother bought it for $10,000.00, and he sold it to the State of Maryland for $20,000.00. There is 125 acres; there is a cemetery on the property where the Wolfe family was buried. My grandfather's name was Clarence Raley, and he was a foreman at the clay mines. He died in 1944. The swamp is now a nature reserve.

Snow

Another story my mother would talk about was a really bad snowstorm when she was little. The snow was piled up so high that they had to go upstairs and climb out the window to go to the barn to feed the animals. It was snowing so bad that they needed to tie a rope around their waist so they could find their way back to the house.

Another story she would tell us is that her grandmother would come and stay with them, and she would smoke a pipe and rub snuff. My mother and father both were from a family of 18 each. I wish I would have known the older generation.

My Story – School

When I was a youngster, I attended a little two-room school in Garrett County, Maryland called Johnson School. This school was about ten miles from the town of Frostburg, Maryland. We lived in a small community called Finzel.

When I started to school I wore homemade dresses and petticoats made out of feed sacks. I stayed home every Monday to help Mom with the younger children while she washed clothes.

When I attended this school everybody walked to school, and the kids who lived the closest got to be selected to be the janitor for half the year and got paid $50.00! So my older brother and I were selected together, and we just lived up over the hill. I was in charge of the lower room and he did the upper grade room, but he was in charge of building the fire. The school had two classrooms, one library closet, and a cloakroom with a water cooler. The chores included building the fire, bringing in wood and coal, shoveling snow, sweeping the floors, and dusting the chalkboards and desks, bringing in water for the water cooler, and cleaning the outhouses (one for boys and one for girls). When we got our pay, this was used to help the family.

My journey to school was not a long one, but to me it was a spooky trail through the big wood, especially in the winter when the ice would hang on the trees, pulling them down to the ground, making them sound and look like ice cold monsters waiting to 'snatch' me up. Today I am still leery of ice on the trees, but I wouldn't trade my memories for anything.

Custodians of the School
By Maxine M. Bond of Frostburg, Maryland
Born 1939

Back in 1950 and 1951, I was in the sixth grade at a two-room school in a little town of Finzel, Maryland, located in Garrett County, the westernmost county in Maryland. My cousin, Eileen, and I were custodians that school year. She was in the seventh grade. The name of the school was Johnson School, and it had grades one through seven. There was no kindergarten back then.

Our responsibility was to keep the school warm by building a fire in the pot-bellied stove, and we also had to keep the rooms clean. Each room had a pot-bellied stove. We had to "bank" the fires each evening; that's what we called it back then. In other words, we had to cover the fire with coal so the fire wouldn't go out overnight.

The next morning I would put some kindling on the fire to get it started and then put lumps of coal on it to get it burning. The teacher, Mrs. Kathleen Layman, would take care of the fire during the school day. I would go to my grandfather's house after school each day to get kindling. He would cut it for me and tie cord around it so it was easier to carry. We also had to go outside and into the cellar to fill the coal bucket with coal several times a day.

We had a crock type cooler in the cloakroom where we hung our coats and put our lunch boxes. The cooler is what we put the water in for drinking. We had to go outside down behind the school and pump the water into a bucket and then carry it back into the cloakroom and pour it into the cooler. This had to be done several times a day. We made our drinking cups out of notebook paper.

After school each day, I would sweep the classroom, the cloakroom, and a very small room where our reading materials and books were stored. The chalkboards had to be cleaned and also the windows on the inside. The outside windows were too high for me to reach.

There were no indoor restrooms, so we had to use the outhouses, which were behind the school, one for the boys and one for the girls. I had to make sure there was enough paper in each. We had to wade through deep snow and bitter cold to get to them, so you tried to limit your water intake for the day.

Back then, we didn't have any 'snow days' or days when school was called off because of bad weather. I remember one time when my uncle, my cousin, Eileen's father, helped us to school by carrying our kindling. We had a bad ice storm, and he wanted to help us. Uncle Harry was a big man, six feet four inches and about 200 pounds.

We walked to school every day. The school was about one half mile away. We walked up the road, down through some woods, and then came to a clearing at the top of a steep hill. Needless to say, Uncle Harry fell down the hill and kindling went everywhere. After we realized he wasn't hurt, we had a good laugh. Uncle Harry had to trudge back up that hill to get home. We also had to pick up all the kindling, which was scattered everywhere.

Back then, we didn't have field trips on buses like kids do today. We'd walk about two miles to a nearby farm to watch the sheep being sheared. We didn't have a cafeteria, so everyone packed their lunch, unless they lived close by and could go home for lunch.

My cousin and I still reminisce about those days at Johnson School, and we're grateful that the board of education and our teacher believed in both of us enough to let us do that job. We didn't disappoint them! By the way, at the end of the school year, we were each paid $50.00, and we thought we were very rich.

Johnson School

My Shotgun Carrying Grandma
By Hilda Jane Dunham of Glengary, West Virginia
Born 1937

The following stories are about my grandma, Lula Virginia Butts, born August 18th, 1877. She lived in the Arden, Needmore, and Gerrardstown area of Berkeley County.

She had a goiter on her neck from a thyroid condition at birth. At twelve years of age, she was thrown from the back of a load of apple props, knocking her kneecap off to the side of her leg. Because of the economic situation of the time, medical treatment was not affordable.

My grandmother was a midwife. She delivered many babies in the Arden, Needmore, and Gerrardstown communities. She delivered me on November 4, 1937. I was the last baby she delivered. She declared her desire to throw me out the upstairs window because there were too many women in the world.

My grandfather, Charles Barrett, was born on September 23, 1875 and died on January 1, 1922. The day of his funeral, a huge snowstorm stopped the hearse from reaching the Needmore Cemetery. A team of horses and a sleigh were borrowed and the casket was transported from RT 45 to the cemetery. His life as an orchard worker and truck garden farmer was ended when an untreated thorn wound in his hand turned to blood poison after finding that my grandfather had diabetes. It was too late to save his life.

My grandmother was left with three children to raise, including a baby who was born before my grandfather's death and died at thirteen months of age. One day a week for a whole year after my grandfather's death, my grandmother changed to her black mourning clothes and walked to Needmore Cemetery to visit my grandfather's grave and her babies buried there.

My mother was born in 1903, May 16th. She weighed two pounds. She was born at home, no hospital, no baby nursery. She was delivered at home by a local doctor whose instructions were to wrap her in swaddling clothes, big wide strips of sheet cloth, put her in as small a container as could be found, and feed her first mother's milk and honey three times a day. Her first bed was a cushion and a

Charles, Lula, Bessie, Martha, Mazie, and Alonca

box her father had purchased a pair of boots in. Though blind in one eye and deaf in one ear, she lived to raise four children and died at 73.

My grandmother carried a shotgun. When her brother-in-law's chickens got loose on her property, she shot them.

She had a horse named Old Bird. She sold the horse to a neighbor. My uncle was very fond of the horse. He would slip through the woods to see if the horse was being treated right. The neighbor, of questionable reputation, with a pulley and chain had hung Old Bird by his front legs and head in a tree. When my uncle ran home to tell my grandmother, she grabbed her shotgun and paid her neighbor a visit. She ordered him to let the horse down or she would shoot him. With tobacco juice flying, he pointed his gun at her head and threatened to shoot first. My grandmother stood her ground. The standoff ended when the front door of the house opened and his wife appeared with a gun cocked to fire. She ordered her husband to get the horse down or she would fill him full of buckshot and he could eat his meals from the mantle.

When the same neighbor stole my grandmother's chickens, she would step on the porch, fire her shotgun in the air, and holler, "Who's stealing my chickens? I'm going to shoot you!" At Christmas time, a country ham would be lying at the front door and my grandmother would say, "That's JM paying me back for the chickens he stole."

My grandmother's death notice, found in the family Bible, states that 500 people attended her funeral. I have no way of verifying this but being a midwife, perhaps it could be true.

Grandma and Poppie's Farm
By Linda C. Burgess of Flintstone, Maryland
Born 1948

Oh! My life as a child was very much memorable. My mom left us three kids: I was seven, with a five and a half year old sister, Shocky, and a nine-month-old brother, Ricky. She walked out and never looked back, so I had my dad and grandmother, Nora, to teach me. Great!

I took care of the kids for about three to four years, while going to school. I fixed dinner, did laundry, and made sure the baby had a sitter while I was in school. That was my Aunt Juanita.

My grandma taught me a lot. We would go to the farm on weekends. My grandparents had a big farm in Wiley Ford, West Virginia. It was called Kline's Dairy Farm.

Back to cleaning, if I'd find a penny, nickel, or dime, or whatever, Grandma would say, "Keep it," so I did and saved my money. I bought me my first pair of white tennis shoes for $1.00. Wow! I was so proud of my shoes and kept care of them.

Back then, in the '50s snowstorms were bad. I remember walking the clothesline to the bus stop. Seeing my dad's head bobbing up and down, as he would shovel the line was funny.

Later my dad, Billy, found an old car with a rumble seat. We would put old hats on, go riding through Wiley Ford, West Virginia, and just have a ball because we too had an old car just like a few others we knew. We were very proud of our dad.

Boy, when weekends came I was so glad to go to Grandma and Poppie's farm. Fun – yes. Poppie would say go get the cows in. Well, we lived next to the ole Potomac River, so instead of getting the cows in, my aunts, Tiney and Shocky, and Cousin Donna, and I would go skinny-dipping. Poppie or Daddy would come after us. Wow!

On Saturday evenings, Poppie took all of us to Moon Glow Skating Rink in the ole pink and brown Wrangler station wagon. We always had fun and treats, ice cream from Queen City Dairy in Cumberland, Maryland.

My poppie was a big shipper of milk since he had a big dairy farm. He delivered milk to the dairy our ice cream came from. Poppie was a big shipper of milk up and down the east coast too. Good cream!

After four years, my dad found a new

Linda's Poppie and Grandma's farm in 1950

Linda Kline and her aunt, Tiney Kline in 1949

wife in Florida on vacation. Her name was Judy. They were married 38 years. She passed March 1, 1995. She was great to us but Shocky was her pick.

I got put out two weeks before my graduation with nowhere to go. I called Mom. She took me in if I got a job. I did at GC Murphy's in Cumberland, Maryland. It was located on our famous street called Baltimore Street. It was very busy with people all the time.

I have so many memories, like all the family reunions, eating watermelon, getting juice all over myself, and eating mustard sandwiches or onion sandwiches because Grandma said they would "keep me from getting a cold," but then we'd have bad breath. Yuck!

Well, most of my folks are gone. My dear dad passed on my 18th anniversary, September 21, 2009; grandparents 1966 – 1984. I adored my grandparents, always giving to all the grandkids and us kids. My mom, Ilene, is still living. She is 82 years old and lives in Cumberland, Maryland.

My life was great and to remember all I have been through. I would not change a thing. I've been married now 23 years to Chester Dale Burgess, Sr. and we live in Flintstone, Maryland. We have a lot of memories too.

Index A
Year of Birth and Hometown

Doms J. Clutter	1942	Accident	Maryland	49
Ralph F. Miller	1947	Accident	Maryland	50
Robert E. Drury	1931	Allison Park	Pennsylvania	20
Loretta F. Barlow	1941	Arlington	Virginia	164
Darlene Thompson	1949	Asheville	North Carolina	78
Maggie Gensel	1939	Atlantic Beach	Florida	50
Angeline W. McPeak	1923	Augusta	West Virginia	208
John E. (Eddie) Racey	1950	Augusta	West Virginia	173
Robert C. Moats	1940	Aurora	West Virginia	183
Barbara Walker Welty	1953	Bakerton	West Virginia	171
Sandra Bailey	1942	Baltimore	Maryland	172
Anne Hampton	1946	Baltimore	Maryland	30
Linda Sechler	1944	Barberton	Ohio	75
Bud Poland	1935	Barboursville	Virginia	152
Reba Deremer	1942	Barton	Maryland	101
Mark A. Zembower	1957	Bedford	Pennsylvania	73
Zona H. Apple	1927	Berkeley Springs	West Virginia	28
Karen L. Barker	1961	Berkeley Springs	West Virginia	97
Leonard B. Barron	1930	Berkeley Springs	West Virginia	52
Judy Compton	1943	Berkeley Springs	West Virginia	148
Barbara Corbett	1939	Berkeley Springs	West Virginia	304
Mary Donna Didawick	1937	Berkeley Springs	West Virginia	81
Judy Mallow Footen	1952	Berkeley Springs	West Virginia	199
Laura Ann H. Glascock	1972	Berkeley Springs	West Virginia	288
Ronnie L. Grove	1944	Berkeley Springs	West Virginia	245
Chuck Hampe	1951	Berkeley Springs	West Virginia	216
Donna J. Pierce	1953	Berkeley Springs	West Virginia	161
Mary Ellen Rich	1940	Berkeley Springs	West Virginia	310
Joseph Petrone	1942	Berryville	Virginia	106
Patricia A. Henson	1942	Big Pool	Maryland	221
Normand R. Fitzgerald	1941	Bloomington	Maryland	92
Jack W. Furbee	Unknown	Bourbonnais	Illinois	180
Sandra D. Butcher	1938	Broadway	Virginia	175
Andrew C. Agnew, Sr.	1933	Burlington	West Virginia	61
Leon Amtower	1944	Burlington	West Virginia	86

Name	Year	City	State	Page
Verda Davy	1929	Burlington	West Virginia	145
Harry W. Meek	1946	Burlington	West Virginia	107
Sidney W. Gooding	1938	Campobello	South Carolina	293
Diana Carbonaro Brown	1950	Capon Bridge	West Virginia	59
Ila Slonaker	1923	Capon Bridge	West Virginia	23
Wanda R. D. Himelrick	1946	Cayce	South Carolina	143
Jerry Timbrook	1945	Chambersburg	Pennsylvania	158
Miller Celia	1940	Chapel Hill	North Carolina	67
CarolynJames-McKenzie	1948	Charles Town	West Virginia	63
Violet Lowery	1940	Charles Town	West Virginia	138
Richard A. Zigler	1955	Charles Town	West Virginia	249
Margaret Boyd	1948	Cherokee	Oklahoma	210
Sharon Carr Phares	1945	Circleville	West Virginia	286
Pauline Sponaugle	1939	Circleville	West Virginia	188
Margaret Whitacre	Unknown	Clear Spring	Maryland	262
Ronald Abe	1935	Clearville	Pennsylvania	111
Forest David Bowers	1941	Coalton	West Virginia	53
Virginia C. Harr Smith	1921	Columbus	Ohio	213
Anna Maxine Dishong	1926	Corriganville	Maryland	268
Gary Fadley	Unknown	Cresaptown	Maryland	46
Clara O. Mynhier	1929	Cresaptown	Maryland	138
Margaret Boggs	1948	Cumberland	Maryland	66
Dixie L. Brinkman	1934	Cumberland	Maryland	23
Theodore W. Clark	1922	Cumberland	Maryland	106
Irene Hughes	1929	Cumberland	Maryland	76
Sharon F. Keefer	1938	Cumberland	Maryland	17
Jacqueline Kerns	1933	Cumberland	Maryland	28
Janet Light	1950	Cumberland	Maryland	93
Marna Meyers Morris	1938	Cumberland	Maryland	34
Marilyn Perdew	1954	Cumberland	Maryland	285
Paul David Powers	1952	Cumberland	Maryland	57
Mildred Roach	1935	Cumberland	Maryland	69
Dr. Carleton A. Shore	1931	Cumberland	Maryland	108
Darrah Speis	1920	Cumberland	Maryland	283
Laverne Stewart	Unknown	Cumberland	Maryland	138
Donna M. Turner	1935	Cumberland	Maryland	146
Edith Wilson	1917	Cumberland	Maryland	45
P. D. Wilson	1951	Cumberland	Maryland	109

Harold L. Winters	1944	Cumberland	Maryland	106
Vicky Miller	1958	Danville	West Virginia	229
Carl Harr	1946	Davis	West Virginia	89
Mary E. Higgins	1935	Davis	West Virginia	190
Ferrie A. Ball	1954	Denton	Maryland	139
Audrey Hedrick Nelson	1947	Dry Fork	West Virginia	265
Betty Workman Hohman	1941	Elkins	West Virginia	155
Robert Glen Schoonover	1927	Elkins	West Virginia	193
Wanda Sharp	1939	Elkins	West Virginia	33
Ernest Huey Smith	1932	Elkton	Maryland	295
Ruby Nell Smith	1921	Elkton	Maryland	294
Barbara Shroyer	1944	Ellerslie	Maryland	41
Edna Hargett	1943	Fairfax	Virginia	236
Ruby O. Teets	1936	Fairfax	Virginia	80
Harold E. Adams	1933	Fairmont	West Virginia	151
Jerome E. Burch	1937	Fairmont	West Virginia	276
Linda C. Burgess	1948	Flinstone	Maryland	319
Donald L. Snyder	1942	Fort Ashby	West Virginia	95
Stanley Kile	1925	Franklin	West Virginia	278
Phyllis A. Lambert	1946	Franklin	West Virginia	38
Deloirs Simmons	1944	Franklin	West Virginia	288
Loretta Hoover	1952	Friendville	Maryland	25
Cecil Kelley	1933	Friendville	Maryland	92
Floyd W. Wakefield	1930	Friendville	Maryland	18
Samuel L. Wakefield	1950	Friendville	Maryland	139
Sylvia Baer	1938	Frostburg	Maryland	91
Maxine M. Bond	1939	Frostburg	Maryland	317
Susan P. Carey-Powell	1960	Frostburg	Maryland	285
Mary M. Fike	1941	Frostburg	Maryland	316
Charlotte A. Folk	1931	Frostburg	Maryland	168
Marlene Stevens Perkins	1947	Frostburg	Maryland	170
James A. Poland	1933	Frostburg	Maryland	178
Mary Ritchie	1947	Frostburg	Maryland	74
Iris B. Stegmaier	1935	Frostburg	Maryland	96
John Sherrick	Unknown	Ft. Ashby	West Virginia	51
Mary Ann McCauley	1938	Gerrardstown	West Virginia	208
Martha Palmer	1937	Gerrardstown	West Virginia	205
Hilda Jane Dunham	1937	Glengary	West Virginia	318

Name	Year	City	State	Page
Jean Catharine Durst	1935	Grantsville	Maryland	287
Harry Handwerk	1940	Grantsville	Maryland	189
William J. Martin	1925	Grantsville	Maryland	118
Beverly Day	1954	Great Cacapon	West Virginia	311
Vivian E. Helsley	1945	Green Spring	West Virginia	22
Lana J. Koontz	1947	Green Spring	West Virginia	195
Louise Smith Crist	1928	Hagerstown	Maryland	270
Jessie Snyder	1940	Hagerstown	Maryland	185
Marlyn Angus	1935	Hancock	Maryland	67
Bill Sterner	1954	Hancock	Maryland	239
Thelma Wagner	1952	Hancock	Maryland	144
B. (Bo) Bolyard	1960	Harpers Ferry	West Virginia	55
Evelyn James	1923	Harpers Ferry	West Virginia	146
Patsy Morgan-Runkles	1945	Harpers Ferry	West Virginia	77
Richard Runkles, Jr.	1951	Harpers Ferry	West Virginia	147
Raymond E. Litten	1928	Hedgesville	West Virginia	299
H. Ward Nicklin	1923	Hedgesville	West Virginia	99
Elsie Mae Parsons	1935	Hedgesville	West Virginia	70
Junior W. Rickard	1944	Hedgesville	West Virginia	264
Evelyn E. Sims	1938	Hedgesville	West Virginia	209
Kenneth Sims	1945	Hedgesville	West Virginia	217
John D. Arthur	1936	High Springs	Florida	214
E. Jean Hast	1943	Hyndman	Pennsylvania	53
Helen M. Lewis	1941	Hyndman	Pennsylvania	212
Viola M. Logsdon	1935	Hyndman	Pennsylvania	115
Eva Sager	1926	Hyndman	Pennsylvania	314
Cherly Kilgore	1950	Inwood	West Virginia	117
Jim Harr	1953	Jackson	Ohio	228
Richard Aaron Pownall	1940	Jarrettsville	Maryland	206
Darlene Ash Gaston	1945	Johnstown	Pennsylvania	296
Patsy Dopson	1937	Kearneysville	West Virginia	157
Sandra Earp	Unknown	Kearneysville	West Virginia	197
Zack T. Fleming	1944	Kearneysville	West Virginia	126
Patt L. Welsh	1941	Kearneysville	West Virginia	153
Joe Etta Caldwell	1938	Keyser	West Virginia	190
Leoda Cox	1923	Keyser	West Virginia	255
Judy Dolechek	1948	Keyser	West Virginia	206
Ruth Gift	1923	Keyser	West Virginia	231

Barbara S. Miller	1943	Keyser	West Virginia	36
Bob Poland	1942	Keyser	West Virginia	238
Faith E. Poland	1941	Keyser	West Virginia	68
David Shapiro	1938	Keyser	West Virginia	112
Joe Winebrenner	1935	Keyser	West Virginia	44
Bernadine Evans	1937	Kitzmiller	Maryland	192
Diana Marine	1959	Lancaster	California	65
Robert M. Laughlin	1939	Lantana	Florida	44
Donna Beal	1953	Lighthouse Point	Florida	230
Victoria Younker	1952	Little Orleans	Maryland	137
Vivian Moore	1952	Lonaconing	Maryland	128
Norma Lee Muir	1936	Lonaconing	Maryland	256
Shirley J. Ravenscroft	1943	Lonaconing	Maryland	124
Evelyn S. Webster	1934	Lost City	West Virginia	193
Barbara L. Epperson	1942	Martinsburg	West Virginia	39
Barbara Moore	1945	Martinsburg	West Virginia	147
Richard Neal	1932	Martinsburg	West Virginia	253
Maxine Souder	1928	Mathias	West Virginia	146
Annabelle Vance	1935	Mathias	West Virginia	273
Anna Mary Fratz	1932	McHenry	Maryland	186
James E. Spinks	1933	Mechanicsville	Virginia	236
Mary Arlene Currence	1948	Mill Creek	West Virginia	149
Hubert Nestor	1930	Moatsville	West Virginia	284
Robert Eugene Lambert	1940	Monterey	Virginia	191
Margaret Meadows	1933	Montrose	West Virginia	87
Iona Crites Bergdoll	1928	Moorefield	West Virginia	198
Rosco E. Bergdoll	1947	Moorefield	West Virginia	313
Sue Bergdoll	1950	Moorefield	West Virginia	291
Kay B. Halterman	1945	Moorefield	West Virginia	135
Janet Hammond	1947	Moorefield	West Virginia	315
Joanne Hesse	1938	Moorefield	West Virginia	207
Billy Jenkins	1949	Moorefield	West Virginia	148
Judy (Bergdoll) Jenkins	1954	Moorefield	West Virginia	201
Sally Arlene A. Stump	1942	Moorefield	West Virginia	261
Jean Warren	1933	Moorefield	West Virginia	43
James Bohn	1943	Mt. Savage	Maryland	113
Cora Carter	1938	Mt. Savage	Maryland	102
Dottie Hughes	1940	New Creek	West Virginia	15

Name	Year	City	State	Page
Betty J. Taylor	1927	New Franklin	Ohio	194
Willard Sheppard	1925	Norfolk	Virginia	142
Marion E. Caldwell	1944	Oakland	Maryland	259
Helen Cottrill Fitzwater	1927	Oakland	Maryland	281
Dorothy P. Glotfelty	Unknown	Oakland	Maryland	196
Alma Maxine Hebden	1925	Oakland	Maryland	291
Paul W. Hoye, Jr.	1930	Oakland	Maryland	137
Elsie Lewis	1943	Oakland	Maryland	162
Johnny Logan	1951	Oakland	Maryland	301
Nina V. Miller	1932	Oakland	Maryland	139
Harriett M. Moon	1932	Oakland	Maryland	150
Sidney Ray Nazelrod	1957	Oakland	Maryland	175
Glenda D. K. Newcomb	1948	Oakland	Maryland	251
Roger Roderick	1943	Oakland	Maryland	240
Mona R. Schultz	1933	Oakland	Maryland	149
Joyce E. Skidmore	1928	Oakland	Maryland	307
Hallie M. Snyder	1939	Oakland	Maryland	140
Nettie G. Bright	1938	Parsons	West Virginia	91
Kathy Hovatter	1958	Parsons	West Virginia	72
John Smith	1947	Parsons	West Virginia	260
Mayo L. Eaton	1943	Paw Paw	West Virginia	292
Alice Sipes Lease	1925	Paw Paw	West Virginia	168
Diana Murphy	1945	Paw Paw	West Virginia	48
Susan B. Shambaugh	1952	Paw Paw	West Virginia	202
George B. Funk	1940	Pennsboro	West Virginia	293
Virginia George	1930	Petersburg	West Virginia	136
Darlene/Frances Kesner	1942	Petersburg	West Virginia	220
Wilma Lee Ketterman	1949	Petersburg	West Virginia	254
Juanita B. Mullenax	1938	Petersburg	West Virginia	215
Roseanna Rexrode	1949	Petersburg	West Virginia	290
Glona Jean Smith	1944	Petersburg	West Virginia	237
Rose Elizabeth Vance	1921	Petersburg	West Virginia	294
James H. Burkett	1936	Points	West Virginia	298
Shirley J. Burkett	1938	Points	West Virginia	166
Pat McKnew	1940	Points	West Virginia	68
Don Stilwell	1930	Princeton	West Virginia	169
Freeda E. Davy	1935	Purgisville	West Virginia	72
Ruby Froman	1937	Pylesville	Maryland	149

Name	Year	City	State	Page
Nina I. Mahoney	1936	Ranson	West Virginia	241
Reba Wilt	1932	Ranson	West Virginia	104
Therman W. Rexroad	1917	Rawlings	Maryland	204
Carol Ann Smith Teter	1948	Red Creek	West Virginia	223
Eileen V. Capel	1935	Ridgeley	West Virginia	95
Madeline Fisher	1930	Ridgeley	West Virginia	140
Kathryn Moreland	1932	Ridgeley	West Virginia	83
Arlene Snyder	1937	Ridgeley	West Virginia	69
Ernie & Betty Racey	1947	Rio	West Virginia	222
Ethel M. Bland	1939	Riverton	West Virginia	205
Susan Kilgore Hill	1942	Roanoke	Virginia	31
Anonymous	1941	Romney	West Virginia	257
Mary Alice Blizzard	1920	Romney	West Virginia	150
Calvin Flanagan	1946	Romney	West Virginia	133
Carolyn Marie Grapes	1936	Romney	West Virginia	189
Ralph E. Riley	1934	Romney	West Virginia	79
Enid Saville	1922	Romney	West Virginia	292
Carolyn R. Cooper	1938	Salem	West Virginia	64
Gary L. Cooper	1939	Salem	West Virginia	211
Susan Meyer	Unknown	San Antonio	Texas	234
EveLina Crouse	1952	Shanks	West Virginia	94
Janice M. Carper	1931	Shepherdstown	West Virginia	67
George Myers	1939	Short Gap	West Virginia	44
Carolyn R. Bobo Rinker	Unknown	Smyrna	Delaware	26
Cheston H. Browning	1942	Spring Hill	Florida	225
Beverly A. Horn	1941	Springfield	West Virginia	109
Phyllis Malone	1946	Springfield	West Virginia	33
Charlotte Eye Hartman	1930	Springville	Utah	84
William Euene Bowers	1937	St. Peters	Missouri	233
Violet R. Eye	1941	Sugar Grove	West Virginia	131
Norma Eisner	1936	Summit Point	West Virginia	45
Barbara Heilig	1952	Swanton	Maryland	71
Betty R. Ream	1935	Swanton	Maryland	254
Betty Rader	1941	Thomasville	North Carolina	242
Robert Armentrout	1943	Upper Tract	West Virginia	121
Janice Cooper Barnes	1949	Waldorf	Maryland	218
Phyllis Garcia	1949	Waldorf	Maryland	154
Betty J. Baum	1928	Warfordsburg	Pennsylvania	35

Linda K. Poole	1942	Warfordsburg	Pennsylvania	114
Wayne C. Ward	1946	Warfordsburg	Pennsylvania	134
Betty Wertz	1935	Warfordsburg	Pennsylvania	243
James Michael	1950	Westernport	Maryland	107
Stephen Michael	1954	Westernport	Maryland	30
Kitty Reeves	1939	Westernport	Maryland	32
Hazel Mason	1926	Winchester	Virginia	253
Delores Ann Snyder	1937	Winchester	Virginia	247
Nada Murphy	1936	Woodbridge	Virginia	238